Is a Law Degree Still Worth the Price?

Is a Law Degree Still Worth the Price?

It Depends on What the Law School Has to Offer You

Creola Johnson
Professor of Law,
Moritz College of Law,
The Ohio State University

Carolina Academic Press
Durham, North Carolina

Library of Congress Cataloging-in-Publication Data

Johnson, Creola.
Is a law degree still worth the price? : it depends on what the law school has to offer you / Creola Johnson.
pages cm
Includes bibliographical references and index.
ISBN 978-1-61163-371-9 (alk. paper)
1. Law schools--Economic aspects--United States. 2. Law--Study and teaching--Economic aspects--United States. 3. Law--Vocational guidance--United States. I. Title.

KF272.J58 2013
340.071'173--dc23

2013018726

Carolina Academic Press
700 Kent Street
Durham, North Carolina 27701
Telephone (919) 489-7486
Fax (919) 493-5668
www.cap-press.com

Printed in the United States of America

To Shelly, Joy & Reneé

Contents

Preface

In April 2012, I sat in my usual chair in the faculty lounge as I waited for a scholar's workshop presentation to begin at The Ohio State University Moritz College of Law. Professor Brian Tamanaha had given the faculty two chapters of his then-pending book FAILING LAW SCHOOLS for us to review. I was stunned as I heard him describe the abject failure of law schools in multiple ways. The one failure that absolutely floored me was his accusation that law schools had engaged in a widespread practice of misrepresenting employment and salary data about the success of their graduates. As a result, law schools were partially to blame for enticing students to enroll in law school and for ultimately leaving many of them in the predicament of not being able to find jobs as attorneys.

As a scholar who writes about consumer protection and predatory lending issues, my ears naturally perk up anytime I hear something about deceptive practices targeted to consumers. My reaction to his presentation was to research the alleged reporting of deceptive employment and salary data. I've spent my career writing and publishing academic papers exposing the deceptive practices of lenders and other for-profit businesses. To my complete surprise, I discovered law graduates had filed lawsuits leveling allegations of deceptive practices against 15 law schools. A few schools were even accused of bait-and-switch scholarship practices where the schools supposedly awarded more merit-based scholarships than could possibly be retained by the students because of minimum-GPA requirements for scholarship retention. I also uncovered other lawsuits filed against several law schools alleging, among other things, that they had misrepresented their accreditation status, committed negligence in their enrollment practices, and unlawfully dismissed students for unsatisfactory academic performance.

My research about the foregoing accusations led me to write this book. I have come to the very uncomfortable conclusion that many law schools have crossed the line of merely "advertising" what they have to offer and have engaged in practices that a layperson—the average law-school applicant—would find deceptive. I distinguish the layperson's perspective from the judicial perspective because, to date, several of the above-mentioned lawsuits have been dismissed as no judge has found a school's practice to be in violation of consumer protection laws. One judge even had the audacity to label all prospective law students "sophisticated"! Instead of sending the message "liars beware," the judges have sent the message "buyers beware" to all future law students.

The fact that *some* law school personnel may engage in deceptive practices should not be reason alone to discourage anyone from going to law school. Why do I say that? Just think of all the dreams we seek to accomplish even though this world is rife with unscrupulous characters. Most of us go on dates in pursuit of a loving, lasting romantic commitment even though many men and women lie about all sorts of things. Most of us still try to buy a car even though car salespeople are infamous for perpetrating deceptive sales tactics. Most of us want to become homeowners despite the subprime foreclosure crisis arising from the predatory lending practices of mortgage brokers and banks.

I wrote this book to encourage students who have already decided to go to law school and need to be empowered with the necessary information to make a wise investment. I show prospective law students how to indeed become sophisticated and conduct thorough research about a law school and analyze all information obtained about that school. That research must begin by looking at the employment data about a school's recent graduating class.

The American Bar Association ("ABA") yielded to extreme pressure and adopted in 2012 new standards mandating that law schools disclose certain employment data. As a result of the new reporting requirements, we now know that many graduates, even the majority of graduates at some schools, did not find fulltime, permanent attorney jobs and, therefore, did not get what they bargained for when they enrolled in law school. Rather than earning six-figure salaries, the majority of graduates earn mid-level, five-figure starting salaries. As you read this book, you will learn that although the ABA's standards force greater disclosures, the ABA's standards allow law schools to continue to exploit gaps in the standards to overstate the success of their law graduates in finding jobs.

Besides calling out the ABA, I challenge the *US News & World Report* rankings system. Based on the research that I've compiled, I urge prospective law students to not make enrollment decisions based on the *US News* rankings system because it is flawed for several reasons, including that it takes into account factors that are *unimportant* and does not give sufficient weight to other factors.

Take as a case in point the *US News*' published ranking[1] of five Florida law schools in its 2014 Best Law Schools Report. The University of Florida is ranked the highest in the first tier at No. 46, followed by Florida State University at No. 48, by the University of Miami in the second tier at No. 76, by Florida International University in the third tier at No. 105, and by Stetson University at No. 109. Yet if you look in Appendix A where I compare the employment outcomes of the 2012 graduates of all ABA-accredited law schools, the highly-ranked University of Florida has the smallest percentage, only 56.8%, of its 2012 graduates employed in fulltime, permanent jobs that require passage of the bar exam—the actual attorney jobs. Moreover, of these ranked Florida schools, the University of Florida has the highest percentage, 8.7%, of unemployed graduates seeking employment. As a result, if the prospective student wants to attend a Florida law school and wants to become employed as an attorney, the University of Florida may not be the best choice even though it's ranked the highest.

Law school applications have steadily decreased in the last four years, yet prospective students continue to apply for admission to several law schools. Many of them will get multiple admission offers. Because a law school education is likely to result in six-figure student loan debt, an applicant's decision regarding where to enroll must be based on a comprehensive analysis of what each school has to offer and not simply use *US News* rankings to make an enrollment decision.

For prospective students who are fortunate enough to have competing offers of admission, I demonstrate how to determine which school has (1) the lowest rate of students lost to attrition, (2) the lowest number of students who transfer out, (3) the most academic support services, (4) the highest rate of graduates who pass the bar exam the first time, (5) the highest percentage of graduates employed fulltime as attorneys, and (6) the lowest number of unemployed graduates seeking employment. All of this information will help

1. Note that *US News* did not reveal the ranking place of six Florida schools that are in the fourth-tier of law schools. My discussion is strictly about the schools with a published ranking number.

prospective students to enroll in the law school where they have the greatest chance of successfully matriculating and graduating on time, of obtaining a license to practice law, and of becoming a fulltime, permanently-employed attorney.

I also show prospective students how to figure out the full cost of a legal education, by taking into account all scholarship offers and the likelihood of retaining merit-based scholarships. The point here is that the prospective student wants to select the school that not only has the greatest employment rate as discussed above, but the school that offers the most in scholarships, grants, etc., and that will result in the student borrowing the least amount of money. I provide an in-depth discussion of student loan forgiveness and payment reduction programs as well as the feasibility of filing bankruptcy to deal with student loan debt. I warn students to borrow money wisely because an enormous amount of debt could prevent a graduate from obtaining a license to practice law.

Armed with my roadmap of how to do a comprehensive analysis, the prospective student will be able to select the school that is right for him or her. Pre-law academic advisors can also use the roadmap to help undergraduates who are sure of their decision to pursue a law degree but need to have realistic expectations about a legal career. My hope is that the legal profession will continue to have an influx of new attorneys who are satisfied with their decision to go to law school.

Acknowledgments

I thank all of the people at The Ohio State University Moritz College of Law that have contributed in various capacities towards the completion of this book. However, I want to send a special thanks to a few people.

First, I am grateful to Professor Katherine Kelly for sacrificing her time to read several chapters of the book and provide me with comments. Her passion for academic success programs made her a wonderful sounding board for my ideas about wise-decision making when selecting a law school.

I thank law librarians Susan Azyndar, Matt Cooper, and Ingrid Matteson for giving immediate attention to my research requests, even though they were often demanding. I want to thank administrative assistants Susan Edwards and Allyson Hennelly for all their help, especially their assistance in completing the tables in the book. Of course, any mistakes are my own.

Associate Dean Donald Tobin was helpful in providing me with a budget to conduct a survey of recent law school graduates. That research helped to crystalize the issues that I address in this book.

Patrick Bauer, Martha Chamallas, and Deborah Merritt deserve special recognition for being my mentors as well as for providing feedback about how to proceed with this enormous undertaking.

I'd like to thank Michelle Alexander, a dear colleague and author of The New Jim Crow. As I grew weary sometimes, I would frequently remember Professor Alexander, as she worked two doors away from my office into the wee hours of the morning to finish her book. Her unassuming presence was a force of nature and an inspiration to me.

I thank the following former law students who provided valuable research and other services: Jill Fridley, Shea Gordon, Bryan Jenkins, and Quendale Simmons. I wish them much success as young attorneys.

Special thanks to Carlie Boos for volunteering to read and comment on earlier drafts of the book. Thank you for helping to paint a picture of the challenges faced by law graduates in their post-recession quest for gainful legal employment.

I thank the law graduates who completed my online survey. Many of you told me about your struggles to manage your law school debt while trying to achieve the middle-class dream. Your struggles gave me a needed boost to persevere to complete this book. I hope that the future law students who read this book will avoid some of the mistakes that you have made and will go on to enjoy fulfilling careers as attorneys and other professionals.

I am immensely grateful for my mom, Shelly, and Aunt Winnie. Though they could not understand my need to work long hours, they were, nevertheless, supportive in taking care of my children. I thank my kids for giving me hugs, kisses, and comic relief.

Is a Law Degree Still Worth the Price?

Chapter 1

The Legal Academy Is in Trouble

I opened an email message from a friend and read the incendiary words: *Why Attending Law School Is the Worst Career Decision You'll Ever Make.*[1] It was an online article by J. Maureen Henderson at *Forbes*' website. My first thought was: Who is this "J. Maureen Henderson" and who made her an authority on the subject?! It turns out no one. She is an online blogger who claims to write about "early career issues." However, she has no law degree and has never worked in the legal profession.[2]

So what's the problem? Because *Forbes* is considered a reputable magazine, Ms. Henderson's inflammatory article could turn away prospective students from pursuing a law degree.

I suppose some Americans have always disliked and will continue to dislike *all* lawyers. Some dislike only lawyers who represent a contrary interest, such as lawyers who advocate for consumer protection. News articles like Ms. Henderson's indicate that it is open season for the "haters" of lawyers to dump on the legal profession and take delight in the misery of recent law graduates who are trying to find attorney jobs. At first, the *New York Times* and other media outlets started reporting in late 2008 that recent law school graduates were having trouble finding law firm jobs.[3] Such reporting was understandable because the start of the Great Recession[4] was having a negative impact on most employment sectors. But then, in 2010, the news stories began to take a decidedly negative turn when they started reporting that the law schools had been accused of publishing deceptive employment and salary data to entice prospective law students into enrolling in law school.[5]

---

1. Ms. Henderson's short bio on Forbes's website states: "Former policy wonk. Current business strategist. I write about higher ed and early career issues. Pithily. I used to care about Gen Y, but I stopped when I realized that would probably lead to premature wrinkles." See www.jmaureenhenderson.com.

2. *Id.*

3. *See, e.g.*, Jonathan D. Glater, *The Lawyer Squeeze: Layoffs and Closings in a Field Thought to Resist Downturns*, N.Y. Times, Nov. 12, 2008, at B1 (discussing the financial crisis's impact on the legal job market and identifying layoffs at and mergers of several prominent law firms as well as the collapses of Thelen LLP and Heller Ehrman LLP).

4. Jeff Sovern, *Preventing Future Economic Crises Through Consumer Protection Law or How the Truth in Lending Act Failed the Subprime Borrowers*, 71 Ohio St. L.J. 761, 832 (2010) (stating that "[t]he subprime crisis precipitated the worst economic decline since the Great Depression" and stating that current economic crisis "has earned the sobriquet 'the Great Recession'").

5. *See, e.g.*, John Eligon, *Jobs Data More Vital to Her Than Food*, N.Y. Times, Aug. 27, 2010 *available at* http://cityroom.blogs.nytimes.com/2010/08/27/jobs-data-more-vital-to-her-than-food/ (reporting about a law graduate claiming that she started a hunger strike on August 5, 2010, as her way of urging greater law school transparency and career counseling reform).

Is the Reporting of Incomplete Employment Data Really a Serious Issue?

To frame the gravity of the issue of reporting deceptive employment data, I want to compare it to the advertising practice of a fictitious company, Drug-Co Pharmaceuticals. Assume that Drug-Co is the manufacturer of a drug call Pain-B-Gone and that on TV, radio, etc., Pain-B-Gone is marketed as a drug that eliminates or substantially reduces headache pain. A 10-tablet supply of Pain-B-Gone is $150. Assume further that every single form of adverting boasts that "94% of the consumers who take Pain-B-Gone feel better!" However, it turns out that Drug-Co's internal data about the effectiveness of the drug shows that only 50% of consumers who took the drug reported that it eliminated or substantially reduced their headache pain. Drug-Co derived the 94% rate by counting consumers who reported that pain in other parts of their bodies was eliminated or reduced (e.g., knee pain went away). Drug-Co was also able to achieve the 94% feel-better-rate by counting consumers who reported that they noticed a benefit not related to headache pain. For example, Drug-Co included consumers who reported that swelling in their hands went down or a toenail fungus went away after taking Pain-B-Gone for three days.

Because Pain-B-Gone is marketed as a drug that alleviates or eliminates headache pain, do you think it is misleading for Drug-Co to boast that the drug has 94% feel-better-rate? Most likely you do, and I bet most people would feel Drug-Co's ads are misleading. No doubt, Drug-Co would sell less Pain-B-Gone if the public knew that only 50% of consumers who took the drug had their headache pain reduced or eliminated. At $15 per tablet, Drug-Co's sales would plummet if consumers also learned that serious negative side effects from taking Pain-B-Gone were commonplace. For some, the costs to the wallet and to the body of taking the drug would far outweigh the potential benefit (i.e., a 50% chance of eliminating or reducing head pain).

When I have presented this hypothetical or similar ones to a few law professors, they readily agree with me that Drug-Co's ads boasting a 94% feel-better-rate would be misleading and, therefore, deceptive. But when I switch gears and try to get them to see this is what many law schools have done, I encounter resistance.

Like Drug-Co, most law schools have boasted that 90% or more of their graduates are employed 9 months after graduation. But at almost half of the law schools, it turns out that, 9 months after graduation, 50% or less of their graduates have full-time, long-term jobs that require passage of the bar exam. I call such jobs the "real attorney jobs" because (1) only those who want to become licensed attorneys have to pass the bar exam and (2) most people want full-time long-term employment. Because research consistently shows the majority of people attend law school to become lawyers, one would naturally assume that reported employment rates would be comprised only of graduates who got attorney jobs or that law schools would simultaneously disclose the percentage of graduates with real attorney jobs.

Law schools have been technically correct about the 90%-or-better employment rate because they counted graduates employed in *ANY* capacity, including those employed as paralegals or employed temporarily in university-funded positions. However, many, if not most, law students and graduates find this method of inflating the employment rate to be misleading. Incredibly, many law school personnel seem to be tone deaf and blind to accusations that such reporting is misleading.

As discussed more fully later, law schools should not be blamed entirely for the predicament of their unemployed and under-employed graduates. However, by consistently reporting a 90%-or-better employment rate, law schools perpetuated a fallacious message that there are enough attorney jobs for nearly all law graduates. This message enticed some people to come to law school. Had law schools fully disclosed the truth, some people would have decided not to go to law school. Consequently, law schools are partially to blame for the fact that the demand for attorney jobs substantially exceeds the supply.

Even though the reporting of misleading employment data was purportedly done by only a few law schools, the entire legal academy is now suffering the consequences. Similar to the predicted reaction of consumers who learn the truth about Pain-B-Gone, many potential law students are avoiding law school because they now realize that attending law school may impose greater harms than benefits: it may put graduates in a tremendous amount of debt ($150,000) and leave them unemployed or under-employed after graduation. While consumers can expect the US Food & Drug Administration to adequately deal with Drug-Co, the American Bar Association ("ABA") has yet to sanction any law school for reporting misleading employment data.[6]

In Addition to Misleading Employment Reporting Practices, Other Problems Exist

The accusation that many law schools have been misrepresenting data is only one among numerous accusations that have been leveled against the legal academy since the start of the Great Recession. In case you have been consumed with undergraduate studies or have been struggling with the trials of day-to-day living, let me summarize for you below what has taken place in the legal academy and the legal job market:

The following has been occurring in the legal academy:

1) Law school graduates have accused law schools of reporting suspiciously high employment rates and salary averages;
2) Law school graduates have filed lawsuits alleging that the high employment and salary data are misleading in violation of consumer protection laws;[7]
3) Two well-regarded law schools have reported inflated LSAT scores and undergraduate GPAs;[8]
4) A growing number of academic voices are decrying law school reporting practices;[9]
5) A shrinking number of test-takers are sitting for the Law School Admission Test (LSAT);[10]

6. The ABA has authority over all ABA-accredited and provisionally-approved law schools.

7. The claims in these lawsuits are fully discussed in Chapter 2.

8. For a full discussion, please read Chapter 7 where I discuss the inflating of admissions data at University of Illinois College of Law and Villanova University School of Law.

9. *See, e.g.*, Brian Tamanaha, Failing Law Schools 72–73 (2012) (explaining over time how "goosing" the numbers became a pervasive practice among law schools but that some schools were more ruthless than others in goosing the numbers).

10. The number of prospective students taking the LSAT is down three years in a row. Ed Wesoloski, *October LSAT: Number of Takers Down 38 Percent from Three Years Ago*, Michigan Lawyers Weekly,

6) A decreasing number of prospective students are submitting applications to law schools;[11] and

7) A declining number of first-year students are enrolling in accredited law schools.[12]

What has happened in the legal job market in the last five years:

1) Law firms have laid off thousands of lawyers;[13]

2) Law firms have reneged on job offers made to some new graduates and postponed the start date of others;[14]

3) Law graduates are having difficulty finding traditional attorney jobs;[15]

4) Many graduates are working in temporary document-review jobs, in non-legal, non-professional jobs, and in various other under-employed positions;[16]

5) Law firms have lowered the starting salaries for entry entry-level attorney positions;[17] and

6) The number of traditional, entry-level attorney jobs is not expected to return to their pre-recession peak levels as firms continue hiring freezes and layoffs.[18]

Nov. 27, 2012, *available at* http://milawyersweekly.com/milwblog/2012/11/27/october-lsat-number-of-takers-down-38-percent-from-three-years-ago/.

11. Law school applications are down by double-digit percentages for the last three years. *See* Three-Year ABA Volume Comparison, Law School Admission Council, http://www.lsac.org/lsac resources/data/three-year-volume.asp (last visited Feb. 14, 2013) (stating that as of Feb., 8, 2013, the number of applicants are down by 19.1% and the number of applications are down by 21.8% in comparison to the same time period in 2012).

12. *See* Debra Cassens Weiss, *1L Enrollment Dropped at Three-Fourths of Accredited Law Schools This Year, Preliminary Stats Show*, ABA Journal, Nov 28, 2012, *available at* http://www.abajournal.com/news/article/enrollment_dropped_at_three-fourths_of_accredited_law_schools_this_year_pre/. While fewer first-year law students enrolled in fall 2012, the decrease in enrollment is not due to an insufficient number of students wanting to get in law school. Many law schools chose to purposely decrease their class sizes to maintain their historically median LSAT score so they can maintain their *US News* rankings status. *See* Joe Palazzolo and Chelsea Phipps, *With Profession Under Stress, Law Schools Cut Admissions*, Wall Street Journal Online, June 11, 2012, http://online.wsj.com/article/SB10001424052702303444204577458411514818378.html (Professor William Henderson (Indiana University Maurer School of Law) states that law schools "are trying to get a class [with a median LSAT score] that mirrors prior classes, but with fewer applicants and enrollees.").

13. Ameet Sachdev, *Fewer Applying to Law Schools*, Chi. Trib., Mar. 23, 2012, at B1 ("The largest and most prestigious law firms that pay six-figure salaries to first-year lawyers laid off thousands of attorneys and have not resumed hiring from law schools at pre-recession levels."). For a full discussion, please read Chapter 9.

14. *See, e.g.*, Ameet Sachdev, *Careers on Hold, Lawyers Do good*, Chi. Trib., April 4, 2010, at B1. See Chapter 14 for a discussion of one graduate's struggle to survive after learning that a Chicago-area law firm revoked its job offer to her.

15. The National Association of Law Placement ("NALP") has reported several times that starting salaries at law firms continue to plummet and that law graduates face the worst legal job market in decades. *See, e.g.*, Press Release, *Law School Grads Face Worst Job Market Yet—Less Than Half Find Jobs in Private Practice*, Nat'l Association of Law Placement, *available at* http://www.nalp.org/2011selectedfindingsrelease.

16. For a full discussion, please read Chapter 10.

17. *See, e.g.*, Janet Cho, *Jones Day Lays Off Workers, Says Technology Takes Up Slack*, Plain Dealer (Cleveland), June 23, 2010, at C1 (identifying several law firms by name and the number of attorneys and staff workers laid off at these firms and stating that "law firms nationwide [are] cutting thousands of staff, cutting salaries, imposing hiring freezes and postponing start dates for new lawyers").

18. *See, e.g.*, Catherine Ho, *Patton Boggs Lets go 65 Attorneys and Staff*, Wash. Post, March 2, 2013, at C1 (stating that 65 workers laid off at international law firm Patton Boggs consists of 30 lawyers and 35 staff employees, including a public policy adviser and several paralegals).

What the ABA and other third parties are doing that impact the legal academy and the legal job market:

1) Law school graduates and others maintain dozens of anti-law-school blogs;[19]
2) Third parties are increasingly demanding that law schools accurately and fully disclose employment and salary information;[20]
3) The number of new law schools is continuing to expand;[21]
4) The number of new law schools with ABA accreditation or provisional approval is continuing to expand;[22]
5) The ABA imposed sanctions on two law schools for reporting inflated admissions data;[23]
6) Law School Transparency filed a complaint with the ABA against Rutgers School of Law-Camden for allegedly violating ABA standards when its associate dean sent recruiting emails to prospective students containing allegedly misleading employment and salary data;[24]
7) The ABA adopted in 2012 new standards mandating that law schools disclose certain employment data.[25]

I suppose that if former Vice President Dan Quayle has heard about some the above problems, he is somewhere laughing and feeling vindicated for saying our nation has "too many lawyers." Because of all the events that have transpired in the last five years, Quayle's assertion of "too many lawyers" has morphed into something ugly—too high tuition costs, too much student loan debt, too few attorney jobs, too many law schools, too many deceptive practices, etc. Despite all of the foregoing, those interested in becoming lawyers should not be easily deterred from going to law school. America continues to need lawyers, especially lawyers committed to doing public service as a great gulf exists between low-

19. Dozens of websites exists where regular posts can be found by angry graduates and students. I explain in subsequent chapters why hostility directed at some law schools may be justified. Below are just a few active websites:

Third Tier Reality: http://thirdtierreality.blogspot.com/
Above the Law: http://abovethelaw.com/
But I Did Everything Right!: http://butidideverythingrightorsoithought.blogspot.com/
Sh*t Law Jobs: http://www.shitlawjobs.com/
Epic Fail: Averting Law School Disaster: http://lawschoolfail.blogspot.com/#sthash.iJuJayOx.dpbs
Attorney to (Temporary) Temp: http://attorneytotemp.blogspot.com/
Subprime JD: http://subprimejd.blogspot.com/
Outside the Law School Scam!: http://outsidethelawschoolscam.blogspot.com
The PresTTTigious Legal "Profession": http://prestttigious.blogspot.com/
Super-Duper: The Non-traditional Law Student Confidence Game: http://dupednontraditional.blogspot.com/.

20. These third parties include US senators. The new standards are discussed thoroughly in Chapter 4.

21. See Chapter 5.

22. Id. An increasing number of ABA-accredited or approved schools are for-profit schools and/or stand-alone law schools (not connected to any university).

23. For a full discussion of the standards, please read Chapter 7.

24. Daniel Wiessner, *Group Claims Rutgers-Camden Law Used Misleading Employment Data*, Thomson Reuters News & Insight, Dec. 31, 2012, http://newsandinsight.thomsonreuters.com/Legal/News/2012/12_-_December/Group_claims_Rutgers-Camden_Law_used_misleading_employment_data/. A copy of the complaint is available at Law School Transparency, http://www.lawschooltransparency.com/documents/509_Enforcement/Rutgers_Camden_Complaint_12-31-2012.pdf.

25. See Chapter 4 for a full discussion.

to-moderate income families in need of affordable legal service and lawyers capable of providing it.

Without question, the legal profession is in crisis. Numerous parallels can be drawn between the mortgage foreclosure crisis and the legal job-market crisis, but I will mention only three for now. The two crises have occurred in part due to erroneous assumptions. First, brokers, lenders, and prospective homeowners incorrectly assumed that housing values would continue to rise and, thereby, concluded incorrectly that homeownership was a completely safe, wealth-building strategy. Similarly, lawyers, law school applicants, and others have incorrectly assumed that six-figure salaries were the norm for new lawyers and that salaries would continue to rise and, as a result, concluded incorrectly that the benefits of a law degree *always* outweigh the cost of obtaining it. As I will show later, the median salary for new law graduates is in the mid-five-figure range and graduates of 81 law schools have a 50% or less chance of getting a full-time, long-term attorney job.[26]

A second parallel to draw from the foreclosure crisis is regarding the disdain heaped on homeowners and law graduates. Radio and TV pundits as well as many ordinary Americans have berated homeowners in crisis for foolishly "buying more home than they could afford" and have argued that they do not deserve any help from the government (even though we bailed out the banks who are partially to blame for the mortgage foreclosure crisis). Similarly, unemployed and under-employed graduates, burdened with six-figure student loan debt, are regularly ridiculed for complaining about their predicament and for asking the courts for relief. Those who ridicule feel that the graduates should not have gone to a low-ranked law school or should not have gone to law school at all. For example, when the Wall Street Journal reported online about the lawsuit against Thomas M. Cooley Law School ("Cooley") being dismissed, many of the 26 comments were unsympathetic. One person, going by the name "But Really", wrote the following: "So why do we excuse the self-imposed ignorance of law applicants regarding details when the amount [of debt] is ten times what you'd spend on a car? If it took 3 years and $150,000 to imbue some concept of 'due diligence' in you, you probably shouldn't have become a[n] attorney in the first place."[27]

The last parallel that I want to draw from the foreclose crisis is that consumers have put too much trust in third parties when making crucial decisions. During the housing bubble, homeowners and prospective borrowers naively trusted mortgage brokers and lenders to make final decisions about home equity and home purchase loans. Likewise, prospective law students and others have *and* continue to put too much trust in a third party—*US News & World Report* ("*US News*") and its yearly rankings—to make law school application and enrollment decisions. As will be explained later, even at a few first-tier law schools, less than 50% of their graduates are able to secure full-time, long-term attorney jobs nine months after graduation. If a graduate of a third-tier school is just as likely to be unemployed or under-employed as a graduate of a first-tier school, then the *US News* rankings system has failed to accurately measure law schools regarding a factor that will matter to many prospective law students.[28]

---

26. Please read Chapter 11.

27. Chelsea Phipps, *Cooley Law Grads' Lawsuit Dismissed*, WALL STREET JOURNAL ONLINE (July 20, 2012), http://blogs.wsj.com/law/2012/07/20/cooley-law-grads%e2%80%99-lawsuit-dismissed/ (last visited Nov. 10, 2012).

28. Unlike the *US News*, the *National Jurist* has developed its own ranking system where post-graduate success accounts for 50% of the methodology formula. For a critique of the *National Jurist* ranking system, *see* Paul Caron, National Jurist Law School Rankings, Feb. 12, 2013, *available at* http://taxprof.typepad.com/taxprof_blog/2013/02/national-jurist.html.

Clarion Call

This book is a clarion call urging prospective law students to stop engaging in default-decision making—using the *US News'* rankings system as the sole or almost exclusive basis for making a law school selection decision. Such default-decision making is a primitive way to make life-altering choices. The *US News'* rankings system is based on a methodology that weighs 12 criteria, and the employment outcomes of each law school is one of those criteria.[29] However, as you will see in later chapters, *US News* has simply relied on the employment reporting practices used by some law schools to hide under-employed graduates.[30] For that reason alone, the *US News'* rankings system should not be used to make enrollment decisions. Besides being widely criticized by law school deans, academics and others,[31] the Honorable Richard Posner,[32] a prominent US federal court judge, makes it clear that reliance on the *US News'* ranking system is "a low-cost, low-benefit method of evaluation—cheap but crude."[33] Notice that he said "low-benefit." That is because a decision based on this ranking system alone can do a student more harm than good.[34]

---

29. Robert Morse and Sam Flanigan, Methodology: Law School Rankings, US News & World Report, March 12, 2012, *available at* http://www.usnews.com/education/best-graduate-schools/top-law-schools/articles/2012/03/12/methodology-law-school-rankings.

30. As explained thoroughly in Chapters 3 and 4, when law schools published their *overall* employment rates, many law school applicants thought that the law schools were reporting the percentage of graduates who had secured full-time jobs as attorneys. It turns out that law schools were counting in their *overall* employment rates graduates employed in *any* capacity (*e.g.* sales associate at Kohl's). Because the ABA in 2012 forced law schools to breakdown the overall employment rate for the classes of 2010 and 2011, we now know that at dozens of law schools less than half of their 2010 and 2011 graduates were employed full-time as attorneys. To see how *US News* justifies its reliance on the data supplied to it by law schools, read the following. Robert Morse, *US News Challenges ABA on Law School Employment Data Standards*, US News & World Report, Jan. 13, 2011, available at http://www.usnews.com/education/blogs/college-rankings-blog/2011/01/13/us-news-challenges-aba-on-law-school-employment-data-standards.

31. Going back as far as 1998, one can find articles (1) criticizing the *US News* ranking system, (2) explaining why its methodology is fundamentally flawed, and (3) urging law school applicants to not rely on it. *See*, e.g., Brent E. Newton, *The Ninety-Five Theses: Systemic Reforms of American Legal Education and Licensure*, 64 S.C. L. Rev. 55, 76 (2012) ("The US News & World Report ranking system is fundamentally flawed, and its influence on legal education has been malignant."); Randall T. Shepard, *From Students to Lawyers: Joint Ventures in Legal Learning for the Academy, Bench, and Bar*, 31 Ind. L. Rev. 445, 449–50 (1998) (discussing a letter sent by the Law School Admission Council to over 70,000 law school applicants criticizing the methodology of the *US News* ranking system); Paul L. Caron & Rafael Gely, *What Law Schools Can Learn From Billy Beane and the Oakland Athletics*, 82 TEX. L. REV. 1483, 1522 (2004) (discussing a letter sent by 164 law school deans to applicants that warned applicants not to rely on rankings because "rankings leave many important variables out of account, arbitrarily weight others, and are generally unreliable as a guide to those qualities of different schools that an applicant should consider when applying to law school").

32. Richard Posner is a U.S. Court of Appeals judge for the 7th Circuit, a senior lecturer at the University of Chicago Law School, and a prolific writer.

33. Richard A. Posner, *Law School Rankings*, 81 IND. L.J. 13, 13 (2006).

34. In the wake of accusations that law schools have published deceptive employment data, even US News warns prospective law students to consider factors other than a school's ranking. Robert, Morse, *Recent Law School News Focuses On Rankings*, US NEWS & WORLD REPORT, July 5, 2012, *available at* http://www.usnews.com/education/blogs/college-rankings-blog/2012/07/05/recent-law-school-news-focuses-on-rankings ("US News urges law school applicants not to heavily rely on the rankings as the basis for where to apply or to attend. Applicants need to strongly consider cost, location, course offerings, and job prospects. The rankings should only be one tool in application process.").

Has the Student Loan Bubble Burst?

A decision based solely or almost exclusively on *US News* rankings or even on the advice of ill-informed relatives and friends is unwise because such decision-making ignores current realities in the legal profession. The first market reality is that student loan debt is an enormous burden for recent graduates and, therefore, the means of paying for a legal education must become a major factor in the law school selection process. Higher education analysts argue that similar to the housing bubble, we are in the midst of a student loan bubble in higher education, and the bubble's bursting is imminent.[35] That means that students will begin defaulting on their student loans at higher rates and in record numbers because they are unable to secure jobs paying well enough for them to cover living expenses and make their monthly student loan payments.[36] As a result of students incurring debt beyond their ability to repay, their defaults will become another drag on the economy. Because the majority of student loans are guaranteed by the United States Government, taxpayers are eventually going to be on the hook for uncollected debt if the borrowers never repay.[37]

Besides the student loan bubble, the law school bubble has burst. American law schools produce approximately 45,000 new graduates each year; however, only 25,000 jobs as attorneys are expected annually.[38] These law graduates carry an average student loan debt in excess of $100,000. Many cannot find attorney jobs so that they can start repaying their loans. As a result of the contraction in the legal job market and the rising cost of a legal education, law schools are now facing dramatic declines in LSAT test-takers, application submissions, and first-year enrollments. Reeling from the domino effect of these declining numbers, many law schools will have to cope with substantial revenue shortfalls. Analysts, therefore, predict that a few law schools will shutter their doors for good.

Several Law Schools Have Been Sued for Reporting Deceptive Employment Data

Some law graduates are so aggrieved about their student loan debts and their meager job prospects that they have filed lawsuits alleging that their law schools have committed

35. Rick Newman, *How Student Debt Is Slowing the Recovery*, US News & World Rep., Apr. 9, 2012 ("Some analysts are even starting to worry about a student loan bubble that could burst and bring a damaging wave of defaults, similar to the subprime meltdown that helped cause the recent recession.").

36. The default rate is already growing. *See generally*, National Consumer Law Center's Student Borrower Loan Assistance Project, Borrowers on Hold: Student Loan Collection Agency's Complaint Systems Need Massive Improvement (May 2012), *available at* http://www.studentloanborrowerassistance.org/blogs/wp-content/www.studentloanborrowerassistance.org/uploads/File/borrowers-on-hold.pdf.

37. William S. Howard, *The Student Loan Crisis and the Race to Princeton Law School*, 7 J.L. Econ. & Pol'y 485 (2011) (arguing that "the consequences from [the bursting of] the student loan bubble could be just as disastrous" as the bursting of the housing bubble). For example, Stafford Student Loans are guaranteed by the U.S. Government. *Id.* I agree with Howard's conclusion that when "the government guarantees a loan, the lender no longer needs to concern themselves with the full risk of default and is willing to make loans regardless of the borrower's ability to repay."

38. Brian Tamanaha, Failing Law Schools (2012).

deceptive and other unlawful practices. Unfortunately, these law graduates are unlikely to get relief from the courts based on the reporting practices of their law schools and their inability to find traditional attorney positions. In March 2012, Judge Melvin Schweitzer dismissed a lawsuit filed against New York Law School ("NYLS") for allegedly reporting deceptive employment and salary data.[39] This dismissal was followed by Judge Gordon Quist's dismissal of the lawsuit filed against Cooley. Three other lawsuits have recently been dismissed. These dismissals do not bode well for graduates who still have pending cases.

Both Cooley and NYLS proclaimed victory after the dismissal of the cases against them;[40] however, this proclamation of victory should serve as a wakeup call for prospective students and their parents. I include parents here because parents are increasingly dipping into savings or taking out private student loans to finance their adult child's education and are, therefore, stakeholders who should play an active role in the law school selection process. Law school applicants and other stakeholders need to do comprehensive and extensive research when deciding whether to accept a law school's offer of admission.

Optimism Bias Hinders Optimal Decision-Making

Before explaining how to perform a comprehensive analysis of a law school, I need to urge prospective students to recognize and overcome optimism bias and other cognitive problems that hinder optimal decision-making. Optimism bias is a social science term that explains that consumers fail to make the most advantageous decision because they selectively interpret the information provided to them in a favorable, and not objective, light.[41]

Let's see how optimism bias could be a factor in the law school selection process. In the complaint filed by nine law graduates against NYLS, the graduates alleged that NYLS misrepresented its statistics regarding its post-graduation employment and salary data.[42] NYLS consistently reported that around 90% of its graduates were employed within nine months of graduation even though several large New York law firms had laid off hudreds of attorneys and had decreased hiring.[43] The complaint alleged that NLYS's data implied

39. Gomez-Jimenez v. N.Y. Law Sch., N.Y.S.2d, 2012 WL 934387, at *14 (N.Y. Sup. Ct. Mar. 21, 2012).

40. For example, NYLS published on its website a summary of the Wall Street Journal's article about the dismissal of the lawsuit. http://www.nyls.edu/news_and_events/new_york_law_school_in_the_news.

41. Prepared Testimony of Robert J. Meyer, the Gayfryd Steinberg Professor of Marketing, The Wharton School, University of Pennsylvania, Before the Senate Commerce, Science, and Transportation Committee Hearing on Aggressive Sales Tactics on the Internet and Their Impact on American Consumers, Nov. 17, 2009, *available at* http://www.gpo.gov/fdsys/pkg/CHRG-111shrg54917/pdf/CHRG-111shrg54917.pdf and on Westlaw at 2009 WLNR 23261838 (explaining "[o]ptimism biases that cause consumers' to selectively interpret the information provided by the firm in a favorable (or trusting) light").

42. *See* Amended Complaint, Gomez-Jimenez v. New York Law School, Case No. 652226/2011 (Sup. Ct. of N.Y. Nov. 21, 2011) (hereafter, "NYLS Complaint").

43. Gomez-Jimenez, 943 N.Y.S.2d 834, 857 (Sup. Ct. 2012).

that its graduates were employed in permanent, full-time positions for which a JD[44] was required or preferred. The complaint alleged that, in reality, the post-graduation employment rate was grossly inflated because it included temporary positions funded by NYLS and part-time and temporary positions that were not in the legal field.

The complaints filed against NYLS and other law schools refer to the alleged deceptive employment reporting practices as "cooking the data"[45] and expose some of the dirty little secrets[46] in legal academia. Let's consider the practice of counting in the employment rate graduates employed in temporary, university-funded positions. It is no secret that recent graduates are employed in these positions because one can walk into almost any law school and find recent graduates working temporarily as research assistants, admissions recruiters, or career counselors. One dirty secret is that law schools counted these temporarily-employed, university workers to boost the overall employment rate, which created the impression in the minds of some that these graduates included in the employment rate were successfully employed as attorneys.

In addition to inflating the employment rate, the NYLS complaint alleged that the reported salary data was misleading because it implied the graduates had a greater earning potential than what all the graduates actually had. In Chapters 4 and 8, I describe the various ways law schools presented their salary data, and I leave it to the reader to decide whether the presentation of the data is misleading.

Unfortunately, for the NYLS graduates, Judge Schweitzer, in dismissing the complaint, found that NYLS did not expressly claim that its employment numbers consisted *solely* of graduates obtaining full-time, long-term employment as attorneys and found that NYLS had disclosed the fact that only 20–25% of graduates responded with salary information. Even though the judge tossed out the case, the graduates were right that the majority of NYLS's graduates do not have attorney jobs. Consider the fact that only 35.5% of NYLS's 2011 graduates had secured full-time, long-term attorney positions—the "real" attorney jobs—nine months after graduation.[47]

Optimism bias could have caused the NYLS graduates, at the time when they were prospective students, to fail to "read between the lines" when looking at the data and ignore the very real possibility that they would be unable to obtain an attorney position at a large law firm that paid a six-figure salary. Because most first-year law students have stellar undergraduate records, they assume they will graduate in the top 10% of their law school classes and, therefore, be one of the graduates obtaining a high-paying job as an attorney at a law firm. Moreover, optimism bias could have caused the students to not appreciate the fact that NYLS's salary data were based on a very small number of graduates responding to NYLS's questionnaire. Consequently, clouded by optimism bias, some prospective students incorrectly concluded that a six-figure salary was the norm. Thus, the prospective students would not have taken into account the possibility of ending up in the bottom half of the class and the probability of being unemployed or under-employed in a low-paying job after graduation.

---

44. A juris doctor, or doctor of jurisprudence, is abbreviated as JD and is the degree conferred by law schools to students completing all requirements for the degree.

45. *See, e.g.*, NYLS Complaint, paragraph 10.

46. I call these practices dirty little secrets because when I first heard about them, I felt that they were not intellectually honest. It is like taking a bath with your clothes on—you might be going through the right motions but you know there's something wrong with that.

47. *See* Chapter 2 for a full discussion. Also see Tables 1-1 and 1-2 in Appendix A.

A Comprehensive Analysis Must Provide Answers to Five Main Questions

To help prospective students overcome optimism bias, I demonstrate for them how to comprehensively analyze not only a school's employment and salary data but numerous other factors. Such an analysis should provide concrete answers to the following questions:

1. What are your chances of successfully matriculating[48] and ultimately graduating? To answer this question the current or prospective student would look at a school's admissions policy, attrition rate,[49] transfer-out data,[50] and academic support program.[51] A high attrition rate or high transfer-out number might suggest that the law school has insufficient academic support to help students to successfully matriculate and graduate.
2. How likely are your chances of passing the bar exam? Students who actually want to become attorneys need to look at the school's bar passage rate for first-time test takers. Bar passage is an absolute necessity in order to obtain a license to practice law. In addition to the bar passage rate, prospective and current students need to find out whether the school provides formal or informal bar-passage support. While students can pay for commercial courses, law-school-funded bar passage programs are recognized as an important method of instructing graduates, especially those at the bottom of the graduating class, about how to pass the bar exam the first time. The lower a person's LSAT score, the higher the probability that the person will not pass the bar exam on the first try. A school with a relatively-low bar passage rate and lacking a bar passage support program would not be a good option for students with low LSAT scores.
3. What are your job prospects? A student should ask about available career support services and should analyze the school's employment data. Under new standards adopted by the ABA, law schools are required to post on their websites employment data that reveal employment outcomes by status (e.g., full-time job requiring bar passage), by type (e.g., law firm position), and by duration (i.e., temporary

48. In the technical sense, matriculating means the act of enrolling in school. I use the terms matriculating or matriculation to broadly mean that a student enrolls in school and continues enrollment until the school's degree requirements have been satisfied. *See, e.g.*, Academic Regulations, AR 3-1.4, George Mason University School of Law, http://www.law.gmu.edu/academics/regulations (last visited Oct. 18, 2012) ("Maintenance of matriculation requires regular class participation and attendance, registration in the course of study required for the status and program the student has selected, successive registration for each fall and spring term of each academic year until study is completed, and compliance with all other relevant requirements.").

49. Attrition rate means the number of students that either flunkout or dropout. When I use the word "flunkout," I am not suggesting that the student in that position actually earned an "F" in one or more courses. A student can "flunkout" or be forced to leave if his or her cumulative GPA falls below 2.0. A dropout could have chosen to withdraw from law school for non-academic reasons, such as serious illness.

50. Transfer-out data means the number of students who withdraw from one law school and enroll in another law school. A high transfer-out rate may suggest that something is going on at that law school that is problematic and may be a signal to prospective students not to enroll in that law school.

51. Academic support programs are various programs directed primarily at first-year students to help them become acclimated to the demands of law school and the methods of successful study habits and exam-taking skills.

or long-term). I explain in Chapter 4 that although the new standards will lead to greater transparency, the prospective or current student should ***not*** take reported employment data at face value. Because the ABA failed to adequately address how each employment type and status can be manipulated, some schools will be able to hide in the employment data the graduates who are under-employed and, thereby, paint a rosier picture than the actual numbers indicate. For example, NYLS claims to have 10 graduates from its 2011 Class working in academia. Some visitors to its website will erroneously conclude these graduates employed in "academia" have faculty positions. Because it's highly unusual for a graduate to get a law professor position straight out of law school, one could reasonably conclude that some or most of the graduates that NYLS claims are working in academia are actually working in non-faculty positions, such as admissions counselors or research assistants.

4. What is your salary potential? Unfortunately, the ABA did not adopt new standards regarding the reporting of salary data. That means some law schools can continue the same salary reporting practices that some graduates found misleading. Moreover, some schools will elect not to disclose on their websites any salary information. As a result, prospective and current students must look to other third-party sources to attempt to assess the earning potential for graduates of a particular school. A very popular resource for such information is the National Association of Law Placement ("NALP"), which reports annually the starting median salaries for law graduates. NALP's salary data is only regional and not specific for the graduates of any particular law school. Consequently, even after performing a thorough research, students will still have to take the salary data obtained with a huge grain of salt and assume that they will earn less than the reported averages.
5. What resources does the law school have available to help you pay for your legal education? To answer this question, prospective and current students must first determine how much money is needed to cover tuition fees, book purchases, and cost of living expenses to obtain a legal education at the targeted law school. The students also need to find out if the law school has work-study positions for eligible law students and has programs available to help students find jobs during the summers and the school year to decrease the amount of borrowing. Next, students should apply for scholarships based on low-income status, leadership experience, or prior academic success. Assuming they qualify for one or more scholarships, the prospective and current students should look at the school's scholarship retention rates. Under new ABA standards, law schools must disclose their scholarship retention rates. The standards, however, do not require the school to disclose the minimum GPA or other requirements that the student must satisfy to retain a scholarship. As result, students that are offered a scholarship need to gain as much information as possible to assess how difficult it will be for them to retain the scholarship and decide how the loss of a scholarship will increase the amount of money that the students may have to borrow.

The above comprehensive analysis should be done for each school making an offer of admission. Rankings may be considered only *after* all other pertinent information has been obtained and assessed.

Applicants fortunate enough to have a high LSAT score are in the best position to borrow the least. With LSAT test-taking down and law school applications down and on-track for a 30-year low, law schools will be fighting over high-scoring applicants and offering them scholarships to get them to enroll. However, as I will explain more fully later, applicants need to make sure they enroll in a school that has a high percentage of graduates employed as full-time attorneys. A full scholarship may be meaningless from a school with a very low percentage of graduates employed as attorneys.

Although my comprehensive analysis requires students to do a cost-benefit analysis, the proverbial saying "you get what you pay for" does not hold true for some schools. Consider that NYLS charges high tuition cost in comparison to the majority of law schools; yet, my analysis of its employment data in Chapter 4 shows that a graduate of NYLS has a small chance of getting an attorney position. Consequently, a JD from NYLS would probably not be worth the price for students wanting such a position.

In this book, I will discuss all aspects of assessing whether a law degree is worth the price in this tough legal job market. I discuss numerous lawsuits asserting various legal theories by law graduates and former students against their law schools. If you are a prospective student, current law student, or recent law graduate, this book is worth reading because I analyze the five types of cases recently filed by distressed law students and graduates. They accuse law schools of the following: (1) negligently enrolling students, (2) misleading students about their lack of accreditation, (3) deceiving students about the employment and salary data of recent graduates, and (4) unlawfully dismissing students with poor academic performance. The fifth set of cases involves law students and graduates trying to get their student loan debt discharged—wiped out—in bankruptcy. The chapters will unfold as follows.

In Chapter 2, I discuss in depth the lawsuits accusing law schools of disseminating deceptive employment and salary data.[52] I analyze a state court judge's opinion dismissing the lawsuit filed against NYLS, and I explain why I believe this case was wrongly decided. Judge Melvin Schweitzer's decision is particularly alarming because he unequivocally concludes that all prospective law students are "sophisticated consumers," without basing his conclusion on any legal authority. Therefore, he seems to have zero tolerance for law graduates claiming they were deceived. He expects law school applicants to find and carefully examine all sources containing information about the law schools on their wish list. I am highly troubled at his conclusion that prospective law students are sophisticated consumers and, consequently, should be held to a higher standard than other consumers. In the pending lawsuits against other law schools, some judges may be tempted to follow Judge Schweitzer's flawed reasoning.

While Judge Gordon Quist did not "necessarily agree" with Judge Schweitzer's conclusion that law school applicants are sophisticated consumers, Judge Quist, when he dismissed

52. The following schools have been sued for reporting deceptive employment and salary data: Albany Law School at Union University; Brooklyn Law School; California Western School of Law; ITT Chicago-Kent College of Law; DePaul University College of Law; Florida Coastal School of Law; Golden Gate University School of Law; Hofstra University Maurice A. Deane School of Law; New York Law School; Texas Southern University Thurgood Marshall School of Law; The John Marshall Law School; Thomas M. Cooley School of Law; Thomas Jefferson School of Law; University of San Francisco School of Law; Southwestern Law School; and Widener University School of Law.

the Cooley lawsuit, suggested that some applicants failed to use their common sense. Although he stated that Cooley's employment reports were "inconsistent, confusing, and inherently untrustworthy,"[53] the graduates' lawsuit had to be dismissed for failing to prove fraud under Michigan law. He ended his opinion by declaring a mantra well known by lawyers: *caveat emptor*—let the buyer beware. Consequently, he puts the burden on prospective students to find out whether the law school is hiding relevant information to lure students.

Because the dismissal of the Cooley and NYLS lawsuits could mean bad news for graduates of other law schools, I feel this book is necessary to warn prospective and current law students. By examining NYLS's employment and salary data for 2009, I show that despite Judge Schweitzer's conclusion, a reasonable person could conclude that NYLS was misleading prospective students. In a later chapter, I explain how, in comparison to highly-ranked schools, like Cornell University Law School, NYLS continues to publish data that can be construed as misleading salary and employment information.

While I see some merit in these lawsuits, many see them as frivolous litigation, which may be condensed into the following simplistic argument:

> Dear Law Schools,
>
> You tricked us into accepting your offers of admission by claiming you are or would soon be accredited. Moreover, you bamboozled us into accepting by grossly inflating the success of your graduates in obtaining real attorney jobs. You should not have enrolled us in the first place because you should have known that we would not be able to accomplish our ultimate goal of becoming a lawyer. After you enrolled us, you should not have dismissed us from school after the first year of law school. Whether we got kicked out or we graduated, we are now strapped with a boat load of student loan debt and no prospects of getting a well-paying job. We have no choice but to file bankruptcy and try to convince a judge to wipe out our student loan debts because it poses too much of a hardship for us.
>
> Thanks For Nothing,
>
> Former Students

In commenting on the lawsuits asserting deceptive practices, Star Jones, a former prosecutor turned-TV-personality, suggested that the law graduates focus their energies, not on suing, but on finding jobs, and thereby implied that they were just a bunch of whiners.[54] I disagree with Star. I have built a reputation as an academic who writes about predatory lending and consumer protection issues. I condemn deceptive practices by many, including mortgage brokers and payday lenders.[55] I have even written about deceptive

53. John T. MacDonald Jr., et al., v. Thomas M. Cooley Law School and Does 1–20, No. 1:2011cv00831, U.S. Dist. LEXIS 100785, at *8 (W.D., Mich. Jul. 20, 2012) ("Sometimes hope and dreams triumph over experience and common sense.").

54. David Lat, *Are Disgruntled Law School Graduates a Bunch of 'Whiners'?*, Above the Law (Feb. 29, 2012), http://abovethelaw.com/2012/02/are-disgruntled-law-school-graduates-a-bunch-of-whiners/ (quoting Star Jones as saying "I hate whiners!").

55. Payday loans are single-payment, high-interest (typically more than 400%), small-dollar (e.g., $500), short-term (typically two weeks) loans that are due on the consumer' next payday. Payday loans are considered so predatory that Congress passed "a federal law that restricts payday lending by bank and non-bank lenders to military personnel in several ways, including capping the APR at 36% on loans to active-duty military members and their dependents." For more information, *see* Creola Johnson, *America's First Consumer Financial Watchdog is on a Leash: Can the CFPB Use its Authority to Declare Payday Loan Practices Unfair, Abusive, and Deceptive?*, 61 Catholic U. L. Rev. 381, 387 (2012).

practices perpetrated by fake online schools and for-profit colleges and universities.[56] The legal academy does not get a pass. While I believe most law professors across the country did not know personnel in career services were creating reports that obscured the number of graduates employed as attorneys,[57] law schools should still be held accountable for their employment reports. To the extent law schools have engaged in deceptive practices, they should be held liable by the courts or at least reprimanded by the ABA! Because the legal academy purports to teach the next generation of lawyers to practice law with high ethical standards, law schools should be held to that the highest standard when reporting their employment and salary data.

Some professors argue that I'm being too hard on law schools because they have not violated ABA standards. In Chapter 2, I explain to the reader that while it is true that law schools have not technically violated ABA standards by counting any graduate employed in *any* capacity, they have violated the spirit of the ABA standards to fairly and accurately report "basic consumer information." By failing to disclose the actual number of graduates who have successfully obtained jobs as attorneys, law schools have deprived law school applicants of valuable information in deciding which school to attend or in deciding not to attend at all.

Recognizing that the courts have largely sided with the legal academy, I feel that it is my duty to help prospective students to actually become sophisticated consumers. Even though the number of applications has declined steadily from a high of 87,500 applications in 2010 to only 59,426 as of August 2013, prospective students, in keeping with conventional wisdom, apply for admission to several law schools in hopes of getting an offer from at least one. According to the Law School Admission Council data, the 2013 applicants submitted 385,358 applications to ABA-approved schools for an average of 6.5 applications per applicant.[58] No doubt, many of these applicants, especially those with high LSAT scores, will get multiple admission offers. Because a six-figure student loan debt is no laughing matter, an applicant's enrollment decision should be made only after performing a comprehensive analysis of what each school has to offer.

---

56. *See* Creola Johnson, *Degrees of Deception: Are Consumers and Employers Being Duped by Online Diploma Mills and Universities?*, 32 J.C. & U.L. 411 (2006); Creola Johnson, *Credentialism and the Proliferation of Fake Degrees: The Employer Pretends to Need a Degree: The Employee Pretends to Have One*, 23 Hofstra Lab. & Emp. L.J. 269, 288–93 (2006).

57. The reason why I assert that most law professors did not know what was going is because most regular (non-dean) law professors are too busy preparing for classes and trying to research and write to publish law review articles. Generally-speaking, career services personnel do not hold law faculty positions and do not come from the ranks of regular faculty members. See Sample Career Services Job Description, Nat'l Assoc. of Law Placement, http://www.nalp.org/samplecareerservicesjobdescription#dir1 (last visited March 27, 2013). I believe career services personnel are operating in almost a black-box like environment, and law school deans are the only ones that actually know or should know what's going in the black box. *See* Paul Horwitz, *What Ails the Law Schools?*, 111 Mich. L. Rev. (2013) ("Faculty members have little involvement in a variety of increasingly bureaucratized functions like career services, loans, and budgeting; they have relatively little knowledge about what most of their students do after graduation; and they have little personal incentive to devote time to structural reform."). Many law professors learned for the first time that career services personnel were accused of misrepresenting employment data when David Segal wrote about it in 2011. *See* David Segal, *Is Law School a Losing Game?*, N.Y. Times, Jan. 9, 2011, at BU1.

58. *See* Three-Year ABA Volume Comparison, LSAC, Aug. 8, 2013, http://lsac.org/docs/default-source/data-(lsac-resources)-docs/three-year-volume-2013.pdf (indicating that the tally of 59,426 is likely the final count for applications for admission to the Fall 2013 entering class); Shawn P. O'Connor, Look for These 3 Law School Trends in 2012, US News & World Rep., Jan. 2, 2012 (describing 9.6% decrease in LSAT test-takers as well as a 9.9% decrease in law school applications to 78,900 in 2011 to from 87,500 in 2010).

In Chapter 3, I explain how to do a comprehensive, sophisticated analysis of a school's data, including employment and salary data, if a prospective student is considering a school's offer of admission or if a current law student is considering transferring to that law school. This book is *not* about how to apply for admission or how to succeed once enrolled in law school. It is about how to decide whether a school's admission or transfer offer is worth accepting. Table 1-1 below identifies 21 factors that should be considered when doing a comprehensive analysis. Note that the school's ranking is not on the table. Later in book, I discuss the *limited* contexts in which a school's ranking can be considered.

Table 1-1. Factors to Consider

Broad Considerations	Individual Factors to Consider
1. Matriculation & Graduation Success	1. Admission policy 2. Attrition rate 3. Transfer-out number 4. Diversity of those in the attrition and transfer out numbers 5. Academic support programs
2. Bar Passage Likelihood	1. Bar-passage rate 2. University-provided bar-exam prep support
3. Employment Prospects	1. Employment status for last 3 years 2. Employment type for last 3 years 3. Overall employment rate for last 3 years 4. Career services support
4. Salary Potential	1. Salary data for employment type or status 2. Salary data published by NALP and others
5. Pre-Law School Assessment of How to Pay for Education	1. Cost of tuition and cost of living expenses 2. Scholarship offers 3. Scholarship retention rate 4. Curve for retention of scholarships 5. Work available during semesters and summers 6. Work-study availability and criteria 7. Student loan amount 8. Loan forgiveness or payment-reduction programs

To demonstrate how a sophisticated analysis can be done, in Chapter 3, I compare Cooley with the University of Cincinnati College of Law ("Cincinnati"). Cooley is America's largest producer of law graduates from its five campus locations and was sued for allegedly reporting deceptive employment and salary data. My analyses of both schools demonstrate that, if one totally ignores rankings, Cincinnati, a second-tier[59] school, is a better value than Cooley, a fourth tier school, but not for obvious reasons. The reader should not jump to the conclusion that this comparison of Cooley and Cincinnati confirms the *US News* rankings system. In a later chapter, I compare a first-tier school with a second-tier school and demonstrate that an education from the latter school is a better value.

59. *US News* ranks law schools into four tiers in descending rank, with the first tier comprising schools considered to be the best law schools.

My comprehensive analyses are not meant to deter people from going to law school if they have a desire to become a lawyer. Instead, I want law school applicants to become the sophisticated consumers some courts presume them to be. I do not want future law school applicants to wind up like the unhappy law graduates who sued Cooley and NYLS as well as the many unhappy, unemployed and under-employed graduates of first and second-tier schools. Some law graduates have gotten into a lot of debt pursing a law degree only to end up earning a salary that is no better than or even less than what they had earned in their pre-law-school positions. Becoming sophisticated consumers is, therefore, paramount.

In Chapter 4, I discuss the ABA's attempt to require law schools to be more transparent when disclosing data relevant to law school applicants. Unfortunately, the ABA's new standards still leave law schools with a lot of discretion—"wiggle room"—and, therefore, law school applicants cannot simply accept employment data at face value but must try to decipher what the numbers actually mean. For example, in Chapter 4, I compiled a list of the top 17 "expensive" law schools, ranked in order of highest tuition. I compare Cornell to NYLS (ranked first and seventeenth, respectively) and I show that Cornell has more transparent information that appears to comply almost perfectly with the new ABA standards. NYLS's reports now disclose more information, but they may still leave the reader wondering if the numbers are reported in a manner that hides potentially negative results. Similarly, when analyzing the data reported on the websites of other law schools, I demonstrate that some schools could do a better job of disclosing relevant data.

In Chapter 5, I shift the discussion from ABA-approved schools to unaccredited law schools, a category of schools that can pose much greater risks to prospective law students. I describe one lawsuit where a former student makes a unique claim of negligent enrollment—that an unaccredited law school should have never allowed the student to matriculate. This rare lawsuit is very important because it will allow me to discuss a huge issue that has received very little media attention: is attending an unaccredited law school too risky and, therefore, not worth the price? The lawsuit involves Duncan School of Law at Lincoln Memorial University, which recently lost its ABA provisional approval. The risks of attending an unaccredited law school such as Duncan are numerous—including the graduate's inability to take a state's bar exam and inability to become a licensed attorney in most states. Duncan is one of several newly opened law schools. The University of Massachusetts at Dartmouth, for instance, recently acquired a previously unaccredited law school. Cooley opened its fifth location in Tampa, Florida in May 2012 and its Ann Arbor, Michigan campus recently became ABA accredited. Because the economic downturn has not stopped the proliferation of law schools, prospective law students must cautiously assess whether a newly-accredited or non-ABA-accredited law school is a wise investment.

In Chapter 6, I move the discussion from alleged bad practices to entice an applicant to enroll to alleged practices that result in the "weeding out" of law students. In a lawsuit by two former students alleging that Thurgood Marshall School of Law unlawfully dismissed them, the former students argued that they should have been permitted to remain in school even though their cumulative GPAs at the end of the first year fell below 2.0. This lawsuit serves as a warning to prospective students that they should *not* get swept away in the excitement of receiving an offer of admission, but should look at a law school's attrition rates, transfer rates, and academic support services. Otherwise, an applicant could enroll in a law school thinking it was a good option but later be forced to withdraw and become burdened with student loan debt and no viable job prospects. While students forced out for academic reasons may draw little sympathy, prospective students need to consider the possibility that they could be in that position. Therefore, prospective students need to find out how committed a law school is to working with students striving earnestly to bring up their grades so that they can graduate.

In Chapter 7, I discuss recent scandals where admissions personnel at two different law schools falsified the undergraduate GPAs and LSAT scores of entering first-year students to make them appear more accomplished than they actually were. These scandals allow us to peek into the world of frenzied attempts by law schools to improve, by any means necessary, their spot in the *US News* rankings. I discuss how the ABA fined Illinois $250,000 and sanctioned it for submitting false admissions data and how this is a step in the right direction for the ABA. In keeping with my recommendation that prospective students should do a comprehensive analysis of each targeted law school, I compare Illinois, one of the schools admitting to the admissions scandal, with the University of Nebraska College of Law ("Nebraska"). Through this comparison, I show that even though Illinois still has a higher *US News* ranking than Nebraska, Illinois is not a better value if one has to borrow money to pay for the legal education. I come to that conclusion because (1) Illinois costs substantially more than Nebraska, (2) Illinois has a higher percentage of unemployed graduates than Nebraska, and (3) Illinois has a lower employment rate than Nebraska.[60]

Like a graduate of Illinois, a graduate of Villanova University School of Law may not fare well in comparison to lower-ranked schools in the second tier because Villanova is another school exposed in an admissions scandal. Because Illinois and Villanova manipulated numbers to achieve higher rankings, both schools have slipped in the *US News* rankings, opposite of their intended effect. Note these are just the schools that got caught. If these two schools, which previously enjoyed very good reputations, were inflating GPAs and LSAT scores, one has to wonder what is happening at other law schools. The ABA relies on the honesty of law schools to submit accurate information and does not audit the information submitted. As a result, law school applicants need to ignore or heavily discount a school's ranking with *US News* when deciding whether to enroll in the law school.

In Chapter 8, I summarize what actions the ABA has taken regarding its oversight of ABA-approved schools, and I explain how the ABA's actions leave much to be desired. Even though it has authority over ABA-approved law schools, the ABA has failed in some respects and, therefore, places students at the mercy of law schools to disclose truthful information. For example, the ABA has no standards for schools to follow when establishing programs concentrating in specialized areas of the law and offering certificates for students completing the coursework for those programs. That means the schools can advertise these specialty programs in a way that conveys the impression that students who complete their programs have better employment opportunities than graduates of a law schools lacking such programs.[61] The ABA also lacks standards for establishing and operating advance law degree programs, most of which confer a master's of law, commonly referred to as a LL.M. degree. Because the ABA does not impose any standards for employment outcomes for LL.M. programs, law schools can cleverly market their LL.M. programs and, thereby, entice people who already hold JDs to borrow as much as $60,000 to obtain an LL.M. degree even though that degree may not make them any more employable.

In Chapters 9 through 11, I stress three main points for consideration by prospective and current law students who still have a strong desire to practice law. First, while the

60. The employment data is about the success of the 2011 graduates from both schools.

61. I am intentionally choosing not to mention any program here because I do not want to appear to be unduly critical of any school in particular.

US has too many lawyers who want traditional law firm jobs, the US does not have enough lawyers willing and capable of representing low-to-moderate income families by providing free or affordable legal services. Second, current and prospective law students who want traditional law firm jobs need to wake-up to the reality that many of those jobs are gone and will never return. Post-recession, the legal job market has experienced a surge in staff, contract, and temporary attorney jobs that pay substantially less than traditional, entry-level, law-firm jobs. Another post-recession reality is that more and more graduates are forced into solo practice. My third point, which builds on the first and second points, is that law schools need to expand clinical programs that produce "practice-ready" graduates trained with basic skills expected of practicing attorneys and need to create incubator programs that prepare graduates to start successful solo practices.

I introduce the real life stories of recent law graduates in Chapter 12. The narratives[62] in this book provide cautionary tales as well as glimmers of hope. The narratives tell the stories of law graduates with a range of diversity that goes beyond race and gender. Some of the narratives are from graduates of highly-ranked law schools as well as schools that have lawsuits pending against them. This suggests that while some graduates feel that they were deceived by their law schools, other graduates of those schools do not feel the same way. Instead, some graduates believe that they must work harder to find legal jobs in an economy still recovering from the recession.

Why narratives? I use narratives to challenge prospective and current law students to ***not*** be driven by optimism bias in their law school selection process. If students assume they will graduate in the top 10% or that enrollment in a highly-ranked school guarantees employment at a big law firm, the students may fail to examine crucial factors that should be considered when selecting a law school. This book uses narratives because a book that only describes the objective facts about the legal job market will be ineffective in getting some prospective students to weigh all factors in the law school selection process. Research shows that narrative evidence is more effective than statistical evidence in increasing one's chances of acting in his or her own best self-interest. For example, in a study of men at risk for Hepatitis B, the men accurately perceived their risk of Hepatitis B infection to be greater—and showed higher intentions to get vaccinated—after reading about someone else's personal experience with Hepatitis B than after simply reviewing statistical evidence.[63]

In this book, you will read the story of Ted,[64] the No. 2 graduate in 2007 from Thurgood Marshall School of Law, who took a non-legal job paying only $10.00 per hour because he did not get any job offers from Houston-area law firms. He now has a well-paying job as an attorney, but, for a while, he questioned the wisdom of going to law school.

Anita's[65] story reflects a frequent outcome for graduates of 1st and 2nd tier law schools. Even though Anita graduated in 2007 from a 2nd tier law school, she has only been able to find steady work as a project attorney, hired through a legal temp agency, doing mostly

62. The narratives are under fictitious names because several of the graduates are not employed in optimal job situations and, therefore, want to preserve their ability to apply for any future promising job opportunities.

63. John de Wit et al., *What Works Best: Objective Statistics or a Personal Testimonial? An Assessment of the Persuasive Effects of Different Types of Message Evidence on Risk Perception*, 27 Health Psychology 110 (2008).

64. Ted is a fictitious name.

65. Anita is a fictitious name and her alma mater has not been revealed to preserve her identity.

document review[66] for big firms in New York City. Because the work has been steady, Anita is content. However, some consider her "under-employed" because she is only a temporary attorney who is unable to use the full range of her legal knowledge and skills, and she has no employer-provided health insurance and other benefits associated with being a permanent law-firm attorney.

Similarly, Tara,[67] who graduated from a first-tier law school, was hired by a law firm as a "staff attorney" in a non-partner track position. This means that Tara does the same work as an entry-level attorney hired in a partner-track position, but Tara's starting salary was less than half the salary of a new attorney in the partner-track position, and Tara can never become a profit-sharing partner in the firm. Like Anita, some would consider Tara under-employed. But unlike Anita, Tara is unhappy with her employment status because she has no passion for the work. When she could not find a job specializing in the area of law that she was passionate about, she felt compelled to take the staff attorney job so she could start paying back her six-figure student loan debt.

You will read several other riveting stories. Some stories may appear at times depressing. They are intended to make prospective students critically think about whether the time is right to go to law school and, if so, which law school delivers the best legal education for an affordable price. Two of the narratives showcase students who transferred to higher ranked schools. I use their stories to show when transferring may be a wise decision. After each narrative, I give my analysis regarding what lessons could be learned from each graduate and what the graduates could have done, if anything, to achieve more desirable outcomes.

Hopefully, after the reading the narratives in this book, prospective students considering enrolling in law school and current students considering transferring to another school will be able to correctly prioritize the factors that should be considered before becoming indebted for more than $100,000.

Because the burden of becoming a sophisticated buyer of legal education involves a huge financial decision—how much should one borrow—I want to apprise all law school applicants, current students, and recent graduates about the various ways of dealing with substantial student loan debt. In Chapter 13, I discuss filing bankruptcy as a means of dealing with stratospheric student loan debt. I discuss several cases, including one involving Carol Todd, a woman who has Asperger's Syndrome and who accumulated $320,000 in student loan debt after attending numerous institutions, including the University of Baltimore School of Law. She was able to meet the hardship test to get her student loan debt discharged because her disease and other ailments made her unemployable. Her case should be understood as an exception, not the rule. Although bankruptcy is the proper venue for trying to get student loan discharged, the standard for discharge is to show a substantial "hardship," and this is very difficult to prove.

Most law graduates will not be able to meet that hardship standard; therefore, I think the better approach is for law school applicants to learn early on in the process about various loan forgiveness programs for law graduates working in certain types of positions and payment-reduction programs for graduates earning salaries below a certain amount. I explain in Chapter 14 how students can qualify for loan forgiveness or reduced-payment

66. Document review is a term used to describe work where an attorney identifies, retrieves, reviews, and produces documents that are potentially relevant to the claims in a pending litigation. The majority of document review work is now done on a computer. Most lawyers consider this work mind-numbing and unsatisfactory. I have done this work before, and I concur based on my experience.

67. Tara is a fictitious name and her alma mater has not been revealed to preserve her identity.

programs designed to address the needs of lower-income graduates. I assert that because student loan debt can be an enormous burden, students cannot afford to put off until after graduation a strategy for dealing with student loan debt. Such debt must be considered before, during, and after attending law school. I urge students to consider loan forgiveness programs, of which there are several. For example, the federal government has two types of programs: Income Based Repayment ("IBR") and Public Service Loan Forgiveness ("PSLF"). Graduates with large debt relative to income are eligible to pay a much smaller monthly loan payment than under a standard 10-year repayment plan. I explain fully the limitations of the IBR program, but that generally-speaking, graduates following the IBR payment plan can have any remaining loan balance forgiven after 25 years of payment.

Similarly, PSLF helps graduates who take public interest jobs, which are the lowest-paid jobs of traditional attorney positions. Those who are committed to public service can take public interest jobs without fearing their modest salaries will prevent them from handling their student loan debts. To qualify, these law graduates must work in public service for 10 years and make 120 qualifying monthly payments. After this 10-year payment period ends, all debt is forgiven, which is much faster forgiveness than under the IBR program.

One major down-side of qualifying for either the IBR or PSLF program is that only federal loans can be dealt with through these programs. As a result, graduates still have to make all required payments for *private* student loans. Therefore, students should avoid, if at all possible, getting private loans while in law school.

Another option for graduates is Loan Repayment Assistance Programs ("LRAPs"). Some schools, 17 states, and the federal government have LRAPs, but requirements differ for each program. Unfortunately, LRAPs have limited funding and are at risk of being defunded. As a result, graduates should always seek to qualify for federal IBR and PSLF programs. Because bankruptcy is not an option for most law graduates,[68] law students must vigorously pursue loan forgiveness and payment-reduction programs. I conclude Chapter 14 by urging those who still want to be lawyers to enroll in law school because viable ways of dealing with student loan debt exist.

Lest anyone thinks that I'm advocating that students not worry about how much debt they amass, I strongly urge students in Chapter 15 to borrow as little money as possible. That's because too much debt could pose an obstacle to a graduate obtaining a license to practice law. In order to become a licensed attorney in any state, the applicant must pass a character and fitness test. Increasingly, bar examiners and courts are scrutinizing an applicant's level of indebtedness and whether the applicant has a plan that adequately addresses how to pay off the debt. The reason why I'm a devoting a whole chapter to this issue is because several state courts have recently denied applicants the ability to take the bar exam or to be admitted even though they have passed the bar exam.

An opinion by the Ohio Supreme Court is especially troubling because it did *not* approve of a graduate's handling of his student loan debt and, therefore, denied him the ability to sit for the bar exam. Tom Smith,[69] who graduated in 2008 with $170,000 in student loan debt, did what many graduates are doing in this tough legal job market. He held on to his part-time job at a public defender's office that paid only $12 an hour in hopes that he

68. Bankruptcy *is not* a good option if a person's primary motivation is to convince a court to wipe out the student loan debt. However, bankruptcy *is* a good option for those who frequently cannot pay their bills and who want to file bankruptcy to create a feasible payment plan for repaying student loan debt.

69. Although this case is a matter of public record, I have decided to use a fictitious name to prevent any further embarrassment or harm to Mr. Smith.

could parlay it into a full-time attorney job once he passed the bar exam and got a license to practice law. Because his part-time income was too low to make student loan payments, the Ohio Supreme Court decided that Mr. Smith had no plan to repay his debts and implied that he should abandon his *part-time legal* job and get a *full-time* ***non-legal*** job to pay back his student loan debt. Even though Mr. Smith had no criminal record and no problem with drugs or alcohol, the Court kicked an under-employed law graduate when he was already down—denying him the chance to take the Ohio bar exam until he got a satisfactory plan to deal with his debt. I hope his tragic story as well as others will help law students avoid being put in a catch-22 situation—unable to get a law license due to student loan debt and unable to then get the attorney job that would help you pay down the debt.

Now, let's turn to Chapter 2 where we will pull back the curtain and discover the shady reporting practices among some law schools that enables them to inflate the employment outcomes of their graduates. You will learn that some high-price law degrees may turn out to be a "vanity degrees"—they look good in the picture frames but they do not make you employable as an attorney.

Chapter 2

The Judges' Message Is "Let the Buyer Beware," Instead of "Let the Liar Beware"

Caveat Emptor is a well-known phrase among lawyers, and it is Latin for "let the buyer beware." It was the law of the land in the early part of the 20th century. By the 1970s, state and federal courts and lawmakers had abandoned that old rule in favor of a more forgiving approach. Today, "*[c]aveat emptor* has no place in modern society, which demands disclosure, honesty and good faith."[1] When discussing passage of a federal consumer protection statute, the United States Supreme Court stated that the law's passage "reflect[ed] a transition in congressional policy from a philosophy of 'Let the buyer beware' to one of 'Let the seller disclose.'"[2]

Instead of holding New York Law School ("NYLS")—the seller of legal education—accountable for failing to disclose material information about the employment outcomes of its graduates, Judge Melvin Schweitzer let the law school off the hook for hiding potentially negative data from its reports. Without citing any legal authority, Judge Schweitzer assumes all law school applicants are sophisticated consumers and, therefore, should not have been misled by NYLS's employment reports. Judges in two other cases add insult to injury by implying that the law graduates of two law schools were lacking in "common sense." These judges' decisions, even if correctly decided under the law, send the wrong message to prospective law students. That message is that while prospective students should expect some law schools to hide negative facts just as quickly as a used car salesman, the burden is nevertheless on the students to not be tricked by their practices.

The Lawsuits

Since 2011, law graduates and former law students have filed lawsuits against seventeen different law schools located in eight different states.[3] The following schools have been sued for allegedly reporting deceptive data, unlawfully dismissing students, and negligently enrolling a student: Albany Law School at Union University; Brooklyn Law School;

1. Plaintiffs' Memorandum of Law in Opposition to Defendants' Motion for Summary Judgment, Krumholz v. AJA, LLC, No. 08-cv-12137-JLT, 2009 WL 5046211 (D. Mass. Aug. 19, 2009). Harris v. M & S Toyota, Inc., 575 So.2d 74, 78 (Ala.1991) (explaining that modern law shifts the paradigm from "let the buyer beware," to "let the liar beware").

2. Mourning v. Family Publications Service, Inc., 411 U.S. 356, 378 (1973).

3. The law schools that have been sued are located in California, Delaware, Florida, Illinois, Michigan, New York, Tennessee, and Texas.

California Western School of Law; ITT Chicago-Kent College of Law; DePaul University College of Law; Florida Coastal School of Law; Golden Gate University School of Law; Hofstra University Maurice A. Deane School of Law; Lincoln Memorial University's John J. Duncan Jr. School of Law; New York Law School; Texas Southern University Thurgood Marshall School of Law; The John Marshall Law School; Thomas M. Cooley School of Law; Thomas Jefferson School of Law; University of San Francisco School of Law; Southwestern Law School; and Widener University School of Law.[4]

In the majority of the recently-filed lawsuits, law graduates alleged that their laws schools violated state law by reporting deceptive and false statements as to the employment rates and salaries of their schools' graduates. This chapter will focus on the lawsuits filed against Thomas M. Cooley School of Law ("Cooley") and NYLS because they are representative of the majority of the lawsuits that have been filed and because their dismissals signal bad news for law graduates seeking relief from the courts.

In Table 2-1 (next page), I identify the schools accused of reporting deceptive data and the range of employment rates that they have claimed for three or more years. As indicated in column three, except for Cooley, most of the law schools claimed to have an employment rate of 90% or better during at least one of the relevant years discussed in the complaints.

Note that a majority of the schools sued made admission offers to more than 50% of the applicants, nearly all of the schools had attrition rates[5] greater than 10%, and some had relatively low bar passage rates for first-time takers.[6] Unlike these law schools, highly selective schools—those that admit a small percentage of applicants—usually have much higher rates of graduates employed as attorneys, have much lower attrition rates, and have higher bar passage rates. In later chapters, I will analyze available information about the law schools that have been sued and show the negative implications of these attending schools. As more fully discussed later, it turns out that at most of these schools, **less than 50%** of their 2011 graduates (nine months after graduation) had full-time, long-term jobs that require passage of the bar exam—the actual attorney jobs.

In March 2012, the lawsuit brought by the graduates of NYLS was the first of the lawsuits alleging deceptive employment data to be dismissed. It was quickly followed by the dismissal in July 2012 of the lawsuit filed against Cooley.[7] I will first start my discussion with the Cooley case. Although both lawsuits were dismissed, the legal bases for dismissal differ substantially.

I will discuss applicable Michigan and New York laws so that you can understand why I assert that one case was correctly decided and the other was wrongly decided. As a result this chapter is for those who want something more than media sound bites. Prospective and current law students should be keenly interested in case law that impacts future law graduates. This chapter lays the groundwork for my assertion in Chapter 8 that law schools can continue to report misleading data even under newly-revised ABA standards for reporting by law schools.

---

4. For those who care about rankings, most of these law schools are ranked in the second, third and fourth tier by U.S. News. Lincoln Memorial University's John J. Duncan Jr. School of Law is not ranked because it is not approved by the ABA at this time.

5. The attrition rate means students who withdraw for failing to satisfy the minimum GPA requirement and who withdraw for other reasons.

6. Note that one's passing of the bar exam is not a guarantee of finding traditional employment as an attorney.

7. The lawsuits filed against Albany, Chicago-Kent, DePaul, and John Marshall-Chicago have been dismissed.

Table 2-1.

Law Schools Sued for Reporting Deceptive Data	Alleged Employ't Rates Claimed by Schools√	FT Applicants+	FT Offers+	FT Offer Rate	# of FT Enrollees+	Full-Time Tuition Resident & Non-Resident+	1st Time Bar Passage Rate**	1st Year Overall Attrition Rate*	2nd Year Overall Attrition Rate*
Albany Law School	90–97%	2,572	1,234	48.0%	236	$40,120	82.89%	2.7%	5.4%
Brooklyn Law School	88–98%	5,053	1,447	28.6%	417	$46,635	87.97%	6.3%	0.4%
Cal. Western Law School	90–93%	2,628	1,228	46.7%	355	$40,780	77.93%	18.8%	1.0%
Chicago-Kent Law School	90–97%	3,340	1,573	47.1%	248	$40,050	95.17%	10.5%	2.1%
Cooley School of Law	76–82%	4,221	3,553	84.2%	260	$30,644	77.41%	14.8%	14.9%
Depaul Law School	88–98%	5,109	2,094	41.0%	257	$39,350	92.39%	9.1%	0.3%
Florida Coastal Law School	80–95%	6,021	4,174	69.3%	782	$34,712	78.77%	21.4%	6.8%
Golden Gate Law School	80–95%	2,276	1,326	58.3%	268	$38,375	64.16%	20.6%	2.6%
Hofstra Univ. Law School	91–96%	4,851	1,922	39.6%	355	$43,660	76.54%	13.7%	4.4%
John Marshall Law School	90–100%	2,941	1,385	47.1%	437	$36,920	85.11%	23.5%	3.6%
New York Law School	90–92%	3,685	1,821	49.4%	520	$46,460	81.14%	10.6%	0.9%
San Francisco Law School	90–95%	4,163	1,350	32.4%	184	$38,800	78.33%	12.7%	4.1%
Southwestern Law School	97–98%	3,383	980	29.0%	295	$39,110	61.23%	9.3%	11.0%
Thomas Jefferson L.S.	56–92%	2,776	1,375	49.5%	318	$19,350	48.15%	31.4%	6.1%
Widener Law School	OVER 90%	1,869	1,096	58.6%	259	$34,890	85.85%	25.4%	0.0%

Data Source: 2012 LSAC Guide.

* Attrition—2009 first-year students who dropped out or flunked out; + Data by LSAC for entering class of Fall 2010; ** For Grads who took bar exam during 2009; √ Alleged in lawsuits filed by Grads.

Compliance with the ABA as a Defense

Before discussing the specifics cases, I want to address the ABA's pre-2012 standard regarding disclosure of information. Prior to the adoption in August 2012 of final revisions to ABA Standard 509, the ABA failed to identify precisely what employment data law schools had to disclose. The pre-2012 version of Standard 509 stated the following: "A law school shall publish basic consumer information. The information shall be published in a fair and accurate manner reflective of actual practice."[8] ABA Interpretation 509-1 stated that basic consumer information included, among other things, "placement rates and bar passage data." Interpretation 509-4 obligated law schools to "fairly and accurately" report consumer information, but it failed to identify any particular placement data that law schools must disclose.[9] As a result, even though law students and graduates are understandably upset over the fact that law schools have boasted very high overall employment rates, the pre-2012 version of Standard 509 did not expressly obligate law schools to disclose the *actual* number of graduates employed as long-term, full-time attorneys. Therefore, the law schools that have been sued are defending their reporting practices on the basis that they have complied with the ABA standards and, thus, are not liable for wrongdoing. As discussed later in this chapter, one judge described the ABA's pre-2012 reporting requirement as "so vague and incomplete as to be meaningless."[10] That means that if law graduates are going to succeed in lawsuits against their schools, they cannot rely on the ABA's pre-2012 reporting requirement but must instead convince a court that state consumer laws have been violated.

Cooley Grads Cannot Sue under Michigan's Consumer Protection Law

John T. MacDonald, Jr., along with eleven other Cooley graduates, filed a complaint alleging that Cooley deceived, defrauded, and misled the graduates about their employment prospects when the school's officials repeatedly reported grossly inflated employment and salary data about its graduates. The graduates alleged that such practices resulted in Cooley committing fraud and violating Michigan's consumer protection statute. My discussion of Judge Gordon Quist's opinion first begins with his assessment of the graduates' fraud claim against Cooley.

---

8. *Standards and Rules of Procedure for Approval of Law Schools 2011–2012*, ABA Section of Legal Education and Admissions to the Bar 40–41, http://www.americanbar.org/content/dam/aba/publications/misc/legal_education/Standards/standardsarchive/2011_2012_standards_and_rules_complete_book.authcheckdam.pdf (last visited Dec. 20, 2012).

9. Prior to the 2012 revisions, Interpretation 509-4 provided the following:

> Standard 509 requires a law school fairly and accurately to report basic consumer information whenever and wherever that information is reported or published. A law school's participation in the Council-designated publication referred to in Interpretation 509-2 and its provision of fair and accurate information for that book does not excuse a school from the obligation to report fairly and accurately all basic consumer information published in other places or for other purposes.

Id. at 41–42.

10. MacDonald v. Thomas M. Cooley Law School, U.S. Dist. LEXIS 100785, at *9 (W.D., Mich. Jul. 20, 2012).

Under Michigan law, in order to prove fraud based on false representation, the graduates needed to show that they had reasonably relied on Cooley's employment reports. I will discuss this in more detail below, but to prevail, the students had to prove by clear and convincing evidence that without Cooley's skewed employment reports, they would not have attended Cooley. The graduates did not persuade Judge Quist of this and so their only remaining hope was to rely on Michigan's state consumer protection law to prove their case

In order to prevail using Michigan's consumer protection law, the graduates had two hurdles to cross: first, they needed to prove that the law applied to the purchase of a legal education and then, second, prove that Cooley had violated that law.

The Michigan Consumer Protection Act ("MCPA") declares as unlawful "[u]nfair, unconscionable, or deceptive methods, acts, or practices in the conduct of trade or commerce," which is defined as "providing goods, property, or service primarily for personal, family, or household purposes."[11] Based on this statutory language, Michigan courts hold that "if an item is purchased primarily for business or commercial rather than personal purposes, the MCPA does not supply protection."[12] The purpose for which an item is purchased is important. Accordingly, protection under the MCPA depends on how the consumer puts the product to use.[13]

In applying the above legal standard, Judge Quist found that the Cooley graduates did not have a claim under the MCPA. Judge Quist held that people entering into law school do so primarily for a *business* purpose because they "purchase a legal education in order to make money as lawyers." Consequently, the graduates failed to cross the first hurdle and their claim that Cooley violated Michigan's consumer protection statute had to be dismissed. To use an analogy, Judge Quist provided an example about the purchase of a woodworking machine: "purchasing a new woodworking machine might make the owner of a small furniture company more productive, more money, and, therefore, happier, but the purchase is still for business or commercial rather than for personal purposes." To drive home the point even further, Judge Quist stated that, "[e]ven the president of a major company of one type or another may receive personal pleasure from the acquisition of another company or machine, but this would not change the fundamental purpose of the purchase—'primarily for business or commercial.'"[14]

11. Mich. Comp. Laws Ann. § 445.903 (West 2012).

12. MacDonald v. Thomas M. Cooley Law School, U.S. Dist. LEXIS 100785, at *2 (W.D., Mich. Jul. 20, 2012).

13. Zine v. Chrysler Corp, 236 Mich. App. 261, 273, 600 N.W.2d 384, 393 (Mich. Ct. App. 1999); Sautner v. Fleetwood Enters., No. 05-73252, 2007 U.S. Dist. LEXIS 33564, 2007 WL 1343806, at *7 (E.D. Mich. May 8, 2007).

14. MacDonald, U.S. Dist. LEXIS 100785, at *14.

Judge Quist Never Reached the Merits of the Consumer Protection Claim

What prospective students need to understand is that Judge Quist never reached the merits of the graduates' consumer protection claim. A lawsuit based on statutory law has two components: (1) the plaintiffs demonstrating that the law applies to them and (2) the plaintiffs proving that the defendant actually broke that law. The Cooley decision means that because the claim was dismissed before even getting to the second part; the graduates never got to introduce evidence proving that Cooley's employment reports were deceptive and, therefore, in violation of Michigan law. I argue that if their claim had been covered under the Act (i.e., they had gotten over hurdle number one), it is possible they would have been successful jumping hurdle two.

The MCPA requires a plaintiff to show an act or practice is deceptive by showing that the business "[f]ail[ed] to reveal a material fact, the omission of which tends to mislead or deceive the consumer, and which fact could not reasonably be known by the consumer."[15] The graduates' argument, taken as a whole, is that Cooley has omitted material facts about the number of graduates employed in temporary and permanent jobs and in part-time and full-time employment, thereby violating the MCPA. At the time this case was filed, such information was not obtainable by the general public. However, law schools like Cooley already had this information because they submit to NALP detailed employment data that differentiates between temporary and permanent jobs, between part-time and full-time employment, and between legal and non-legal jobs. Unfortunately, NALP does not make the data for individual schools available to the public. Instead, NALP compiles all of the data submitted by the schools and then reports the aggregate data for all law schools. As Judge Quist noted, because Cooley and other law schools already compile this data and disclose it to NALP and other third parties, Cooley could have disclosed to its prospective students more information than what it chose to reveal.[16] As a result, the graduates would have argued that since some of the detailed employment figures were notably unfavorable to Cooley, its failure to make such information available is a failure to disclose a material fact in violation of state law.

While the raw data Cooley submitted to NALP was unavailable to the graduates when they were prospective students, the court could have examined Cooley's public reports for the last 7 years to determine whether there was a pattern of concealing negative information and obscuring data. As shown below, in the year 2005, Cooley reported that it had five graduates employed in a category called "Banking/Financial" and identified an employer, Beacon Hill Staffing Group, which is a temp agency that finds temporary positions in various fields, including law.[17] A reasonable interpretation is that at least one graduate in the "Banking/Financial" category was working temporarily.

15. Mich. Comp. Laws Ann. § 445.903(s) (West 2012).

16. *MacDonald*, U.S. Dist. LEXIS 100785, at *14.

17. *Specialties*, Beacon Hill Staffing Group, http://www.beaconhillstaffing.com/OurSpecialties/Introduction/tabid/196/Default.aspx (last visited Jun. 21, 2012) ("Our specialty groups provide direct hire, executive search, temporary staffing, contract consulting and temp/contract-to-hire solutions to emerging growth companies and the Fortune 500 across all market sectors and industries.").

2005 BUSINESS Percent Employed: 16% Average Starting Salary: $60,000			
TYPE OF BUSINESS		*BUSINESSES EMPLOYING COOLEY GRADS*	
Banking/Financial	5	Beacon Hill Staffing Group	Boston, MA
Entertainment	1	Blue Cross Blue Shield of Michigan	Detroit, MI
Insurance	4	Chicago Title Insurance Company	Indianapolis, IN
Consulting	2	Global Holding & Investment Co., LLC	Fairfield, NJ
Technology	2	LawyerLink LLC	Chicago, IL
Trade Association	1	Lexis Nexis	Miamisburg, OH
Other Business	25	Michigan Bankers Association	Lansing, MI
Unknown	4	Stevens, Cooper & Burditte	Atlanta, GA

In the 2006 report below, Cooley reported that it had eight graduates employed in a category called "Legal Temporary Agency." The only reasonable interpretation here is that these graduates were employed in jobs that were not long-term or permanent. Thus, in 2006, Cooley was willing to disclose this negative information.

2006 BUSINESS Percent Employed: 20% Average Starting Salary: $61,000			
TYPE OF BUSINESS		*BUSINESSES EMPLOYING COOLEY GRADS*	
Accounting	2	Allstate Insurance Company	Yonkers, NY
Banking/Financial	7	American Standard Companies, Inc.	Piscataway, NJ
Entertainment	1	Blue Cross Blue Shield of Michigan	Lansing, MI
Insurance	9	Dow Corning	Midland, MI
Technology	7	Equity One	Miami, FL
Trade Association	1	LexisNexis	Miamisburg, OH
Legal Temporary Agency	8	NASCAR	Daytona Beach, FL
Other Business	41	Paradigm Talent Agency	Beverly Hills, CA
Unknown	6	Special Counsel	Washington, DC

However, if one compares the 2006 report to the 2010 report below, one can see that Cooley has eliminated completely the "Legal Temporary Agency" category even though those knowledgeable about the legal job market have to admit many graduates were hired by temp agencies to do temporary legal work.[18] Because of this omission, a prospective student could have concluded that Cooley's employment outcomes had improved so dramatically that it did not have any graduates working in temporary positions.

2010 BUSINESS Percent Employed: 18% Average Starting Salary: $71,470			
TYPE OF BUSINESS		*BUSINESSES EMPLOYING COOLEY GRADS*	
Accounting	1	J.P. Morgan Chase	Chicago, IL
Banking/Financial	4	American Electric Power Noble Energy, Inc.	Columbus, OH Denver, CO
Insurance	5	General Motors Corporation	Warren, MI
Management Consulting	9	Decorum Consulting Group	New York City, NY
Technology	4	Texas Oil and Gas	Fort Worth, TX
Publishing	2	Assets International, LLC	Southfield, MI
Other Business/In-house	72	M. Lee Smith Publishers	Nashville, TN

Given the state of the legal job market in 2010, it stands to reason that Cooley must have had graduates working temporarily. Therefore, Judge Quist could have concluded that Cooley's decision to eliminate the temp category was a failure to disclose a material fact and would have been misleading to some prospective law students. In other words, when determining whether a business has engaged in a deceptive practice, the court should look at the business' reporting practice over time, not focus exclusively on one single report.

As a result of Cooley's elimination of the temporary job category, the reader is left wondering where Cooley has accounted for in the 2010 report the number of temporarily employed graduates or wondering whether Cooley deleted this unfavorable information altogether. As one can see, in the years 2005 and 2006, Cooley reported that it had 25 and 41, respectively, graduates employed in a category called "Other Business." In 2010, the category had been changed to "Other Business/In House" and, when compared to the 2006 report, has almost doubled in number to 72 graduates. Perhaps, Cooley put in that new category some of its graduates doing temporary legal work. Moreover, because of the word "In-house," an applicant could have interpreted it to mean that many of these graduates are doing some type of professional "in-house" work. None of Cooley's reports explains each category and why it chose to eliminate or change some categories. Thus, Judge Quist could have determined that Cooley's reports over time reflect material omissions of relevant facts.

To satisfy the final component of the MCPA, the graduates had to show that the omitted fact could not have been reasonably known by the consumer.[19] Looking at the 2010 report, law school applicants could not have been expected to know the number of graduates Cooley hid in other categories due to its elimination of the "Legal Temporary Agency" category. Consequently, Judge Quist could have found that Cooley's reporting practice,

18. For a full discussion of the dramatic rise in legal temp jobs for law graduates, please read Chapter 10.

19. Mich. Comp. Laws Ann. § 445.903(s) (West 2012).

over time, demonstrates that it knowingly chose to stop revealing the number of its graduates doing temporary work, and it also knew that law school applicants could not have found that information anywhere else.

Too bad the case was dismissed because the graduates could not establish that their legal education was purchased for a "personal" purpose, otherwise Judge Quist could have actually analyzed the reports like I have done. Had the graduates gotten past the personal-purpose hurdle, Judge Quist could have denied Cooley's motion to dismiss so the graduates could have gathered more evidence to try to prove that Cooley had engaged in a deceptive practice under Michigan consumer protection law.

Now that I have explained how the court could have been receptive to the graduates' consumer protection claim had they been able to cross the personal-purpose hurdle, let me move on to explain the dismissal of the graduates' civil fraud claim. Under a civil (common law) fraud claim, a plaintiff must prove that the defendant knowingly made a material misrepresentation on which the plaintiff relied to his or her detriment and that such reliance was reasonable. Note that this fraud claim requires a heavier burden of proof than a statutory consumer protection claim because the plaintiff has to prove reasonable reliance.

Judge Quist first examined the 2010 report below and noted that Cooley reported 70 graduates were self-employed.

Theodore Souris, Augustus B. Woodward, and James Witherell classes (September 2009, January 2010, and May 2010)	
Number of graduates with employment status known	780
Percentage of graduates employed	76%
Average starting salary for all graduates	$54,796

PRIVATE PRACTICE Percent Employed: 50% Average Starting Salary: $52,318			
SIZE OF FIRM		*FIRMS EMPLOYING COOLEY GRADUATES*	
Self Employed	70	Sullivan, Ward, Asher & Patton, PC	Southfield, MI
2 to 10 Attorneys	157	Graff & Associates	Columbus, OH
11 to 25 Attorneys	21	Heavner, Scott, Beyers & Mihlar, PC	Chicago, IL
26 to 50 Attorneys	7	Alstock,Witkin,Kreist, & Overholtz	Pensacola, FL
51 to 100 Attorneys	5	Ryley, Carlock & Applewhite	Phoenix, AZ
101 to 250 Attorneys	7	Thompson, Meier & King, PC	Canton, GA
251 to 500 Attorneys	2	Plunkett Cooney	Bloomfield Hills, MI
501+ Attorneys	2	Hoeppner, Wagner & Evans, LLP	Valparaiso, IN
Firm Size Unknown	14	Marinosci Law Group Stewart, Greenblatt, Manning & Baez	Fort Lauderdale, FL New York, NY

He then explained that through a process of deductive reasoning, the graduates should have realized that some of these self-employed graduates were working part-time because a new graduate just starting a law firm does not have enough clients to keep him or herself working full-time. As a result, "a reasonable person [should have concluded] that the employment statistic includes all employed graduates, not just those who obtained or started full-time legal positions." The court stated further, "[e]ven though Plaintiffs plead that they thought that the statistic referred to only full-time legal jobs, their subjective misunderstanding of information ... cannot mean that Cooley has committed" fraud.

After dismissing the part of the fraud claim based on the employment data, Judge Quist dismissed the graduates' claim that the salary data constituted a fraudulent misrepresentation. Below is the first part of the 2010 report.

Number of 2010 graduates	934
Number of graduates with employment status known	780
Percentage of graduates employed	*76%*
Average starting salary for all graduates	*$54,796*

The Cooley graduates alleged that with the phrase "Average starting salary for all graduates," Cooley's represented that $54,796 is the median salary for *all* 934 graduates. The judge agreed that Cooley's descriptor was false and, therefore, a material misrepresentation. However, Judge Quist pointed out that the graduates still needed to show their reliance on this misrepresentation was reasonable. He determined that Cooley had no way of knowing the starting salaries of graduates who did not respond to the survey since the report indicated that only 780 of 934 graduates responded and that it did not indicate how many graduates supplied their salary information. As a result, Judge Quist concluded that "[t]he number of graduates who responded and indicated their starting salaries is impossible to determine from the Employment Report." This conclusion was a fatal blow to the graduates' claims: "It is quite apparent from a reading of an Employment Report, without blinders as to a particular statistic, that all of the representations in the Employment Report cannot simultaneously be true."

To make Judge Quist's reasoning easier to follow, assume that Betty asks to try on a ring that is in the fine jewelry section of a department store. Assume that the asking price for the ring is $2,000, and that it has a tag which has written on one side "Cubic Zirconia" and on the other side ".50 Carat Genuine Diamond." Betty should realize immediately that both sides of the tag cannot be true and, therefore, she should realize that the ring might not be worth anywhere near $2,000.

Similarly, Judge Quist is essentially telling the Cooley graduates that they should have known that the contradictory salary information that they relied on could not all be reasonably inferred as true. As a result, Judge Quist stated that "[w]ithout question, the [Cooley] Employment Reports are inconsistent, confusing, and inherently untrustworthy." Thus, according to Judge Quist, no reasonable law school applicant should have relied on them: "[w]ith red flags waiving and cautionary bells ringing, an ordinary prudent person would not have relied on the statistics to decide to spend $100,000 or more" to attend Cooley.[20]

---

20. *MacDonald*, U.S. Dist. LEXIS 100785, at *6–*9. Relatedly, Judge Quist did not find that Cooley negligently misrepresented information to the Cooley graduates because such a claim requires reasonable reliance, which as stated above did not occur.

Perhaps, Judge Quist hinted at the graduates' optimism bias when he stated: "Sometimes hope and dreams triumph over experience and common sense."[21]

In the lawsuit filed against DePaul University, Judge Neil Cohen, when he granted DePaul's motion to dismiss, piled on the law graduates by also stating that "common sense should have allowed" the law graduates to properly interpret DePaul's salary statistics.[22]

After Judge Quist's opinion was released, the Wall Street Journal reported that Cooley's Legal Counsel, James Thelen, stated that they were "satisfied" with the result—that the case was thrown out for failure to establish fraud.[23] I do not believe Mr. Thelen or anyone employed at Cooley should be satisfied or pleased,[24] especially in light of Judge Quist's conclusions about Cooley's employment reports and about the school itself. Besides calling Cooley's reports "inconsistent, confusing, and inherently untrustworthy," Judge Quist stated that "the bottom line is that the statistics provided by Cooley and other law schools in a format required by the ABA were **so vague and incomplete as to be meaningless and could not reasonably be relied upon** [emphasis added]." He also called Cooley "a bottom-tier law school with the lowest admission standards in the country."[25] I explain in a later chapter that this last statement about Cooley is true. I will close this section by repeating a comment posted by one person who responded to the WSJ article and Mr. Thelen's statement: "There is no honor in this most noble profession when those who stand at the gates can lie, cheat and fraudulently entice those who seek entrance. Shame on you, Cooley!"[26] Cooley may have won a victory in a Michigan state court, but it may have lost in the court of public opinion.[27]

The Lawsuit Filed against NYLS Was Dismissed

Like the Cooley graduates, the graduates who sued NYLS were unsuccessful. Alexandra Gomez-Jimenez, along with eight other NYLS graduates, alleged as misleading NYLS's practice of representing an extremely-high overall employment rate for graduates and failing to disclose that this rate included part-time, temporary, and non-legal jobs.[28] The graduates asserted that they relied on these statistics when choosing to attend NYLS. As

21. The full context of his comment can be found in his opinion, which is available at my website, lawdegreevalue.com.

22. Phillips et al. v. DePaul University, No. 12-CH-3523, (Sept. 11, 2012 Cook County Circuit Court). I chose not to discuss Judge's Cohen decision because his reasoning regarding the law graduates' claim of fraud is very similar to Judge Quist's reasoning.

23. Chelsea Phipps *Cooley Law Grads' Lawsuit Dismissed*, WSJ Blog (July 20, 2012, 7:03 PM), http://blogs.wsj.com/law/2012/07/20/cooley-law-grads%E2%80%99-lawsuit-dismissed/.

24. *Federal Judge Tosses Out Jobs-Reporting Lawsuit Against Cooley Law School*, Thomas M. Cooley Law School (July 20, 2012), http://www.cooley.edu/news/2012/federal_judge_tosses_out_jobs_reporting_lawsuit_against_cooley_law_school.html (quoting Don LeDuc, Cooley's president and dean, as stating "[w]e're obviously pleased with this decision").

25. *MacDonald*, U.S. Dist. LEXIS 100785, at *9.

26. Phipps, *supra* note 23 (comment posted by a reader going by the pseudonym "DontGoto-LawSchool").

27. A quick Google search reveals many bloggers or websites posting negative comments about Cooley. Moreover, enrollment for the fall of 2012 dropped dramatically. *See Cooley Law Enrollment Falls Amid Skepticism*, Lansing State Journal (Lansing, MI), Aug. 19, 2012.

28. *Gomez-Jimenez*, 943 N.Y.S.2d at 857.

a result of their reliance, the graduates now find themselves either unemployed or "under-employed" in jobs not involving traditional attorney positions. Judge Melvin Schweitzer of the Supreme Court of New York on March 21, 2012, granted a motion to dismiss the lawsuit filed against NYLS, stating "[t]he court does not view these post-graduate employment statistics to be misleading in a material way for a reasonable consumer acting reasonably."[29]

Below I discuss why I believe Judge Schweitzer is incorrectly holding law school applicants, as consumers, to a higher standard than is required by the statutes that make deceptive business practices unlawful. I cannot discuss every aspect of the opinion; therefore, I urge each reader to find and read in full Judge Schweitzer's opinion, which is easily available at my website.[30]

The Legal Standard for Proving That a Practice Is Deceptive

In New York, the legal standard for deceptive practices is covered under New York General Business Law § 349(a) ("GBL 349"), which states that "[d]eceptive acts or practices in the conduct of any business, trade or commerce or in the furnishing of any service in this state are hereby declared unlawful."[31] This statute is patterned after a provision in the Federal Trade Commission Act ("FTC Act"), which "prohibits unfair or deceptive acts or practices in or affecting commerce."[32] The New York City Administrative Code provides that GBL 349 is to be construed so as to supplement the rules, regulations, and decisions of the FTC and the courts interpreting certain provisions of the FTC Act.[33]

Interpreting GBL 349, Judge Schweitzer first articulated the legal standard for proving deception as follows: "To state a cause of action under GBL 349, a plaintiff must allege that the defendant's conduct was: (1) consumer oriented; (2) deceptive or misleading in a material way; and (3) that plaintiff suffered injury as a result."[34] Ignoring the issue of damages and assuming that NYLS's employment data was consumer oriented, the main issue for Judge Schweitzer regarding this claim was whether the employment and salary data marketed by NYLS were deceptive or misleading in a material way under GBL 349. In determining whether an act is misleading, the New York Court of Appeals has adopted an objective test, which limits misleading acts to those likely to mislead a reasonable consumer acting reasonably under the circumstances.[35] The FTC Act similarly defines as deceptive or misleading a representation that is likely to mislead consumers acting reasonably under the circumstances.[36]

---

29. *Id.* at 843.

30. Lawdegreevalue.com.

31. N.Y. Gen. Bus. Law § 349 (McKinney 2012).

32. *See* 15 U.S.C. § 45(a). See also Matter of State of New York v. Colorado State Christian Coll. of Church of Inner Power, 76 Misc.2d 50, 54, 346 N.Y.S.2d 482, 487 (1973) ("It is thus clear that the legislative purpose in [New York] enacting § 349 of the General Business Law was to follow in the steps of the Federal Trade Commission with respect to the interpretation of deceptive acts and practices outlawed in Section 5 of the Federal Trade Commission Act (15 U.S.C.A. s 45)").

33. 21 N.Y. Jur. 2d Consumer and Borrower Protection § 7 (2012).

34. *Gomez-Jimenez*, 943 N.Y.S.2d at 840.

35. Oswego Laborers' Local 214 Pension Fund v. Marine Midland Bank, N.A., 647 N.E.2d 741, 745 (N.Y. 1995).

36. F.T.C. v. Gill, 71 F. Supp. 2d 1030, 1045 (C.D. Cal. 1999) aff'd, 265 F.3d 944 (9th Cir. 2001).

Analyzing Schweitzer's Conclusions

Applying the above legal standard, Judge Schweitzer found that the employment statistics for two years were not misleading.[37] Below is a copy of NYLS's 2009 employment and salary report, which was attached to the complaint filed by the graduates. Note the visual presentation of the salary ranges placed immediately next to percent of graduates employed in a particular practice area. Observe also that immediately above the first table are words indicating that only 20% of the graduates supplied salary data.

Class of 2009 Employment Statistics

The employment rate for the Class of 2009 within nine months of graduation is 89.7%, with 94% of the graduates reporting employment information.

Approximately 20% of our 2009 graduates reported salary information. The salary range (minimum to maximum) and median salaries by employment category are:

Practice Area	Percent	Salary Range Min.–Maximum	Average
Private Practice	45.6%	$28,000–$160,000	$120,197
Corporate/Business	23.7%	$50,000–$96,000	$75,167
Government	8.2%	$41,000–$72,000	$56,054
Public Interest	16%	N/A	N/A
Judicial Clerkship	3.4%	$42,000–$58,200	$45,887
Academic	3.1%	$40,000–$45,000	$42,500

Of those graduates in private practice reporting salary information, the minimum—maximum and median salaries by firm size are as follows:

Firm Size	Percent	Salary Range Min.–Max.	Average
501+	20%	$145,000–$160,000	$159,500
251–500	6%	$120,000–$160,000	$155,000
101–250	4%	$90,000–$160,000	$136,667
51–100	4%	$62,000–$90,000	$81,750
26–50	3%	$55,000–$55,000	$55,000
11–25	11%	$47,000–$65,000	$57,000
2–10	51%	$28,000–$80,000	$54,583
Unknown	1%		

37. Gomez-Jimenez, 943 N.Y.S.2d at 840.

Judge Schweitzer focused on the sentence indicating the low response rate regarding the salary data and concluded that this sentence was sufficient to put prospective students on notice that the salaries reported were not representative of salaries earned by all graduates. He also found that the salary statistics for other years were not misleading even though they lacked any written disclaimer regarding the response rate.

If Judge Schweitzer had properly given deference to the FTC's interpretation regarding what may be misleading, he would have analyzed NYLS's disclosure of its salary data by focusing on whether some students would have found the disclosure misleading. The FTC Policy Statement on Deception provides: "An interpretation may be reasonable even though it is not shared by a majority of consumers in the relevant class, or by particularly sophisticated consumers. A material practice that misleads a significant minority of reasonable consumers is deceptive."[38] Applying this standard to NYLS's disclosure of its salary data, Judge Schweitzer could have recognized that a minority of applicants could have been misled by NYLS's visual presentation and in doing so correctly concluded NYLS violated the law. By juxtaposing the percent employed in various firm sizes, by claiming a 94% employment response rate and by reporting average salaries for each firm size, NYLS's employment report implied that these law firm jobs were full-time attorney jobs. Because how else could it claim an average salary of $120,197 for a paralegal or part-time attorney job for a graduate employed in private practice?

In order for a prospective student to not have been misled, the prospective student would have to already know that a low response rate means most graduates who fail or refuse to supply salary information usually earn substantially less than those who choose to supply that information. Judge Schweitzer totally ignored the fact that NYLS's disclosure of salary data for two previous years did not have any information regarding the low response rate. From this visual presentation, a prospective student could have incorrectly concluded that NYLS's graduates are earning much greater salaries than what all graduates actually earned. Consequently, Judge Schweitzer could have concluded that the disclosures for those years were misleading.

Is NYLS's Post-Graduate Employment Data Likely to Mislead a Reasonable Consumer?

While I can force myself to accept Judge Schweitzer's ruling about the salary data, even though I believe NYLS could have done a better job of accurately disclosing the salary data, I cannot accept his ruling about the employment data because it went too far. Let's look again at NYLS's 2009 report as it relates to employment. NYLS fails to include any asterisk or small-font statements explaining the nearly 90% employment rate it claimed. Because of the lack of at least an asterisk or a footnote and accompanying sentences further explaining the 89.7% employment rate, NYLS's report would lead some prospective students to believe that all these graduates are employed in full-time, long-term jobs for which a law degree was required or preferred.

38. FTC Policy Statement on Deception, appended to Cliffdale Associates, Inc., 103 F.T.C. 110, 174 (1984), *available at* http://www.ftc.gov/bcp/policystmt/ad-decept.htm.

The table below is how NYLS categorized its employed graduates. The second column totals 100%.

Practice Area	Percent	Salary Range Min.–Maximum	Average
Private Practice	45.6%	$28,000–$160,000	$120,197
Corporate/Business	23.7%	$50,000–$96,000	$75,167
Government	8.2%	$41,000–$72,000	$56,054
Public Interest	16%	N/A	N/A
Judicial Clerkship	3.4%	$42,000–$58,200	$45,887
Academic	3.1%	$40,000–$45,000	$42,500

Because we now know that since the start of the Great Recession many recent law school graduates around the country are employed not as lawyers but as legal assistants or paralegals, NYLS has to be counting as employed in the "Private Practice" category graduates working at law firms, but not in traditional attorney positions. Likewise, some graduates employed in the "Corporate/Business" category could be working, not as corporate attorneys, but as sales associates at retail establishments or baristas at Starbucks. Moreover, none of these categories reveal that some graduates are employed in temporary or part-time positions and, thus, could create the impression that all graduates are employed in full-time, long-term positions. Most law school students did not know about the widespread practice of law schools' counting employed graduates who are working in *any capacity* just so a school can claim to have an extremely high employment rate.

Instead of focusing his analysis on what NYLS actually disclosed and failed to disclose, Judge Schweitzer focused his attention on whether the omitted information was misleading within the context of *all information that was publicly available to the plaintiffs*. He opined that "[o]ne would think that reasonable consumers, armed with the publicly available information from *U.S. News* that plaintiffs cite, thus would avail themselves of plaintiffs' own logic as stated in their complaint when it comes to evaluating their chances of obtaining the full-time legal job of their choice." Judge Schweitzer seems to imply that the NYLS applicants must have been willfully blind to the mediocre job opportunities available to graduates of a low-ranked law school: "NYLS applicants, as reasonable consumers of a legal education, would have to be wearing blinders not to be aware of these well-established facts of life in the world of legal employment."

Judge Schweitzer's opinion emphasizes that the plaintiffs could have discovered that NYLS's employment rates included part-time, temporary and non-legal jobs if they had consulted other resources or had some knowledge of the general state of the market for legal employment. In his opinion, other resources may have also provided a better idea of the employment prospects for full-time attorney positions for NYLS graduates. Instead of actually analyzing whether NYLS's employment reports themselves were misleading, Judge Schweitzer expresses his disbelief that law school applicants could be that ignorant about the state of the legal job market.

Judge Schweitzer assumes, without citing to any evidence or legal precedent, that all law school applicants are sophisticated and, thereby, exculpates NYLS from possible liability for disseminating employment data that some applicants found misleading:

> **By anyone's definition, reasonable consumers — college graduates — seriously considering law schools are a sophisticated subset of education consumers,** capable of sifting through data and weighing alternatives before making a decision regarding their post-college options, such as applying for professional school. **These reasonable consumers have available to them any number of sources of information to review when making their decisions** [emphasis added].[39]

Judge Schweitzer assumes that all law school applicants know about NALP and other sources and would not have relied *solely* on NYLS's employment reports. His opinion never considers the possibility that some applicants do not know about these other sources. He completely glosses over the fact the information reported by NALP is aggregated data for all law schools and not specific for each school.[40] His opinion never highlights the fact that NALP, *U.S. News*, the ABA, and other third parties rely on information self-reported by the law schools and do not independently audit or verify the accuracy of the information reported by the law schools.[41]

Omissions Can Be Misleading

Judge Schweitzer should have analyzed NYLS's *omission* of information regarding the number of graduates employed in temporary, part-time and non-legal positions. The New York Administrative Code defines deception to include a material omission, which includes the "failure to state a material fact if such use deceives or tends to deceive."[42] Judge Schweitzer's opinion does not dispute that a material omission can be deceptive under GBL 349. However, Judge Schweitzer simply chose not to discuss whether NYLS's omissions were material and likely to mislead. One could reasonably expect some prospective students to be misled by NYLS's omission of the number of graduates employed in temporary, part-time and non-legal positions when it reported an 89.7 percent or better employment rate.[43] Some prospective students would incorrectly conclude that the NYLS's employment rate only included graduates working in permanent, full-time jobs involving the practice of law.

---

39. Gomez-Jimenez, 943 N.Y.S.2d at 846.

40. *See, e.g.*, Andrew P. Morriss & William D. Henderson, *Measuring Outcomes: Post-graduation Measures of Success in the U.S. News & World Report Law School Rankings*, 83 Ind. L.J. 791, 830 (2008) (stating that although NALP collects data from each school, "[u]nfortunately these data are not available to the public as school-level data").

41. *See, e.g.*, *Law Sch. Admissions Council & Section of Legal Educ. & Admissions to the Bar, Am. Bar Ass'n*, *in* ABA-LSAC Official Guide to ABA-Approved Law Schools 509 (2012) ("Neither the ABA nor LSAC conducts an audit to verify the accuracy of the information submitted by the law schools."); Anthony Ciolli, *The Legal Employment Market: Determinants of Elite Firm Placement and How Law Schools Stack Up*, 45 Jurimetrics J. 413, 415 n. 11 (2005) ("U.S. News does not verify employment data or distinguish between legal and nonlegal jobs.").

42. N.Y. ADC. LAW § 20-701(a)(2) *available at* http://codes.lp.findlaw.com/nycode/ADC/20/5/1/20-701.

43. We will never know how low the actual rate is since the judge tossed out the lawsuit against NYLS. However, as explained in a later chapter where I compare the reported employment rates of low-ranked law schools to much higher ranked law schools, one could reasonably believe that NYLS's actual rate of graduates employed in permanent, full-time, bar-passage required jobs is much lower than what its 2009 report suggests.

While American common law[44] generally does not impose liability for fraud based on the failure to disclose, modern consumer protection statutes have alleviated the harshness of the old standards required under common law fraud.[45] In general, today, where the parties do not have equal access to pertinent facts, sellers must reveal material facts known only to them that would substantially undermine the fairness of the bargain.[46] American courts have developed three different views as to when it is deceptive to withhold material information from consumers.[47] The most conservative view would impose liability for nondisclosure only when the seller had actual knowledge of the omitted facts and intentionally failed to communicate this information to buyers.[48]

Law schools—sellers of legal education—have actual knowledge of the employment figures that students want to know. They report the number of graduates employed in full-time attorney positions to NALP every year, and that proves that the law schools have this data available.[49] Moreover, law schools have had actual knowledge of the number of graduates employed in part-time, temporary and non-legal jobs for many years but have failed to disclose that information to the public. One plausible interpretation is that NYLS's failure to disclose was intentional especially since Law School Transparency and others have been for years calling for greater transparency in the disclosure of employment data. Therefore, even under a conservative interpretation of the non-disclosure of material facts, Judge Schweitzer could have concluded that a jury could find that NYLS failed to disclose material information to prospective students and that this non-disclosure was intentional.

The requirement that the omission is "likely to mislead" requires a showing of probable deception. For example, advertising that is capable of being interpreted in a misleading way should be construed against the advertiser.[50] The FTC has stated that when a representation is targeted at a specific group of consumers, it will determine the effect of that practice based on a reasonable member of that group. In the current context, the test asks whether a member of the group of law school applicants could have been misled by the nearly 90% employment rate in NYLS's 2009 report.[51] The answer is yes. Judge Schweitzer, instead, decided that all law school applicants are sophisticated and, therefore, the NYLS graduates could not have been misled. He never analyzed the four corners of the employment reports and assessed whether a reasonable consumer could be misled.

---

44. Black's Law Dictionary defines "American common law" as the "body of English law that was adopted as the law of the American colonies and supplemented with local enactments and judgments." BLACK'S LAW DICTIONARY (9th ed. 2009).

45. MARY DEE PRIDGEN, CONSUMER PROTECTION AND THE LAW § 2:3 (2011) (Westlaw).

46. *Id.*

47. *Id.* at § 3:7.

48. *Id.*

49. At the time of Judge Schweitzer's opinion, new ABA disclosure standards had not been adopted. *Council Proposes Changes to Standard* 509, American Bar Association, http://www.americanbar.org/publications/syllabus_home/volume_43_2011-2012/spring_2012/council_proposeschangestostandard509.html (last visited Jun. 21, 2012). The new standards now require law schools to disclose more thorough information to consumers than what many law schools voluntarily chose to disclose prior to 2012.

50. *Gill*, 71 F. Supp. 2d at 1045.

51. Matter of Cliffdale Associates, Inc., 103 F.T.C. 110 1984 WL 565319, at *47(1984).

When Did All Law School Applicants Become Sophisticated Consumers?

Where did Judge Schweitzer get the idea that all law school applicants are sophisticated?[52] I am not sure. However, contrary to Judge Schweitzer's erroneous conclusion, many law school applicants are naïve about legal education and the job market. I will use myself as an example. When I applied to law school in 1991, I knew nothing about law schools and almost nothing about the practice of law other than what I saw on television. Then and now television *never* portrays law graduates as struggling to find attorney jobs. I was not friends with any attorneys. I grew up in poverty and was a first-generation college graduate from a very large extended family, where almost no one has attended college, much less graduated from college. Thankfully, the legal academy had a good reputation back then, and I do not feel that I was deceived by the promotional materials that I read. If I had seen NYLS's report back in 1991, I would have been misled because I would have believed the 89.7% employment rate actually reflected graduates employed in traditional attorney jobs, not jobs as paralegals or temporary jobs working as a research assistant or performing document review. It would *never* have occurred to me that I must assume that law schools withhold material information from their promotional materials for their own gain. Now, as a law professor who has read the files of applicants seeking admission to law school, some applicants have backgrounds similar to my own and are, therefore, not sophisticated. Educated does not equal sophisticated!

Unfortunately, Judge Schweitzer's opinion stands for the proposition that prospective students should distrust what the law schools have disclosed. How *low* has the legal profession sunk that law school applicants cannot trust law school deans and professors—the educators who are supposed to teach them how to become ethical lawyers? Should applicants expect law school personnel to lie to them at the very outset? Although the plethora of law bloggers would suggest that the legal academy's reputation has decreased in recent years, law schools do not have the reputation of used car dealers. If one envisions the typical law school applicant as being 22 years old, one would expect a 22-year-old to know that he or she cannot trust a used car salesmen. No doubt, 22-year-old consumers have seen numerous TV commercials with fast-talking car salesman yelling "no money down; no credit, no problem" and have heard their parents say "you can't trust them." Also, news reports and TV shows periodically have secretly recorded shady car salesmen and reported about the lies they tell consumers. As a result, many 22-year-olds would be very suspicious of a car sales pitch. Unlike car dealerships, law schools generally do not

52. Judge Schweitzer has had a distinguished career. In 1966, he graduated with from the highly-ranked New York University. *See* Judge Schweitzer's biography at http://www.nycourtsystem.com/applications/judicialdirectory/Bio.php?ID=7030088. In 1969, he obtained a law degree from Fordham University School of Law, a very reputable private law school, where he had the distinction of being an Ed Sullivan Scholar. Hired that same year at the prestigious law firm of Rogers & Wells LLP (now Clifford Chance US LLP, a firm that is not known for representing consumers), Melvin Schweitzer started off as an associate attorney, made partner, and eventually became of counsel. *See* Clifford Chance, http://www.cliffordchance.com/home.html (last visited April 15, 2013) (boasting "Clifford Chance is one of the world's leading law firms, with 34 offices in 24 countries and some 3,200 legal advisers"). He has been admitted to practice before the United States Supreme Court since 1976. From 2001 and in 2005, he operated his own law firm, M.L. Schweitzer & Associates, P.C., until he was appointed by Governor George Pataki, as a judge serving on the Court of Claims. He held this position until 2009, when he became a judge on the Supreme Court of New York. http://www.nycourtsystem.com/applications/judicialdirectory/Bio.php?ID=7030088.

advertise on TV or radio; therefore, Judge Schweitzer was wrong to assume that all law school applicants should know they should be suspicious of a law school's employment report.

Most American law schools are a part of established, traditional universities, and students have trusted these higher education institutions for centuries. Consequently, law school applicants who do not know about the accusations lodged against law schools should not be expected to distrust or be suspicious of law schools.

I could not find any cases where a New York court has held that a reasonable consumer is expected to consult outside sources when evaluating a representation made by a business. Judge Schweitzer's decision is, therefore, dangerous because of its implications in requiring all consumers to do their own independent investigations. He chose to penalize pre-law students for having higher education despite the fact that they did not have the type of specialized knowledge that would have allowed them to make a well-informed assessment of the value of a law degree from NYLS.

Applying an objective standard, a jury could have found NYLS's employment reports were likely to mislead a reasonable consumer pursuing legal education. A fair interpretation of NYLS's 2009 employment report is that it implied that 89.7% of its graduates were employed in traditional, full-time attorney or law-related positions. The standard for a motion to dismiss required that the court accept plaintiffs' allegations as true and accord the complaint all favorable inferences. In close cases, the judge should deny the motion. At this early stage of litigation, the graduates' complaint should have survived NYLS's motion to dismiss, at least as to the deceptive practices claim. The question of whether the employment data was misleading should have been based on all of the facts after the graduates had access to the discovery process and were able to uncover more details about what information NYLS had at its disposal but chose not to disclose. Rather than allowing the case to continue so that the graduates could build their case based on facts uncovered, Judge Schweitzer's opinion now shifts to future law school applicants the burden of discovering the "holes" in a law school's employment and salary reports.

Appellate Court Upholds Dismissal of NYLS Lawsuit

The Appellate Division, First Department, upheld Judge Schweitzer's dismissal of the $200 million class action lawsuit filed against NYLS.[53] In a written opinion for the five-judge panel, Judge Ronaldo Acosta stated that "we recognize that students may be susceptible to misrepresentations by law school" and, therefore, did not necessarily agree that law school applicants were sophisticated in making career decisions. Nevertheless, Judge Acosta held that because NYLS's employment reports did not contain an explicit false statement, NYLS did not make a deceptive statement in violation of NY's General Business Law. In other words, NYLS's overall employment data contain no statements indicating whether the jobs were full or part-time; therefore, NYLS did not make a false or misleading representation. Judge Acosta stated that the reports were "unquestionably incomplete" and noted

---

53. Gomez-Jimenez v. New York Law School, (Dec. 20, 2012) N.Y. Slip Op 08819, 2012 WL 6620602, *aff'g* 36 Misc.3d 230, 943 N.Y.S.2d 834 [Sup Ct, N.Y. County].

that some students could make erroneous assumptions based on the incomplete information. In other words, Judge Acosta is saying that while laymen could call NYLS' employment reports deceptive, the law does not.

Judge Acosta also concluded the relevant omitted information—the percentage of grads with actual attorney jobs—cannot constitute a deceptive act because the graduates failed to show that a special relationship existed between them and the school or the school had "a fiduciary obligation requiring a duty of full and complete disclosure." Judge Acosta never explains why a special relationship or a fiduciary duty must exist in light of the NYC Administrative Code, which mentions neither. General Business Law § 349 is patterned after the FTC Act, which does not require a special relationship or fiduciary duty to prove that an omitted material fact constitutes a deceptive act.

All hope is gone for the NYLS graduates because New York's highest court denied the graduates' request for appeal.[54] Meanwhile, in a lawsuit filed against Albany Law School for allegedly reporting deceptive data, the trial court dismissed the suit by basing its reasoning on Judge Acosta's analysis.[55] Writing the opinion for the court, Judge Richard Platkin, himself a 1993 Albany Law School graduate, refused to take himself off the case. Judge Platkin took note that law school applicants are "a reasonably well-educated (though not necessarily sophisticated) group of consumers who are called upon to make major life decisions" and that this case has a group of consumers that is different from cases brought by the general public. The implication is that law school applicants should have done more to assess the representations made by Albany Law School and should not have assumed the employment rate included only graduates with full-time jobs where a law degree is required or preferred.

A Revival of Caveat Emptor?

The New York cases appear to be resurrecting the doctrine of *caveat emptor*—"let the buyer beware." Caveat emptor is a doctrine from common law that limited legal remedies for deceit to only the most egregious cases of intentional fraud.[56] However, modern consumer protection statutes mitigate the harshness of this doctrine and, therefore, make it considerably fairer for consumers to obtain legal redress. Professor Mary Dee Pridgen, a recognized consumer law expert, explains the modern approach used by courts: "[c]ontrary to the requirement of caveat emptor that buyers independently investigate anything the seller tells them, modern statutory cases allow buyers to rely on the honesty of the businessperson in a consumer transaction."[57] For example, in a Massachusetts case where a real estate developer misrepresented the future use of a lot adjoining plaintiffs' property, the plaintiffs were not barred from pursuing their case despite the fact that they had failed to check the public records regarding the then-lawful use of the lot.[58]

As noted by the Supreme Court of the United States *in Federal Trade Commission v. Standard Education Society*,

54. Gomez-Jimenez v. New York Law School, 2013 N.Y. Slip Op. 68698, 2013 WL 1235500, (N.Y. Mar 28, 2013).

55. Austin v. Albany Law School, 2013 NY Slip Op 2300. Under the legal doctrine known as *stare decisis*, a trial court is obligated to honor the precedents of higher courts in its state on the same issue. In other words, Judge Platkin had to apply the law as interpreted by Judge Acosta.

56. Pridgen *supra* note 45, at § 2:1.

57. *Id.* at § 3.4.

58. *See* Brandt v. Olympic Const., Inc., 449 N.E.2d 1231, 1233 (Mass. App. Ct. 1983).

> [l]aws are made to protect the trusting as well as the suspicious. The best element of business has long since decided that honesty should govern competitive enterprises, and that the rule of caveat emptor should ***not*** be relied on to reward fraud and deception.[59]

One could argue that Judge Schweitzer's opinion is a step backwards to an age where deceit and deception were condoned. He certainly has burdened all law school applicants with a duty to independently investigate the employment statistics published by law schools even though such a duty is not a part of the legal standard in New York or under the FTC Act. The test is whether the omission is likely to mislead a reasonable consumer; it does not force a reasonable consumer to become an authority on sleazy sales techniques by consulting outside sources before entering into a contract. The graduates-plaintiffs allegedly relied on the honesty of NYLS, an institution that is supposed to educate ethical and honest lawyers. To ask law school applicants to distrust the law school and be skeptical of all representations it makes is to revive *caveat emptor*, an outdated doctrine from a previous legal era.

Now if you have not read Judge Quist's opinion, you may be wondering why I am making a big deal out of *caveat emptor*. At the end of Judge Quist's opinion that dismissed the case against Cooley, he issued the following warning: "as put in the phrase we lawyers learn early in law school—*caveat emptor*."[60] However, it is noteworthy that Judge Quist was making this statement after dismissing the graduates' common law fraud claim. Caveat emptor is not the standard when the claim is based on a consumer protection statute prohibiting deceptive acts and practices. In other words, consumers' relying on such a statute do ***not*** have an obligation to investigate the veracity of a seller's representations in order to prove a violation of the statute.

Unlike Judge Quist's *caveat emptor* warning, Judge Acosta made it clear that he does not condone the reporting practices of law schools. He wagged the proverbial finger of shame in the legal academy's face for its unethical behavior:

> "In the last analysis, the law is what the lawyers are. And the law and the lawyers are what the *law schools* make them." Defendant [New York Law School] and its peers owe prospective students more than just barebones compliance with their legal obligations. Defendant and its peers are educational not-for-profit institutions. They should be dedicated to advancing the public welfare. In that vein, defendant and its peers have at least an ethical obligation of absolute candor to their prospective students.[61]

Kudos to Judge Acosta for calling on law schools to embrace the highest ethical standards in their reporting practices. As succinctly stated by Jason Dolin, an adjunct professor at Capital University Law School, "[m]ost of us went to law school to become barristers, not baristas"; therefore, law schools should "[p]ublish in a conspicuous, easy-to-find place on [their] websites the percentage of graduates for each graduating class who found jobs that were JD[-]required, full-time and non-temporary."[62]

---

59. F.T.C. v. Standard Educ. Soc., 302 U.S. 112, 116 (1937) (emphasis added).

60. *MacDonald*, U.S. Dist. LEXIS 100785, at *9.

61. Gomez-Jimenez v. New York Law School (Dec. 20, 2012) N.Y. Slip Op 08819, 2012 WL 6620602, *aff'g* 36 Misc.3d 230, 943 N.Y.S.2d 834 [Sup Ct, N.Y. County] (omitting internal footnotes and citations) (emphasis added).

62. Jason M. Dolin, *Deciphering Law Schools' Post-Graduate Employment Data*, Ohio Lawyer, Nov./Dec. 2010, *available at* https://www.ohiobar.org/NewsAndPublications/News/OSBANews/Pages/OSBANews-1385.aspx.

In the next chapter, I will revisit Judge Schweitzer's opinion when I demonstrate to prospective law school students how they should do a sophisticated analysis of available information about a law school to assess whether a law degree at that law school is worth the price. I also discuss in Chapter 3 the employment data now available about each of the schools that have been sued for reporting misleading employment reports. A gross disparity exists between their reported overall employment rates and actual percentage of graduates who obtained real attorney jobs. Thus, despite any judge's ruling, it is now evident that these schools omitted the truth about the success of their graduates in obtaining such jobs.

Chapter 3

"S" Is for Sophisticated, Not Special

"[C]ollege graduates—seriously considering law schools[,] are a sophisticated subset of education consumers...."[1] Judge Melvin Schweitzer

In June 2012, English teacher David McCullough, Jr., delivered a commencement speech at Wellesley (Mass.) High School's graduation that shocked the nation. Recounting the numerous ways and many years in which helicopter parents and others have heaped accolades on the graduating seniors, McCullough gave them a heavy dose of reality when he told them at least six times "**You're not special!**" Mr. McCullough's speech went viral and has been viewed by 1.8 million on YouTube.[2]

In comparison to Mr. McCullough's shocking speech, Judge Melvin Schweitzer's opinion dismissing the lawsuit against New York Law School ("NYLS") has garnered little media attention but was nevertheless shocking to some, including me. Judge Schweitzer, with a broad brush, painted all law school applicants as sophisticated and exculpated law schools from liability for disseminating misleading employment and salary data. The message to prospective law students is: "You're not special; you're sophisticated!" For some prospective law students, it may be difficult for them to accept being told they are not special. However, a simple Google search will reveal numerous bloggers asserting that today's young wannabe law students, sometimes called 0Ls, suffer from Special Snowflake Syndrome.

Judge Schweitzer turns on its head the meaning of "special" by implying that if you are special enough to get into law school, then you are sophisticated enough to do your own research and not rely on self-serving statements contained in a law school's recruitment materials![3] He places squarely on the shoulders of all law school applicants the burden of "discover[ing] their realistic post[-]graduation employment prospects by consulting the many [available] sources of information."[4] On appeal, Judge Acosta affirmed the dismissal of the lawsuit even though it was clear that NYLS omitted material information—the percentage of graduates with full-time, long-term attorney jobs.

---

1. *Gomez-Jimenez*, 943 N.Y.S.2d at 857. For a full discussion of the opinion, read Chapter 2.
2. *See You Are Not Special Commencement Speech from Wellesley High School*, YouTube.com, *available at* http://www.youtube.com/watch?v=_lfxYhtf8o4 (last visited March 16, 2013).
3. *Gomez-Jimenez*, 943 N.Y.S.2d at 853 (describing graduates suing NYLS as "among the select segment of students accepted into an American law school").
4. *Id.*

To put Judge Acosta's opinion regarding omissions in perspective, let me tell the true story about dating a guy, who by all appearances did not have any children. I never saw any photos of children in his apartment, in his car, or his office. While I was dating him, I ran into a mutual friend, who said to me "So did Ron tell you about his son he had with Dana?"[5] My mouth fell open because I also knew Dana. Until this point in time, Ron never discussed having to spend time with a child and he never hinted that he was the father of a child. Ron conveniently neglected to tell me that Dana had pegged him as the father and that he was paying monthly child support payments to her. When I confronted him about it, he exclaimed, "Well, *she* says the baby is mine!" Of course, Michael Jackson's Billie Jean song popped in my head!

I believe almost everyone would agree that his failure to tell me about his son was an "omission of material information." Why would he choose to do that? Maybe he was afraid that the disclosure of his son would put him in a negative light or would lead me to dump him and move on to other dating prospects. Had I married him and later discovered the truth, no doubt I would have been harmed financially by his obligation to make monthly child support payments—less money in our home to meet our needs.

Similar to Ron, law schools with low percentages of graduates employed in long-term, full-time attorney jobs have omitted the actual number of graduates with these jobs. Most law students and graduates believe this information is material and believe law schools should have disclosed it. Regardless of their stated reasons for failing to disclose this information to applicants, many law schools knew that if some applicants had known the truth, they would have turned down the schools' admission offers and would have chosen to attend another law school or not attend at all. Graduates of NYLS and the other schools that have been sued assert that they have been harmed financially by the law schools' omission of material information because they are now strapped with enormous student loan debt and are unemployed or under-employed.

Judge Acosta does not condone NYLS's reporting practice; however; he simply concludes that under his interpretation of the New York law, NYLS could produce an incomplete employment report and allow prospective students to make the wrong assumptions. Ouch!

The bottom line is that while many would agree that what Ron and these law schools have done is unethical, it is not unlawful. They did not make a false statement such as "I have no children" or "The 94% employment rate consist of only graduates with fulltime, long-term attorney jobs." We all know that when it comes to dating, most people conceal the negatives, which forces us to become sophisticated when assessing an individual for romantic or marital purposes. Similarly, prospective law students must now become sophisticated when assessing a law school for enrollment purposes because some schools have negative data they attempt to hide.

Professor Johnson's Framework for a Sophisticated Analysis

To empower prospective students to do what Judge Schweitzer and Judge Acosta expect of law school applicants, I fully explain below a very sensible way of researching and

5. Their real names have been changed.

weighing all available criteria before deciding which law school's offer of admission to accept. Towards the end of the chapter I demonstrate that law schools that have been sued for reporting deceptive employment data have a very low percentage of graduates employed in full-time attorney jobs when compared to the very high overall employment rates they claimed to have.

Succinctly, applicants should gather the following information when doing a comprehensive analysis of a school and when weighing a school's offer of admission:

Factors to Consider

Broad Considerations	Individual Factors to Consider
1. Matriculation & Graduation Success	1. Admission policy 2. Attrition rate 3. Transfer-out number 4. Diversity of those in the attrition and transfer out numbers 5. Academic support programs
2. Bar Passage Likelihood	1. Bar-passage rate 2. University-provided bar-exam prep support
3. Employment Prospects	1. Employment status for last 3 years 2. Employment type for last 3 years 3. Overall employment rate for last 3 years 4. Career services support
4. Salary Potential	1. Salary data for employment type or status 2. Salary data published by NALP and others
5. Pre-Law School Assessment of How to Pay for Education	1. Cost of tuition and cost of living expenses 2. Scholarship offers 3. Scholarship retention rate 4. Curve for retention of scholarships 5. Work available during semesters and summers 6. Work-study availability and criteria 7. Student loan amount 8. Loan forgiveness or payment-reduction programs

To demonstrate a sophisticated comprehensive research, I will analyze available data from two law schools: Cooley and the University of Cincinnati College of Law ("Cincinnati"). Currently, there are 200 fully-ABA-accredited law schools, and they are ranked by *US News*, which divides the schools into four tiers, with each tier comprising 50 law schools and with the first-tier comprising the most-highly ranked schools.[6] I chose to compare Cooley with Cincinnati because a person getting an offer from a third or fourth tier law school could very well also get an offer from a second tier law school like

6. Actually more than 50 schools are in the first tier because some schools are tied for the same spot.

Cincinnati. An unknown number of students with offers from first and second tier schools are accepting offers from third and fourth tier law schools frequently because they are awarded full scholarships from a school in one of the two bottom tiers. In fact, some students who do very well on the LSAT are offered full scholarships from schools to which they have never applied because law schools are able to take advantage of the Candidate Referral Service for recruiting purposes.[7] As explained in detail below, a law applicant with multiple offers of admission and scholarships should seriously consider numerous criteria, not just a school's ranking or scholarship award, before making a final decision on which school's admission offer to accept. Every student's needs are unique, and, therefore, applicants should try to select the school that best satisfies their needs.

Cooley is ranked in the fourth tier and is the nation's largest law school, producing the greatest number of graduates from its five campuses, four of which are located in Michigan and one in Florida. As discussed extensively in Chapter 2, Cooley was sued for allegedly publishing deceptive employment and salary data. Cincinnati, which has not been sued, is ranked in the second tier at 69 in 2012 by *US News* and is one of the smallest law schools because its entering first-year class is usually less than 150 students.

Analyzing Cooley's Employment Report

Although the case against Cooley was dismissed, I have carefully scrutinized Cooley's employment report below and provided an explanation for Judge Quist's statement that the report was inherently untrustworthy.[8] Moreover, a careful scrutiny of Cooley's employment data should put an applicant on notice that if becoming a lawyer is the desired goal, enrollment in Cooley is statistically *highly unlikely* to lead to a traditional law firm job.

As sophisticated consumers, law school applicants must first realize that Cooley and other law schools include in their overall employment rate graduates employed in *any* capacity, including non-legal, non-professional positions or undesirable legal positions. Only a small percentage of consumers attend law school to obtain non-legal positions;[9] yet a law school applicant trying to find an accurate number of graduates employed as lawyers may find it challenging.

Applicants are forced to do some speculating about the meaning of the data obtained and hope to come to the correct conclusion. For example, Cooley's 2010 report, which contained employment and salary data for students who graduated between September

7. *See* Daria Roithmayr, *Barriers to Entry: A Market Lock-in Model of Discrimination*, 86 Va. L. Rev. 727, 770 (2000) (stating that CRS, "which is designed to select students according to descriptive information—e.g., LSAT score, GPA, racial/ethnic or geographic background—for law schools to recruit"). By registering with CRS, law school applicants consent to the Law School Admission Council's release of their information to law schools and related entities. http://www.lsac.org/llm/choose/llm-crs.asp.

8. Judge Quist opined that, "[w]ithout question, the [Cooley] Employment Reports are inconsistent, confusing, and inherently untrustworthy." *MacDonald*, U.S. Dist. LEXIS 100785, at *9.

9. *Executive Summary: "Inside the Minds of Law School Applicants"*, Veritas Prep (2011), http://www.lawschoolpodcaster.com/wp-content/uploads/2010/10/FINAL_Executive-Summary_2011-Law-School-Applicant-Survey.pdf.

2009 and May 2010,[10] indicated that 15% of its graduates were employed in "government jobs" and 18% in "business jobs." As pointed out by others, the government category can include graduates working in positions that do not involve the practice of law even though the graduate preferred an attorney position, and the business category could include graduates working as sales associates[11] because they could not find an attorney position. There is nothing stopping Cooley or any other law school from including in the "government" category a law graduate employed as a paralegal or including in the "business" category a graduate working as a pharmaceutical salesperson. Therefore, one can reasonably conclude that the actual percentages of graduates employed as *attorneys* in government and business jobs are less than what Cooley has reported.

As shown below, Cooley's 2010 employment report states that 76% of all graduates supplying employment information are employed. But that employment rate should not be taken at face value for three reasons.

Theodore Souris, Augustus B. Woodward, and James Witherell classes (September 2009, January 2010, and May 2010)	
Number of 2010 graduates	934
Number of graduates with employment status known	780
Percentage of graduates employed	76%
Average starting salary for all graduates	$54,796

First, notice that only 780 of 934 graduates reported their employment information. That is a response rate of 83.5%. The plaintiffs in the Cooley complaint allege that this rate is "relatively paltry" in comparison to the 97% or better rate obtained by many higher ranked law schools.[12] A sophisticated law applicant needs to wonder why 154 graduates did not respond to Cooley's questionnaire and what are they doing now. They may not all be employed. To be safe and make a conservative conclusion, a sophisticated law school applicant should assume that some of the 154 graduates are unemployed and some are employed in positions that are undesirable. A few may have enrolled in another graduate school program—perhaps going deeper into debt—to avoid the prospect of being unemployed and being responsible to repay law school loans. As Professor Tamanaha points out in his book, graduates are reluctant to admit they are unemployed or under-employed.[13] Therefore, one can reasonably assume that a significant number of these graduates were too embarrassed to let Cooley's career director know about their employment status.

The second reason why the 76% employment rate cannot be taken at face value is that an overall employment rate includes graduates who have undesirable jobs. Prior to reading this book, many of you would assume that an overall employment rate consisted of graduates with actual attorney positions. Without being warned that this data may be

10. Exhibit 2, MacDonald, No. 11-cv-00831 (Aug. 8, 2011).

11. Back in 1994, when the legal job market was fairly good, some graduates still had difficulty finding attorney positions. I knew of one graduate who worked at a large sales department store. The anti-law-school bloggers report that many graduates, after the start of the 2007 recession, are doing similar non-professional, non-legal work.

12. Amended Complaint at 27, MacDonald, No. 11-cv-00831 (W.D. Mich. Nov. 09, 2011).

13. Brian Tamanaha, Failing Law Schools 147-4 8 (2012).

unreliable, would it have occurred to you that a law school would include in the employment rate graduates employed as paralegals, secretaries, and recruiters—jobs that one could get without a law degree? Ignore for the moment that nearly one in four (24%) of Cooley's graduates reported that they are unemployed—a shocking admission in itself. Because an employment designation has more than one interpretation, sophisticated law school applicants must realize that the reported employment rates alone just are not informative enough to help them predict their post-graduation outcomes.

A third reason to be suspicious of the 76% employment rate is that Cooley fails to disclose the numerator and denominator used to get this employment rate. In reality, the 76% employment rate was achieved taking 593 and dividing it by 780, the number of graduates that supplied employment information.[14] But since Cooley had a large number of graduates unaccounted for, a sophisticated, cautious consumer should factor into the equation an unfavorable view of the 154 unaccounted-for graduates by assuming they are all unemployed or have undesirable jobs. So instead of dividing 593 by 780 and getting an employment rate of 76%, as reported by Cooley, a prospective student should divide 593 by 934, which yields an overall employment rate of 63%.

Now, let's revisit Cooley's claim that 50% of its graduates are employed in private practice. Because we know that 593 of the graduates have jobs, you would then expect approximately 297 of the 593 graduates to be employed in private practice.

PRIVATE PRACTICE Percent Employed: 50% Average Starting Salary: $52,318			
SIZE OF FIRM		*FIRMS EMPLOYING COOLEY GRADUATES*	
Self Employed	70	Sullivan, Ward, Asher & Patton, PC	Southfield, MI
2 to 10 Attorneys	157	Graff & Associates	Columbus, OH
11 to 25 Attorneys	21	Heavner,Scott, Beyers & Mihlar, PC	Chicago, IL
26 to 50 Attorneys	7	Alstock,Witkin,Kreist, & Overholtz	Pensacola, FL
51 to 100 Attorneys	5	Ryley, Carlock & Applewhite	Phoenix, AZ
101 to 250 Attorneys	7	Thompson, Meier & King, PC	Canton, GA
251 to 500 Attorneys	2	Plunkett Cooney	Bloomfield Hills, MI
501+ Attorneys	2	Hoeppner, Wagner & Evans, LLP	Valparaiso, IN
Firm Size Unknown	14	Marinosci Law Group Stewart, Greenblatt, Manning & Baez	Fort Lauderdale, FL New York, NY

But if you add up the figures reported on the left side under the heading "SIZE OF FIRM," you will see the sum total is only 285 graduates, not 297. Where are 12 of the graduates accounted for? I don't know. If you are starting to get confused, I'm not the

14. The figure 593, which was obtained by multiplying 780 by 76%, differs from the number in Cooley's official report to the ABA. If you go to the ABA's website where each ABA-accredited school now has an employment report for 2010 graduates, you can see that Cooley reported that 586 of its 2010 graduates were employed. http://employmentsummary.abaquestionnaire.org. The two figures are slightly off; however, Cooley's report does not provide an explanation of the discrepancy between the report it published to prospective law students and what it eventually reported to the ABA.

one confusing you. If one divides 285 by 780, then only 36.5% of the graduates who responded are employed in private practice, not 50%. In other words, you should see that the visual presentation creates the impression that 50% are employed; however, when you do the actual math, you can see that only 36.5% of the graduates who supplied employment information have jobs as attorneys.

A sophisticated analysis has to go even further to dissect the private practice setting. If you think that all of the 297 or 285 (whichever is correct) graduates employed in private practice are actually working as lawyers, you had better think again. Nowhere in Cooley's report does it state that these jobs require a law degree or bar passage. It is common knowledge among lawyers that, since the downturn in the legal market in 2007, some law graduates are doing document review working in temporary legal jobs and some are working as paralegals or legal assistants.[15] Although many graduates with these jobs have passed the bar exam, passage of the bar exam is not a requirement to do these jobs. As a result, an applicant needs to realize that some of the Cooley graduates working at law firms do not have traditional attorney positions because many graduates today are working temporarily in law firm offices as document reviewers.[16] When analyzing Cooley's 2010 data, an applicant needs to compare this report with reports for prior years. If one did that, one would notice that prior to 2010, Cooley had a sub-category for "Legal Temporary Agency" listed in its employment report, but that sub-category was eliminated in the 2010 report.[17] To live up to Judge Schweitzer's sophisticated consumer standard, an applicant should question why this category was eliminated. Therefore, a sophisticated applicant should recognize the possibility exists that a substantial number of the graduates reflected in the 2010 report could be employed in temporary legal jobs. Thus, the actual percentage of graduates employed in permanent positions as attorneys in private practice could be substantially less than 36.5%.

Of the 285 graduates Cooley reported are working in private practice, 70 are self-employed. That means 24% (70/285) of the graduates working in private practice are solo practitioners. Some, if not most, of these self-employed graduates are not in this position by choice, as alleged by one of the plaintiffs in the Cooley lawsuit. In its official report to the ABA, Cooley reported that 86 of its 2010 graduates are self-employed, and as a result, Cooley had the largest number of self-employed law graduates out of all the law schools.[18] Based on the official report, nearly 1/3 (86/285) of its 2010 graduates in private practice are trying to survive as entrepreneurs.

There is nothing wrong with becoming a solo attorney. However, self-employed attorneys are responsible for finding their own clients, running both the business and legal sides of the practice, hiring secretarial or paralegal support, paying for their own health insurance policies, and handling many other responsibilities. These are not easy tasks to accomplish with zero "real world" experience, and many solo practices fail for this reason. Furthermore,

15. *See, e.g.*, Daniel Fisher, *Class-Action Firms Capitalize On Wretched Market For Law-School Grads*, Forbes, Jan. 4, 2013, *available at* http://www.forbes.com/sites/danielfisher/2013/01/04/class-action-firms-capitalize-on-wretched-market-for-law-school-grads/.

16. *Id.* (describing how many graduates are actually hired by legal temp agencies and sent to the law firms to do document review work, which is basically examining documents to determine which ones should be referred to senior attorneys who are preparing for litigation). I did this work one summer after my first year of law school. Even though temp agencies and law firms require document reviewers to have a law degree and have passed the bar exam, document review work could be done by paralegals or legal secretaries.

17. *See supra* Chapter 2, pp. 30–34 for tables from Cooley's employment reports.

18. The ABA's website has an Excel spreadsheet with all of the 2010 graduation data for each law school. http://employmentsummary.abaquestionnaire.org. If you click on the link to generate the 2010 report and use the sort & filter command (largest to smallest), Cooley is number one.

solo and small-firm attorneys are more likely to get in trouble for violating rules of professional responsibility because they neither have the time nor the resources to adequately represent their clients.[19] Therefore, most law graduates do not aspire to become solo practitioners straight out of law school. Unlike Cooley, Harvard Law School, which is reputed by some to produce the brightest and most capable lawyers, has no recent law graduates working as solo practitioners. As a result, a sophisticated law applicant needs to be concerned about Cooley's high number of self-employed graduates.

Besides the 70 self-employed graduates, some of the 157 graduates that Cooley claims are working in firms with a size of 2 to 10 attorneys may also be self-employed in office-sharing arrangements or in small firms formed by a partnership of two or more recent graduates. Thus, savvy law applicants should realize that if they attend Cooley, they are very unlikely to obtain a job at a law firm with a size greater than 10 because only 44 of 285 (15%) graduates are employed in private practice at firms with a size greater than 10. Cooley graduates have to face the real possibility that they may wind up self-employed straight out of law school if they really want to practice law. Remember, self-employed does not necessarily mean the graduate is turning a profit. As I write this section, I am thinking about a recent conversation with a self-employed graduate who told me that she barely brings in enough legal fees to pay her bills and is often unable to do that.

So, exactly how many Cooley graduates in the 2010 report were working as full-time attorneys in permanent jobs? The exact number cannot be determined from the report disclosed by Cooley to the public. The plaintiffs' in the lawsuit filed against Cooley alleged that the number of graduates employed as "real" attorneys may be 25% or less.[20] That percentage is plausible based on my full analysis of Cooley's 2010 report. If you compare the 2010 report to the 2011 report, you will see that the continuing trend of a low rate of graduates being employed as fulltime attorneys. Cooley's official report to the ABA regarding its 2011 graduates show that only 37.5% (375 of its 999) of the graduates had full-time, long-term jobs as attorneys and that 80 of the graduates are self-employed. Consequently, law applicants should conclude that if they want attorney positions at traditional law firms, they have a low chance of getting such a position if they graduate from Cooley. Because Cooley's 2011 report is in compliance with the new ABA standards, it serves as a glaring example as to why new standards were necessary for reporting employment data to prospective students. As will be discussed in Chapter 4, the new standards for law schools to follow when reporting employment data do not go far enough.

Comparing Employment Data from Different Schools

Even under the ABA's pre-2012 lax standards, some law schools disclosed more detailed employment data than what Cooley did. One law school with a very different reporting

19. Ted Schneyer, *On Further Reflection: How "Professional Self-Regulation" Should Promote Compliance with Broad Ethical Duties of Law Firm Management*, 53 ARIZ. L. REV. 577, 626 n. 268 (2011) ("Evidence bears out the common belief that solo practices and small firms tend to be at greater risk for ethics violations than large firms.").

20. Prior to August 2012, the ABA did not require employment information to be disclose in a certain format. Nor did it require the employment information to contain a minimal amount of information. Amended Complaint at 3, MacDonald, No. 11-cv-00831 (W.D. Mich. Nov. 09, 2011).

method is the University of Cincinnati College of Law ("Cincinnati"). Cincinnati's website contains employment data for students graduating between December of 2009 and May of 2010.[21] While Cincinnati's employment report contains less overall information than Cooley's report, Cincinnati's report contains more relevant information. Table 3-1

Table 3-1.

	Cooley	Cincinnati
Number of Graduates	927	129
Overall Employment %	76%	87%
% of Graduates Reporting Employment Data	780/934 or 83.5%	112/129 or 87%
% Employed in Private Practice	50%???	Unknown
% Employed—Bar Passage Req'd	Unknown	56.69%
% Employed—Bar Passage Req'd Fulltime	Unknown	48%
% Employed by Their Law School	Unknown	7%
Average Salary	$54,796	$62,918
% of Graduates Reporting Salary	Unknown	22%

summarizes the post-graduate employment information that I found in June 2012 on the law schools' websites for the class of 2010. Prior to August 2012, the ABA did not require employment information to contain specific details or that it be disclosed in a certain format.

As you can see, comparing these two schools is not an easy task. First, one can see that Cincinnati reports a substantially greater overall employment rate of 87% in comparison to Cooley's 76%. At first glance Cincinnati's data may be disappointing because only 48% of its graduates are working in full-time positions that require bar passage. However, we do not know what percentage of Cooley graduates are employed in those positions just by looking at the report Cooley disseminated to the public.

Luckily, a prospective student is not left to speculate about these figures as reported on the schools' websites. As part of the new reporting requirements, the ABA now has at its website employment reports for each ABA-approved school starting with the year 2010. I have replicated below the "employment status" sections of both schools as reported at the ABA's website.[22]

If one divides 375 by 927, only 40.5% of Cooley graduates are employed in long-term positions. By contrast, 58.9% (76 ÷ 129) of Cincinnati's graduates are employed long-term. Cooley reported that 14.2% (132 ÷ 927) of its graduates were unemployed and that 16.7% (155 ÷ 927) of its graduates' employment status was unknown. As I have previously pointed out, a sophisticated applicant must assume that the latter figure is comprised of unemployed and undesirably-employed graduates. Therefore, 30.9% (14.2% + 16.7%)

21. *Employment Statistics*, UNIV. OF CINCINNATI COLL. OF LAW, http://www.law.uc.edu/prospective-students/admissions/employment-statistics (last visited Jun. 18, 2012).

22. To get a school's report, the reader can go to http://employmentsummary.abaquestionnaire.org/. The reader can probably tell that the rows do not add up to the first number in the row. The format that the ABA required for the 2012 reports (about the 2011 graduates) has been modified dramatically and makes more sense—the numbers add up—and will be discussed in Chapter 4.

THOMAS M. COOLEY LAW SCHOOL
EMPLOYMENT SUMMARY FOR 2010 GRADUATES

EMPLOYMENT STATUS	NUMBER	LONG TERM	SHORT TERM
Employed	586	375	61
Pursuing graduate degree FT	22		
Unemployed—not seeking	32		
Unemployed—seeking	132		
Employment status unknown	155		
Total graduates	927		

EMPLOYMENT BY LAW SCHOOLS	NUMBER	LONG TERM	SHORT TERM
Of employed—# law school funded	4	3	1

UNIVERSITY OF CINCINNATI COLLEGE OF LAW
EMPLOYMENT SUMMARY FOR 2010 GRADUATES

EMPLOYMENT STATUS	NUMBER	LONG TERM	SHORT TERM
Employed	112	76	31
Pursuing graduate degree FT	6		
Unemployed—not seeking	2		
Unemployed—seeking	7		
Employment status unknown	2		
Total graduates	129		

EMPLOYMENT BY LAW SCHOOLS	NUMBER	LONG TERM	SHORT TERM
Of employed—# law school funded	10	0	10

of Cooley's graduates have unacceptable employment outcomes. Cincinnati, on the other hand, only has 0.05% (7 ÷ 129) of its graduates unemployed and 0.02% (2 ÷ 129) of its graduates with an unknown employment status and, thereby, has a total of 0.07% graduates with unacceptable employment outcomes.

When one compares the law firm information below from each school, the predicament of Cooley graduates is very troubling. An astonishing 28% (86 ÷ 305) of Cooley's graduates employed at law firms are solo practitioners, but only 8% (3 ÷ 37) of Cincinnati's graduates are solo attorneys.

Cooley has a much greater percentage (53% or 163 ÷ 305) of graduates employed at firms with a size of 2–10 people than Cincinnati does (30% or 11 ÷ 37). However, as explained previously, some of those graduates are likely working together in two-person firms, and that means they are self-employed. Moreover, some were probably hired by solo practitioners in non-attorney positions, such as paralegals or legal secretaries. Cooley

THOMAS M. COOLEY LAW SCHOOL
EMPLOYMENT TYPE FOR 2010 GRADUATES

EMPLOYMENT TYPE	NUMBER	LONG TERM	SHORT TERM
Law Firms			
Solo	86	62	1
2–10	163	110	7
11–25	22	15	3
26–50	8	6	0
51–100	5	3	0
101–250	9	6	2
251–500	2	1	0
501+	2	1	1
Unknown	8	3	1

CINCINNATI, UNIVERSITY OF
EMPLOYMENT TYPE FOR 2010 GRADUATES

EMPLOYMENT TYPE	NUMBER	LONG TERM	SHORT TERM
Law Firms			
Solo	3	1	1
2–10	11	10	1
11–25	6	3	3
26–50	4	4	0
51–100	6	4	1
101–250	1	1	0
251–500	3	3	0
501+	1	1	0
Unknown	2	1	1

has a much smaller percentage (16% or 48 ÷ 305) of graduates employed at firms with a size of 11–501+ attorneys than Cincinnati does (57% or 21 ÷ 37).[23]

In addition to the employment data, law school applicants should attempt to compare salary figures. The ABA does not require law schools to report salary data and it does not have such data at its website. As reflected in Table 3-1 above, Cooley claims its graduates earn an average salary of $54,796. The problem here is that Cooley never discloses how

23. I excluded the graduates whose firm status is unknown.

many graduates supplied the salary information. Cincinnati reports that its 2010 graduates enjoy a median salary of $58,000 and an average of $62,918, but only 29 of its 112 graduates provided their salaries. Because a small percentage of Cincinnati's graduates reported their salaries and an unknown percentage of Cooley's graduates reported such information, the salary data is unhelpful and has the potential to be misleading.

After critically analyzing the numbers the schools placed on their websites and submitted to the ABA, one has a better idea about the employment prospects of graduates from Cooley and Cincinnati and should take the salary data with a HUGE grain of salt. A sophisticated analysis should cause law school applicants to realize that Cooley graduates have a very low probability of getting an attorney position at a mid-size or large law firm and a high probability of being a solo attorney. Because attorneys at mid-size-to-large law firms tend to earn higher salaries than attorneys who are self-employed or are at small firms, a law school applicant needs to weigh the risk of incurring six-figure student loan debt at Cooley for a small shot at earning a higher salary at a mid-size-to-large law firm.

Comparing Data About ABA-Approved Law Schools in the ABA-LSAC Official Guide

A sophisticated analysis should not simply end after looking at employment and salary data. Rather than only relying on information supplied by law schools on their websites, prospective law students need to consult a resource that displays the information about different law schools in a standard format because that will be more useful when comparing schools. The Law School Admission Council (LSAC) is the nonprofit organization that prepares and administers the LSAT and publishes several useful resources.[24] The *ABA-LSAC Official Guide to ABA-Approved Law Schools: 2013 Edition* ("LSAC Guide") has a standard format for displaying important statistics for every ABA-Approved law school. I doubt very seriously if more than a small percentage of law school applicants know about the LSAC Guide. You now know because you are reading this book. The same information reported in the LSAC Guide is also available on LSAC's website.[25] The LSAC Guide contains some of the information that the law schools report on their own websites, but it also contains several important statistics that the school's websites do not provide.

To continue explaining how a sophisticated law school applicant should conduct research, I will look at the official data for Cooley and Cincinnati supplied by them to the ABA and reported in the LSAC Guide.[26] The data in the 2013 LSAC Guide represents the class of 2010 and bar exam test-takers during the 2010 calendar year.

---

24. *About the Law School Admission Council*, Law School Admission Council, http://www.lsac.org/aboutlsac/about-lsac.asp (last visited Sept. 28, 2012).

25. *Official Guide to ABA-Approved Law Schools*, Law School Admission Council, https://officialguide.lsac.org/release/OfficialGuide_Default.aspx (last visited Jun. 18, 2012).

26. Law School Admission Council, ABA-LSAC Official Guide to ABA-Approved Law Schools 208–209, 748–749 (2012) (hereinafter "LSAC Guide").

Table 3-2.

	Cooley	Cincinnati
First-Time Bar Passage Rate	71.92%	100%
First-Year Attrition Rate	16.3%—124 academic; 211 other	4.2%—zero academic; 6 other
Second-Year Attrition Rate	12.1%—33 academic; 87 other	Zero
Transfers In/Out	11 in/227 out	9 in/3 out
Tuition	$34,340 Full-time for both residents and non-residents $22,090 Part-time	$22,204 Resident—Full-time $38,720 Nonresident—FT No Part-time program
Total % Receiving Grants	55.0%	70.6%
Median Grant Amount	$9,017 Full-time $6,558 Part-time	$6,500 Full-time

Table 3-2 above summarizes some of the important information in the 2013 LSAC Guide about Cooley and Cincinnati.

The first conclusion a prospective student should come to from looking at this information is that she needs to look at the LSAC Guide to see the data reported to the ABA and not simply look at what the law schools have posted on their websites! It is not in the law school's interest to advertise negative information such as high attrition rates. Prospective students should also notice that it is easier to compare schools because the data is presented in the same format for every school. However, the LSAC Guide does not clearly disclose everything an applicant needs to know and, as a result, an applicant still needs to be aware of what is lurking beneath the surface of these statistics.

A School's Bar Passage Rate Is Relevant

A savvy law school applicant should look at a school's bar passage rates. As indicated in Table 3-2, the first-time bar passage rate for Cooley graduates is only 71.92% compared to Cincinnati's rate of 100%. That means nearly 30% of the Cooley graduates were unable to become licensed practicing attorneys due to failing the bar exam. Cooley's average bar passage rate is also low in comparison to the average passage rate for test takers in Michigan.[27] If some of Cooley's bar-failing graduates were already employed as attorneys, their failing would negatively impact their employment. For example, they would not be able to appear in court on behalf of a client and may be assigned unchallenging legal work until they pass the exam. If these graduates were not employed as attorneys, their failure will prevent most of them from securing attorney positions. Cooley's bar passage rate is troubling

27. *See* 2013 LSAC Guide, (reporting that Cooley's average passage rate is 74.35% while the average passage rate for the state is 84.53%).

because the nearly 30% of the graduates who failed the bar exam have already incurred substantial student loan debt due to the tuition fees (over $34,000 per year) and are now responsible for repaying those loans or figuring out a way to defer repayment.

Professor Jane Yakowitz's study of graduates who fail the bar exam shows that five to ten years after graduating, these graduates "lag *well* behind lawyers on every measure—earnings, employment stability, even marriage and divorce rates."[28] Her study also found that these graduates "fare worse than college graduates [who never went to law school], despite their better-than-average undergraduate grades."[29] No doubt, most law school applicants believe they will pass the bar exam the first time, they should nevertheless weigh a school's low passage rate into their overall analysis of that school.

Attrition and Transfer-Out Rates Must Not Be Ignored

Besides the bar passage rate, law school applicants need to determine a school's attrition rate. The LSAC Guide defines attrition rate in two ways: (1) "academic attrition," which refers to students discontinuing their legal studies for academic reasons, and (2) "other attrition," which includes students who transfer and who leave for other reasons.[30] These attrition definitions appear to be intentionally vague. Let me make it plain—the academic attrition rate is the percentage of students who fail to satisfy the minimum GPA requirement, which is usually a 2.0. I do not mean to sound harsh, but I call that the "flunk out" rate even though the student may not have received a "F" or "E" grade. The "other attrition" rate is the percentage of students who drop out or withdraw for reasons other than academic failure. In the 2013 LSAC Guide, the total attrition rate for Cooley's first year law students was 16.3% (or 335 students) while the total attrition rate for Cincinnati's first-year students was only 4.2% (or 6 students). The attrition rates for second-year law students at Cooley and Cincinnati were 12.1% (120 students) and 0% (zero students) respectively.

Prospective law students might be wondering "why should I care about a school's attrition rate since I expect to do well?" The attrition rate may signal a difference in philosophies regarding access to law school and the process of "weeding out" students who are not likely to do well. Cooley prides itself on being accessible to all,[31] particularly to minorities.[32] Perhaps in keeping with that philosophy, Cooley makes admission offers

---

28. *See* Jane Yakowitz, *Marooned: An Empirical Investigation of Law School Graduates Who Fail the Bar Exam*, 60 J. Legal Educ. 3, 4 (2010). She estimates that 170,000 graduates have never passed the bar exam even though they have tried. *Id.* at 15–17.

29. *Id.* at 4. Her study finds that bar-failing graduates "spring back and out-perform the average college graduate in the latter half of their careers." However, bar-failing graduates never catch up with their peers who pass the bar exam the first time.

30. 2013 LSAC Guide.

31. *History*, Thomas M. Cooley Law School, http://www.cooley.edu/about/history.html (last visited Jan. 10, 2013) ("Thomas Cooley is also committed to providing a legal education to people from all walks of life.").

32. Michael Sasso, *Law School Breaks Ground in Riverview*, Tampa Trib., Sept. 21, 2011, *available at* 2011 WLNR 18951542 (quoting Jeff Martlew, the associate dean of the Cooley's Tampa Bay campus, as stating "Cooley Law prides itself on its appeal to minorities, and it believes it will find strong demand

to most of its applicants. As indicated in the 2013 LSAC Guide, Cooley made admission offers to 3,230 of its 4,032 applicants or 80%. Many of these applicants, however, have LSAT scores and GPAs that are too low for them to gain admission at first and second tier law schools. Longstanding research shows that a low LSAT score is a predictor of low first-year grades in law school and of difficulty in passing the bar exam on the first try.

Cooley's attrition rate has been high consistently. For example, in the 2012 LSAC Guide, Cooley had an attrition rate of 14.8% for first-year students and 14.9% for second-year students.[33] That means that the matriculation process[34] at Cooley resulted in nearly 30% (or 430) of the admitted students either flunking out or dropping out. If a student has to borrow to cover tuition ($30,644 for full-time for the year 2009) and living expenses ($13,800), $44,444 per year is a lot of money for a student to borrow just to have access to a legal education at an institution with a high attrition rate and relatively low employment rate. A student who either flunks or drops out of Cooley now has a burdensome debt load without enjoying an increase in employability as a traditional attorney.

Looking at Table 3-3 (next page), a prospective law student can see how Cooley fares in comparison to the top-ten least selective schools for the class of 2009.

The schools on this list make admission offers to the majority of people that apply, and Cooley tops the list. Except for University of Puerto Rico School of Law, which is a public school that charges very low tuition, all of the other schools are private schools and have relatively high tuition rates. Cooley, along with, five other schools on the list of the top-ten least selective schools have double-digit attrition rates.

Cincinnati, on the other hand, makes admission offers to only 43% of its applicants and has an extremely low attrition rate.[35] The 2012 LSAC guide shows that in 2009 Cincinnati received 1,823 applications, made 775 admission offers, but only 144 students matriculated. Because Cincinnati admits a significant number of students with high LSAT scores, etc., one could describe Cincinnati's admission policy as selective, exclusionary or elitist. Given this example of the difference in admission policies between Cincinnati and Cooley, a sophisticated applicant needs to assess how she feels about open and selective admission policies in light of a school's attrition rate. If racial diversity is important, the student can consult the LSAC Guide to see the percentages of admitted students based on race.

In addition to its attrition rate and admissions policy, Cooley's transfer rate is alarming because 153 students transferred from Cooley to other law schools. However, *only one* student transferred from Cincinnati to another law school. Keep in mind that Cooley is nearly ten times the size of Cincinnati. Note that many of the students who transferred may also be counted in Cooley's attrition rate. Nevertheless, it is still obvious that a substantial number of Cooley students are eager to transfer to a different school. A sophisticated law school applicant has to wonder why they wanted to get out of Cooley so badly and enroll in another law school. If the applicant considers that Cooley has a large

---

among blacks and Hispanics in the Bay area"). He also stated that one of Cooley's mottos is "big, cheap and good."

33. 2012 LSAC GUIDE, at 749 (reporting that 107 first-year students withdrew due to academic failure and 183 withdrew for other reasons, thereby yielding a total attrition rate of 14.8 and also reporting that 64 second-year students withdrew due to academic failure and 76 withdrew for other reasons, thereby yielding a total attrition rate of 14.9).

34. *See supra* note 48, in Chapter 1 where I define matriculation broadly to mean enrolling in law school and completing all of the school's JD degree requirements.

35. 2012 LSAC GUIDE.

Table 3-3. The Top 10 Least Selective Schools in 2010

	Full-Time Applications+	Full-Time Offers+	Full-Time Offer Rate	Transfer Out Rate	Full-Time Tuition Resident	Full-Time Tuition Non-Resident	1st Year Academic Attrition*	1st Year Other Attrition*	1st Year Overall Attrition Rate
Cooley Law	4211	3553	84.4%	153	$30,644	$30,644	107	183	14.8%
Phoenix Law	2350	1682	71.6%	30	$36,036	$36,036	26	37	17.6%
Florida Coastal Law	6021	4174	69.3%	91	$34,712	$34,712	57	85	21.4%
Valparaiso Law	1350	921	68.2%	25	$36,800	$36,800	8	33	19.2%
Puerto Rico Law	243	162	66.7%	0	$7,611	$9,437	5	0	1.3%
Roger Williams Law	1501	949	63.2%	9	$38,010	$38,010	5	14	8.7%
Charlotte Law	3328	2065	62.0%	18	$34,990	$34,990	21	29	18.1%
New England Boston	2734	1680	61.4%	18	$39,990	$39,990	20	34	13.5%
Appalachian Law	1368	816	59.6%	12	$28,325	$28,325	0	11	8.7%
Vermont Law	1056	628	59.5%	11	$42,220	$42,220	0	12	5.2%

Data Source: 2012 LSAC Guide.

+ Data for entering class of Fall 2010; * Attrition figures are for first-year students who dropped out or flunked out in 2009.

number of students transferring, flunking, or dropping out in the first two years of law school, the applicant can then understand why Cooley graduates accused the school of having "lackluster retention rates" in their lawsuit.[36]

Scholarships and Tuition Costs Are Crucial Factors to Consider

Along with the attrition and transfer rates, a law school applicant must consider a school's tuition costs and scholarship offers when choosing among competing admission offers. According to the 2012 LSAC Guide, Cooley awarded grants and scholarships covering full tuition to 149 students while Cincinnati awarded only one full-tuition scholarship. However, the scholarship information provided in the LSAC Guide does not contain a few of the most important details a student should know when accepting an admission offer based on a scholarship award. Before making any decisions, a sophisticated applicant needs to find out what the minimum requirements are that must be met to retain the scholarship. Schools usually require a student to maintain a certain GPA to keep a merit-based scholarship for the second and third years of law school. Therefore, an applicant needs to discover the school's grading curve.

The ability to sustain a 3.0 GPA at one school can mean something completely different at another school. Each law school has its own grading curve. Moreover, achieving high grades in law school is substantially more difficult in comparison to grade performance in undergraduate school. Grades for many courses in law school are based on *only* one exam taken at the end of the semester. Consequently, a scholarship recipient cannot assume that a 3.2 GPA requirement can easily be satisfied just because the recipient always maintained at least a 3.5 GPA as an undergraduate student. If the law school applicant discovers, for example, that he or she needs to be in the top 50% of the class to keep a scholarship, the applicant needs to consider the risk he or she is taking. Applicants must, therefore, factor into the total education expenditure the cost of paying tuition for the second and third years just in case a scholarship is lost.

In a lawsuit filed against Golden Gate University School of Law ("Golden Gate"), graduates accused the school of awarding scholarships to 57% of the first-year students and alleged that under the school's grading curve only 33% of them could possibly earn the GPA required to maintain their scholarships.[37] Some law students naively assume that they will finish in the top ten-percent of their classes because they have been excellent students their entire lives. They gloss over the fact that they will be competing with an entire class of high-achieving students who also expect to earn top grades. If one connects the dots of losing a scholarship to dropping out of law school, a sophisticated law school applicant could conclude that one reason why students may drop out of law schools such as Golden Gate and Cooley is because their GPAs for the first year were insufficient to retain their scholarships, and, therefore, they chose to drop out instead of paying full tuition for the last two years of law school.

36. Amended Complaint at 24, MacDonald, No. 11-cv-00831 (W.D. Mich. Nov. 09, 2011).

37. Class Action Complaint at 10, Arring v. Golden Gate Univ., No. CGC-12-517837 (Cal. Superior Feb. 1, 2012).

Law school applicants or transfer students who are racial minorities or come from economically disadvantaged backgrounds should also inquire about the demographics of those who drop out, voluntarily or otherwise, and those who lose scholarships. The LSAC Guide does not disclose the race or socio-economic status of those who drop out or lose scholarships.

The reason applicants and transfer students should make this inquiry is that if a school claims to have an open admissions policy or a generous scholarship program to increase admission of students from more diverse backgrounds, the policy or program may be suspect if, for example, a disproportionate number of racial minorities drop out or lose their scholarships. Suspect open admissions policies and generous scholarships may deprive minorities of their investment in human capital when a disproportionate number of minorities drop out with large student loan debt and no ability to be employed as lawyers.

Now let's return to the comparison of Cooley and Cincinnati to consider the cost of a legal education at each school. If the law school applicant gets admitted to both and will have to pay out-of-state tuition, a legal education will cost more at Cincinnati than at Cooley. Tuition and cost of living for 2012–2013 academic year are estimated at $54,476 for full-time enrollment at Cooley[38] and $41,872 for residents enrolling full-time at Cincinnati.[39] For non-residents enrolling at Cincinnati, the costs are estimated at $59,380.[40] If the applicant attends Cincinnati as a non-resident, that amounts to an estimated additional expense of up to $14,712 over the course of three years when compared to Cooley.[41] However, the additional expense may be worth the investment. Based on the above, thorough analysis of the available data from each school, Cincinnati has extremely low attrition and transfer rates, a much better first-time bar passage rate, a substantially higher employment rate for graduates employed in private practice, and a substantially higher overall employment rate. Therefore, a JD from Cincinnati offers its graduates better outcomes than Cooley does and might be worth the price if the applicant strongly desires to become a practicing lawyer.

While I have done a detailed comparison of Cooley and Cincinnati, this comparison does not confirm the *US News* ranking system. In Chapter 7, I provide a comparison of the University of Illinois College of Law and the University of Nebraska College of Law that demonstrates that Nebraska, although ranked lower than Illinois by *US News*, is a better value and, thus, proves the limitations of this ranking system.

My Story

Consider how I decided which law school to attend even though I did not have the benefit of the LSAC Guide and other resources. In 1991, I got offers of admission from all six of the law schools to which I applied, but I did not know anything about law schools or how to pick the best one. I was a first-generation college student, and I did not have

38. $39,750 tuition + $14,726 COL = $54,476. *See* Estimated Academic Expenses 2012–13, http://www.cooley.edu/finaid/tuition_incoming.html (last visited Sept. 28, 2012).

39. $23,536 tuition + $18,336 COL = $41,872. *See* Tuition and Budget Information, http://www.law.uc.edu/prospective-students/financial-aid/tuition-and-budget-information (last visited Sept. 28, 2012).

40. $41,044 tuition + $18,336 COL = $59,380. *Id.*

41. A student may incur substantially less over 3 years at Cincinnati if the student is able to secure in-state residency for the last two years of law school.

any friends or relatives who were lawyers. Contrary to Judge Schweitzer's opinion, I was not sophisticated by any stretch of the imagination. Nevertheless, I used my accounting background to do a cost-benefit analysis and chose to go to West Virginia University College of Law ("WVU") because the school gave me a full tuition scholarship. I did not know anything about rankings. It would not have mattered because, back then, rankings existed for only the top 20 law schools. However, based on today's rankings, I received offers from schools, including Cincinnati, ranked higher than WVU.

At the time I applied, I knew I would work hard and expected to secure a job as an attorney after graduation. However, I had no idea about how large my post-graduation salary would be. Therefore, I could not take a chance on going to a place like Cincinnati, where I would have had to borrow $60,000 to pay for my education but could end up getting a job with insufficient income to pay my debts and enjoy a decent lifestyle. I grew up as a very poor kid in New Orleans, and I lived a life of subsistence for many years. I was not about to incur what I perceived to be a staggering amount of debt just to pursue a law degree and wind up struggling to survive. So WVU was the only logical choice for me. After three years of law school, my salary as an attorney at a Pittsburgh law firm doubled what I was making as accountant prior to law school. Attending WVU law school was, therefore, worth the price for me.

I attended WVU with a flexible mindset when it came to employment, and I was willing to make West Virginia my home. Some graduates today are not able to take advantage of all job opportunities because they inflexible when it comes to job location. For example, they attend law school in Ohio knowing all along that they only want to practice in highly-competitive job markets like Chicago or New York City, areas with the largest numbers of local and regional law schools. Because I was flexible, I interviewed extensively the fall semester of my third year of law school, and I received an offer from a law firm in Pittsburgh, Pennsylvania.

Even if I had not been able to secure a law firm job, I believe I still would have been happy with my decision to go to WVU because I had incurred very little debt to obtain a great legal education. Because I got to attend law school and incur so little debt, I was empowered to pursue a more rewarding career. All of the jobs that I have had since graduating from law school have been more rewarding than my job as an accountant for a Fortune 500 company.

Loan Assistance Programs Must Be Considered

I had so little to weigh when I made my decision to go to law school, but today's applicants have to weigh a lot more factors given that they will most likely incur a six-figure student loan debt. A law school applicant should also consider whether the preferred law school is located in a state that has loan forgiveness or repayment programs or if the school itself has such programs. According to the ABA's website, 24 states have loan repayment assistance programs (LRAPs).[42] Due to lack of funding, LRAPs in four other

42. The following jurisdictions have LARPs: Arizona, District of Columbia, Florida, Illinois, Iowa, Louisiana, Maine, Maryland, Massachusetts, Minnesota, Mississippi, Montana, New Hampshire, New Mexico, New York (two programs), North Carolina, Ohio, Oregon, Pennsylvania, South Carolina, Texas, Vermont, and Virginia. *See* State Loan *Repayment Assistance Programs*, AM. BAR ASSOC., http://

states have been substantially curtailed or suspended altogether.[43] Some loan forgiveness or repayment programs are income based while others are dependent on the eligible graduate being employed for a specified number of years in a public service position (e.g., legal aid attorney or public defender). Some law schools[44] and non-profit organizations have their own loan repayment assistance programs, and, as a result, a law graduate may be able to take advantage of more than one program simultaneously. Please read Chapter 14 for a more thorough explanation of eligibility requirements for programs designed to enable graduates to make affordable loan payments. The good news is that law school applicants do not have to shun law school for fear of incurring insurmountable debt. Moreover, these programs provide a ray of hope for law school applicants who are committed to doing public service, but are worried about how they will be able to repay their student loan debt based on a public servant's salary.

What Are the Employment Rates for the Schools That Have Been Sued?

As promised earlier, I compare in Table 3-4 (next page) all the schools that have been sued for allegedly reporting deceptive employment data. I want the reader to see how their pre-2012 overall employment rates compare to the rates that schools are forced to disclose under Revised Standard 509.

The number of graduates employed in full-time, long-term jobs that require passage of the bar exam is indicated in column three of the table above and I refer to them as "Permanent Bar-Passage Required Jobs." This job categorization is the best descriptor of graduates who have traditional attorney jobs because bar-exam passage is a requirement only for practicing attorneys. I have arranged the 15 schools from the lowest percentage[45] of graduates employed in Permanent Bar-Passage Required Jobs. As you can see, Golden Gate has the lowest rate of 22% (42 out of 191 graduates) followed by Thomas Jefferson, which has a rate of 26.7% (63 out of 236 graduates). Observe that in the fourth column, most of these schools claimed, for several years, to have an extremely high employment rate because they counted all graduates employed in *any* capacity, including jobs that most law students consider to be *unsuccessful* employment.

---

www.americanbar.org/groups/legal_aid_indigent_defendants/initiatives/loan_repayment_assistance_programs/state_loan_repayment_assistance_programs.html (last visited Jan. 10, 2013).

43. *State Loan Repayment Assistance Programs*, Am. Bar Assoc., http://www.americanbar.org/groups/legal_aid_indigent_defendants/initiatives/loan_repayment_assistance_programs/state_loan_repayment_assistance_programs.html (last visited Jan. 10, 2013) (stating that "Kentucky and Washington are providing assistance to current recipients, but will not be taking applications, and LRAP in Indiana, Missouri and Nebraska have been suspended").

44. For example, Stanford Law School typically appropriates $2 million for its loan repayment assistance program for graduates employed in public service jobs. Karen Sloan, *Stanford Dips into Savings to Meet Financial Aid Promises*, Nat'l L. J., Sept. 27, 2012.

45. The denominator is the total number of graduates.

Table 3-4. Law Schools Sued for Reporting Deceptive Data

Schools Ranked from Lowest Rate of Grads with FTLT Bar-Passage Required Jobs	Total # of 2011 Grads	2011 Grads Employed-FTLT Bar-Passage Required	% of Grads Employed-FTLT Bar-Passage Required	Lawsuits Allege Employ't Rates Claimed by Schools^Δ	2011 Grads Employed-FTLT JD Advantage	2011 Grads Un-employed-Seeking	% of 2011 Grads Un-employed-Seeking	2011 Grads with Unknown Employ't Status	% of Grads w/Unknown Status
Golden Gate Law School	191	42	22.0%	80–95%	15	34	17.8%	3	1.6%
Thomas Jefferson Law School	236	63	26.7%	56–92%	13	74	31.4%	8	3.4%
San Francisco Law School	222	76	34.2%	90–95%	17	26	11.7%	13	5.9%
Southwestern Law School	298	103	34.6%	97–98%	53	30	10.1%	25	8.4%
New York Law School	515	183	35.5%	90–92%	59	75	14.6%	23	4.5%
Florida Coastal Law School	451	165	36.6%	80–95%	20	61	13.5%	1	0.2%
Cooley School of Law	999	375	37.5%	76–82%	63	110	11.0%	263	26.3%
Cal. Western Law School	285	112	39.3%	90–93%	8	34	11.9%	31	10.9%
Depaul University Law School	319	129	40.4%	88–98%	35	66	20.7%	11	3.4%
Hofstra Univ. Law School	297	121	40.7%	91–96%	20	27	9.1%	19	6.4%
John Marshall Law School	401	174	43.4%	90–100%	51	56	14.0%	12	3.0%
Widener University Law School	252	119	47.2%	OVER 90%	19	20	7.9%	22	8.7%
Brooklyn Law School	455	215	47.3%	88–98%	32	108	23.7%	9	2.0%
Albany Law School	236	118	50.0%	90–97%	14	26	11.0%	4	1.7%
Chicago-Kent Law School	332	169	50.9%	90–97%	19	33	9.9%	14	4.2%

Data Source: http://employmentsummary.abaquestionnaire.org/.
FTLT: Full-time, Long-term; ^Δ See complaints filed by graduates.

Because the ABA now forces disclosure of the number of Permanent Bar-Passage Required Jobs, prospective students can now see how small of a chance they may have of obtaining such employment if they go to one of these schools. Moreover, most schools have 10% or more of their graduates who are unemployed and seeking employment.

Observe that Albany and Chicago-Kent have an employment rate that is not far off from the national percentage of graduates with Permanent Bar-Passage Required Jobs. In its Class of 2011 National Summary Report,[46] NALP reports 65.4% of 2011 graduates have bar-passage-required jobs. However, as depicted in Chart 3-1, this percentage was achieved by using as the denominator only the number graduates with a known employment status and not the total number of all 2011 graduates.

Chart 3-1.

No. of 2011 Grads with Bar-Passage-Required Jobs (includes full and part-time and temporary jobs)	27,224
No. of 2011 Grads with Known Employment Status	41,623
No. of 2011 Grads with Bar-Passage-Required Jobs (includes full and part-time and temporary jobs)	27,224
Total No. of All 2011 Grads	44,495

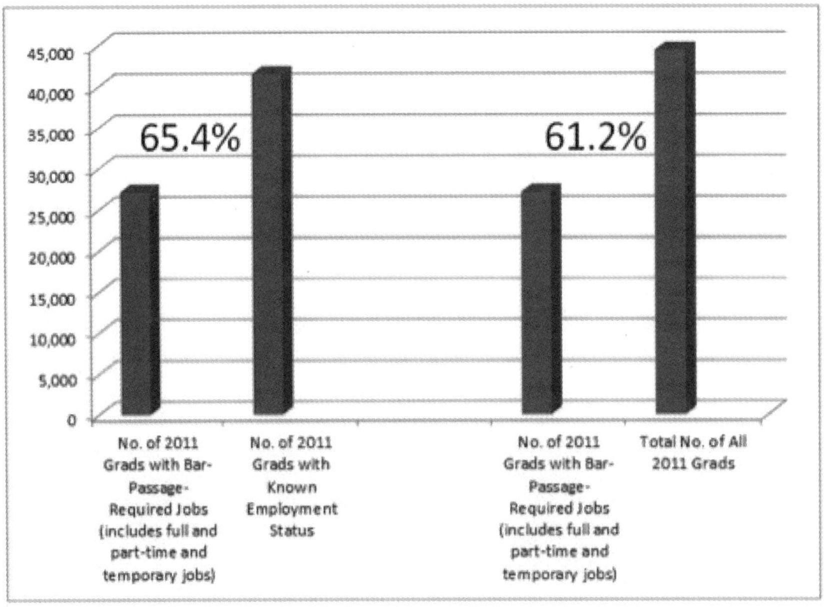

I've already explained that the sophisticated applicant should assume unaccounted for graduates are either unemployed or under-employed and factor them into the calculation. The NALP report does *not* provide the exact number of graduates with both full-time and long-term jobs requiring bar passage. It does, however, indicate that 24,902 graduates have full-time, bar-passage-required job. If you divide that number by the total number (44,495)

46. *Class of 2011 National Summary Report*, NALP, http://www.nalp.org/classof2011 (last visited January 8, 2013).

Table 3-5. Bar-Passage, Attrition, and Tuition Data

Law Schools Sued for Reporting Deceptive Data	Full-Time Tuition Resident & Non-Resident+	1st Time Bar Passage Rate**	1st Year Overall Attrition Rate*	2nd Year Overall Attrition Rate*
Albany Law School	$40,120	82.89%	2.7%	5.4%
Brooklyn Law School	$46,635	87.97%	6.3%	0.4%
Cal. Western Law School	$40,780	77.93%	18.8%	1.0%
Chicago-Kent Law School	$40,050	95.17%	10.5%	2.1%
Cooley School of Law	$30,644	77.41%	14.8%	14.9%
Depaul Law School	$39,350	92.39%	9.1%	0.3%
Florida Coastal Law School	$34,712	78.77%	21.4%	6.8%
Golden Gate Law School	$38,375	64.16%	20.6%	2.6%
Hofstra Univ. Law School	$43,660	76.54%	13.7%	4.4%
John Marshall Law School	$36,920	85.11%	23.5%	3.6%
New York Law School	$46,460	81.14%	10.6%	0.9%
San Francisco Law School	$38,800	78.33%	12.7%	4.1%
Southwestern Law School	$39,110	61.23%	9.3%	11.0%
Thomas Jefferson L.S.	$19,350	48.15%	31.4%	6.1%
Widener Law School	$34,890	85.85%	25.4%	0.0%

Data Source: 2012 LSAC Guide.

* Attrition—2009 first-year students who dropped out or flunked out; ** Grads who took the bar exam during 2009; + Data by LSAC for entering class of Fall 2010.

of graduates, you discover that only 56% of the 2011 graduates have full-time bar-passage required jobs. Therefore, the 56 percentage for all graduates is relatively close to the percentage of graduates of Albany and Chicago-Kent with Permanent Bar-Passage Required Jobs.

So now let's assume for the sake of further comparisons that Samantha, a prospective student, has admission offers from Widener, Brooklyn, Albany, and Chicago-Kent and that she considers them to have very similar employment rates for the Bar Passage Jobs and that they are close in line with the national rate. Thanks to the ABA's new reporting standard and the LSAC Guide, Samantha has resources to easily compare the schools on other factors. Look again at the Table 3-4 on page 67. When Samantha compares these four schools, she can see that Brooklyn has a large number (108 or 23.7%) of graduates who are unemployed and seeking. However, as shown in Table 3-5 above, Widener-Delaware has a large first-year attrition rate (25.4%) and a relatively low bar passage rate (85.85%) for first-time takers. In comparison to Widener, Albany has a very low attrition rate.

Albany may, therefore, be the best of the four schools, especially if Samantha's LSAT score puts her in the bottom 25th percentile, and she is worried about being at risk of either flunking or dropping out.

Just because Albany may appear to be the best based on the four factors above, Samantha cannot stop her analysis there. The problem now is that she will have to talk to personnel at the four law schools to gather other important information to be certain that Albany gives her the most "bang for her buck." In Chapter 8, I discuss the limitations in getting truthful information not available in the LSAC Guide. If Albany offers her a full scholarship and she wants to practice in New York, than Albany may be the best choice.

To summarize, law school applicants are expected to be sophisticated consumers and, therefore, cannot rely on rankings when choosing to accept an offer of admission. A few schools can claim a higher ranking using a ranking system other than the one published by *U.S. News*.[47] For example, one of the founders of Cooley has devised his own rankings system reflected in a report titled "Judging the Law Schools." In the 2010 report, Cooley is ranked in second place, right behind Harvard University Law School![48] The *National Jurist* recently announced its list of Best Law Schools 2013, where Stanford received the highest final GPA of 3.90, making it number one on the list. Harvard received a final GPA of 3.20, making it No. 24 on the list.[49]

Rather than rely on any rankings system, applicants must critically analyzed a law school's employment data, attrition rate, admission rate, transfer rate, first-time bar passage rate, scholarship retention rate, tuition fee, cost-of-living expense, and loan forgiveness program. The applicant must assess all of these factors in light of the applicant's reason for going to law school and in light of the applicant's current employment status. Some law graduates have become very unhappy after incurring six-figure debt, but earning only a mid-level five-figure salary.

In the next chapter, I show how the ABA's new reporting standards can be exploited to hide under-employed graduates. I also revisit NYLS by showing that, even after its victory in getting the lawsuit dismissed, NYLS continues to report data that could be interpreted as misleading, especially when compared to reporting done by much higher ranked law schools.

47. Because the *US News* ranking system is considered flawed for various reasons, several others have created their own ranking system.

48. *Harvard Number 1, Cooley Number 2. Here's How* (Feb. 7, 2011), *available at* http://www.cooley.edu/news/2011/020411_judging_the_law_schools.html.

49. *See Best Schools Revisited*, NAT'L JURIST MAG., Mar. 2013, Vol.22, No.6, pp. 27–31.

Chapter 4

A Lot of Wiggle Room Remains in the ABA's New Disclosure Standards

"[B]arely 65% of 2011 graduates had landed law-related employment within nine months of graduation, the lowest rate since NALP began reporting in 1985. Even the 65% number is suspect, given the powerful, rankings-driven incentives schools have to cook the figures."[1] James Huffman, Dean *Emeritus* of Lewis & Clark Law School

Law schools have been widely criticized for a lack of transparency in reporting employment and salary data. Professor Tamanaha argues that game theory may be in play amongst law schools, keeping everyone from engaging in ethically sound behavior.[2] Allow me explain game theory in the context of steroid abuse and then compare it to the problem of misrepresenting employment information. The temptation for players to use steroids is high because (1) steroids are effective in enhancing sports performance, (2) detection of steroids is often difficult, and (3) the payoff of steroid usage is great. "Once a few athletes choose to break ranks and violate the rules to gain a competitive advantage, this induces others to do so as well."[3] Similarly, law schools benefit from counting every graduate who is employed in *any* capacity so that they can claim to have very high employment rates. Furthermore, the ABA has not acted to punish any law school for deceptive reporting practices, and *US News* simply relies on employment data submitted by the law schools to create the "top law schools" list. Because prospective students have no way to access a school's raw employment data, it is impossible for them to detect misleading employment reports. This means that so long as even one school is benefiting from the practice of hiding under-employed graduates, some law schools will want to engage in this practice to level the playing field.

As you saw in the last chapter, although no state court judge has held law schools liable for their reporting practices, judges recognize the fact that law schools have engaged in reporting practices that are seriously lacking in transparency and want law schools to do better.[4] As discussed briefly below, prior to these lawsuits, many had been calling for

1. James Huffman, Commentary, *Perverse Incentives of the Lawyers Guild*, Wall Street Journal, at A13, Feb. 21, 2013, *available at* http://online.wsj.com/article/SB10001424127887324162304578305710253751052.html?mod=googlenews_wsj.

2. Dionne Koller, *From Medals to Morality: Sportive Nationalism and the Problem of Doping in Sports*, 19 Marq. Sports L. Rev. 91, 94 (2008).

3. *Id.* at 94.

4. *See, e.g.*, *MacDonald*, U.S. Dist. LEXIS 100785, at *9 (Judge Quist stated that "the bottom line is that the statistics provided by Cooley and other law schools in a format required by the ABA were so vague and incomplete as to be meaningless and could not reasonably be relied upon."); *Gomez-Jimenez*, 943 N.Y.S.2d 834. ("The fact is, however, that all data collection starts with the law schools themselves, and it is this court's fervent hope that all the heat generated around this issue over this last year will be replaced with a renewed sense of responsibility to prospective applicants and students, starting at the law school level.").

law schools to provide full and accurate disclosures. After years of a rising tide of criticisms lodged against the ABA and its law schools, the ABA finally reacted and revised its standards in August 2012. Unfortunately, its standards do not go far enough to address the criticisms.

Pre-2012 Voices Demanding Full Accurate Disclosures[5]

One of the most outspoken and dedicated pre-2012 voices is that of Law School Transparency (LST). Established in 2009, LST is a nonprofit legal education policy organization that works to improve information given to consumers, and it advocates for reform to current law school models.[6] LST consists of Kyle McEntee, Patrick Lynch, Derek Tokaz, Natalie Reyes,[7] an advisory board consisting of formal advisory board members, law professors, current students, recent graduates, and attorneys, and other volunteers.[8] In April 2010, Mr. McEntee and Mr. Lynch posted online a white paper explaining why the employment reports published by law schools were misleading and setting forth their proposed model for reporting employment data.[9] In this paper, eventually published in a law journal,[10] the authors explain the "LST Proposal," which would require schools to report a host of information, including the graduates' employer type, employer name, and position name as well as whether the job requires bar exam passage and is full-time, part-time, temporary or permanent. The LST Proposal was not unreasonable because NALP already collected this information from each school but only disclosed to the public general aggregated information.

After finding that law schools were slow to respond to calls for transparency, LST created the Data Clearinghouse, a user-friendly online database of employment and salary information about ABA-approved law schools.[11] The data that LST publishes is compiled from information supplied by the ABA, *U.S. News*, school websites, and NALP reports that have been cross referenced and reconciled to provide a more accurate set of statistics for the public.[12] This Data Clearinghouse is already having a positive effect on the legal landscape. Now some law schools actively seek to update the information accumulated

5. Amended Complaint at 26, MacDonald, No. 11-cv-00831 (W.D. Mich. Nov. 11, 2011).

6. *Mission*, Law School Transperncy, http://www.lawschooltransparency.com/about/mission/ (last visited Jan. 8, 2013) (hereinafter "Law School Transparency Mission").

7. *Our Team*, LawSchoolTransparency.com, http://www.lawschooltransparency.com/about/team/ (last visited Jan. 8, 2013) (each of these individuals obtained their JD from prestigious schools and are currently practicing attorneys).

8. *Id.*

9. David Lat & Elie Mystal, *Increasing Transparency in Employment Reporting by Law Schools: What Is To Be Done?*, Above the Law, Apr. 2010, http://abovethelaw.com/2010/04/increasing-transparency-in-employment-reporting-by-law-schools-what-is-to-be-done/.

10. Kyle McEntee & Patrick Lynch, *A Way Forward: Transparency at American Law Schools*, 32 Pace L. Rev. 1 (2012) (initially posted, April 10, 2010, on the Social Science Research Network at http://papers.ssrn.com/sol3/papers.cfm?abstract_id=1528862#.pdf).

11. Law School Transparency Mission, *supra* note 6.

12. *LST Score Report, available at* http://www.lawschooltransparency.com/clearinghouse/ (last visited Jan. 8, 2013).

by LST.[13] For example, after making the 15 Worst Law Schools list based on employment data in LST's Data Clearinghouse, two law schools contacted LST with correct information, and, as a result, these schools were removed from that list.[14]

Many voices in the legal community have taken notice of the usefulness of LST. *Above The Law* readers recognized LST as lawyers of the year in 2010 for their work.[15] When referring to the dismal state of the U.S. legal market, *Law Fuel*[16] relied on the analysis of data reported by the ABA and gathered by LST.[17] The *National Jurist*,[18] whose main audience is current and prospective law students,[19] derived a grading scale to reflect the level of transparency that a law school has based on feedback from, among other entities, LST.[20] Under the *National Jurist's* grading scale, 41% of law schools received a failing grade and an additional 15% received a D. Schools that reported only what the ABA requires received a C. Six schools received an A+, nine received an A, and eleven received an A–. Along with simply failing to report certain information, schools were penalized if they presented misleading data. Beth Kransberger, the associate dean for student affairs at Thomas Jefferson School of Law (which received one of the highest rankings in the report), remarked that the trend towards greater transparency is a positive one for law schools.[21]

LST and the *National Jurist* are not the only pre-2012 voices to show concern over the ABA requirements for law school employment statistics. In March of 2011, *U.S. News* admitted that it "agrees with the efforts of Law School Transparency to improve employment information from law schools and make the data more widely available" and that "more still needs to be done by all parties."[22] The *New Republic* in April of 2011 acknowledged the need for more and better information for prospective law students, and that while such information "will make law school look like a far worse investment than it does at present," it is needed to protect consumers.[23] In 2011, in a letter to former ABA president Stephen N. Zack, United States Senator Barbara Boxer requested a detailed summary of the ABA's plans for information reform due to the increasing number of news articles

---

13. *Data Clearinghouse Updates*, Law School Transparency, http://www.lawschooltransparency.com/2012/05/data-clearinghouse-updates/ (last visited Jan. 8, 2013).

14. *Americans Like the Rich, and the Rich Benefit America*, TaxProf Blog, http://taxprof.typepad.com/taxprof_blog/2012/05/page/4/ (last visited Jan. 8, 2013). The reader needs to scroll down the page and find the link to a posting titled "The 15 Worst Law Schools."

15. David Lat, *ATL's Lawyer of the Year (2010): The Winner*, Above The Law, http://abovethelaw.com/2011/01/atls-lawyer-of-the-year-2010-the-winner/ (last visited Jan. 8, 2013).

16. *About*, LawFuel.com, http://www.lawfuel.co.nz/about (a website operating since 2001 to provide law news and information on law job sites) (last visited Jan. 8, 2013).

17. *The End of the Golden Era ... For Lawyers*, LawFuel.com, http://www.lawfuel.co.nz/news/340/the-end-of-the-golden-era-for-lawyers (last visited Jan. 8, 2013).

18. *About*, The National Jurist, http://www.nationaljurist.com/content/about (last visited Jan. 8, 2013) (A magazine which provides news regarding legal education).

19. Joanna L. Grossman, *Feminist Law Journals and the Rankings Conundrum*, 12 Colum. J. Gender & L. 522, 531 (2003).

20. *Law School Transparency Rankings*, TaxProf Blog (Mar. 22, 2012), http://taxprof.typepad.com/taxprof_blog/2012/03/law-school.html.

21. Elizabeth Ewing, *Are Law Schools Failing When it Comes to Employment Transparency?*, National Jurist, Mar. 2012, at 22–23 *available at* http://www.nxtbook.com/nxtbooks/cypress/nationaljurist0312/#/22.

22. Robert Morse, *U.S. News Urges Law School Deans to Improve Employment Data*, U.S. News & World Rep.: Educ. (Mar. 9, 2011), http://www.usnews.com/education/blogs/college-rankings-blog/2011/03/09/us-news-urges-law-school-deans-to-improve-employment-data.

23. Paul Campos, *Served: How Law Schools Completely Misrepresent Their Job Numbers*, The New Republic (Apr. 25, 2011, 12:00 AM), http://www.tnr.com/article/87251/law-school-employment-harvard-yale-georgetown.

about the reporting of admissions and post-graduation information.[24] Senator Charles E. Grassley sent a similar letter requesting information and attention by Mr. Zack.[25] Bill Hebert, the president of the State Bar of California, published an article in response to the growing concern over the responsibilities of law schools that addressed guidelines to which future law school applicants should look.[26]

Even at the ground level, inside law schools, there has been an effort for reform in the reporting of information by law schools. In 2011, The University of Chicago Law School voluntarily offered more detailed employment data for prospective law school students.[27] The Dean, Michael Schill, was delighted and proud of its employment statistics and its stance promoting transparency.[28] In the same year, the student body presidents of 55 law schools across the country called for enhanced accuracy and transparency in the reporting of data pertaining to legal education.[29]

All of the forgoing voices represent the discontent with the lack of transparency shown by the ABA and accredited law schools across the nation.

The ABA Reacts to Criticisms of Lack of Transparency

The ABA's Council of the Section of Legal Education and Admissions to the Bar accredits law schools, and it is responsible for setting various standards for law schools to follow. Under ABA Standard 509, "[a] law school shall publish basic consumer information. The information shall be published in a fair and accurate manner reflective of actual practice."[30] In response to much criticism and calls for action, the ABA, at its March 2012 meeting, unanimously voted to make changes to Standard 509 in an effort to improve transparency in the reporting of information by law schools.[31] The revisions were published for Notice and Comment, and a final version of the revisions was approved at the June 2012 council

---

24. Press Release, Boxer Calls on American Bar Association to Ensure Accurate and Transparent Data Reporting by Law Schools, U.S. Senator Barbara Boxer California (Mar. 31, 2011) *available at* http://boxer.senate.gov/en/press/releases/033111b.cfm.

25. Letter from Charles E. Grassley, U.S. Senator, to Stephen N. Zack, ABA President *available at* http://www.grassley.senate.gov/about/upload/2011-07-11-Grassley-to-ABA.pdf.

26. Bill Hebert, *What is the Value of a Law Degree?*, Cal. St. B.J., Feb. 2011, *available at* http://www.calbarjournal.com/February2011/Opinion/FromthePresident.aspx.

27. David Lat, *The University of Chicago Law School Offers Detailed Employment Data: Will Other Schools Follow Suit?*, Above The Law (Dec. 14, 2011) http://abovethelaw.com/2011/12/the-university-of-chicago-law-school-offers-detailed-employment-data-will-other-schools-follow-suit/.

28. *Id.*

29. *55 Student Body Presidents Call for Legislation to Force Law Schools to Submit Data to Feds* (May 18, 2011) http://taxprof.typepad.com/taxprof_blog/2011/05/55-law-student-body.html.

30. *2011–2012 Standards and Rules of Procedure for Approval of Law Schools*, ABA Section of Legal Education and Admissions to the Bar (2011), *available at* http://www.americanbar.org/content/dam/aba/publications/misc/legal_education/Standards/standardsarchive/2011_2012_standards_and_rules_complete_book.authcheckdam.pdf.

31. American Bar Association Section of Legal Education and Admissions to the Bar, *Council Proposes Changes to Standard 509*, *available at* http://www.americanbar.org/publications/syllabus_home/volume_43_2011-2012/spring_2012/council_proposeschangestostandard509.html (last visited Jun. 21, 2012).

meeting.[32] The ABA House of Delegates approved the revisions at its August 2012 meeting, thereby obligating ABA-approved law schools to comply with the revisions (hereafter "Revised Standard 509").[33]

The Revised Standard 509

The Revised Standard 509 mandates that "[a]ll consumer information that a law school reports, publicizes, or distributes shall be complete, accurate and not misleading to a reasonable law school student or applicant." The revision also states that violations of Standard 509 may result in sanctions under Rule 16, which include probation and removal from the list of ABA-approved law schools.[34]

Subsection(d) and (e) are new additions to Revised Standard 509 and read as follows:

> (d) A law school shall publicly disclose the employment outcomes of its JD graduates on its website.
>
> > (1) The employment outcomes shall be posted on the school's website each year by March 31 or such other date as the Council may establish.
> >
> > (2) The employment outcomes posted must be accurate as of February 15th for persons who graduated with a JD degree between September 1 two calendar years prior and August 31 one calendar year prior.
> >
> > (3) The employment outcomes posted shall remain on the school's website for at least three years, so that at any time at least three graduating classes' data are posted.
> >
> > (4) The employment outcomes shall be gathered and disclosed in accordance with the form, instructions and definitions approved by the Council.
>
> (e) A law school shall publicly disclose on its website, in the form designated by the Council, its conditional scholarship retention data. A law school shall also distribute this data to all applicants being offered conditional scholarships at the time the scholarship offer is extended.

Based on the foregoing, Revised Standard 509 covers disclosures in three areas: scholarship retention, employment data, and salary data. I will discuss them in that order. More accurate scholarship information enables law school applicants to better assess how

---

32. ABA Section of Legal Education and Admissions to the Bar Standards Review Committee, *Proposed Standard 509* (June 2012).

33. Debra Cassens Weiss, *No Fudging: Revised Standard Bars Law Schools from Publishing Misleading Consumer Info*, ABA Journal, Aug. 6, 2012, *available at* http://www.abajournal.com/news/article/no_fudging_revised_standard_bars_law_schools_from_publishing_misleadin/. A redline version of the changes is available at http://www.americanbar.org/content/dam/aba/migrated/2011_build/legal_education/committees/standards_review_documents/actions/20120120_src_action_s509_redlined.authcheckdam.pdf.

34. *Id.* at 1. Subsection a of Revised Standard 509 now reads as follows:

> (a) All consumer information that a law school reports, publicizes or distributes shall be complete, accurate and not misleading to a reasonable law school student or applicant. Schools shall use due diligence in obtaining and verifying consumer information. Violations of these obligations may result in sanctions under Rule 16 of the Rules of Procedure for Approval of Law Schools.

much student loan debt they will have to incur. The more accurate employment and salary data are, the more empowered law school applicants will be to predict their job prospects and their salary potential.

Disclosure of Scholarship Retention Rate

Senator Grassley, in a 2011 letter to then-ABA President Stephen Zack, questioned why no one knows what the scholarship retention rates are at law schools and expressed that he "was extremely disturbed to find that the ABA does not exercise stronger oversight controls over its membership on this critical issue."[35] As part of the uniformed disclosure required under Revised Standard 509, each law school must now disclose on its website conditional merit scholarship retention data. Moreover, this information must be distributed to all applicants that are offered scholarships at the time the scholarship offer is made. The purpose of such disclosures is to allow law school applicants the opportunity to evaluate their chances of losing their scholarships.

The ABA needed to address scholarship disclosure practices because law schools have been criticized for failing to report statistics regarding the number of students unable to retain their scholarships after the first year. Law schools, particularly lower-ranked schools, have an incentive to provide scholarships in order to attract students with high LSAT scores and GPAs because these are factors considered by *U.S. News* when ranking the law schools.[36] Some law schools have been accused of "bait and switch" scholarship practices, which arguably benefit these law schools in the ranking game but actually harm students who amass more debt than they had anticipated. Under the bait-and-switch practice, law schools are accused of offering more scholarships than can possibly be renewed because of the minimum GPA students must maintain in order to keep the scholarships. In other words, the curves these schools have in place effectively reduce the number of students who can meet the minimum GPA requirements. The law schools then tell the students who lose their scholarships that they must find other resources to pay for law school.

Students who lose their scholarships must choose unsavory options, such as borrowing substantially more money to complete the two remaining years of law school or withdrawing from law school completely. Those who lose their scholarships could try to transfer to another school. However, transferring to another law school is highly unlikely for such students because their first-year GPAs signal that they may be struggling academically.

The ABA now imposes on law schools the required disclosure format below to address scholarship retention rates:

35. Grassley Letter, *supra* note 25.

36. *See, e.g.*, David Segal, *Law Students Lose the Grant Game as Schools Win*, N.Y. Times, Apr. 30, 2011, at A1, *available at* http://www.nytimes.com/2011/05/01/business/law-school-grants.html?pagewanted=all&_r=0 ("Why would a school offer more scholarships than it planned to renew? The short answer is this: to build the best class that money can buy, and with it, prestige. But these grant programs often succeed at the expense of students, who in many cases figure out the perils of the merit scholarship game far too late.").

Scholarship Retention Data

Students Matriculating in	# Entering with Conditional Scholarships	# Whose Conditional Scholarships Have Since Been Reduced or Eliminated
Previous Academic Year		
Previous Academic Year—1		
Previous Academic Year—2		

This format forces disclosure of useful information but does not address all the concerns raised by some during the ABA's comment period regarding revisions to Standard 509. For example, Drucilla Ramey, Dean at Golden Gate University School of Law,[37] wanted the chart to include a column allowing a school to indicate the number of second-year and third-year students who did not receive scholarships upon enrolling initially but that were able to obtain scholarships based on their successful first-year performances in law school.[38]

Similarly, Andrew Horwitz, the Associate Dean of Academic Affairs at Roger Williams University School of Law, criticized the chart for lacking a column for law schools to report the number of students who have received unconditional scholarships—that is, those not dependent on the student maintaining a certain GPA or ranking in the class.[39] He believes the format required under Revised Standard 509 will incentivize some schools to make all scholarships conditional and establish low retention standards, so that it will appear that the school has a high scholarship retention rate. Moreover, he is concerned that some schools may be tempted to under-report the loss of a scholarship. For instance, if a student has more than one scholarship but loses only one for failing to satisfy the minimum GPA requirement, the school may not count that student as having lost a scholarship.

Like Dean Horwitz, Mr. McEntee at LST is concerned about the possibility of a law school under-reporting and, therefore, obscuring the true retention rate and leading to confusion among law school applicants.[40] Assume, for example, that Ashley, a hypothetical law student, received a $15,000 scholarship upon enrolling as a first-year student and that she earned a 2.0 GPA at the end of her first semester. Assume, further, that she realizes that it will be nearly impossible for her to pull her GPA up enough to keep her scholarship because retention is dependent upon her having a cumulative GPA of 3.2 at the end of her first year. Consequently, she drops out of law school without starting the second semester. Will her law school choose not to count her as having lost her scholarship even

37. Golden Gate University School of Law is being sued by several graduates who assert that it misrepresented its employment and salary data.

38. Comment from Andrew Horwitz, the Associate Dean of Academic Affairs at Roger Williams University School of Law to ABA Section of Legal Education & Admissions to the Bar (Apr. 23, 2012) (on file with ABA). A single PDF file containing all the comment letters is on the ABA's website at http://www.americanbar.org/content/dam/aba/administrative/legal_education_and_admissions_to_the_bar/council_reports_and_resolutions/june_2012_council_open_session/2012_src_memo_to_council_re_509_and_16_w_comments.authcheckdam.pdf (last visited Oct. 11, 2012) (hereafter "ABA Comment Letters").

39. *Id.* He states that his school grants some unconditional scholarships to some students because they "bring something interesting to our class."

40. *Id.*

though her first-semester GPA was a strong indicator that she would not have been able to satisfy the GPA requirement to keep her scholarship? Revised Standard 509 is not clear on this point. Because the ABA chose not to adopt a disclosure chart to reflect the concerns mentioned above, the burden is on scholarship recipients to make additional inquiries by contacting the law school personnel in charge of scholarship data.

The ABA does not require disclosure of the age, race or socio-economic status of those who lose their scholarships. Consequently, prospective and transfer students who are older students, racial minorities, or come from economically-disadvantaged backgrounds should also inquire about the demographics of those who lose scholarships. A generous scholarship program may be used to increase admission of students from more diverse backgrounds, but it may do more harm than good if, for example, a disproportionate number of racial minorities lose their scholarships.

Despite the requirements of Revised Standard 509, some schools could be doing what Countrywide and Wells Fargo have been penalized for doing. These lenders claimed they were opening the doors of homeownership to African Americans and Latinos through their mortgage loans, but, in actuality, they gave them horrible subprime loans that led them into foreclosures at a rate several times that of similarly-situated white borrowers.[41] Like lenders that have stripped wealth from minority communities via their discriminatory lending, law schools with suspect scholarship retention rates may deprive minorities of their investment in human capital because a disproportionate number of minorities who lose their scholarships will drop out with large student loan debt and no ability to be employed as lawyers.

I am not accusing law schools of discriminatory practices. However, the legal academy should be concerned if schools with very low admission standards are using scholarships to recruit minority students with low LSAT and undergraduate GPAs and are boasting about the diversity of their student bodies. Such students are not only more likely to lose their scholarships but are at greater risk of academic failure or of not passing the bar exam after graduation. Rather than helping minority students in the long run, these "temporary" scholarships primarily benefit the law schools—they have a diverse student body which helps the school's public image and future recruitment prospects.

Revised Standard 509 does not account for attrition or transfer rates in scholarship retention reporting requirements. Thus, to properly weigh a scholarship offer, prospective students must analyze the scholarship retention information along with the school's attrition rate and transfer-out rate. Consider Golden Gate University School of Law, which is being sued for reporting misleading employment and salary data. In the lawsuit filed against it, several graduates allege that Golden Gate offered academic scholarships to 57% of the entering class while knowing that only 33% of the students could retain

41. *See, e.g.*, Press Release, Dep't of Justice, Justice Department Reaches $335 Million Settlement to Resolve Allegations of Lending Discrimination by Countrywide Financial Corporation (Dec. 21, 2011), *available at* http://www.justice.gov/opa/pr/2011/December/11-ag-1694.html (stating that Countrywide charged "more than 200,000 African-American and Hispanic borrowers higher fees and interest rates than non-Hispanic white borrowers in both its retail and wholesale lending"); Press Release, Dep't of Justice, Justice Department Reaches Settlement with Wells Fargo Resulting in More Than $175 Million in Relief for Homeowners to Resolve Fair Lending Claims, *available at* http://www.justice.gov/opa/pr/2012/July/12-dag-869.html (stating "between 2004 and 2008, Wells Fargo discriminated by steering approximately 4,000 African-American and Hispanic wholesale borrowers, as well as additional retail borrowers, into subprime mortgages non-Hispanic white borrowers with similar credit profiles received prime loans").

the scholarships due to the school's strict grading curve.[42] To an unsophisticated, uninformed, or even misled law school applicant, a retention rate of 33% may appear good because of optimism bias—"I've made at least a 3.8 GPA my whole life so getting a 3.0 should be a piece of cake." However, an applicant may not be impressed by a 33% retention rate after learning that that 24.6% of Golden Gate's first year students either flunked or dropped out in 2008 and 20.6% did the same in 2009.[43] Moreover, 23 students transferred out of the school while only two students transferred into Golden Gate. A sophisticated applicant, therefore, needs to consult LSAC's most recent guide regarding a school's transfer and attrition rates and also question the school's administration to find out what percentage of those who either dropped out or transferred did so because of the loss of an academic scholarship. Simply reviewing a school's reported data, as required by Revised Standard 509, would not necessarily give an accurate picture to the applicant.

Ms. Alexandra Leumer, a 2009 graduate of Golden Gate, was quoted in a *New York Times* article as feeling "snookered" because instead of graduating from law school with very little debt, she had to borrow an additional $60,000 to cover tuition costs after losing her scholarship at the end of the first year.[44] In her second year at Golden Gate, she started hearing complaints among classmates who had also lost their scholarships. At that point, Alexandra realized that loss of her scholarship was a real possibility from the outset. While she may have felt snookered, Alexandra's comments also revealed her optimism bias: "I didn't give [the possibility of losing the scholarship] much thought ... I didn't think it would be a challenge."

Professor Jerome Organ has been at the forefront of exposing the loss of merit-based scholarships and showing the negative effects of merit-based scholarships on the individual who loses the scholarship and on the student body as a whole.[45] Professor Organ is keeping a watchful eye on whether law schools are complying with Revised Standard 509. His preliminary research suggests that 47% of law schools are not supplying scholarship data in compliance with the standard and that the scholarship retention rate averages at 69% for the schools that made scholarship retention data public.[46] That means a substantial number of students are losing their scholarships.

Professor Organ's research emphasizes the need for applicants to obtain full and accurate scholarship retention data. By failing to do so, law school applicants or transfer students who are offered scholarships could grossly underestimate the cost of getting a legal education and end up feeling that the JD was not worth the price. In summary, although Revised Standard 509 forces disclosure of scholarship retention rates, those who are offered scholarships must assess other critical factors and gain as much information as possible before enrolling in a school making a generous scholarship offer.

---

42. Class Action Complaint at 10, Arring v. Golden Gate University, No. CGC-12-517837, (Cal. Superior Feb. 1, 2012).

43. Note that "other" attrition rate may also include students who dropped out and then transferred to another school. *See* 2012 LSAC Guide. The most recent edition of the LSAC Guide is available at https://officialguide.lsac.org.

44. David Siegel, *Behind the Curve*, N.Y. Times, May 1, 2011, at BU1.

45. *See* Jerome Organ, *How Scholarship Programs Impact Students and the Culture of Law School*, 61 J. Legal Educ. 173, 188 (2011) ("[A] significant percentage of their students are going to experience a 'double-whammy' of inadequacy. Not only are they not 'measuring up' in terms of getting the types of grades to which they were accustomed as an undergraduate (getting Bs and Cs instead of As and some Bs), they are now being told they are 'unworthy' of continued scholarship assistance as a result.").

46. *See* Mike Stetz, *Cloak of Darkness Fades on Merit Scholarships*, Nat'l Jurist Mag., Mar. 2013, Vol.22, No.6, pp. 10–11 (reporting that 50% of the 2012 scholarship recipients lost their merit-based scholarships at Golden Gate).

New Requirements for Reporting Employment Data

In addition to requiring disclosure of scholarship retention rates, Revised Standard 509 makes major changes regarding law schools' disclosure of employment data. Under Revised Standard 509, law schools must display employment data in a uniform chart that discloses whether employment is full-time or part-time, temporary or long-term, and whether it requires bar passage or favors law school graduates.[47] Below is the part of the ABA-uniform chart related to employment status.

Class of ___ Employment Report at 9 Months after Graduation

		Full Time		Part Time	
Employment Status	Number	Long	Short	Long	Short
Employed Bar Passage Required	##/%	##	##	##	##
Employed JD Advantage	##/%	##	##	##	##
Employed Professional Position	##/%	##	##	##	##
Employed Non Professional Position	##/%	##	##	##	##
Employed Job Category Undeterminable	##/%	##	##	##	##
Pursuing Graduate Degree Full Time	##/%				
Unemployed Start Date Deferred	##/%				
Unemployed Not Seeking	##/%				
Unemployed Seeking	##/%				
Employment Status Unknown	##/%				
Total graduates	##/100%				
Law School/University Funded Position					
Of Employed Law School/ University Funded		##	##	##	##

47. ABA Section of Legal Education and Admissions to the Bar Standards Review Committee, *Proposed Standard 509*, at 6 (June 2012).

Accounting for Graduates in University-Funded Positions

During the comment period for Revised Standard 509, several individuals submitted comments intended to require law schools to disclose the most complete and accurate information regarding employment outcomes of their graduates, particularly for graduates working in university-funded positions. Ann Reed, a member of the Board of Directors of the University of North Carolina Law Alumni Association, focused her comments on the reporting of university-funded positions, stating "some law schools have instituted programs (1) to pay otherwise-unemployed graduates a modest stipend in exchange for otherwise unpaid legal work, (2) to treat those graduates as 'employed,' and (3) thereby to create the impression that these graduates have succeeded in finding full-time, permanent, non-University-funded employment."[48] At the time of Ms. Reed's comments, the proposed employment chart had a category of employment status labeled "Law School/University Funded Position" that would have forced disclosure of the number of graduates in these positions and whether their positions were long or short term and full-time or part-time.[49] Ms. Reed supported the-then proposed changes and felt that they would better serve prospective students seeking to predict their employment outcome.[50]

While Ms. Reed's comments were reflected in Revised Standard 509, the problem is that a graduate working in a university-funded position is still accounted for in the first part of the chart and can be counted in the "Bar Passage Required" category simply because the school created a written job description that requires bar passage for the university-funded position. Moreover, it is common knowledge *in the legal academy* that law schools around the country regularly employ recent graduates working as recruiters, admissions counselors, and research assistants. Based on the standardized chart, law school applicants would have no way of knowing if some portion of the graduates employed in "Bar Passage Required" jobs truly had jobs they would consider worth incurring over $100,000 in student loan debt to get a law degree. With that in mind, the question becomes is it nonetheless ethical to count graduates working in these university-funded positions in various employment categories, including the JD-Advantage category?

What Is a JD-Advantage Job?

During my research of the definition of these various categories, I found online a memorandum, dated November 8, 2011, from Arthur Gaudio, the Dean of Western New England School of Law.[51] In his capacity as the 2010–2012 Chair of the ABA Questionnaire

48. *See* ABA Comment Letters, *supra* note 38.

49. ABA Section of Legal Education and Admissions to the Bar Standards Review Committee, *Proposed Standard 509*, at 6 (June 2012).

50. *See* ABA Comment Letters, *supra* note 38.

51. Memorandum from Dean Art Gaudio, Chair, Questionnaire Committee, to Council of the Section of Legal Education and Admissions to the Bar (November 8, 2011) *available at* http://www.americanbar.org/content/dam/aba/administrative/legal_education_and_admissions_to_the_bar/council_reports_and_resolutions/2011_questionnaire_memo_re_placement.authcheckdam.pdf (hereafter, "ABA Memo").

Committee,[52] Dean Gaudio wrote this memorandum (hereafter the "ABA Memo"), and it defines each "employment status" and "employment type" category. The ABA Memo defines the JD-Advantage position as follows:

> **A position in this category is one for which the employer sought an individual with a JD, and perhaps even required a JD, or for which the JD provided a demonstrable advantage in obtaining or performing the job, but itself does not require bar passage, an active law license, or involve practicing law.** Examples of positions for which a JD is an advantage include a corporate contracts administrator, alternative dispute resolution specialist, government regulatory analyst, FBI agent, and accountant. **Also included might be jobs in personnel or human resources, jobs with investment banks, jobs with consulting firms, jobs doing compliance work for business and industry, jobs in law firm professional development, and jobs in law school career services offices, admissions offices, or other law school administrative offices.** Doctors or nurses who plan to work in a litigation, insurance, or risk management setting, or as expert witnesses, would fall into this category, as would journalists and teachers (in a higher education setting) of law and law related topics. **It is an indicator that a position does not fall into this category if a JD is uncommon among persons holding such a position.**[53]

Unfortunately, many prospective law students who do not read this book will not realize that the JD-Advantage category may include numerous jobs they would consider unsuccessful employment upon graduation from law school. For example, as a result of this definition, a law school can clearly count admissions personnel or career counselors in the JD-Advantage category. Many directors and assistant directors of admissions and career services offices have JDs and have intentionally chosen to leave the practice of law to pursue these positions. However, it is well-known in the legal academy that the entry-level positions in admissions and career services are often filled by recent graduates who could not find jobs as lawyers.

As a result of Revised Standard 509 and the accompanying definition described above, law school applicants should realize that the JD-Advantage category may include graduates who feel that they are under-employed.

The definition for the JD-Advantage category is silent about what to do with research assistants. Consequently, some schools could include graduates working as research assistants in the JD-Advantage category. Moreover, these research assistants may be accounted for as long-term, full-time employees if they work 35 hours per week and there is no definite time frame in which the job is expected to end. Is this practice really ethical given the applicants' expectations when viewing reported data regarding the JD-Advantage employment? I have hired 3L students as research assistants and had them resume working for me after taking time off for the bar exam. However, the fact that these research assistants had a JD was not crucial or a factor for their continuing to work as research assistants. I simply wanted a 3L student who could research and write well.

There are differences between the JD-Advantage definition in the ABA Memo and in NALP's Employment Report and Salary Survey form ("NALP's Survey Form") that further

---

The memorandum was addressed to Council of the Section of Legal Education and Admissions to the Bar, the entity in charge of ABA-law schools and responsible for creating standards for the schools to follow. I refer to that entity as the ABA.

52. General Information, Faculty, Professor Arthur R. Gaudio, W. New England Univ., http://www1.law.wne.edu/faculty/index.cfm?selection=doc.9735&uid=165.

53. *See* ABA Memo, *supra* note 51 (emphasis added).

complicate a prospective law student's ability to have a clear picture of a law school's employment data. The last sentence in the ABA Memo's definition of the JD-Advantage category states: "It is an indicator that a position does not fall into this category if a JD is uncommon among persons holding such a position."[54] This last sentence does not appear in the definition section of NALP's Survey Form.[55] Grads who choose to provide their employment information online must use NALP's Survey Form. Career counselors for law schools also use this form if they complete NALP's Survey Form. I tried to reconcile the differences between the definitions in NALP's Survey Form and the ABA Memo by contacting the ABA and NALP but could not get clarity from either organization to share with the reader. Apparently, there was a rift between the two over the collecting and reporting of employment data, but they have patched up their differences, thereby suggesting the definitions should be viewed as identical.[56]

Nevertheless, I argue that it is uncommon for someone with a JD to be employed as a research assistant, as that position is still usually held by matriculating law students. In recent years, however, more and more law graduates are working temporarily as research assistants until they find permanent jobs. As a result, some law schools will include research assistants in the JD-Advantage category. My point here is simply that because the ABA did not provide a precise, long list of jobs that should be included in each of the employment "status" categories, law schools have the discretion to account for graduates working in university-funded positions in a manner that some prospective students will find unethical or misleading.

The JD-Advantage definition is also problematic in other ways as well. The JD-Advantage definition is broad in that the graduate does not have to be engaged in the practice of law. However, the "spirit" of the definition is that the JD must give the graduate "a demonstrable advantage in obtaining or performing the job."[57] The problem I have with the definition is that if the law school's career counselor is inputting the graduate's employment information, the counselor could take leeway and put in the JD-Advantage category graduates for whom a JD has no demonstrable advantage. One way that the ABA could have given better guidance regarding the JD-Advantage category would have been to articulate a "but-for test"—that is, but for the graduate possessing a JD, another candidate would have most likely been chosen.

To illustrate how the JD-Advantage category can be manipulated, assume Sasha was a police officer with the Boston Police Department ("BPD") prior to going to law school and that after graduating from law school, she returned to the BPD as a police officer because she could not find a job as an attorney. Because Sasha has earned an advanced degree, she would automatically be entitled to a 25% raise.[58] Assume further that she conveyed this salary increase information to the law school career counselor. The law school could then count Sasha in the JD-Advantage category even though she may not count herself as having obtained an employment position as a result of her JD. Presumably,

---

54. *See* ABA Memo, *supra* note 51.

55. NALP's Employment Report and Salary Survey form is *available at*, http://www.nalp.org/uploads/ERSS/2012GraduateSurvey_and_FAQs_Dec2012.pdf (hereinafter, "NALP's Survey Form").

56. ABA, NALP Bury the Hatchet on Law School Placement Data Reporting, http://taxprof.typepad.com/taxprof_blog/2011/08/more-on-the-aba-nalp-.html.

57. *See* ABA Memo, *supra* note 51.

58. *Boston Police Department Officer Requirements*, CRIM. JUSTICE DEGREE SCH., http://www.criminaljusticedegreeschools.com/criminal-justice-resources/police-departments-by-metro-area/boston-police-department-officer-requirements/ (last visited Oct. 3, 2012).

she got her old job back based on her years of experience as a police officer, not her possession of a JD diploma. Sasha may also count herself as unsuccessful in the job market because she has incurred over $100,000 in student loan debt just to get a 25% raise in a job she had before law school. My main point here is that prospective students need to realize that a school's JD-Advantage category may include graduates who could have gotten the job *without* getting a law degree.[59]

What could happen if Sasha, and not the career counselor, completes the survey form? If Sasha inputs the information herself and she is embarrassed about her predicament, she could check the box for "JD-Advantage" on NALP's Survey Form.[60] She may feel compelled to do so because she does not want to appear to have failed. She could rationalize her JD-Advantage selection because she now has the ability to be a better cop since she took a constitutional law course and learned about lawful stop-and-frisk searches. Regardless of her rationale for self-identifying as having a JD-Advantage job, it is clear that the broad definition for this category allows for a great deal of leeway in the kinds of employment it reflects, and a prospective law student would not know this information when applying.

What about the "Employed-Professional" Category?

The ABA Memo's definition of the "Employed-Professional Position" is as follows, and NALP's definition is essentially the same:

> A position in this category is one that requires professional skills or training but for which a JD is neither required nor a demonstrable advantage. Examples of persons in this category include a math or science teacher, business manager, or performing arts specialist. Other examples include professions such as doctors,

59. *ABA to Ask Law Schools for More Extensive Job-Placement Data*, Reuters, Dec. 6, 2011, *available at* http://newsandinsight.thomsonreuters.com/Legal/News/2011/12_-_December/ABA_to_ask_law_schools_for_more_extensive_job-placement_data/ (Richard Revesz, dean of New York University School of Law, stated that the new categories such as JD-Advantage "can be ambiguous because it is not always clear which individuals benefit from having a law degree when working outside the legal profession"); *A Couple of Class of 2011 Placement Charts*, Inside the Law School Scam (March 15, 2012), http://insidethelawschoolscam.blogspot.com/2012/03/couple-of-class-of-2011-placement.html (Anonymous posted the following comment "What does 'JD-advantage' mean? Both schools report over 30 graduates in this category. My guess is that this is a scam category that includes grads who snagged white collar nonlaw jobs due to preexisting contacts or skills. Nonlaw employers no longer 'prefer' a JD—the market-flooding behavior of the law schools has destroyed any 'mystique' the degree once had."); These Data Will Fundamentally Reshape the Legal Education Industry, The Legal Whiteboard, June 26, 2012, http://lawprofessors.typepad.com/legalwhiteboard/current-events/ ("Many [in the JD-Advantage category] are likely compromise jobs—not as good as practicing law, but better than non-professional alternatives."); Matt Leichter, *Who Are American University's 79.6 Percent?*, The Law School Tuition Bubble (Nov. 12, 2012), http://lawschooltuitionbubble.wordpress.com/2012/11/12/who-are-american-universitys-79-6-percent/ (arguing that the JD-Advantage Professional categories allow American University to make superficial arguments about the versatility of a JD).

60. This NALP survey is available for all graduates to use to report their employment information. However, many graduates do not bother to complete the survey. These graduates are tracked down (via Facebook, LinkedIn, etc.) by career service employees who gather the information from the graduate over the phone or through email.

> nurses, engineers, or architects, if a JD was not demonstrably advantageous in obtaining the position or in performing the duties of the position.[61]

Assume that Paul was a math teacher prior to law school and went back to his old teaching job after graduating, he fits the definition of an "Employed-Professional." Assume further that he got an automatic raise as result of getting an advanced degree. No doubt, many, if not most, law schools would correctly put him in the Employed-Professional category because his law degree gave him no advantage in getting his old job or in performing his duties as a math teacher. However, the law degree did not help him get this "professional" job. Moreover, this was not the desired outcome in pursuing a law degree.

The potential for manipulation of the Employed-Professional category is great for graduates who attended law school *part-time* while maintaining full-time employment. Nearly 90 law schools have part-time JD programs,[62] and the students enrolled in such programs usually retain their full-time positions.[63] To prove my point, let's return to the example of Sasha, the police officer. If she kept her full-time job as a police officer while attending law school and maintained that position because she could not find a job post-graduation as a prosecutor, how would the law school count her in its employment report?

She should be characterized as Employed-Professional because the "JD was not demonstrably advantageous in [her] obtaining the position." However, I am certain that many law schools would put her in the JD-Advantage category (for the reasons described in the previous section) even though it is uncommon for police officers to hold JDs. In this tough legal job market, I would imagine that a significant number of graduates of part-time programs have been unable to find traditional attorney jobs and, therefore, have elected to keep the same jobs that they had while in law school. I have anecdotal stories that this is the case. However, these graduates will very likely be accounted for in a manner that incorrectly conveys the impression that these graduates found their jobs after graduating from law school. Because several law schools have very sizeable part-time programs, their inclusion of graduates who have retained the same jobs in either the JD-Advantage or Employed-Professional categories can *significantly* increase the overall employment rate. Therefore, the ABA should have had required law schools to create a separate category for graduates of part-time programs so as to not mislead prospective students into believing these graduates "found" their jobs after graduation.

---

61. *See* ABA Memo, *supra* note 51.

62. Robert Morse & Sam Flanigan, *Methodology: Part-time Law School Rankings*, U.S. NEWS & WORLD REP. (Mar. 12, 2012), http://www.usnews.com/education/best-graduate-schools/top-law-schools/articles/2012/03/12/methodology-part-time-law-school-rankings ("This year, *U.S. News* presents the rankings of the 85 accredited law schools offering part-time programs.").

63. *See, e.g.*, David F. Chavkin, *Clinic Under the Stars: Giving Part-time Students their Due*, 13 CLINICAL L. REV. 719, 734 (2007).

Can the "Employment Type" Categories Be Manipulated?

Now let's return to the uniform chart that law schools must follow. As you can see, immediately below the "Employment Status" section is a section labeled "Employment Type."

			Full Time		Part Time	
Employment Type		**Number**	**Long**	**Short**	**Long**	**Short**
Law firms		##	##	##	##	##
Solo		##	##	##	##	##
2–10		##	##	##	##	##
11–25		##	##	##	##	##
26–50		##	##	##	##	##
51–100		##	##	##	##	##
101–250		##	##	##	##	##
251–500		##	##	##	##	##
501+		##	##	##	##	##
Unknown		##	##	##	##	##
Business & industry		##	##	##	##	##
Government		##	##	##	##	##
Pub. Int. (inc. Pub. Def.)		##	##	##	##	##
Judicial Clerkships		##	##	##	##	##
Federal		##	##	##	##	##
State & local		##	##	##	##	##
Other		##	##	##	##	##
Academia		##	##	##	##	##
Employer Type Unknown		##				
	Total	##	##	##	##	##
			Full Time		**Part Time**	

The Employment Type category is broken down into the following six subcategories based on the type of employer: law firms, business & industry, government, public interest, judicial clerkships, and academia.

The ABA apparently chose to ignore or otherwise disregard the suggestions submitted by Mr. McEntee, the executive director of LST, regarding the manipulation of the categories under employment type. For example, his comments reflected his concern that the term "Academia" under the "Employment Type" section could be misleading. Mr. McEntee stated that this number implies that graduates are working as law professors or academics at universities when in reality some may be working as research assistants for professors. He advised that the council disaggregate, eliminate, or rename this category to avoid misleading prospective students.[64]

Using information that I obtained from the University of Illinois College of Law's website, I will explain how the employment type category for "Academia" can be misleading to prospective students if the law school provides no explanation of the category. Below is how the University of Illinois College of Law disclosed (in June 2012) its employment outcomes for its 2011 graduates by type of employment.[65]

Areas of Legal Practice

Area	Number
Law Firm	
Solo	1
2–10	21
11–25	9
26–50	6
51–100	4
101–250	9
251–500	4
501+	13
Unknown Size	1
Business & Industry	30
Government	26
Public Interest	10
Judicial Clerkships/Federal	9
Judicial Clerkships/State & Local	0
Academia	9

What a prospective law student cannot determine from this display of "Areas of Legal Practice" is how Illinois accounted for the law graduates working in university-funded positions, but not as professors. A few inches above this disclosure of the numbers, the law school states that of 34 positions classified as short-term, "11 of [them] were funded in some manner by the University of Illinois."[66] It is a mystery to the law school applicant how Illinois has accounted for the eleven graduates in the employment type categories. I know that Illinois has included these eleven graduates because the total numbers by employment type add up to 100% of its law graduates. All eleven graduates cannot be in the

64. ABA Comment Letters, *supra* note 38.

65. *Student Employment Data: Class of 2011*, UNIV. OF ILL., http://www.law.illinois.edu/career-services/student-employment-data (last visited July 29, 2012). *See also* Am. Bar Ass'n Sect. of Legal Ed. & Admissions to the Bar, Employment Summary Report, http://employmentsummary.abaquestionnaire.org/ (hereinafter "Illinois Employment Data").

66. *Id.*

"Academia" category as that category has only nine graduates. Furthermore, such a large number of graduates employed in academia cannot be taken at face value. It is extremely rare for a law graduate to obtain a job as a law professor only a few months after obtaining a law degree.[67] A less-savvy law school applicant (a) may not see the note about the law school employing recent graduates, and (b) may not understand that many of the positions in academia are quite possibly employed as research assistants or otherwise working in positions for which they did not need a law degree.

How Is Academia Defined?

NALP's Survey Form has a job section labeled "ACADEMIA/EDUCATION," and its instructions for completing the form states:

> ACADEMIC: Positions may be at any level, from elementary to higher education, including at your own law school, and within either the private or public sector, e.g., private colleges, state universities, and local public education.[68]

The definition in the ABA Memo is even broader than NALP's Survey Form:

> Academic positions include those at any academic level, including elementary, secondary, and higher education, and regardless of whether they are at private or public institutions. **Positions include faculty member, teacher, librarian, and administrator; positions also include law school funded positions such as research "fellow" and clinic staff attorney.** Positions outside the academic sphere of an educational institution, such as positions at university hospitals and similar university related entities, should be reported as a position in business and industry if the institution is a private institution or government if the institution is public. This category only includes employment in an academic institution; it does not include pursuing a degree or being enrolled in an academic program at an academic institution.[69]

As a result of the ABA's definition, one or more of Illinois' graduates included in the Academia category could be career counselors or admissions recruiters (or even elementary school teachers). The ABA should have created two categories: "Academia-Law Professor" and "Other Academia." Such distinctions would then make it clear to prospective students the number of graduates who became law professors. Unfortunately, the generic Academia category has too much potential for law school applicants to incorrectly assume that graduates in that category are law professors.

My next point is crucial, so do not gloss over it. It is relatively easy for those reporting this data to conflate employment *type* with employment *setting*. The reason why NALP and the ABA can keep the Academia sub-category under the Employment Type category and resist revising it to fit Mr. McEntee's recommendation is because the "Employment Type" does not mean what kind of job the graduate has but what type of entity the graduate's employer is. Stated differently, if Michael works as a law librarian at the

---

67. A law graduate who also has a Ph.D. is the type of graduate capable of getting a professor position shortly after graduating from law school.

68. NALP's Survey Form.

69. *See* ABA Memo, *supra* note 51.

University of Texas, his employer is a public academic institution; thus, he is employed in Academia. It is accurate that his employer is an academic institution, but this may not be the type of employment an applicant would expect in this category. To avoid creating confusion about this, the ABA should have labeled the "Employment Type" category as "Employment Setting."

The Potential to Mislead Prospective Students about Law Firm Positions

Below is a side-by-side comparison of the definitions of and instructions regarding the "Law Firm" subcategory in the ABA's Memo[70] and NALP's Survey Form.[71]

ABA's Definition of and Instructions about "Law Firm"	NALP's Definition of and Instructions about "Law Firm"
A law firm is a group of attorneys practicing law together regardless of their specific legal relationship. Any job in a law firm, including associate, law clerk, law firm librarian, paralegal, and clerical position is included. A law firm is included if it is a private, for-profit firm even though it may perform substantial public interest work. However, a firm whose practice primarily involves under-represented clients, or groups that advocate for community interests, is included in Employment Type, Public Interest, below. A graduate hired by, and working directly for, a law firm on a contract basis is included. However, a graduate working at a law firm but employed by an agency that places attorneys in temporary positions is included in Employment Type, Business and Industry, below. Questions 1–8 ask for the total number of attorneys in the entire firm. If the firm has multiple offices, this includes the total of all attorneys in all of the offices. All attorneys employed in all offices should be included regardless of their status in the firm. The category of "solo practice" applies to a graduate who has truly established his or her own solo practice. It does not apply to a graduate who is unemployed, but who may be willing to take an occasional client while still seeking employment. If the graduate is a clerk or associate for a solo practitioner, the firm size should be "Law firm—2–10."	This category includes all jobs in private practice, including jobs as an associate, law clerk, paralegal, or other professional or clerical staff. Private practice includes public interest law firms, which are private and for-profit firms distinguished from other private firms in that a majority of their practice involves clients that are typically underrepresented, or groups that advocate for community rather than corporate interests. Sliding fee cases, attorney fee cases, and contingent fee cases are common. Typical areas of practice for public interest law firms include plaintiff's employment discrimination, civil rights, union representation, and environmental law. Firm size refers to the total number of attorneys firm-wide counting all senior and junior partners, of counsel, staff attorneys, senior and junior associates, and the like. Use the solo practice category only if you have established your own solo practice; if you are working for another single lawyer report the firm size as 2–10.

70. *Id.*
71. NALP's Survey Form.

As the reader can see, the definitions and instructions about the Law Firm category are strictly about trying to determine the size of the law firm where the graduates work, not whether the graduates are actually attorneys at those firms. Consequently, a graduate working in a two-person firm may actually be working as a paralegal for a solo practitioner.

Additional Examples of How Law Schools Can Obscure Employment Realities

Because of the ABA and NALP definitions, law schools with lackluster employment rates can use the both the "employment type" and "employment status" categories to obscure graduates working in under-employed positions. For example, a law school could report that it has 15 graduates employed in the "Judicial Clerkships/Federal" employment type and 31 graduates employed in "Government"; however, some of these jobs could be *non*-traditional positions for entry-level lawyers. For example, I know one graduate[72] who for a period of time worked in a full-time position performing data entry work for a local judge. The law school's career counselor could count this job as a full-time, long-term JD-Advantage position if the judge prefers to hire JD holders for that position to help them secure better employment. The position was long-term in the sense that the judge had not set a date when the position would end. While the graduate was grateful for the chance to earn a paycheck, make no mistake, he was very unhappy that this was the only job remotely related to the legal profession that he could secure after graduating with honors. I wonder how many law schools would categorize his employment status as JD-Advantage or even as Bar-Passage-Required? Would he be placed in "Employed—Professional Position" because the job did not require a J.D? If the job did not require special skills or training, he should be included in the Non-Professional category.[73] Would some law schools avoid asking too many questions so that as soon as they hear that a graduate is working as a clerk for a judge or a law firm, they can categorize as many graduates as possible as JD-Advantage?

This same graduate working as a data entry clerk could be accounted for in either the "Government" or "Judicial Clerkship" subcategory of the "Employment Type" category of the chart. A data entry clerk is not a judicial clerk by any reasonable interpretation; yet a school could put him in the Judicial Clerkship subcategory and technically comply with the ABA's reporting requirements. The law school applicant must, therefore, be a little skeptical of these categories particularly if the school has come under fire for publishing misleading reports.

Along with hiding under-employed graduates in the employment status and employment type categories, law schools, under Revised Standard 509, could continue to convey the incorrect impression that that information supplied is representative of a class and,

72. This person did not graduate from Illinois.

73. *See* ABA Memo, *supra* note 51 (defining the "Employed—Non-Professional Position" as "one that does not require any special professional skills or training."); *See also* NALP Survey, *supra* note 55 (defining an "Employed—Non-Professional" position as "any professional skills or training, or is one that you may not view as part of your career path.").

therefore, it should be considered incomplete, inaccurate, or misleading by those receiving the data.[74] For instance, some schools display employer lists, which provide the names of law firms and other employers where past graduates have obtained work. So for instance, assume that a graduate is doing document review at the Chicago office of Jones Day, but her actual employer is a legal temp agency. This graduate should actually check the "Business & Industry" subcategory box. If the graduate is physically present in office space at Jones Day in Chicago and checks the Law Firm box on NALP's Survey Form, a law school could display an employer list identifying Jones Day as an employer simply because of how the graduate completed the form.[75] Consequently, an employer list could be misleading to applicants who do not know about the submission of data that is either intentionally or unintentionally misleading.

Besides employer lists, some schools prominently feature information that is not relevant if a prospective student is seeking to find out the *actual number* of graduates employed permanently in full-time attorney positions. For example, Charlotte School of Law, a for-profit, recently-ABA-accredited law school, has a webpage titled "Student Outcomes and Disclosures." It has two charts, both of which take up a significant amount of web-page space. One chart is about Charlotte's bar passage rate and the other I have duplicated below and it begins with the following sentence:[76]

> Our program prepares graduates for the following positions listed by the Standard Occupational Classification (SOC)

SOC Code	Occupation	O*Net
23-1011	Lawyers	http://www.onetonline.org/find/quick?s=23-1011
23-1021	Administrative Law Judges, Adjudicators, and Hearing Officers	http://www.onetonline.org/find/quick?s=23-1021
23-1022	Arbitrators, Mediators, and Conciliators	http://www.onetonline.org/find/quick?s=23-1022
23-1023	Judges, Magistrate Judges, and Magistrates	http://www.onetonline.org/find/quick?s=23-1023
25-1112	Law Teachers, Postsecondary	http://www.onetonline.org/find/quick?s=25-1112

This chart is not required by the ABA. Every law school could claim that they are preparing students to get the jobs identified in the chart. In a paragraph above this chart, Charlotte claims, among other things, that its 2011 graduates have an employment rate of 82.47%, but Charlotte fails to mention what percentage have permanent, full-time bar-passage-required jobs. Therefore, an unsophisticated prospective student may conclude

74. AM. BAR ASSOC., Revised Standard 509 (2012).

75. While NALP or the ABA may double check with a school to amend some clearly inaccurate reporting (like a graduate inadvertently indicating he is Unemployed—Not Seeking but is actually working full-time in a law firm), they likely do not double check everything and take much of the reporting by law schools at face value.

76. *Student Outcomes & Disclosures*, CHARLOTTE SCH. OF LAW, http://www.charlottelaw.org/admissions/student-outcomes-disclosures (last visited Oct. 17, 2012).

this prominently-featured chart is important or required and may be impressed by the 82.47% employment rate.

Rather than including a chart on its webpage about its actual employment outcomes, Charlotte has left it up to prospective students to identify the correct hyperlink containing this information. A prospective student may not notice a hyperlink labeled as "Employment Outcomes—Class of 2011" because the hyperlink is presented in a smaller font than the other large, bold headings on the webpage. This hyperlink is easy to overlook, but it contains the most valuable information about employment outcomes for graduates of this school. The hyperlink directs the website visitor to the actual chart required under Revised Standard 509 and allows prospective students to see the number of Charlotte graduates employed in bar-passage-required jobs. By looking at the report Charlotte submitted to the ABA, a prospective student would discover that 42 of the 97 (or 43%) graduates in 2011 had full-time, long-term, bar-passage required jobs and that most (25 out of 31) of the graduates reported to be at law firms were either solo practitioners or employed at very small firms with a size of 2–10 attorneys.[77] To prevent schools from making it difficult for prospective students to find the uniform chart required under Revised Standard 509, the ABA should have required law schools to prominently feature at their websites the uniform chart disclosing all required employment information.

Differences in How Law Schools Choose to Comply with Revised Standard 509

To drive home the point that law schools can continue to hide graduates working in potentially under-employed positions, let's revisit New York Law School ("NYLS") and its reporting practice before and after Revised Standard 509. Recall that Judge Schweitzer dismissed the lawsuit filed against NYLS. I compiled in Table 4-1 (next page) various facts about the top fifteen law schools that charge the most expensive tuition rates ("Top 15 List of Schools with the Highest Tuition") based on 2009 information.

Do you remember the saying, "you get what you pay for"? Well, that saying does not hold true for all of the schools making the Top 15 List of Schools with the Highest Tuition. Unlike most of the schools on this list, NYLS has a very low rate (35.5%) of graduates employed in full-time, permanent jobs for which bar passage is required and yet its tuition was $47,800 for full-time students. It also has a high attrition rate (10.6%)—i.e., the percentage of students who flunk out or drop out. For the entering class of 2009, the NYLS's attrition rate was based on 21 students flunking out and 56 students dropping out. I decided to compare the employment figures of NYLS, which is number 15 on the 2009 list, with the employment figures of Cornell University Law School, which is in first place on the list.[78]

Now let's see how NYLS disclosed the employment outcomes for its 2009 graduates.

---

77. By looking at the report submitted to the ABA, a prospective student would discover that 42 of the 97 (or 43%) graduates in 2011 had full-time, long-term, bar-passage required jobs and that most (25 out of 31) of the graduates reported to be at law firms were either solo practitioners or employed at firms with a size of 2–10 attorneys. To see Charlotte's report, search for the school's name at http://employmentsummary.abaquestionnaire.org/.

78. Note that the Business Insider, using 2011 data, ranked Columbia as number one on the list of the most expensive law schools with a total yearly costs of $81,950. Jennifer Polland, *The 10 Most*

Table 4-1. Schools Ranked in Order of Most Expensive Tuition Fee

School's Name	2011 Grads Employed, Bar Req.	2011 Grads Employed, JD Advantage	2011 Grads Employed, Professional	Tuition	Cost of Living	Total 3 Yrs.	Attrition*	Transfers In*	Transfers Out*	Bar Passage*
Cornell Univ.	179/201 = 89.1%	0/201 = 0%	2/201 = 1.0%	$53,150	$19,460	$217,830	7.8%+	0	15	99.00%
Columbia Univ.	437/456 = 95.8%	6/456 = 1.3%	2/456 = 0.43%	$52,902	$20,680	$220,746	0%	78	2	96.06%
Yale Univ.	183/205 = 89.3%	8/205 = 3.9%	5/205 = 2.4%	$52,525	$20,080	$217,815	0.50%	16	0	96.37%
Northwestern Univ.	235/287 = 81.9%	27/287 = 9.4%	3/287 = 1.0%	$51,920	$24,460	$229,140	4.40%	38	7	94.00%
Univ. of Penn.	235/274 = 85.8%	19/274 = 6.9%	1/274 = 0.36%	$50,718	$21,392	$216,330	0%	25	7	95.72%
Univ. of S. Cal.	150/207 = 72.5%	16/207 = 7.7%	3/207 = 1.4%	$50,591	$23,361	$221,856	0.90%	18	8	90.81%
Univ. of Cal.—Berkeley	263/310 = 84.8%	8/310 = 2.6%	7/310 = 2.25%	$50,163	$22,060	$216,669	0.70%	46	2	91.63%
Duke Univ.	181/207 = 87.4%	13/207 = 6.3%	2/207 = 0.96%	$49,617	$21,871	$214,464	3.50%	5	8	94.20%
Stanford Univ.	177/192 = 92.2%	9/192 = 4.7%	1/192 = 0.52%	$49,179	$27,522	$230,103	1.10%	15	0	94.24%
New York Univ.	424/466 = 90.9%	17/466 = 3.6%	4/466 = 0.86%	$48,950	$22601*	$214,653	1.60%	58	3	96.88%
Harvard Univ.	541/589 = 91.9%**	14/589 = 2.4%**	2/589 = 0.34%**	$48,786	$25,000	$221,358	0.50%	29	0	98.19%
Brooklyn Law School	N/A***	N/A***	N/A***	$48,416	$25,560	$221,928	6.30%	32	24	89.00%
Yeshiva Univ. (Cardozo)	197/380 = 51.8%	15/380 = 3.9%	4/380 = 1.1%	$48,370	$24,778	$219,444	5.20%	39	5	89.52%
Fordham Univ.	246/428 = 57.5%	12/428 = 2.8%	19/428 = 4.4%	$47,986	$26,396	$223,146	0.60%	24	14	89.84%
New York Law School	183/515 = 35.5%	59/515 = 11.5%	28/515 = 5.4%	$47,800	$23,323	$213,369	10.6%^	13	37	81.00%

* Data from ABA LSAC Official Guide to ABA-Approved Law Schools, 2012 Ed. (2011); ** Harvard employment data from the Class of 2010; *** Employment statistics provided could not be formatted to the new ABA Standard; + Cornell's attrition rate is 7.8% due to 16 students dropping out. No students flunked out; ^ New York Law School had 21 students flunk out and 56 students drop out.

NYLS's Class of 2009 Employment Statistics

The employment rate for the Class of 2009 within nine months of graduation is 89.7%, with 94% of the graduates reporting employment information.

Approximately 20% of our 2009 graduates reported salary information. The salary range (minimum to maximum) and median salaries by employment category are:

Practice Area	Percent	Salary Range Min.–Maximum	Average
Private Practice	45.6%	$28,000–$160,000	$120,197
Corporate/Business	23.7%	$50,000–$96,000	$75,167
Government	8.2%	$41,000–$72,000	$56,054
Public Interest	16%	N/A	N/A
Judicial Clerkship	3.4%	$42,000–$58,200	$45,887
Academic	3.1%	$40,000–$45,000	$42,500

The graduates who sued NYLS alleged that the above disclosure misled them, when they were applicants, about the success of NYLS's graduates. In other words, by counting any graduate employed in any capacity, the lawsuit alleges that NYLS created the impression that nearly 90% of its graduates had obtained jobs as attorneys in the various employment settings described above.

Expensive Law Schools In America[:] #1 Columbia Law School, BUS. INSIDER, http://www.businessinsider.com/the-10-most-expensive-law-schools-in-america-2012-9#1-columbia-law-school-10 (last visited Oct. 4, 2012) (It calculated total costs by including tuition, book purchases, miscellaneous school fees, and cost-of-living expenses. Cornell and NYLS were ranked seven and ten, respectively, with yearly costs of $76,680 at Cornell and $74,986 at NYLS.).

Analysis of NYLS's 2011 Employment Report

Now let's examine the employment report on NYLS's website to assess how well it complies with the ABA's reporting requirements under Revised Standard 509.

New York Law School Employment for Class of 2011: Nine Months after Graduation[79]

			Full-Time		Part-Time	
Graduate Outcome and Employment Status	**Number**	**% of Class**	**Permanent**	**Temporary**	**Permanent**	**Temporary**
Employed—Bar Pass Required[1]	229	44.5%	183	7	10	29
Employed—J.D. Advantage[2]	96	18.6%	59	21	8	8
Employed—Professional[3]	45	8.7%	28	7	8	2
Employed—Non-Professional[4]	20	3.9%	6	1	6	7
Employed—Job Type Unknown	10	1.9%				
Pursuing Graduate Degree FT	6	1.2%				
Unemployed—Not Seeking	11	2.1%				
Unemployed—Seeking a Job	75	14.6%				
Employment Status Unknown	23	4.5%				
Total Graduates (class size)	**515**	**100.0%**				

[1] Bar admission is required or anticipated for the position. Includes judicial clerks.

[2] A law degree is a demonstrable advantage in obtaining of performing the job. Includes positions like regulatory analyst, policy manager, corporate compliance, foreclosure specialist.

[3] Professional skills and training are required. Includes positions like business manager, procurement manager, physician, engineer.

[4] Positions that do not require any special training.

79. *New York Law School 2011 Employment Statistics*, New York Law Sch., http://www.nyls.edu/user_files/1/3/4/21/CSRS%20Employment%20Stats%20for%20Web%200511%20v1-rev.pdf (last visited Oct. 4, 2012) (hereinafter "NYLS Employment Statistics").

Contrary to the format provided by the ABA for employment reports, NYLS has not classified separately in the chart the number of graduates employed in law-school-funded positions from the number of graduates employed in full-time, part-time, short-term, or long-term positions. Several inches above the chart, NYLS has a sentence that states it "funded 31 of the positions below."[80] Again, contrary to the ABA's uniform chart, NYLS fails to indicate how many of these 31 graduates are in full-time, part-time, long-term and short-term positions. NYLS has 183 out of 515 graduates or 35.5% employed in full-time, long-term jobs in the category "Employed—Bar pass required." Because these jobs require bar passage, I assume they actually involve the practice of law and are, therefore, the best indicator that a graduate employed in that capacity has an attorney position. However, because NYLS has not provided additional information about the 31 graduates employed in NYLS-funded positions, an applicant may wonder if NYLS may have failed to disclose potentially negative employment information that could cause the rate of 35.5% to be inflated. In other words, slightly less than 35.5% of the graduates may be employed long-term, full-time in *non*-university-funded jobs that involved the actual practice of law.

The reader should take special note that my calculated rate of slightly less that 35.5% contradicts NYLS's 44.5% employment rate claimed in the chart for graduates employed in bar-passage-required jobs. NYLS purported rate of 44.5% was arrived at by excluding from the denominator the graduates who are unemployed and whose employment status is unknown and including in the numerator graduates employed in short-term and part-time positions.[81] My calculation of 35.5% (or slightly less) is more accurate because (1) most law school applicants want full-time, permanent attorney jobs and (2) the lawsuits show that the plaintiffs wanted to know what percentage of ALL graduates actually got this type of job.

Furthermore, several inches above the chart, NYLS states "80.3% (400/498) were employed as of February 15, 2012." This sentence ends with an asterisk directing the reader to a footnote about the number of graduates who were excluded from the denominator. This footnote fails to tell the reader that NYLS included graduates employed in part-time and temporary positions. When I made the numerator contain only graduates employed in permanent, full-time positions and the denominator included all graduates, I determined that NYLS's overall employment for graduates employed in permanent, full-time positions is only 54.8% (282/515).[82] In other words, NYLS only had 54.8% of *all* its graduates employed long-term and full-time regardless of the Employment Status category. After comparing NYLS's reporting practice before and after Revised Standard 509, the reader can understand why the graduates sued NYLS. By using a denominator that does not consist of *all* its graduates, NYLS continues to create the impression that its graduates had more successful employment outcomes than they actually did.

Revised Standard 509 has forced NYLS to disclose the reality that most of its graduates are not employed full-time, long-term in bar-passage-required jobs—they are not practicing attorneys. Again, NYLS has deviated from the uniform chart by failing to provide the specifics about graduates employed in university-funded positions. Moreover, NYLS reports percentages that use math calculations in a manner that obscures the actual employment realities. As a result, if prospective students do not do their own math calculations, they will not accurately assess their chances of getting a full-time, long-term, bar-required job. The reality is that if prospective students want to become attorneys and they enroll

80. *Id.*
81. *Id.* (estimating that a student will incur $72,816 per year in educational and living expenses).
82. The figure 282 is the sum of 183 + 59 + 28 + 6.

in NYLS, they have a small chance (less than 35.5% as explained above) of getting a full-time, long-term, bar-required job and a significant chance of being unemployed (14.6%).[83] These odds may be very unsatisfactory given that students will incur at least $49,225 per year in tuition costs alone[84] and rack up more than $200,000 in student loans if they have to finance their entire legal education.[85]

Now let's compare NYLS's reporting practices to Cornell's. I could not find online Cornell's 2009 report. However, its website has a report comparing employment data for the 2006 to 2010 classes.[86] For the 2009 class, it claimed a 97% overall employment rate, which was the lowest for those years. That is significantly better than the purported 89.7% overall employment rate claimed by NYLS for in its 2009 report.

The question now becomes: how closely does Cornell's 97% employment rate for the 2009 class compare to the percentage of graduates employed in attorney positions in the 2011 class report? I have copied below the "Employment Status" section of the employment report available at Cornell's website. This section complies substantially to the new format required by Revised Standard 509.

Cornell Graduate Employment for Class of 2011: Nine Months after Graduation[87]

Employment Status	Total	Full Time/ Long Term	Law School Funded
Employed	182	156	26
Bar Passage Required	179	153	26
JD Advantage	0	0	0
Professional	2	2	0
Non-Professional	0	0	0
Employed: Job Type Unknown	1	1	0
Pursuing Graduate Degree FT	3	-	-
Unemployed: Start Date Deferred	0	-	-
Unemployed: Not Seeking Job	0	-	-
Unemployed: Seeking Job	11	-	-
Status Unknown	5	-	-
Total Graduates	**201**		

83. This unemployment rate is from dividing 75 by 515.

84. *Tuition and Financial Aid*, N.Y. Law Sch., http://www.nyls.edu/prospective_students/tuition_and_financial_aid (last visited Oct. 4, 2012).

85. *Id.* (estimating that a student will incur $72,816 per year in educational and living expenses).

86. *Final Employment of Cornell Law School Graduates Classes of 2006–2010 by Type of Practice*, Cornell Univ. Law Sch., http://www.lawschool.cornell.edu/careers/aboutus/upload/2010finalstats-2.pdf (last visited Oct. 4, 2012).

87. *Statistics*, Cornell Univ. Law Sch., http://www.lawschool.cornell.edu/careers/aboutus/statistics.cfm (last visited Jan. 11, 2013).

Observe first that Cornell can claim a 90.5% overall employment rate because of its 201 graduates, 182 are employed. Cornell only has 5.4% (11 out of 201) of its graduates that are unemployed and seeking a job. By contrast, NYLS has 14.6% (75 out of 515) of its 2011 graduates that are unemployed and seeking a job. Cornell classifies separately the number of graduates employed in law-school-funded positions from the graduates employed in full-time, long-term positions. Because I am assuming that the status "Bar Passage Required" is the best indicator of graduates employed in jobs involving the practice of law, a prospective applicant can determine that 76.1% (or 153 out of 201) of Cornell graduates are employed in full-time, long-term jobs involving the practice of law. That percentage is more than double the 35% of NYLS graduates with the same employment status. But recall that the 35% rate is most likely not accurate and may be substantially smaller since NYLS did not separately account for 31graduates employed in NYLS-funded positions that require bar passage. Thus, Cornell does a better job of complying with the disclosure format required under Revised Standard 509 and, therefore, prospective students know how Cornell accounted for the graduates working in university-funded positions and can be fairly confident that the 76.1% employment rate for bar-required jobs is accurate. Consequently, law school applicants fortunate enough to get into Cornel have a really good chance of getting a bar-passage-required job and a very small chance of being unemployed and, as a result, can conclude that Cornell is a better value for the $55,220 annual tuition fee it now charges.

Besides differences in the "Employment Status" category, NYLS and Cornell have material differences in the way they disclosed their "Employment Type" categories. Below is the Employment Type chart for Cornell.

Cornell Graduate Employment Type for Class of 2011: Nine Months after Graduation[88]

Employment Type	Total	Full Time/ Long Term	Law School Funded
Law Firms			
Solo	0	0	0
2–10	6	6	0
11–25	7	7	0
26–50	3	3	0
51–100	2	2	0
101–250	8	8	0
251–500	12	12	0
501+	58	58	0
Other			
Unknown	3	3	0
Business & Industry	3	3	0
Government	32	14	18
Public Interest	16	8	8
Federal	16	16	0
State & Local	9	9	0
Academia	1	1	0
Employer Type Unknown	6	6	0
Total	**182**		

Employment Location	State	Number
Largest Employment	New York	74
2nd Largest Employment	California	20
3rd Largest Employment	D.C.	16

Cornell's chart deviates slightly from the format required under Revised Standard 509 because it does not have a column identifying the graduates working in part-time positions. However, this deviation is not misleading because all of Cornell's graduates are employed in full-time, long-term positions. Since almost all graduates want to be employed full-time and long-term, they would only care about the number of graduates in those positions.

Unlike Cornell's chart, NYLS's chart below does not comply with the ABA's uniform chart and makes it difficult to determine the number of graduates employed at law firms

88. *Id.*

in temporary or long-term jobs and employed full-time or only part-time. The difficulty arises from the fact that NYLS conflates Employment Type (NYLS categorizes by "Setting") with NYLS's salary data.[89]

New York Law School Employment Type for Class of 2011: Nine Months after Graduation

Employment Setting*	# of Grads	# of FT Salaries Reported	Minimum	25%	Median	75%	Maximum
Law Firms	164	89	$30,000	$50,000	$60,000	$76,500	$160,000
Solo	2	0					
2–10	94	44	$30,000	$41,850	$50,000	$60,000	$90,000
11–25	32	22	$31,200	$55,000	$65,000	$75,750	$150,000
26–50	16	12	$31,200	$48,000	$67,500	$89,500	$100,000
51–100	6	<5	$65,000				$135,000
101–250	1	<5					
251–500	4	<5	$100,000				$130,000
501+	7	6	$110,000	$136,250	$160,000	$160,000	$160,000
Firm Size Unknown	2	0					
Business & Industry	133	53	$20,800	$53,500	$67,000	$86,600	$200,000
Government	49	31	$40,000	$50,000	$55,000	$62,038	$76,500
Public Interest	27	18	$28,000	$39,500	$48,887	$53,511	$76,000
Judicial Clerkships	14	14	$43,000	$43,437	$46,750	$61,959	$69,000
Academia	10	<5	$45,000				$74,000
Employer Type Unknown	3	0					

* Salary information on this chart does not include compensation reported by those employed part time. For employment settings for which five or fewer graduates reported salaries, salary information is intentionally left blank to protect the privacy of the graduates.

In addition to conflating employment numbers with salary data, NYLS's format obscures the number of graduates employed in part-time and temporary positions. In the second column of the chart, NYLS discloses that 164 graduates have jobs at law firms but fails to disclose how many of these jobs are temporary. The heading at the top of the third column only indicates the number of graduates with fulltime *salaries*, not fulltime jobs. The reality is that a graduate who has fulltime work hours could nevertheless be employed temporarily,

89. NYLS Employment Statistics, *supra* note 79.

as is usually the case with document reviewers. NYLS's chart above has improved over its 2009 report, but it does not conform to the ABA's uniform chart and, therefore, has the potential to be misleading.

A person would have to create a spreadsheet to figure out how NYLS stacks up against Cornell. However, the comparison would still be inadequate because one cannot accurately assess how many NYLS graduates are employed only temporarily or part-time in each of the employment type categories or how NYLS has accounted for graduates working in NYLS-funded positions. At best, an applicant can determine that only 9% of the NYLS graduates with law firm jobs are working at firms with more than 100 attorneys. By contrast, the large majority (83%) of Cornell graduates employed in a law firm setting are working at firms with more than 100 attorneys.

The foregoing demonstrates that while Revised Standard 509 will force greater transparency of employment figures, a law school applicant needs to realize that a lot of "wiggle room" remains for law schools to obscure the actual employment outcomes. As a result, the ABA has left it to the integrity of law school deans and admissions personnel to be make disclosures that are "complete, accurate and not misleading to a reasonable law school student or applicant."

It remains to be seen how strictly the ABA will enforce the disclosure standards or whether it will sanction violating schools to the fullest extent possible. The ABA has amended Rule 16 to allow it to punish law schools in violation of Revised Standard 509 by placing them on probation or removing them from the list of ABA-approved law schools. However, as Mr. McEntee has pointed out, the weakness of Sub-section 509(a) is that it states that the ABA "may" sanction, not "must" sanction.[90] The lack of mandatory enforcement of the general terms was a problem with the prior version of Standard 509. The lack of mandatory punishment that is at least remedial in nature—e.g., conspicuous corrections on law school website and by letters for distributing any incorrect, inaccurate or misleading information—reflects another missed opportunity for the ABA to incentivize all law schools to "do the right thing."

The bottom line is that law school applicants need to be very careful when looking at categories for "Employment Type" and "Employment Status." If a school's numbers strike you as untrustworthy, do not reward it for its lack of transparency by enrolling in that school.

Salary Reporting Can Still Be Manipulated

Perhaps, the most disappointing aspect of Revised Standard 509 is that it does not compel law schools to disclose salary data or, in the event of voluntary disclosure, require law schools to follow a particular format. In 2011, the ABA Young Lawyers Division's (YLD) "Truth in Law School Education" initiative passed a resolution urging, among other things, that the ABA compel law schools to provide salary data in a non-misleading manner. In March 2012, the ABA stated that it "declined to require the collection and publication of salary data because fewer than 45 percent of law graduates contacted by their law schools report their salaries." When YLD learned that the proposed changes to Old Standard 509 did not compel law schools to provide school-specific salary data, the

90. *See* ABA Comment Letters, *supra* note 38.

YLD responded that the ABA should require law schools to achieve a mandatory minimum response rate from graduates regarding their salaries and to disclose the results.[91]

Similarly, Kyle McEntee also urged the ABA to compel disclosure of salary data. He conceded that the disclosure of salary data has the potential to deceive applicants because of the low response rate of graduates willing to supply salary information.[92] However, Mr. McEntee explained that by failing to require disclosure, the ABA has left schools with no incentive to collect salary data from graduates and no incentive to provide the data results to prospective students. This means that prospective students will not be able to fully assess whether a JD is worth pursuing because of a lack of information about salary outcomes for graduates of a particular law school.

Professor Brian Tamanaha also expressed his concern that the ABA's "do nothing" approach allows law schools to refuse to collect or disclose to applicants school-specific salary data: "[l]aw schools with the poorest employment results will undoubtedly prefer that no school specific salary numbers be collected because the city-state averages [based on aggregated salary data] look good by comparison to the actual results for their graduates." Professor Tamanaha, therefore, urged that the ABA take on the task of "collect[ing] the salaries on a school specific basis ... [because] only then can prospective students get a sense of their potential expected earnings at a given school."[93] Perhaps, realizing that this proposed idea will never be adopted, Professor Tamanaha ended his comment by asking the ABA to require law schools to post a warning when law schools disclose salary averages based on a low response rate. He urged that the required warning be a "plain and brief statement advising students that the true average salary is unknown but probably below the reported average salary figure." As Professor Tamanaha has pointed out, it is well documented that salary reporting comes from graduates earning the highest salaries; therefore, a warning requirement is justified.[94]

The ABA rejected the above recommendations that it require law schools to report school-specific salary data or that it require law schools to post a warning if they voluntarily disclose salary data. Although the ABA "felt strongly that the current collection of such data is unreliable and produces distorted information," it stated that Revised Standard 509 still permits law schools to report salary data as long as they "specify the number of respondents and the percentage of graduates the data represents." Note that this was also required under Old Standard 509.

I am surprised that the ABA did not at a minimum require a warning to applicants that they may earn a salary less than the median or average salary due to a low salary response rate. Such a requirement is no different than numerous consumer protection statutes that require certain disclosures designed to warn consumers about the risks associated with a transaction.[95]

Consider how the ABA's failure to require nothing more than what was required under Old Standard 509 has the potential to be misleading. Refer back to charts on pages 94 and 100 to see how NYLS disclosed its salary data for 2009 and 2011. Because both charts

91. *Id.*
92. *Id.*
93. *Id.*
94. *Id.*
95. For example, the Truth in Lending Act requires that lenders disclose the cost of financing a loan as a dollar amount and as an annual percentage rate. *See* 15 U.S.C.A. § 1605(a)(3); *see also* 12 C.F.R. § 226.4(b)(3). Some state payday lending statutes require lenders to include a written disclosure warning the borrower that other forms of credit may be less expensive than a payday loan.

conflate employment type with salaries, some less-sophisticated applicants will erroneously conclude that their earning potential as a NYLS graduate is greater than it actually is. Indeed, that is exactly what the law graduates asserted in their lawsuit against NYLS.

Prospective students must sear it into their subconscious that a school's presentation of its salary data may be grossly misleading because as few as twenty percent of a graduating class may supply their salaries to the schools. The general consensus is that graduates who do not report salary information are the ones who are making lower amounts. The effect is that the average salary data displayed by a law schools is skewed and appears higher than it actually is.

The ABA missed a real opportunity to require law schools to be more transparent by providing school-specific salary data or to at least posting a conspicuous warning next to reported salary data. With no reporting requirements regarding salary data, some law schools that voluntarily disclose salary data will be tempted to leave prospective students with a much rosier salary potential than the actual reported salaries indicate. Law schools that refuse to post any salary information leave prospective students in the dark about their earning prospects upon graduating from those schools.

Points to Take Away

In summary, the ABA's new employment reporting standards will force greater transparency so that prospective students can make a more fully-informed enrollment decision. However, because of the ABA's unwillingness to be aggressive in its role as commander-in-chief of law school disclosures, prospective students cannot take at face value the data reported by law schools. The five main points to remember are as follows. First, because most law graduates do not provide salary information, law school applicants have to discount salary data and expect to earn only a salary in the mid-five-figure range. NALP's June 2013 press release stated that the national median salary for the 2012 graduates was $61,245, which represents a 12.5% decrease in the national median salary from $72,000 for the 2009 class.[96] Furthermore, over the last decade real wages have actually declined dramatically.

The second main point is that the JD-Advantage and Employed-Professional subcategories listed under "Employment Status" will most likely include jobs that many law school applicants consider unsuccessful employment. Third, the six subcategories under "Employment Type" are describing where the graduates work, not what they do. As alleged in over a dozen lawsuits filed against law schools for reporting deceptive data, a significant number of graduates could be working in academic, law-firm, business, and governmental settings as career counselors, paralegals, legal secretaries or other under-employed positions.

The fourth main point is that while the *US News* rankings released in 2013 takes into account employment data disclosed under the new ABA standards, I maintain that the rankings methodology is still flawed. In a March 2013 interview, Lee Pacchia of Bloomberg News, asked Bob Morse, Director of Data Research at *US News*, several questions regarding how it accounted for the new ABA employment data requirements in the latest rankings.[97]

---

96. NALP Press Release, June 20, 2013, p. 3, Law School Class of 2012 Finds More Jobs, Salaries Rise.

97. *New Data "Unmasks" Law Schools, Says Rankings Czar*, BLOOMBERG.COM, (March 12, 2013), *available at* http://www.bloomberg.com/video/new-data-unmasks-law-schools.

Mr. Morse stated that "full weight" was given to jobs classified as JD-advantage and bar-passage-required. He further stated that professional and non-professional jobs were given less than full weight, while part-time and non-long-term jobs were given the least weight. Based on his explanation, Mr. Morse has given some law schools incentives to exploit the ABA's new standards. As I have explained thoroughly in this chapter, the JD-Advantage category can be manipulated; therefore, *US News* should not give JD-advantage jobs full weight as it does with bar-passage-required jobs. Since Mr. Morse announced to the world that both JD-advantage and bar-passage-required jobs are given full weight, law schools have a very good reason to include in the JD-advantage category graduates employed in jobs where the law degree was neither necessary nor a demonstrable advantage. Additionally, *US News* should give zero weight to non-professional jobs because no one incurs six-figure student loan debt in law school to get a non-professional job. Similarly, *US News* should not be according any weight to graduates employed at law schools as part-time research assistants, career counselors or admissions ambassadors as these are not jobs people attend law school to get. Finally, Morse admits that *US News* does not know how law schools are classifying graduates employed in law-school-funded positions. *US News* does not verify any data submitted by the law schools. Thus, although Mr. Morse reports that *US News* has adjusted its rankings methodology to address the new ABA standards, such adjustments do not overcome the criticisms that the methodology is flawed.

Mr. Morse's admissions lead me to the final main point of this chapter. Because only newly-licensed attorneys need to pass the bar exam to practice law, the "Bar Passage Required" category listed in a school's employment report is the best indicator of the number of graduates working as attorneys or as judicial law clerks.[98] As a result, prospective students who believe they want to become lawyers should try to get an offer of admission from a law school with a high percentage of graduates employed in Bar-Passage-Required jobs. Make sure that the employment rate is based on a numerator consisting only of those in permanent full-time Bar-Passage-Required jobs and the denominator includes *all* the graduates, not just the ones who are employed.[99] Prospective students should not count on the ABA to force more accurate disclosures. Be sure to read Chapter 8, where I summarize how much critical information applicants need but for which the ABA has no disclosure standards. Consequently, prospective students are left in the precarious position of having to rely on law school personnel to be truthful.

I will close the chapter with Table 4-2 (next page), which identifies the law schools that had 65% or more of their 2011 graduates employed in long-term, fulltime bar-passage-required jobs.[100] A few schools that made the list may be surprising to some; however, additional information shows that their graduates may not have the outcomes that some law school applicants find acceptable. For example, although Mississippi College made

98. Judicial law clerks usually become licensed attorneys and that is why these clerkship positions are included in the bar-passage-required category.

99. For example, Camden School of Law at Rutgers University has been accused of grossly inflating its employment rate by excluding from the denominator the number of 2011 graduates who are unemployed. *See LST Calls for Dean's Resignation and ABA Investigation*, LawSchoolTransparency.com, http://www.lawschooltransparency.com/2012/05/lst-calls-for-deans-resignation-and-aba-investigation/ (last visited Jan. 11, 2013) (Camden's report "excludes non-employed graduates without indicating that 17.8% of the class has been excluded. Once again, 90% of employed actually means only 74% of the whole class" and only 63.6% are employed in bar-passage-required jobs.).

100. The raw data are from the ABA, and I've rounded up the percentages. ABA Section of Legal Education and Admissions to the Bar, Employment Summary Report, http://employmentsummary.abaquestionnaire.org (last visited Feb. 20, 2013). For a summary of employment outcomes of the 2011 graduates of all ABA-accredited law schools, look at Tables 1-1 and 1-2 in Appendix A.

Table 4-2.

	School's Name	2011 Grads with FT, LT, Bar Passage-Required Job	Total # of 2011 Grads	Percent with FT, LT, Bar-Passage Required Job
1	VIRGINIA, UNIVERSITY OF	357	377	94.7%
2	COLUMBIA UNIVERSITY	429	456	94.1%
3	STANFORD UNIVERSITY	175	192	91.1%
4	NEW YORK UNIVERSITY	420	466	90.1%
5	HARVARD UNIVERSITY	525	583	90.1%
6	CHICAGO, UNIVERSITY OF	179	203	88.2%
7	YALE UNIVERSITY	180	205	87.8%
8	PENNSYLVANIA, UNIVERSITY OF	231	274	84.3%
9	DUKE UNIVERSITY	170	207	82.1%
10	GEORGE WASHINGTON UNIVERSITY	421	518	81.3%
11	LOUISIANA STATE UNIVERSITY	143	176	81.3%
12	CALIFORNIA-BERKELEY, UNIV. OF	248	310	80.0%
13	ST. MARY'S UNIVERSITY	195	249	78.3%
14	ALABAMA, UNIVERSITY OF	128	164	78.0%
15	NORTHWESTERN UNIVERSITY	221	287	77.0%
16	CORNELL UNIVERSITY	153	201	76.1%
17	MICHIGAN, UNIVERSITY OF	286	379	75.5%
18	ARIZONA, UNIVERSITY OF	119	158	75.3%
19	MISSISSIPPI COLLEGE	125	166	75.3%
20	VANDERBILT UNIVERSITY	146	198	73.7%
21	KENTUCKY, UNIVERSITY OF	97	135	71.9%
22	CAMPBELL UNIVERSITY	95	133	71.4%
23	BAYLOR UNIVERSITY	110	157	70.1%
24	TEXAS AT AUSTIN, UNIVERSITY OF	267	382	69.9%
25	FLORIDA STATE UNIVERSITY	194	279	69.5%
26	EMORY UNIVERSITY	155	225	68.9%
27	WEST VIRGINIA UNIVERSITY	86	125	68.8%
28	UTAH, UNIVERSITY OF	92	134	68.7%
29	BOSTON COLLEGE	195	285	68.4%
30	NORTH CAROLINA, UNIVERSITY OF	169	247	68.4%

	School's Name	2011 Grads with FT, LT, Bar Passage-Required Job	Total # of 2011 Grads	Percent with FT, LT, Bar-Passage Required Job
31	ARIZONA STATE UNIVERSITY	137	201	68.2%
32	LOUISVILLE, UNIVERSITY OF	95	142	66.9%
33	MISSOURI-COLUMBIA, UNIVERSITY OF	94	141	66.7%
34	UNIVERSITY OF NEVADA-LAS VEGAS	85	128	66.4%
35	NEW MEXICO, UNIVERSITY OF	68	103	66.0%
36	MONTANA, UNIVERSITY OF	56	85	65.9%
37	TULSA, UNIVERSITY OF	79	120	65.8%
38	IOWA, UNIVERSITY OF	120	183	65.6%
39	SAMFORD UNIVERSITY	97	148	65.5%
40	SOUTHERN CALIFORNIA, UNIVERSITY OF	134	207	64.7%
41	NEBRASKA, UNIVERSITY OF	84	130	64.6%
42	GEORGIA STATE UNIVERSITY	120	186	64.5%

Data Source: Employment Summary Report, http://employmentsummary.abaquestionnaire.org.
FT, LT = Full-time, Long-term.

this list, I reveal in Chapter 11 that 75% of its graduates who are employed at law firms are actually employed as solo practitioners and in extremely small firms (size 2 to 10 attorneys).

To compare a summary of employment outcomes at each law school, please look at Tables 1-1 and 1-2 in Appendix A where I reveal the percentage of 2011 graduates employed in long-term, fulltime bar-passage-required jobs. Also in Appendix A are Tables 5 and 6, which contain employment data about the success of 2012 graduates in securing post-graduation employment. Table 7 compares employment data for 2011 and 2012 graduates. In Appendix B, I have created a matrix for students to use when comparing law schools and have provided a matrix example comparing three law schools.

In the next chapter, I put under the microscope a group of schools ignored by *US News* and by most in the legal academy. Students who attend one of the nearly 40 unaccredited law schools operating in the United States are at risk of spending an enormous amount of money to get a degree that may severely limit their options for practicing law.

Chapter 5

Negligent Enrollment Claim: A Segue to the Risks in Attending Unaccredited Schools

In the previous chapters, I discussed the ABA and some of the risks of attending ABA-accredited law schools with unfavorable statistics, including high unemployment, attrition, and transfer-out rates. Beyond these ABA-approved schools is another category of law schools that applicants should be concerned about. There are currently 37 non-ABA-accredited law schools.[1] The majority of these unaccredited schools are located in California. Unfortunately, I cannot provide any reliable data about how many students graduate from these unaccredited schools because no organization publishes data regarding the enrollment numbers and graduation rates at unaccredited schools. However, in comparison to ABA-accredited schools, much more serious risks are associated with attending these schools, and I will discuss those risks in further detail in this chapter. Despite those risks and the depressed legal job market, new law schools are opening and are recruiting prospective law students. Because many law schools are responding to the decrease in LSAT test-taking and applications for admission by intentionally reducing their class sizes, prospective students who do not have LSAT scores high enough to get in these schools will be targeted by unaccredited law schools. This chapter is in keeping with theme of the previous two chapters in that it recommends that prospective students contemplating attending a non-ABA-accredited school actively search for and analyze available information about that school even before submitting an application to the school.

So why should prospective law students be wary of enrolling in non-ABA-accredited law schools? The primary reason is that having a degree from one of these law schools really limits, and in some cases completely prevents, the graduates of these schools from actually practicing law. Below, you will meet Morgan Crutchfield, who enrolled in one of those schools but later sued it based on a claim of negligent enrollment.

Before going into the specifics of Ms. Crutchfield's lawsuit, I will briefly explain ABA-accreditation. The ABA's Section of Legal Education and Admissions to the Bar (hereafter, the "ABA") is the only recognized accrediting agency by the U.S. Department of Education to accredit JD programs at American law schools.[2] A school's decision to seek ABA-accreditation is completely voluntarily. Several law schools, such as the Nashville School of

1. According to the Law School Admissions Council, there are 37 non-ABA-accredited or provisionally-approved law schools in the U.S. *Choosing a Law School*, Law School Admission Council, http://www.lsac.org/jd/choose/law-school-links.asp#NON-ABA (last visited Jan. 11, 2013). *US News* does not rank non-ABA-accredited schools.

2. *Accreditation in the United States: Specialized Accrediting Agencies*, Dept. of Ed., http://www2.ed.gov/admins/finaid/accred/accreditation_pg7.html (last visited Jan. 11, 2013).

Law, have never sought ABA-accreditation.[3] A preliminary step to receiving ABA-accreditation is for a school to be provisionally approved, and it can only seek such approval until after it has been in operation for one full year.[4] That means that a new school will be operating without ABA-approval for at least one year although the school may have the approval of a state agency or other accrediting organization. To obtain ABA-provisional approval, the school must show that it is in substantial compliance with the ABA's standards and that the school has a plan demonstrating that it will be in full compliance with the standards within three years after being provisionally approved. Once it has received such approval, the school then has five years to demonstrate it has fully met all the ABA's standards in order to receive ABA-accreditation.

The ABA does not establish the rules dictating which graduates are able to sit for a state's bar exam. Instead, each state sets its own minimum requirements that must be met in order to practice law in that particular state. These requirements typically include earning a JD, passing a character and fitness test (which will be discussed in more detail in Chapter 15), and then passing the state's bar exam. In all *fifty* states, a student with a JD from an ABA-accredited law school can seek permission to take the state bar exam. For graduates of unaccredited law schools who want to practice law *outside* of the state where they earned their degree, only a handful of states allow those graduates to take their state exam and only if the unaccredited school is approved by the respective state's authority. These states are Alabama, California, Connecticut, Massachusetts, Michigan, Nevada, and Tennessee.[5] Because of these severe limitations on a graduate's ability to practice law, I consider non-ABA accredited schools to be "unaccredited" in this book even though they may have state approval to operate.

Morgan Crutchfield's Experience at Duncan Law School

Morgan Crutchfield serves a recent example of a student who enrolled in an unaccredited school and may not be eligible to sit for a state's bar exam. In 2012, Morgan filed against Duncan School of Law ("Duncan") a lawsuit alleging that after enrolling in the unaccredited school, she learned that she was not eligible to take the Tennessee bar exam due to the school's negligence.[6] Duncan,[7] which is part of Lincoln Memorial University, is a Tennessee-approved but non-ABA-accredited law school, located in

3. *About the School*, Nashville Sch. of Law, http://nashvilleschooloflaw.net/?page_id=6 (last visited Oct. 12, 2012).

4. *Rules of Procedure for Approval of Law Schools*, Rule 4(c), Am. Bar Assoc., *available at* http://www.americanbar.org/content/dam/aba/publications/misc/legal_education/Standards/2012_2013_aba_rules_of_procedure.authcheckdam.pdf (hereafter, "ABA Rules") ("A law school may not apply for provisional approval until it has completed the first full academic year of its program," unless it qualifies for some limited exception.). http://www.ncbex.org/assets/media_files/Comp-Guide/CompGuide.pdf.

5. Nat'l Conference of Bar Examiners, Bar Admission Requirements 2012, *available at* http://www.ncbex.org/assets/media_files/Comp-Guide/CompGuide.pdf.

6. Crutchfield v. Lincoln Mem'l Univ., Duncan Sch. of Law, No. 182237-1 (Ch. Ct. for Knox Cnty., Tenn. Feb. 14, 2012) (hereafter "Crutchfield Complaint").

7. Duncan is among three law schools that have lost provisional approval by the ABA and is one of the 37 non-ABA-accredited law schools operating in the United States.

Knoxville. While Morgan's claim is rare, her lawsuit is very important because it will allow me to discuss a huge issue: Is attending an unaccredited law school too risky and, therefore, not worth the price?

In the spring of 2009, Morgan received an admission offer to be a part-time student at Duncan as part of its inaugural class. She was excited to be invited to join the graduating class of 2013 and could envision herself in four years[8] walking across the stage to get her law diploma. The location of the law school was just right for her because she would be able to retain her job and would not have to move. As a startup law school, Duncan lacks ABA-approval and accreditation; however, it is approved by the Tennessee Board of Law Examiners. Because Tennessee is among the seven states that permit students from pre-approved, non-ABA schools, to take the bar, Morgan expected to be able to sit for the Tennessee exam and ultimately practice law.

Like many law school applicants, Morgan Crutchfield had applied for law school admission when she was an undergraduate senior and, therefore, did not yet have a bachelor's degree. She was a few credit hours short of obtaining her degree. After speaking with an academic counselor at her undergraduate institution, Pennsylvania State University ("Penn State"), Morgan believed that credit hours that she had earned at another college would be sufficient to meet the foreign language requirement necessary for graduation from Penn State.[9] As a result, she thought that she would receive her bachelor's degree in the summer of 2009, just before the start of law school.[10]

In July 2009, right before she was about to begin her studies at Duncan, Morgan found out that her request for substitute credits was denied and that Penn State had not granted her a bachelor's degree. She e-mailed this seemingly bad news to Paul Carney, the Director of Admissions at Duncan at that time, asking him if it "would be possible for [her] to attend [Duncan] while [she] finish[ed] these Spanish credits ... or if [she would] have to wait an entire year to attend."[11] Mr. Carney subsequently replied to Morgan, by email, informing her that her admission offer was "still valid" contingent upon her completing the foreign language requirement "prior to completion of [her] legal program of study [at Duncan]." Relying then on Mr. Carney's statement that it would be okay for her to finish her credits for her bachelor's degree while simultaneously attending law school, Morgan enrolled in Duncan in the fall of 2009.

What may seem like a minor inconvenience was actually a big problem for Morgan. As discussed above, each state sets its own requirements for applicants seeking to take that particular state's bar exam. In Tennessee, one of those requirements is that students must receive their bachelor's degree ***prior*** to enrolling in law school.

Unfortunately for Morgan, she asserts that she attended Duncan for two full years before the issue of the undergraduate-degree requirement was even approached. Two years after she first enrolled, April Meldrum, Duncan's Associate Dean for Academics, e-mailed Morgan requesting that she provide Dean Meldrum "verifiable information regarding [Morgan's] enrollment in the twelve hours of Spanish and something from [her] undergraduate institution indicating when [her] Bachelor's degree will be conferred." Morgan responded with assurances that her enrollment in Spanish classes would satisfy the graduation requirements for Penn State before graduating from Duncan. Dean

8. Start-up law schools often have part-time programs, which result in attending law school for at least four years for completion of the JD requirements.

9. Attachment B, Crutchfield, No. 182237-1 (Ch. Ct. for Knox Cnty., Tenn. Feb. 14, 2012).

10. *Id.*

11. *Id.*

Meldrum replied to these assurances by stating that she wanted to make sure that Morgan was on track to get her diploma "BEFORE fall 2012."[12]

At this point, Morgan had completed 54 credit hours at Duncan over a span of two and a half years.[13] It was around this time that she found out that she would not be eligible to sit to take the Tennessee bar exam.[14] As a result, Morgan sued Duncan Law School, Paul Carney, and April Meldrum (the "Defendants"), to recover damages amounting to $250,000.[15]

Morgan based her lawsuit on three different legal theories: negligence, breach of contract, and intentional wrongdoing. Essentially, she argues that the school had a duty to know the rules concerning who may sit for the Tennessee bar exam and by allowing her to enroll even though they knew this would disqualify her, they acted negligently. She further asserts that the Defendants fraudulently misrepresented the rules and intentionally induced her to rely on their misrepresentation of the rules. She alleges that these actions constituted a breach of contract because the Defendants failed to provide her with a legal education that would allow her to practice law. She argues that the Defendants' actions caused her to essentially waste two and half years of her life and incur $79,560 in student loans to pursue a legal career that was over before it even started. The problem here is further exacerbated by the fact that because Duncan lacks ABA-accreditation, Morgan may be restricted to taking only the Tennessee bar exam if she graduates.[16]

When the Defendants responded to Morgan's lawsuit they did not dispute the content of the email messages. Instead, they argued that the Tennessee Board of Law Examiners (the "Tennessee Board") could "waive the requirement of graduation from an accredited undergraduate school if the applicant has" met certain requirements.[17] They basically argued that Morgan should remain in school and take a wait-and-see approach, borrowing even more money in hopes that the Tennessee Board would ignore the rules just for her. The Duncan Defendants argued that they had performed their duties, but that Morgan only had herself to blame because she dropped out of school before she found out whether the Tennessee Board would waive the requirement.[18] They further asserted that by dropping out of school, Morgan had made it impossible for them to perform their duties. The bottom line is that the Duncan Defendants maintain that any loss suffered by Morgan was caused by her actions alone.

Morgan's claims of negligence and breach of contract are worth discussing here. A law school applicant would not know and cannot be expected to know about all of the various and complex qualifications a graduate must possess to take the bar exam. However, law schools should be expected to know these requirements because they are preparing students to take the bar exam and fulfill their dreams of becoming lawyers.

---

12. *Id.* Attachment C, Crutchfield, No. 182237-1 (Ch. Ct. for Knox Cnty., Tenn. Feb. 14, 2012). Ms. Crutchfield's complaint does not provide an explanation as to why she had not completed her undergraduate degree even though she had been in law school for two and half years.

13. Crutchfield Complaint ¶ 18.

14. *Id.* at ¶ 19.

15. *Id.* The complaint also names Sydney Beckham, the Dean of Duncan Law School; however, it does not assert that he made any representations to Ms. Crutchfield.

16. Only eight other states allow applicants with out-of-state, non-ABA-accredited degrees to sit for their bar exam and only if the state has approved the school. For example, West Virginia could allow Morgan to sit for its bar exam but only if she met all of West Virginia's eligibility requirements.

17. *Id.*

18. Answer ¶ 20, Crutchfield, No. 182237-1 (Ch. Ct. for Knox Cnty., Tenn. Feb. 14, 2012).

Under breach of contract law, there is a legal doctrine called mitigation of damages. Under this doctrine, in order to succeed on a breach of contract claim, the person filing the lawsuit must take reasonable action to avoid incurring any additional injury or damages. What this means for Morgan is that Duncan is implying that she has a duty to mitigate any damages inflicted by Duncan. In other words, Duncan is not admitting to any wrongdoing but if it had done so, Morgan is obligated to mitigating any damages by borrowing more money to pay tuition to attend law school for three more semesters so she can graduate and apply for the waiver of undergraduate-degree requirement to take the Tennessee bar exam. This argument is really troubling for me because it would seem more reasonable for Duncan to pay for Morgan's remaining semesters of school because had Duncan not admitted her in the first place for failing to possess an undergraduate degree, Morgan may not have ever gone to law school.

How can I come to this conclusion? If Morgan had been told to wait and enroll in the fall of 2010 *after* her undergraduate-degree completion, she most likely would have heard about the problems in the legal job market. By the fall of 2010, several major newspapers had already published news stories about law graduates struggling to find jobs and being heavily indebted.[19] Had she been forced to wait a year, after completing her undergraduate degree, she may have decided that going to law school would be too risky of an endeavor. In the long run, Morgan may be better off pursuing another career because a law degree from Duncan, a non-ABA-accredited school, may be of dubious value, especially in a depressed legal job market.

This lawsuit against Duncan appears to be a rare type of claim in light of the other types of claims pending against several law schools. However, the suit is still relevant because Duncan was and still is an unaccredited[20] law school despite its attempt to earn a provisional accreditation from the ABA.[21] It is important that prospective students understand the differences between accredited and unaccredited schools and the inherent risks associated with attending the latter.

In fact, Morgan's lawsuit was not the first time Duncan found itself in court. A few months before Morgan filed her lawsuit, Duncan filed suit against the ABA for denial of provisional accreditation allegedly in violation of various state and federal laws. Duncan claimed that the ABA "arbitrarily and capriciously denied [it] provisional accreditation" and that the "ABA's decision was motivated by a desire to restrain trade and limit competition among law schools."[22]

19. *See, e.g.*, *Law School Tuition: Value of Degree Cross-Examined with Hiring on Decline, Many Graduates Left with $100,000 in Debt, No Job*, Chi. Trib., Apr. 17, 2010, at 17. I'm assuming that Ms. Crutchfield was in the habit of paying attention to print media. By January 2011, several major newspapers had reported the bad news about legal job market. *See, e.g.*, Anne Lowery, *How Law School Went from Being a Sure Thing to a Bum Deal*, Wash. Post, Oct. 31, 2010, at G04. I take the position that law graduates who enrolled in law school before 2011 should not be blamed for their predicament, especially in light of the credible accusations that employment statistics, as reported by several law schools, were not accurate or transparent.

20. Unless specifically indicated, I characterize a non-ABA-accredited school as unaccredited even if it has passed a state's standard for approval.

21. Complaint ¶ 7, Lincoln Memorial Univ., Duncan Sch. of Law v. The Am. Bar Assoc., No. 3:11-CV-608 (Dist.Ct. E.D. Tenn. Dec. 22, 2011) (hereafter "Duncan Law School's Complaint"). *See also* Dec. of Hullett H. Askew at ¶ 60–72, Lincoln Mem'l Univ., Duncan Sch. of Law v. The Am. Bar Assoc., No. 3:11-CV-608 (D.C. Eastern District of Tennessee Knoxville Division, filed Jan. 3, 2012).

22. Duncan Law School's Complaint ¶ 7, Lincoln Memorial Univ., Duncan Sch. of Law v. The Am. Bar Assoc., No. 3:11-CV-608 (Dist.Ct. E.D. Tenn. Dec. 22, 2011).

The ABA's response to Duncan's lawsuit is an interesting one and, if true, is a clear demonstration of additional risks of attending an unaccredited law school. When Duncan applied for provisional approval in 2011, the ABA sent out a site evaluation team, which spent time at the school and prepared a report. The team allegedly discovered that Duncan's enrollment was 40–45% below the projection that it made in its feasibility study for a new law school.[23] The team also alleges it discovered several other detrimental factors (not disputed by Duncan), including Duncan's low admissions profiles, declining applications from prospective students, declining LSAT scores and undergraduate GPAs for first year students, and employing a Director of Academic Success who did not have training or experience in academic support.[24] This last finding is especially noteworthy because it may be a reference to April Meldrum, Duncan's Associate Dean for Academics, whose email messages to Morgan are relevant in the case. Dean Meldrum's résumé posted online indicates that she had no prior work experience as an academic or in law school admissions.[25] Additionally, the ABA discovered that Duncan had readmitted *one-third* of the students it had previously dismissed for academic reasons.[26] If these students had to borrow additional money to repeat courses they had failed, this finding should make a person considering enrolling in Duncan to question the school's pedagogical skills.

The ABA Accreditation Committee discussed the foregoing with Duncan at a hearing regarding provisional accreditation. The Accreditation Committee concluded that "Duncan had not established ... substantial compliance with each of the Standards and had not presented a reliable plan for achieving full compliance. Specifically, the Committee concluded that Duncan failed to establish substantial compliance with [several] Standards and Interpretations." Based on the foregoing, the Council of the Section of Legal Education and Admissions to the Bar made a decision to deny Duncan provisional approval. Consequently, Duncan remains unaccredited.[27]

The legal and accreditation issues that Duncan has faced raise the broader question of whether it is wise to attend and graduate from an unaccredited law school.

To illustrate the significance of attending a non-accredited law school, further discussion of the Duncan lawsuit is warranted. The general rule for Tennessee is that applicants who want to take the Tennessee bar must graduate from an ABA-approved law school or a law school that is located in Tennessee and approved by the Tennessee Board of Law Examiners ("TBLE").[28] The TBLE has approved Duncan School of Law graduates to apply for and take the Tennessee bar exam even though the ABA has denied accreditation. The TBLE's approval of Duncan is subject to certain ongoing conditions and is approved only until December 31, 2017.[29] However, a fair interpretation of this limited approval granted by

---

23. *Id.*

24. ABA's Brief in Opposition, p. 5.

25. Prior to being employed at Duncan, Dean Meldrum had been a practicing attorney and a juvenile court judge in Clinton, Tennessee.

26. ABA's Brief in Opposition, p. 6.

27. *Id.* at 6–10.

28. *See* Tennessee Board of Law Examiners, http://www.state.tn.us/lawexaminers/BLERequi.html (last visited June 9, 2012).

29. *See* Tennessee Board of Law Examiners, http://www.state.tn.us/lawexaminers/docs/Web%20Notice%20DSOL%20April%202012.pdf (last visited June 9, 2012). The text of this .pdf document reads, in its entirety:

> The Tennessee Board of Law Examiners (TBLE) extends its approval for Duncan School of Law (DSOL) graduates to apply for and take the Tennessee Bar Exam to December 31, 2017. The approval is subject to the Board's continued satisfaction that Duncan School of Law is maintaining and/or improving upon the current mechanisms it has established to strengthen

TBLE is that Duncan could lose approval if Duncan has not received ABA accreditation by that date.

Perhaps, the possibility of losing TBLE-approval motivated Duncan to try another path to accreditation. In October 2012, Duncan dropped its multi-million dollar lawsuit against the ABA, and, by the close of 2012, it made key personnel changes, including replacing the dean of the law school and hiring a director of admissions,[30] and it submitted a new application to the ABA for provisional approval.[31]

No doubt, Duncan faces an uphill battle considering that its first-year class for the 2012–2013 academic year consisted of only 15 students[32] and considering that it has to wait and see how many of the 77 students who graduated in May 2013 can pass the bar exam and, thereby, silence Duncan's critics.[33]

Morgan Crutchfield was not among Duncan's first class of graduates. The chancery court threw out her lawsuit, calling it "not ripe" and "premature" because any alleged damages would be speculative. The court did not agree with her that she had established negligence on the part of Duncan. But even if she had, the court opined that, at this point, she had ***not*** sustained any damage. In other words, until she graduates, applies for the waiver, and is *denied* the waiver, the court cannot award any damages for any proven negligence.[34] That means Morgan is going to have to borrow more money to pursue this route, and come back to court if she is denied the chance to take the bar exam due to the

---

> the law school and cure any deficiencies that may exist in its ABA accreditation process. To that end, the Tennessee Board of Law Examiners will conduct site visits to the DSOL on at least an annual basis and will further review DSOL during this time period. Should DSOL not obtain full ABA accreditation by December 31, 2017, or should DSOL otherwise cause the TBLE to have concerns about its program at any time prior to December 31, 2017, the TBLE may institute proceedings under Supreme Court Rule 7, Section 2.09 relative to noncompliance with applicable standards set forth in Rule 7, Section 2.08. The Tennessee Board of Law Examiners wishes the Duncan School of Law success in its continued efforts to achieve ABA accreditation.

30. *Veteran Law School Dean Parham Williams, Jr., Named Interim Dean at LMU-Duncan School of Law*, Targeted News Serv. (U.S.), Dec. 13, 2012, available at http://www.prweb.com/releases/2012/12/prweb10235736.htm (The President of LMU, in announcing Parham's appointment stated: "The Duncan School of Law has a strong academic program of legal education and I am confident that Parham will continue to enhance the program."); *Mathews Joins LMU-DSOL as Director of Admissions*, Targeted News Serv. (U.S.), Dec. 11, 2012 available at http://lmu1.lmunet.edu/cgi-bin/MySQLdb?VIEW=/news/view_one.txt&newsid=1352 (announcing the appointment of Randy Mathews as Director of Admissions, describing his 18 years of experience with a bar exam preparation company, and asserting that "[h]is education coupled with his work experiences provide him with a unique skill set that is well suited for his new role" at Duncan).

31. Megan Boehnke, *Full Court Press: LMU Law School Working Hard on ABA Reapplication*, Knoxville News-Sentinel, Dec. 19, 2012, available at http://www.knoxnews.com/news/2012/dec/19/full-court-press-lmu-law-school-working-hard-on/ (describing the "war room" crammed with faculty and administrative personnel, who were working very long days just to submit a completed application by the December 31st deadline).

32. Megan Boehnke, *LMU Drops Lawsuit against American Bar Association*, Knoxville News-Sentinel, Oct. 31, 2012, *available at* http://www.knoxnews.com/news/2012/oct/31/lmu-drops-lawsuit-against-american-bar/.

33. Megan Boehnke, *Amid Accreditation Worries, Students Return to LMU Law School LMU Drops Lawsuit Against American Bar Association*, Knoxville News-Sentinel, KnoxNews.com, Aug. 29, 2012 (stating that administrators and students view the bar exam "as a prime opportunity to silence critics" of Duncan).

34. Order, Dec. 21, 2012, Cructhfield v. Lincoln Mem'l Univ., et al., No. 182237-1, (Chancery Court Knox County, TN).

undergraduate-degree requirement. But what will she really gain in the end if Duncan never receives ABA-accreditation?

A prospective student visiting Duncan's website is informed that the school is TBLE-approved and that its admitted students are eligible to apply for federal financial aid. The website, however, does ***not*** disclose, as of June 2013, the fact that Duncan lacks or was denied accreditation by the ABA. Instead, Duncan's website states that it has a "relationship" with the ABA. A visitor to the website is told Duncan "has applied for provisional accredi[t]ation [sic] with the ABA." It then contains the following, which some could construe as a disclaimer regarding its accreditation status:

> The Dean is fully informed as to the Standards and Rules of Procedure for the Approval of Law Schools by the American Bar Association. The Administration and the Dean are determined to devote all necessary resources and in other respects to take all necessary steps to present a program of legal education that will qualify for approval by the American Bar Association. The Law School makes no representation to any applicant that it will be approved by the American Bar Association prior to the graduation of any matriculating student.
>
> If you have any questions regarding the accredi[t]ation [sic] status of DSOL or its potential status with the ABA, please contact Vice President and Dean Sydney Beckman.[35]

Duncan's webpage contains no discussion as to why ABA-accreditation may be important to the applicant's career aspirations as an attorney.

If prospective law students are considering enrolling in an unaccredited law school, they should find out whether the state where they want to practice law has rules limiting bar exam eligibility based on the school's accreditation status. I have uncovered several court cases where graduates of unaccredited schools were denied the ability to take the bar exam or denied a license to practice law in a particular state.[36] As discussed above, bar examination eligibility rules vary from state to state regarding whether a law graduate

35. *A Note on Accreditation*, Lincoln Mem'l Univ., http://www.lmunet.edu/law/accreditation.shtml (last visited June 11, 2013).

36. *See, e.g., In re Galardi*, No. 55165, 2010 WL 5550642 (Nev. Dec. 21, 2010) (The Supreme Court of Nevada refused to grant a waiver of the ABA-accredited-school requirement so that a graduate of Ventura College of Law, a California-approved law school, could take the Nevada bar exam.); *In re Hart*, 183 Vt. 602, 949 A.2d 447, 449 (Vt.2008) (A graduate of an unaccredited law school, Novus School of Law, requested permission to sit for the Vermont bar exam. The Supreme Court of Vermont upheld the bar examiners' denial of the graduate's request not only because Novus was not an approved school in the State of Vermont but also because "there was no evidence by which it could discern the rigorousness of the courses offered at Novus"). An exceptional graduate of an unaccredited school may be able to get bar examiners or a court to waive the ABA-accredited-school requirement. For example, in *Mitchell v. Board of Bar Examiners*, the Supreme Judicial Court of Massachusetts waived the requirement for Mr. Mitchel, a 2004 graduate of Concord Law School, an unaccredited online law school owned by the Washington Post Co. and authorized by the State of California. In granting Mr. Mitchell permission to take the Massachusetts bar exam, the Court based its decision on (1) the possibility that the ABA might change its rule to allow online distance learning schools to become accredited and (2) the fact that Mr. Mitchell had achieved stellar academic performance. *See Mitchell v. Board of Bar Examiners*, 452 Mass. 582, 588–589, 897 N.E.2d 7, 12 (2008) (His performance included receiving awards for best oral advocate and best brief, graduating with highest honors, and passing the California bar exam the first time). The Court made it clear that its ruling does not give blanket approval of online schools: "we are not suggesting that we have decided to accept graduation from an online law school as meeting the educational requirement for taking the Massachusetts bar examination, or indeed to change our ABA-approval requirement." The reader should note that the ABA has not approved any online law school as an accredited law school.

of an unaccredited law school can sit for the bar exam, but in the *majority* of states, graduating from a non-ABA-accredited law school prevents the graduate from being able to take the bar exam in those states.

If the School Eventually Gets Accreditation, I'll Be Fine, Right???

Some students might assume that if the school eventually becomes accredited by the ABA, he or she would be able to sit for any state's bar exam. That, however, would be an incorrect assumption. The National Conference of Bar Examiners provides a chart and explanation of the different state requirements in its Comprehensive Guide to Bar Admission Requirements.[37] This guide does not appear to address the consequences of attending and graduating from a law school that becomes approved or unapproved while a student is attending it. Determining the results of such a situation would require an examination of specific state bar admission rules.

Consider, for example, Pennsylvania Bar Admission Rule 203, which states that if a school was unaccredited at the time the applicant matriculated or graduated, in order to sit for the bar exam the applicant must demonstrate he or she is a lawyer in good standing in another state and that the applicant practiced law (or the equivalent) for five of the past seven years in the other state.[38] This means if a person has not already been practicing law for five of the last seven years in another state, the person's matriculation at an unaccredited school prevents him or her from taking the bar exam in Pennsylvania immediately after graduating from that school. Assume, for example, that "Tony" enrolled in Duncan in 2011 and that by the time he graduated in 2014, Duncan had managed to receive ABA-accreditation. Tony could not take the bar exam in Pennsylvania until after he had already been a licensed practicing attorney in good standing in Tennessee for five of the previous seven years. The New York State Board of Law Examiners Rule 520.5 appears to establish similar requirements as Pennsylvania's bar admission rule.[39] Therefore, a prospective student should not rely on the words of admissions personnel at an unaccredited law school, but should instead contact the state supreme court or the state bar examiner's office to learn about eligibility requirements to take the state's bar exam.

I am not suggesting that a degree from an unaccredited school should never be pursued. A prospective student could consider getting a degree from an unaccredited law school in California if he or she has an unquenchable desire to become a lawyer and cannot get into an ABA-accredited school. Law students enrolled in non-ABA-accredited but California-approved law schools are required to take and pass the First Year Law Students' Examination (FYLSX) before being allowed to continue with their law school studies.[40]

---

37. Comprehensive Guide to Bar Admission Requirements 2012 4–5, http://www.ncbex.org/assets/media_files/Comp-Guide/CompGuide.pdf (last visited June 10, 2012).

38. *Id.* at 12.

39. *Id.* at 11–12.

40. Committee of Bar Examiners, Guidelines for Unaccredited Law School Rules, Division 1.3, *available at* http://admissions.calbar.ca.gov/Portals/4/documents/Education/Unaccredited_Law_School_Guidelines.pdf.

Unless such a student passes this preliminary examination, FYLSX, commonly known as the "baby bar" exam, he or she will not be able to sit for the California bar examination.[41] A California court has pointed out that there is a strong public policy in the baby-bar-exam requirement because it serves a dual purpose of (1) protecting persons who are ill-suited for a legal career from continuing to spend time, money, and effort in an endeavor where they have little chance of success, and (2) affording persons who are better qualified for a legal career an opportunity to measure the quality of their training and education after the first year to better prepare themselves for the general bar examination.[42]

Returning to Morgan's case against Duncan, it is unfortunate for her that Tennessee does not have a baby-bar exam requirement for first-year law students attending Duncan. She has already borrowed more than $79,000 and matriculated two and a half years at Duncan. If the baby bar exam was a requirement, she could take it and then consider re-enrolling in Duncan if she does well on it. Ms. Crutchfield's lawsuit shows that students attending an unaccredited school *without* a baby-bar-exam requirement run the risk of getting in enormous debt for a career they may not be competent to do. Moreover, a student's detrimental reliance on crucial, but incorrect information could prevent the student from becoming a lawyer. This is a hard pill to swallow especially if the student had to borrow a lot of money to pay for the legal education.

Although taking the baby bar exam is a required of students attending an unaccredited school in California, I am not suggesting that this requirement alone is a good reason to enroll in a non-ABA accredited school. A prospective student needs to find out what the passage rate is for the baby bar exam for each unaccredited school in California. The State Bar of California provides statistics regarding the baby bar exam at its website. Historically, the baby-bar passage rate has been very low.[43] For example, of the 108 first-time takers from Concord Law School, only 19 students, or 17.6%, passed the June 2012 baby bar exam.[44]

In addition to experiencing very low passage rates for the baby bar exam, those who graduate from unaccredited schools have low passage rates when they take the regular bar exam. According to the National Conference of Bar Examiners, of the 3,236 graduates of non-ABA-approved law schools who took a state's bar exam in 2011, only 804 graduates passed, resulting in a bar passage rate of 25%.[45]

Because California is home to most of the non-ABA-accredited schools, statistics regarding their bar exam results are relevant. As revealed in Table 5-1 (next page), the annual July bar exam results for the last five years shows that graduates of CA-unaccredited law schools have the lowest passage rate among all first-time takers of the California bar exam.[46]

41. *Id.*

42. *See* Bib'le v. Committee of Bar Examiners, 606 P.2d 733, 737 (Cal. 1980), cert. denied, 449 U.S. 860 (1980).

43. *See* Robert J. Salzer, *Juris Doctor.Com: Are Full-Time Internet Law Schools the Beginning of the End for Traditional Legal Education*, 12 CommLaw Conspectus 101 (2004) ("Statistics show that unaccredited programs generally have a 'baby bar' pass rate of under 30%.").

44. *See* California First-Year Law Students' Examination: June 2012, the State Bar of California, *available at* http://admissions.calbar.ca.gov/Portals/4/documents/Statistics/Junefylsxstats2012_R.pdf (last visited March 14, 2013).

45. *See* National Conference of Bar Examiners, 2011 Statistics, at 10–11, April 9, 2012, *available at* http://www.ncbex.org/assets/media_files/Statistics/2011Statistics.pdf (last visited March 14, 2013) (reporting that 74% of the graduates of ABA-approved law schools passed the bar exam).

46. *See* Statistics for the California bar exam are published by the State Bar of California at http://admissions.calbar.ca.gov/Examinations/Statistics.aspx (publishing results for exams dating back to

Table 5-1. California General Bar Examination Statistics

First-Timers			
	2012		
Law School Type	**Took**	**Pass**	**%Pass**
CA ABA Approved	4107	3157	76.9
Out-of-State ABA	1425	907	63.6
CA Accredited	290	90	31.0
CA Unaccredited	90	20	22.2
	2011		
	Took	**Pass**	**%Pass**
CA ABA Approved	3910	2978	76.2
Out-of-State ABA	1348	891	66.1
CA Accredited	256	89	34.8
CA Unaccredited	89	21	23.6
	2010		
	Took	**Pass**	**%Pass**
CA ABA Approved	3791	2849	75.2
Out-of-State ABA	1381	941	68.1
CA Accredited	272	110	40.4
CA Unaccredited	115	23	20.0
	2009		
	Took	**Pass**	**%Pass**
CA ABA Approved	3723	2953	79.3
Out-of-State ABA	1486	1031	69.4
CA Accredited	360	116	32.2
CA Unaccredited	117	31	26.5
	2008		
	Took	**Pass**	**%Pass**
CA ABA Approved	3745	3114	83.2
Out-of-State ABA	1524	1142	74.9
CA Accredited	344	126	36.6
CA Unaccredited	145	47	32.4

While graduates of CA-accredited schools fair better than graduates of CA-unaccredited schools, graduates of CA-accredited schools still have passage rates that are usually half that of graduates of ABA-accredited schools located in California. Consequently, prospective students considering enrolling in a non-ABA-accredited school need to weigh how strongly they want to become a practicing attorney. If becoming such an attorney is the ultimate goal, then enrollment in an ABA-accredited school with a high bar passage rate is a safer route even though tuition at an ABA-accredited schools is usually substantially higher than tuition at California accredited and unaccredited schools. I wonder what advice Los Angeles Mayor Antonio Villaraigosa would give on this issue. He graduated from Peoples College of Law, a registered unaccredited school in California. He stopped trying to pass the California bar exam after failing it four times.[47] Fortunately for him, he had aspirations that did not depend on his obtaining a license to practice law.[48]

Unaccredited Law Schools Have Been Sued for Other Bad Acts

In addition to having very low bar-exam passage rates, unaccredited law schools have been sued for various kinds of bad behavior. One of the main complaints in these lawsuits is that the schools have misrepresented their unaccredited status or failed to disclose it. For example, in the case of *Goehring v. Chapman University*, three law students who were members of the inaugural class of Chapman University Law School (a then-unaccredited law school in California) separately sued the school for fraud based on misrepresentations that the school made to the students regarding its accreditation status.[49]

At issue in *Goehring* is that in 1995, when the law school opened, Chapman failed to disclose its lack of accreditation and that it had not obtained preliminary approval from the ABA.[50] This lack of disclosure is significant because California law students who attend an unaccredited school must attend law school for four years and must pass the baby bar exam in order to be eligible to sit for the California Bar Exam.[51] Under California law, Chapman had an obligation to obtain signed disclosure statements from its students prior to receiving any tuition. Although the court concluded that the students had failed to satisfy all the elements necessary to prove fraud and negligence, the court found that the students were entitled to a refund of tuition under state law due to Chapman's failure to comply with the state's accreditation disclosure requirements.[52] This case demonstrates that there

---

2007). California tracks bar passage data for three types of law schools: ABA-accredited law schools, California-accredited schools, and California-registered-but-unaccredited schools.

47. Maura Dolan, *A High Bar for Lawyers*, L.A. Times, Feb. 21, 2006, *available at* http://articles.latimes.com/2006/feb/21/local/me-bar21.

48. The Committee of Bar Examiners (CBE) for the State Bar of California adopted a rule that took effect January 1, 2013 and requires all CA-accredited law schools to maintain a minimum bar passage rate of 40% to maintain accreditation. In response, Southern California Institute of Law, a CA-accredited night law school, sued the CBE and others asserting that the new rule is unconstitutional in violation of the Fourteenth Amendment of the US Constitution. *See* Rebekah Kearn, *Night Law School Challenges Bar Examiners*, Courthouse News Service, Feb. 6, 2013, *available at* https://www.courthousenews.com/2013/02/06/54611.htm.

49. Goehring v. Chapman Univ., 121 Cal. App. 4th 353, 358 (2004).

50. *Id.* at 359.

51. *Id.*

52. *Id.* at 387.

is potential relief for students—at least in California—if they can prove that their law school failed to comply with the statutory disclosure requirements regarding accreditation.

Another lawsuit involving students suing an unaccredited law school is the case of *Rodi v. Southern New England School of Law*.[53] Joseph Rodi, a graduate of Southern New England School of Law,[54] could not take the New Jersey bar exam because the school failed to receive ABA accreditation prior to his graduation.[55] Alleging fraud and a violation of a consumer protection statute in his lawsuit, Mr. Rodi asserted that based on the deans' oral false statements regarding the school's accreditation prospects, he remained at the school and passed up other opportunities to do something else. One of the deans sent Mr. Rodi a letter stating, "there should be no cause for pessimism about the school's ultimate achievement of ABA approval." However, Southern New England's brochure contained the following statement: "The Law School makes no representation to any applicant or student that it will be approved by the American Bar Association prior to the graduation of any matriculating student."[56]

The court concluded that the dean's letter constituted a prediction, not a false statement, and the school's brochure disclaimed any promise of accreditation. Moreover, because Mr. Rodi made two attempts to transfer to other schools, the court held that no reasonable jury could find that he relied on the deans' statements and, if he did rely, his reliance was not reasonable.[57] Thus, Mr. Rodi's lawsuit against Southern New England was unsuccessful in providing him relief.

The *Rodi* decision is a warning that students should research all available information about an unaccredited law school before making a decision to attend one. One of the obstacles to finding objective information is that neither *US News* nor LSAC tracks or reports information about these schools.[58] For instance, if one visits LSAC's web link for unaccredited schools and clicks on the link for Concordia University School of Law, the visitor is directed to Concordia's website. Concordia is a 2012 startup, Christian law school operating in Boise, Idaho and approved by the Idaho State Board of Education ("SBOE").[59] However, SBOE provides no information about Concordia other than that it is registered and authorized to provide education in Idaho.[60] A prospective student considering enrolling in Concordia and any other unaccredited school would be advised to contact a reputable local attorney or local judge to learn more about the school and gain some perspective on how the school is regarded.

Another warning to take away from the *Rodi* case is that prospective students should not assume they can easily transfer to another school. Mr. Rodi could not get another law school to accept him as a transfer student. The opinion does not identify these law schools; however,

53. Rodi v. Southern New England School of Law, 532 F.3d 11 (1st Cir. 2008).

54. This school never received accreditation but later was acquired by University of Massachusetts at Dartmouth in 2010 and recently received provisional accreditation. *See infra* note 66.

55. *Rodi*, 532 F.3d at 13.

56. *Id.*

57. *Id.* at 16

58. If one clicks on LSAC's link for an ABA-accredited law school, one can find a wealth of information. *See supra* Chapter 5. However, if one clicks on the link for a non-ABA-accredited school, the visitor is directed to the school's website. http://www.lsac.org/jd/choose/law-school-links.asp. *Id.*

59. *Accreditation Process*, Concordia Univ. Sch. of Law, http://www.concordialaw.com/about/accreditation_process.cfm (last visited Oct. 8, 2012).

60. *Private Colleges & Universities Registered with the Idaho State Board of Education*, Idaho St. Bd. Of Educ. http://www.boardofed.idaho.gov/priv_col_univ/reg_col_univ.asp (last visited Oct. 8, 2012) (stating that "Concordia University is accredited by the Northwest Commission on Colleges and Universities").

I assume they were accredited since Mr. Rodi alleged that Southern New England falsely represented its accreditation prospects. A prospective student of an unaccredited school should realize that, except in California, the probability of transferring from an unaccredited law school to an ABA-accredited law school is highly unlikely. As a result, prospective students should not enroll in an unaccredited school in hopes of transferring to an accredited one. If the ultimate goal is to graduate from an accredited school, then prospective students should study harder to achieve an LSAT score that is sufficient to get into an accredited school.

The bottom line from the *Rodi* decision is that students enrolled in non-ABA-accredited schools may find themselves unable to transfer to an ABA-accredited school and graduates of these unaccredited schools may be unable to sit for a state's bar examination.

Many unaccredited law schools can present problems that prospective students may not know about when applying. For instance, the director and chairman of the board of the American Justice School of Law, a for-profit school located in Paducah, Kentucky, was forced to resign in light of student complaints regarding his performance.[61] In 2007, the ABA denied the school's application for accreditation due to "deficiencies in the library holdings and other areas."[62] The law school then closed just four years after opening.[63] Students admitted during the middle of the provisional period probably had no idea that the money borrowed to pursue a law degree at American Justice School of Law would be a fruitless endeavor.

Novus Law School, an unaccredited school, which provides only online courses and is operated by a corporation located in the Marshall Islands, was sanctioned $10,000 by a bankruptcy court for violating bankruptcy law. Ronnie Moore, the bankrupt graduate, had several unsecured debts discharged—wiped out—including $5,819 that he owed to Novus for unpaid tuition. Novus refused to give Mr. Moore his transcript and degree even though he had completed all the educational requirements necessary for obtaining the degree. Under bankruptcy law, Novus was rightfully sanctioned for trying to hold the degree hostage because such behavior by Novus was an attempt to coerce Mr. Moore's payment of the discharged tuition debt.[64]

Again, law school applicants should do as much research as they can on an unaccredited school. Upon finding negative judicial or administrative opinions about the school, the applicant should consider that to be a red flag and, therefore, carefully weigh the value of a degree from that unaccredited law school.

John Domantay came to the ugly realization that with a degree from an unaccredited school, he would not be able to achieve his goal of becoming a practicing attorney in Georgia. Mr. Domantay graduated from the John F. Kennedy School of Law, a Califor-

61. Bill Bartleman, *Osborne Out at Law School: Director Resigns Hours Before Board Meeting to Remove Him, Says Students Complaints Cause for Concern*, The Paducah Sun, Nov. 09, 2007.

62. *Id.*

63. Dave Thomas & Michelle Weyenberg, *A Law School No More: Barkley School of Law's New Beginning Is Cut Short With the Announcement That it is Shutting Down at the End of the Year*, PreLaw Mag. at 7, Winter 2009, *available at* http://www.nxtbook.com/nxtbooks/cypress/prelaw-winter-09/index.php?startid=7

64. In re Moore, 407 B.R. 855, 861 (Bankr. E.D. Va. 2009) (concluding that Novus "willfully violat[ed] the discharge injunction by refusing to issue the debtor's transcript and certify the debtor's graduate status"). The ability to get student loan debt discharged in bankruptcy is very difficult. In Chapter 13, I discuss a graduate's ability to use bankruptcy to wipe out debt.

nia-approved law school that is not accredited by the ABA, and subsequently applied to take the bar exam in Georgia.[65] The general rule in Georgia is that applicants seeking to take the Georgia bar exam must hold a law degree from an ABA-accredited law school. Mr. Domantay sought a waiver of the rule, but the Georgia Board of Bar Examiners denied the waiver because he had failed to make a showing that his education from John F. Kennedy School of Law was the equivalent of a legal education at an ABA-accredited school. In particular, Mr. Domantay failed to provide any documentation from a dean of an ABA-accredited law school that the John F. Kennedy School of Law provided an equivalent legal education. The Supreme Court of Georgia affirmed the Board's denial of the waiver stating that "[w]hile Domantay provided several references, a transcript, and an admirable history of public service, these alone fall well short of the showing of good cause required by the Rules Governing Admission to the Practice of Law."

Despite the troubles that the students in all of the above-mentioned lawsuits have encountered, the legal academy continues to expand. When I started teaching fourteen years ago, there were only 180 ABA-accredited law schools. Now there are 200 ABA-accredited law schools and three provisionally approved schools, bringing the total of ABA-blessed schools to 203. The aforementioned Southern New England School of Law was acquired by the University of Massachusetts at Dartmouth in 2010, and some believe this acquisition will cost state taxpayers a fortune over time.[66] In 2012, the ABA granted the University of Massachusetts-Dartmouth School of Law provisional approval, but it remains to be seen if it will receive full accreditation. The University of California-Irvine School of Law and the University of LaVerne College of Law in California also recently gained provisional approval from the ABA.[67]

Several law schools have been created and denied accreditation and/or disbanded in the last decade. For example, in 2010, the Maine Supreme Judicial Court for the second time unanimously denied Husson University's request to allow the graduates of its proposed law school to take the Maine bar exam even though Husson stated that it had no intention of seeking ABA-accreditation.[68] Whether the costs of accreditation was a motivating factor in Husson's decision not to seek ABA-approval, the Court found that it was an insufficient reason for allowing graduates of the proposed school to sit for the Maine bar exam.[69] As a result, the financial backers of Husson have ended their attempts at opening the law school. Had they been successful, Husson's law school would have become the second law school in Maine and, presumably, would have afforded non-traditional law students

65. In re Domantay, 285 Ga. 876, 876–77, 684 S.E.2d 628, 629 (2009).

66. Jeff Jacoby, *The Price of UMass Law School*, Boston Globe, Feb. 7, 2010.

67. Memorandum to Deans of ABA-Approved Law Schools regarding Provisional Approval of the University of LaVerne College of Law, dated Mar. 26, 2012, http://www.americanbar.org/content/dam/aba/administrative/legal_education_and_admissions_to_the_bar/council_reports_and_resolutions/2012_university_of_la_verne_provisional_approval.authcheckdam.pdf (last visited Jan. 11, 2013); Memorandum to Deans of ABA-Approved Law Schools regarding Provisional Approval of the University of California, Irvine, School of Law, dated June 14, 2011, http://www.americanbar.org/content/dam/aba/administrative/legal_education_and_admissions_to_the_bar/council_reports_and_resolutions/2011_06_u_of_california_irvine_provisional_approval.authcheckdam.pdf (last visited Jan. 11, 2013).

68. Judy Harrison, *Husson Ends Quest to Have a Law School*, Bangor Daily News Apr. 12, 2010.

69. In re Husson University School of Law, 2010 ME 16, 989 A.2d 754 (Me. 2010) ("Husson's decision not to apply for accreditation from the ABA, whether based on a business or policy decision not to offer tenure, or because such a process would be expensive, provides an insufficient basis for us to take these extraordinary steps, and therefore we decline Husson's request.").

the chance to earn a law degree. Consequently, the University of Maine School of Law remains the only law school in Maine.[70]

At least five proposed law schools have been put on hold or abandoned in recent years for various reasons. For example, St. John Fisher College in Rochester, New York and Wilkes University in Pennsylvania have both abandoned their plans to open a law school.[71] The University of Delaware, SUNY Binghamton, and SUNY Stony Brook have postponed plans to open up law schools.[72]

Incredibly, in spite of the economic downturn and the decrease in law-firm hiring, several law schools have recently opened or are about to open as the demand to attend law school remains sufficiently high. For example, in September 2012, Cooley Law School opened its fifth campus in Tampa, Florida with in inaugural class of 104 students.[73] Cooley's Ann Arbor campus opened in 2009 and received ABA-accreditation in 2012.[74] In August 2012, Atlanta's John Marshall Law School opened the Savannah Law School, located in Savannah, Georgia,[75] with an inaugural class of 45 students out of 508 applicants.[76] The previously-mentioned Concordia University School of Law opened in fall 2012 with an inaugural class of 73 students.[77] The Judge Paul Pressler School of Law at the Louisiana College ("LC") was planning to welcome its first incoming class in August 2013 but is now on hold due to a scandal at LC.[78] Indiana Tech in Ft. Wayne, Indiana welcomed its first incoming class in August 2013 and is also seeking provisional accreditation.[79] The

---

70. *About Maine Law*, UNIV. OF MAINE SCH. OF LAW, http://mainelaw.maine.edu/about/ (last visited Jan. 11, 2013).

71. Sean Carroll, *St. John Fisher Law School Idea Dead*, WHAM ABC 13, May 24, 2012, *available at* http://www.13wham.com/news/local/story/saint-john-fisher-law-school-idea-dead/f7jCxiuHV0e WlcBIAldNoA.cspx (last visited Jan. 27, 2013); *Wilkes University Suspends Law School Planning Initiative*, WILKES UNIV., June 4, 2010, *available at* http://www.wilkes.edu/pages/194.asp?item=58605.

72. *University of Delaware Puts Law School on Hold*, THE FACULTY LOUNGE, http://www.thefaculty lounge.org/2011/05/university-of-delaware-puts-law-school-on-hold-.html (last visited Jan. 11, 2013).

73. Cooley Law School's First Class Reports to New Tampa Bay Campus, http://www.cooley.edu/ timeline/2012.html (last visited Jan. 27, 2013).

74. Karen Sloan, *Cooley's Ann Arbor Campus Wins Accreditation*, NAT'L L. J., June 21, 2012, *available at* http://www.law.com/jsp/nlj/PubArticleNLJ.jsp?id=1202560391679&rss=nlj&slreturn=1 (stating that the "ABA's Council of the Section of Legal Education and Admissions to the Bar voted on June 8 to approve the school's bid for full accreditation, but didn't announce the decision publicly until June 18" but not explaining the delay in the announcement).

75. Alex Bender, *Savannah Law School Opening Delayed*, WTOC-TV, http://www.wtoc.com/story/ 19356425/savannah-law-school-runs-into-unexpected-delay (last visited Jan. 11, 2013) (stating that the school is operating out of the Coastal Georgia Center until its new building is completed). The school's website is at http://www.savannahlawschool.org/.

76. Email from Rose Anne Nespica, Assoc. Dean of Savannah Law School (Oct. 9, 2012) (stating that Savannah is pleased with the enrollment size and that the school is committed to producing public servants such as prosecutors and public defenders).

77. Nick Groff, *Concordia Law Opens its Doors in Boise*, IDAHO PRESS-TRIB. (NAMPA, IDAHO), Sept. 21, 2012, available at http://www.idahopress.com/members/concordia-law-opens-its-doors-in-boise/article_120de81a-039c-11e2-9998-0019bb2963f4.html.

78. Sam Favate, *Louisiana Law School Loses Dean Before Grand Opening*, Wall Street J. Online, Sept. 20 gd, 2012, available at http://blogs.wsj.com/law/2012/09/20/louisiana-law-school-loses-dean-before-grand-opening/ (stating that the recent resignation of the dean may delay the opening of the school in 2013).

79. Indiana Tech has an impressive faculty. *See, e.g.*, *Federal Judge to Join Indiana Tech*, INSIDE INDIANA BUS., Jan. 13, 2013, (announcing that US Bankruptcy Judge Judith Fitzgerald, who is retiring from the bench in summer 2013, will be a full-time faculty member at Indiana Tech Law School in fall 2013).

University of North Texas College of Law in Dallas, Texas, anticipates opening in August 2014.[80] These recently proposed and opened law schools will result in more law graduates having to compete in a still-recovering legal job market.

The ABA takes the position that it is powerless to stop the proliferation of law schools because to do so would be a violation of anti-trust laws, which "ban concerted action to bar entry to a public profession." In Chapter 9, I take the position that despite the growing number of law schools, we do NOT have enough lawyers trained to do public service. While many complain about the expansion in the number of law schools, such expansions will continue as long as the elite and wanna-be elite schools use LSAT scores in manner that excludes public-service-minded students with lower LSAT scores from admission.

Given that start-up law schools will be unaccredited, prospective students like Morgan Crutchfield should become knowledgeable about the targeted unaccredited school's mission and operations and should become fully informed about the potential consequences of graduating from the unaccredited school. The applicants should also try to assess the quality of the education as well as the job prospects of the recent graduates of these schools. This research endeavor will be difficult because the ABA, US News, and LSAC do not report relevant information, such as attrition and unemployment rates, about these schools. One way of discovering valuable information about an unaccredited school is to find and visit the location where a significant number of graduates of these schools are taking bar exam review courses. By talking to these recent graduates, prospective students can discover information about the graduates' educational experiences and job offers.

In addition to the brick-and-mortar unaccredited law schools, prospective students need to do a thorough analysis of online law schools, such as Concord Law School at Kaplan University, California Southern University's School of Law, and California's St. Francis School of Law. The ABA caps the number of credits a student can earn for "distance education," including online courses, at twelve credit hours, so none of these online law schools can qualify for ABA accreditation.[81] Prospective students need to understand that just because these online schools are approved in California does not mean that graduates of these schools will realize their dream of becoming practicing attorneys. Even a Concord law graduate admits the existence of "a significant stigma attached to online, non-ABA law schools that affects hiring practices."[82]

Many excellent law professors have been a part of establishing an unaccredited law school, and I do not doubt their scholarly contributions, their pedagogical skills, or the legal

---

80. *University of North Texas Moves Forward with Dallas Law School Plans*, Nat'l Jurist, Jan. 20, 2012, http://www.nationaljurist.com/content/university-north-texas-moves-forward-dallas-law-school-plans.

81. ABA Section of Legal Education and Admissions to the Bar, 2011–2012 Standards and Rules of Procedure for Approval of Law Schools Standard 306(d) *available at* http://www.americanbar.org/content/dam/aba/publications/misc/legal_education/Standards/2012_standards_chapter_3.authcheckdam.pdf (last visited July 29, 2012) (hereinafter "2011–2012 Standards for Approval of Law Schools").

82. Menachem Wecker, *Online Law Degrees Face Hung Jury*, U.S. News & World Rep., June 7, 2012 (The article quotes Joy Nonnweiler, an attorney who holds a JD from Concord and practices law in Waukesha, Wis. This story also quotes Ms. Linda Doyle, the hiring partner at an international law firm with more than 1,000 lawyers. She stated that does not know of any large firm that hires graduates of online law schools and that "she has never seen an online JD mentioned in the 3,000 law student résumés her firm reviews annually.").

education they impart to their students. For example, the University of California-Irvine School of Law, which recently gained provisional ABA-approval, ranked seventh in a faculty scholarly impact study done by researchers at the University of St. Thomas School of Law.[83]

Law school applicants need to make a distinction between the stellar credentials of the educators at a non-ABA-accredited school and the perception of prospective employers about the value of a law degree from that school. Applicants need to try to find out to what extent graduates of a non-ABA-accredited law school are successful in finding traditional attorney jobs or desirable professional positions. In Chapter 4, I explained in great detail the ABA's new disclosure requirements regarding the reporting of employment data. I explained how these disclosure requirements will force ABA-accredited law schools to be more truthful, especially about the number of graduates employed in full-time, permanent positions that require passage of the bar exam. As far as the non-ABA-accredited law schools, they are not subject to the ABA's employment disclosure standards (or any other ABA standard); therefore, prospective students considering enrolling in a non-ABA-accredited school may not get full disclosures regarding the employment outcomes of its graduates.

I visited the websites of some of the non-ABA-accredited schools and could find little-to-no employment statistics.[84] For instance, under a heading titled "PLACEMENT RATES AND SERVICES," the website for the Nashville School of Law states the following: "The school maintains a registry of students and alumni who are interested in notification of job opportunities. 100% of the 2010 NSL graduates seeking employment are employed. 91% of those who passed the bar are employed in the legal field and 9% non-legal."[85] If the reader recalls my in-depth discussion in Chapter 4 about the employment reporting practices at ABA-accredited schools, the reader should discern that the words "employed in the legal field" does not mean the graduates are employed as attorneys but may mean that a significant number of the graduates are likely to be employ as paralegals or in similar under-employed positions. While some of the schools provided success stories of a few graduates on their websites, these stories are only anecdotal and do not count as *hard* data.

When it comes to start-up law schools, they obviously have no employment data; consequently, any information they provide about possible employment outcomes would be sheer speculation. I am not advising against going to an unaccredited law school but simply urging applicants to proceed with extreme caution.[86] Also, keep in mind that non-ABA-accredited schools have very low bar-passage rates in comparison to ABA-accredited schools. The bottom line is that law school applicants need to be aware that law degrees from start-up law schools and some non-ABA-accredited schools could end up being very expensive "vanity" degrees—the diplomas look lovely framed on the wall, and they make you feel good about yourself, but they may not make you any more employable.

---

83. For example, although a law librarian and I searched, we could not find any employment data at the website for Kaplan University's Concord Law School—a for-profit online law school started in 1998. Under the Student Services tab, I clicked on Career Services, but that page does not include any placement statistics. *See Career Services*, CONCORD LAW SCH., http://info.concordlawschool.edu/Pages/Career_Services.aspx (last visited Oct. 18, 2012).

84. 2011–2012 STANDARDS FOR APPROVAL OF LAW SCHOOLS, *supra* note 81.

85. On the left side of Nashville's home page, there is a list of Quick Links. I found Nashville's summary of its employment outcomes when I clicked on "About Us." http://nashvilleschooloflaw.net/?page_id=6.

86. For a discussion on the advantages of going to an unaccredited law, *see* Howard B. Miller Former President of the State Bar of California, *A Fresh Look at California's Law Schools*, CALIFORNIA BAR J., August 2010, *available at*, http://www.calbarjournal.com/August2010/Opinion/FromthePresident.aspx.

Chapter 6

Unlawful Dismissal Claim: "Weeding Out" vs. Retention and Academic Support

"Look to your left. Look to your right. One of you won't be here next year."[1]

This is a famous quote by the fictitious Professor Charles W. Kingsfield (played by John Houseman) at Harvard Law School in the classic movie *The Paper Chase*. It is a fitting quote because while law schools have programs in place to retain their students, attrition rates at 71 of 197 ABA-accredited schools are equal to or greater than 10%. That translates into more than 3,700 first-year law students withdrawing for academic and other reasons.[2] This chapter begins with a discussion of alleged unlawful practices used to force *out* students with poor academic performance. In a lawsuit filed in 2012 against Thurgood Marshall School of Law at Texas Southern University ("TSU"), Jonathan Chan and Karla Ford, former law students, assert a claim for unlawful dismissal.[3] This lawsuit is very important because it is keeping with the central question in this book: is a law degree still worth the price for today's law school applicants. Law students who are forced to withdraw for failure to satisfy academic standards are usually strapped with substantial student loan debt and are not employable in the legal profession. For them, the pursuit of law degree has not been worth the price. The TSU complaint allows me to inform prospective law students that they should assess a law school's commitment to ensuring that hard-working students succeed after they have been admitted. Readers may determine for themselves whether some law schools are "weeding out" the weak students and whether these institutions are actually committed to the academic success of *all* students enrolled.

Mr. Chan and Ms. Ford attended TSU from fall 2010 through spring 2011 when they were both dismissed from the school.[4] The dismissal occurred after Mr. Chan had received a "D–" and Ms. Ford a "D" in their Contracts II course taught by a visiting law professor, Shelley Smith.[5]

---

1. The Paper Chase (Twentieth Century Fox 1973).

2. *See* Table 2 in the Appendix A (indicating that based on data from the 2013 LSAC Guide, 3,747 first-year students from the entering class of Fall 2010 withdrew for failing to satisfy academic standards or for other undisclosed reasons).

3. Complaint, Chan, et. al v. Bd. of Regents of Texas S. Univ., et. al, No. 4:12-CV-325 (S.D. Tex. Feb. 2, 2012) (hereinafter "Chan Complaint").

4. *Id.* at ¶ 14–15.

5. *Id.* Regents disputes Ms. Ford's Contracts II grade and argues that she actually received a "D–" grade. *See* Motion to Dismiss and for Summary Judgment, Chan v. Bd. of Regents of Tex. S. Univ., No. 4:12-CV-325 at 5 (S.D. Tex. May. 11, 2012).

Both students appealed their grades because they believed that the professor had "arbitrarily issued them a low grade." They argued that the grades were not based upon their performance on the examinations, but instead were to "curve them out" of the law school. According to the students, they had attended the exam review sessions for all three of the Contracts II exams, but they were never informed by the professor how their exams were graded. Moreover, Mr. Chan and Ms. Ford allege that they were not even given a chance to review their final exams to better understand how they were graded. They based their lawsuit against TSU on these claims and stated that the school and Professor Smith had "deliberately withheld all information from [them] regarding the basis for the grades they received ..." even though they requested such information.[6]

The students had a hearing with the Academic Standards Committee regarding their petitions for a grade change, but their appeal was denied, and Mr. Chan and Ms. Ford were informed that the Committee had accepted Professor Smith's report that the grades were accurate. However, the former students were not given any additional information or evidence regarding Professor Smith's grading process. Less than a week after this meeting, the Committee denied the students' petition for a grade change—citing that there was "insufficient evidence" to support the petitions. Claiming that the school's dismissal of them violated the law school's rules and the former students' U.S. Constitutional Rights, Mr. Chan and Ms. Ford asserted that TSU and Professor Smith have destroyed their ability to attend law school or to ever enter the legal profession.[7]

TSU sought to have the suit dismissed, arguing that the students' claims were either barred or contradicted by indisputable evidence. They described the law school's grading and academic policy, citing to a non-waivable academic policy in the law school's Student Rules that declares, "A first year student must achieve a cumulative law school grade point average of 2.0 or above." Because Mr. Chan's first year cumulative GPA was 1.82 and Ms. Ford's was 1.83, TSU argued that the students were both dismissed for valid reasons. They further argued that by providing the students with the opportunity to challenge their grades, they were provided "all the due process owed to them." TSU concluded its argument by stating that the students "are probably not best suited for law school, and would benefit from moving on to find better career paths, rather than dwelling upon this meritless suit."[8]

The lawsuit against TSU shows that by simply enrolling in law school, a student will not automatically graduate with a JD. The Achilles' heel for the former TSU law students' case is that courts do not usually intrude into academic decisions. Many judicial decisions support TSU's contention that academic determinations by a university are entitled to deference by the courts. For example, in the case of *Bd. of Curators of the Univ. of Mo. v. Horowitz*,[9] the United States Supreme Court dismissed substantive and procedural due process claims by a medical student challenging her academic dismissal, noting that courts are ill-equipped to review academic determinations. Similarly, in *Regents of Univ. of Mich. v. Ewing*,[10] the Supreme Court dismissed a university student's challenge to the school's

6. Chan Complaint, *supra* note 3, at ¶ 16–20.

7. *Id.*

8. Motion to Dismiss and for Summary Judgment, *supra* note 5, at 1–7. A number of other procedural motions were filed by plaintiffs and defendants following plaintiffs' complaint and defendants' motion to dismiss. However, enough information has been provided for the reader to get a gist of their arguments.

9. 435 U.S. 78, 89 (1978).

10. 474, U.S. 214, 225 (1985).

academic decisions noting that judges "should show great respect for the faculty's professional judgment" when asked to review the substance of a genuinely academic decision.

A case that is even more comparable to Mr. Chan and Ms. Ford's case is the matter of *Susan M. v. New York Law School.*[11] In this case, law student Susan M. had challenged her dismissal from New York Law School for academic deficiency. When Susan M.'s cumulative GPA fell below the requisite 2.0, she was notified by the law school that it would be considering whether to allow her to continue attending at the school. After responding in writing to this notification and also appearing before the Academic Status Committee to state her case orally, the Committee decided to dismiss Susan M. from the law school due to her poor academic performance.[12]

Like Ms. Ford and Mr. Chan, Susan M.'s lawsuit alleged that the dismissal decision was arbitrary and that her poor grades for the "fourth semester was directly attributable to the irrational testing and grading procedures of three of her four professors." The court held that Susan M.'s allegations were directed at the professors' pedagogical evaluation of her exam performances, "a determination best left to educators rather than the courts" and, therefore, dismissed her lawsuit. Further, the court stated that "[a]s a general rule, judicial review of grading disputes would inappropriately involve the courts in the very core of academic and educational decision making."[13]

Because the lawsuit filed by Ms. Ford and Mr. Chan would also involve the courts in Professor Smith's evaluations of their exams, I do not see any real distinction between their case and Susan M.'s case. As a result, their lawsuit is doomed to be dismissed.

I am sympathetic to the fact that Ms. Ford and Mr. Chan now have significant student loan debt but no law degree to show for it. Prospective students, however, need to realize that the majority of law students are disappointed with their academic performance in law school because earning an "A" average is very difficult as the study of law differs dramatically from academic study in undergraduate school.[14] Students should understand that obtaining a law degree is not like buying a toaster from Wal-Mart because if you get kicked out (like Mr. Chan and Ms. Ford) or do not like the educational and testing methods employed by the professor, you cannot get a refund.[15]

The Chan and Ford lawsuit provides a teachable moment for prospective law students because it raises the issues of attrition rates and academic support services. Prospective and transfer students need to assess how often students are forced to withdraw for academic failure and whether a law school has programs in place to prevent such failure. Prospective and transfer students seeking information about a school's attrition rate should look to the LSAC Guide, which is published annually. Consulting the most recent LSAC Guide is a must because it provides a wealth of information, including negative information that law schools may be unwilling to disclose on their websites or to students individually.

---

11. 76 N.Y.2d 241 (1990). This is the same New York Law School that was sued for disseminating deceptive employment and salary data. Please refer to Chapter 2 for a discussion of that lawsuit.

12. *Id.* at 243–244.

13. *Id.* at 242–44.

14. Many books are targeted towards first-year law students and attempt to prepare them to do well in law school. I suggest that if the reader is about to begin law school, start first with books written by professors with a long track record in teaching legal writing and/or legal reasoning skills.

15. I hope that the former TSU students are not tempted to default on their student loans. Those who default not only negatively impact their creditworthiness and, therefore, their ability to borrow; they can also lose other job opportunities if prospective employers pull their credit reports and discover the defaults.

A School's Attrition Rate Must Be Considered

Let me demonstrate why researching a school's attrition rate is an important factor when doing a comprehensive analysis of a school. According to the LSAC Guide, the "academic attrition" numbers are based on the number of students forced to withdraw for failing to satisfy a school's GPA requirement, and the "other attrition" numbers are based on students who withdraw from law school for other reasons.[16] I explained in Chapter 3 that the "other attrition" category could actually include students who also failed to satisfy the school's minimum-GPA requirement, but the school elected to put the student in the other-attrition category because the student also had personal problems that interfered with the student's performance. Because the law schools decide which attrition category to put their former students in and because LSAC simply relies on the attrition data submitted to it by the law schools, prospective students should always look to see if a school has a high number of students placed in the "other attrition" category.

A school that has high attrition numbers is Cooley Law School, the largest law school in the United States.[17] The 2013 LSAC Guide shows that for the previous school year, Cooley had 124 students withdraw for academic failure and 211 students withdraw for other reasons. Those numbers total 335 students and comprise an attrition rate of 16.3% of the first-year class. For that same year, Cooley had a total of 120 (12.1%) second-year students withdraw for academic failure and other reasons. The attrition rate for both classes means that Cooley lost 28.4% (16.3% + 12.1%) of its students for academic failure or other reasons.

Cooley's attrition rate in the previous LSAC guide is also nearly 30%. In the 2012 LSAC Guide, Cooley had a 14.8% attrition rate for its first-year students and a 14.9% attrition rate for its second-year students. These rates amount to a total attrition rate of 29.7% of Cooley's students either flunking out or dropping out. To put Cooley's attrition rates into perspective, one has to compare it to the overall attrition rate for all ABA-approved law schools. The ABA tracks the total attrition rate for students enrolled in JD programs. For the year 2010–2011, the ABA reported that the total number of students withdrawing was 6,794, which includes 5,177 first year students.[18] In 2010–2011, the total number of JD enrollees was 147,525.[19] Therefore, the overall attrition rate was 4.6% during the 2010–2011 school year among all JD students. When one compares this 4.6% rate to the double-digit attrition rates at many law schools, one should see consistently high attrition rates as a red flag.

---

16. Law School Admission Council, ABA-LSAC Official Guide to ABA-Approved Law Schools (2013) (hereinafter "LSAC Guide"). The most recent version of the LSAC Guide is available online

17. Cooley Law School is one of the schools that was sued for allegedly reporting deceptive employment and salary data. The 2008 to 2010 LSAC Guides revealed the following attrition rates for the 2006 to 2008 first-year entering classes at Cooley: 26% (or 483 students), 26.1% (or 533 students), and 31.8% (or 576 students). In Chapter 2, I discuss the judge's opinion dismissing that case. In Chapter 3, I compare Cooley to another law school to demonstrate how to do a comprehensive analysis of a school to determine if pursuing a law degree at the school is worth the price.

18. Total J.D. Attrition 1981–2010, *available at* http://www.americanbar.org/content/dam/aba/administrative/legal_education_and_admissions_to_the_bar/statistics/jd_attrition.authcheckdam.pdf.

19. Enrollment and Degrees Awarded 1981–2010, *available at* http://www.americanbar.org/content/dam/aba/administrative/legal_education_and_admissions_to_the_bar/statistics/enrollment_degrees_awarded.authcheckdam.pdf.

Like Cooley, TSU has consistently had a relatively high attrition rate. I have consulted the LSAC Guide to obtain information about TSU's entering classes for 2006–2010 and discovered that it has the following rates of attrition for the entering first-year classes:

Texas Southern University, Thurgood Marshall School of Law JD Attrition Rates

Year	Academic	Other	Total	Total Percent
2010	30	0	30	14.2%
2009	26	6	32	15.8%
2008	19	20	39	20.2%
2007	37	19	56	22.0%
2006	22	20	42	17.9%

I am assuming that Ms. Ford and Mr. Chan never researched TSU's attrition rates or if they did, they assumed they would never be forced out for academic failure.

Prospective law students cannot assume they will achieve outstanding academic success in law school and, therefore, should inquire into a school's academic support programs after discovering it has a high attrition rate. Before returning to the discussion of my assessment of the attrition rates at Cooley and TSU, I thought it would be helpful to explain what an academic support program ("ASP") is. Typically, law school ASPs are fall into four different categories: pre-law school academic support, first-year academic support, upper-class academic support, and post-law school academic support.[20] "Most [ASPs] are designed to help students become acclimated to the demands and methods of law school study and are typically offered prior to or during the first year of law school."[21] The method of support varies from school to school.[22] For example, some programs consist of tutoring by upper-level students and professors or by staff hired specifically to tutor. Some programs teach students how to do in-depth legal analysis, particularly in the context of writing essay examinations so that students can improve their test-taking skills.[23] Some ASPs do all of the foregoing in a course offered *only* to students deemed at risk of not performing satisfactorily or students who have already earned a first-semester GPA that puts them below 2.0.

Despite not having a strong consensus among law schools as to which type of ASPs are most effective, there are several justifications for having such programs—especially when they are properly utilized. For instance, it has been argued that ASPs are effective because they "help humanize the law school environment [b]y providing a source of encouragement and assistance"[24] Stated differently, by having ASPs, the law school is signaling to students that it cares about students' success and is committed to helping them persevere.

Academic support programs are not only relevant to students at risk of academic failure but should also be of interest to admitted law students who have received scholarships

---

20. *Id.* at 278.

21. Cynthia Schmidt and Ann Iijima, *A Compass for Success: A New Direction for Academic Support Programs*, 4 CARDOZO PUB. L. POL'Y & ETHICS J. 651, 653 (2006).

22. *Id.*

23. *Id.*

24. Louis N. Schulze, Jr., *Alternative Justifications for Law School Academic Support Programs: Self-Determination Theory, Autonomy Support, and Humanizing the Law School*, 5 CHARLESTON L. REV. 269, 272 (2011).

that are contingent upon maintaining a certain GPA. If scholarship recipients earn first-semester grades that put them at risk of losing their scholarships, they need to know whether the school has academic support to aid them in pulling up their grades so that they can keep their scholarships.

After experimenting for almost three decades, virtually all law schools now have some type of ASP,[25] but the reader needs to know that some programs may not be that helpful for some students.

Now that I have provided an overview of ASPs, let's return to my discussion of Cooley and TSU. Since Cooley has high attrition rates, I thought it would be useful to the reader to find out if Cooley offers an ASP to its students. According to the welcome message from Cooley's president and dean, Cooley proclaims that it has an "academic support program second to none."[26] WOW! Poor academic performance may be attributable to factors that Cooley cannot fix through its ASP. However, law school applicants seeking to live up to Judge Schweitzer's sophisticated consumer standard should question the successfulness of Cooley's ASP.

By way of comparison, at the law school where I teach—The Ohio State University Moritz College of Law—we have a long history of offering ASPs to our students.[27] According to the 2013 LSAC Guide, Ohio State's attrition rate for first-year students was 2.2%, consisting of five students who withdrew for non-academic reasons; no students withdrew due to academic failure. According to the 2012 LSAC Guide, Ohio State had a zero attrition rate because no students withdrew.[28]

To determine whether Ms. Ford and Mr. Chan could have obtained academic support information at TSU's website at the time they applied, I used "Wayback Machine."[29] My research indicates that until July 20, 2011, TSU had a webpage discussing academic support programs, and it indicated that Associate Dean Patricia Garrison, a TSU law graduate in 2007, was in charge of academic support. Since July 20, 2011, TSU has had a webpage titled "Academic Support Programs,"[30] and it states that TSU has an "Academic Support Team" consisting of three instructors along with Associate Dean Garrison and an administrative assistant.

According to TSU's website, two out of the three academic support instructors are 2010 graduates of TSU, and the majority of the support offered appears to be directed towards helping graduates prepare for and pass the bar exam.[31] I am not implying that TSU's academic support for first-year students was insufficient prior to Mr. Chan's and Ms. Ford's enrollment. I am simply stating that the information about such support

---

25. *Id.* at 651.

26. *Welcome Message from President and Dean Don LeDuc*, Thomas M. Cooley Law School, http://www.cooley.edu/about/welcome.html (last visited Jan. 28, 2013).

27. *See e.g.*, Katherine Silver Kelly, Assistant Clinical Professor of Law and Director, Academic Support Program, Ohio St. Univ. Moritz Coll. of Law, http://moritzlaw.osu.edu/faculty/bios.php?ID=889 (last visited Jan. 11, 2013).

28. 2013 LSAC Guide, *supra* note 16.

29. The Wayback Machine enables Internet users to view historical versions of captured webpages and to study whether webpages at websites have changed or no longer exist. I enlisted the help of information technology personnel to help me use Wayback Machine and other means of studying TSU's current and former web pages.

30. Academic Support Programs, Tex. S. Univ. Thurgood Marshall School Of Law, http://www.tsulaw.edu/academics/academic_support/asp_team.html (last visited Jan. 11, 2013).

31. Prospective and transfer students should also determine whether a school has academic support programs gear towards bar-exam passage because such support is very important for graduates at risk of not passing the bar exam.

evidently did not exist at TSU's website for all law school applicants to see prior to Mr. Chan's and Ms. Ford's enrollment at TSU. Moreover, the ASP team was a fledgling group when these students enrolled in 2010. TSU's double-digit attrition rate for the most recent reporting year may be an indication that the ASP still needs more improvement, especially since the head of the ASP, Associate Dean Patricia Garrison, a white female, has filed a discrimination suit against TSU, a historically-black university.[32] Stated differently, because the head of the ASP is claiming racial discrimination and the ASP employees she supervises are African-Americans, a law school applicant should assess whether TSU has a work environment that negatively impacts the effectiveness of its ASP team.

A High Transfer-Out Rate May Be a Red Flag

Law school transfer-out rates may be related to attrition rates and may provide clues to prospective law students as to how current law students feel about the law school they attend. Although students transfer schools for a number of reasons, a common reason given is to attend a higher-ranked school that will hopefully lead to better job opportunities. When pressed for additional reasons for wanting to transfer, students frequently identify something negative about the school they want to leave. As a result, I urge law school applicants, when evaluating a school, to research whether the school has a large number of law students wanting to transfer to another school. According to the 2013 LSAC Guide and 2012 LSAC Guide, Cooley had 227 students and 153 students transfer out for the respective reporting years.[33] To put this all in to perspective for the reader, consider that Cooley's 227 transfer-out number is larger than an entire first-year class of students at some law schools. Having such a high transfer-out rate does not speak well of any law school.

In keeping with the sophisicated consumer standard, prospective students should consider a law school's attrition rate, transfer rate, and academic support program. Once enrolled, law students have to learn to read critically and analyze complex laws and apply them to multi-faceted scenarios. The same is true for prospective law students in researching law schools. Prospective students must learn to search for and read all available data about law schools critically during their selection process in order to avoid having a devastating experience like Mr. Chan and Ms. Ford had.

After filing the lawsuit against TSU, both Mr. Chan and Ms. Ford told a reporter that they were upset about being dismissed from law school after their first year. Ms. Ford described the situation by saying that "[t]here is a lot of embarrassment and shame. It took a toll." She said further, "When you believe that you are doing fairly well and you get a grade you feel you don't deserve, it's devastating." Similarly, Mr. Chan said "[C]oming from an Asian family, failing is a tough thing to bring up ... [t]he only words I can think of are shameful and disgraceful."[34]

---

32. *TSU Employee Files Discrimination Lawsuit*, KPRC Houston, Click2Houston.com (Nov. 10, 2011, 1:54 PM), http://www.click2houston.com/news/TSU-Employee-Files-Discrimination-Lawsuit/-/1735978/4718210/-/8jt6ylz/-/index.html.

33. 2012 and 2013 LSAC Guide, *supra* note 16.

34. Monica Rhor, *Former TSU Law Students Take Grade Dispute to Court*, Houston Chron. (Feb. 7, 2012), *available at* http://www.chron.com/news/houston-texas/article/Former-TSU-law-students-take-grade-dispute-to-3128943.php.

In hindsight, perhaps Ms. Ford and Mr. Chan could have avoided this whole scenario. Unquestionably, publicly available information about TSU could have given them further insight about their possibility of success. A *proactive* student would have inquired about TSU's attrition rate and would have also asked about the availability of ASPs. Not knowing whether Mr. Chan and Ms. Ford acted in such a manner, they are now unfortunately in a *reactive* posture—suing their law school after displaying a poor academic performance.

The legal documents that the students filed in the TSU matter do not provide information about how Mr. Chan and Ms. Ford performed academically prior to law school or what their LSAT scores were. However, according to the 2012 LSAC Guide, TSU's admitted class had only sixteen students that had LSAT scores above 160 and none above 170.[35] In fact, 498 of the 672 admitted students scored between 145 and 154 on the LSAT. Perhaps Ms. Ford and Mr. Chan fell into the category of admitted students who scored above 160. If, however, they fell into a lower percentile, they were at risk of not performing well academically.

Research shows a strong correlation between a student's LSAT score and the student's first-year law school performance as measured by his or her by GPA; a student with a low LSAT score has a greater likelihood of performing poorly. Additional research has taken into account learning styles. Students with learning styles that reflected a low preference for abstract conceptualization tend to not only have relatively low LSAT scores, but also tend to have low GPAs for the first year of law school. However, those with very high LSAT scores and a high preference for abstract conceptualization were not guaranteed success.[36]

My point in discussing the research is not to make prospective students fear performing poorly in law school, but for them to realize that if they have scored in the bottom 25th percentile on the LSAT, it is imperative that they do as much research as possible about the school's commitment to academic success of all enrollees. Prospective students need to consult the LSAC guide online[37] (or at their local law library) for the last five years to analyze the targeted law school's attrition rates and transfer-out rates. Prospective students need to ask to speak to the person in charge of the law school's ASPs. Moreover, these students should request to be put in touch with former participants in the school's ASP to get their feedback about how effective they thought the program was. Prospective students should not simply accept representations made by admissions personnel. Such personnel may not really know how a school's ASP is conducted and may be tempted to mislead since the performance of admissions personnel is often linked to how many students they can persuade to actually enroll.

When prospective students are assessing whether to enroll in a particular law school, they must have a level head and must do their research in a manner that takes into account the possibility of being in the bottom half of their law school class and, therefore, having a more difficult time finding traditional attorney positions that pay a decent salary. Research shows most students think that they will perform well in law school. Professor Emily Zimmerman conducted a three-year empirical study that investigated the expectations and attitudes of law students regarding their grades. What she found is that, on average, students expected to earn a GPA over 3.30. Furthermore, "in all three survey years, the most frequently predicted grade point average was 3.50. In each survey year, however,

---

35. *Id.*

36. Eric A. DeGroff, *Training Tomorrow's Lawyers: What Empirical Research Can Tell Us about the Effect of Law School Pedagogy on Law Student Learning Styles*, 36 S. Ill. U. L.J. 251, 269 (2012). Professor DeGroff's research also show a correlation as it relates to passing the bar exam: "failure by law students to adapt more fully to abstract learning modes may inhibit their performance on the bar exam."

37. Law School Admission Council, https://officialguide.lsac.org/.

the average reported grade point average was closer to 3.00."[38] The difference between 3.0 and 3.50 is huge. That means the majority of students expected to earn an "A–" average, but they actually earned a "B" average!

Students need to understand how the curve works. For example, the website for Ohio State University Moritz College of Law states that professors are encouraged to use a 30/60/10 grading scale.[39] If I have ten law students who each had high LSAT scores and high undergraduate GPAs, three of them will get As, six will get Bs, and one will get a C or below. At the end of the day, half of them will be in the bottom of the class. A student who writes a good essay exam answer may still earn a B– because the grade is not based solely on what the student knows, but how the student articulates his or her knowledge in a three-hour exam period and how the student's answer compares with others in the class.

I am not known for using sports analogies but allow me to use one. Each year, thousands of high school football players hope they will be recruited by one of the Big Ten schools because they reputedly have the best coaches, facilities, resources, scholarships, and bowl game opportunities. According to the NFL Players Association, of 100,000 annual graduating high-school players, only 9,000 become college football players and only 215 go on to make to an NFL roster.[40] That means only 0.2% of the college players realized their dreams of becoming an NFL player. Does that mean the 8,785 who did not make it to the NFL were bad players? Of course not. But in relation to their peers, the 215 new players emerged as the best athletes to play in the NFL.

Similar to the NFL roster outcome, simple mathematics tell us that 90% of law students will not make it to the top 10%. The professor's evaluation of each exam, in light of the grading curve, is intended to reveal to the big law firms which graduates presumably will make the best entry-level lawyers because many law firms use the top-ten-percent status as a proxy for analytical ability and heavily factor it into their hiring decisions. The graduates hired by these firms usually have the highest entry-level salaries and tend to have the greatest earning potential. However, as with star college football players who do not make it to the NFL, students who do not graduate in the top ten percent can be just as capable attorneys as the 10-percenters and can go on to rewarding legal and non-legal careers.

Unfortunately, athletes and law students whose performance put them at the bottom of the class need to be concerned.

TSU and Cooley are not the only schools with high attrition rates. Table 6-1 (next page) identifies the schools that lost 15% or more of the 1L students in the fall 2010 entering class to attrition. The source of the attrition data is the 2013 LSAC Guide.

As the reader can see, 40 ABA-accredited law schools in the 2013 LSAC Guide have 1L attrition rates at 15% or more. At some schools, the overall attrition rate may appear small until one looks at the actual number of the first-year students who were forced to withdraw for academic reasons. For instance, 59 Western State students, 60 Whittier students, and 124 Cooley students were forced to withdraw. Furthermore, it is alarming that at 40 law schools, a total of 1,019 students had to withdraw for failure to meet the schools' academic standards. Equally troubling is the 1,622 students who withdrew for "other" reasons. It makes me wonder what kind of support these law schools could have provided to the students to enable some of them to stay in school. No doubt, most of

38. *See* Emily Zimmerman, *Do Grades Matter?*, 35 Seattle Univ. L. Rev. 305 (2012).

39. *Grading Policy*, The Ohio St. Univ. Moritz Coll. Of Law, http://moritzlaw.osu.edu/academics/grading_policy.php (last visited Jan. 11, 2013).

40. *NFL Hopeful FAQs*, https://www.nflplayers.com/About-us/FAQs/NFL-Hopeful-FAQs/.

Table 6-1. School's Ranked from Highest 1L Attrition Rate

		1L Academic Attrition #	1L Other Attrition #	Total 1L #s	% of 1L Class
1	Univ. of LaVerne Col. of Law	21	51	72	43.6%
2	Western State Col. of Law	59	24	83	34.9%
3	Whittier Law Sch.	60	33	93	31.0%
4	Widener Univ. Sch. of Law—Pennsylvania	23	32	55	30.9%
5	Nova Southeastern Univ.—Broad Law Center	66	44	110	28.0%
6	Thomas Jefferson Sch. of Law	32	67	99	28.0%
7	Faulkner Univ., Thomas Goode Jones Sch. of Law	20	18	38	26.0%
8	Liberty Univ. Sch. of Law	19	15	34	25.8%
9	Florida A&M Univ. Col. of Law	37	37	74	25.7%
10	Florida Coastal Sch. of Law	26	114	200	25.5%
11	Western New England Univ. Sch. of Law	7	34	41	24.1%
12	Touro Col.—Jacob D. Fuchsberg Law Center	14	55	69	23.8%
13	Capital Univ. Law Sch.	26	31	57	23.7%
14	Widener Univ. Sch. of Law—Delaware	34	57	91	23.5%
15	Golden Gate Univ. Sch. of Law	24	50	74	23.2%
16	Univ. of San Francisco Sch. of Law	18	38	56	22.3%
17	Willamette Univ. Col. of Law	12	24	36	22.2%
18	Pontifical Catholic Univ. of Puerto Rico	16	42	58	21.4%
19	Univ. of Detroit Mercy Sch. of Law	13	45	58	21.2%
20	New England Law—Boston	10	73	83	21.2%
21	Barry Univ. Dwayne O. Andreas Sch. of Law	23	32	55	21.1%
22	The John Marshall Law Sch.	44	63	107	21.0%
23	Univ. of District of Columbia—Clarke Sch. of Law	5	21	26	20.6%

		1L Academic Attrition #	1L Other Attrition #	Total 1L #s	% of 1L Class
24	The Univ. of Toledo Col. of Law	6	33	39	20.6%
25	Oklahoma City Univ. Sch. of Law	14	31	45	20.0%
26	St. Thomas Univ. Sch. of Law	29	24	53	19.4%
27	Charlotte Sch. of Law	47	48	95	19.3%
28	North Carolina Central Univ. Sch. of Law	26	12	38	18.5%
29	Southern Univ. Law Center	54	5	59	18.4%
30	Valparaiso Univ. Law Sch.	5	33	38	18.4%
31	Univ. of New Hampshire Sch. of Law	4	20	24	18.3%
32	Cleveland-Marshall Col. of Law, CSU	12	22	34	17.5%
33	Ave Maria Sch. of Law	8	27	35	17.4%
34	California Western Sch. of Law	27	30	57	17.4%
35	Regent Univ. Sch. of Law	15	13	28	16.7%
36	Catholic Univ. of America, Columbus Sch. of Law	5	40	45	16.4%
37	The Thomas M. Cooley Law Sch.	124	211	335	16.3%
38	Santa Clara Univ. Sch. of Law	19	32	51	15.6%
39	Univ. of Dayton Sch. of Law	7	24	31	15.3%
40	Washburn Univ. Sch. of Law	8	17	25	15.2%
		1,019	1,622	2,701	

the 2,701 students incurred substantial student loan debt but have not increased their employment potential.

Please look at Table 2 in Appendix A, where you will see that 39 of the 40 schools had a 1L attrition rate of 10% or greater in the 2012 LSAC Guide. Most schools had 1L attrition rates exceeding 15% for two consecutive years. That should make any person applying for admission to these schools question whether the schools have a pattern of allowing students to flunk out of law school. Many of the 40 schools also have high transfer-out numbers. Finally, at the majority of these schools, less than 50% of the 2011 graduates secured a long-term, fulltime bar-passage-required job nine months after graduation. As more fully discussed in Chapter 11, the majority of the graduates of these schools who are employed at law firms are actually self-employed as solo practitioners and at firms with a size of 2–10 persons. Thus, a full analysis of all available data shows that students enrolled in these schools not only have a significant probability of flunking or dropping out, but a high probability of experiencing *undesirable* employment outcomes.

The main point I want to emphasize is that prospective law school students cannot rest on their laurels and assume that past magna-cum-laude status is a predictor of landing in the top-ten percent of the law school class. Some students will earn GPAs that put them at the bottom of the class and may be forced out for failure to satisfy a school's academic standards. I believe it is okay to dream big, but prospective students need to discover, before enrolling, what the targeted law school will do if they enroll and earn a 1.99 GPA. Will the law school provide various resources to support the students' effort to stay in school and graduate or will the law school kick out the students? Unlike college football programs, which tend to invest numerous resources into helping their athletes to overcome injuries or improve academically, some law schools will not do the same to help their law students achieve a satisfactory GPA. By looking at the schools attrition and transfer-out rates, a prospective student can better gauge the school's actual commitment to academic support.

Update: As I was nearing the completion of the book, the court dismissed the TSU lawsuit on the grounds that I articulated. Prior to this, Ms. Ford was hopeful: "[Y]our dream doesn't stop because of something like this ... Is it a roadblock? Absolutely. But, in my heart, this is where I want to be, what I want to do."[41] I sincerely hope that things will work out for the best for both Ms. Ford and Mr. Chan.

Weeding Out Students: Is It Consumer Protection or Educational Malpractice?

A few months ago, I listened to presentation where a retired law professor argued that it was educational malpractice not to flunk students whose exam answers showed insufficient competency regarding the subject matter of the course. He feels this move is necessary to protect the public from incompetent attorneys. When he started teaching decades ago, it was common practice for law schools to flunk out a substantial percentage of the first-year class. However, I was troubled by his contention that today's legal academy should be flunking out students who by the end of their first year have often amassed as much as $60,000 in student loan debt. I take the position that we should *not* admit students who we think cannot succeed. Isn't it educational malpractice—or even worse a scam—for law schools to admit students they have reason to believe will fail and profit in the form of tuition revenue from their failed endeavor? Once a student is admitted, I believe law schools should marshal all resources necessary to help a struggling, hard-working student prevail.

My advice is that if you choose to go to law school, make sure the law school has an actual commitment to academic support. Look at the number of faculty members and other resources in place to help students succeed academically. Also, look up the school's attrition data in the LSAC Guide for last five years and make sure the attrition rates are very low or at least steadily declining.

41. Rhor, *supra* note 34.

Chapter 7

Reliance on *US News'* Rankings Is Not Justified and May Be Harmful

> *"Today, rankings facilitate laziness. The illusory comfort of an unambiguous numerical solution is easier than engaging in critical thought and exercising independent judgment. Forgotten along the way is the computer science maxim 'garbage in, garbage out.'"*[1] Stephen J. Harper

The last chapter described the sad story of two law students forced to withdraw for failing to satisfy TSU's academic requirements. I suspect that Jonathan Chan and Karla Ford most likely did not know about TSU's relatively high attrition rate when they chose to enroll. Like the majority of law school applicants, Mr. Chan and Ms. Ford may have decided to enroll into the highest ranked school from which they received an offer. In this chapter, I argue that students should not be obsessed with rankings in the enrollment decision-making process.

As I am writing this chapter, I am conducting an online survey directed to recent law graduates.[2] As of January 27, 2013, I have collected 255 responses. In the survey, I ask a series of questions designed to uncover what factors the graduates considered when they were prospective students and had to make an enrollment decision. Of the graduates who solicited advice from persons (other than law school personnel), the graduates' responses showed that the two groups most solicited for advice were parents and practicing lawyers or judges. In response to the question "did you feel that the person advising you to select a law school based on the highest ranking believed that the ranking of the school was a decisive factor for enrolling in a particular school," 80% answered yes. I also asked the following question: "Regarding the law school you ultimately decided to attend, which of the following did you place the MOST WEIGHT on when making your decision to attend that school?" The number one answer was the law school's ranking in *US News*.[3]

Each year, *US News* publishes the "*US News* Best Law School Rankings," where it ranks roughly 200 ABA-accredited law schools. They are divided into four tiers, with each tier comprising 50 law schools and the first-tier comprising the highest ranked schools. According to Judge Richard Posner,[4] the *US News'* ranking system is "a low-cost, low-

---

1. Stephen J. Harper, "Gaming the Reporting"?, March 13, 2013, http://thelawyerbubble.com/2013/03/13/gaming-the-reporting/.
2. The survey is called "Value of a Legal Education Survey" and is available at this website https://www.surveymonkey.com/s/lawdegreevalue. Graduates from the years 2006 to 2013 are encouraged to take the survey.
3. This finding of primary reliance on rankings is consistent with other studies.
4. Richard Posner is a U.S. Court of Appeals Judge for the Seventh Circuit, a senior lecturer at the University of Chicago Law School, and a prolific writer.

benefit method of evaluation—cheap but crude."[5] I argue that this crude decision-making process has and will continue to harm many graduates.

Let me provide one anecdotal story to illustrate how a heavy reliance on the *US News* rankings can be harmful. In 2003, Niko Marneris enrolled in John Marshall Law School, a Chicago school then-ranked in the fourth tier. After the first semester, his 3.9 GPA put him comfortably in the top 10% and earned him a spot on the school's law journal. He decided to transfer to Chicago-Kent College of Law, which was and still is ranked in the second tier.[6] In an ABA Journal news story, Mr. Marneris described his motivation for transferring to Chicago-Kent as follows: "The move 100 percent came down to fear of having a diploma from a lower-ranked versus a higher-ranked school."[7] He further stated, "I thought that for the rest of my career I'd have this black mark, despite the great reputation of graduates from my school among local judges and lawyers." In 2006, he wound up graduating from Chicago-Kent in the middle of the pack and could not find a job as an attorney. His first job was at a law firm, but he was employed in a marketing position. His rankings obsession caused him to forfeit being considered John Marshall's cream of the crop—graduating in the top 10% and with law journal experience. Had he stayed at John Marshall, I am confident that he would have been hired as an attorney by one of John Marshall's numerous alumni located in the Chicago area.[8]

Mr. Marneris failed to realize that he was already in a legal job market that some believe is over-saturated with law schools and lawyers. Illinois has nine law schools alone, and Chicago is within a five-hour or less driving distance of several first-tier schools, such as University of Iowa, University of Michigan, and Ohio State University. However, John Marshall has regional strengths despite its low *US News* ranking.

In retrospect, Mr. Marneris regrets the transfer but has decided to turn lemons into lemonade. He started his own law firm but he admits that his student loan debt is a heavy burden. He advises prospective students not to base a transfer or enrollment decision solely or primarily on rankings.

The reader may be wondering why there is such an obsession with the *US News* ranking system. Under the *US News* methodology, the median LSAT scores of a law school's entering class accounts for 12.5 percent of each law school's *US News* score.[9] The median undergraduate grade point average ("UGPA") for the entering class accounts for 10 percent.[10] Law schools believe that the other criteria considered by *US News* in its ranking methodology are largely beyond the control of law schools and that, therefore, improving the median LSAT score and UGPA are the primary ways for schools to improve their ranking positions.[11] Moreover, because the differences in rankings among law schools can

5. Richard A. Posner, *Law School Rankings*, 81 IND. L.J. 13, 13 (2006).

6. Note that both John Marshall and Chicago-Kent were sued for allegedly reporting deceptive employment data. These lawsuits were filed long after Niko graduated in 2006 from law school.

7. William D. Henderson and Rachel M. Zahorsky, *The Pedigree Problem: Are Law School Ties Choking the Profession?*, 98 ABA J. 36 (July 1, 2012, 5:20 AM), *available at* http://www.abajournal.com/magazine/article/the_pedigree_problem_are_law_school_ties_choking_the_profession/#correction.

8. I discuss later in this chapter research showing that John Marshall is among the top ten law schools with graduates as partners in big Chicago-area law firms.

9. Robert Morse & Sam Flanigan, *Methodology: Law School Ranking*, US NEWS AND WORLD REP. (Mar. 12, 2012), http://www.usnews.com/education/best-graduate-schools/top-law-schools/articles/2012/03/12/methodology-law-school-rankings.

10. *Id.*

11. *See* Alex M. Johnson, Jr., *The Destruction of the Holistic Approach to Admissions: The Pernicious Effects of Rankings*, 81 IND. L.J. 309 (2006) ("[O]f the objective and subjective variables that are used to evaluate the law schools there are very few that a dean can control with some degree of certitude.

be explained primarily by the median LSAT score of the entering classes, law schools and their deans of admission feel tremendously pressured to admit students with high LSAT scores.[12] Generally-speaking, the higher the LSAT scores, the higher the ranking of the law school. This in turn means that the higher-ranked schools receive a greater number of applications, especially from prospective students with high LSAT scores. In response, law schools compete to attract such students in order to improve their relative ranking.

An official from the Law School Admission Council, which administers the LSAT, stated that "[c]olleges overemphasize test scores in admissions decisions because they can easily be quantified, and because higher LSAT scores make schools look better to those who try to rank America's law schools, like *US News & World Report* magazine."[13] The Council has warned law schools against over-relying on LSAT scores in the admissions process, and many academics have heavily criticized law schools for such over-reliance in an attempt to go up in the rankings.[14] Moreover, rightly or wrongly, the *US News* rankings system has been criticized for this trend. The main criticisms are as follows: "the [*US News*] system decreases incentives for innovation, measures the wrong things, has a deleterious impact on admissions decision and diversity, is unreliable, contributes to the escalation of law school costs, is unrelated to the quality of education provided by the institution, and is not individualized for the needs of each student and offerings of a particular school."[15] Arguably, the most damning criticism is that the ranking system creates such immense pressure that "schools frequently manipulate the rankings by reporting false data."[16] Despite the warnings and criticisms, admission officers believe they must raise median LSAT scores and undergraduate GPAs ("UGPA").

Scandals involving the inflation of admissions data have revealed that a few schools are desperate to do whatever it takes to maintain or improve their rankings.[17] A *New York Times* article noted this trend when it stated that "repeated revelations of manipulation

---

The one variable that can be reliably improved (but not without cost) is the median LSAT. Given the near-perfect correlation between the median LSAT score and the school's ranking, a school may raise its median LSAT score and presumably ranking by rejecting students with lower LSAT scores.").

12. *See, e.g.*, Marjorie M. Shultz & Sheldon Zedeck, Identification, Development, and Validation of Predictors for Successful Lawyering 86 (2008) (reporting the results of a study indicating that the median LSAT scores of the entering classes explains roughly 90 percent of the differences in law school rankings published by *US News*). *See also* Pamela Edwards, *The Shell Game: Who is Responsible for the Overuse of the LSAT in Law School Admissions?*, 80 St. John's L. Rev. 153, 157 (2006). To a lesser extent, law schools also try to admit as many students as possible that have very high UGPAs as a way to improve in the rankings system.

13. Floyd Weatherspoon, *The Status of African American Males in the Legal Profession: A Pipeline of Institutional Roadblocks and Barriers*, 80 Miss. L.J. 259, 288 (2010).

14. Edwards, *supra* note 12, at 158.

15. Lauren Carasik, *Renaissance or Retrenchment: Legal Education at a Crossroads*, 44 Ind. L. Rev. 735, 803–804 (2011); Michael Sauder & Ryon Lancaster, *Do Rankings Matter? The Effects of US News and World Report Rankings on the Admission Process of Law Schools*, 40 Law & Soc'y Rev. 105, 105 (2006) (As two professors put it, "the [*US News*] rankings help create rather than simply reflect differences among law schools through the magnification of the small, and statistically random, distinctions produced by the measurement apparatus.").

16. Daniel Thies, *Rethinking Legal Education in Hard Times: The Recession, Practical Legal Education, and the New Job Market*, 59 J. Legal Educ. 598, 599 (2010).

17. Scandals regarding admissions data are not unique to law schools, as *US News* and others provide rankings for colleges and other graduate schools. One liberal arts college was recently found to have inflated SAT scores in an effort to improve its rankings. *Fraud on Campus: Don't Blame the Rankings, Blame the Cheaters,* Chi. Trib. (Feb. 18, 2012), http://articles.chicagotribune.com/2012-02-18/news/ct-edit-claremont-20120218_1_liberal-arts-illinois-and-villanova-rankings (stating that Claremont McKenna College, a liberal arts school in Southern California, admitted to inflating the SAT scores of incoming freshmen for at least six years).

show the importance of the rankings in the minds of prospective students, their guidance counselors, parents, the alumni considering donations, the professors weighing job offers—and, of course, the colleges themselves."[18]

Scandals at Villanova and Illinois

One recent scandal involved Villanova University School of Law ("Villanova"). In 2011, the ABA censured Villanova for inflating the UGPAs and LSAT numbers for incoming first-year classes.[19] Villanova had intentionally and falsely reported a median LSAT score of 162 and median UGPA of 3.44 for the entering class of 2009.[20] As stated previously, these numbers are reported to the ABA and *US News* and together comprise almost one quarter of a school's ranking.[21] Villanova claimed that the scandal was limited to a small number of administrators and admissions staff who were terminated after the scandal was discovered. In censuring Villanova, the ABA stated that the misrepresentation of the admissions data was "reprehensible and damaging" to prospective applicants, law students, and the legal profession.[22] As part of the public reprimand, the ABA ordered Villanova to post the censure on its website for two years, issue a public statement of correction to all law schools, and hire an independent compliance monitor for at least two years to ensure submission of accurate data.[23] In the first *US News* rankings report released after the scandal was exposed, Villanova dropped from 84th to 101st, effectively dropping it from second-tier school status to third-tier status.[24]

The University of Illinois College of Law ("Illinois") perpetrated a similar scheme of manipulating numbers to make the incoming classes appear more academically accomplished than they actually were.[25] The GPAs, LSAT scores, and acceptance rates were all altered for several incoming classes. Spending around $1 million to investigate the scandal, Illinois hired the Jones Day law firm and an outside data analysis firm to determine the extent of the manipulation of the admissions data. The investigation revealed that Admissions Dean Paul Pless single-handedly executed this scandal for six of the last seven years. In an email message to a friend, Pless explained how he could use the school's early-admission program to improve the median LSAT score: I can "[j]ack up the GPA

---

18. Richard Perez Pena & Danielle E. Slotnik, *Gaming the College Rankings,* N.Y. Times (Feb. 1, 2012), at A14, *available at* http://www.nytimes.com/2012/02/01/education/gaming-the-college-rankings.html?_r=1&pagewanted=all.

19. Chris Mondics, *Villanova Law Censured by ABA Over Admissions-data Fraud, but Retains Accreditation,* Philadelphia Inquirer (Aug. 16, 2011), http://articles.philly.com/2011-08-16/business/29892664_1_law-school-american-bar-association-lsat-scores.

20. Robert J. Morse, *Villanova Law School Certifies Accuracy of New Data, US News* & World Rep. (Feb. 17, 2011), *available at* static.usnews.com/documents/education/villanova-letter-us-news.pdf.

21. Morse & Flanigan, *supra* note 9.

22. Press Release, Am. Bar Assoc., ABA Legal Education Section Sanctions Villanova University School of Law for Intentionally Reporting Inaccurate Admissions Data, (Aug. 15, 2011), *available at* http://www.abanow.org/2011/08/aba-legal-education-section-sanctions-villanova-university-school-of-law-for-intentionally-reporting-inaccurate-admissions-data/.

23. *Id.*

24. Katy Hopkins, *In 2013 Best Law School Rankings, Top Schools Switch Spots, US News* & World Rep. (Mar. 13, 2012), http://www.usnews.com/education/best-graduate-schools/top-law-schools/articles/2012/03/13/in-2013-best-law-school-rankings-top-schools-switch-spots.

25. Jodi S. Cohen, *A University of Illinois Law Dean Resigns After Reports Details Manipulations of Admissions Data,* Chi. Trib. (Nov. 8, 2011), http://articles.chicagotribune.com/2011-11-08/news/ct-met-u-of-i-law-school-1108-20111108_1_lsat-score-test-scores-data-analysis.

without risking the low LSAT ... Nice gaming the system; I'm so proud."[26] He admitted to investigators that he later changed the actual GPAs of the students admitted through the early admission program to 4.0.[27] He resigned after an investigation placed the blame solely on him.[28] During his seven-year tenure in admissions, Illinois' ranking improved. Also, during his tenure, Pless's salary increased from $72,000 to $130,051 as a reward for his perceived recruiting success.[29] In 2012, Illinois dropped from 23 to 35 in the *US News* rankings.[30]

At first, it appeared that the only repercussion for Illinois would be the drop in its ranking. However, recently, the ABA imposed sanctions on Illinois.[31] In its censure, the ABA noted that:

> The College of Law lacked effective internal controls and oversight to prevent, deter and detect inadvertent or intentional manipulation of admissions data. The problem came to light in 2011 when a "whistleblower" brought suspicions to the attention of the University of Illinois. This led to prompt internal and external investigations at significant costs. The College of Law has since implemented corrective actions and has come into compliance with the Standards at issue.[32]

The sanctions that the ABA imposed include:

> (1) a public censure; (2) a requirement that the law school issue a public corrective statement; (3) a requirement that the law school hire a compliance monitor to report to the section's accreditation committee on its admissions process and data for the 2012–13 and 2013–14 academic years; (4) a monetary penalty; and (5) termination of a section agreement that allowed the law school to conduct an early-admissions program.[33]

The ABA stated that "[n]o matter what the competitive pressures, law schools must not cheat. The College of Law cheated."[34]

As mentioned above, one of the sanctions imposed on Illinois was a monetary penalty in the amount of $250,000.[35] Issuing such a fine was a first for the ABA regarding a university reporting inaccurate consumer data.[36] The monetary sanction "addresses the

---

26. Jodi S. Cohen, *U. of Ill. Official Boasted of 'Trap'[;] Law Admissions Dean: Program Was Cover for Boosting Ranking*, Chi. Trib., Nov. 9, 2011, at A1.

27. *Id.*

28. *Id.*

29. Jodi S. Cohen, *A University of Illinois Law Dean Resigns After Reports Details Manipulations of Admissions Data*, Chi. Trib. (Nov. 8, 2011), http://articles.chicagotribune.com/2011-11-08/news/ct-met-u-of-i-law-school-1108-20111108_1_lsat-score-test-scores-data-analysis.

30. Hopkins, *supra* note 24.

31. Press Release, Am. Bar Assoc., ABA Legal Education Section Announces Sanctions Against University of Illinois College of Law, http://www.abanow.org/2012/07/aba-legal-education-section-announces-sanctions-against-university-of-illinois-college-of-law/ (hereinafter "ABA Press Release").

32. Council of the Section of Legal Education and Admissions to the Bar of the American Bar Association, University of Illinois College of Law Censure, (June 2012), *available at* http://www.americanbar.org/content/dam/aba/administrative/legal_education_and_admissions_to_the_bar/council_reports_and_resolutions/2012_june_u_illinois_public_censure.authcheckdam.pdf (hereinafter "Illinois Censure").

33. ABA Press Release, *supra* note 31.

34. Illinois Censure, *supra* note 32.

35. Jodi S. Cohen, *U. of Ill. Law School Fined $250,000 for False Admission Data*, Chi. Trib., (July 24, 2012), http://articles.chicagotribune.com/2012-07-24/news/chi-20120724u-of-i-law-school-fined_1_false-admissions-data-lsat-scores-paul-pless.

36. *Id.*

harm to the reputation and standing of legal education and the profession resulting from the College of Law's violations of the Standards."[37] To put this into prospective, the fine sanctioned against Illinois is equal to nearly two times the amount of its then-Dean Pless's salary. However, the fine was a little less than the student loan indebtedness of only *one* graduate who had to finance his or her entire law school education.

The sanctions imposed by the ABA on Illinois also reveal what is at the root of the admissions scandal: The ABA is relying on every law school's integrity to do the right thing by honestly reporting information to the ABA. However, the discovery of Illinois' false reporting did not come to light because of checks and balances put in place by the dean of Illinois or by periodic audits conducted by the ABA. Instead, as mentioned in the ABA censure letter, it was a whistleblower who notified Illinois about possible falsities being included in admissions data. As such, Illinois was placed in a position where they had to react to the problem. Going forward, the ABA should be proactive and conduct random and periodic audits of law schools to verify that the schools are submitting accurate admissions data. Because the ABA has not indicated that it conducts periodic audits, law school applicants need to recognize the possibility that there are other admissions scandals yet to be uncovered as some law schools attempt to game the *US News* rankings system. This crystalizes the point that I am trying to drive home with this book: Since the ABA does not have in place a system to audit admissions departments, prospective students have to do a lot more analysis on their own to figure out if they should enroll in a particular law school.

Given the fraudulent and dishonorable tactics uncovered in well-regarded schools, one has to wonder how many other schools are doing the same but have not been caught. In response to these scandals, some have questioned whether the rankings tempt administrators to cut corners. A report by the National Association for College Admission Counseling (NACAC) harshly criticized the *US News* system:

> They have created a frenzy of competition among campuses that has also added to the frenzy experienced by students who are trying to be competitive to be admitted. They have turned college presidents into CFOs and fundraisers. They have turned admissions efforts into high-level marketers, and forced colleges to manipulate admissions stats, waiting list lengths, and lead students on to get them to apply.[38]

Similarly, 164 deans from ABA-approved law schools signed a letter urging the *US News* to stop ranking law schools because the ranking system inherently flawed.[39] In 2010,

37. Illinois Censure, *supra* note 32.

38. Nat'l Assoc. for Coll. Admission Counseling, A View of the *US News* & World Report Rankings of Undergraduate Institutions from the College Admission Counseling Perspective 10 (May 2011), *available at* http://www.ireg-observatory.org/pdf/USNewRankingsReport_NACAC.pdf.

39. Press Release, Carl C. Monk, Association of American Law Schools Calls On *US News* & World Report To Stop Ranking Law Schools (Feb. 18, 1998), *available at* http://www.aals.org/deansmemos/ranknews.html; *see also* Law School Admissions Council, Deans Speak Out, http://www.lsac.org/Choosing/deans-speak-out-rankings.asp; *see also* David A. Thomas, *The Law School Rankings Are Harmful Deceptions: A Response to Those Who Praise the Rankings and Suggestions for a Better Approach to Evaluating Law Schools*, 40 Hous. L. Rev. 419, 422 (2003) ("[T]he [*US News*] magazine does not publish all the relevant data, does not describe all the measures it takes to ensure the accuracy of the data, and does not describe its methodology in enough detail to enable anyone to actually check the results or to isolate and identify the influence of individual factors on the rankings."); Louis H. Pollak, *Why Trying to Rank Law Schools Numerically Is a Non-Productive Undertaking: An Article on the US News & World Report 2009 List of "The Top 100 Schools"*, 1 Drexel L. Rev. 52 (2009) (In this article,

the Society of American Law Teachers (SALT) issued a statement in support of boycotting *US News* by urging law schools and ABA to withhold the release of LSAT scores to *US News*.[40]

Even in the absence of cheating, the rankings system has to be discounted because of how it can be finessed. Consider for example the Dickinson School of Law, which in 1997 was listed as unranked in the third tier by *US News*. That year Dickinson, located in Carlisle, Pennsylvania, merged with Pennsylvania State University, 100 miles away in State College.[41] By the year 2000, applications for enrollment had increased by nearly 30%, and in 2005, *US News* ranked it at 90. Subsequently, Penn State's Dickinson School of Law opened a second location on Penn State's main campus in State College, and, by 2012, *US News* had ranked "Pennsylvania State University (Dickinson)" in the second tier at 76.[42] This is a major feat, considering that it is very difficult to make substantial movement up in the rankings.

However, in 2013, after recognizing the dramatic drop in law school applications, Penn State's trustees approved a plan to spit the once-unified law school into two separate law schools that will each seek ABA-accreditation. The out-going dean stated that this will result in the smaller of the two, Dickinson Law School, being able to admit "more students under slightly-relaxed academic standards." This move, if taken, is likely to result in Dickinson going down in the *US News* ranking.[43]

Besides dealing with the pressure arising from so much emphasis being placed on the rankings system, law schools now have to grapple with how to maintain their UGPA/LSAT numbers in the face of the declining number of people taking the LSAT exam and applying to law school. Law school applications have decreased by 24% over the last two years.[44] The rates of decline are very similar for male and female applicants and at both public and private law schools. This declining number of applications means that some law schools may struggle to produce as much revenue from the tuition of their incoming classes if they refuse to admit students with lower GPAs and LSAT scores. The potential for revenue shortage is compounded at law schools that are a part of public universities due to decreased funding from various sources, including the state. Some law schools, such as UC Hastings, plan to respond to the declining application rate by significantly reducing their class sizes. Frank Wu, dean of UC Hastings College of the Law, stated that his law school plans to reduce this fall's entering class size by 20% and layoff seventeen non-faculty employees because of the shrinking job market for lawyers.[45] Stating that "[t]here's nobody clamoring

---

US Federal District Court Judge Louis Pollak asserts that the *US News*' ranking of law schools is counter-productive to the health of legal education).

40. *See SALT Issues Statement to Diminish Influence of U.S News Law School Rankings*, SOC'Y OF AM. LAW TEACHERS (Sept. 30, 2010), *available at* www.saltlaw.org/contents/view/321.

41. *See* Elizabeth Chambliss, *Patterns of Organizational Alliance by U.S. Law Schools*, 80 FORDHAM L. REV. 2615 (2012).

42. Best Law Schools, *US NEWS & WORLD REP* (2012), http://grad-schools.usnews.rankingsandreviews.com/best-graduate-schools/top-law-schools/law-rankings (follow page "4" hyperlink); Anthony Bellafiore, *Penn State's Dickinson School of Law Sees Drop in Rankings*, DAILEY COLLEGIAN, March 15, 2012, http://www.collegian.psu.edu/archive/2012/03/15/dickinson_law_dropped_in_rankings.aspx (describing the school's movement in the rankings over the years).

43. *See* Charles Thompson, *Carlisle Law Faculty Gives Qualified Support to Plan for Two, Separate Penn State Law Schools*, PENN LIVE, May 2, 2013, *available at* http://www.pennlive.com/midstate/index.ssf/2013/05/carlisle_law_faculty_gives_qua.html

44. Sam Favate, *Number of Law School Applicants Continues to Slide*, WALL ST. J. (Apr. 9, 2012), http://blogs.wsj.com/law/2012/04/09/number-of-law-school-applicants-continues-to-slide/.

45. Bob Egelko, *UC Hastings Shrinking with Market for Lawyers*, SAN FRANCISCO CHRON. (May 1, 2012, 4:00 AM), http://www.sfgate.com/education/article/UC-Hastings-shrinking-with-market-for-lawyers-3526463.php.

for more lawyers, more law schools, more law students," Dean Wu believes that applications will continue to decline, resulting in a 40% drop over a three-year period.

Reducing class sizes is one way law schools can keep their UGPA/LSAT numbers up in spite of the decrease in applicants. It may be a sensible solution, especially for lower ranked law schools, considering the supply of new lawyers is expected to exceed the amount of new attorney jobs available. However, not all schools will have the option to accept fewer students due the ripple effect from a significant decrease in revenue. If they want to keep their rankings and revenues up at the same time, law schools will have to resort to more creative strategies.

Maintaining Ranking Status and Increasing Revenue via LL.M. Programs

Schools that need to maintain their revenue and do not want to risk dropping in the rankings can increase the number of students enrolled in their LL.M. programs.[46] An "LL.M." is the abbreviation for Master of Laws, which is an advanced law degree, and it often has a designation following the abbreviation indicating that the lawyer has acquired expertise in specified field of law—e.g., "LL.M. in Tax."[47] Over the last two decades, the legal academy has experienced a dramatic increase both in the number and size of LL.M. programs. According to the ABA's website, of the 200-plus ABA-approved law schools, 149 have some type of LL.M. program.[48] Several schools have five or more programs.[49] The tuition for a one-year LL.M. program can exceed $50,000.

Because students enrolled in LL.M. programs already hold some type of law degree,[50] their enrollment does not negatively affect a school's ranking position.[51] In addition to the regular ranking, *US News* ranks specialty programs by combining specialized curricula

46. LL.M. programs are different from joint-degree programs. Eighty-seven percent of law schools have established joint-degree programs. The dual JD/MBA (master's in business administration) degree remains the most popular of the programs. *ABA Curriculum Committee, A Survey of Law School Curricula: 2002–2010* 16 (2011) *available at* www.abanow.org/ ... /1341346391LawSchoolCurricul-aSurveyExecSummary.pdf., *See* Press Release, Am. Bar Assoc., ABA Survey Highlights Changes in Law School Curricula (July 5, 2012), *available at* http://www.abanow.org/2012/07/aba-survey-highligh-ts-changes-in-law-school-curricula/. These programs are generally seen as cost effective for students because they develop cross-disciplinary expertise in a non-legal discipline while simultaneously pursuing a JD. *See* Robert J. Rhee, *On Legal Education and Reform: One View Formed from Diverse Perspectives*, 70 Md. L. Rev. 310, 311 (2011).

47. Some schools have master's degree for non-lawyers, and its abbreviation may be M.S. for Master of Science or M.P.S. for Master of Professional.

48. *Post J.D. Programs by School*, Am. Bar Assoc., https://www.americanbar.org/groups/legal_education/resources/llm-degrees_post_j_d_non_j_d/programs_by_school.html (last visited Jan. 14, 2013).

49. *Id.* (For example, University of Miami has the following specialized LL.M. programs: Comparative Law, Estate Planning, Inter-American Law, International Law, Ocean and Coastal Law, Real Property and Land Development, and Taxation).

50. American law schools create LL.M. programs for two different groups: international students who already hold some type of law degree and students who hold a JD from an American law school.

51. The *US News* ranking system takes into account the LSAT scores and GPAs of regular law students, i.e., those enrolled in JD programs.

at the JD and LL.M. level. For instance, in its latest *US News* tax law rankings, ten schools that emphasize tax law but that lack a tax LL.M. program moved up in the rankings while six schools with a tax LL.M. program moved down in the rankings.[52]

What Is Good for the Goose Is Not Necessarily Good for the Gander?

Just because LL.M. programs may help law schools boost or maintain revenue without negatively affecting their rankings does not mean a LL.M. degree is worth pursuing. It is understandable that some graduates or third-year law students may be interested in pursuing a LL.M. degree because they are having difficulty securing a full-time, long-term legal job. Proponents of LL.M. programs argue that the advance degree will boost the graduate's employability. However, prospective LL.M. students need to realize that the degree may increase their indebtedness by another $60,000 to $80,000 if they have to borrow money to pay for the degree. Cornell, for example, estimates that its one-year, general LL.M. degree will cost $78,720, which includes a tuition fee of $59,260.[53]

Law graduates who are unable to find attorney positions need to be careful before deciding that enrolling in a LL.M. is the right course of action to increase their employability. The ABA does not accredit LL.M. programs. Instead, the ABA simply acquiesces to the existence of LL.M. programs on the basis that it does not interfere with the basic JD experience:

> The ABA reviews post-JD degree programs only to determine whether the offering of such post-JD program would have an adverse impact on the law school's ability to maintain its accreditation for the JD program. If no adverse impact is indicated, the ABA acquiesces in the law school's decision to offer the non-JD program and degree. Acquiescence in a post-J.D. program does not constitute ABA approval or endorsement of such a program.[54]

The ABA does not impose any admissions standards or require law schools to report information about their LL.M. programs.

Because the ABA does not impose any standards regarding LL.M. programs and exercises no oversight over the programs, some in the legal community view LL.M. programs with suspicion and question whether such programs are primarily a revenue booster.[55] This suspicion shows that not everyone considers an LL.M. degree as a requirement to succeed.

---

52. *New 2012 US News Tax Rankings*, TaxProf Blog (March 16, 2011), http://taxprof.typepad.com/taxprof_blog/2011/03/new-2012.html.

53. *Tuition and Expenses*, Cornell Law School, http://www.lawschool.cornell.edu/admissions/tuition/tuition_expenses.cfm (last visited Jan. 14, 2013).

54. *Council Statements*, Am. Bar Assoc., http://apps.americanbar.org/legaled/accreditation/Council%20Statements.pdf (last visited Jan. 29, 2013).

55. *See* Carole Silver, *What We Don't Know Can Hurt Us: The Need for Empirical Research in Regulating Lawyers and Legal Services in the Global Economy*, 43 Akron L. Rev. 1009, 1044 (2010) ("But the absence of ABA oversight has resulted in bar admission authorities being suspicious of LL.M. programs, and they are quick to point to the absence of standardization in LL.M. programs as justification for their mistrust. Suspicion also is fueled among overseas students, who worry that LL.M. programs are more a source of revenue and only secondarily the substantive focus of their U.S. law schools.").

While some employers may view an LL.M. as a valuable instrument, others believe an LL.M. "might indicate that applicants were unfocused in their studies or felt they had to bolster their JD credentials."[56] According to Steven John, a managing director at Major, Lindsey & Africa, a legal recruiting firm, big law firms have never demanded that attorneys hold advanced law degrees.[57] Mr. John stated further that, "advanced degrees in law—with the exception of LL.M.s for foreign-trained attorneys and tax LL.M.s—can actually hurt job candidates, because they may signal uncertainty about their career paths or attempts to avoid the reality of a difficult job search."[58] Even *US News* has warned students to proceed with caution because LL.M. graduates may increase their student loan debt but not their chances of getting the desired job.[59] In the end, the amount of loan indebtedness may outweigh any reward.

It is extremely rare to find online employment data regarding the specific employment outcomes of a school's LL.M. graduates;[60] therefore, I urge those interested in LL.M. programs to demand answers regarding the employment outcomes of a school's LL.M. graduates. Prospective LL.M. students should also do their best to independently assess the local or regional reputation of a law school's LL.M. program. First, look at the websites of local and regional firms to see how many LL.M. graduates of the targeted school are employed at the firms. Second, watch a local trial and strike up a conversation with the judge or one of the lawyers after the trial is over to get their opinion of the LL.M. program. Finally, go to a meeting of the local chapter of the ABA's YLD (Young Lawyers' Division) or the YLD sections of the state and local bar associations to find graduates with LL.M. degrees to assess their opinion of the degrees.

In summary, because the ABA does not have standards, and because data about LL.M. programs is not reported in the LSAC Guide, there is no objective information available to assess a program's quality and the potential benefits it may offer. My advice is to focus on LL.M. programs that are rare. For example, St. John's bankruptcy LL.M. program remains the only one of its kind. The fewer the number of schools with a particular program, the more likely there may still be jobs for that LL.M. specialization.

---

56. Menachem Wecker, *Though Controversial, LL.M.'s Can Lead to Specialized Legal Jobs: In Areas Such as Tax or Securities Law, Experts Say an LL.M. Can Add Value to a J.D.*, US NEWS: EDUC. (Feb. 6, 2012), *available at* http://www.usnews.com/education/best-graduate-schools/top-law-schools/articles/2012/02/06/though-controversial-llms-can-lead-to-specialized-legal-jobs.

57. Karen Sloan, *Big Law Firms Don't Care About Your LL.M., Recruiter Warns*, NAT'L L.J. (Jan. 10, 2012). Mr. John made his comments during a panel discussion at the 2012 annual meeting of the Association of American Law Schools and, therefore, a room filled with law school administrators heard him say that the big law firms do not seek graduates with LL.M. degrees.

58. *Id.*

59. Wecker, *supra* note 56.

60. With the exception of Philip Postlewaite, Professor of Law and Director of Northwestern' s Tax Program, I did not uncover any other law school that publishes online specific employment outcomes of its LL.M. graduates. A link to employment statistics can easily be found at Professor Postlewaite's homepage for the Tax Program, and it has data for years 2007 to 2011. LLM Tax, Northwestern Law, http://www.law.northwestern.edu/career/statistics/llmtax.html (last visited Jan. 14, 2013). Unlike the websites that have an overall employment rate, which, I've explained, one has to view with suspicion, Professor Postlewaite identifies the number and percentage of graduates employed at accounting firms, law firms and other businesses. He actually has a separate category labeled "Underemployed" which includes those who are self-employed or are working part-time or in temporary positions. Therefore, one can be confident that the 85% employment rate for the 2011 tax-LL.M. graduates accurately reflects the number of graduates with successful employment outcomes.

I know some in the legal academy will disagree with me, but I would avoid a general LL.M. program. Hanover Research, a Connecticut-based firm, identified the increase in LL.M. programs as a revenue-generating strategy for law schools.[61] The president and dean of Vermont Law School reported that it has experienced a budget shortfall of $3.3 million due to the dramatic drop in enrollment of first-year law students and that he plans to boost revenue by to increasing "the number of LL.M and certificate programs it offers."[62] You have to appreciate his honesty. Nevertheless, this book's mission is to warn prospective and current law students to be sophisticated and to look out for their own best interests. Because some law schools may be using LL.M. programs as a cash cow to make up for deficits arising from the drop in JD enrollments, I remain skeptical that such programs can increase a graduate's employability. Until you see some hard statistics about the employment outcomes of these programs, you should likewise remain skeptical.

Increasing the Number of Transfer Students without Affecting the Rankings

To maintain their rankings position and to boost their revenue, law schools could also admit more transfer students from lower ranked schools. Students transferring to another school after their first year are not considered part of the incoming first-year class for the *US News* rankings and, therefore, their UGPA and LSAT numbers do not play a role in a school's ranking. As a result, law schools can afford to accept transfer students with below-median UGPA and LSAT numbers, and receive tuition from them, without fearing that their rankings will take a hit.

One law professor has criticized this practice:

> The current ABA reporting and *US News* ranking systems create an incentive to harvest transfer students [from lower-ranked schools]. If some portion of the pool of transfers occurs solely from an effort to enhance rankings, then the cost of transfers in that respect is not tied to any intrinsic improvement in legal education but only to a hollow effort to appear better.[63]

A counter argument is that law schools that use transfer strategically are getting students have already been "tested" by another school and have succeeded. Therefore, these transfer students are a low-risk admit because they are likely to graduate and pass the bar exam.

It has also been reported that some law schools actually pursue transfer students to improve the diversity of the student body.[64] I think diversity is a good goal to pursue, but I am concerned that higher-ranked schools are "stealing" students that lower-ranked schools were willing to admit as entering first-year students.

---

61. Revenue Generation Strategies for Law Schools, Hanover Research (Aug. 2011), *available at* http://www.hanoverresearch.com/wp-content/uploads/2012/10/Revenue-Generation-Strategies-for-Law-Schools-Membership.pdf.

62. Karen Sloan, *New Vermont Law School Dean Taking on $3.3M Budget Shortfall*, Nat'l L.J. (Nov. 26, 2012), *available at* http://www.law.com/jsp/nlj/PubArticleNLJ.jsp?id= 1202579363738&New_Vermont_Law_School_dean_taking_on_M_budget_shortfall&slreturn=20121112091858.

63. Jeffrey L. Rensberger, *Tragedy of the Student Commons: Law Student Transfers and Legal Education*, 60 J. Legal Educ. 616 (2011).

64. Wendy Espeland & Michael Sauder, *Rankings and Diversity*, 18 S. Cal. Rev. L. & Soc. Just. 587 (2009).

Because some schools may be using transfers in a crafty manner, it has been advocated that law schools should provide more information about transfer students so that prospective law students can make more informed choices about which law school to attend.[65] Prospective students should research whether a law school has a high transfer-in rate. Not only does a high transfer-in rate mean that the total number of students attending the law school are not included in *US News*' ranking statistics, it could also mean that these transferees will alter the class rankings—more students competing to be in the top 10%—and affect opportunities to grade-on to the law journals. A high number of transfer-in students could increase the stress-level in the law school environment as the transfer-in students compete with the rest of the student body to find employment in a depressed legal job market. To avoid any surprises, prospective students should ask law school admissions personnel how transfer students affect matters like class-ranking and journal opportunities.

Law school is an investment—for most people an enormous investment—and knowing the costs (tuition, etc.) and expected return (job prospects) is a necessity for any wise investor.

The ABA's Position on Rankings

Prospective students need to understand that the ranking is not the be-all end-all measurement of evaluating a law school. The ABA does not endorse any ranking system and encourages applicants to consider numerous criteria:

> No rating of law schools beyond the simple statement of their accreditation status is attempted or advocated by the official organizations in legal education. Qualities that make one kind of school good for one student may not be as important to another. The American Bar Association and its Section of Legal Education and Admissions to the Bar have issued disclaimers of any law school rating system. Prospective law students should consider a variety of factors in making their choice among schools.[66]

Unfortunately, not enough prospective students are listening to the ABA. Too much emphasis on rankings can tempt some law schools to do things that are not related to improving the legal education of their students.

An Offer from a Top-14 School Is a Big Deal

If I were to create a bright line rule, I would say that unless an applicant has an admission offer from a "Top 14" law school ***and*** is seeking to work at a nationwide law firm, the ranking of the law school needs to be one among *numerous* criteria to be considered before enrolling. Since the inception of *US News* rankings system, the law schools making the Top 14 list have been fairly consistent and *US News* annually reports about the schools making the list. My reason for a cutoff at the Top 14 is that graduates

---

65. Rensberger, *supra* note 63.

66. *ABA-Approved Law Schools*, Am. Bar Assoc., http://www.americanbar.org/groups/legal_education/resources/aba_approved_law_schools.html (last visited Jan. 14, 2013).

of these schools have a high probability of getting a job as a traditional attorney and a very low chance of being unemployed. As explained in depth in Chapter 4, under the ABA's Revised Standard 509, law schools are supposed to use a uniform format to report employment outcomes and have to specifically identify the number of graduates employed in full-time, long-term jobs that require passage of the bar exam (hereafter "Permanent Bar-Required Jobs"). I take the position that the category of Permanent Bar-Required jobs is the best measure of the number of graduates who have permanent full-time jobs that involve the practice of law because bar passage is only required for practicing attorneys. I realize that the "JD-Advantage" category may include other sought-after jobs that do not involve the practice of law. I nevertheless discount the JD-Advantage category as an accurate measure of the kind of jobs that prospective students want because, as explained fully in Chapter 4, law schools can easily manipulate that category to count under-employed graduates.

In 2012, *US News* ranked three schools tied in seventh place on its Top 14 list. As indicated in the Table 7-1 (next page), the majority of the 2011 graduates of the Top 14 schools were able to secure Permanent Bar-Required Jobs; however, the schools are ***not*** equal in terms of results.

If 80% is the minimum percentage of Permanent Bar-Required jobs that an applicant is willing to accept, Michigan, Northwestern, Georgetown, and Cornell did not make the cut. Law school applicants should not make a final decision about these four schools until *after* they have read Professor Theodore Seto's 2011 study of partners at America's 100 largest law firms (hereafter, the "NLJ 100").

Professor Seto conducted a study of the NLJ 100 firms to determine which schools have the greatest number of graduates employed as junior and mid-level partners and where they are located. What he discovered is that the NLJ 100 partners who graduated from years 1986 to 2011usually came from schools located in only one major job market.[67] Let me explain further by using Georgetown as an example. Based on the employment data that it submitted to the ABA, Georgetown, in comparison to the other Top 14 schools, has the lowest percentage of graduates employed in Permanent Bar-Required jobs. However, Professor Seto's study of the NLJ 100 partners in the Washington, DC market reveals that Georgetown is number one on the list of feeder schools with 286 of its graduates as NLJ 100 partners.[68] Yale, on the other hand, is number one on the Top 14 list from *US News* but comes in at number seven on the feeder school list with only 66 graduates as NLJ 100 partners employed in the DC market. Stanford did not even make the list of the top-ten feeder schools in the DC market. After studying 11 major markets for the NLJ 100 firms, Professor Seto concludes that hiring at the NLJ 100 firms "is astonishingly local" and that very few law schools are "truly national" when it comes to hiring and partnering. The data analyzed from all markets reveal that only Harvard and Georgetown are truly national schools, coming in at number one and two, respectively, on the top-50 feeder schools for NLJ 100 firms nationwide.[69]

---

67. Theodore P. Seto, *Where Do Partners Come From,* 62 J. LEGAL EDUC. 242 (Nov. 2012).

68. *Id.* at 248, Table 3-Top Feeder Schools: Washington, D.C.

69. *Id.* at 243 ("Harvard and Georgetown are standouts; Yale and Stanford are not."). The reader should also consider several postings by another law professor who has criticized Professor Seto's methodology for failing to account for schools with larger class sizes. *See* Robert Anderson, *A Last Word on the Seto Rankings,* WITNESSETH: LAW, DEALS, & DATA (Dec. 23, 2012), http://witnesseth.typepad.com/blog/2012/12/a-last-word-on-the-seto-rankings.html (asserting that the "failure to control for class size provided a rankings boost for larger schools simply for being larger, distorting the results from the top school to the bottom school").

Table 7-1. Summary of 2011 Employment Outcomes at Top 14 Law Schools

US News Ranking		# of 2011 Grads	# with F/T, L/T Bar-Required Jobs	% with F/T, L/T Bar-Required Jobs	# with F/T, L/T JD-Advantage Jobs	% with F/T, L/T JD-Advantage	% of Bar-Required plus JD-Advantage	# of 2011 Grads Seeking & Unemployed	% Seeking & Unemployed
1	Yale	205	180	88%	7	3%	91%	1	0%
2	Stanford	192	175	91%	9	5%	96%	3	2%
3	Harvard	583	525	90%	21	4%	94%	13	2%
4	Columbia	456	429	94%	6	1%	95%	1	0%
5	University of Chicago	203	179	88%	14	7%	95%	2	1%
6	NYU	466	420	90%	17	4%	94%	10	2%
7	UC Berkeley	310	248	80%	8	3%	83%	7	2%
7	U Penn	274	231	84%	18	7%	91%	7	3%
7	University of Virginia	377	357	95%	5	1%	96%	2	1%
10	University of Michigan	379	286	75%	39	10%	86%	13	3%
11	Duke	207	170	82%	11	5%	87%	3	1%
12	Northwestern	287	221	77%	22	8%	85%	11	4%
13	Georgetown	644	403	63%	55	9%	71%	35	5%
14	Cornell	201	153	76%	0	0%	76%	11	5%

Data Source: Employment Summary Report, http://employmentsummary.abaquestionnaire.org.

As shown in Table 7-2 below, ranking based on the number of partners nationwide at NLJ 100 firms is not in sync with the *US News*' Top 14 ranking in 2012.

Table 7-2.

US News Ranking	Top 14 Law Schools	NLJ 100 Rank
1	Yale	16
2	Stanford	17
3	Harvard	1
4	Columbia	5
5	University of Chicago	8
6	NYU	3
7	UC Berkeley	14
7	U Penn	11
7	University of Virginia	4
10	University of Michigan	7
11	Duke	19
12	Northwestern	10
13	Georgetown	2
14	Cornell	21

US News ranks Harvard at No. 3; however, Professor Seto ranks Harvard at No. 1 because it has 946 graduates employed as partners in the NLJ 100 firms, and it made the top-ten list of feeder schools for all eleven markets studied. Ranked No. 2, Georgetown has 729 graduates employed as NLJ 100 partners, and it made the top-ten list of feeder schools in eight of the eleven markets. Law school applicants should also take note (in Table 7-3) the schools that did not make the *US News*' Top 14 but that made the nationwide Top 20 list of feeder schools for NLJ 100 Partners.

Table 7-3.

NLJ Ranking	Schools in the NLJ Top-20 List That Did Not Make US News' Top-14 Law Schools
6	George Washington
9	Univ. of Texas
12	Boston University
13	Fordham
15	UCLA
18	UC Hastings
20	Boston College

In light of Professor Seto's findings, let's revisit the story about Niko Marneris, who enrolled in John Marshall, then-ranked in the fourth tier, and later transferred to Chicago-Kent. He was fearful that his John Marshall degree would not lead to an attorney position even though he had a 3.9 GPA at John Marshall that put him in the top 10% and earned him a law journal spot. Professor Seto's study of partners at NLJ 100 firms located in the Chicago market revealed that John Marshall has 59 partners at NLJ 100 firms and, therefore, made number nine on the list of the top-ten feeder schools. Chicago-Kent came in at number eight with 91 of its graduates as NLJ 100 partners. Professor Seto's study confirms my assessment that Niko should have stayed at John Marshall where he most likely would have graduated with honors and would have, therefore, been able to capitalize on John Marshall's regional reputation by getting hired by one the firms with John Marshall alumni.

Based on the foregoing, my final conclusion is that if a prospective student wants to get hired at a big law firm ***and*** the student has an *admission offer* from a Top 14 law school, the student needs to make sure that the school is on the list of the top-ten feeder schools in the city where the student wants to practice law. Only then will the student have the best chance of benefiting from the Top 14's high rate of employment. For those who have an admission offer from a school that is ***not*** on the Top 14 list, I recommend that the prospective students do a full-scale analysis of the strengths and weaknesses of that school before making an enrollment decision. Below, I compare two schools to illustrate why rankings alone is not a good basis on which to make an enrollment decision.

Comparison of Illinois and Nebraska

To provide a comparison that demonstrates the limitations of the law school rankings, I will analyze employment data provided by Illinois and the University of Nebraska College of Law ("Nebraska") along with other important factors to consider when evaluating law schools. In the 2013 *US News*' law school rankings, Illinois was tied with William & Mary Law School for 35th place and Nebraska was tied with six other law schools for 89th place.[70] Because Illinois is a first-tier school, those who place great importance on the *US News* rankings would heavily favor enrolling in Illinois over enrolling in second-tier Nebraska. However, a prospective student should consider the employment outcomes at each school. The employment data displayed on each law school's website for the class of 2011[71] are summarized in Table 7-4 (next page).

70. *Best Law Schools* (2012), *US News & World Rep.*, http://grad-schools.usnews.rankingsandreviews.com/best-graduate-schools/top-law-schools/law-rankings (last visited Jan. 14, 2013).

71. While visiting a school's website is a good idea, prospective students should always go to the official website maintained by the ABA for employment reports. *See* http://employmentsummary.abaquestionnaire.org

Table 7-4.

Sources: Schools' Websites	**Illinois—1st Tier Ranking at 35**	**Nebraska—2nd Tier Ranking at 89**
Number of Graduates	190	130
Overall Employment %	152/187 or 81.3%	115/127 or 90.6%
% of Graduates Reporting Employment Data	187/190 or 98.4%	127/130 or 97.7%
% Employed in Law Firms	68/152 or 44.7%	56/115 or 48.7%
% Employed—Bar Passage Req'd	118/152 or 77.6%	84/115 or 73.0%
% Employed—Full-time	133/152 or 87.5%	108/115 or 93.9%
% Employed—Long-term	118/152 or 77.6%	110/115 or 95.7%
% Employed—Position Funded by Their University	19/152 or 12.5%	1/115 or 0.01%
% Unemployed Seeking Work	30/187 or 16%	9/130 or 6.9%
Average Salary	Unknown	$54,188
% of Graduates Reporting Salary	Unknown	72/115 or 62.6%

Overall, the employment prospects for Illinois and Nebraska may seem similar. Nebraska, however, gets a slight edge primarily because it has a much smaller percentage of graduates who are unemployed and seeking work. Nebraska has a higher overall employment rate of 90.6% for the class of 2011 compared to Illinois' rate of 81.3%. However, a prospective student should realize that both of these rates contain graduates employed in non-legal jobs. Both schools have a high employment response rate so the information is representative of the class. Both schools also do a good job of disaggregating employment data into categories that are important to law school applicants.

The percentage of graduates employed in jobs that require bar passage is a very important statistic and both schools have impressive numbers. While Illinois has a higher percentage of employed graduates that work in jobs that require bar passage, Nebraska makes up for this with its higher overall employment rate. Nebraska also discloses that all of its graduates in positions that require bar passage are in full-time jobs. Nebraska does not categorize jobs into temporary or permanent positions but does state that only two graduates are doing temporary attorney work and one graduate is doing temporary law clerk or paralegal work. It is not clear if these are the only graduates who are working temporary jobs.

Nebraska's higher overall employment rate is even more impressive when one considers that 93.9% of employed graduates are in full-time jobs. Furthermore, while Illinois does not disclose salary data, Nebraska's salary statistics are based on a sample that is fairly large when compared to many other schools' salary data. However, because only 37% of Nebraska's graduates did not supply their salary information, prospective or transfer students cannot assume that their salaries post-graduation will be as good as the average salary data provided.

The most troubling statistic for Illinois is that it has 16% of its grads reporting that they are unemployed and seeking work. Keep in mind that the admissions scandal at Illinois was being investigated and discussed in the media while many of the 2011 graduates were looking for jobs. Now that the new rankings have come out and Illinois has slipped from 23 to 35, employers may be more cautious about hiring Illinois graduates, especially those ranked in the bottom half of their class. This plunge in the rankings could be particularly damaging given the abundance of competition for new attorney positions in the state of Illinois, which has *nine* ABA-accredited law schools and *two* of them (Northwestern and University of Chicago) are ranked in the Top 14.[72] On the other hand, Creighton University School of Law (located in Omaha) is the only other law school located in Nebraska. Considering all of the factors that are available, an applicant can see that Nebraska's numbers are better than Illinois'. Moreover, an applicant could surmise that the drop in the rankings by Illinois and the high amount of in-state competition could hurt the employment outlook for Illinois graduates in the future.

Comparing the ABA Data

The LSAC Guide is a useful resource for comparing law schools and has information that is not available or difficult to find on a law school's website. Absent a specific disclosure requirement by the ABA, law schools do not have an incentive to disclose potentially negative information. That means prospective law students must consult the LSAC Guide to discover information that may raise a red flag.[73]

Along with the schools' employment statistics, I will analyze some other important criteria that students must consider when choosing a law school. Additional relevant information on Illinois and Nebraska for the class of 2009 in the LSAC Guide is summarized in Table 7-5.

Table 7-5.

Source: LSAC Guide	Illinois	Nebraska
Overall Employment %	165/192 or 85.9%	118/132 or 89.4%
% of Graduates Reporting Employment Data	192/192 or 100%	132/134 or 98.5%
% Employed in Law Firms	110/165 or 66.7%	71/118 or 60.2%
First-Time Takers' Bar Passage Rate	95.45%	90.91%
Attrition Rate for 1st Two Years Combined	5.3%	6.6%
% of Students with Full Tuition or More Scholarships	8.8%	12.2%
% of Graduates Employed In State	101/165 or 61.2%	88/118 or 74.6%
Tuition	Resident—$36,420 Nonresident—$43,420	Resident—$13,337 Nonresident—$28,649

72. Although Illinois is ranked in the first tier, University of Chicago Law School and Northwestern University School of Law are ranked in the top 12 and are considered more reputable by many than Illinois.

73. The LSAC Guide is available in print or online. LAW SCHOOL ADMISSIONS COUNCIL, https://officialguide.lsac.org/release/OfficialGuide_Default.aspx.

If one dissects the 2009 data in the LSAC Guide, one can see that it paints a picture that is slightly more favorable to Illinois. However, note this data came before the admissions scandal was disclosed to the media. While Nebraska has a higher overall employment rate for its 2009 graduates, Illinois fares better in the percentage of graduates employed in law firms. Illinois has a better first time bar passage rate, but this could be explained by variations in state bar exams. Most Nebraska students take the bar in Nebraska, where the state's average passage rate for first-time takers is 86.86%. In Illinois, the state's average first-time passage rate is 90.52%. So in comparison to the respective state averages, each school's students do comparably well in passing the bar exam. Neither school has a high attrition rate. A large majority of Nebraska's graduates work in Nebraska, which could deter some prospective law students from applying if they do not wish to live in that state. Geographical preference is an individual decision, but being unable to find a job can make this preference seem much less important than being employed.

Nebraska has a slightly higher overall employment rate for 2009 when compared to Illinois' overall rate. Observe that if one compares the employment rates in both tables above, Nebraska's overall employment rate increased from 89.4% for its 2009 graduates to 90.6% for its 2011 graduates, while Illinois' decreased from 85.9% to 81.3% for the same years. Illinois also saw a dramatic increase in unemployed-but-seeking employment numbers—from 0.5% for the class of 2009 to 16% for the class of 2011. Illinois' negative numbers may be attributed to the admissions scandal. Some employers may feel that they have been deceived into valuing Illinois graduates more than they should have in light of Illinois' reporting of false median UGPA and LSAT numbers in previous years. At the end of the day, Nebraska is a more attractive option than Illinois due to Illinois' decrease in overall employment rate and increase in percentage of its graduates that are unemployed and seeking work.

Even if one assumes that the two schools are roughly equivalent in terms of employment prospects without any scandal, one can see the scales tip in favor of Nebraska when it comes to the cost of a legal education at each school. The out-of-state tuition ($28,649) at Nebraska is about two-thirds of the out-of-state tuition ($43,420) for Illinois. If a student is able to become an in-state resident for the last two years of law school, their tuition will be cut by more than half at Nebraska. Illinois does not offer a comparable discount for in-state residents. Assuming that an out-of-state student gets in-state residency after the first year of law school, the total tuition paid for three years at Nebraska would be $55,323. If an out-of-state student gets in-state residency in Illinois after their first year, the total three-year tuition bill will be $116,260. That is more than twice the amount of debt with no better employment prospects. The fact that Illinois has a cost-of-living that is $2,300 more than Nebraska is also significant. Over the course of three years that is an extra cost of $6,900. It is easy to see why Nebraska made the top-ten list of schools where graduates carry *the least* amount of debt, with an average indebtedness of $52,396.[74] Illinois' 2011 graduates who had to incur student loan debt had an average indebtedness of $90,432.[75] Note that residency rules vary so prospective students considering an out-of-state law school should find

74. Ryan Lytle, *10 Law Schools That Lead to the Least Debt*, US NEWS & WORLD REP., http://www.usnews.com/education/best-graduate-schools/the-short-list-grad-school/articles/2012/03/22/10-law-schools-that-lead-to-the-least-debt (last visited Jan. 14, 2013).

75. *Whose Graduates Have the Most Debt?*, US NEWS & WORLD REP., http://grad-schools.usnews.rankingsandreviews.com/best-graduate-schools/top-law-schools/grad-debt-rankings/page+6 (last visited Jan. 14, 2013).

out how easy it is to obtain in-state residency status when estimating the cost of attending that school.

Given that the above analyses demonstrate that Nebraska graduates have a slightly better employment rate and carry substantially less student loan debt, a law school applicant or transfer student should see that Illinois does not yield a better result for its high price and that, therefore, *US News*' high ranking of Illinois may be meaningless.[76] Knowing how much a legal education will cost and how likely one is to receive a desirable job should be among the most important criteria considered by law school applicants or transfer students.

If Illinois offered the student a substantial scholarship, that offer could tip the scales in favor of Illinois. For the hypothetical out-of-state student who gets in-state residency after the first year of law school, Illinois would have to offer a scholarship that covers full tuition or close to this amount to make it a more attractive option financially than Nebraska. If Illinois offered a scholarship that only covered half of tuition, an education at Illinois would still cost slightly more than Nebraska and the student would incur a higher cost-of-living expense in Champaign, Illinois. Given that the job prospects for Illinois graduates are to some extent poorer and may not dramatically improve after its drop in the rankings, a prospective or transfer student could decide a legal education at Illinois may not be a better financial investment even if a scholarship is offered.

As I neared the completion of this book, *US News* released in March 2013 its rankings list where Illinois slide further from 35 to 47. That amounted to the largest drop of any first-tier school. Bob Morse stated that Illinois' 2011 employment data played a factor in Illinois' fall.[77] While Mr. Morse did not identify how each employment figure was weighted, it apparently mattered that Illinois was ranked among the top 50 schools with the highest number of unemployed 2011 graduates seeking jobs.[78]

Can Cooley's Name Change Boost its Rankings?

While Illinois has gone down dramatically in the *US News* rankings, Cooley may go up in the rankings. Since the case against Cooley was dismissed, Cooley continues to have a non-published spot in the fourth tier, the lowest tier in *US News*' rankings of law schools. Cooley's enrollment numbers have declined substantially. Perhaps to combat this decline, Cooley officially became affiliated in September 2013 with Western Michigan University

76. Please consult Tables 1-1 and 1-2 in Appendix A where I reveal the percentage of 2011 graduates employed in long-term, fulltime bar-passage-required jobs. In Appendix B, I have created a matrix for students to use when comparing law schools and have provided a matrix example comparing four law schools.

77. Johnathan Hettinger and Lauren Rohr, *UIUC College of Law drops 12 spots in national rankings?*, The Daily Illini, Mar 13, 2013, *available at* http://www.dailyillini.com/news/campus/article_8cc3a898-8b9a-11e2-b45b-001a4bcf6878.html#user-comment-area.

78. *Id.* Note this news story stated Illinois is number 31. Please see Table 3 in Appendix A for a list of the top 50 schools ranked from highest to lowest *number* of unemployed-but-seeking 2011 graduates. In Table 3, Illinois is ranked at 34. Had I ranked the schools starting with the highest *percentage* of unemployed graduates, Illinois would have been ranked at 31.

and is now the Western Michigan University Thomas M. Cooley Law School. Because of Western Michigan's relatively better standing in *US News'* college rankings, the name change may benefit Cooley by improving its public perception—people shorten the name to the WMU Law School or people see the first part of the name—Western Michigan—and never notice "Cooley" in the official name.[79] As a result of operating under its new name, Cooley may boost its standing in *US News'* law school rankings like Dickinson did when it became part of Penn State. Critics are skeptical that the name change will improve Cooley's standing. In either case, prospective students should not let the name change *alone* influence their enrollment decision.

My Advice: Don't Rely on *US News*; Do Your Own Analysis

In summary, I hope the reader is persuaded by my in-depth analyses of Nebraska and Illinois that a host of factors must be considered before deciding which school's offer should be accepted. While the differences in employment for graduates of both schools is arguably somewhat similar, the rankings difference in 2012 was huge—55 places—and Illinois's tuition was dramatically more than Nebraska's. The US rankings system does not deserve the heavy weight that most law school applicants give it. Don't get me wrong; I would not recommend turning down an offer from Harvard just because a fourth-tier school offered a full scholarship. Harvard graduates enjoy a very high employment rate, and Harvard is truly a national school because it is a top-ten feeder school in all major legal job markets. However, most law school applicants are not going to get an offer from Harvard or any of the other Top 14 law schools. As a result, most students, after doing a careful analysis of each school making an offer of admission, may find that the job prospects for schools with different rankings are similar while the amount of debt the student will incur can be drastically different. Prospective law students should look to bar association directory to see whether a substantial number of graduates of the targeted school are employed as attorneys at mid-size and large law firms. The bottom line is that, when assessing competing offers, an applicant's goal should be to accept an offer from the school that has the best employment outcomes and overall data ***and*** that is located in the state where the applicant wants to practice law or is open to practicing law.[80]

79. For a discussion of the name change and its impact, *see Cooley Weathering Decline in Enrollment*, Lansing State J. (Lansing, Mich.), Aug. 18, 2013, at A1.

80. Too many law students go to out-of-state schools when they know they intend to go back home to practice law and tragically find out that it is very difficult to get a job back home due to a lack of strong job connections to legal employers in the home state. Therefore, Professor Seto's research is worth considering in detailed to see which schools are top feeder schools for the 11 major legal job markets he studied.

Chapter 8

The ABA Leaves Much to Be Desired

"In a year when a number of lawsuits alleging consumer protection law violations have been filed against ABA law schools, when major newspapers have devoted thousands of words to problems with law school reporting practices, and when two United States Senators have encouraged significant changes to [ABA] policies, it is surprising that the ABA is resorting to half measures instead of tackling a major problem head on."[1] U.S. Senator Barbara Boxer

Senators Barbara Boxer (D-CA), Charles Grassley (R-IA), and Tom Coburn (R-OK) have tried to get the ABA as well as the US Department of Education to address the lack of transparency problem in the legal academy and to address the ABA's alleged lack of adequate oversight of ABA-accredited law schools.[2] One of the major changes that Senator Boxer called for was for the ABA to create a mechanism for "independent oversight and auditing of statistics reported by law schools." That did not happen. At this point in the book, the reader should realize that the new ABA standards make more transparent employment data available to law school applicants. However, the ABA's performance of its role as commander-in-chief of law-school disclosures is lacking. The ABA is the entity that is truly responsible for this task given that it is the only entity approved by the US Department of Education to accredit American law schools and to exercise oversight over accredited law schools. The ABA has not sanctioned any law school for reporting deceptive employment data,[3] and the courts are largely unreceptive to lawsuits filed by law graduates.

1. Press Release, Boxer Urges American Bar Association to Take Stronger Steps to Protect Law School Students, U.S. Senator Barbara Boxer (D-CA) (Oct. 6, 2011) *available at* http://boxer.senate.gov/en/press/releases/033111b.cfm (including letter dated Oct. 6, 2011, to William Robinson III, then-president of the ABA, urging him to implement changes to protect law students from misleading reporting practices by law schools).

2. Besides Senator Boxer, Senator Grassley also wrote a letter to the ABA president, and in it, Senator Grassley expressed his concern that, among other things, the ABA "was barely granted renewed recognition by the U.S. Department of Education's accreditation experts." *See* Letter from Charles E. Grassley, U.S. Senator (R-Iowa), to Stephen N. Zack, ABA President *available at* http://www.grassley.senate.gov/about/upload/2011-07-11-Grassley-to-ABA.pdf. Senators Boxer and Coburn wrote a letter to the U.S. Department of Education's Inspector General asking Kathleen Tighe to provide information about law school job placement, bar passage and loan debt statistics in light of serious concerns raised about the accuracy and transparency of information being provided to prospective law school students. *See* Dennis Cariello, *Senators Coburn and Boxer Request OIG Examination of American Law Schools*, Educ. Industry Reporter, Oct.14, 2011, *available at* http://www.educationindustryreporter.com/2011/10/senators-coburn-and-boxer-request-oig-examination-of-american-law-schools/.

3. At this time, the ABA has not responded to a formal complaint filed by Law School Transparency against Rutgers School of Law-Camden for allegedly violating ABA standards when its associate dean of enrollment sent recruiting emails containing allegedly misleading employment and salary data. *See*

That means a heavy burden is on prospective students to become fully informed about a school before making an enrollment decision. As a result of the ABA's failure to establish a system to independently audit law school reporting practices and its failure to require full disclosure about a number of matters, the ABA will prevent prospective students from acquiring accurate information critical to enrollment decisions.

The purpose of this chapter is to show the reader that despite recent actions taken by the ABA and despite the availability of standardized reporting of law school data in the LSAC Guide, prospective students must continue to rely on law schools and third parties for information and must figure out how to interpret the information obtained. Although this chapter is short, I feel it is necessary to highlight for prospective students how much information students still cannot find from an independent source.

Table 8-1 (next page) is an expansion of the table from Chapter 3, and I revised it to demonstrate which information is published in the annual LSAC Guide and which information must be obtained from law schools and other third parties.

Omissions From Employment and Salary Data

Most of Chapter 4 is devoted to explaining to the reader why Revised Standard 509 is not sufficient to lead to full disclosure of all facts regarding a school's employment and salary data. However, I think it is important to briefly reiterate a few key points. Because of definitions provided by the ABA and NALP, law schools can manipulate categories for employment type and employment status to create higher employment rates. That means prospective students still have to contact the schools and make additional inquiries. For example, prospective students need to ask the career services director where the law school accounted for graduates working temporarily as research assistants for professors. Were the research assistants included in the category for bar-passage-required jobs or for JD-advantage jobs? Inclusion in the former category would be misleading as passage of the bar exam is not necessary to perform the job. The format required by Revised Standard 509 does not force law schools to disclose the number graduates actually working as *lawyers* at law firms in bar-passage-required jobs. Therefore, prospective students need ask law school personnel for that figure. If prospective students want to know, for example, about the median salary of graduates working in law firms with a size less than 51 attorneys, they will have to ask law school personnel. Note, however, that law schools have no obligation under Revised Standard 509 to collect or disclose salary data.[4]

Complaint Filed With ABA Against Rutgers—Camden, Law School Transparency, Dec. 29, 2012, http://www.lawschooltransparency.com/2012/12/complaint-filed-against-rutgers-camden/.

4. In March 2012, the ABA stated that it "'declined to require the collection and publication of salary data because fewer than 45 percent of law graduates contacted by their law schools report their salaries.'" A single PDF file containing comment letters regarding revisions to Standard 509 is on the ABA's website at http://www.americanbar.org/content/dam/aba/administrative/legal_education_and_admissions_to_the_bar/council_reports_and_resolutions/june_2012_council_open_session/2012_src_memo_to_council_re_509_and_16_w_comments.authcheckdam.pdf (last visited Oct. 11, 2012) (hereafter "ABA Comment Letters").

Table 8-1.

Broad Considerations	Individual Factors to Consider	Recent ABA Action	LSAC Guide Has Info	Rely on Law School and Others to Provide Info
1. Matriculation & Graduation	1. Admission Policy or Practices	Sanctioned Illinois and Villanova	✓	✓
	2. Attrition Rate		✓	
	3. Transfer-out Number		✓	
	4. Diversity of attrition/transfer out numbers			✓
	5. Academic support programs	No ABA Standards		✓
2. Bar Passage Likelihood	1. Bar-passage rate		✓	
	2. University-provided bar-prep support			✓
3. Employment Prospects	1. Employment status for last 3 years	New ABA Standards	✓^	
	2. Employment type for last 3 years	New ABA Standards	✓^	
	3. Overall employment rate for last 3 years	New ABA Standards	✓^	
	4. Career services support			✓
4. Salary Potential	1. Salary data for employment type or status	Unchanged#		✓*
	2. Salary data published by NALP and others			✓*
5. How to Pay for Education	1. Cost of Tuition and COL expenses		✓	✓
	2. Scholarship offers		✓	✓
	3. Scholarship Retention Rate	New ABA Standards		✓
	4. Curve for retention of scholarships			✓
	5. Work available during semesters/summers			✓
	6. Work Study			✓
	7. Student loan amount			✓
	8. Loan forgiveness/ payment-reduction programs			✓

* Reported salary data must be taken with a grain of salt. Most graduates are not going to earn six-figure salaries; ^ Must consult each year's LSAC Guide; # The ABA chose not to mandate salary disclosures even though several parties urged it to do so.

Applicants should not be surprised if they cannot get accurate and complete answers from some schools about their employment and salary data. As part of my research for this book, I had a difficult time getting a few law schools to provide seemingly non-controversial data, such as the number of students enrolled in a start-up law school. If prospective students make greater demands for relevant information, law schools will start to provide it.

Shortcomings of Matriculation-Related Data

In addition to the ABA's shortcomings in disclosure requirements for employment and salary data, the ABA does not require schools to disclose any additional matriculation-related data than what is already available in the LSAC Guide. This Guide displays information regarding each law school's attrition rates, transfers-out numbers, and bar-passage rates.[5] As a result of the foregoing published information, a prospective student will be able to determine whether a school has high attrition rates, high transfer-out numbers, and low bar-passage rates. However, the prospective student will not learn from the LSAC Guide whether these negative statistics have a disparate impact based on race, ethnicity, gender or age. For instance, a prospective student who is a 55-year-old Hispanic female cannot tell if (1) women disproportionately withdraw for family reasons, (2) older students disproportionately lose their merit-based scholarships, or (3) minorities disproportionately flunk out of that law school. Anyone seeking such information must ask a law school representative. Unfortunately, at schools with substantially-negative, matriculation-related data, the representative's statements may be incomplete and, therefore, misleading. Recall in Chapter 2 that a few courts have held that law schools owe no duty to applicants to fully disclose all the facts. Consequently, prospective law students should be guarded.

Negative matriculation-related data should naturally lead a prospective student to ask about a school's academic support programs. The ABA has no standards or disclosure requirements regarding academic support services geared towards matriculating students. As a result, prospective students need to search for information about a school's academic support outreach. I recommend that students speak directly to the persons in charge of academic support services and not to admissions personnel, who may be uninformed and may be inclined to oversell the qualities of the law school or what it has to offer students. Prospective students should ask to be put in touch with former participants in these various services to determine whether they thought such services were helpful in improving their GPAs. Additionally, while the LSAC Guide discloses each school's first-time and overall bar-passage rates, it does not contain any information about a school's

---

5. *After the JD: First Results of a National Study of Legal Careers*, THE NALP FOUNDATION FOR LAW CAREER RESEARCH AND EDUCATION & THE AMERICAN BAR FOUNDATION (2004), *available at* http://www.americanbarfoundation.org/uploads/cms/documents/ajd.pdf. I have not talked about some data provided by the LSAC Guide, such as LSAT scores, because that information may be relevant for deciding whether a law school worth applying to in the first place. My discussion assumes a prospective student has multiple offers of admission and needs to understand what data are available and relevant in deciding which offer to accept.

bar-exam support services. Therefore, prospective students must once again rely on law schools to provide accurate information about such services.

Accuracy of Information from Career Support Services

Prospective students must rely on law schools to truthfully describe their career support services to aid them in finding permanent and temporary positions, including work-study jobs and summer associate positions. The LSAC Guide does not provide information regarding career support services. News organizations have reported that there is perhaps a misunderstanding among students regarding the purpose of a career services office. Some students may believe that it is up to career services officers to find them a job. In my fourteen years of teaching, I have even heard about a few parents complaining that the career services office had not done enough to help their adult children find jobs. Perhaps, the name change should be a clue as to the office's purpose because the term "career *placement* office" has long ago been replaced by the "career *services* office." Most career services offices believe their role is to support students in their preparation for the job hunt as well as for the hunt itself, but, ultimately, the students are the ones who are responsible for securing a job. Bloggers have taken a very negative view of law school career services offices, claiming, for instance, that they "fundamentally fail because most focus not on building student skills in long-term career development and professionalism, but rather in short-term job application skills."[6]

Many students feel that career services support help only those in the top ten or twenty percent of the class and that little-to-nothing is done to help those in the bottom half of the class.[7] I do not envy the people employed in career services because at any given point in time they have a good amount of critics no matter how good the job market is. Some career services personnel are, however, justifiably the recipients of anger from unemployed graduates if their schools "cooked" the employment data. But career services personnel should not be blamed for the depressed legal job market. At the end of the day, students have to realize that they have to do a fair amount of networking themselves in order to find jobs. My point here is not to defend any law school's career services office, but to tell prospective students that relying on a school's reported data is not enough—they need to interview the career services director, along with current students at the school and even alumni, to assess the extent of the school's career services support. Recognize that a school may actually offer various services that are helpful but that participation in those services could be low. Too often, students fail to take advantage of services available to them and erroneously believe the services do not exist.

---

6. Aaron Street, *Law School Career Services Fail, But there are Fixes*, LAWYERIST.COM (Jan. 5, 2010), *available at* http://lawyerist.com/law-school-career-services-fail/.

7. Laura A. Calloway & Brad Carr, *Summary Report: Survey of New Admittees Regarding Law Student Debt and Post-law School Employment*, 72 ALA. L. REV. 193, 196 (May 2011) (reporting survey results of recent graduates admitted to the Alabama bar and describing a number of survey comments, including "[c]areer services was only helpful to the top 10 percent of the class").

Information Regarding the Cost of the Legal Education

Unlike information about career services, information relevant to the cost of legal education is available through a variety of sources. Cost of tuition and cost of living expenses are reported in the LSAC Guide and on the law schools' websites. Because tuition costs and related information are reported in the LSAC Guide and on law schools' websites, prospective students may feel they are able to accurately assess how much a legal education will cost them if they enroll in a particular law school. While it seems that such information is straightforward and has no potential to mislead, that conclusion may not be correct. For example, both Capital University and The Ohio State University have law schools in urban areas of Columbus, Ohio. In the 2013 LSAC Guide, Capital University's cost of living is listed as $13,785 while Ohio State's cost of living ("COL") is $20,900. For those unfamiliar with Central Ohio, Capital University's law school is not on the university's main campus, but rather is located in downtown Columbus, minutes from the state capital. Housing is not widely available in downtown Columbus, so students must either rent an expensive downtown apartment or rent further-away inexpensive housing and commute to school.[8] While Ohio State is also an urban campus, it is not in the downtown area and has plenty of typical (i.e., more affordable) housing near the law school.

Knowing the city, I cannot reconcile the $7,115 difference in cost of living between the two law schools. Conceivably, Ohio State's COL would be lower given the greater number of affordable student housing options and lower cost of commuting one might assume. However, it could be that Ohio State's COL figure assumes students will reside in a high-end apartment because an expensive apartment complex is only one block away from the law school and was built to accommodate law students in particular.[9]

My point is not to quibble about which school's COL figure is more accurate but to tell prospective students to accurately assess the tuition and COL figures so that they correctly assess how much money they may need to borrow. Prospective law students must then carefully compare the cost of education not just between schools located in different regions but also between schools located in the same region. Prospective students should also visit the campuses and consult apartment guides to locate affordable housing in low-crime areas.

Related to the cost of education is the issue of scholarships. For each school, the LSAC Guide reports the number of grants and scholarships awarded to full and part-time students. Some of the schools that have been sued are known to award a substantial number of scholarships, but a few are accused of offering more scholarships to first-year students than can possibly be retained for the remaining years of law school. Under the ABA's revision of Standard 509, schools must now disclose to scholarship recipients the number of conditional scholarships awarded and retained for each class. Such disclosures can be by personal letter and not on the school's website. The ABA does not mandate that the school disclose the GPA a student must maintain to retain the scholarship or any

8. Commuting via public transportation is a relatively cheap option compared to driving one's own vehicle.

9. An unfurnished one-bedroom apartment in the Gateway complex is currently $860.00 per month. Some students get furnished apartments, which cost more than $1,000 per month. While that may not be considered a high price in New York or Los Angeles, it is in Columbus, Ohio.

information about how difficult it is to retain a scholarship. Furthermore, schools do not have to disclose if certain groups disproportionately lose their scholarships. Consequently, prospective law students must obtain that information from the law schools about these issues. This is not a good position for prospective students to be in, because some schools may be tempted to hide or misrepresent the truth or simply say nothing and allow students to draw erroneous conclusions, such as incorrectly concluding that a 3.2 GPA-requirement is easy to obtain in law school. As a result, prospective students could completely underestimate the amount of borrowing necessary to pay for their education and regret pursuing a law degree if they had to unwittingly incur six-figure debt to obtain it.

The Predicament of Information That Is Grossly One-Sided

The ABA has no standards or disclosure requirements regarding a number of matters critical to making a wise enrollment decision. The ABA's failure or refusal to take action or impose standards in the areas above is the main reason why I've entitled this chapter "The ABA Leaves Much To Be Desired." I am not suggesting that the ABA has not accomplished anything meaningful, but I have demonstrated how its inaction puts prospective students in the position of having to rely on the integrity of law school personnel to make truthful disclosures about the information desired. Some schools have incentives to misrepresent or hide relevant information.

Prospective students must now be aggressive in finding accurate information that is not reported by the ABA, LSAC, or NALP. Accurate information may be obtained by talking to alumni as well as members of various student organizations. Law schools, for instance, have numerous affinity groups based on religion, race, ethnicity, gender, sexual orientation, and other characteristics (*e.g.*, Middle Eastern Law Students Association). Other organizations focus on specialized areas of law or on social issues (e.g., Student Animal Legal Defense Fund). Connecting with students and alumni of these organizations may provide more accurate information than raw data provided by the schools. In summary, prospective students should seek to talk to as many people as possible to get a wide range of perspectives.

In the next two chapters, I paint a picture of the legal job market that prospective law students must be prepared to face. The legal job market is suffering from a substantial decrease in the number of traditional entry-level attorney jobs and a dramatic increase in the number of second-class, lower-paying legal jobs. However, there is a growing need for lawyers capable of providing low-cost legal services and law schools need to do more to prepare graduates for such service.

Chapter 9

Do We Have Too Many Lawyers?

Media reporting and online blogging about the tough legal job market can be framed as a debate regarding supply and demand. Many argue that we have too many lawyers. In this Chapter, I demonstrate that we do not have *enough* lawyers. We have an abundance of lawyers who want to work at *private-sector* law firms because these employers historically pay the highest wages and offer the most job security. While businesses have attorneys lined up to do their bidding, consumers in need of legal services are hard-pressed to find an attorney to represent them. Due to major funding cuts to traditional legal aid organizations and government employers, we have a severe shortage of public interest lawyers to represent poor and moderate-income families and individuals accused of crimes.

The thousands of laid-off lawyers in both the private and public sectors are now in fierce competition with each other as well as with new law graduates to find *any* attorney position. In the midst of this fierce competition, more and more lawyers are forced to attempt solo practice just to bring in income. Meanwhile, the legal bar complains that most law schools have not done enough to prepare law graduates for the actual practice of law. As fully explained in Chapter 11, a small but increasing number of law schools have gotten off the sidelines and have expanded their skills-based courses that give students practical training and have created "incubator" programs that train recent law graduates to successfully start solo practices. This chapter paints for the reader an accurate picture of the supply and demand realities in the legal job sector so that the reader can understand why I later argue for the expansion of programs that prepare graduates for solo and small-firm practice to represent those in need of affordable legal services.

Job Losses since the Start of the Great Recession

From January to August 2012, legal sector jobs whipsawed between adding jobs—offering hope—and losing jobs—exacerbating the despair among unemployed and under-employed law graduates.[1] Although September and October experienced a bump in jobs, bringing a net-gain of 6,000 jobs to legal job sector, those gains do not come close to replacing the thousands of jobs lost since the start of the Great Recession. The net gain means that about 1.12 million people are now employed in the legal job sector; however, that amounts to roughly 50,000 less people employed since the pre-recession average of

1. Claire Zillman, *Legal Sector Lost 1,400 Jobs in August, Nearly Wiping Out July Gains*, THE AM. LAWYER, Sept. 7, 2012, *available at* http://www.americanlawyer.com/PubArticleALD.jsp?id=1202570521518&Legal_Sector_Lost_1400_Jobs_in_August_Nearly_Wiping_Out_July_Gains&slreturn=20120813152941.

1.17 million people employed. Thus, the recession has demonstrated that the legal job sector is subject to downturns in the economy just like other job sectors.

The Decrease in Demand for Traditional Entry-Level Positions

The majority of jobs lost have occurred in the private sector, particularly at large law firms. When the Great Recession hit, businesses drastically cut back on the amount of legal work that was usually contracted out to the big law firms. That it turned led to massive layoffs of thousands of lawyers at US law firms.[2] Many firms closed[3] while other firms delayed the start date of recently hired graduates by as much as a year. Even though the Great Recession is officially over, many law graduates remain unemployed and underemployed in paralegal and other non-attorney positions. That's not surprising with continuing layoffs, including a 2013 layoff announcement by Weil, Gotshal & Manges, an elite large law firm, that it planned to fire 170 employees, including 60 attorneys, and cut the salaries of 30 partners. Businesses have decided that they must keep legal fees to a minimum and have, therefore, changed how they pay for legal services. To cut their own cost, some businesses have been and continue to pressure law firms to agree to receive a flat-rate retainer fee covering all work contracted out to them and have refused to agree to the customary hourly-billing structure, which is far more costly for businesses.

In addition to insisting that law firms agree to less-expensive fee structures,[4] many businesses are outsourcing low-level legal work to legal temp agencies.[5] For example, instead of paying the firms' high hourly rates to have junior associate attorneys review legal documents in preparation for trial, many businesses and law firms hire these same attorneys via legal temp agencies and, thereby, greatly reduce their costs. Stated differently, newly-minted attorneys are getting paid as little as $15 per hour from the legal temp agencies instead of six-figure salaries from law firms who used to charge their business clients hourly rates of $200 or more for those attorneys to review documents.[6] Moreover, some businesses are achieving even greater savings by outsourcing routine legal work to

---

2. *See, e.g.*, Tamanaha, Failing Law Schools, at 167 (estimating that "9,500 lawyers were let go from the 250 largest law firms" in 2009 and 2010). Although not an official labor statistic source, Lawshucks, which tracks layoffs, states that as December 2011, approximately 13,435 attorneys and staff have been laid off at major law firms since January 1, 2008. *See Lawshucks: Life In and After Biglaw*, *available at* http://lawshucks.com/layoff-tracker/ (last visited Feb. 15, 2013).

3. *See, e.g.*, Jeff Blumenthal, *Large Law Firms Shuttering Offices to Reduce Overhead*, Philadelphia Bus. J., May 6, 2011, *available at* http://www.bizjournals.com/philadelphia/print-edition/2011/05/06/large-law-firms-shuttering-offices-to.html?page=all; Jay Hancock, *Debt Hounds Wind Up Chasing Their Own Tails*, Baltimore Sun, Jan. 20, 2010, *available at* http://articles.baltimoresun.com/2010-01-20/business/1001190048_1_debt-collection-consumer-debt-debt-collectors (discussing the shutdown of Mann Bracken, one of the nation's largest debt-collection law firms).

4. For a more thorough discussion of various fee structures, *see, e.g.*, Terrence T. Murphy, *Legal Competition—How to Manage Legal Costs*, Metropolitan Corp. Counsel, at 39, June 1, 2012.

5. *See, e.g.*, Janice Fioravante, *Contract Lawyers in Hot Demand*, Crain's N.Y. Bus. 15, Jan. 9, 2012.

6. *See, e.g.*, *id.* (stating that "[c]orporations are refusing to pay $250 an hour for first- or second-year attorneys," that graduates of elite law schools are finding it difficult to secure jobs paying six-figure salaries, and that some new graduates are getting paid as little as $25 per hour as temp attorneys).

non-US firms, such as Pangea3 which charges businesses only $25 to $35 per hour for attorneys in Mumbai, India, to draft contracts.[7]

All the foregoing is good news for Corporate America because it has found cost-effective measures for reducing its legal bills. This news is, however, bad for recent law graduates who wanted to secure traditional law-firm or in-house counsel positions. As firms and companies slowly increase their hiring for permanent positions, recent law graduates will have to compete with lawyers who were laid off and are still unemployed or under-employed.

Impact of the Recession on Public Interest Lawyers

While massive layoffs at law firms have not hurt Corporate America's ability to secure legal services, layoffs among public interest firms have negatively impacted the ability of working poor and middle-class families to find affordable legal services. According to a 2005 study conducted by the Legal Services Corporation ("LSC"),[8] 80 percent of low-income individuals in need of legal services do not receive them.[9] This study confirmed the existence of the "Justice Gap," which is the disparity between the number of low-income people in need of the legal assistance and the capacity of legal aid organizations to meet those needs. The Justice Gap has only gotten worse since the recession hit. According to census data from 2010, over 46 million Americans now live at or below the poverty level, and that is an increase of 2.6 million persons from 2009 and constitutes an overall poverty rate of 15.1%.[10] That increase in the poverty rate means that nearly 1 in 5 Americans, approximately 60 million people, qualify for free legal assistance because their income is at or below 125% of the poverty level. That number is projected to grown to 62 million Americans by the end of 2015.[11]

Even though the demand for public interest lawyers has increased, the supply of public interest attorney positions has decreased. I define "public interest" or "public service" lawyer broadly to include civil legal aid attorneys, public defenders, civil rights attorneys and prosecutors along with attorneys who serve as counsel for governmental agencies. In comparison to the widespread media coverage about layoffs at law firms, the media has given little attention to the layoffs of public interest lawyers. For example, due to budget cuts, prosecuting attorney offices around the country have let go hundreds of

7. Ameet Sachdev, *Outsourcing Firms Court Corporate Work*, Chi. Trib., Dec. 28, 2010.

8. LSC is a congressionally-created and partially, federally-funded nonprofit organization that provides legal assistance in civil matters to low-income families.

9. *Documenting the Justice Gap in America*, Legal Serv. Corp. 17 (2005), *available at* http://www.lsc.gov/press/documents/LSC%20Justice%20Gap_FINAL_1001.pdf. *See also* Rebekah Diller & Emily Savner, *A Call to End Federal Restrictions on Legal Aid for the Poor*, Brennan Center for Justice 1 (2009), *available at* http://brennan.3cdn.net/7e05061cc505311545_75m6ivw3x.pdf ("Study after study finds that 80 percent of the civil legal needs of low-income people go unmet.").

10. *See* U.S. Census Bureau, U.S. Dep't of Commerce, Ser. No. P60-239, Income, Poverty, and Health Insurance Coverage in the United States: 2010, at 2, 14 (2011), *available at* http:// www.census.gov/prod/2011pubs/p60-239.pdf.

11. Memorandum from LSC President J. Sandman, July 19, 2013 *available at* http://www/lsc.gov/sites/lsc.gov/files/LSC/pdfs/Management_sRevisedfy2015BudgetRequestRecommendation(7-19-2013).pdf

attorneys,[12] including 36 prosecutors laid off over a five-year period by the King County Prosecuting Attorney's Office in Seattle, Washington.[13] While some prosecutors have created unique programs that allow law students to handle misdemeanor cases,[14] other prosecutors are sometimes forced to let misdemeanor cases go due to insufficient staff, and their ability to successfully prosecute felony cases can be overwhelming.[15]

Besides prosecutors being laid off due to budget cuts, public defenders in various jurisdictions have been laid off, including 15 attorneys let go in 2010 by the San Joaquin County's Public Defender's Office in California,[16] as well as 60 public defenders laid off in Minnesota since 2008.[17] The loss in public defender jobs has left the remaining public defenders with a staggering caseload that threatens the effectiveness of the legal representation they can provide. As one public defender put it, "his lawyers are too overburdened, understaffed and underfunded to effectively represent poor people."[18] Even though many public defender offices are outsourcing thousands of criminal cases to private attorneys to deal with the backlog of cases, many of these private lawyers have no criminal defense experience. Some of these private attorneys volunteer to take the cases on a paid or pro bono (i.e., free) basis while others are forced into representing people accused of crimes due to local rules imposed on licensed lawyers.[19] In either scenario, it is logical to

---

12. I could not find any exact figures, but as a result of finding numerous news stories about layoffs at prosecuting attorney offices, it seems the job loss is in the hundreds. *See, e.g.*, Greg Bluestein, *State Budget Cuts Clog Criminal Justice System*, Oct. 26, 2011, *available at* http://www.msnbc.msn.com/id/45049812/ns/us_news-crime_and_courts/t/state-budget-cuts-clog-criminal-justice-system/ ("The National District Attorneys Association estimates that hundreds of millions of dollars in criminal justice funding and scores of positions have been cut amid the economic downturn, hampering the ability of authorities to investigate and prosecute cases.").

13. *See* Bob Young, *Some Fees Up Under County's 2013 Budget*, SEATTLE TIMES, at B3, Nov. 14, 2012 (stating that due to a budget cut of $875,000, 10 positions would be lost in the King County Prosecuting Attorney's Office).

14. For example the city attorney for the City of Columbus has created a "Prosecution Resource Unit," which is a mediation program for minor misdemeanors to be resolved without criminal prosecution. *See* City of Columbus, *Columbus City Bulletin 2011 Annual Report*, at 16, *available at* http://council.columbus.gov/uploadedFiles/City_Council/Gutters/Most_Requested/2011%20Annual%20Report.pdf (last visited Feb. 16, 2013) ("In 2011, this program operated in the evenings with mediators from the [Ohio State University] Moritz College of Law, Capital University Law School, and members of the alternative dispute resolution community in an effort to resolve disputes without resorting to criminal prosecution. The Program scheduled 302 mediation hearings in 2011, resulting in 184 hearings conducted. Of these 184 mediation hearings, 75% resolved with an agreement.").

15. *See, e.g.*, Mark Gilger, *ADA Laid Off*, NEWS-ITEM (SHAMOKIN, PA.), Feb. 1, 2012 (discussing the layoff of an assistant district attorney with years of experience and quoting District Attorney Tony Rosini as saying "[h]andling misdemeanors is also important, but given the staff cuts we have had, it is impossible to cover all cases").

16. *See* Merrill Balassone, *Cases in the Hundreds Anger Stanislaus County Public Defenders*, MODESTO BEE, Oct. 3, 2010, *available at* http://www.modbee.com/2010/10/03/1366221/cases-in-the-hundreds-anger-stanislaus.html.

17. *See* John Brewer, *More Fines and Fewer trials? Public Defenders Ask Relief*, ST. PAUL PIONEER PRESS (MINN.), at A1, Sept. 16, 2010.

18. *See* David Ovalle, *Public Defender's Office: Cutback in Public Defender Caseloads Disputed*, MIAMI HERALD, at B1, Mar. 30, 2009 (quoting Carlos J. Martinez, the Public Defender for Miami-Dade County).

19. *See, e.g.*, John Simerman, *Judge Taps New Orleans Noteworthies to Handle Criminal Cases*, NEW ORLEANS TIMES PICAYUNE, Feb. 15, 2012, *available at* http://www.nola.com/crime/index.ssf/2012/02/judge_taps_new_orleans_notewor.html (Martha Castillo, an in-house attorney for an insurance company, tried but was unsuccessful in getting removed from a case where she was required to represent a defendant in drug case. She told the judge "I have no experience or skills. I never tried a criminal case.").

conclude that some defendants represented by inexperienced private attorneys are getting ineffective legal representation, resulting in devastating consequences, such as wrongful conviction and imprisonment.[20]

Like public defender offices, legal aid organizations have laid off hundreds of legal aid lawyers, who provide free legal representation in civil cases to eligible poor people. In 2010 and 2011 alone, several legal aid offices closed.[21] During that same time frame, legal aid organizations let go hundreds of attorneys and other staff employees, and those layoffs contributed to a total job loss of 833 legal aid employees by the end of 2011.[22] Chairman Levi expects that number to grow to 1,500 lost positions by the end of 2012.[23] He concludes that the Justice Gap has now become the "Justice Chasm" since the start of the Great Recession, leaving millions of Americans eligible for free legal representation but unable to obtain it.[24]

The Justice Gap is expected to get worse for several reasons. First, federal and other funding sources to LSC programs have been cut dramatically,[25] resulting in fewer legal aid lawyers available to serve low-income consumers. Second, future funding for LSC programs face an uncertain future depending on how the battles over budget cuts play out in Congress in 2013.[26] In 2007, the ratio of *all* lawyers providing legal services to all persons was one lawyer to 429 persons. However, for that same year, the ratio of legal aid lawyers serving low-income persons was one legal aid lawyer to 6,415 low-income persons.[27] Since the recession, that ratio has gotten worse due to the layoff of legal aid attorneys and the increase in Americans living at the poverty level.

Besides low-income families, many middle-class consumers cannot afford legal representation.[28] By one estimate, the majority of the US population make too much to qualify for free legal aid but cannot afford traditional attorney's fees when legal representation is

---

20. The situation in St. Louis is so bad that now some people accused of crimes are ineligible to be assigned a public defender. They have to wait to see if volunteer attorneys will step up to take their cases. Donna Walter, *St. Louis Judge Allows Public Defenders to Decline Many Cases*, Missouri Lawyers Media, Oct. 2, 2012, *available at* http://molawyersmedia.com/blog/2012/10/02/public-defenders-will-decline-hundreds-of-new-cases/ ("The St. Louis Circuit Court is looking for volunteer attorneys to represent more than 1,500 defendants a year who will not be represented by public defenders under new caseload rules.").

21. See, e.g., John Wester, *An Overlooked Crisis: Not Enough Legal Aid for the Poor*, Charlotte Observer, Dec. 8, 2011 (reporting that due to major cuts in federal and state funding in 2011, the Legal Aid of NC in Charlotte had to close four offices and let go 30 employees and predicting that budget cuts in 2012 will lead to further job eliminations).

22. Legal Services Corp, *Updates: Staff Reductions Hit Legal Aid Programs* (Feb. 2012) http://www.lsc.gov/media/lscupdates/2012/lsc-updates-february-8-2012.

23. Chairman Levi's Remarks to the ABA.

24. John G. Levi, *Losing Access to Legal Aid*, News & Observer (Raleigh NC), Oct. 1, 2012.

25. LSC's Fiscal Year 2013 Budget Request, *available at* http://www.lsc.gov/congress/funding/lscs-fiscal-year-2013-budget-request (stating that "Federal appropriations for basic field grants have declined by 18 percent between FY 2010 and FY 2012.").

26. In August of 2011, Representative Austin Scott (R-GA) proposed a bill (HR 2774) that sought to not just reduce funding for LSC, but to get rid of the LSC by repealing the LSC Act entirely. Congress drastically reduced federal funding to the LSC in 2012. Additionally, even the GOP lost seats in the US Senate and the House in the November 2012 election cycle, republicans are still insisting on balancing the budget by reducing or eliminating funding to many organizations, which would presumably include the LSC.

27. Quintin Johnstone, *Law and Policy Issues Concerning the Provision of Adequate Legal Services for the Poor*, 20 Cornell J.L. & Pub. Pol'y 571, 573 n.5 (2011).

28. *See* Gillian K. Hadfield, *The Price of Law: How the Market for Lawyers Distorts the Justice System*, 98 Mich. L. Rev. 953 (2000).

needed.[29] For instance, the average hourly rate for a lawyer in La Crosse County, Wisconsin is $150,[30] but it is $250 per hour for a lawyer in Arizona.[31] Depending on the firm size or the type of legal representation sought and the region where it is sought, lawyers charge fees that are beyond what many families can afford to pay. In a 2009 study of Texas attorneys, the State Bar of Texas found that the median hourly rate charged by solo attorneys was $198 while firms with 201 to 400 attorneys charged a median hourly rate of $368.[32] Consider as a case in point that before major changes to the federal bankruptcy law in 2005, the average attorney fee for a Chapter 7 case was $712; however, two years later, it increased to $1,078.[33] The U.S. Bankruptcy Court in Miami reported that a Miami attorney charges consumers an average Chapter 7 fee of $1,500, which is cost prohibitive for many consumers, and is linked to the drop in bankruptcy filings in the Miami area.[34]

The high cost of traditional attorney fees has led more and more consumers to resort to companies, such as LegalZoom, Rocket Lawyer, Nolo, and Quicken WillMaker Plus, that provide online do-it-yourself ("DIY") forms and instructions for creating wills, powers of attorney, limited liability companies, etc. However, in study of DIY wills from several online companies, Consumer Reports found that unless a consumer is leaving his or her entire estate to a spouse, these wills are no match for one done by a competent lawyer and that the language in some of the wills could lead to unintended results.[35]

Law schools can do more to increase the number of lawyers committed to public service so that consumers do not have to rely solely on do-it-yourself companies. Many law schools have reduced their class sizes by following an admission strategy of admitting students that have LSAT scores high enough to help the schools maintain their historical median LSAT scores so that they can retain their ranking status with *US News*.[36] The problem with this admission strategy is that it can result in the exclusion of students who can do well in law school and have a demonstrated commitment to public service and want to use the law degree to serve under-represented populations.

Law schools can look to several pipeline programs to find students who may have a

---

29. Billie Tarascio, *A New Breed of Practitioner*, LAW PRACTICE MAGAZINE, August 2011.

30. Jessica Larsen, *Justice for All: Clinic Offers Free Legal Advice*, LA CROSSE TRIB. (Wisconsin), Nov. 17, 2011.

31. Christine Harvey, *Lawyers Say Increased Use of Do-It-Yourself Legal Services Risky*, BUS. J. (Phoenix), Sept. 30, 2011.

32. DEP'T. OF RESEARCH AND ANALYSIS, STATE BAR OF TEXAS, *2009 Hourly Fact Sheet*, *available at* http://www.texasbar.com/AM/Template.cfm?Section=Research_and_Analysis&Template=/CM/ContentDisplay.cfm&ContentID=11240.

33. *See* U.S. GOV'T ACCOUNTABILITY OFFICE, GAO-08-697, DOLLAR COSTS ASSOCIATED WITH THE BANKRUPTCY ABUSE PREVENTION AND CONSUMER PROTECTION ACT OF 2005, (Jun 27, 2008), *available at* http://www.gao.gov/products/GAO-08-697.

34. *See* Daniel Bortz, *Are You Too Broke to Go Bankrupt?*, U.S. NEWS & WORLD REP., July 26, 2012.

35. *See Legal DIY Websites Are No Match for a Pro*, CONSUMER REP. MAG., (Sept. 2012), *available at* http://www.consumerreports.org/cro/magazine/2012/09/legal-diy-websites-are-no-match-for-a-pro/index.htm (Consumer reports asked to serve as experts "three law professors—Gerry W. Beyer of Texas Tech University School of Law, who specializes in estates and trusts; Richard K. Neumann of Hofstra University, a contract specialist; and Norman Silber, an expert in consumer and commercial law at Hofstra and Yale—to review in a blind test the processes and resulting documents.").

36. *See* Joe Palazzolo and Chelsea Phipps, *With Profession Under Stress, Law Schools Cut Admissions*, Wall Street Journal Online, June 11, 2012, http://online.wsj.com/article/SB10001424052702303444204577458411514818378.html (Professor William Henderson (Indiana University Maurer School of Law) states that law schools "are trying to get a class [with a median LSAT score] that mirrors prior classes, but with fewer applicants and enrollees.").

propensity towards public service.[37] Pre-law-school pipeline programs were initially established to prepare minorities for legal careers in order to increase diversity in the legal profession but today focus on preparing students of all races who come from socio-economically disadvantaged backgrounds.[38] The City University of New York (CUNY) School of Law created in 2006 the Pipeline for Justice Program, which is a unique approach to finding public-service minded students and preparing them for admission to law school.[39] From the pool of applicants that CUNY rejected because their LSAT scores were too low, CUNY identifies the applicants with a record of public service and invites them to participate in an intensive LSAT preparation course. The course has two parts and runs from October to June. During the first part, students take a minimum of fifteen practice LSAT exams. During the second part, students participate in an intensive course designed to improve their critical reading and writing skills. Students also re-take the LSAT. Associate Dean Mary Lu Bilek, who co-teaches the course, finds that students who initially scored low can often substantially improve their LSAT score "not by gaming the test, but by actually learning new ways to think critically." CUNY admits the students who successfully complete the course. Because these admitted students have a track record of public service prior to taking the course, CUNY'S Pipeline for Justice Program helps it to further its "mission to provide access to the profession for historically underserved groups."

A survey of all the pipeline programs is beyond the scope of this book; however, the reader should be aware that the number of various pipeline programs is growing. Academics knowledgeable about these programs are offering ideas about how to make them more effective.[40] I simply urge the legal academy to create more of them and to use the pipeline programs as a vehicle of discovering, admitting, and preparing public-service-minded individuals to represent consumers who cannot afford the fees typically charged by law firms.

In summary, businesses have various cost-effective ways of getting their legal service needs taken care of, but low-income and middle-class families are largely left to face their legal problems alone.[41] While there appears to be an abundance of lawyers in general, the bottom line is that the demand for public interest lawyers far exceeds the supply of them. In other words, we have a *severe* shortage of lawyers that can represent low-income families who qualify for legal aid and middle-class families who cannot afford average legal fees. In the next two chapters, I will discuss the dramatic increase in "second class" entry-level attorney jobs and what law schools can do to produce more "practice ready" graduates who are committed to public service and are trained them to provide low bono services.

---

37. Another pipeline program that is popular in Ohio is the Law and Leadership Institute (LLI) pipeline program. http://www.lawandleadership.org/home. This program allows high school students from under-served urban communities throughout Ohio to become familiar with the legal profession by participating in an intensive college preparatory program in law and leadership. The Ohio State University's Moritz College of Law participates in this pipeline program, and it is becoming increasingly important for other law schools to partake of similar pipeline programs.

38. E. Christopher Johnson Jr., *Increasing Diversity and Creating Responsible Citizens and Leaders*, 91 Michigan Bar Journal 32 (2012).

39. City Univ. N.Y. Sch. of Law, The Pipeline to Justice: CUNY Law Enhances Access to the Profession 8, *available at* http://www.law.cuny.edu/academics/social-justice/pipeline/pipeline.pdf.

40. *See, e.g.*, Laura Rothstein, *Shaping the Tributary, the Why, What and How of Pipeline Programs to Increase Diversity in Legal Education and the Legal Profession*, 40 Journal of Law & Educ. 551 (2011).

41. *See, e.g.*, Chairman Levi's Remarks to the ABA, *supra* (Chairman Levi states that "[LSC] legal service programs are forced to turn away over 50 percent of those seeking help because of inadequate" funding); Lisa Brodoff, *Lifting Burdens: Proof, Social Justice, and Public Assistance Administrative Hearings*, 30 J. of the Nat'l Assoc. of the Admin. Law Judiciary 601 (2010) (citing to a study in the Washington state that "found that 87% of low-income households experience a civil legal problem each year, 8% experience a public benefits problem, and 88% of low-income people face their legal problems without help from an attorney").

Chapter 10

Post-Recession Rise in Déclassé Legal Jobs

"BigLaw is Heaven.
Document review is Purgatory.
Insurance defense is the 7th Circle of Hell."[1]

Although businesses have an increased need for legal services now that the economy is rebounding, businesses are still insisting on the most cost-efficient fee structure to pay for legal work done by American law firms. As a result, some law firms are hiring again but not at the pre-recession levels and a significant amount of new hires are in "second-class" or déclassé law firm jobs, such as document review jobs (explained later). This trend in legal hiring is bad news for you if you are a prospective or current law student with aspirations of getting that big law-firm job.

I do not intend to offend anyone by stating that the staff and career attorney positions are déclassé jobs. I distinguish these various déclassé attorney jobs for new law graduates from jobs taken by experienced attorneys who *voluntarily* work in non-partner positions at the law firms or as specialized experienced contract attorneys hired either by the firms directly or legal staffing agencies.[2]

Rather than being hired as associate attorneys in traditional, partnership-track positions, many new law graduates are being hired as "staff" or "career" attorneys. For example, Orrick, Herrington & Sutcliffe, a large law firm based in San Francisco, bought and renovated a building in Wheeling, West Virginia, where it houses an operations center consisting of 300 employees. They perform various functions, including serving the firm's 1,000-plus attorneys. Of the 300 employees, 17 are "career" attorneys who are not on the partnership track and who handle routine functions for the firm's traditional associate attorneys and partners. Also, 26 attorneys review documents in preparation for trial. By moving document-review and routine functions to West Virginia, Orrick boasts that it achieves an estimated "savings of over $5 million annually primarily as a result of lower salaries and real estate expenses than it would pay in San Francisco or other major met-

---

1. Akshen, Urban Dictionary, posted July 7, 2006, http://www.urbandictionary.com/define.php?term=document%20review&defid=1849729. This online dictionary is content-generated by users who can provide real or fictitious names. I could not find Akshen's identity.

2. Lawyers in the latter category may be proud members of the National Association of Freelance Legal Professionals. At the end of the following news story, Lisa Solomon posted a comment taking issue with the author making it appear that all contract attorneys were forced into undesirable employment positions and stated that "[t]o distinguish themselves from contract lawyers, an increasing number of lawyers who provide services to law firms as independent contractors call themselves 'freelance lawyers.'" *See* Janice Fioravante, *Contract Lawyers in Hot Demand*, Crain's N.Y. Bus., Jan. 8, 2012, *available at* http://www.crainsnewyork.com/article/20120108/SMALLBIZ/301089988.

ropolitan cities." These staff and career attorneys are paid substantially less than traditional associate attorneys and are not eligible to make partner, which means they will never have an ownership interest in the firm or get a share of the firm's profits. Nevertheless, Orrick maintains these are not "second class" lawyers.[3]

Similar to Orrick, the Pittsburgh-based office of Reed Smith opened a customer center in downtown Pittsburgh that houses 300 employees to assist the firm's 1,700 attorneys worldwide. Of the 300 employees, 75 are "staff" attorneys who are not on the partnership track and who perform document reviews and other legal work. Gary Sokulski, the chief operating officer for Reed Smith, stated that "[i]nstead of hiring a $130,000-a-year new lawyer, we get these people for *less than half that number*."[4]

According to a 2011 survey of 200 of the nation's largest law firms, the National Association of Women Lawyers ("NAWL") found that 75% of the firms employ staff and/or career attorneys who are not on the partnership track.[5] Moreover, the majority of the staff/career attorney positions are held by women.[6] Therefore, female law students need to be aware that these non-partner-track jobs may be disproportionately offered to them.

In the face of criticism that the entry-level career and staff attorney jobs are second-class positions, law firms try to put a positive spin on the fact that these attorneys will never make partner and have relatively low salaries. The firms claim these attorneys get to do the same work as traditional partnership-track associate attorneys, but they work fewer hours and have less responsibility, thereby making them ideal jobs "for mothers, adjunct faculty lawyers and those who volunteer time to boards or civic organizations."[7] However, the déclassé law-firm attorney jobs discussed here are not the jobs most new graduates *prefer* to have no matter how much the partners at law firms try to recast them as desirable employment.

Several news stories cut to the chase and have identified these jobs as a second-class group of lawyers.[8] Describing the staff attorneys at Orrick, one author depicted the reality of the situation:

> The nation's biggest law firms are creating a second tier of workers, stripping pay and prestige from one of the most coveted jobs in the business world. Make no mistake: These are full-fledged lawyers, not paralegals, and they do the same work traditional legal associates do. But they earn less than half the pay of their counterparts—usually around $60,000—and they know from the outset they will never make partner.[9]

So how is a new law graduate supposed to deal with six-figure student loan debt and struggle to make it on a much-lower-than-expected salary? As explained in Chapter 14,

---

3. Joyce Gannon, *Law Firm's Operations Center Helps Revitalize West Virginia Mill Town*, Pitt. Post-Gazette, Aug. 13, 2012, at A12, *available at* http://www.post-gazette.com/stories/business/news/law-firms-operations-center-helps-restore-an-old-building-revitalizes-west-virginia-mill-town-648761/ (last visited Nov. 13, 2012).

4. *Id.* (emphasis supplied).

5. *See 7 Disturbing Trends for Female Lawyers*, Missouri Lawyers Media, Fed. 14, 2012 (finding that "[w]omen lawyers are more likely to occupy positions that are not on a partner track" and "[w]omen represent 55 percent of staff attorneys").

6. *Id.*

7. *See, e.g.*, Chad Halcom, *Alternative Career Paths Rising: Firms Divided on Trend*, Crain's Detroit Bus., June 27, 2011, *available at* http://www.crainsdetroit.com/article/20110626/FREE/306269985/off-the-law-partner-track-alternative-career-paths-rising-firms-divided-on-trend#.

8. *Id.*

9. *See* Catherine Rampell, *At Well-Paying Law Firms, a Low-Paid Corner*, N.Y. Times, at A1, May 24, 11, *available at* 2011 WLNR 10317647 (Westlaw).

these relatively-low paid staff/career attorneys may be eligible for a federal repayment assistance program so that they can reduce their student loan payments to an affordable amount. Under this program, if these low-paid private-sector attorneys remain in such a position for 25 years and make the required loan payments during that time, they will have any remaining student loan debt wiped out—forgiven. What that means is that law firms are in the long-run shifting their "savings" from creating career/staff attorney positions onto to the taxpayers!

Unlike the graduates who obtain entry-level career/staff attorney positions, graduates who work for temp agencies have it the worst because they can get paid as little as $15 per hour to review documents and do not receive benefits, such as paid vacation time or health insurance. Just like the law firms, the temp agencies who hire recent law grads to do document review try to cast these déclassé jobs as desirable employment. In a recent a job posting for document review positions, one legal temp agency stated that the job was "a great opportunity to earn significant income" and describe it as follows:

> Law school graduates who have earned a Juris Doctorate but have not yet been admitted to any state Bar association are needed for several upcoming "JD" Document Review projects at our Atlanta metro review facility. JD Document Reviewers may be reviewing client materials in legal matters for relevance or specific issues and respond to interrogatories or comply with civil investigative demand letters, Second Requests and subpoenas in litigation, investigations or regulatory matters.[10]

The job posting never mentions the salary. By outsourcing document review work to legal temp agencies, law firms can cut the cost of such work by more than half because the reviews are done using sophisticated electronic-discovery software and the law graduates get paid very low wages in comparison to traditional associate attorneys.[11]

The Drudgery of Document Review

The reader needs to get a sense as to why document review can be extremely undesirable legal work even if one is satisfied with getting paid $20 per hour to review about 70–100 documents per hour—doing work that someone without a law degree can do. In a news story entitled "Attorney at Blah," one law graduate describes his experience as a temporary document reviewer at a law firm:

> The project started at 9 a.m. on a Monday in a conference room with a nice view, where a lawyer from the firm gave the 20-odd temps an overview of the case (it was a company investigating itself, in anticipation of a Department of Justice investigation—I can't say more, or I'll violate a confidentiality agreement ...). The

10. *See Job: Law School Graduates/JD's needed for Document Review Projects* (Atlanta), Jobing.com, http://atlanta.jobing.com/law-school-graduates-jdandapos-s-needed-for-document-review-projects-atlanta/job/employment/39129207 (last visited Nov. 21, 2012) (starting salary is not mentioned). The "employer" is actually DTI, a legal temp agency specializing in hiring workers to do discovery work. *See Career Opportunities*, DTI, http://ch.tbe.taleo.net/CH14/ats/careers/requisition.jsp?org=DTIGLOBAL&cws=1&rid=4807 (last visited March 16, 2013).

11. *See, e.g.*, Valerie Valentine, *Saving Time, Money and Face with E-Discovery*, Information Management, Aug. 3, 2011. I've heard that some graduates who do document review work do not complain about getting paid as little as $15 per hour because they have never had a job that paid that much or because they hope the job will turn into permanent employment.

> lawyer handed us binders with more information about the case—about how we'd discern the relevant documents from the irrelevant—and then a member of the administrative staff told us not to use the Internet too much, or we'd be in trouble....
>
> [W]e [the temp lawyers] were trained on the particular computer program we'd be using, then got clicking. Relevant. Not relevant. Not relevant. Not relevant. Two staff attorneys—full-time lawyers hired by the law firm to oversee the temp document reviewers—sat at a table in the front of the room, watching us click in this quiet, quiet room. Mostly quiet room....
>
> This was the easiest job I'd ever had, the only job that was neither physically nor intellectually taxing, and I was making nice money. Every day was the same, every day was quiet, every day was a combination of angst and contentment, until the day that one of the two staff attorneys—the more chatty one—unexpectedly stood up and said the documents had all been reviewed, and it was time for us to go home.[12]

From the excerpt above, temp attorneys obviously are in a precarious situation, not knowing from day-to-day when the current gig will end or how soon they will get assigned to a new case just so they can keep earning a paycheck. Despite the precarious situation, graduates take the temporary document review job because it is better than no job.

While Attorney at Blah stated that the document review job was not physically or mentally taxing, other attorneys have had different experiences. Descriptions of the mental toll include extremely boring and soul crushing.[13] Descriptions of the physical toll include tendonitis and carpal tunnel syndrome due to mouse-clicking eight or more hours a day.[14]

Temp attorneys hope their work will lead to a permanent attorney position at the firm where they do document reviews. However, the president of a legal staffing firm in New York City admits that such jobs "infrequently" lead to permanent jobs. That confirms my suspicion because I've heard that many lawyers have been doing temp work long-term—more than a year—since the Great Recession started. It is better, therefore, to get hired as permanent career/staff attorney than to be a temp lawyer.

One final observation from Attorney at Blah's story is that even though the staff attorneys hired by the firm were not actually doing document review, they were hired to "watch" the temp workers to make sure they did. Consequently, both groups lacked client interaction and were not using the legal skills acquired in law school.

Hopefully, career/staff attorneys who start off doing document review (or overseeing others who do) will eventually get to perform traditional attorney work. Nevertheless, their long-term career potential at a law firm is stunted. Because they can never make partner, they may not get the quality of legal work that usually prepares traditional associate attorneys to become partners. One may reasonably conclude that some career/staff attorneys, as long as they stay at the firm, may remain underutilized and unfilled in the declassee law-firm jobs.

---

12. *See* Arin Greenwood, *Attorney at Blah*, WASH. CITY PAPER, Nov. 8, 2007.

13. *See, e.g.*, *First-Year Corporate Lawyer Can't Believe His Job Is THIS Soul Crushing*, BUS. INSIDER, Nov. 28, 2012, *available at* http://www.businessinsider.com/first-year-associate-hates-his-job-2012-11#ixzz2OIFfL81b (An entry-level attorney hired by a big law firm stated that "[d]oc review is the most boring experience of your life, but strangely nerve-wracking because you know you're messing it up, but you just can't bring yourself to care that you're messing it up.")

14. *See, e.g.*, Katie Battle, Healthy Tips for Document Review Attorneys, July 28, 2011, http://lawyerist.com/healthy-tips-for-document-review-attorneys/ (advising document review attorneys to stretch and bring their own wrist guards and chair cushions to avoid injuries).

Besides law firms, some corporate legal departments have let go attorneys and are using contract attorneys to perform document review. Some corporate legal departments have been affected by the recession and have had to downsize, but the number of layoffs have been much smaller than the layoffs at the law firms.[15] In 2011, the Association of Corporate Counsel, a professional association for lawyers who serve as in-house counsel, conducted a survey that found, among other things, that approximately 34% of the 876 corporate legal departments surveyed had used "contract" attorneys in the previous fiscal year to perform primarily document review. Apple, Inc., is a larger than life example. In its litigation battle against Samsung Electronics over patents for HTC smartphones, Apple amassed a team of in-house and outside lawyers, including contract attorneys proficient in Korean because Samsung is headquartered in South Korea.[16] Notably, the Korean-speaking attorneys were hired to do document review and were paid in the same price range as non-attorney translators. In other words, these foreign-language proficient attorneys are viewed as a real "bargain" because "you get more bang for your buck!"[17] If these attorneys had to incur six-figure student loan debt to get this temporary gig, I can only imagine what expletive they would use to describe their predicament. One 2010 law graduate described his experience as a bilingual contract attorney as being less tedious than regular document review work because "the potential is there to learn new vocabulary, and it helps me stay focused more than it might in English."

The chart below summarizes the type of déclassé jobs new graduates must be prepared to accept because of the dramatic decrease in traditional attorney positions.

	Career/Staff Attorney	**Contract Attorney**	**Temporary Attorney**
Paid Less Than Traditional Associate Position	√ (could be far less)	√ (could be far less)	√ (only a fraction)
Document Review	√	√	√
Routine Legal Work	√	Maybe	Maybe
Non-Partnership Track	√	√	√
Benefits	Most likely	Maybe	No
Promotions	Maybe	Probably Not	No
Long-Term (several months or more) Work	√	Maybe	No
Short-Term/Seasonal Employment		√	√

15. For instance, major corporations located in Missouri got rid of several attorneys through layoffs and buy-outs in 2009. See Heather Cole, *In-house Legal Departments in Missouri Slim Down*, Missouri Lawyers Media, Dec. 21, 2009 (discussing the downsizing of legal departments at several companies, including Monsanto Co. and Anheuser-Busch Cos).

16. *See* Susan Decker & Adam Satariano, *Apple's Krall Leads Samsung Win in Jobs' Global Smartphone War*, Bloomberg News, Sept. 10, 2012, *available at* http://www.bloomberg.com/news/2012-09-10/apple-s-krall-leads-samsung-win-in-jobs-global-smartphone-war.html; Jennifer Smith, *Wanted: Temp Attorneys With Foreign-Language Skills*, Wall St. J., at B1, July 24, 2012.

17. Smith, *supra* note 16.

Based on the job characteristics identified above, career/staff attorneys have it better than the contract and temp attorneys not only because they have long-term employment with benefits, but because they have the potential to be assigned legal work that allows them to put to use their legal writing and research skills. I've found news stories indicating that contract attorneys may be attorneys with specialized legal skills and, therefore, more highly paid; however, other stories indicate that entry-level contract attorneys typically do document review work and other routine work on a short-term or long-term basis. Moreover, even if the entry-level contract attorneys are employed directly by a corporate legal department or a law firm, as opposed to a temp agency, these attorneys are not permanent employees. The bottom line is that newly-minted law graduates need to face the reality that they may start their careers doing mind-numbing document review, whether they are called career, staff, contract, or temp attorneys. They also need to accept the fact that these are mid-level, five-figure salary positions, not the six-figure salary jobs enjoyed by only a few entry-level attorneys.

Déclassé Lawyers Should Do Pro Bono Work

To combat the lack of fulfillment and intellectual stimulation, I urge all entry-level déclassé lawyers, whether hired by corporate legal departments, law firms, or legal temp agencies, to do pro bono work. Rather than feeling like their law degree was a waste of time and money, déclassé attorneys can, for example, volunteer as attorney for numerous taskforces created or expanded post-recession to help consumers in crisis. For instance, the Legal Aid Center of Southern Nevada has created the Pro Bono Project, which trains private-sector attorneys who volunteer their time to aid consumers facing various legal problems, including those who need to file bankruptcy and resolve a foreclosure crisis. Volunteer attorneys receive free continuing legal education courses and mentoring from experienced attorneys.[18]

Besides the pro bono projects established by legal aid organizations, the Pro Bono Institute ("PBI"), a nonprofit based in Washington DC, assists corporate legal departments and law firms in their pro bono efforts. PBI has gotten 134 large law firms (50 or more attorneys) to sign the Law Firm Pro Bono Challenge, which sets the standards and definitions for pro bono work and reflects each firm's institutional commitment to providing pro bono services. PBI's 2011 data shows 50,795 attorneys from these firms performed a total of 4,476,866 hours of pro bono work and that the firms donated $28.7 million to legal services organizations.[19] PBI has also gotten over 100 companies to become signatories to the Corporate Pro Bono Challenge. Moreover, PBI has partnered with the Association of Corporate Counsel (ACC) to create the Corporate Pro Bono Project (CPBO) to expand the number of in-house pro bono programs to approximately 300 in 2010, a stratospheric rise from roughly 10 in 2001.[20] PBI also works with ACC and other organizations to remove impediments to corporate lawyers and law-firm attorneys being able to perform pro bono legal work.

18. *See Volunteer Opportunities*, Pro Bono Project, Legal Aid Center of Southern Nevada, http://www.lacsn.org/images/stories/Lawyer_Volunteer_Feb_2011.pdf (last visited Nov. 20, 2012).

19. *See Report on the 2011 Pro Bono Institute Law Firm Pro Bono Challenge® Statistics*, Pro Bono Institute http://www.probonoinst.org/images/pdfs/2011_challenge/2011-challenge-report.pdf (last visited Nov. 29, 2012).

20. *See In-House Pro Bono at a Glance: 2010 Benchmarking Survey March 2011*, Pro Bono Institute.

The foregoing partnerships mean that lawyers, whether employed at law firms or corporations, can make meaningful contributions to the lives of those in need of legal services. For instance, Steven Fus, who is a transactional and compliance attorney in the legal department at United Continental Holdings Inc., forgets about the airline company when he volunteers monthly at the Expungement Help Desk operated by Cabrini Green Legal Aid in the Circuit Court of Cook County's office.[21] Mr. Fus meets with individuals seeking to clear their criminal records of arrests or minor convictions. This expungement program is necessary because many employers automatically exclude from the job applicant pool anyone who has been arrested or convicted, no matter if the arrests were unwarranted or the convictions were overturned or were based on minor offenses from years ago.[22] By getting these records sealed, Mr. Fus and other volunteer attorneys help consumers who were previously unemployed find jobs.

At first, Mr. Fus was uncomfortable volunteering because he knew nothing about criminal law and had rarely interacted with poor people. However, he quickly got passionately invested. He likes the challenge of resolving legal matters for United, but he says "it pales in comparison to being able to help someone make a life change" through expungement of a criminal record.[23] Four years later, Mr. Fus is still volunteering at the Expungement Help Desk and started in 2012 an official pro bono project for United's attorneys and paralegals to devote their time to helping consumers.

In summary, while a significant number of new law graduates can expect to be hired by corporate employers, law firms, or temp agencies in various déclassé attorney jobs, graduates must seize numerous opportunities to do pro bono work[24] and thereby remain passionate for justice.[25] They must find a way to meaningfully contribute to justice even though they are not highly-compensated or lack power and prestige. Déclassé attorneys will receive lower salaries and may suffer indignities, such as being called "coders"[26] or being "watched." Those in entry-level déclassé jobs should, nevertheless, pay it forward by volunteering to do pro bono work because millions of low-income and middle-class families are desperately in need of legal services[27] and various partnerships and organizations have made it easier for lawyers to volunteer their time. In the next chapter, I will discuss how law schools should admit more public-service minded students into law school and should play a bigger role in making pro bono services available to those in need of legal assistance.

---

21. *See* Claire Bushey, *Charity Begins at the Office*, CRAIN'S CHICAGO BUS., at 25, Aug. 20, 2012.

22. *Id. See also 81% of clients who visit the Expungement Help Desk are either unemployed or underemployed*, CABRINI GREEN LEGAL AID, http://www.cgla.net/criminal-records (last visited March 16, 2013) ("Most individuals served at the Help Desk have either no convictions or only minor, non-violent convictions from years ago with no intervening arrests. Our clemency clients have had no arrests or convictions for a period of at least 10 years and have demonstrated significant life changes.").

23. *See* N.Y. Comp. Codes R. & Regs. tit. 22, § 520.16 (2012).

24. The ABA's Standing Committee on Pro Bono and Public Service provides a National Pro Bono Opportunities Guide, which has a wealth of information about pro bono opportunities in all 50 states and Washington, DC. *See* http://www.probono.net/aba_opps/.

25. I am aware that some law firms and companies severely limit the type and amount of pro bono work junior attorneys can do. Therefore, students who get job offers from law firms or corporate legal departments and who want to do pro bono work should make sure the organizations are institutionally committed to supporting and facilitating pro bono opportunities for junior attorneys.

26. *See, e.g.*, Vanessa O'Connell, *Lawyers Settle... for Temp Jobs*, WALL ST. J., at B1, July 15, 2011 (stating that Chevita Phifer, a 2009 law graduate who has had several document review assignments, overheard an attorney for the firm refer to her as a "coder").

27. For a full discussion of the millions of Americans in need of legal services, *see* Chapter 9.

Chapter 11

It's A Small World After All: A Big Firm Job Is a Mirage for Most Law Grads

In June 2012, John H. Musser IV, a sole practitioner in New Orleans and the 72nd president of the Louisiana State Bar Association (LSBA), declared his one-year tenure as "The Year of the Solo." Acknowledging that some graduates choose to go into solo practice, Mr. Musser noted that an increasing number of recent graduates are forced into solo practice. Musser stated that these new lawyers "are unprepared" and "don't know how to maintain trust accounts, conduct effective discovery and all that goes into shouldering the simultaneous burdens of operating a firm and handling a case."[1] In Louisiana[2] and many other states, 50% or more of the practicing bar is comprised of solo and small-firm attorneys, and the ABA estimates that 48% of attorneys in private practice are solo practitioners.[3] These are the type of attorneys—not big-firm attorneys—who usually represent individuals in cases involving probate matters, personal injury, criminal defense, family matters, real estate transactions, personal bankruptcy, and debt collection.[4]

In this chapter, I make the case that law schools should invest substantial resources into creating courses and programs to prepare graduates for solo and small-firm practice. Such an investment is justified because the statistics show that the majority of law graduates end up as solo practitioners or as lawyers in very small firms and because these are the lawyers most likely to serve low-to-moderate income families in need of legal services.

"Making Lawyers Out of Law Students"[5]

Public-service-minded students in particular,[6] and law students in general, need to be prepared by graduation day to do tasks expected of entry-level lawyers. The legal bar and

---

1. *See* Ben Myers, *State Bar President Placing Emphasis on Solo Practitioners*, New Orleans City Business, June 19, 2012.

2. *Id.*

3. *See* Hanover Research, Solo Practice: Obstacles and Resources, Sept. 2012, *available at* http://www.hanoverresearch.com/wp-content/uploads/2012/10/Solo-Practice-Obstacles-and-Resources-Membership.pdf (stating that the ABA estimates that America has 435,000 solo attorneys and that they make up 48% private-practice attorneys).

4. *Id.*

5. Timothy Casey & Kathryn Fehrman, *Making Lawyers Out of Law Students: Shifting the Locus of Authority*, Perspectives: Teaching Legal Research and Writing (Winter/Spring 2012).

6. By public-service-minded students, I mean students who are motivated by social justice and want to attend law school to serve the public in various capacities, such as county prosecutors, legal

law students have been begging law schools to teach more practical skills. The majority of law schools have responded by expanding the number of skills-based courses and clinical programs. The ABA occasionally reports about all the skills-based courses and programs law schools have in place to give students practical experience. In its "A Survey of Law School Curricula: 2002–2010," the ABA reported that the majority of law schools have been influenced to adopt curricula changes as result of the job market and that 50% of law schools offer professional skills courses.[7]

Calling on law schools to place more emphasis on legal skills is not a novel idea. In an ABA publication, widely-known as the MacCrate Report, the ABA outlines the lawyering skills law schools should seek to impart to students.[8] The MacCrate Report is credited for prompting law schools to expand skills-based courses and clinical programs to impart practical training and to give law students hands-on experience in helping real clients. However, the gap between what legal employers want and what new law graduates can actually do persists because legal employers, especially law firms, no longer want to spend the resources necessary to mentor to new lawyers.[9] Many employers want—from day one—new graduates to be "practice-ready" so that they can "hit the ground running."[10] Indeed, new law grads, feeling the crushing weight of six-figure-student loan debt, frequently complain that their law schools did not do enough to prepare them to go fend for themselves. Since the MacCrate Report, two major studies, commonly referred to as the Carnegie Report[11] and the Best Practices Report,[12] not only recommend the further expansion of programs and courses designed to impart lawyering skills but that these skills be weaved into the regular courses that teach black letter law.[13]

Although a discussion of these reports is beyond the scope of this book, the reports explain that some academics have been and continue to be resistant to the idea that practical lawyering skills need to be infused throughout the curricula and would rather

---

aid attorneys, public defenders or other public service positions. However, because of budget cuts, many public-service-minded students will not be able to find these traditional jobs. Nevertheless, law schools should create programs to enable public-service-minded students to start their own law firms and work for social justice.

7. Am. Bar Assoc., A Survey of Law School Curricula: 2002–2010 (Catherine L. Carpenter, ed. 2012).

8. Peter A. Joy, *The Cost of Clinical Legal Education*, 32 B.C.J.L. & Soc. Just. 309, 326 (2012); Margaret Martin Barry, *Practice Ready: Are We There Yet?*, 32 B.C.J.L. & Soc. Just. 247, 274 (2012).

9. Am. Bar Assoc., Sec. Legal Educ. and Admissions to the Bar, Legal Education and Professional Development—An Educational Continuum, Report of the Task Force on Law Schools and the Profession: Narrowing the Gap (1992) (hereinafter the "MacCrate Report").

10. *See, e.g.*, Michele L. Bendekovic, Reply to Law Schools from Law Firms, Univ. of Tulsa College of Law, Jan. 10, 2013, http://www.utulsa.edu/academics/colleges/college-of-law/About%20the%20College%20of%20Law/News%20Events%20and%20Multimedia/News/2013/January/Reply%20to%20Law%20Schools%20from%20Law%20Firms.aspx (Ms. Bendekovic, the Director Attorney Recruiting & Professional Development for the law firm Steptoe & Johnson, argues that law students should acquire skills in law school that enable them to be well-equipped associate attorneys because "[e]ntry level associates will do much more than just writing [sic] research memos").

11. William M. Sullivan et al., Educating Lawyers: Preparation for the Profession of Law (2007) (hereinafter "Carnegie Report").

12. Roy Stuckey et al., Best Practices for Legal Education (2007), *available at* http://law.sc.edu/faculty/stuckey/best_practices/best_practices-full.pdf (hereinafter "Best Practices").

13. Black letter law is the "informal way of referring to basic principles of law." West's Tax Law Dictionary § B550 (2011–2012 ed.).

that such skills training be taught in clinical programs.[14] This resistance is sometimes based on the opinion that law schools are not "trade schools" and that the push towards more skills training would dumb down legal education by robbing graduates of the ability to "think like a lawyer." Some resistance is also brought on by the legal bar itself for failing to reward law schools who have made dramatic curricula changes to impart practical skills. One common complaint by law school administrators is that law firms continue to hire those in the top 10% instead of hiring the clinic-trained graduates with lower GPAs. As such, law school administrators are left to wonder why they should continue to put more resources into making curricula changes if clinic-trained graduates are not successful in getting law firm jobs.

Even President Barack Obama believes curricula change is necessary and suggested that the first two years of law school consist of classroom instruction and the third year consist of practical experience. He believes this curriculum change would also reduce the cost of a legal education. Anticipating pushback, he stated: "Now, the question is can law schools maintain quality and keep good professors and sustain themselves without that third year. My suspicion is, is that if they thought creatively about it, they probably could."[15]

Besides President Obama, a growing number of academics have embraced the notion that law schools must change to adapt to an ever-changing legal job market. For example, the Boston College Law School's Journal of Law and Social Justice held a symposium in Spring 2012, entitled "The Way to Carnegie: Practice, Practice, Practice—Pedagogy, Social Justice, and Cost in Experiential Legal Education."[16] Academics participating in the symposium presented and published papers proposing a host of alternative clinical programs and "practice ready" curricula to better prepare students to perform their jobs as lawyers after graduation from law school.

Prospective Students Need to Inquire about Skills-Based Courses

When considering which school to apply to or enroll in, prospective law students should inquire about how extensive the school's skills-based course offerings are and about clinical programs directed towards preparing graduates for solo and small-firm practice. Such research is necessary because a substantial number of America's attorneys are solo practitioners. By one conservative estimate, 32% of lawyers in private practice are solo attorneys.[17] NALP's report about 2011 law school graduates indicates that the number of solo attorneys is on the rise.[18] Many, maybe even the majority, are not in solo practice by choice. Therefore, prospective students should also find out to what extent the targeted law school offers clinical courses and programs that are available to *all* students. Because

---

14. *See* Carnegie Report, *supra* note 10; *see also* Best Practices, *supra* note 11.

15. Transcript of Remarks by the President in Town Hall Meeting at Binghamton University, Office of Press Secretary, The White House, Aug. 23, 2013, http://www.whitehouse.gov/the-press-office/2013/08/23/remarks-president-town-hall-binghamton-university.

16. Jane H. Aiken et al., *The Way to Carnegie: Practice, Practice, Practice—Pedagogy, Social Justice, and Cost in Experiential Legal Education*, 32 B.C.J. L. & Soc. Just. 215, (2012), *available at* http://www.bc.edu/content/dam/files/schools/law/lawreviews/journals/bcjlsj/32_2/JLSJ_32_2_web.pdf.

17. The Hanover Research Report discussed conservative estimates and compared them to the number estimated by the ABA. *See* Hanover Research, *supra* note 3 (stating that the ABA estimates that America has 435,000 solo attorneys and that they make up 48% private-practice attorneys).

18. NALP, *Class of 2011*, *available at* http://www.nalp.org/classof2011 (last visited Feb. 19, 2013).

clinical programs can be expensive to operate and faculty to teach skills-based courses may be difficult to find, not all students interested in them are able to participate.[19]

Despite the greater availability of skills-based courses, many still complain that law students are not practice-ready.[20] This may be because law schools fail to have outcome-based measurements of effectiveness. The ABA has no standards regarding the measurable expected outcomes of student learning—what students have actually learned and should be capable of doing. The Society of American Law Teachers ("SALT") and other groups are urging the ABA to adopt outcome measurement standards that include a core skill set that law schools must teach students. SALT would like the required skill set to include proficiency in client counseling, negotiation, and fact-finding investigation as well as the ability to work collaboratively and communicate effectively with others from diverse backgrounds.

Until the ABA adopts outcome measurement standards, prospective students must seek to interview former students who have participated in a school's various skills-based courses, externships, clinics, etc. to assess how much practical training they may actually receive in such programs. Regardless of whether the ABA adopts new, outcome based standards, law schools need not to wait for direction from the ABA to decide that each of their graduates should have a core set of practical skills.

Practical lawyering skills may be particularly important for those public-service minded students that I want law schools to focus on admitting. The reality is that if law schools admit more students dedicated to public service, many of these graduates will not find traditional attorney jobs at governmental or legal aid organizations due to widespread budget cuts and hiring freezes. However, if properly trained through skills-based courses in law school, many public-service-minded graduates can go out and start their own solo or small practice firm. Law schools should view as a mandate the duty to prepare such graduates to work for themselves and use their skills to serve people who cannot afford to get legal representation from big firms. By doing so, law schools will be training the type of lawyers that are severely needed.[21]

Grads from a Small Number of Schools Get Most Big Firm Jobs

If you are a prospective law student that expects to secure a big-law-firm job, you are setting yourself up to be disappointed unless you graduate from a small select group of schools. For the majority of law graduates, landing a big law firm job is a mirage. Of the 2011 graduates who are employed at law firms, NALP reports that 21.2% are employed

19. *See* Quintin Johnstone, *Law and Policy Issues Concerning the Provision of Adequate Legal Services for the Poor*, 20 Cornell J.L. & Pub. Pol'y 571, 613 (2011) (stating that clinical courses are more expensive than regular courses because enrollment in such courses has to be limited to a small number of students in order for them to be adequately supervised by clinical staff).

20. *See, e.g.*, David Segal, *What They Don't Teach Law Students: Lawyering*, N.Y. Times, Nov. 19, 2011, at A1, *available at* http://www.nytimes.com/2011/11/20/business/after-law-school-associates-learn-to-be-lawyers.html?pagewanted=all (quoting Jeffrey W. Carr, the general counsel of FMC Technologies, as stating that law schools produce "lawyers in the sense that they have law degrees, but they aren't ready to be a provider of services").

21. *See* Chapter 9 for a discussion regarding the shortage of lawyers capable of serving low-to-moderate-income families.

at law firms with more than 500 attorneys ("501-plus"). This percentage at first glance may not seem so bad to prospective students biased by optimism that they will graduate in the top 10%, which is typically the pool of graduates with the greatest chance of getting a big firm job. However, if you look at the data for each school, you will see the odds of getting that job is *much* smaller at the majority of law schools.

In Table 11-1 (next page), I identify the top 30 ABA-approved law schools with 2011 graduates employed at a 501-plus firms.

As the reader can see, 78% (2277 out of 2932) of the 2011graduates employed at 501-plus firms graduated from these law schools.[22] That means most of the 2011 graduates at 501-plus firms come from *only* 15% (30 out of 197) of the law schools. In contrast, 50 out of 197 law schools did not have any 2011 graduates at a 501-plus firm and 28 law schools had *only one* graduate employed at a 501-plus firm. Consequently, graduates of 40% (78 out of 197) of the law schools have zero or a near-zero chance of getting a big law firm job.

Likewise, a small number of schools account for the majority of 2011 graduates at firms with 250 to 500 attorneys ("large-size firm"). Harvard tops this list of such schools in Table 11-2 (page 189). As the reader can see, 33 (or 17%) of law schools accounted for 65% (569 out of 880) of the 2011 graduates employed at large-size firms. In contrast, 54 (or 27%) of the law schools had *zero* graduates at a large-size firm and 36 (or 18%) schools had *only one* graduate. As a result, at 45% of the schools, a graduate has zero or a near-zero chance of getting a large-size firm job.

Based on the foregoing, one can reasonably conclude that landing a 501-plus or large-firm job is a fantasy for most graduates. In other words, unless you graduate from a small number of select schools, you should *not* enroll in law school expecting to land a job at a 501-plus or large-firm after graduation.[23]

It's a Solo or Very Small Firm World

A sizeable and increasing number of graduates are solo attorneys or are employed in extremely small firms. According to NALP, in comparison to the immediate pre-recession class of 2006, the percentage of 2011 graduates self-employed as solo attorneys more than doubled, going from 2.9% to 6.1%.[24] Moreover, the percentage of graduates employed in very small firms (2–10 attorneys) rose from 33.4% for the class of 2006 to 44% for the class of 2011. However, these statistics do not paint the full picture.

Table 11-3 (page 190) demonstrates that out of 197 law schools, 28% (or 56 out of 197) have 70% or more of their 2011 grads in solo or very small firms. Moreover, when I focused my research on which schools have a simple majority of graduates employed in solo and very small firms, I discovered that 127 (or 65%) of the law schools have 51% or more of their graduates employed in such firms. Table 4 in Appendix A reveals that at the majority of law schools, law graduates should expect to be self-employed or employed at very small

22. The table is derived from employment data for each school that is now available at ABA Section of Legal Education and Admissions to the Bar, Employment Summary Report, http://employmentsummary.abaquestionnaire.org (last visited Feb. 20, 2013).

23. *Id.*

24. *See*, NALP, *Class of 2011 Has Lowest Employment Rate Since Class of 1994*, NALP Bulletin, (July 2012), *available at* http://www.nalp.org/0712research.

Table 11-1. Top 30 Schools with Grads at Largest Law Firms

	Schools Ranked from Highest # of Grads Employed at 501-Plus Firms	# of 2011 Grads at 501-Plus Size Firms
1	COLUMBIA UNIVERSITY	236
2	HARVARD UNIVERSITY	226
3	NEW YORK UNIVERSITY	168
4	GEORGETOWN UNIVERSITY	162
5	PENNSYLVANIA, UNIVERSITY OF	125
6	NORTHWESTERN UNIVERSITY	116
7	VIRGINIA, UNIVERSITY OF	96
8	CALIFORNIA-BERKELEY, UNIVERSITY OF	92
9	CHICAGO, UNIVERSITY OF	83
10	MICHIGAN, UNIVERSITY OF	82
11	STANFORD UNIVERSITY	76
12	GEORGE WASHINGTON UNIVERSITY	72
13	FORDHAM UNIVERSITY	67
14	TEXAS AT AUSTIN, UNIVERSITY OF	67
15	DUKE UNIVERSITY	66
16	CALIFORNIA-LOS ANGELES, UNIVERSITY OF	64
17	CORNELL UNIVERSITY	58
18	YALE UNIVERSITY	52
19	SOUTHERN CALIFORNIA, UNIVERSITY OF	51
20	BOSTON COLLEGE	44
21	BOSTON UNIVERSITY	37
22	WASHINGTON UNIVERSITY	31
23	YESHIVA UNIVERSITY	30
24	CALIFORNIA-HASTINGS, UNIVERSITY OF	29
25	VANDERBILT UNIVERSITY	29
26	AMERICAN UNIVERSITY	26
27	NORTH CAROLINA, UNIVERSITY OF	24
28	EMORY UNIVERSITY	24
29	SANTA CLARA UNIVERSITY	23
30	LOYOLA MARYMOUNT UNIVERSITY-LOS ANGELES	21
	Total # of 2011 Grads from Top 30 Schools	**2,277**
	Total # of 2011 Grads from All Law Schools	**2,932**

Table 11-2. Top 33 Schools with 2011 Grads at Firms with 251 to 500 Attorneys

	School's Name	# of 2011 Grads Employed at 251–500 Size Firms
1	HARVARD UNIVERSITY	42
2	GEORGETOWN UNIVERSITY	38
3	COLUMBIA UNIVERSITY	31
4	VIRGINIA, UNIVERSITY OF	31
5	FORDHAM UNIVERSITY	29
6	CALIFORNIA-BERKELEY, UNIVERSITY OF	27
7	MICHIGAN, UNIVERSITY OF	27
8	NEW YORK UNIVERSITY	26
9	GEORGE WASHINGTON UNIVERSITY	23
10	NORTHWESTERN UNIVERSITY	22
11	PENNSYLVANIA, UNIVERSITY OF	21
12	VANDERBILT UNIVERSITY	20
13	MINNESOTA, UNIVERSITY OF	18
14	SOUTHERN CALIFORNIA, UNIVERSITY OF	15
15	TEXAS AT AUSTIN, UNIVERSITY OF	15
16	DUKE UNIVERSITY	13
17	WASHINGTON UNIVERSITY	13
18	WILLIAM MITCHELL COLLEGE OF LAW	13
19	BROOKLYN LAW SCHOOL	12
20	CORNELL UNIVERSITY	12
21	SOUTHERN METHODIST UNIVERSITY	12
22	HOUSTON, UNIVERSITY OF	11
23	BOSTON COLLEGE	10
24	EMORY UNIVERSITY	10
25	OHIO STATE UNIVERSITY	10
26	ALABAMA, UNIVERSITY OF	9
27	INDIANA UNIVERSITY-INDIANAPOLIS	9
28	INDIANA UNIVERSITY MAURER SCHOOL OF LAW	9
29	YESHIVA UNIVERSITY	9
30	AMERICAN UNIVERSITY	8
31	LOUISIANA STATE UNIVERSITY	8
32	STATE UNIVERSITY OF NEW YORK AT BUFFALO	8
33	SUFFOLK UNIVERSITY	8
	Total # of 2011 Grads from Top 33 Schools	**569**
	Total # of 2011 Grads at Large-Size (251–500) Firms	**880**

Table 11-3.

	Schools Ranked from Highest % of Grads Employed in Solo or Very Small Firms (last column)	2011 Grads Who Are Solo	2011 Grads at Very Small Firms (2–10)	Total # of Grads at Solo & Very Small Firms	Total # of 2011 Grads at Law Firms	% of Grads at Solo or Very Small Firms
1	SOUTH DAKOTA, UNIVERSITY OF	2	9	11	11	100%
2	APPALACHIAN SCHOOL OF LAW	4	26	30	32	94%
3	CITY UNIVERSITY OF NEW YORK	1	18	19	21	90%
4	SOUTHERN UNIVERSITY	12	22	34	38	89%
5	ATLANTA'S JOHN MARSHALL	21	32	53	60	88%
6	ELON UNIVERSITY	6	38	44	50	88%
7	REGENT UNIVERSITY	7	28	35	40	88%
8	TEXAS SOUTHERN UNIVERSITY	31	35	66	76	87%
9	PHOENIX SCHOOL OF LAW	5	46	51	59	86%
10	AVE MARIA	2	21	23	27	85%
11	ST. MARY'S UNIVERSITY	29	101	130	153	85%
12	TOLEDO, UNIVERSITY OF	6	22	28	33	85%
13	WESTERN NEW ENGLAND	6	26	32	38	84%
14	FAULKNER UNIVERSITY	7	38	45	54	83%
15	MONTANA, UNIVERSITY OF	2	33	35	42	83%
16	WESTERN STATE	6	28	34	41	83%
17	HAMLINE UNIVERSITY	3	55	58	70	83%
18	TEXAS WESLEYAN UNIVERSITY	21	58	79	96	82%
19	NORTHERN ILLINOIS UNIVERSITY	3	29	32	39	82%
20	VALPARAISO UNIVERSITY	5	49	54	66	82%
21	NORTH CAROLINA CENTRAL.	13	27	40	49	82%
22	THOMAS M. COOLEY LAW	80	190	270	332	81%
23	QUINNIPIAC UNIVERSITY	4	34	38	47	81%
24	CHARLOTTE SCHOOL OF LAW	9	16	25	31	81%
25	NEW ENGLAND SCHOOL OF LAW	15	60	75	94	80%
26	BARRY UNIVERSITY	11	54	65	82	79%
27	WILLAMETTE UNIVERSITY	14	29	43	55	78%
28	NEW MEXICO, UNIVERSITY OF	4	35	39	50	78%

	Schools Ranked from Highest % of Grads Employed in Solo or Very Small Firms (last column)	2011 Grads Who Are Solo	2011 Grads at Very Small Firms (2–10)	Total # of Grads at Solo & Very Small Firms	Total # of 2011 Grads at Law Firms	% of Grads at Solo or Very Small Firms
29	LIBERTY UNIVERSITY	5	16	21	27	78%
30	WASHBURN UNIVERSITY	14	31	45	58	78%
31	VERMONT LAW SCHOOL	2	36	38	49	78%
32	IDAHO, UNIVERSITY OF	2	29	31	40	78%
33	CHARLESTON SCHOOL OF LAW	1	52	53	69	77%
34	OREGON, UNIVERSITY OF	8	35	43	56	77%
35	CAMPBELL UNIVERSITY	13	43	56	73	77%
36	DRAKE UNIVERSITY	11	47	58	76	76%
37	THOMAS JEFFERSON	10	47	57	75	76%
38	NORTH DAKOTA, UNIVERSITY OF	0	22	22	29	76%
39	SO. ILLINOIS-CARBONDALE	10	34	44	58	76%
40	SOUTHWESTERN LAW SCHOOL	12	68	80	106	75%
41	MAINE, UNIVERSITY OF	1	20	21	28	75%
42	MISSISSIPPI COLLEGE	14	49	63	84	75%
43	UNIVERSITY OF LA VERNE	1	32	33	44	75%
44	SOUTH TEXAS COLLEGE OF LAW	21	131	152	203	75%
45	CALIFORNIA WESTERN	11	95	106	143	74%
46	LOUISVILLE, UNIVERSITY OF	5	35	40	54	74%
47	ARKANSAS, LITTLE ROCK	5	49	54	73	74%
48	ARIZONA STATE UNIVERSITY	10	53	63	86	73%
49	WIDENER UNIVERSITY	7	64	71	97	73%
50	CAPITAL UNIVERSITY	7	40	47	65	72%
51	GONZAGA UNIVERSITY	4	40	44	61	72%
52	FLORIDA COASTAL	13	85	98	136	72%
53	WYOMING, UNIVERSITY OF	1	18	19	27	70%
54	ALBANY LAW SCHOOL	3	68	71	101	70%
55	LEWIS AND CLARK COLLEGE	8	45	53	76	70%
56	MCGEORGE SCHOOL OF LAW	7	71	78	112	70%

firms.[25] As explained in full in Chapter 2, some of those employed at the very small firms may not even be attorneys. They could very well be paralegals. Of those who are actually attorneys, a significant number could simply be two or three graduates who decided to start a firm together. A quick Google search shows that some graduates chose to partner together and start a law firm after they could not find jobs. That means some of these graduates are also self-employed and not employees at a small but well-established law firm.

The above-data may be surprising to the reader but not to law schools, and yet very few law schools have courses or programs designed specifically to prepare law students to start or successfully run a solo or small firm practice.[26] And more importantly to me, law schools have done very little to prepare public-service-minded graduates to represent consumers in a solo or small-firm setting to close the justice gap.[27] While many law schools offer consumer law and poverty law courses, such courses do not actually teach lawyering skills necessary to represent consumers and operate a small business.

Because starting a solo practice is a business endeavor, law schools need to actually teach lawyering skills, such as client interviewing and counseling, as well as office management skills, such as marketing and basic accounting. A few schools have created "incubator" programs. Through these innovative programs, recent law graduates receive skills training and mentoring that allow them to successfully start a solo practice.

Incubator Program Prepares Grads for Solo Practice

Before discussing the law-school-based incubator programs, I thought the reader should know about one bar association's stellar incubator program. Recognizing that the legal academy is not doing enough to prepare graduates to become practicing attorneys in this tough legal job market, the Columbus Bar Association[28] has begun the first-of-its kind program called "Columbus Bar inc." The "inc" is short for incubator (hereafter "CBA Incubator Program") and is a year-long program that offers graduates of any Ohio law school who have passed the Ohio bar exam[29] the chance to transition from law student

25. *See* Appendix A, Table 4, which ranks ABA-accredited schools starting with the school with the highest percentage of graduates employed at law firms as solo attorneys and as small-firm practitioners.

26. *See* William Hornsby, *Challenging the Academy to a Dual (Perspective): The Need to Embrace Lawyering for Personal Legal Services*, 70 Md. L. Rev. 420, 437 (2011) (discussing available information regarding courses that prepare students for solo practice and "[c]rudely extrapolating from this information, in a profession where students are four times more likely to maintain a solo practice than to practice in a large firm, at best, only 3,000 law students per year (out of more than 100,000) have any exposure to law practice management through their course work."); Debra Moss Curtis, *Teaching Law Office Management: Why Law Students Need to Know the Business of Being a Lawyer*, 71 Alb. L. Rev. 201, 206 (2008) (surveying law school websites for courses teaching law-firm office management and finding fewer than one-third of U.S. law schools appear to offer such a course).

27. *See* Chapter 9 for a discussion of the shortage of lawyers willing and capable of providing affordable legal services to low-to-moderate income families.

28. The CBA is located in Columbus, Ohio.

29. When it was first started, the CBA Incubator Program was limited to only graduates of Capital University Law School and Ohio State University Moritz College of Law, both located in Columbus, Ohio. Now applicants must be a graduate of an Ohio law school and be admitted to Ohio bar in the last two years.

to successful solo practitioner. The incubator program is analogous to residency programs for medical school graduates.

In exchange for a promise to pay a small monthly fee (currently $350) and a promise to take at least one pro bono case, graduates selected for the CBA Incubator Program get office equipment (e.g., fax machine) and office space in the same building where the Columbus Bar Association is located (downtown Columbus, Ohio).[30] Most importantly, the incubating attorneys participate in educational training tailored for solo attorneys[31] and receive on-site mentoring from several seasoned volunteer attorneys and retired judges.[32] The incubating attorneys also receive referrals through the Columbus Bar Association's Lawyer Referral Service as well as the Lawyers for Justice Program. The former helps any individual who contacts the CBA to find a lawyer while the latter helps low-income families eligible for pro bono legal services.

The CBA Incubator Program has been successful and is well-supported by the Ohio bar and the legal community at large. Six of the eight incubating attorneys in the 2011 inaugural group have graduated.[33] In its second year, the CBA Incubator Program has eight participants. They benefit from a cadre of attorneys, judges, and other legal professionals who donate their time as mentors or as educators. Moreover, the CBA Incubator Program has received a $25,000 grant from the Columbus Law Library Association and a $50,000 grant from the Columbus Bar Foundation to cover the cost of developing the program over a two-year period.[34] It has also received numerous in-kind (non-cash) donations, including office space, office furniture, and software licenses. The CBA Incubator Program is frequently mentioned in the media as a success story, and it received the 2012 Solo and Small Firm Project Award from the ABA's Solo, Small Firm and General Practice Division.[35] This award recognizes successful implementation of a program targeted to solo and small-firm attorneys.

I have two points to drive home with my lengthy discussion of the CBA Incubator Program. First, the program demonstrates that the legal profession does not have to wait for a "market correction" and sit idly by watching new law graduates undergo a baptism by fire to see who can make it as a solo practitioner. The CBA Incubator Program shows that graduates who receive three key ingredients—training, mentoring, and networking—can be successful as solo attorneys. Second, the CBA Incubator Program makes the participants aware of the justice gap and inculcates in the participants a public-service commitment to provide pro bono representation to underserved communities.

I wish I could report that other bar associations are following the Columbus Bar Association's initiative and creating similar incubator programs. While bar associations across the country have various mentoring programs and online resources for solo and small-firm attorneys,

---

30. *See* Columbus Bar Assoc., Columbus Bar inc: A Professional Development Center, http://www.cbalaw.org/_files/Columbus%20Bar%20inc%20Sponsorship%20Packet.pdf.

31. *Id.* (stating that the training subjects include "client intake, billing practices, law office management, law firm marketing, case management, court rules, and discovery").

32. *Id.* (stating that the office space is reserved for the attorneys who volunteer as mentors and that they must commit to holding regular office hours there as well as to taking phone calls and responding to emails when they are off-site).

33. Debbie Briner, *Hands-on Help*, Columbus CEO, (October 19, 2012), http://www.columbusceo.com/industry_news/legal/article_be0b2394-1a1c-11e2-bcaf-0019bb30f31a.html.

34. *See id.*; *see also* Columbus Bar inc., *supra* note 30.

35. Press Release, ABA Now, Columbus Bar Association to Receive ABA General Practice, Solo and Small Firm Division 2012 Solo and Small Firm Project Award, (May 18, 2012), *available at* http://www.abanow.org/2012/05/columbus-bar-association-to-receive-aba-general-practice-solo-and-small-firm-division-2012-solo-and-small-firm-project-award/.

none at this time have an incubator program except the Columbus Bar Association.[36] Hopefully, the CBA Incubator Program will serve as model that other bar associations will soon follow.

Law-School-Based Incubator Programs Promote Access to Justice

Unlike the legal bar, the legal academy has several incubator programs. One academic defines law-school incubator programs as "in-house law firms created and supported by law schools to serve low- and middle-income clients and to help recent graduates learn how to start their own practices."[37] In 2007, CUNY launched the first incubator program, called the Incubator for Justice, as part of CUNY's Community Legal Resource Network (CLRN). Via the CLRN, graduates selected for CUNY's Incubator for Justice Program receive support in setting up and running solo and small-firm practices and are required to devote hours to serving low-income communities that lack access to legal representation. This model creates a "low bono" firm, as opposed to a "pro bono" firm because the clients they serve can pay a modest legal fee but usually earn too much money to qualify for pro bono legal assistance. The discounted fee is a bargain compared to the hourly rates charged by traditional law firms.

Just like the CBA Incubator Program, CUNY's Incubator for Justice Program provides graduates with training, mentoring, and networking.[38] Graduates participating in CUNY's Incubator for Justice Program get Manhattan office space for $500 a month in exchange for their agreement to work a minimum of 12 hours per month providing representation in civil matters to underserved individuals at the bargain rate of $75 per hour. Graduates can incubate for up to 18 months. Since its inception, 16 participants have completed CUNY's Incubator for Justice Program and nine are currently enrolled.

CUNY's pioneering incubator program is the brainchild of CUNY Professor Fred Rooney, who has consulted with other law schools interested in creating incubator programs. To date, he has helped establish or been influential in establishing an incubator program at California Western School of Law[39] and Thomas Jefferson School of Law.[40] In addition to these, the following law schools have also created incubator programs: Brooklyn

---

36. Hanover Research, *supra* note 3 (providing an in-depth discussion of incubator programs and that the CBA Incubator Program is the bar-association created program).

37. Elizabeth Chambliss, *Organizational Alliances by U.S. Law Schools*, 80 Fordham L. Rev. 2615, 2649 (2012).

38. I could not find where the Columbus Bar Association gave credit to CUNY for being the model for the CBA's Incubator Program. However, I assume that because CUNY's Incubator for Justice Program pre-dates the CBA program, the CUNY model was considered in formulating the model for the CBA Incubator Program.

39. *CUNY Expanding Incubator Program for New Grads with Cal Western, Thomas Jefferson*, The Nat'l Jurist, (Oct. 12, 2012) *available at* http://www.nationaljurist.com/content/cuny-expanding-incubator-program-new-grads-cal-western-thomas-jefferson.

40. *Id.*; *TJSL Launches Solo Practice Incubator Program*, Thomas Jefferson School of Law, (Nov. 1, 2012), http://www.tjsl.edu/news-media/2012/7888?fb_action_ids=10100503205703596&fb_action_types=og.likes&fb_source=other_multiline&action_object_map=%7B%2210100503205703596%22%3A170878809716754%7D&action_type_map=%7B%2210100503205703596%22%3A%22og.likes%22%7D&action_ref_map=%5B%5D (hereinafter "*TJLS Launches Incubator Program*").

Law School,[41] Charlotte School of Law,[42] Florida International University College of Law, Illinois Institute of Technology Chicago-Kent College of Law, University of Maryland School of Law, University of Missouri-Kansas City School of Law, and Pace University Law School.[43]

Almost all of the law-school-based incubator programs have "access to justice" as one of their core missions in that the incubating attorneys are required to provide a certain amount of pro bono or low-cost legal services to under-represented populations.[44] Professor Rooney strongly favors a social-justice incubator model and explains that by using such a model "we help our graduates become successful social entrepreneurs who contribute to improving access to justice while enabling them to make a living." A few incubator programs take Professor Rooney's social justice vision one-step further by imparting to the incubating attorneys specialized legal knowledge and skills needed by under-served populations who, in the absence of the incubator program, could not afford such an attorney. For example, Thomas Jefferson's incubating attorneys are afforded office space at the National Family Justice Center and provide pro bono representation for victims of domestic violence.[45]

Nearly all of the foregoing incubator programs are making small inroads in bridging the justice gap by providing free or low-cost legal services to traditionally underserved populations. The Legal Services Corporation ("LSC") is seeking funding from Congress to expand social-justice incubator programs; however, we must wait to see how congressional budget battles will affect LSC's funding.[46]

The Legal Bar Should Lobby for a Pro Bono Service Requirement for New Grads

Since the legal bar regularly complains that law graduates lack practical training, bar associations around the country should lobby for new law graduates seeking bar admission

41. *The Real World of Law Practice, Brooklyn Law Incubator & Policy Clinic*, Brooklyn Law School, http://www.brooklaw.edu/academics/clinicalprogram/blip/More%20About%20BLIP.aspx (last visited Feb. 20, 2013) (hereinafter "Brooklyn Law School Incubator Clinic").

42. *Small Practice Center Launches*, Charlotte School of Law, (Sept. 21, 2012), http://www.charlottelaw.org/about/small-practice-center-launches (hereinafter "Small Practice Center Launches").

43. Hanover Research, *Solo Practice: Obstacles and Resources*, (Sept. 2012), *available at* http://www.hanoverresearch.com/wp-content/uploads/2012/10/Solo-Practice-Obstacles-and-Resources-Membership.pdf.

44. Brooklyn's incubator program does not have access to justice as a core mission of its program. *Brooklyn Law School Incubator Clinic*, *supra* note 41 ("BLIP functions like a full-service, technology-oriented law firm in which students provide transactional, policy, some litigation and general legal support to tech-oriented startup clients, innovators and entrepreneurs."). Charlotte, which is a for-profit school, launched its program in September 2012, but its website fails to mention any access-to-justice component to its mission. *See* Small Practice Center Launches, *supra* note 37.

45. *TJLS Launches Incubator Program*, *supra* note 40.

46. *Pro Bono Task Force report: 'If we don't do it, who will?'*, Harvard Law School, http://www.law.harvard.edu/news/2012/10/27_lsc_pro_bono_task_force_report.html (last visited Feb. 21, 2013). Arizona State University Sandra Day O'Connor College of Law is planning the start-up of its incubator program in 2013. *See* Karen Sloan, *Think of It as a Residency for Lawyers*, N.Y.L.J., (June 5, 2012) http://www.newyorklawjournal.com/PubArticleNY.jsp?id=1202557309020&Think_of_It_as_a_Residency_for_Lawyers&slreturn=1.

to have to fulfill a pro bono service requirement before applying for admission to the state bar. Why? Because if graduates have to fulfill such a requirement, then law schools will be forced to create incubator programs and/or other skills-based programs that qualify as pro bono service to enable their graduates to be qualified for admittance.

Let's consider New York, a state that has a few law-school-based incubator programs. New law graduates seeking admission to the NY bar will have to complete 50 hours of qualifying pro bono work before filing an application.[47] The pro bono requirement seeks to accomplish two goals: (1) close the gap "in access to justice" by providing low-income individuals and families with legal representation, and (2) "help[] prospective attorneys build valuable skills and imbue[] in them the ideal of working toward the greater good."[48] Of the 15,000 applicants who seek admission to the New York bar each year, roughly 9,000 are admitted. Can you imagine how many low-income families and individuals can be helped if these applicants provide 500,000 or more hours in free legal services in their quest to become licensed attorneys in New York?

The new pro bono requirement will not only increased the skills of bar applicants, but will improve the lives of low-income families nationwide and even world-wide. That's because two-thirds of the applicants seeking admission are not graduates of New York law schools and their qualifying pro bono service can be performed "in any state or territory of the United States, the District of Columbia, or any foreign country." Law schools in and around the state New-York that lack an incubator program or a similar access-to-justice program will be behind the eight ball when it comes to preparing their graduates to meet the pro bono service requirement. I suspect that all law schools that have a significant number of graduates seeking admission to the New York bar will create and expand programs that not only serve the legal needs of low-income families but provide skills for their graduates. At this time, New York is the first and only state to require pro bono service from new attorneys seeking admission. However, several other states are considering adopting a pro bono service requirement.[49]

More Law Schools Should Create Incubator Programs

For now, prospective students with an offer from a law school with a high percentage of graduates employed in solo and small law firms need to find out whether the school has an incubator program or concrete plans to start one. If the school lacks an incubator program, or at a minimum opportunities to receive training in clinical programs, the prospective student should see that as a possible red flag. What kind of law school knows that a lot of its graduates will be forced to pursue the solo practitioner route but willingly

47. *See* Advisory Committee on New York State Pro Bono Bar Admission Requirements, Report to the Chief Judge of the State of New York and the Presiding Justices of the Four Appellate Division Departments, Sept. 2012, *available at* http://www.nycourts.gov/attorneys/probono/ProBonoBarAdmissionReport.pdf (last visited Mar. 22, 2013). The roughly 160,000 attorneys already licensed in the state of New York are exempt from the pro bono service requirement.

48. *Id.*

49. *See* James Podgers, *New York's New Rule Requires Bar Applicants to Perform 50 Hours of Pro Bono Work*, ABA Journal, March, 2013 (stating that Massachusetts, California, and New Jersey are considering adopting a pro bono service requirement).

allows its graduates to take another enormous gamble in life without any support from the school? Entrepreneurial acumen does not come naturally for most graduates; therefore, law schools with a high number of self-employed graduates should be committed to providing training to aid their graduates in becoming successful social-justice-minded, solo practitioners.

Other Services Available for Solo Attorneys

Even if the targeted law school does not have an incubator program, services are available for lawyers who choose or are forced to start a solo practice. For instance, in 2009, Susan Liebel started Solo Practice University, where graduates, for a $295 quarterly fee or $695 annually, have access to training courses covering topics such as marketing and office management and receive mentorship about operating a solo law firm.[50]

While seemingly slow to respond to the needs of the growing number of solo attorneys, the ABA launched in January 2012 the Solo and Small Firm Resource Center, which offers training materials to attorneys in solo and small-firm practice.[51] One of the founders of the Center stated that "[w]e have tried to collect in one place a useful 'toolkit' for those of you considering entering into a new solo or small firm."[52] ABA President William Robinson III stated that the Center was created to offer *free* resources to solo and small-firm attorneys "to level the playing field" so that lawyers who work alone or in small settings will have access to the same online information available to attorneys at big law firms.[53] The ABA has also created SoloSez, which the ABA reports is its "most active email listserv," and it has roughly 3,000 solo and small-firm attorneys as subscribers who discuss everything from "tech tips and legal opinions to what to wear to court."[54] Similar to the ABA, many state and local bar associations also offer online resources for start-up and current solo and small-firm attorneys.[55]

I do not know how effective the foregoing resources are, but I thought they were worth brining to the attention of current and prospective law students for their consideration.

---

50. *Susan Cartier Liebel*, Solo Practice University, http://solopracticeuniversity.com/faculty/susan-cartier-liebel/ (last visited Feb. 21, 2013) (hereinafter "*Susan Cartier Libel*"). Prices for various plans are available at http://solopracticeuniversity.com/signup/.

51. *The ABA Solo and Small Firm Resource Center*, Am. Bar Assoc., http://ambar.org/soloandsmallfirms (last visited Feb. 21, 2013) (stating that "[s]olo and small firm attorneys have unique needs, and the ABA Solo and Small Firm Resource Center was created especially for you"). The Center is supposed to provide the follow:

> The Solo and Small Firm Resource Center provides online articles, CLE programming, a discussion list for solo and small firm lawyers and other information from groups throughout the ABA, including the ABA General Practice, Solo and Small Firm Division and Law Practice Management Section. The website offers practice management advice, business development strategies, career guidance, advice for handling problem cases and clients, technology reviews, networking events and more.

Hanover Research, *supra* note 3.

52. *Susan Cartier Liebel*, *supra* note 50.

53. Press Release, ABA Now, ABA Serves Solo and Small-Firm Lawyers With New Online Resource Center, Jan. 19, 2012, http://www.abanow.org/2012/01/aba-serves-solo-and-small-firm-lawyers-with-new-online-resource-center/.

54. *Welcome to the ABA GPSolo Solosez Home*, Am. Bar Assoc., http://www.americanbar.org/groups/gpsolo/resources/solosez.html (last visited Feb. 21, 2013). Solosez is free to subscribers.

55. *Solo and Small Firm Practice*, Texas Bar CLE, http://www.texasbarcle.com/cle/LPDirectory.asp?lCategoryID=3 (last visited Feb. 21, 2013).

If you are a prospective student with an admission offer from a school where the majority of its graduates go into solo or small-firm practice, before enrolling in that school, make sure it is actually devoting *more* resources to prepare graduates for the reality of solo and small-firm practice. These are law schools that are on a mission to prepare all of their graduates to be successful, not just the ones capable of landing entry-level positions at law firms.

Is It Educational Malpractice to Leave Students Ill-Prepared for Solo Practice?

In 1948, of the roughly 152,600 attorneys working in the U.S. in private practice, 66.2% were solo practitioners.[56] Much has happened in the intervening 65 years. Unlike then, law students expect law schools to help them find jobs. However, post-recession, many traditional entry-level, law-firm jobs have been permanently eliminated. Although hiring has resumed in the both the private and public sectors, such hiring is not expected to return to the pre-recession peak levels. Consequently, an increasing number of graduates have been and will be forced into solo or small-firm practice if they want to become practicing attorneys. Only graduates of roughly three-dozen law schools can expect to be hired at the large-size and 501-plus firms. Therefore, most law schools need to train students to create their own jobs and not sit around waiting until a legal employer offers them a job.

For law schools to not make substantial changes to the curricula to reflect reality—that many graduates are going to be forced into solo or very-small practice—is to commit educational malpractice. Oh, I'm not saying a court would make that finding. I am asserting that unemployed and under-employed graduates should not be asked to spend money for continuing legal education courses to learn how to operate a solo or small firm practice; they should have been able to get that crucial training when they were enrolled in school and borrowed more than $100,000 to get a legal education.

Prospective students, you now have the power to decide which law schools will go the way of Woolworth Stores, Borders Books, and Montgomery Ward. These were iconic stores that failed to effectively respond to market forces and competitors, like Wal-Mart and Amazon, with updated and superior business models. If you cannot get into the select group of schools where most of their graduates find jobs as attorneys, then make sure the school you enroll in has courses and programs to help their graduates become successful solo and small-firm attorneys.

Legal eaglets should not be flung into the job market ill-prepared to become successful attorneys.

---

56. William D. Henderson, *A Blueprint for Change*, 40 Pepp. L. Rev. 461 (2013); Patricia Kay Oliver, Justice For All, 40 Pepp. L. Rev. 509, 470 (2013).

Chapter 12

Narratives of Recent Graduates

If you're a prospective law student and you've made it this far in the book, you must still have an interest in attending law school. In this chapter, graduates tell their stories of setbacks and triumphs and describe to what extent they have struggled to find ideal employment since the start of the recession.

Although these narratives are not intended to persuade anyone to go to law school, I need to say few things to provide context for prospective students who may be discouraged by media reporting. Media reports about the plight of recent law grads have been so negative that they either imply or explicitly state that attending law school is a bad idea. Such reporting assumes that people who possess only a bachelor's degree and who do not attend law school have many other viable alternatives to attending law school. Many young people who are now afraid to attend law school can expect to be under-employed in jobs that require very little skills and that pay very low wages—wages that are often lower than the wages of low-paid law graduates.

In January 2013, the Center for College Affordability and Productivity released a study showing that 11% of college graduates are employed in jobs that require less than a four-year college degree but more than a high school diploma and, even more disturbing, 37% are employed in jobs that do not even require a high school diploma.[1] That means 48% of US college graduates are under-employed. Moreover, substantial disparities exist in the starting salaries of those fortunate to be using their degrees in professional occupations. For instance, electrical engineering majors have an average median salary of over $60,000 per year while social work majors have an average median salary just under $34,000 per year. That's because not all majors are equal nor are all degree-granting universities. Graduates of elite private schools tend to have higher starting salaries than graduates of public and non-elite private universities. However, recent college graduates are really suffering. A 2012 Rutgers University study found that 11% of students who graduated between 2006 and 2011 are unemployed and only half had fulltime jobs.[2]

Forecasts signal an even more competitive job market for finding jobs that pay well and require higher education. Of the 30 occupations with the largest projected growth for the 2010–2020 decade, according to the Bureau of Labor Statistics, 10 of those jobs

---

1. Richard Vedder, Christopher Denhart, & Jonathan Robe, *Why Are Recent College Graduates Underemployed? University Enrollments and Labor Market Realities*, Ctr. for College Affordability and Productivity (Jan. 2013), *available at* http://centerforcollegeaffordability.org/uploads/Underemployed%20Report%202.pdf (basing conclusions based in part on information obtained from the US Bureau of Labor Statistics).

2. Charley Stone, Carl Van Horn, & Cliff Zukin, Rutgers Univ., John J. Heldrich Ctr. for Workforce Dev., Chasing the American Dream: Recent College Graduates and the Great Recession (May 2012), http://www.heldrich.rutgers.edu/sites/default/files/content/Chasing_American_Dream_Report.pdf ("Those who graduated during the recession-era labor market (2009 to 2011) earned $3,000 less on average in their first job than those who graduated before the recession began.").

will require less than a high school diploma, 12 will require only a high school diploma, and only 4 will require a doctoral or professional degree.[3]

Despite the widespread number of college graduates working in under-employed positions, the low starting salaries for many professional occupations, and the projection of largest growth in jobs that require a high school diploma or less, the mainstream media is not suggesting that young people should avoid college on the basis that the student loan debt burden is too high to justify the investment in attaining a bachelor's degree. Media reports may assert that certain majors are not worth the investment, but they are *not* urging young people to avoid college. Why? Research consistently shows that over a lifetime, four-year bachelor's degree holders usually earn substantially more than those who possess only a high school diploma or an associate's degree.

Likewise, many who obtain a law degree are going to earn substantially more over a lifetime than those who possess only a bachelor's degree, especially those with a liberal arts degree. Although they have taken a lot of criticism, two professors have done a detailed economic analysis demonstrating that the majority of law graduates will earn on average of $1,000,000 over the course of a lifetime.[4] As a result, the media should not be urging people to avoid law school. To the contrary, those interested in becoming lawyers need to first assess their skills, long-term goals, and desire to become an attorney. If they still want to go to law school, they need follow the advice provided in this book so that they can enroll in the law school that offers the best educational opportunities for the right financial aid package, which includes scholarships and not just loans. As explained more fully in Chapter 14, law students need to consider enrolling in loan forgiveness and assistance programs that help them to obtain affordable loan payments. In summary, prospective students who have a desire to become attorneys need to develop a strategy to gain the best legal education with the least amount of student loan debt.

Now let's turn to the narratives. I used fictitious names to conceal the identities of the graduates giving the narratives. Becasue several of the graduates are not satisfied with their employment situation, their anonymity is necessary to preserve their ability to pursue promising job opportunities. As you will see, some graduates made the mistake of not adequately considering student loan debt and how to minimize borrowing. The narratives are here to help prospective students give meaningful consideration to issues that they may have, heretofore, either ignored or glossed over in their excitement about attending law school.

Anita: "Temping" Too Long

I decided to go to law school primarily because I thought it would be good for expanding my career options. I did not have a strong desire to be a lawyer but was definitely interested in it. I took the LSAT in fall 2003. I then applied to ten law schools and was accepted to four.

---

3. C. Brett Lockard & Michael Wolf, *Occupational Employment Projections to 2020*, 135 Monthly Lab. Rev. Online 84, 100 (2012), *available at* http://www.bls.gov/opub/mlr/2012/01/art5full.pdf (projecting the largest growth in jobs as personal care aides and home health aides, both of which do not require a high school diploma).

4. Michael Simkovic & Frank McIntyre, The Economic Value of a Law Degree, *available at* http://papers.ssrn.com/sol3/papers.cfm?abstract_id=2250585 (uploaded April 13, 2013) (finding that when compared to those who only have a bachelor's degree, "even at the 25th percentile, toward the bottom of the income distribution, a law degree confers a much larger increase in earnings").

I contacted admissions personnel about my competing offers and asked them for information and advice to better help me decide which offer to accept. Before applying, I did not conduct any research on the state of the legal job market. My sense was that the job market was strong.

Ultimately, I decided to go to a second-tier law school in the south ("Southern Regional Law School"), where I graduated with a JD in 2007. Scholarship offers and tuition costs were the most important factors in my decision of which law school to attend, followed by reputation, ranking, and the location of the school as it relates to the cost of living. The scales tipped in favor of my going to Southern Regional Law School because its cost of living estimates were low in comparison to the other schools from which I received offers. The low cost of living coupled with scholarships that covered a substantial amount of tuition meant that I could keep my student loans to a minimum. In my cultural upbringing, my immigrant parents placed heavy emphasis on avoiding borrowing money.

During my 1L year at Southern Regional Law School, I began to doubt my decision to go to law school. This doubt was partially due to the fact that law school seemed very heavy on theory. I had a hard time seeing how what I was learning was going to help me to be an effective lawyer. However, I stuck it out and remained in school. I ended up graduating just outside of the top half of my class, and I passed the bar exam on my first attempt.

I am currently working for a legal staffing agency that places me with law firms that are seeking to hire lawyers for temporary work. Typically, I am placed at large NYC law firms who hire me through the agency to review voluminous documents in preparation for upcoming trials. The length of time that I am placed at a particular firm varies depending on the project to which I am assigned. Being placed at a law firm is not a guaranty of future employment. If a graduate's work is not satisfactory to the firm, then the firm's HR people will tell the temp agency not to send the graduate back to that firm. The pay that I receive is much less than an entry-level attorney would make at these large law firms, but the work that I do is not difficult as it strictly deals with reviewing documents. Fortunately, I have been able to maintain steady fulltime employment almost every month since passing the bar exam in 2007.

The hours that I have to work each day are often very long. It would not be out of the ordinary for me to work from 9:30 a.m. to 8:00 p.m. Monday thru Friday and sometimes work on the weekend. Because of the hours, it makes it more difficult to socialize and have fun outside of work. However, because I live in New York City, a lot of places are open late and, therefore, I have many places where I can socialize when I am not too tired from work. The truth be told, I am not even sure what I would do if I didn't work such long hours because I have grown accustomed to them.

I've learned that some people who started law school around the time that I did believe their law schools misled them about the employment success of the schools' graduates. I do not believe I was misled or received false statements. However, at the time I enrolled in law school, I did expect that post-graduation I would be able to obtain a fulltime, permanent job that required a JD and involved the practice of law. Because I graduated in 2007, a few months before the start of the Great Recession, I think it played a significant role in the inability of many law graduates—including me—to obtain the job they envisioned obtaining when they first enrolled.

Looking back on the enrollment decision-making process, I would have placed greater emphasis on the location of the school as it related to future career plans and less emphasis on scholarships and other cost factors. Southern Regional Law School, although considered very reputable in its state, has carried no weight in my pursuit of a permanent job in the

New York area. Although I occasionally hear of a few graduates who are brave enough to venture into solo practice, nothing in my law school experience would lead me to take that route. Consequently, my hope is that one of the law firms that I have done temp work for will soon hire me permanently as an attorney. Despite accumulating a substantial amount of debt (less than $50,000), overall, I am happy with my decision to go to law school. That's because my income is higher than what I was earning prior to my enrollment in law school. My steady employment, even as a "temporary" lawyer, has allowed me to adequately handle my debt and live a comfortable lifestyle.

Lessons to Learn from Anita's Story

Anita realized that her diploma from Southern Regional Law School could not get her a permanent attorney job in New York City. The reader may recall from Chapter 7 my discussion of Professor Seto's research and published paper entitled "Where Do Partners Come From?" He studied several regions of the country to discover who becomes a partner at America's top 100 largest law firms (known as the "NLJ 100"). The top ten law schools that are feeder schools for the NLJ 100 in New York City are as follows: NYU, Columbia, Harvard, Fordham, Georgetown, The University of Pennsylvania, Brooklyn, St. John's, Boston University, and Yale.

Because Anita was able to get into Southern Regional Law School, a second-tier school, she probably could have gotten admitted to Brooklyn, which is also a second-tier school. Professor Seto's research shows that Brooklyn, ranked number seven as a feeder school, has 88 partners at NLJ 100 firms in New York City. Because Anita knew she wanted to practice law in New York City, she should have tried to get into Brooklyn, which has a large number of partners she could have tried to connect with to increase her employment potential. I would encourage prospective students to look at Professor Seto's research to find out which NLJ 100 firms are feeder schools for the city in which employment is desired.

Let's assume for the sake of argument that Anita could not have gotten into Brooklyn, I encourage students to determine to what extent the targeted school has course offerings and programs tailored to prepare graduates for solo and small-firm practice. In Chapter 11, I discuss at length the push from the legal bar to get more schools to offer courses and programs to make their graduates "practice ready." The backdrop for this discussion is the fact that many predict many of the law-firm jobs lost during the Great Recession will never return. Law schools, therefore, need to do more to prepare their graduates to fend for themselves.

Denise: An Equal Justice Works Fellow Makes a Difference

I graduated from a mid-west university without incurring any student loan debt. I was able to do this through a combination of merit-based scholarships, part-time jobs, and parental assistance. After taking the LSAT and applying to several law schools, my enrollment decision focused on two schools. Both are located in the mid-west. One school is ranked in the first tier and the other in the third tier. The third-tier law school offered me a full-ride scholarship that included a stipend for living expenses. After consulting with my undergraduate academic advisor and discussing the value of a degree from a third-tier law school, I instead chose to attend the first-tier law school. I now have approximately $160,000 in student loan debt.

I became involved with nonprofit and consumer rights work very early in law school and worked very hard to become familiar with and competent about consumer protection issues. I worked both summers in fulltime clerkship positions and worked part-time during my last year of law school. All of my employment was at either governmental or non-profit organizations and allowed me to perform either indirect or direct service to consumers. All three of these were unpaid but immensely valuable. I was, however, able to subsidize this work by cashing out savings, entering writing contests, and obtaining fellowship sponsors.

Based on this experience, I was fortunate to obtain a position as an Equal Justice Works AmeriCorps Legal Fellow at a legal aid organization. In exchange for full-time service as an AmeriCorps member, I not only earned a monthly salary, but also earned two $5,000 Segal AmeriCorps Education Awards, which could be used to pay back qualified student loans or used to help pay for higher education. The EJW-AmeriCorps Legal Fellowship is slightly different from the traditional AmeriCorps program in that it comes with a higher salary and is specifically tailored for attorneys. All EJW-AmeriCorps fellows practice law in some way, and their sponsoring organizations determine the community's need and/or how their funding will be specifically applied. The funding from my sponsoring organization allowed me to represent borrowers facing foreclosure. I eventually expanded this scope to include all consumer rights issues.

When I started my EJW-AmeriCorps fellowship, I was immediately handed a full caseload of clients that eventually grew to be larger than more experienced attorneys on the consumer team at the legal aid organization. I ultimately became very successful in my practice and was placed in charge of the most complex cases. During my two years as an EJW-AmeriCorps Legal Fellow, I saved 54 clients from losing their homes in foreclosure, and I recovered approximately $150,000 in monetary damages for my clients. I never lost a case. I know this sounds like I'm bragging, but I did become somewhat of an authority in the foreclosure defense field. I routinely trained other attorneys. To become a more-well rounded attorney, I also did non-legal work, including acting as a member of firm's law clerk recruiting committee and establishing a new community outreach program.

As I neared the end of my two-year fellowship, I was hoping that the legal aid firm would be able to hire me as a permanent full-time attorney because I loved my job and was learning and growing as an employee. However, in January 2012, it became clear that it would not be possible considering the firm's budget and the continuing economic trouble affecting all legal service organizations.

Between January and August, when my grant officially expired, I applied for over fifty legal positions and was only offered one interview. The vast majority of employers refused to review my resume because I did not have the minimum number of years of experience they required.

The most difficult part of my post-fellowship experience has been expanding my job search to include jobs that I simply did not want. I went to law school to become a public interest attorney, but vacancies for those jobs are so few. Those currently employed as legal aid attorneys are holding onto their positions, and there is fierce competition for the few available positions.

The same week my grant expired, I forced myself to take a non-legal position with a state agency. The work is very administrative and not challenging for a competitive person like myself. Honestly, my job is unfulfilling even though I'm thankful to be gainfully employed. I cannot quantify for the reader the emotional and psychological impact of being under-employed—not working in the legal profession as an attorney. I recently started volunteering for a legal aid firm just so that I could feel like I'm doing something, anything, worthwhile with my law degree.

I credit the EJW-AmeriCorps Legal Fellow program for letting me practice my passion for two years. Without it, I would never have known how rewarding this work could be. I was incredibly happy for two years, and I became a skilled attorney because of the fellowship. I know I made a difference in my clients' lives, and helping them made a difference in my life.

Although times are tough right now in the legal job market, I am not going to give up on my dream of being a fulltime, permanent legal aid attorney.

Gaining Perspective from Denise's Story

First, I need to say that Denise's experience is heart-breaking for me, as a professor, to hear because the legal profession desperately needs lawyers like her who are committed to serving low-income families. Some students incorrectly assume that their law professors do not care. It simply is not true. I can tell you that, without a doubt, law professors around the country are extremely troubled by the fact that recent graduates have so much debt but face a legal job market where the number of permanent attorney positions have shrunk and starting salaries have decreased. I also know that some undergraduate professors and law professors are advising undergraduate students not to go to law school. I simply cannot give that advice without knowing much more about each individual's skills, strengths, and passion for the law.

Like Denise, I too found the practice of law to be much more rewarding than my pre-law school career. It bothers me that if I had wanted to go to law school today, others would automatically discourage me from pursuing a legal career that makes me excited to get up in the morning. When I worked as a legal aid attorney in the 1990s, I only earned $29,000 a year. That was less than the amount of money I earned as an accountant prior to going to law school. When I compare the two careers, I would never want to be an accountant again.

The law school Denise attended is on the high end of tuition for its region. So her debt of $160,000 is within the realm of reasonable debt. I have not asked her about her lifestyle during law school, and I don't want to know in order to preserve her anonymity. I would suspect that in retrospect she could have cut more corners.

I can tell you that in my 15 years of teaching, it appears to me that most law students live a "middle-class lifestyle." I've talked to numerous professors, and they have made the same observation, which is contrary to our experience of living frugal lifestyles while in law school. By middle-class lifestyle, I mean that law students often live in apartments where the rent is in the mid-to-high range, they regularly eat out at restaurants, and they frequently spend money for truly discretionary services (e.g., getting pedicures). For example, near the Ohio State College of Law is an apartment complex where the rent is $1,000 or more. If a student chose instead to live in a $600 apartment, he or she could save nearly $15,000[5] in rent year while obtaining the degree, and avoid paying thousands

5. A monthly saving of $400 ($1000 minus $400) translates into a savings of $14,000 (36 months times $400) over a three-year period if one assumes that there are no increases in the rent.

more in interest after graduating from law school. Again, I am not assuming that Denise lived a middle-class lifestyle and neither should the reader make that assumption.

I am using Denise's story to make the point that law students should lower their standard of living while enrolled in law school and should strategically use their student loans. The seeming inability of law students to spend money only for true necessities is what some behavioral economists would refer to as the problem of delayed gratification. I hate to keep using myself as an example, but I think it would be helpful to the reader. While in law school, I was fortunate to have a scholarship that paid me a monthly stipend of $888 during the nine-month school year. I had a car note of $425. I found, near the campus, a tiny apartment where the monthly rent was $250. If I would not have been able to find an apartment that cheap, I was prepared to sell my car and walk to school so that I could live within my $888 budget and avoid getting student loans.

It doesn't take an accountant to figure out that I didn't have much money left after paying $675 for the rent and the car loan. At the time, I had been told that I could probably qualify for food stamps, but I never pursued it. With the remaining monthly stipend ($213), I had to cover all other expenses, such as utility costs and gas for my car. As result, I lived a Spartan lifestyle. I did not have cable and picked up only one channel clearly with the antenna. I purchased groceries based solely on very good specials offered at the local grocery stores. For instance, I never bought bananas unless they cost 25 cents per pound. I bought loaves of bread from the "day old" bread store for two or three loaves per dollar, and I would freeze the loaves until needed. I packed my lunches and cooked my dinners. I very rarely ate at a restaurant. When I did, it was usually to get a cheeseburger at McDonald's, not to eat pricier items at Buffalo Wild Wings or similar restaurants that I see frequented by today's law students.

I know you may be thinking my life style is not realistic today. How could today's law student borrow only $10,000 for living expenses in law school or survive post-graduation on the salary of an AmeriCorps Legal Fellow? If a person is single and has no dependents and is willing to make sacrifices—delay gratification while obtaining the degree—the person can do it. Think about it. Law students are "the cream of the crop" as they say. Instead of being like their peers who never went to college or who ended their academic pursuit after getting an undergraduate degree, law students commit to three more years of study. Unlike their peers who regularly party and attend concerts or sporting events, law students miss out on a lot of fun activities because they are preparing for a better future—higher income, greater job security, and a more fulfilling career. Just like they delay using their nights and weekends for fun time-consuming activities, law students need to delay making some discretionary purchases so as to make smarter lifestyle choices with the money they borrow.

A law student's ability to delay gratification from partying to pursue a legal education has to be applied to spending habits. So, for example, if law students borrow the recommended amount for living expenses but then get a roommate or secure a similar cost-saving living arrangement, law students could save a substantial chunk of their student loans to tide them over during the summer if they cannot find summer clerkship positions that pay. By the third year, students can then request less student loan money and minimize their overall borrowing or could take out the maximum to cover their living expenses while studying for the bar exam. These cost-saving ideas are just suggestions.

I know students who have graduated from law school with less than a $100,000 in debt because they opened up their eyes and took advantage of available opportunities. For instance, I know students who became resident assistant/advisers ("RA") in undergraduate dormitories because that position carried with it free room and board. Some RA positions even get paid a monthly stipend. I know another law student who was a dorm mother at a sorority house to get free room and board in exchange for keeping an eye on the "naughty girls!" She kept that position for a while post-graduation to minimize her expenses until she found a permanent legal position. Have you heard the expression "where there's a will, there's a way"? Law students have to adopt that as a mantra when it comes to spending wisely and follow it.

Let me move on to my final observation about Denise's experience. I don't want anyone to jump to the conclusion that she should have gone to the third-tier law school just because it offered her a full-ride scholarship. This school, as well as many other lower-ranked law schools, offers such scholarships to attract prospective students with LSAT scores high enough to get admitted to first-tier schools. However, as I explained in detail in Chapter 4, many of those scholarships are lost after the first year because the GPA that must be maintained to keep such scholarships is usually high. Therefore, Denise would have probably lost that scholarship and would have wound up borrowing at least $70,000 for the remainder of her years at that third-tier law school. I have no doubt that the reputation of her first-tier law school played a factor in her ability to get the jobs that she secured while in law school as well as her job as an AmeriCorps Legal Fellow.

I don't pretend to offer a magic pill that helps prospective students immediately figure out where to enroll. I refer prospective law students to previous chapters where I discuss a multiplicity of factors that must be considered in the enrollment decision-making process. In Chapter 14, I will talk about how law graduates can take advantage of income-based reduced-payment programs that can reduce their student loan debt. In Chapter 13, I will also talk about when filing bankruptcy can be an option for dealing with debt.

Ted: When Graduating No. 2 in the Class Isn't Good Enough

In 2002, I graduated with a B.S. degree from Trinity University in San Antonio, Texas. I financed my education at Trinity by taking out student loans and working part-time at a restaurant and a package courier company. I had an interest in going to law school because of the influence of my father, who has been a lawyer in Texas for over 30 years. Despite his influence, I wasn't sure I wanted to take the leap. So after graduating from Trinity, I worked for two years, going from part-time to full-time employment status at both my jobs. Between these two jobs, I was averaging over 70 hours per week. I then started to get restless and knew that if I was ever going to go to law school, I needed to go ASAP while I still knew how to prepare and study diligently.

I took the LSAT, but my score wasn't that great because I was stressed out due to a family crisis that arose just before I took the test. I applied to John Marshall Law School, South Texas Law School, Southern Methodist University School of Law, Texas Southern University Thurgood Marshall Law School ("TSU"), and the University of Houston Law School. Despite not having an excellent LSAT score, TSU and John Marshall offered me acceptance. I decided to go to TSU because it offered me the best overall scholarship package, which covered my entire tuition fees. Choosing TSU made sense also because I already lived in Houston. As a result, I could keep one of my jobs and work part-time while attending law school, and, therefore, I would not have to take out as much student loan debt.

I knew that TSU, a low-ranked law school, was not regarded as well as some of the other Texas law schools. Therefore, I knew I could have a problem finding a job in Texas if I didn't do very well in law school. I suspect through osmosis or otherwise, I was capable of good analytical reasoning prior to going to law school because I grew up in a household with a lawyer. With my dad's encouragement to work hard, I believed that I would graduate at or near the top of my class. Therefore, I did not consider TSU's reputation to be an obstacle to my getting a job as an attorney. If my expectation of doing very well academically materialized, I believed TSU's reputation would not hinder my ability to get that job at a big firm!

While at TSU, I maintained a stellar academic record even though I was working part-time at the restaurant. I was in the top 10% at the end of my first year and, consequently, was offered a spot on the Thurgood Marshall Law Review.[6] Because I was working part-time, I didn't have additional free time to devote to both being a member of the law review and to studying for classes. So I declined the offer of membership.

I maintained my academic intensity and, as a result, was ranked number two in my class during my second year of law school. My academic record allowed me to obtain an internship at a law firm during the summer of 2006.

In fall 2006, at the beginning of my 3L year, I did the usual on-campus interviews with the big firms. As the No. 2 person in the class, I was sure that I was going to get an offer. I met the most stringent criteria in the job announcements by being in the top 10%. However, days turned into weeks and weeks turned into months with no job offer forthcoming. By the time graduation rolled around, I did not have any job offers. I guess maybe I wasn't saying the exact words the hiring partners wanted to hear during the interviews.

Without a job offer, I focused on passing the bar exam. I quit my job and moved in with my parents. In addition to the typical student loans I had already incurred in law school, I was forced to get a "bar" loan to pay for bar exam prep courses, testing fees, and living expenses to get me through three months of no employment. I studied intensely because I wanted to put myself in the best position to get an offer after the exam. I realized that some employers, particularly governmental employers, do not hire until after bar passage results are published.

After I passed the bar exam on my first try in 2007, I expanded my job search and applied for attorney positions at all types of legal employers, not just law firms. A local bankruptcy trustee hired me, not as a law clerk, but as a case analyst, which was a non-legal, data entry job that paid roughly $10/hour. Although this job allowed me to get some work experience and to make some contacts, I was extremely discouraged that this was where I ended up after doing so well in law school. Through the trustee and a contact that I had made while at this job, I was offered my first attorney position at a small law firm. Despite my starting salary of about $45,000, I was excited about the opportunity to be a lawyer. I never took a bankruptcy law course in law school, but I started work in the area of consumer bankruptcy. I am still working at this firm today. I love what I do and my salary has risen dramatically over the last four years.

---

6. All accredited law schools have "law journal" or "law review," which is a journal publication "containing scholarly articles, essays, and other commentary on legal topics by professors, judges, law students, and practitioners." Black's Law Dictionary (9th ed. 2009). Most law reviews are edited by law students, and membership to law review is usually offered to students ranked in the top 10% at the end of the first year of a law school. This is called "grading-on" to the journal. Most journals also reserve a percentage of additional membership spots to those who do well in a write-on competition.

My post-graduation experience differs greatly from the expectations I had when I started law school. Before going to law school, I expected to obtain an attorney position at a big law firm in Texas and that it would pay me over $100,000 per year. As I mentioned above, the $10/hour job that I got right out of law school was a far cry from these expectations. This was a hard pill to swallow due to the fact that my accumulated student loan debt exceeded $100,000—$60,000 from undergrad and $45,000 from law school. Such a huge amount of debt has interfered with my ability to do certain things because my monthly student loan payments total more than $700 per month.

Despite my student loan debt, I wanted to buy a house. However, because this debt was so large, I was forced to search extensively for a mortgage company or bank willing to give me a loan even though I had a very high credit score. Eventually, I saved enough down-payment money to satisfy one lender and was able to qualify for a first-time home-buyer program. I am grateful for my home; however, that nice dream car that I wanted before law school is still out of reach. I have never taken a vacation outside of the city in which I live. I have even delayed getting married to my fiancée because I don't want to saddle her with the debt issues created by my decision to attend, and successfully complete, law school.

If I could do law school all over again based on the knowledge gained by my experiences, I do not think that I would have re-taken the LSAT to get into a higher ranked law school. Had I gone that route and gotten into a higher ranked school, I would have amassed an even larger amount of debt than I have now. However, in retrospect, I am certain that I should have participated in law review. This would have greatly increased my chances of being offered, by graduation day, an entry-level attorney position at one of the area law firms.

Gleaning Wisdom from Ted's Story

What lessons should prospective students learn from Ted's experience? First, I don't think it's advisable to work while being a first-year law student. In Ted's case, he had the benefit of having a father as a lawyer. So for him, the transition from undergraduate study habits to law school study habits were not a problem. While Ted's part-time employment did not hinder his ability to excel academically, I believe that working limited the time he had available to develop meaningful connections during his first year. Had he connected with any of his professors and mentioned law review, all would have told him that he should join law review.

This leads me to the next lesson. If you have the opportunity to join law review, you absolutely should do it. Even if students cannot "grade-on" to law review, most journals have "write-on" competition so that students who do well in the competition may become members of law review.[7] My advice has always been that sometimes a part-time job while in law school has to take a back seat to making a career-maximizing move. Based on that advice, Ted should have stopped working or reduced his hours so that he could have devoted time to being a student editor on law review.

Traditional law firms and many governmental employers, in the recruiting process, rely very heavily not only on a student's grade point average and class ranking, but on the student's law review participation. Because being a law review editor requires that the student engage

---

7. Write-on competitions are now widespread because the automatic grade-on system was viewed as flawed and unfair. For example, some people who grade-on are very good test takers, not the best writers.

in editing and other writing skills, these employers view law review participation as a good proxy for strong writing skills. Because Ted was so highly ranked but not on law review, prospective employers could have viewed that very negatively. For example, a partner could have interpreted Ted's lack of law review participation as unwillingness to work very hard. Thus, Ted miscalculated how important law review participation was and, therefore, did not accept it, and this most likely prevented him from getting a big firm job.

The third lesson to take away from Ted's experience is that students need to prepare for various interviewing techniques. The days of showing up at interview and saying "hire me because I'm in the top 10%" are over. One of the biggest law firms in the country is Jones Day, and one of its partners, Steven Bennett, indicated that "paper" credentials—GPA, ranking, and law review—are not enough these days to get a big firm job. He states that because clients are insisting on more "bang for their buck," big law firms can no longer hire legions of entry-level attorneys. This has partially led to an increase in "behavioral interviewing," which Mr. Bennett describes as employers asking job candidates "specific questions about how they have handled difficult circumstances in the past."[8] The student's answers are used by the employer to predict how the student will respond to future problems that may arise on the job. Mr. Bennett also says that the student has to be prepared to explain how the students' specific job experiences relate to the needs of the law firm in serving its clientele.

Because the number of entry-level attorney jobs has shrunk and is not expected to ever return to pre-recession levels, prospective students need to check out the career placement office at the targeted law school. Prospective students must assess what efforts are being taken by the career placement office (1) to get *more* legal employers to participate in on-campus recruiting and (2) to help students get ready for interviews. For the student, having a career counselor edit a resume is no longer enough. The law school should have career placement staff dedicated to helping students do mock interviews to get them prepared to put their best foot forward and be prepared to adequately respond to behavioral interviewing techniques used by legal employers.[9]

Ted's inability to get hired at one of the big law firms in Texas was most likely due the absence of TSU alumni in partner positions. Professor Seto's research about law graduates who become partners at top law firms in Houston shows that TSU is not among the top ten feeder law schools.[10] As result, Ted already had an uphill battle trying to persuade partners at these law firms to hire him over top graduates from their alma maters.

Ted's experience also is a lesson in persistence. Because the legal job market has an abundance of law graduates seeking attorney jobs, new graduates need to be prepared to do an extensive job search and take advantage of networking opportunities. Lastly, new graduates need to be willing to accept an under-employed position if it has a reasonable prospect of leading to a permanent attorney position. Since embarking on this book project, I have heard numerous stories of graduates who take positions as paralegals and volunteer unpaid internships and were subsequently able to turn those positions into permanent attorney positions.

---

8. Steven C. Bennett, Practising Law Institute, Winning Strategies for Managing Your Career 2010 (March 24, 2010).

9. I did not do an extensive search but I did find a few law schools that had online information about how law students can be prepared for behavioral interviewing techniques. *See, e.g.*, Patricia White, *Building Interview Skills: What to Tell Students about the Behavioral Interview*, NALP Bulletin (Jan. 2005), *available at* http://www.law.ou.edu/career/handouts/Building%20Interview%20Skills.pdf.

10. For a longer discussion of Professor Seto's research, refer to Chapter 7.

As for Mr. Paul's student loan debt, I would like to direct the reader to Chapter 14 where I discuss loan payment assistance programs that are based on one's income. During the period when his income was low, Mr. Paul would have been eligible to have his student loan payments lowered to only 15% of his discretionary income. I want prospective and current students to be aware of these programs so that they can adequately manage their student loan debt. Note that private student loans are not covered by these programs; therefore, private loans should be avoided if at all possible.

Larry: The Transfer That Saved My Career

I graduated from Michigan State University ("MSU") in 2005 with a bachelor's degree in criminal justice. While at MSU, I was a member of Reserve Officers' Training Corps ("ROTC"), which is a college-based program for training commissioned officers who want to serve in the United States Armed Forces. I took an interest in law very early during undergraduate studies at MSU. In my senior year at MSU, I took the LSAT and decided to apply for admission at MSU Law School and Cooley Law School. As I waited for possible offers, I also applied for and landed a paid internship in State Farm's litigation group. I was offered admission to Cooley and awarded a fairly sizeable scholarship that covered about half of my tuition. My ability to keep the scholarship was contingent on my maintaining a minimum GPA. I decided to accept Cooley's offer. I obtained student loans to cover my living expenses and the rest of my tuition.

During my time at Cooley, I worked very hard and did well academically. Before enrolling in Cooley, I knew that I would have to work hard to do well. At the new student orientation, the incoming students were advised to work hard in order to achieve academic success. Students were also advised to take only nine-credit-hour course load during the first semester if they were concerned about doing well in law school. I was confident that I had the discipline to study and do well, so I decided to take the normal twelve-credit-hour load for fulltime students. After my 1L year, I had an "A" average and ranked number eight in my class.

Overall, my time at Cooley was a positive experience. For example, I appreciated how Cooley stressed to its students the importance of reading critically and outlining my notes to be prepared for class in order to succeed. Cooley's professors were exceptional teachers, despite the inherent difficulties of teaching a large class size, which is the norm. Cooley's facilities were magnificent and provided top-of-the line technology. For example, Cooley provided students with DVDs of the lectures if we missed a class. Additionally, we had microphones for students to use to project their voices when answering questions in the classroom.

The main drawback to attending Cooley is that it is a fourth-tier law school, and I discovered I had very limited employment options as a Cooley law student. I applied for a summer job that was posted by Cooley's career services department. I got an interview with the firm, but it did not make me an offer. I decided to get very aggressive in my search for a legal job for summer. Despite sending out dozens of resumes and cover letters to legal employers in Michigan, I did not get any interviews. Instead, I received lots of "Dear John" letters thanking me for applying. With no prospects for a legal job, I discussed my lack of job success with one of Cooley's instructors, and she recommended I take an unpaid summer intern position at the Michigan Supreme Court. Because I needed income,

I opted to take a job unloading trucks at a warehouse. I was extremely disappointed that despite being ranked eighth in the class, I did not receive a single offer for paid legal position. In retrospect, I wish I had known more about this negative consequence of going to a fourth-tier school like Cooley.

After not getting any job offers for a summer position, I realized that I needed to change schools if I wanted to improve my employment opportunities. Because I am from Arizona and have family living there, I decided to pursue a transfer to the law schools at both the University of Arizona and Arizona State University. I asked three of my professors to serve as references as required in the transfer application process. To my surprise, I encountered pushback from my professors when I told them that I wanted to transfer to increase my chances of getting a job. One professor flat out refused to write a recommendation letter for me even though I took two courses from this professor and was a very active participant in his classes. The other two professors tried to talk me out of transferring. I quickly realized that I needed to modify my reason for wanting a transfer if I was going to convince them to write the recommendation letters. When I approached them again, I emphasized that I wanted to go home to Arizona and be near my family. They eventually agreed to write the letters. Both Arizona schools offered to accept me as a transfer student, but I decided to transfer to the University of Arizona College of Law (hereafter "Arizona") because it was ranked higher than the other school.

After enrolling in Arizona, I noticed an enormous improvement in my job opportunities. For example, I was granted interviews with several of the top law firms in the Phoenix area during the on-campus interviewing ("OCI") sessions. Many of the employers were impressed with my eighth place ranking, despite my resume reflecting that I obtained it at Cooley. As a result of OCI interviews, I received a couple of offers for summer employment between my second and third year. I accepted a summer associate position at the Phoenix office of a national law firm with over 500 attorneys. I was very satisfied that I was able to obtain a paid legal position where I could gain practical experience.

In addition to my summer position, I worked during the second semester of my 2L year at Arizona. I applied for and obtained an internship with the Arizona Legislative Council ("ALC")[11] where I gained valuable experience doing mostly legal research and writing. Typically, a state representative or senator would receive a complaint or concern from a constituent, and he or she would then send ALC a research request to determine how other states handled the complaint or concern. As a result, my research allowed me to play a role in state politics: working for a representative or senator to attempt to resolve a problem for Arizona citizens. This internship paid my tuition for the spring semester of my second year. Also I was paid a monthly stipend and earned credit for class. This internship was very important because as a result of it, I did not feel bad about losing my scholarship from Cooley. My borrowing for my 2L year at Arizona was roughly equal to the amount of borrowing I did to cover my year at Cooley. I continued to receive job opportunities at Arizona. During my 3L year, I worked as a law clerk for a county prosecutor in the civil litigation division. I was really grateful for this job opportunity because litigation is where my passion lies.

---

11. The Arizona Legislative Council is a statutory committee that serves both house of the Arizona Legislature. *See Welcome To The Arizona Legislative Council*, http://www.azleg.gov/az_leg_council/default.htm (last visited Feb. 24, 2013) (stating that the Council provides "a variety of nonpartisan bill drafting, research, computer and other administrative services to all of the members of both houses of the Legislature").

I graduated from Arizona in 2008 in the top 20% of my class with the distinction of cum laude. I took the California bar exam and passed it on my first attempt. As a result of my academic record at Arizona and passing the bar exam, I was offered and accepted a position at a very good law firm in California. I held that job for approximately one year before joining the United States Army JAG Corps.

I started my JAG Corps career as a legal assistant attorney and worked my way up to a trial counsel position, which I hold today. In this position, I am essentially a government prosecutor where I prosecute rape, attempted murder, and complex crimes against military personnel charged with crimes under the military code.

Professor Johnson asked me to describe any drawbacks I encountered after transferring to Arizona. When I first transferred to Arizona, I did not realize that there would be some potentially negative consequences of transferring. For example, I did not realize that my ranking position would be lost and, therefore, I did not automatically qualify to join the Arizona law review. Moreover, one's GPA does not carryover from the school that you transfer from. I had to start over to earn a GPA that would put me near the top of the class. Of course, I worked hard and did that. As previously stated, I graduated in the top 20% of the class.

I have been informed about the lawsuit filed against Cooley accusing it of misleading prospective students with its employment and salary data. Upon reflection, I do not feel that Cooley provided me with information that was misleading or deceptive. To the extent Cooley's materials could be construed as deceptive, I believe I avoided being deceived because I am by nature mistrusting and, therefore, seek to always read between the lines. For example, I discovered online a report or some type of survey where Cooley was ranked fairly high. However, I took this information with a huge grain of salt because I was already aware of *US News* rankings and that it is considered by most to be reputable.[12]

I have been asked to address my student loan debt. All told, the student loan debt that I incurred during law school was between $80,000 and $90,000. If I add the student loans that I obtained during my undergraduate years at MSU, the total amount of my student loan debt was roughly $115,000. Despite this student loan debt, I am absolutely happy with my decision to go to law school, and I love being a lawyer. To me student loans are just a necessary evil of getting an education that greatly improves one's chances of finding a meaningful and fulfilling career. Because of my JAG Corps position, I earn a fairly good salary with very good benefits, and I qualify for a loan payment and forgiveness program as a member of the military. As a result, I am on track to have my student loans paid off within 10 years of graduating from law school.

Conclusions to Draw from Larry's Story

Larry's story is compelling on its own; however, I do have a few points to highlight. First, he did not forgo his dream of being an attorney just because he did not get an offer

12. While most law school applicants think the *US News* ranking system is reputable, that is not the case among academics. The *US News* ranking system has been widely criticized for decades. For a more full discussion, please refer to Chapter 7. The premise of my book is that unless an applicant gets an offer from one of the Top 14 law schools, the US News ranking system should *not* be used to make an enrollment decision. For an interesting discussion of the various rankings systems, read *Ranking the Rankings*, PRAWFSBLAWG, (Jan. 30, 2013), http://prawfsblawg.blogs.com/prawfsblawg/2013/01/ranking-the-rankings.html.

from a higher ranked law school. Second, when he enrolled at Cooley, Larry, who was already a member of ROTC, had made plans to apply for admission to the Army JAG Corps while in law school. That meant that in comparison to the typical law student, he had more than one avenue to pursue a job as an attorney. Third, Larry tried to be vigilant in limiting the amount he borrowed. He was motivated to accept Cooley's offer because it offered him a substantial scholarship. When he got to Arizona, he was employed most of his time there; yet he did not allow his employment during the school year to hamper his ability to excel academically. He also obtained an internship that paid his tuition for one semester. Through Larry's story, I am trying to get prospective students to strike a proper balance between being confident, on the one hand, and having an actual strategy, on the other hand, for accomplishing the long-term goal of becoming an attorney while minimizing student loan borrowing.

Look Before You Leap

Finally, I do not want prospective students to that think that a transfer to higher ranked school is always the best option. A transfer is advisable if a student winds up like Larry—very highly-ranked but no employment prospects—and the targeted law school has much higher employment outcomes than the current school. Look below to see how Cooley's 2011 graduates compare to the graduates of Arizona State and University of Arizona in securing full-time, long-term, bar-required jobs.

Comparison of Cooley to the Targeted Schools

2011 Data	LT, FT, BR Job	Total # of Grads	% Employed
U of AZ	119	158	75%
AZ State	137	201	68%
Cooley	375	999	38%

Assuming that the employment outcome for the Arizona schools where much better than Cooley's in the year Larry sought a transfer, his transfer was the right move because he had much better chance of getting an attorney position as a graduate of the Arizona schools than as a graduate of Cooley.[13]

While Larry' transfer led to the desired result, other transfer students have not fared so well. Recall that in Chapter 7, I told the story of Niko Marneris, who enrolled in John Marshall, then-ranked in the fourth tier, and later transferred to Chicago-Kent. Fearful that John Marshall's *US News* ranking status would prove fatal, he transferred to Chicago-Kent even though he had a 3.9 GPA at John Marshall that put him in the top 10% and earned him a law journal spot. As the reader see can below, Chicago-Kent's employment success is minimally better than John Marshall for the 2011 graduates.

13. I could not provide the data for the year in which Larry sought a transfer because the ABA standards forcing greater transparency did not go into effect until 2012 for the class of 2011. As explain in previous chapters, the high overall employment rates reported by Cooley before the new ABA standards took effect were completely unreliable in assessing the actual percentage of graduates who had fulltime, longterm jobs as attorneys.

2011 Data	LT, FT, BR Job	Total # of Grads	% Employed
Chicago-Kent	169	332	51%
John Marshall	174	401	43%

Mr. Marneris' academic performance at Chicago-Kent was insufficient and he graduated ranked in the middle of the pack. He did not receive any offer for an attorney position. I am confident that if Niko had stayed at John Marshall where he would have graded on to the law journal and most likely would have graduated with honors, he would have been able to capitalize on John Marshall's regional reputation and found a job as a lawyer.

It is better to be very highly-ranked and stay put than to transfer to a school with only marginally better employment outcomes and risk graduating with a mediocre academic record. The latter position is a recipe for unemployment.

Tara: Graduating from a Top 14 School Is No Guarantee

My name is Tara, and I graduated from a Top 14 law school (hereafter "My T-14 School").[14] I wanted to tell my story because many people are under the misconception that all graduates of a Top 14 law school can write their ticket to wherever they want to go.[15] That turned out to not be true for me as well as for some of the people who graduated from My T-14 School.

I've always wanted to do public interest legal work and was excited about the opportunity to get a law degree to served under-represented populations. I did well on the LSAT and applied for admission to several law schools. I got an offer from a law school ranked at the low end of the first-tier, and it awarded me a scholarship that would have covered all of my tuition. I also got an offer from My T-14 School. Because of the ranking of My T-14 School and its reputation among public interest firms, I believed that my ability to secure a public interest job would be better if I graduated from My T-14 School than if I had graduated from the other law school. However, I was very concerned about how much debt I would incur at My T-14 School, which did not offer me a scholarship.

I explained my dilemma to an admissions worker at My T-14 School. She told me that I would be able to qualify for the school's loan forgiveness program if I took a public

14. Professor Johnson discusses the Top 14 law schools in Chapter 7.

15. Please do not confuse "Tara" with a 2013 candidate for graduation of another Top 14 school. Dana Tapper, a 3L student at University of Virginia School of Law, appeared recently on the Ellen DeGeneres Show where Ellen gave Dana $20,000 to help her pay some of her debts. *See* Staci Zaretsky, *UVA Law Student Wins Money For Loan Debt On Live TV*, Above the Law, Feb. 28, 2013, *available at* http://abovethelaw.com/2013/02/uva-law-student-wins-money-for-loan-debt-on-live-tv/?show=comments#comments. Ms. Tapper, who has incurred nearly six figures in student loan debt, stated that she has been struggling to find a public interest job despite applying for one on a daily basis. When asked whether she was worried about lacking a job offer even though she goes to a Top 14 law school, she responded: "Yes and no. UVA has been very, very supportive, especially those from the school's Public Service Center. Because of their help, I haven't been as terrified about not having a job as [I] should be. The school is really working hard to help everyone who's interested in pursuing public interest careers find a job that suits them."

interest job. Moreover, after 10 years in that public interest job, I would be able to wipe out any remaining student loan debt. That was good news to me because that meant that I could enroll in the higher ranked school and not have to worry about how I would eventually pay back the student loan debt on a public interest salary.

During my time at My T-14 School, I turned down job offers from law firms and only took public interest jobs during the summers. Although the firm jobs paid far more than the public interest jobs, I only wanted to do public interest work since I had a great passion in that area.

I graduated from law school during the economic downturn. Public interest firms were not just refusing to hire but they had started laying off people. Therefore, I could not find a public interest job even though I graduated from My T-14 School. I contemplated getting a non-legal job at a public interest firm so I could qualify for the school's loan forgiveness program. During law school, I had gotten several federally-guaranteed student loans as well as private loans. I inquired about how I could qualify for My T-14 School's loan forgiveness program. I was flabbergasted when I learned for the first time that my private loans would not be covered even if I could find a qualifying public service job. Because my private loans under the standard monthly repayment plan would be huge, I was sickened to realize I had no way to get the payments reduced under the school's loan forgiveness program.

Desperate to find employment to deal with my student loan debt, I started interviewing with law firms. However, I could not gain any traction in the interviews because my resume reflected an interest only in public service. In other words, I could not convince a law firm that I was interested in traditional law-firm practice.

Even a year after graduating from law school, I still could not find a traditional law-firm attorney job. A few months later, I learned about a job opening as a "staff attorney" at a law firm. I interviewed for the position and got it. So what does "staff attorney" mean? It means I do the same work as an entry-level associate attorney hired in a partner-track position, but my starting salary was less than half the salary of the attorney in the partner-track position. I am not on the partnership track and, therefore, never can become a profit-sharing partner—the ones who make the biggest bucks at the law firm. I consider myself to be under-employed. As a graduate of a Top 14 law school, I should have been able to secure a six-figure salary at one of the large law firms. I also consider myself under-employed because I'm not satisfied with my employment status. I have no passion for the work, but I felt compelled to take the job so I could start paying back my six-figure student loan debt.

Gaining Insight from Tara's Story

First, would-be students should not simply rely on rankings but should assess other data about each law school making an offer. If the data, particularly the employment data, turns out to be positive, the prospective student should then focus on the school's reputation in the legal job market where the school is located. Recall that Tara turned down the offer from the first-tier law school that made her a full-tuition scholarship offer. Research suggests that legal hiring is astonishingly local. That means that the ideal option may be to go to the best law school located in the region where the prospective student eventually wants to end up practicing law. It could be that the lower-ranked first-tier law school had better regional reputation when it comes to public interest jobs, than the far-away Top 14 law school that Tara chose to attend.

The second take-away from Tara's story is that prospective law students should give careful consideration to a first-tier school making a scholarship offer. While a few schools ranked in the lower tiers have been accused of offering bait-and-switch scholarships, I have not seen similar accusations lodged against first-tier schools. By accepting scholarships on the front-end, prospective students can minimize student loan borrowing over the course of three years. It's better to be in a position of having borrowed less than to have borrowed a lot in hopes that a loan forgiveness program can wipe out the debt. Had Tara attended the lower-ranked first-tier school, she would have emerged with far less debt than she incurred at the Top 14 school. Also, she would have avoided private loans and would have been well-situated to accept a lower-paying, but satisfying public-interest job. She would have then qualified for the loan forgiveness programs available to graduates with public service jobs, even if they are non-legal.

Third, prospective students should not rely on the words of admissions personnel when it comes to scholarships and post-graduation loan assistance and forgiveness programs. There are too many stories of admissions personnel going to any length to get the right people admitted. Personnel that are directly in charge of the scholarships and the school's loan forgiveness programs should be consulted to gain accurate information.

Once enrolled, students should pay attention to what's happing in the marketplace as well at the law school itself. Adjustments may need to be made. For instance, Tara should have taken a summer job at a law firm just in case public interest jobs turned out to be hard to come by. She was not prepared for the unstable legal job market because she had not positioned herself to be attractive to law firms, which hire far more graduates, than public interest organizations.

The New Normal

Because of Tara's story, I have to warn future law students that "staff" or "career" attorneys are the new normal. As explained in Chapter 10, the recession has resulted in a spike in déclassé attorney positions that pay graduates sometimes less than half the salary of traditional associate attorneys. These jobs may involve an associate doing routine legal work, doing the same work as an entry level, partner-track associate, or doing monotonous document review. I know about a recent graduate who took a staff attorney position out of fear that he might not find a permanent attorney position. I explained in Chapter 10 that prospective students need to realize that the traditional entry-level, partnership-track jobs that pay six-figure salaries are out of reach for the majority of graduates. Realize that some graduates take "career" or "staff" attorney jobs because those are the only jobs that they can find after graduation. However, while the déclassé jobs are sometimes not fulfilling, the salary for one of these jobs may be high enough to cover the bills and provide a comfortable lifestyle.

If offered a career or staff attorney job, graduates should consider taking it because they can provide graduates the opportunity to practice law in a sophisticated capacity without the pressures of a traditional partner-track job. These career and staff attorney jobs are often touted as "lifestyle jobs," and, for some attorneys, these jobs are good lifestyle positions for those who want more time to devote to family activities or volunteer work. Moreover, not everyone is cut out to work 60–80 hours a week, as is usually required of traditional partner-track associates. Others have no desire to taken on the pressure to bring in business, as law firms expect their attorneys to eventually become "rainmakers."

Whether a career or staff attorney position is taken by choice or out of desperation, I encourage law graduates employed in such jobs to do pro bono legal work that positively impacts the lives of consumers and to remain passionate about the law.

Liz: Transferring to a Top 10 School Opened Many Doors

I grew up in a small, conservative, non-diverse town in the mid-west before attending the University of Notre Dame, where I graduated magna cum laude with a B.A. While at Notre Dame, I had a sense that I would go to law school, but I didn't want to go straight to law school. In 2003, I moved to New Orleans after graduation for a "real world" experience. For the next three years, I worked full-time as a paralegal and part-time as a bartender to supplement my income. My work as a paralegal cemented my decision to go to law school; I quite enjoyed the research and writing aspect of the job. Moreover, even though I was exposed to the less-glamorous, routine life of lawyers at the law firm, I was still convinced this was the career I wanted.

By my third year of working in New Orleans, I felt the time was right to go to law school. Hurricane Katrina had devastated New Orleans a few months before, and the people of New Orleans were reeling from the aftermath. The city I grew to love was in a state of disrepair, and I realized it would be good time to become a lawyer as New Orleans needed all sorts of help. In 2006, I was accepted to Tulane University Law School and was waitlisted at Vanderbilt Law School. I didn't want to wait so I decided to enroll in Tulane. Selecting Tulane was a logical choice because it was the highest ranked law school that I got an offer from, and I was already living in New Orleans. Moreover, enrolling in Tulane would allow me to avoid relocation expenses, and I could still work as a paralegal during law school.

My first year of law school was very challenging for me. I had to learn to manage my time wisely to prepare for class while holding down my part-time paralegal job. Tulane was also challenging because the environment at the law school was dramatically different from my expectations. After three years of living in New Orleans, I took for granted that I was constantly surrounded by a diverse group of friends with very progressive attitudes about race and equality. New Orleans is a very diverse city, in terms of its native population. Moreover, tourists from all over the world add to the culture of diversity. However, I was shocked at what I encountered at Tulane. While I developed some very close and enduring friendships with several classmates at Tulane, I was also confronted with a level of racism among my peers that I was in no way prepared for. On many occasions, I encountered students making racist remarks and behaving in a racially-insensitive manner, the likes of which I had witnessed far too often growing up as a white female in an almost exclusively white Midwestern city. As a result, the environment at Tulane led to a lot of angst among some of the members of the student body.

Despite this environment and the challenges it presented, I finished my 1L year in the top 20% of my class, was invited to join the Tulane Law Review, and was elected as an officer of no less than four law school organizations. Even with these accomplishments and the many close friendships I had developed over the past year, as well as my love for New Orleans, I was exhausted by the thought of spending two more years in an environment I perceived as racially insensitive. I knew this was the last time I would be in school and

I wanted to truly love the experience. So I started thinking that it was time to a transfer to another school for a better experience.

It wasn't just the atmosphere at Tulane that made me want to leave. I started to question whether Tulane had the nationwide appeal necessary for the career I wanted. By the end of my 1L year, I was focused on pursuing a career in environmental law and from what I could discern, recruitment at Tulane was limited to regional employers (e.g., Louisiana, Mississippi, Georgia, etc.), and very few, if any, of these employers had robust environmental law practices. While *US News* ranked Tulane's program among one of the top five environmental law programs in the country, the law school as a whole did not seem to offer the national recognition I had expected when enrolling. I didn't want my job prospects in environmental law to be limited.

After my second semester at Tulane, I sought a transfer and was accepted at both Vanderbilt University and the University of Michigan Law School. While it was a tough decision, Michigan's ranking as a top 10 law school and excellent reputation, combined with the administration's friendly and helpful attitude, persuaded me to enroll sight-unseen. Once I arrived, I was immediately impressed with the faculty, the staff, and with my classmates. In contrast to Tulane, I found that Michigan facilitates an atmosphere of inclusivity where the importance of diversity is touted as one of the school's primary achievements; prejudice of any type, be it based on race, gender, sexual preference, etc., was not tolerated. Consequently, I felt much more comfortable at Michigan than I did at Tulane.

Transferring to the University of Michigan was one of the best, if not the best, decisions of my career. For one, Michigan offered more environmental law courses than Tulane (surprising, given that Tulane has a much more established, and recognized, environmental law program). As a result, I could focus my academic energy on learning all that I could about environmental law. Unlike Tulane, Michigan did not have a lot of required upper-level courses. I, therefore, had complete liberty to take courses of interest to me.

Another thing that I really liked about Michigan was that it offered an externship program where students could work abroad full-time for one semester to gain practical legal experience, without having to take law school classes. During the last semester of my third year, I was afforded an opportunity to work in Geneva, Switzerland, at a non-governmental organization based in Washington, DC. My environmental law work experience in Switzerland was invaluable.

In addition to my work experience abroad, I was very involved in several organizations at Michigan, and I was also fortunate enough to be selected as a member of the Michigan Journal of Race & Law's Editorial Board.

Because of the stature of Michigan Law School, I was able to interview with several employers from around the country during OCI (on-campus interviewing) season, which draws between 400–500 employers each year. Tulane could not compare as they drew far fewer employers at OCI. Michigan's OCI interviewing process was unique in that students are able to choose the employers that they wanted to interview with, and the employers cannot learn, prior to the interview, the student's grades or class ranking. Moreover, employers do not have a say in selecting the students they interview. I discovered that many employers were just eager to hire a Michigan Law graduate. When I interviewed with an environmental law firm in the State of Washington, the hiring partner asked about Tulane on my resume and asked me where Tulane was located. I was astonished at his lack of familiarity with Tulane, which some Louisianians often refer to as the "Harvard of the South." This was just another confirmation that transferring to Michigan was the right course of action for me.

As a result of Michigan's OCI process, I received numerous job offers in my third year of law school. I ultimately decided to accept an offer to work at a large, boutique environmental law firm.

Looking back at my time in law school, overall I am happy that I decided to go, and especially happy that I transferred to Michigan. I firmly believe that much of my success in law school can be attributed to the environment in which I learned. I graduated magna cum laude in the top 4% of my law school class, as a member of the Phi Kappa Phi Honor Society, and as a member of the Michigan Chapter of the Order of the Coif. Michigan Law School opened up so many doors for me, and I remain in contact with a network of friends and faculty.

I recently left the environmental law firm in the fall of 2012 to start a one-year federal clerkship in a very prestigious district. This clerkship experience will provide me with litigation opportunities and experience from behind the scenes in the courtroom, while also providing me with sound legal writing experience.

Despite my student loans—$40,000 from undergrad and $150,000 from law school—I still think that having a law school degree was the right choice for me. I advise future law students to make sure that they *really* want to go to law school, in light of the debt that it leaves you in and the diligence required to succeed.

Lessons to Learn from Liz's Story

Rather than going straight from undergraduate school to law school, I recommend that prospective law students work for two or three years like Liz did. If the goal is to become a lawyer, prospective law students should pursue employment in a legal environment. Pre-law-school work experience, particularly with a legal employer, will give a would-be law student time to decide whether getting a law degree is really desired and whether the time is right. Also, for prospective students who have been dependent on familial support, work experience will give them time to become financially independent and will help them feel the pinch of having to deal with student loan debt already acquired. This money management experience puts prospective students in a better position to borrow wisely. Otherwise, those who go straight to law school may not get a reality check regarding how much student loan debt reduces a person's disposable income.

I wanted to share Liz's experience with prospective students so that they can decide ahead of time if a certain type of diverse environment is necessary for a person's overall well-being. Assuming the racism was only expressed by a small minority of students, Liz, a white female, still felt that the racism she and her African-American classmates observed at Tulane to be sufficiently negative that it was a factor in her decision to pursue transfer to another school. For some students, a certain type of diversity and a climate accepting of such diversity is really important. For example, if one searches online the terms LGBT and "law school," one can find law students and graduates who self-identify as gay, lesbian, bisexual or transgender asserting that they experienced LGBT discrimination or bashing from fellow law students. There are three studies showing that self-identified LGBT students experienced discrimination in law school on the basis of their sexual orientation.[16] Moreover, I imagine that discrimination from

16. Kate Nace Day & Russell G. Murphy, *"Just Trying To Be Human in This Place": Storytelling and Film Inside the First-Year Law School Classroom*, 39 Stetson L. Rev. 247 (2009) (discussing the studies

classmates continues to be experienced by other "outsider" students, such as Arab American law students since 9-11.[17]

I am not suggesting that students make the diversity of the law school's environment a determinative factor in making an enrollment decision. I feel that discrimination from "majority" groups can make one a stronger person and a better advocate. I went to West Virginia University College of Law, which is located in a state where almost everyone is white. I anticipated experiencing racial discrimination at the law school and in the community and did experience it. For me, getting a quality legal education at the least possible expense was determinative, not the extent to which I would encounter a racially hostile environment. By the way, I found the environment at WVU to be mostly positive.

Throughout this book, I have emphasized a school's employment data as being very important in making an enrollment decision. Because the ABA has forced more accurate disclosures of the type of data prospective students want to know, one can see that Michigan grads enjoy a much greater employment rate than Tulane grads. Liz's dramatic increase in employment opportunities at Michigan makes sense due to Michigan's ranking among the Top 14 law schools[18] and is confirmed by a comparison of the employment reports for Michigan and Tulane. As reported in Table 1-1 of Appendix A, 75% (286 of 379) of Michigan's 2011 graduates obtained the coveted fulltime, long-term, bar-passage-required jobs. In contrast, only 58% of Tulane's 2011 graduates obtained such jobs. As indicated in Tables 6 and 7 of Appendix A, both schools experienced a significant jump in these rates for their 2012 grads. It is also not surprising that Liz wound up at a large law firm because 76% of Michigan's 2011 graduates were employed at law firms with a size greater than 100. Tulane, on the other hand, only had 21% of its graduates employed at 100-plus size firms.

I realize everyone cannot get into Michigan. However, as explained in Chapter 14, prospective students who have strong desire to be an attorney should not forgo law school just because they did not get an admission offer from a Top 14 law school. Law graduates who take advantage of loan payment assistance and forgiveness programs can reduce their student loan debt and, thereby, enjoy a decent lifestyle.

---

and concluding that "[i]t seems beyond dispute that many outsider students are silenced in the first-year classroom").

17. *See, e.g.*, Matthew L.M. Fletcher, *The Legal Fiction of Standardized Testing*, 21 Law & Ineq. 397, 414 (2003) (stating that an Arab American law student told his professor that "a couple of white male law students stopped him in the hallway to tell him that he was an Affirmative Action law student and they didn't think he was smart enough to study with them").

18. The top 14 law schools are based on *US News* ranking and are discussed in Chapter 7.

Chapter 13

In Limited Circumstances, Bankruptcy Is an Option for Eliminating Student Loan Debt

Bankruptcy Cannot Relieve Most Grads of Burdensome Student Loan Debt[1]

Because I have practiced and taught bankruptcy law for years, I occasionally meet people who feel that their debt is insurmountable and wonder if filing bankruptcy can help them. A graduate who has amassed unmanageable student loan debt can file bankruptcy to reduce or eliminate the debt *but only* if the graduate's financial situation poses an "undue hardship." Unfortunately, this undue hardship burden is impossible for most graduates to prove. Therefore, I recommend that indebted students read Chapter 14 where I discuss various loan forgiveness or reduced-repayment programs that graduates can apply for to alleviate student loan indebtedness. You can skip this chapter if you have a sense that your debt load will ***not*** be insurmountable. Below I describe three cases to show the reader how bad a debtor's circumstances must be to persuade a court to discharge—*i.e.* wipe out—the debt.[2]

---

1. *Editorial: It's Smart to Let Needy Students Shed Loan Debt in Bankruptcy*, Baylor Lariat, (Baylor University) Feb. 14, 2013, *available at* http://baylorlariat.com/2013/02/14/editorial-its-smart-to-let-needy-students-shed-loan-debt-in-bankruptcy/.

2. Under the U.S. Bankruptcy Code, an educational debt that "impose[s] an undue hardship on the debtor and the debtor's dependents" can be discharged so long as it is one of the following types of debts:

> (A)(i) an educational benefit overpayment or loan made, insured, or guaranteed by a governmental unit, or made under any program funded in whole or in part by a governmental unit or nonprofit institution; or
>
> (ii) an obligation to repay funds received as an educational benefit, scholarship, or

Disabled Debtor Gets Nearly $340,000 in Student Loans Discharged

Carol Todd made legal and business news headlines in 2012 when she convinced a U.S. bankruptcy court in Maryland to discharge nearly $340,000 in student loan debts.[3] To provide some background about how Ms. Todd amassed such a large amount of debt over a 20-year period, a brief summary of her educational history is necessary. Ms. Todd obtained a GED at 39 and pursued higher education as part of a rehabilitation program.[4] She then obtained an associate's degree in art from Villa Julie College (now Stevenson University). Later, she received a full scholarship to the University of Baltimore School of Law, attended the school for a period of time, but dropped out subsequently.[5] She obtained a bachelor's degree in philosophy from the College of Notre Dame in Baltimore, then went to Towson University where she received two master's degrees. Having completed all that, Ms. Todd was still not done pursuing higher education. She participated in a six-year doctoral program at Regent University in Virginia. Although she did not receive a degree there, she did receive a doctoral degree from an unaccredited online university. The bankruptcy judge described Ms. Todd's educational endeavors as an "academic odyssey."[6]

At the end of this academic odyssey, Ms. Todd wound up unemployed at the age of 63. On a monthly social security check of $768, she could not pay both her student loan debts and her living expenses. To support her claim of undue hardship, Ms. Todd had her physician testify that she suffers from Aspergers syndrome, "a disorder considered on the high-functioning end of the autism spectrum."[7] The doctor described the neurological disorder by way of example to demonstrate that Ms. Todd was incapable of interacting and functioning as normal employee: "A person with [an] intellectual disability may be able to bus tables at McDonald's[,] but after 10 minutes[,] the person may walk out the door and do something else." The doctor stated further that unless an employee with Aspergers syndrome has a supervisor standing nearby constantly telling the employee what to do, the employee will not be able "focus on a task and execute an eight hour day of something productive in order to be paid for doing it."[8]

Based on the doctor's testimony, Judge Robert Gordon found that Ms. Todd was unable to obtain sufficient employment each time she completed a degree even though she desperately sought permanent full-time employment.[9] In fact, the only job that Ms. Todd

---

stipend; or

(B) any other educational loan that is a qualified education loan, as defined in section 221(d)(1) of the Internal Revenue Code of 1986, incurred by a debtor who is an individual ...

11 U.S.C. 523(a)(7) (2012).

3. *See, e.g.*, Leigh Jones, *Asperger Syndrome Prompts Court to Forgive Former Law Student's Debt*, Nat'l Law J., May 21, 2012, *available at* http://www.law.com/jsp/nlj/PubArticleNLJ.jsp?id=1202555456097&slreturn=20130127170518; Kristi Tousignant, *U.S. Bankruptcy Court in Maryland Discharges Autistic Student's Loans*, Daily Record (Baltimore, MD), May 22, 2012, *available at* 2012 WLNR 12481230.

4. In re Todd, 473 B.R. 676 (Bankr. D. MD. 2012).

5. *Id.* No reason is provided as to why she withdrew from law school.

6. *Id.* at 684.

7. *Id.*

8. *Id.* at 681–82.

9. *Id.*

was able to obtain was that of an adjunct professor[10] for three public universities in West Virginia over four years.[11] Judge Gordon held that Asperger syndrome made it impossible for Ms. Todd to hold a job and, thus, repay her loans.

Some may question how Ms. Todd could have been smart enough to obtain multiple degrees, but be deemed non-employable, and thereby excused from paying back her student loans. Judge Gordon concluded that "[w]hile Ms. Todd can focus with intensity academically, Autism will not allow her to function in a normal job setting and generate meaningful income."[12]

Due to her inability to gain employment, Ms. Todd was able to meet what is known as the *Brunner* Test for undue hardship.[13] Without getting too technical, the *Brunner* Test requires proof "(1) [t]hat the debtor cannot maintain ... a 'minimal' standard of living ... if forced to repay the loans; and (2) [t]hat additional circumstances exist indicating that this state of affairs [will] persist for a significant portion of the repayment period of the student loans."[14] Courts have stated that the gist of the *Brunner* test requires a debtor to prove that a "certainty of hopelessness, [exists,} not simply a present inability to fulfill financial commitment."[15] The bankruptcy judge ruled that Ms. Todd passed this test. Taking into account Ms. Todd's autism, together with her osteoporosis and post-traumatic stress disorder, Judge Gordon found that her "autism and other ailments serve—like a metaphysical prison cell—to limit and restrict her lifestyle in a thoroughly potent way."[16] Ms. Todd's story is illustrative of what is needed to discharge of student loan debt based the debtor's disability and physical ailments.

Unemployed Graduate of Unaccredited Law School Gets Loans Discharged

The reader may be wondering if it is possible to meet the hardship test in the absence of a disability or substantial illness. Yes, it is possible to prove an undue hardship without a disability or illness. In some jurisdictions, courts follow a test known as the "totality of the circumstances" test (the "TOC Test") to prove an undue hardship.[17] The TOC Test is less stringent than the *Brunner* Test because, among other things, the debtor does not have to prove under the TOC Test a certainty of hopelessness.[18] For example, in *In re*

10. An adjunct professor is a part-time instructor position where the professor teaches a semester-long course for a very low salary that lacks any benefits. Once I got paid $3,000 to teach one course as an adjunct professor. When I taught the course, I was still employed full-time as an attorney.

11. In re Todd, 473 B.R. at 681–82.

12. *Id.*

13. *Id.* Brunner v. New York State Higher Educ. Servs. Corp., 831 F.2d 395 (2d Cir.1987) (per curiam). The *Brunner* test is a three-prong test requiring that the debtor show (1) an inability to pay the student loan debt, at her current level of income and expenses, and maintain a minimal standard of living; (2) the likelihood that this inability will persist for a substantial part of the loan repayment period; and (3) the existence of debtor's good faith efforts to repay the loans.

14. In re Todd, 473 B.R. at 687.

15. Brightful v. Pa. Higher Educ. Assistance Agency, 267 F.3d 324, 328 (3d Cir.2001).

16. In re Todd, 473 B.R. at 682.

17. In re Bronsdon, 435 B.R. 791 (B.A.P. 1st Cir. 2010).

18. *Id.*

Bronsdon, a 64-year-old, single woman, Denise Bronsdon, did not suffer from any disability or debilitating illness. Ms. Bronsdon obtained a bachelor's degree at age 50 from Wellesley College in 1994. In 2005, she graduated from Southern New England School of Law, a start-up law school that never received accreditation, and was acquired in 2010 by the University of Massachusetts at Dartmouth.[19] Although Ms. Bronsdon graduated in the top half of her law school class, she failed the state's bar exam three times.[20] By the time she had filed her bankruptcy petition, Ms. Bronsdon had worked briefly as a receptionist and then temporarily as a patent prosecution secretary. As a means of getting more sustainable income, she had tried securing a patent for an invention and publishing a book but was unsuccessful in both endeavors. After filing bankruptcy, Ms. Bronsdon's only source of income was a monthly social security check of $946.00. Moreover, she had moved into her father's house to cope with her debts.

Before deciding Ms. Bronsdon's fate, the court rejected the *Brunner* Test by deciding that the test asked the debtor to prove too much and was not warranted by the language of the Bankruptcy Code. Although the TOC test has three prongs, the court distilled the test into "one simple question: Can the debtor now, and in the foreseeable future, maintain a reasonable, minimal standard of living for the debtor and the debtor's dependents and still afford to make payments on the debtor's student loans?"[21] The Bankruptcy Appellate Panel of the First Circuit Court took into account Ms. Bronsdon's history of seeking fulltime employment and upheld the bankruptcy court's decision that she could ***not*** keep up her monthly student loan payments and maintain a minimal standard of living.

The lender argued that Ms. Bronsdon should be barred from receiving a discharge due to her failure to agree to a reduced loan payment plan, even though under that plan she would have been required to make zero payments. The Bankruptcy Appellate Panel rejected this argument and agreed with the bankruptcy court:

> [S]hackling the Debtor [Ms. Bronsdon] to the [plan] would be ... a pointless exercise. Although her current payments under the [plan] would be zero, interest would continue to accrue despite the fact that the Debtor's chances of ever repaying any portion of the loan are virtually non-existent. The Debtor is now 65 years old, has failed to pass the Massachusetts bar examination three times.... Debtor has attempted unsuccessfully to find employment as a secretary and has sought to publish a novel. These efforts demonstrate her good faith.... Nor are circumstances likely to improve for the Debtor. But for the ability to live in the den of her father's home, the Debtor, without some sort of financial aid, could easily become homeless. In view of her age and work history, her prospects for a better financial future are dim. To subject her to a meaningless repayment plan when she clearly does not have the ability to repay these student loans now or in the foreseeable future is not required by [the Bankruptcy Code].[22]

The reader should be able to discern that although the Bankruptcy Appellate Panel is relying on the TOC test, its application of that test to Ms. Bronsdon's situation shows that she was in a hopeless situation as required under the *Brunner* Test.

---

19. *See* Chapter 5. *See also About UMass Law*, UNIV. OF MASS. SCH. OF LAW, http://www.umassd.edu/law/about/ (last visited Feb. 28, 2013) ("The Massachusetts Board of Higher Education established the University of Massachusetts School of Law—Dartmouth in 2010, thereby creating the state's only public law school. UMass Law has its roots in the Southern New England School of Law, founded in 1981.").

20. In re Bronsdon, 435 B.R. at 794.

21. *Id.* at 798.

22. *Id.* at 803. See Chapter 5 where I discuss low bar-exam passage rates as a risk among several risks associated with attending an unaccredited law school.

Law Graduate Employed in Non-Legal Job Must Repay $85,000

The last case that I will discuss here is similar to Ms. Bronsdon's case in that an under-employed law graduate also sought discharge of his student loan debt. However, the case is different because the court decided that the debtor's struggle was due, in part, to his own lifestyle choices and not to market forces. In *Hedlund v. Educational Resources Institute, Inc.*,[23] Michael Hedlund sought to discharge student loans totaling $85,245.87.[24] Mr. Hedlund, a 1997 graduate of Willamette University College of Law,[25] spent the past nine years trying to get his student loans discharged. His case went from the bankruptcy court to the appellate level and then back down to the bankruptcy court.

To make a long story short, Mr. Hedlund was living with his wife and child in Klamath Falls, Oregon when in 2002, after over two years of nonpayment to one his student loan creditors, his paycheck was garnished to pay the student loan creditor $258 per month. Mr. Hedlund did not try to stop the garnishments; therefore, they continued for over a year. Then, in 2003, a second student loan creditor garnished more than $1,000 from his bank account. Mr. Hedlund could not survive on the money left after garnishments from two different creditors, and, consequently, he had to file bankruptcy to make the garnishments stop.[26]

I describe Mr. Hedlund as under-employed because he has been working not as an attorney but as a juvenile counselor at the Klamath County Juvenile Department. He twice failed the bar exam. As a result, he could not get a license to practice law and could not work as an attorney with his father and brother, both attorneys in the father's law firm.

Even though Mr. Hedlund did not fight the garnishment of his paycheck for 16 months and proposed a settlement of $5,000 to one his creditors, the court found that he had not met the *Brunner* test for a hardship discharge. Why? First, the Honorable Ann Aiken, Chief Judge for the U.S. District Court of Oregon, decided that despite Mr. Hedlund's settlement offer, he had failed to make any real attempts to enter into a negotiated reduced payment plan despite being aware of this plan option. Moreover, his wife, Mrs. Hedlund, worked at a flower shop only for six hours, one day per week because she preferred to be a stay-at-home mother for their daughter, who was at least 10 years old at the time Judge Aiken rendered her decision in March 2012.[27] Judge Ann Aiken made it clear that this voluntary one-wage-earner arrangement was unacceptable:

> While this Court is dismayed by the circumstances faced by the majority of today's law school graduates, Hedlund's case is distinguishable. He graduated in 1997, which was a period of great prosperity and rapid economic growth for the United States. Thus, even without passing the bar exam, Hedlund was able to obtain relatively high-paying, steady employment. Further, Hedlund and his wife chose to be a single-income family, which is a lifestyle that few today can afford,

---

23. *See* Hedlund v. Educ. Res. Inst., Inc., 468 B.R. 901 (D. Or.2012).

24. I say "has" instead of "had" because the battle is not over. After losing this case, Mr. Hedlund filed an appeal to the US Court of Appeals for the Ninth Circuit.

25. *Id.*

26. A person's filing for bankruptcy relief obligates all creditors to cease collection efforts. Creditors which seek to continue debt collection actions must seek express approval from the bankruptcy court. The bankruptcy court, then, decides what each creditor is entitled to under bankruptcy law.

27. Hedlund, 468 B.R. at 905. The opinion states that the daughter was born in 2001.

> especially when free child care is available [from the grandparents]. Therefore, Hedlund's financial circumstances are, in part, a by-product of his life choices rather than market forces.[28]

Judge Aiken found that the above circumstances were not beyond Mr. Hedlund's reasonable control; consequently, he had not established an undue hardship and his student loan debt would not be discharged.

The lessons prospective students and law graduates should take away from the above cases are as follows. First, whether a court uses the TOC test or the *Brunner* test, a graduate will have a very difficult time proving circumstances that constitute an undue hardship if they are able to secure steady full-time employment. Second, graduates should make every effort to negotiate a workable payment plan with their lenders before resorting to filing bankruptcy. Third, graduates need to secure the best employment possible even if the job is non-legal. A graduate's failure to pass the bar exam is no excuse for failing to maximize his or her employment potential. The final lesson is that the graduate's spouse certainly has the choice to refuse to work but such a choice may count against the graduate in bankruptcy court!

Snapshot Summary of Cases

On the next page, I have put together a table summarizing the cases I've discussed so that the reader will get a snapshot of the difficulty of obtaining a student loan debt discharge. The picture shows that if you are employable and can minimize your expenses or increase your household income to make student loan payments, you will not get your student loan debt discharged.

Judge Aiken Expresses Concern for Recent Law Graduates

Unlike Judge Quist and Judge Schweitzer who evidenced little, if any, sympathy[29] when they tossed out the lawsuits filed against Cooley and NYLS, respectively, Judge Aiken used a large part of her opinion in the *Hedlund* case to castigate law schools for saddling law graduates with a staggering amount of student loan debt. According to Judge Aiken, the student loan debt crisis unfolds as follows. First, stratospheric increases in law school tuition have been occurring for decades. Citing to *Forbes Magazine*, Judge Aiken noted that law school tuition has increased 317% from 1989 to 2009. While lawyers who graduated in the 1970s and 1980s could have saved or worked to pay for tuition, Judge Aiken recognized that, "with the exception of the independently wealthy, students must take out loans in order to finance their degrees." She emphasized the national average student loan indebtedness for law graduates at $100,000 as well as the indebtedness for graduates of Oregon law schools ranging from $91,347 to $105,928 in 2010.

28. *Id.* at 916.
29. *See* Chapter 2.

Debtor's Name	Carol Todd	Denise Bronsdon	Michael Hedlund
Student Loan Debt	$339,361.68	$82,049.45	$85,245.87
Current Employment Status	Unemployed; receives $768 in Social Security Disability payments and $200 in food stamps	Unemployed; receives monthly Social Security check of $946	Employed consistently
Age	63	64	33
Marital Status	Single	Single	Married with a child
Gender	Female	Female	Male
Disability	Yes	No	No
ABA-Accredited School?	Yes	No	Yes
Law School Graduation Status	Dropped out	Graduated but failed the bar exam 3 times	Graduated but failed the bar exam 2 times
Efforts to Find Better Employment to Maximize Income	Tried, but disability interfered with job prospects	Tried, but was unsuccessful	Maintained steady employment; wife only worked one day per week
Efforts to Minimize Expenses	Not clear from opinion	Lived with her father	Could have decreased expenses but such a decrease would not allow him to pay the monthly student loan payments in full
Attempts to Negotiate a Reduced Payment Plan	No	No	Not good enough; "Hedlund ceased any efforts to renegotiate a repayment schedule"
Was Student Loan Discharged?	Yes, under *Brunner* Test	Yes, under TOC Test	No, under *Brunner* Test because Hedlund could not show good faith because his hardship stemmed from his personal life-style choices

After discussing the average six-figure indebtedness incurred to pay skyrocketing law school tuition rates, Judge Aiken described the dismal job outlook for recent law graduates. Citing to various sources, Judge Aiken emphasized the fact that the number of entry-level jobs has shrunk even for graduates of top-tier law schools. Moreover, despite improvement in the overall economy, Judge Aiken stated that 2011 graduates have "even fewer employment opportunities, as those graduates must compete against unemployed graduates from previous years for the same limited number of entry-level positions." As a case in point, Judge Aiken stated that almost 383,000 applications were submitted by law graduates for *only* 874 federal clerkship positions in 2010. Note that only 44,258 law students graduated in 2010.[30] And just when graduates were hoping things could not get any worse, Judge Aiken, citing to NALP's 2010 report, discussed the dramatic drop in starting salaries both for public and private sector jobs.

The high tuition rates, high student loan debts, poor job prospects, and lower salaries led Judge Aiken to one inescapable conclusion: "the current higher education system has become untenable and unsustainable; as a result, increasing numbers of students will be forced to file for bankruptcy."

Student Loan Debt Can Be a Life Sentence

I, along with many others, have described student loan indebtedness for law graduates as a mortgage. But because student loans are almost impossible to discharge, some academics are now calling student loan debt a life sentence. As Professor Jean Braucher has said, "[t]he non-dischargeability of student-loan debt absent [proof of] undue hardship is permanent, a life sentence."[31] Now this might sound like hyperbole, but I can assure you it is not!

Until 1976, student loans were dischargeable in bankruptcy just like any other unsecured debt. At that time, Congress made student loans dischargeable five years after they became due. Then in 1990, Congress extended the waiting period to seven years and then eliminated the waiting period altogether in 1998. That elimination means that unless a debtor can satisfy the undue hardship exception, student loan debt cannot be discharged in bankruptcy, and the debtor may be strapped with student loan debt for decades. The final blow to students came in 2005, when major changes to Bankruptcy Code added private student loans, not just government-backed student loans, to the category of non-dischargeable educational loans. Some private student lenders can be just as predatory as some of the subprime mortgage lenders whose actions led to the very recession that continues to impact law graduates today. Professor Braucher suspects that aggressive lobbying by private lenders led to private student loans being non-dischargeable in bankruptcy.

It is indisputable that in 1976, when student loans were first made non-dischargeable only for a five-year period, college graduates could pay off their debt in a relatively short period of time (a few years or less) because the amount borrowed was relatively small due to low tuition rates. That was the case even into the 1980s. For example, in a recent law review article, Professor Paul Campos stated that he paid, in 1986, $4,420 as in-state (resident) tuition at the University of Michigan Law School. If that figure was adjusted only for inflation, the rate would be about $9,000 in 2011 dollars. However, the 2012–2013 tuition for first-year Michigan law students was $48,012, which is more than a ten-fold increase *after* adjusting for inflation.[32]

The sad fact is that large and rapid increases in tuition costs are not isolated to a few elite schools like Michigan. Professor Campos' article shows that "[s]ince the mid-1980s, private law school tuition has increased by 155.8 percent in real, inflation-adjusted terms,

30. *Class of 2010 National Summary Report*, NALP, *available at* http://www.nalp.org/uploads/NationalSummaryChartforSchools2010.pdf (last visited Feb. 28, 2013).

31. Jean Braucher, *Mortgaging Human Capital: Federally-Funded Subprime Higher Education*, 69 Wash. & Lee L. Rev. 439 (2012).

32. Paul Campos, *The Crisis of the American Law School*, 46 U. Mich. J.L. Reform 177 (2012).

while public law school resident tuition has increased by an astounding 428.2 percent over inflation." He states that resident tuition at public law schools increased from $3,746 in 1985 to $7,201 in 1995, $13,944 in 2005 and $19,788 in 2012. For private law schools, the corresponding median tuition amounts in 2012 dollars for the same years were $15,438, $24,988, $33,021 and $39,496. Unfortunately, this increase is not expected to stop, with tuition at roughly a dozen law schools expected to exceed $70,000 by the year 2020.[33]

Professor Campos goes on to show how wages for American households have remained relatively stagnant over the last 40 years. After analyzing the rise in wages in comparison to the rise in tuition, Professor Campos shows that law students have to incur in enormous amount of debt for a small increase in salaries. The total cost of a legal education exceeds $150,000 at most law schools, "[m]eanwhile, the average American family enjoys $17 more per month in income than it did four decades ago."[34]

Perhaps the rise in law school tuition rates would not be so bad if graduates were able to obtain traditional legal employment, which historically meant job security. However, according to the National Association for Law Placement, which tracks employment trends for law graduates, nine months after graduation only 56% of total number of 2011's graduates were employed in full-time positions requiring passage of the bar exam.[35] These are the most sought after jobs because most people attend law schools to become lawyers. Not only has the employment rate for bar-required jobs decreased since the recession, entry-level salaries for law graduates have gone down dramatically. In a recent press release, NALP stated:

> The median starting salary for new law school graduates from the Class of 2011 fell 5% from that for 2010 and has fallen nearly 17% just since 2009. The mean salary fell 6.5% compared with 2010, and since 2009 the mean has plunged almost 16%.... The research also reveals that the median starting private practice salary fell over 18% from 2010 and since 2009 has fallen an astonishing 35%. These are among the most dramatic findings that were released ... from NALP's Employment Report and Salary Survey for the Class of 2011.[36]

While the drop in salaries may have been expected after the recession, the pervasiveness with which starting salaries are dropping is surprising.[37] NALP's Executive Director James Leipold believes that "[n]early all of the drop can be attributed to the continued erosion of private practice opportunities at the largest law firms." According to Professor Brian Tamanaha and others, many of those big firm jobs are never coming back.[38] This means that future law graduates need to realize that most of them will not find jobs paying six-figure salaries. Professor Campos' research shows that an estimated 15% of law graduates

---

33. *Id.*

34. *Id.* at 182.

35. *See* Press Release, NALP, Class of 2010 National Summary Report, (June 2011), *available at* http://www.nalp.org/uploads/NationalSummaryChartforSchools2010.pdf. Note that my 56% figure is arrived at by dividing 24,902, the number of known graduates with fulltime, bar-required positions, by 44,495, the *total* number of graduates in the class of 2011. NALP reports that 70% of the 2011 class have these jobs, but that percentage is based on a denominator of 35,278, the *known* number of grads with both full-time and part-time jobs.

36. *Median Private Practice Starting Salaries for the Class of 2011 Plunge as Private Practice Jobs Continue to Erode*, NALP (July 12, 2012), *available at* http://www.nalp.org/classof2011_salpressrel.

37. *Id.*

38. Tamanaha, Failing Law Schools, at 169 (discussing how law firms now hire temporary contract attorneys and use legal temp agencies to hire law graduates to do document review work and discussing a survey where "[a]bout half of the law firms polled admit to using contract attorneys and expect that it will remain a permanent part of their staffing").

presently are securing high-paying entry-level legal jobs, while another 25% land legal jobs paying in the mid five-figures.[39] Similarly, Professor William Henderson's analysis of salary data shows that very few graduates obtain entry-level jobs paying above the median salary.[40] Consequently, a solid majority of graduates earn near or substantially ***below*** the mid-five-figure salary range. Some graduates may see their salaries grow to six figures over the course of a career, but the majority of recent graduates should *not* expect to earn six-figure salaries for entry-level attorney positions.

My point in describing all of the above bad news is not to conclude that law school is no longer worth the price. The main point here is that because getting a hardship discharge is almost impossible, law graduates have to expect to pay back their student loan debt for a very, very long time; therefore, it amounts to life-long indebtedness.

Bankruptcy Law Treats Student Loan Debt Worse than a Mortgage Loan

Student loans are now worse than mortgage loans. In general, if a debtor can no longer keep up with his mortgage payments, he can file bankruptcy, surrender the home to the lender, and have discharged any remaining mortgage loan balance after the house is sold at the foreclosure sale. But a law graduate who is stuck in a low-paying job has to keep trying to figure out how to minimize expenses and maximize income, even if that means taking on two jobs just to be able to make the student loan payments. This scenario for law graduates is not expected to change, as Congress has been resistant to calls to reform the non-dischargeability of student loans. Because the current legal job market is not expected to return to the plentiful high-paying jobs of the early 2000s, it strikes me as fundamentally unfair to deny law graduates a more reasonable test for proving an undue hardship. Most recent law graduates do not have lucrative six-figure salaries to match the $100,000-plus in student loans that they have to incur. As a result, the legal profession and the legal academy need to push for expansion of loan forgiveness and payment-reduction programs.[41]

Mr. Hedlund's Case Is an Example of Life-Long Indebtedness

Now let's revisit Mr. Hedlund's attempt to discharge $85,000 in student loan debt to show that he is now faced with life-long indebtedness. At the bankruptcy court level, Mr. Hedlund was not entirely unsuccessful. The bankruptcy court granted Mr. Hedlund a partial discharge of $30,000. As a result, the bankruptcy judge felt that Mr. Hedlund could

39. Campos, *supra* note 32, at 204.

40. *See* William Henderson, Distribution of 2006 Starting Salaries: Best Graphic Chart of the Year, Empirical Legal Study, (Sept. 4, 2007), *available at* http://www.elsblog.org/the_empirical_legal_studi/2007/09/distribution-of.html.

41. *See* Chapter 14.

pay off the remaining $55,000 by making monthly payments of $465, instead of the $800 monthly payments required by the student loan creditor, the Pennsylvania Higher Education Assistance Agency ("PHEAA"). Unfortunately for Mr. Hedlund, Judge Aiken reversed the bankruptcy court's decision on appeal, thereby leaving Mr. Hedlund on the hook for the entire student loan balance.

Immediately before the trial in bankruptcy court, PHEAA had offered to settle the case by offering Mr. Hedlund three different payment options. Under option one, Mr. Hedlund would pay $417.67 each month for 359 months and make one final payment of $414.79. The grand total of this payment option is $150,358.32 to repay is outstanding student loan of roughly $85,000. Moreover, these payments would last 360 months, which is 30 years, the same repayment period typical of mortgage loans. The other two payment options required Mr. Hedlund to make monthly payments varying between $307 and $446 per month for a thirty-year term. Mr. Hedlund was 33 when this case was rendered. All of these payment options, of course, assume the best case scenario—that Mr. Hedlund will maintain good health and keep his jobs, and Mrs. Hedlund will secure substantially more work hours to help Mr. Hedlund make his student loan monthly payments. Mr. Hedlund rejected all of the payment options offered by PHEAA. Recall that Mr. Hedlund is employed as a juvenile counselor, not an attorney, and he did not need a law degree to obtain that position. As a result, a reasonable conclusion is that he is financially worse off than the other counselors who did not obtain graduate degrees and, thereby, avoided being indebted to the tune of $85,000, and avoided 30 years of making student loan payments.

Mr. Hedlund's case is a perfect example as to why we need loan forgiveness or repayment assistance programs. The opinion hinted that the Hedlunds wanted to have a second child. However, the costs associated with having and rearing a second child make expansion of their family a financially unwise decision. Moreover, the court's description of his monthly expenditures does not indicate that he is saving for retirement. Therefore, a fair interpretation of his financial situation is that his student loan debts impede his ability to save for retirement and, perhaps, save for a rainy day. Furthermore, a recent report by the advocacy group, Young Invincibles, shows that many graduates with student loan debt cannot qualify for mortgages to buy a home because their debt-to-income ratio is too high.[42]

High Student Loan Payments Can Make Survival on a Modest Salary Difficult

Because Judge Aiken failed to specify Mr. Hedlund's exact salary, I must provide an example to show readers how much a monthly student loan payment can eat up a graduate's gross monthly income. Assume that Mary, a single 25-year old woman who lives alone in a cheap apartment, owes $150,000 in student loan debt. Assume further that this debt is comprised of a Stafford Loan of $61,500 with fixed rate of 6.8% and a Graduate PLUS loan of $88,500 with a fixed rate of 7.9% and that she is required to follow the industry's standard 10-year plan. Table 13-1 (next page) shows the median annual salaries for 2011

42. *See* Jen Mishory & Rory O'Sullivan, *Denied?: The Impact of Student Debt on the Ability to Buy a House*, Young Invincibles, http://younginvincibles.org/wp-content/uploads/2012/08/Denied-The-Impact-of-Student-Debt-on-the-Ability-to-Buy-a-House-8.14.12.pdf (last visited Feb. 28, 2013).

Table 13-1.

Median Salary by Job Type	Average Annual Salary	Salary per Month	Monthly Payment under Standard 10-yr Plan	Loan Payment's % of Monthly Income	Monthly Payment under Standard 30-yr Plan	Loan Payment's % of Monthly Income
Law firm	$85,000.00	$7,083.33	$1,771.00	25%	$1,048.00	15%
Government	$52,000.00	$4,333.33	$1,771.00	41%	$1,048.00	24%
Public Interest	$45,000.00	$3,750.00	$1,771.00	47%	$1,048.00	28%
Clerkships	$52,000.00	$4,333.33	$1,771.00	41%	$1,048.00	24%

Data Source: NALP's 2011 Report.

graduates employed at law firms or employed in governmental, public interest, and judicial clerkship jobs. Let's further assume that Mary is employed in a public interest job, which is consistently the lowest-paid category of jobs for law graduates.

As the reader can see, if Mary has an annual salary of $45,000 for her public interest job, she would have monthly gross income of $3,750 and a monthly student loan payment of $1,771 under a standard 10-year plan. This payment plan would consume nearly 50% of Mary's monthly gross income. Even if Mary obtains a 30-year payment plan, the student loan payment would consume 28% of her gross monthly income. Plus, she would pay well over $100,000 in *additional* interest under a 30-year plan.[43] Under either payment plan, Mary will never be able to save the required 20% down payment on a modest home because her student loan payments consume too much of her gross income.

Debt management experts recommend that students with annual salaries in the range of $40,000 should not incur student loan debt requiring more than 8 to 13 percent of their income.[44] There are two problems with this advice. First, a legal education is so expensive, that there is no way for the typical law student to borrow at the recommended level. For example, if Mary knew at the time she entered law school that she wanted to be a public interest lawyer, she should have borrowed only $5,850 (13% of $45,000). Even if Mary received full-tuition scholarships, Mary could never limit her borrowing to the recommended level due to the cost of living expenses while in law school. The second problem is that even if Mary strongly desired a big-law-firm job where she could earn a salary large enough to comfortably pay back a six-figure student loan debt, she could have never accurately predicted, at the time she entered law school, her chances of getting such a job.

Luckily, there are several different debt relief programs that law graduates may qualify for that can provide help with student loan debt. For law graduates with high debt burdens and low incomes, these programs can be lifesavers. Therefore, those with strong desires

43. *See* Philip G. Schrag & Charles W. Pruett, *Coordinating Loan Repayment Assistance Programs with New Federal Legislation*, 60 J. LEGAL EDUC. 583, 586 (2011) (Using almost the exact same figures, the authors showed that "[a] 30-year repayment plan for the same debt and interest rate would reduce the annual payments by nearly half to $12,576, but the borrower would still be paying more than a quarter of gross income toward loan repayment and would have to pay an additional $164,359 over the life of the loan.").

44. *Id.*

to become lawyers should still consider pursuing a law degree. The next chapter will discuss programs designed to alleviate the burden of student loan debt for law graduates.

As this book was headed to print, I learned that a decision was made regarding Mr. Hedlund's appeal.The Ninth Circuit Court of the Appeals (the "9th Circuit") reversed Judge Aiken's decision by applying a different legal standard, called "clearly erroneous," when assessing whether Mr. Hedlund had acted in good faith.[45] Because the bankruptcy court's interpretation of the facts was rational, the 9th Circuit concluded that it would affirm the bankruptcy court's partial discharge of $30,000 in student loan debt. The 9th Circuit did not, however, endorse the actions of Mr. Hedlund and his spouse. For example, the 9th Circuit viewed with skepticism the Hedlunds' claim that their two cell phones and new car lease were necessary expenses. Furthermore, the 9th Circuit described Mr. Hedlund's effort to negotiate a repayment plan of his student loan debt as "minimal." Because of the 9th Circuit's criticisms, the reader needs to realize that had the bankruptcy court concluded Mr. Hedlund had acted in bad faith, the 9th Circuit would have also upheld the bankruptcy court's conclusion as a fair interpretation of the facts. As a result, my advice remains the same: debtors who seek to get a student loan debt discharged in bankruptcy need to prove good faith by showing they have minimized their living expenses, have maximized their income, and have made serious efforts to get a reasonable repayment plan with the lender.

The main point of this chapter is that bankruptcy cannot be used by most consumers to eliminate student loan debt. However, filing bankruptcy is a viable option if someone is making IBR payments and is, nevertheless, falling behind on other debts. Because a person can follow a repayment plan in a Chapter 13 bankruptcy case, bankruptcy can give a graduate substantial breathing room to get into a better financial situation. That's because during the three-to-five-year repayment period of a Chapter 13 case, Sallie Mae or any other student loan creditors cannot call you, cannot send you letters, cannot garnish your paycheck, and cannot seize your tax refund. So if you find yourself still struggling to repay your debts even after qualifying for an IBR program, consult a good bankruptcy attorney.

45. Hedlund v. Educ. Res. Inst. Inc., 718 F.3d 848, 855 (9th Cir. 2013). Because of the Court's decision, Mr. Hedlund now has to repay only $55,000.

Chapter 14

IBR, PSLF, LRAP, and Other Acronyms That Can Save You Thousands

> *"LRAP [Loan Repayment Assistance Program] has been a lifesaver ... A lot of nonprofits can't afford to pay competitive salaries, which wouldn't be a big of deal if I hadn't graduated with over $100,000 in debt. LRAP was a gamechanger for me to be able to stay here for so long, be able to do the work I love...."* Lauren Onkeles-Klein[1]

Law graduates who find themselves unemployed or under-employed are struggling greatly to repay their student loans. Even before they graduate, some students can see a looming student-loan repayment crisis and try to prepare for it. Consider the story of Paraisia Winston, who entered and won a financial fitness contest while in law school.[2] Her prize consisted of receiving free advice from a certified financial planner. At the time, Ms. Winston was a second-year law student at the Loyola University Chicago School of Law, and she then estimated that she would have $180,000 in student loan debt upon graduating from law school. She had received a job offer from a law firm paying an annual salary of $145,000. Ms. Winston was faced with a dilemma: Should she accept this offer simply because it would pay her enough to cover her debts and live comfortably, or should she pursue her dream of becoming a criminal attorney in the public sector despite the fact that it would pay a salary that was only a fraction of what the law firm was willing to pay. Because she had an enormous student loan debt, along with $20,000 in credit card debt, Ms. Winston decided that the only financially-wise decision was to accept the law firm's offer.[3] After graduating in 2009, she was dealt a heavy blow when the law firm rescinded the offer because of cutbacks. She has since then worked briefly as a prosecutor and is currently holding down two jobs, one as an associate attorney at a small law firm and one as general counsel for a Cook County commissioner in Chicago.[4] Presumably, she has figured out a sensible plan to pay back her student loan debt.

---

1. Catherine Ho, *D.C. Bar Foundation's Loan Repayment Program Falling Short*, Wash. Post, Mar. 15, 2012. Ms. Onkeles-Klein is a recipient of a LRAP (Loan Repayment Assistance Program) grant from the DC Bar Foundation. She used the grant to reduce the six-figure student loan debt incurred while attending Georgetown Law Center. She is the Senior Supervising Attorney at the Children's Law Center, Inc., and has been an attorney there for eight years.

2. Sheryl Nance Nash, *What Matters Most?*, Black Enterprise, May 1, 2008, at 70, *available at* http://www.blackenterprise.com/mag/what-matters-most/.

3. Sheiresa McRae & Sheryl Nance Nash, *Reaching the Next Level*, Black Enterprise 63, Dec. 1, 2009, *available at* 2009 WLNR 26387480.

4. Paraisia Winston, LinkedIn Profile, http://www.linkedin.com/pub/paraisia-winston/1a/7a2/b1b (last visited Feb. 28, 2013).

This chapter offers hope to law graduates and students burdened or about to be burdened with six-figure student loan debt. I will explain various programs that lessen the financial burden of student loan debt and will focus on the federal programs that can reduce monthly payments and possibly offer debt forgiveness. In addition to the federal programs, I will discuss non-federal repayment assistance programs that are offered by some law schools, states, and employers and have varying requirements and benefits. To give the reader a practical understanding of these important options, I will provide detailed hypothetical situations to demonstrate how these programs work and how much money they can save.

Student Loans 101

Before getting into the specifics of various loan assistance and forgiveness programs, let's start with a quick primer on loans. Keep in mind that my explanation has been greatly simplified to avoid confusion. ***This is not a "how to" section but merely an overview to provide the reader with general information. If you have specific questions about your student loans or loan forgiveness programs, please contact your financial aid officer or Equal Justice Works.***

A person who holds an undergraduate degree that was financed primarily through student loans, often has a basketful of student loan products. Most will be federal loans and examples include Direct Loans,[5] Stafford Loans,[6] Perkins Loans,[7] and Parent-PLUS Loans.[8] Some of these loans are subsidized while others are not. An unsubsidized loan begins to accrue interest from the time of disbursement to the student and continues to accrue interest while the student is enrolled in school and even when the student has received a deferment of the loan payments.[9] For the subsidized loan, the government will pay the interest charges while the student is still in school. Besides the federal loans, many prospective law students have in their basket private student loans, which usually tend to be more expensive than federal loans and have less favorable terms.[10] Some private loans carry fixed interest rates while others carry variable interest rates.[11]

---

5. Direct Loans are loans made directly by the federal government (*i.e.*, U.S. Department of Education), and they can be subsidized or unsubsidized loans. *See Glossary*, FED. STUDENT AID, http://www.direct.ed.gov/glos.html (last visited Fed. 28, 2013).

6. The Stafford Loan is a federal low-interest loan made to students on the basis of financial need and guaranteed by the federal government. *College Loans*, SCHOLARSHIPS.COM, http://www.scholarships.com/financial-aid/student-loans/college-loans/ (last visited Feb. 28, 2013). Undergraduate students can borrow annually from $5,500 and $12,500, depending on whether they qualify as dependent or independent students. Graduate and professional students can borrow as much as $20,500 annually.

7. *College Loans*, SCHOLARSHIPS.COM, http://www.scholarships.com/financial-aid/student-loans/college-loans/ (last visited Feb. 28, 2013) ("Federal Perkins Loans are low-interest loans for both undergraduate and graduate students with high financial need. The Federal Perkins Loan program is administered by individual colleges and universities who contribute a share to the program alongside funding from the federal government.").

8. Parent-Plus loans are federal unsubsidized loans obtained by parents of dependent undergraduate students in the parent's name to help pay for their children's college education. *See Glossary*, FED. STUDENT AID, http://www.direct.ed.gov/parent.html (last visited Feb. 28, 2013).

9. *Id.*

10. *See College Loans*, SCHOLARSHIPS.COM, http://www.scholarships.com/financial-aid/student-loans/college-loans/ (last visited Feb. 28, 2013) (stating that students and their parents often resort to obtaining private loans when their federal loans are insufficient to pay for the student's education).

11. *Id.*

Once enrolled in law school, most students will add to their basket of student loan debt Federal Unsubsidized loans and Grad-PLUS loans,[12] and some students will add private loans. The Grad-PLUS loan is an unsubsidized loan guaranteed by the federal government and it allows a graduate or professional student to borrow up to the cost of attendance, minus any other financial aid received. Since the creation of the Grad-PLUS program in 2006, graduate students have been able to borrow the entire cost of attending graduate school through direct loans or loans guaranteed by the federal government. So theoretically, a law student should not have to borrow from a private lender.

Below is a chart intended to be a simplified example describing features of the type of loan products (obtained both in college and in law school) commonly found in the student loan basket after graduating from law school.

Loan	Features
Stafford	• Borrow up to $20,500/year, total of $138,500. • Fixed interest rate. • Repayment begins 6 months after graduation. • Interest starts accruing on day borrowed. • Typical 10-year repayment. • Repayment options, interest-gathering deferments, and forbearances available.
Perkins	• Borrow up to $8,000/year, total $60,000. • Repayment begins 9 months after graduation. • Typical 10-year repayment. • Fixed interest rate, interest paid by government while in school. • Special forbearance and other repayment options available.
Parent PLUS	• Creditworthy, eligible parents can borrow everything other loans don't cover. • Typical 10-year repayment. • Repayment can begin 60 days after loan disbursed. • Fixed interest rates. • Forbearance and deferment options available.
Grad PLUS	• Creditworthy eligible students can borrow everything other loans don't cover. • Typical 10-year repayment. • Repayment begins 6 months after graduation. • Fixed interest rates. • Interest-bearing forbearance and deferment options available.
Private Loans	• Borrowing ability limited by credit worthiness. • Interest rates may be fixed or variable, rates vary widely. • Repayment term often 10-years, but varies widely. • Repayment structures vary widely, not eligible for public programs.

Loans are obtained each academic year, and all of these loans count as separate loans. Typically, each semester of enrollment results in a disbursement of half of the total loan for that school year. Each loan is reported to the federal government, and consequently, a student could have a basket consisting of 20 loans. Because it is often a nightmare for a graduate to keep track of all these loans and disbursements, many students will consolidate some or all of their eligible federal loans before starting or after graduating from law school. The primary reason for consolidating is to make it convenient for the student to

12. *Id.*

keep track of their loans and pay them in a timely fashion. Generally speaking, consolidation does not have a huge financial impact unless the graduate was able to convert some variable-interest-rate loans into one fixed-interest-rate loan. For most graduates, consolidation is a very good idea. By consolidating, a graduate typically gets an interest rate reduction of .25 percent. But keep in mind that some loans cannot be consolidated.

As one can see from the chart on the previous page, the typical loan-repayment term is 10 years. If we assume that I graduated today with a grand total of $75,000 in student loan debt, and it was consolidated into one loan with a fixed-interest rate of 9%, my monthly student loan payment would be $950. That is a large student loan payment, and it exceeds the monthly mortgage payment for many homeowners. Over a 10-year period, I will have to pay $114,000 to extinguish the debt. Because law graduates carry an average student loan debt that is around $100,000, a law graduate's student loan payment can easily top $1,300 per month. Such a high payment is a staggering monthly burden, especially in light of the weak job market and the inability of many law graduates to find high-paying jobs.

Now that I have painted a portrait of the types of student loan debts law graduates carry and the enormity of the monthly payments, the reader is well-positioned to see what the various loan assistance and forgiveness programs can do for the graduates.

Debt Relief Programs— A Light at the End of the Tunnel

Income-Based Repayment

In 2007, Congress passed the College Cost Reduction and Access Act ("CCRAA") for the stated purpose of making college education more affordable and, therefore, more accessible.[13] Two provisions of the CCRAA made significant changes to the way graduates could repay student loans.[14] The first provision is called Income-Based Repayment ("IBR"). Under this payment option, a student's monthly loan payment is determined by analyzing their income and their family size. It's often called the "pay what you earn" plan because it is designed for graduates whose loans are hefty in comparison to their income.[15]

Only loans made directly by the federal government (i.e., Direct Loans) or loans guaranteed by the federal government are eligible for an IBR plan.[16] That means that a law graduate's direct unsubsidized loans and Grad-PLUS loans are eligible for an IBR plan. However, it is unfortunately common for law graduates to come to law school already burdened by types of student debt that will not qualify for IBR upon graduation. Recall that I stated that a student may have a private loan in his student loan basket because he was forced to obtain the loan while in undergraduate school to help pay the costs of college. Private student loans do not qualify for an IBR plan; for this reason, as well as

---

13. Jennifer R. Stoller & Stephanie M. Jackson, *Student Loans, in* Ohio Consumer Law § 22.2 (Julie Khoury Robie ed., 2012).

14. Philip G. Schrag & Charles W. Pruett, *Coordinating Loan Repayment Assistance Programs with New Federal Legislation*, 60 J. Legal Educ. 583, 591 (2011).

15. *Id.* at 591.

16. *Id.*

their high costs, students should avoid borrowing from private lenders if at all possible. Moreover, some students' parents obtained Parent PLUS loans to help defray the costs of undergraduate school. Because Parent-PLUS loans are in the name of the parent, they do not qualify for an IBR plan.

Under the IBR formula, law graduates can have their student loan payments lowered depending on the ratio of their incomes to their qualifying student loan debts. The required payment under the IBR plan is 15% of borrower's discretionary income, which is defined as the borrower's adjusted gross income minus 150% of the federal poverty level for a family the size of the borrower's family.[17] I will later provide a series of examples. As a general guideline, this usually makes the monthly payment about 10% of the borrower's gross income.

The benefit of an IBR plan to the law graduate is that, in comparison to the monthly payment required under the standard 10-year loan repayment term, the graduate has a smaller monthly student loan payment. For example, if John is a single law graduate whose income is no greater than 150 percent of the federal poverty level (now $17,235 for a single-person household),[18] John would not have to make a payment until his income takes him above that amount. If John is a single law graduate with $123,200 in education debt at 6.8% interest and an income of $50,000, his payment can be reduced from $1,417, the payment required under a standard 10-year repayment plan, to $421 under an IBR plan.[19] Since John's IBR payment of $421 is less than his standard payment of $1,417, John has a "partial financial hardship," which is required for IBR plan eligibility. Because the IBR formula bases the payment on the borrower's income, if John's income increases then his payment will increase as well. If at any point he would pay more under the IBR plan than under the standard repayment plan, he can go back to paying the standard plan amount.

While the IBR plan allows the graduate to benefit from the lower payment option, the IBR plan does have drawbacks. Most importantly, it extends the repayment period and can cause accrual of interest. Luckily, this can be mitigated by another feature of the IBR program which forgives any remaining loan balance after 25 years. Under current law, this forgiveness of debt would be taxable income, but the law could be changed by the time the debt is forgiven. In John's example, if we assume, he receives 4 percent annual salary increases, the government would forgive $96,464 of remaining debt in the 25th year.[20] The higher one's debt is and the lower one's income is, the greater the chance that some of the debt will be forgiven after 25 years.

The only requirements for an IBR plan are that the loans are issued or guaranteed by the federal government and that the borrower's debt amount and income level allow the borrower to qualify for the partial hardship as described in the above example. There is no requirement under the IBR plan that the borrower work in public service. This makes the provision especially important for law graduates working in the private sector. Graduates who have low income jobs at small law firms, graduates who have only found temporary or part-time work at law firms, or graduates not even working in the legal profession (but still looking for work) may all consider using an IBR plan to reduce their

17. *Id.*

18. *2013 Annual Federal Poverty Guidelines*, Families USA, *available at* http://www.familiesusa.org/resources/tools-for-advocates/guides/federal-poverty-guidelines.html (last visited Feb. 28, 2013).

19. Schrag & Pruett, *supra* note 14, at 591.

20. *Id.*

monthly payments. For IBR purposes, income is determined based on the borrower's most-recently filed tax return. However, if the tax return does not accurately reflect the graduate's current income (because he just graduated, is self-employed, or has income that fluctuates from year-to-year), the graduate may use alternative documentation, like paystubs, to determine income.[21]

For married borrowers in two-income families, it is usually better to file separate tax returns to get the maximum benefit of under an IBR plan.[22] That is because the IBR plan disadvantages married borrowers in cases where each person has outstanding loans, they file a joint Federal tax return, and both qualify for the IBR plan. In such a case, the married borrowers could pay up to double the monthly loan payments of two unmarried borrowers.

Unfortunately, only a small number of graduates eligible for the IBR plan are enrolled in it. This low participation rate is due in part to the complexity of the IBR enrollment process and the fact that graduates are forced to consolidate eligible loans to be qualify for the IBR plan.[23] Consolidation is complex because there are many different types of loans and loan servicing companies, and there are many options for consolidating loans. However, only the loans consolidated through the Federal Direct Consolidation Loan Program retain federal protections like income-driven repayment plans and forgiveness programs that I am describing in this chapter.

President Obama issued a Presidential Memorandum directing the Secretary of Education to simplify, by September 30, 2012, the process by which graduates become eligible for the IBR plan.[24] The Memorandum stated that the Secretary "shall create a streamlined online application process for IBR that allows student loan borrowers with federally held loans to import their Internal Revenue Service income data directly into the IBR application."[25] On September 26, 2012, the Department of Education announced the availability of an Electronic Income-Based Repayment (IBR) Application on its StudentLoans.gov web site, and this "Electronic IBR Application streamlines the application process for the majority of borrowers who choose to repay their eligible" federal student loans.[26] It is too new for me to report whether it actually streamlines the process.

---

21. U.S. Dept. of Educ., Fed. Student Aid, Income Based Repayment Program Questions and Answers 5 (Feb. 7, 2011), *available at* http:// studentaid.ed.gov/sites/ ... /income-based-repayment-common-questions.pdf (hereinafter "Fed. Student Aid Q&A").

22. *Id.* at 593.

23. Equal Justice Works, *Significant Student Debt Reforms Quietly Take Flight*, U.S. News & World Rep., Jun. 13, 2012, *available at* http://www.usnews.com/education/blogs/student-loan-ranger/2012/06/13/significant-student-debt-reforms-quietly-take-flight.

24. Press Release, The White House Office of the Press Secretary, Presidential Memorandum—Improving Repayment Options for Federal Student Loan Borrowers (Jun. 7, 2012), *available at* http://www.whitehouse.gov/the-press-office/2012/06/07/presidential-memorandum-improving-repayment--options-federal-student-loan.

25. *Id.*

26. William Leith, *Loan Servicing Information—Electronic Income-Based Repayment Application*, Fed. Student Aid, Sept. 26, 2012, *available at* http://ifap.ed.gov/eannouncements/092612EleIncBasedRepayApplication.html (last visited Oct. 19, 2012).

Public Service Loan Forgiveness

The other provision of the CCRAA[27] that enables students to effectively handle their student loan debt is a provision that is generous to graduates that choose to work in public service jobs for 10 years. At an average salary of $38,500, public interest lawyers are the lowest paid category of attorneys; a fact that discourages many law grads from taking public interest jobs.[28]

While many law school applicants wish to obtain a law degree as a means to serve the poor and marginalized, very few actually enter the public interest field upon graduation. For example, at the University of Texas School of Law, only 4% of 2007–2009 alumni work in public service.[29] The low compensation provided by public interest jobs and the hefty burden of student loan debt makes it difficult for law students to follow through on their promise to work for the underserved. Meanwhile, the need for greater legal representation for low-income individuals was recognized by the American Bar Association and the National Legal Aid and Defender Association which highlighted the following three initiatives designed to increase access to justice:

> 1) heightening awareness of the public, legislature, and the legal community about the need to expand civil legal assistance to persons of limited means; 2) increasing federal, state, and private funding for legal aid; 3) founding or growing loan repayment assistance programs to reduce obstacles to debt-encumbered law school graduates accepting legal positions serving low-income populations.[30]

Across the nation, there is on average one legal aid attorney available to serve 6,415 poor people while there is one private sector attorney available to serve 429 people in the general population.[31] The ABA Commission on Loan Repayment and Forgiveness observed the need for more public interest lawyers, stating that, "society suffers when its poor and moderate-income residents are unable to obtain legal assistance. Their inability to find a lawyer can have dire consequences in their everyday lives and impact the communities in which they live."[32] The difficulties in attracting the most qualified lawyers to public interest jobs has significant negative consequences for consumers that rely on these attorneys to represent them. It is generally known in the legal community that unrepresented consumers,

---

27. Besides the IBR plan, there is an older income-based program known as the income-contingent repayment (ICR) plan. I chose not to discuss the ICR plan because most of the time when one uses the calculation formula for each plan, IBR payments are lower than ICR payments. One scholar who has written about the subject does not believe any borrower would need to elect to pay through an ICR plan now that the IBR plan is available. Schrag & Pruett, *supra* note 14, at 606, n. 60. For a discussion of the shortcomings of ICR and the necessity of the PSLF program, *see* Philip G. Schrag, *The Federal Income-Contingent Repayment Option for Law Student Loans*, 29 Hofstra L. Rev. 733 (2001). For a further discussion on the differences between IBR and ICR plans, *see* Fed. Student Aid Q&A, *supra* note 21.

28. Scott Cummings, *Reframing Public Service Law: Innovative Approaches to Integrating Public Service into the Legal Profession*, 33 U. Ark. Little Rock L. Rev. 355, 359 (2011).

29. W. Lawson Konvalinka, *More Than A Poor Lawyer: A Study in Poverty Law*, 89 Tex. L. Rev. 449, 450 (2010).

30. Peter C. Alexander & Gary S. Gildin, *Bankruptcy Pro Bono Legal Assistance Programs: An Update*, 2007 Ann. Surv. of Bankr.Law 15 (2007).

31. Jill Lynch Cruz, Melinda S. Molina & Jenny Rivera, *Hispanic National Bar Association Commission on the Status of Latinas in the Legal Profession Study on Latina Attorneys in the Public Interest Sector la Voz de la Abogada Latina: Challenges and Rewards in Serving the Public Interest*, 14 CUNY L. Rev. 147, 161 (2010).

32. *Id.*

or those who represent themselves, are no match against companies represented by private-sector lawyers, particularly those from big law firms.

Luminaries in the legal profession also recognized the need to attract law graduates to public service jobs by highlighting the consequences arising from actions by lawyers who are not well-suited for legal service. For instance, Barry Scheck, one of the founders of the Innocence Project, stated that "[n]othing more surely guarantees the conviction of innocent defendants than an incompetent, underfunded, or ineffective lawyer."[33] Since 1992, the Innocence Project has exonerated 292 people in the United States through DNA testing, including 17 who served time on death row.[34] These people served an average of 13 years in prison before exoneration and release.[35] These wrongfully-convicted individuals ultimately benefited from lawyers dedicated to and well-suited for public service but not until they suffered greatly from the incompetent lawyers ill-fitted for the difficult task. The current state of public defenders leaves much to be desired:

> [A] severe lack of funding; excessive and rising public defender caseloads coupled with inadequate support personnel; insufficient attorney compensation, leading to increased pressure to plead cases; arbitrary and capricious payments to assigned counsel, failures to inform of the right to counsel; acceptance of improper waivers of counsel in misdemeanor cases; and the increased use of contracts for defense services based primarily on cost, not quality considerations.[36]

As a result, payment-reduction programs are necessary to attract more qualified lawyers to do public defense work that could help decrease the number of wrongful convictions.

Programs such as IBR and Public Service Loan Forgiveness ("PSLF") can allow more recent law graduates to enter public service without fear that massive student loan payments will swallow up a huge portion of their modest salaries. An ideal PSLF program combines both the reasonable monthly payments of an IBR plan and complete student loan forgiveness after 10 years. As a result, a PSLF plan can allow young lawyers to fulfill their desire to serve the public while still working off their debt. An increased supply of public interest attorneys can improve the quality of legal representation received by the poor and underprivileged. PSLF gives recent graduates this opportunity with the added benefits of doing work that helps the least served segments of the population and can be more rewarding personally than private sector work.

The PSLF program has more requirements for eligibility than an IBR plan; however, due to the immense benefits it offers, qualified graduates should not be deterred by the paperwork. The first limitation is that the federal PSLF program only covers Direct Loans. Second, all loans that are guaranteed by the federal government must be consolidated into Direct Loans to be included in the PSLF program. Consolidation has usually been a long and complicated process that should be started immediately upon graduation. Hopefully, the process will go more quickly due to the availability of the Department of Education's creation of the Electronic IBR Application via StudentLoans.gov. Because private loans are not eligible for consolidation, they cannot be eliminated by PSLF. This is another reason I strongly urge students to not get private loans even though lenders

---

33. Rick Jones, *The New Frontier in Indigent Defense—Big Firms in State Trial Courts*, The Champion (Jun. 2009), *available at* http://www.ndsny.org/pdf/NACDL_NEW_FRONTIER.pdf (last visited Feb. 28, 2013).

34. *Mission Statement*, Innocence Project, http://www.innocenceproject.org/about/Mission-Statement.php (last visited Feb. 28, 2013).

35. *Id.*

36. Jones, *supra* note 33.

are aggressively trying to market them as comparable to federally-guaranteed loans.[37] As of June 2010, students can obtain federal direct loans for the full amount of their education debt.[38]

The final requirement for participation in the PSLF program is that the borrower makes 120 qualifying, on-time monthly payments. After these payments are made, the remaining balance of the debt will be forgiven, tax-free.[39] In other words, the amount forgiven under the PSLF program does not have to be counted as income in the graduate's tax return. Another benefit of the PSLF program is that payments do not need to be consecutive; therefore, borrowers can take time off for parental leave to start a family or can work for a for-profit organization and then resume qualifying payments when they return to work in a public service position. Qualifying payments do not need to be made using the IBR formula, but such IBR payments will usually be the only type of payments that make sense for most public service workers.[40] Assuming a graduate who is employed in a qualifying service job timely makes the required payments under a standard ten-year plan, the graduate would have no remaining debt as it would be forgiven under the PSLF program.

By making payments under the IBR formula for ten years, a borrower can have a significant portion of their education debt forgiven under the PSLF program. For example, assume that Jane is a single law graduate with $123,200 in education debt and that during her first year of employment, she earns $50,000 in a qualifying public service job and receives thereafter 4% annual pay increases. Under the PSLF program with an IBR component, she will pay $62,111 over a ten-year period of making IBR payments.[41] The government will then forgive the $144,685 in debt she still owes after ten years of payments. The ten-year period for forgiveness under PSLF gives the borrower a much greater chance of having debt forgiven and considerably increases the amount that will be forgiven when compared to the twenty-five year forgiveness period under IBR.

Slowly but surely, some graduates are combining the advantages of IBR and PSLF to handle their enormous federal student loan payments.[42] Consider, for example, Sara Pic, a 2005 graduate of Northeastern University School of Law, who amassed $175,000 in student loan debt from both Northeastern and Smith College, her undergraduate school. Her career path led her to Health Law Advocates of Louisiana, where she is now litigation director for this non-profit organization that helps low-income consumers to obtain medical care and to manage their medical debts. With a starting salary of only $45,000,

---

37. For example, I have a brochure that an employee at Fifth Third Bank handed out during a presentation for Ohio State University employees. *See Private Student Loan vs Plus Loan for Graduate Students*, Fifth Third Bank, *available at* my website lawdegreevalue.com. Fifth Third claims in the brochure that its private loan can carry an interest rate as low as 2.25%, which is lower than the 7.5% fixed-interest rate for a Grad-PLUS loan. The brochure fails to indicate that the borrower probably needs an extremely high credit score well over 700 to qualify for 2.25% rate and fails to state whether this rate is variable. Because of my background as an accountant and a bankruptcy attorney, I doubt very seriously if many students can qualify for private loan at such a low interest rate. Students are better off getting the Grad-Plus loan for numerous reasons, including the fact that they are loans covered under the IBR and PSLF programs, but private loans are not.

38. Schrag & Pruett, *supra* note 14, at 597.

39. All documentation needs to be retained as proof.

40. Heather Jarvis, *What Every Lawyer Should Know About the Economic Realities of a Legal Education*, 19 Educ. & Practice 1, 3–4 (Fall 2011).

41. Schrag & Pruett, *supra* note 14, at 592.

42. Hudson Sangree, *To Forgive is Divine*, Northeastern Law Mag., at 22, Winter 2012, *available at* http://viewer.zmags.com/publication/56efa8ec#/56efa8ec/22.

Ms. Pic needed help managing her own major debt—student loans. She enrolled in the IBR plan and pays less than $400 a month on the $100,000 portion of student loan debt because they are comprised of federal loans. Because she is working full-time at a non-profit organization, her position should qualify as a public service job and, as a result, she should be able to have the unpaid portion of her federal loans eliminated after 10 years of IBR payments. Unfortunately, $75,000 of Ms. Pic's $175,000 student loans was from private lenders, and does not quality for inclusion in the IBR plan. Still struggling to manage her private loans, Ms. Pic describes them as "crippling." Again, I cannot stress enough that current and prospective students should avoid getting private loans.[43]

The benefits of IBR and PSLF are not limited to law graduates. Any graduate can use IBR and PSLF if they satisfy the requirements, even if they only borrow for undergraduate education.[44] Moreover, if law graduates cannot find public-service attorney positions, they can work in other public service positions and still qualify under the PSLF program. Everyone from social workers to corrections officers can enjoy the benefits of these programs. The large amount of debt that can be forgiven under the PSLF program creates a huge incentive for law graduates to stay in public service for at least ten years. If you consider the $144,685 that Jane had forgiven in the previous example, that amounts to an additional $14,468.50 per year in tax-free income that she earned during her ten years of public service.

Finally, PSLF comes with burdens and risks other programs to not. For example, borrowers are responsible for maintaining documentation to prove their work qualified as public service for the forgiveness program. Because the amount of loan forgiveness will not be determined until the tenth year, the law graduates may have a lot of paperwork that must be maintained. Moreover, although this may only be a theoretical concern, there is nothing stopping Congress from eliminating the PSLF program. The only good news for now is that there are no rumblings or rumors indicating that the program is in jeopardy.

The amount forgiven via PSLF is not a handout; this is delayed compensation for those who followed through on a 10-year commitment to serve their fellow Americans in various capacities.

Those interested in PSLF should be aware that public interest work is no cakewalk and that these attorneys work hard to earn their debt forgiveness. PSLF does help to make up for the low salaries public interest lawyers earn and partially level the playing field between private and public sector employment. The higher the amount of debt and the lower the income of the borrower, the more benefit they can receive from PSLF. Generally speaking, PSLF makes public service jobs more attractive financially than small law firm jobs. Why do I say that? If the salary is relatively the same for a lawyer at a legal aid organization and a lawyer at a small firm, the law graduate working in the legal aid position will get loan forgiveness after 10 years, but the graduate working at the small firm will have to work for 25 years.

Changes to IBR and President Obama's New Initiative

Since passing CCRAA in 2007, Congress has passed reforms to make the IBR program even more helpful to graduates with education debt, and it will be particularly helpful to

43. Adam Minsky, a 2010 Northeastern graduate, has started his own law office that helps individuals deal with their student loan debts. He finds that many people do not know about the federal IBR plan or do not understand how it could benefit them. Mr. Minsky educates clients about the federal programs. *Id.*

44. Schrag & Pruett, *supra* note 14, at 595.

future law graduates in low-income, private-sector jobs. As you may recall, under the original IBR program, graduates' monthly payments are based on a formula using 15% of their monthly discretionary income and can get loan forgiveness after 25 years of payments. The 2010 legislation made the IBR payment formula and forgiveness date more liberal; however, these 2010 changes are effective only for graduates who take out their first federal loans after July 1, 2014.[45] The revised IBR formula calculates payments based on 10% (rather than 15%) of discretionary income, which turns out to be about 6.7% of actual income, and loan forgiveness can be obtained with only payments of 20 years rather than 25 years. As a result of this revised formula, future law graduates who are employed in the private sector and have low incomes and high federal loans will have lower payments and have more debt forgiven in a shorter period of time. The reduced payment would benefit those using PSLF as well. Using again the above example of Jane with $123,200 in debt and making $50,000 with 4% annual pay increases, she will pay $41,407 (rather than $62,111) over ten years and have $165,569 forgiven under PSLF.[46] Just remember that the 2010 reforms will not apply to those who obtain their first federal loan prior to July 1, 2014.

In addition to the 2010 changes to the IBR program, in October 2011, President Obama announced that his administration would accelerate to 2012 many of the benefits of the plan Congress passed in 2010.[47] This "Pay as You Earn" initiative ("PAYE") would allow borrowers to make payments amounting to 6.7% of income and qualify for loan forgiveness after 20 years, just like the 2010 IBR program. The main distinction between the two programs is that borrowers who are not eligible for the 2010 IBR program—which requires the first federal loan to be obtain after July 1, 2014—will qualify for the PAYE-IBR if borrower has obtained at least one federal loan in 2012.

Loan Repayment Assistance Programs

In addition to the federal IBR and PSLF programs, loan repayment assistance programs ("LRAPs") are offered by many schools, bar associations, employers, states and even the federal government to provide funds to help student loan borrowers make monthly payments as they are due.[48] The main difference between LRAPs and the federal programs (i.e. IBR and PSLF) is that LRAPs provide funds to the graduate to make the IBR or other loan payments. Recall Sara Pic, the graduate who amassed $175,000 in student loan debt, but only $100,000 of the debt is from federal loans. Because of her enrollment in the IBR program, her payments are less than $400 a month based on her public interest salary of $45,000 annually. Some LRAPs would give Ms. Pic the $400 per month to make the payments under the IBR program. Other LRAPs would permit her to use its funding to pay down her $75,000 in *private* student loans.

LRAPs are generally available based on different public interest professions. In 2008, 76 of the nation's 190 accredited law schools had LRAPs, and there were enormous variations among their eligibility criteria, income criteria, and levels of support.[49] Six of

45. *Id.*
46. Schrag & Pruett, *supra* note 14, at 597.
47. Schrag, *supra* note 27, at 2.
48. Equal Justice Works, Take Control of Your Future: What You Should Know About Educational Debt 9 (2012), *available at* http://files.equaljusticeworks.org/ed-debt/ejw-ed-debt-toolkit_3-21-12.pdf.
49. Schrag & Pruett, *supra* note 14, at 588.

these schools were responsible for 70% of the nationwide funds used for LRAPs.[50] Yearly payments vary from $500 to full loan repayment.[51] Because of the tremendous variation between each school LRAP, students and graduates should consult their schools to determine if they have a LRAP and what the requirements are.

Seventeen states also have LRAPs.[52] State LRAPs get their funding from various sources. For example, Pennsylvania's LRAP is funded by the *pro hac vice* fees instituted by the Supreme Court.[53] These are fees from licensed out-of-state-lawyers who are permitted to represent a client in a Pennsylvania court case without first having to obtain a Pennsylvania law license. LRAPs can be particularly helpful for those that have private loans that do not qualify for the federal programs. For example, the Ohio Legal Assistance Foundation noted that when referring to the total LRAP funds of $75,000 that an individual can receive, "[l]owering their federal payments and having their federal loans forgiven after ten years will help many participants maximize their $75,000 for payment of their private loans."[54] Graduates should check with their state's supreme court as well as with state and local bar associations to determine what LRAPs are available. Some employers also offer LRAPs and graduates should ask employers about these programs and what the qualifications are.

Graduates that work for the federal government may qualify for the federal LRAP. Federal agencies are authorized to provide up to $10,000 in loan repayment assistance per year for federal loans with a total lifetime cap of $60,000 per employee.[55] In exchange for each year that an employee accepts this benefit, she or he must commit to working for the federal government for an additional three years. If an employee accepts this benefit and leaves before this period expires, she or he must repay the full amount. Many agencies offer this benefit, but not all do so. Thus, graduates should discuss this with human resources representatives at the agency they are interested in working for.

Unfortunately, LRAPs often have limited funding and are at risk of being defunded. One federal program, the funding for Civil Legal Assistance Attorney Student Loan Repayment Program, was taken away by Congress in 2011.[56] LRAPs in several states have been and are currently suspended while Kentucky and Washington continue to assist current recipients but are not taking applications from new graduates.[57] Law students

50. *Id.*

51. Judge Advocate Gen. Corps., U.S. Navy, Student Loan Relief Programs 2 (Aug. 2011), *available at* http://www.jag.navy.mil/documents/Careers/Student%20Loan%20Relief%20Programs.pdf.

52. Univ. of Wisc. Law Sch., 2012 Graduation Guide 23 (2012), *available at* http://www.law.wisc.edu/current/commencement/images/2012_grad_guide_w_cover2.pdf.

53. Susan Jacobs Jablow, *Lieber Appointed to Term on ABA IOLTA Commission*, 13 Lawyers J. (the Journal of Allegheny County Bar Association), Oct. 7, 2011, at 8, *available at* http://www.acba.org/ACBA/pdf/TLJ/TLJv13-20-100711.pdf.

54. Ohio Legal Assistance Foundation Making a Critical Difference: Ohio Legal Assistance Foundation's Loan Repayment Assistance Program 14 (Jan. 2010), *available at* http://www.olaf.org/public/files/program/lrap/lrap-report.pdf.

55. NALP, 2010–2011 Federal Legal Employment Opportunities Guide 14, *available at* http://www.wcl.american.edu/career/government/documents/NALP_Federal_Legal_Employment_Opportunities_Guide_-_2010-11.pdf.

56. Equal Justice Works, *Law Students Can Find Ways to Pay Off Debt*, U.S. News & World Rep. (Jun. 8, 2011), http://www.usnews.com/education/blogs/student-loan-ranger/2011/06/08/law-students-can-find-ways-to-pay-off-debt.

57. *State Loan Repayment Assistance Programs*, Am. Bar Assoc., http://www.americanbar.org/groups/legal_aid_indigent_defendants/initiatives/loan_repayment_assistance_programs/state_loan_repayment_assistance_programs.html (last updated Sept. 21, 2012).

should be aware that more LRAPs could be defunded. The defunding of state LRAPs and the fact that many states do not have LRAPs makes the federal programs even more important. The good news is that the federal IBR and PSLF programs are thought to be relatively secure and not likely to be eliminated.[58]

IBR and PSLF programs, which are federal programs, do not preclude graduates from participating in LRAPs, but the reverse is not always true.[59] Some LRAPs do not allow graduates to participate in either the IBR or PSLF program, or both, while other LRAPs require graduates to first pursue IBR or PSLF eligibility. These restrictions are counterintuitive and limit the impact of local LRAP programs. If the LRAP is combined with the federal programs, it could allow law schools to help more graduates and increase the bang for their buck. The savings would then allow law schools with limited funds to improve or expand their LRAPs. As one law journal article stated, "[t]he central idea behind coordinating LRAP and federal benefits is to restructure LRAP programs so that the federal programs do most of the heavy lifting, allowing the most effective use of limited law school LRAP funds."[60] For example, Georgetown expects LRAP applicants to repay their loans using IBR and has qualifications for its LRAP that are similar to the requirements for PSLF.[61] If a graduate working in public interest has a $400 monthly IBR payment, Georgetown's LRAP can cover this payment for 10 years, at which point the remaining debt will be forgiven under PSLF. As a result, a Georgetown graduate employed in a public service job can contribute zero out-of-pocket funds to the repayment of her student loans. Of course, not every law school even has an LRAP and each one has its own requirements. If you are a prospective law student, especially one that may want to work in public service, find out about the LRAPs at each school you are considering.

How IBR and PSLF Could Work for Law Graduates

I realize that I have provided a lot of information; therefore, some more detailed examples of how the federal programs could work for law graduates can help demonstrate their benefits. First, consider that Ted, a single law graduate, works in a qualifying public service job for ten years. Assume that he has a federal student loan debt of $150,000 (one loan is for $60,000 at 6.8% interest rate and the other loan is for $90,000 at 7.9% interest rate), and he has a starting salary of $50,000 with 4% annual pay increases. Table 14-1 (next page) displays the payment obligations under three repayment plans: the standard 10-year plan, the IBR plan, and new IBR plan initiated by President Obama that will begin in July 2014 under his "Pay as You Earn" initiative.

58. *Loan Repayment Assistance Programs*, Equal Justice Works, http://www.equaljusticeworks.org/ed-debt/post-grad/loan-repayment-assistance-programs (last visited Feb. 28, 2013) ("It also may be possible to use LRAPs in conjunction with some federal relief programs."). *See also* Schrag & Pruett, *supra* note 14, at 598–99 ("Specifically, law schools ... can tie their programs to IBR, PSLF ... by requiring their graduates to use those programs.... These schools would never provide a graduate with a larger amount of money than the graduate was required to pay, assuming that the graduate elected IBR. In other words, schools can use their own limited funds to supplement the federal programs, not replace them.").

59. Jarvis, *supra* note 40, at 4.

60. Schrag & Pruett, *supra* note 14, at 598.

61. *Id.* at 599.

Table 14-1. $150,000 Debt, $50,000 Starting Salary, Public Service[62]

	Standard 10 Year Repayment Plan	IBR Plan	New IBR Plan
First Monthly Payment	$1,777	$416	$277
Max Monthly Payment	$1,777	$616	$411
Total Amount Repaid	$213,287	$61,234	$40,823
Total Loan Forgiveness	$0	$200,666	$221,077

This table illustrates the huge amount of money a graduate in public service can save using both the IBR and PSLF plans. Under the IBR-PSLF combination, Ted would end up paying less than a third of what he would have had to pay under a standard repayment plan. The monthly payments are significantly smaller. In the first year, the monthly payment of $416 is 10% of Ted's monthly income. The standard monthly payment of $1,777 is 43% of the Ted's monthly income in the first year and, as such, would severely limit his ability to live a decent lifestyle. The IBR plan makes monthly payments much more manageable and the PSLF forgives most of the total debt ($200,666) after 10 years. Remember that debt forgiveness under PSLF is tax-free. Because of his commitment to public service for 10 years, Ted is receiving his delayed compensation in the form of loan forgiveness.

Under the standard plan, Ted would only have available to him $28,680 of his gross annual income in his first year of debt payments. However, if Ted enrolls in the IBR plan and takes advantage of a LRAP offered by his law school, employer, or state, he could further maximize the income that would be left to handle his other living expenses and save towards buying a home.

The New IBR plan (passed by Congress in 2010) is even more generous because of the lower percentage of income (6.7% vs. 10%) for each payment. Compared to the standard plan, Ted will pay less than 20% of the total student loan debt under the New IBR over a 10-year period. This plan will take effect for graduates that take out their first loans after July 1, 2014, but the Obama "Pay as You Earn" initiative could make some or all of the New IBR benefits apply to graduates that received their first federal loan in 2008 or later and had at least one federal loan in 2012.

Next consider a graduate working at a small or medium sized law firm. This example would also apply to a public service lawyer that does not stay in public interest for the full ten years. Once again assume $150,000 in debt, a $50,000 starting salary and 4% annual pay increases. While the graduate does not receive PSLF, Table 14-2 (next page) shows that the graduate still benefits from IBR and would greatly benefit from the New IBR.

62. *See Calculators*, FINAID.ORG, http://www.finaid.org/calculators/ (last visited Feb. 28, 2013).

Table 14-2. $150,000 Debt, $50,000 Starting Salary, Private Practice[63]

	Standard 10 Year Repayment Plan	IBR Plan for 25 Years	New IBR Plan for 20 Years
First Monthly Payment	$1,777	$416	$277
Max Monthly Payment	$1,777	$1,176	$633
Total Amount Repaid	$213,287	$220,713	$103,869
Total Loan Forgiveness	$0	$207,572	$269,931

While the standard repayment plan remains the same, the IBR plan is not as beneficial here as it was to a graduate that qualifies for PSLF. Under the IBR plan, Ted will actually end up paying slightly more than under the standard plan. However, Ted will be paying this amount over 25 years instead of 10 years. For many law graduates, it will make a lot more sense to pay a slightly larger amount off over a much longer period of time because the monthly payments will be much smaller and allow a more comfortable lifestyle. While more interest accrues under the IBR plan due to the small payments, a substantial amount of the debt is still forgiven after 25 years. This example illustrates why the IBR plan is helpful but not nearly as advantageous to a low-income attorney at a law firm when compared to a public service attorney that qualifies for a PSLF plan.

The New IBR plan will provide a smaller monthly payment and forgiveness after 20 years instead of 25. The result is that Ted will pay less than half of what he would have to pay under the standard plan or the old IBR plan. This New IBR plan should help many new law graduates deal with the lower salaries that law firms are now paying. The New IBR plan will benefit public service attorneys as well; however, it is has a primary benefit of improving the financial situation of graduates that do not qualify for PSLF but earn low-incomes in private-sector jobs.

A final example will deal with the payment obligations of a law graduate that is temporarily unable to find a full-time attorney position. This is a common situation for law graduates, who find themselves employed in temp jobs, working in part-time attorney positions, or even working as sales associates or at other non-legal jobs. For the purposes of this example, it is irrelevant whether the graduate is doing contract legal work or working in a non-legal position. Table 14-3 below assumes $150,000 in debt, a $20,000 starting salary that jumps up to $50,000 in year three (when the grad finds full-time legal work), with 4% pay increases.

Table 14-3. $150,000 Debt, $20,000 Salary for 2 Years, Then $50,000 Salary, Private Practice[64]

	Standard 10 Year Repayment Plan	IBR Plan	New IBR Plan
First Monthly Payment	$1,777	$41	$27
Max Monthly Payment	$1,777	$1,055	$567
Total Amount Repaid	$213,287	$189,123	$87,286
Total Loan Forgiveness	$0	$240,382	$286,514

63. *Id.*
64. *Id.*

This example shows the flexibility provided by the IBR plan. First, note that Ted's monthly payment under the 10-year payment would exceed his monthly income until he gets the attorney position. He would, therefore, be in default and would have to ask the lenders for a deferment if he does not know about the IBR program. Thankfully, during the first two years after graduation when Ted has not yet found an attorney position, the IBR plan gives Ted a very low monthly payment on account of his low income. Even this $41 monthly payment counts towards the 25 years of payments required to receive forgiveness. While in this example Ted had a low income just after graduation, any dips in income at any time will result in a lower payment under the IBR plan. As income increases, the payments increase as well. A standard repayment plan does not provide this kind of flexibility, making it difficult to manage for those that find themselves temporarily unemployed or under-employed. However, everyone's individual situation will be different and IBR will not be the best choice for everyone. Current students and recent graduates should use the calculators at ibrinfo.org, and finaid.org to determine if the IBR plan will be a good option.

Tips on Managing Student Loan Debt

For Law Students and Law Graduates:

- **Find out if your law school, state, or employer has a LRAP.** If they do, find out what the requirements are and if you qualify.
- **Find out if you qualify for IBR or PSLF.** If your loans are direct federal loans or guaranteed by the federal government, you may qualify for IBR if your debt is high enough relative to your income. While millions could probably benefit from IBR, fewer than 450,000 currently participate in an IBR plan.[65] If you work in public service for 10 years and have federal direct loans or direct consolidation loans, you may qualify for PSLF. See ibrinfo.org for more information and for the IBR calculator to estimate your payments under IBR.
- **Consider LRAPs, IBR, and PSLF during your job search.** The availability of these programs can be a significant factor in determining whether a job will provide you with enough financial resources to live comfortably. If the employer offers a low-income but allows you to use one of these programs, then it may be a better option than a higher paying job that does not qualify you for a debt relief program. See the financial calculators at http://www.finaid.org/calculators/ibr.phtml.

For Potential Law Students:

- **Find out if each law school you are applying to has an LRAP and what the qualifications are.** Even if you hope to earn a high income, you may find yourself in a low-income job and needing assistance from an LRAP. Some LRAPs are now income based. The main point is to find out what your options will be now before making an enrollment decision.
- **Get federal loans, not private loans.** As of June 30, 2010, borrowers can get the full amount of their education loans in federal direct loans. Private loans do not qualify for IBR and PSLF. Parent PLUS loans also do not qualify for these programs. See ibrinfo.org for more information on how to qualify for IBR and PSLF.

---

65. Jarvis, *supra* note 14, at 3.

- **Consider the availability of these programs when estimating the total cost of law school.** While IBR will likely be available as long as you have federal loans, do not assume you will get a job that will qualify you for LRAPs or PSLF. However, you should still factor in the possible availability of debt assistance when choosing a law school.

Chapter 15

Can Student Loan Debt Get between You and a License to Practice Law?

In the two previous chapters, I explained how bankruptcy can be used to eliminate debt for graduates in extreme hardship situations and how loan forgiveness and assistance programs can lessen the burden of student loan debt for many law graduates, especially those in public service jobs. This chapter is my dire warning to prospective and current law students to borrow as little money as possible to finance a legal education so that they can avoid becoming like the graduates described later in this chapter. As the reader will see, student loan debts became an albatross around the necks of these graduates and, in some instances, state bar examiners and courts have used the debts as a basis for preventing these graduates from realizing their dream of becoming licensed attorneys. These "gatekeepers" to the legal profession have treated indebted law graduates as criminals, unfit to practice law.

As I wrote this chapter, the 2012 Olympic Games were taking place in London. I mused about how the sacrifices and trials of Olympic athletes often mirrored the tribulations of many law students. I began to see the process of obtaining a legal education as having numerous hurdles that must be crossed in order to reach the ultimate goal of becoming a lawyer. Unfortunately, unlike the sports we know and love, the legal profession race is poorly regulated and the rules largely undefined. Moreover, many of the runners are unaware of the new obstacles constantly being placed in their way. Even more troubling, some future lawyers face more barriers than others, making theirs a race without a fair outcome.

While the high cost of attending law school and the dismal job market are certainly among those hurdles affecting recent grads, an additional hurdle—the character and fitness test—is imposed by the legal industry itself. Every state sets its own requirements that applicants must meet in order to practice law in that state. The character and fitness test is used by state bar examiner committees to assess whether an applicant is fit to practice law. Some state bar examiners require the applicants to pass this test prior to taking the bar, while other examiners only require that applicants pass it before becoming a licensed attorney.

The term "test" is a bit of a misnomer here. All bar exam applicants have to take a multiple choice ethics exam known as the MPRE. However, the character and fitness test is not so much a test, but rather a series of disclosures to the state's bar examiner committee, which then uses these disclosures to decide whether the applicant is morally fit to become a lawyer. The specific requirements vary from state to state, but applicants are typically required to disclose conduct such as prior arrests, illegal drug use, mental illness, academic honor code violations, and terminations from employment. Students are often forced to undergo rigorous references checks that sift through decades of their personal lives and undergo interviews with senior attorneys and state bar staff.

In addition to the above disclosures, bar examiner committees want applicants to disclose the types and amounts of their debts. Student loan debt, the very debt that is a prerequisite for the majority of people to obtain higher education, may now be seen as a character flaw. This so-called flaw can be used as a reason to prevent someone from practicing law. Several states, including Ohio, Kentucky, and New York, have already denied graduates admittance to the bar solely on the basis that the graduates did not have a feasible plan for repaying their student debt. Some states have included student loan debt among the reasons for denying candidates admission and, thereby, are potentially using such debt as a factor to tip the scale against admitting the candidate to the practice of law.

State bar committees essentially decided that having excessive student loan debt should be treated like a DUI or other criminal offenses to be used to prevent someone from becoming a licensed attorney. There are several problems with this line of thinking. First, some may argue that people facing financial difficulties are more likely to commit crimes. However, there is no empirical evidence showing that people with large student loan debt are more likely to commit crimes in general, or white-collar crimes in particular. A 2011 study, though not directly on point, supports the law graduates because it found that there was no correlation at all between poor credit scores and the propensity to commit financial crimes at work.[1] It may be fair for bar examiners to conclude that law graduates with large student loan debts are more likely to have poor credit scores, but it is not fair to conclude they are more likely to defraud their clients and, therefore, lack the fitness to practice law.

Low-Income Law Students Usually Carry More Debt

Another problem arising from the bar examiners' refusal to admit applicants with large student loan debt is that this standard most likely disproportionately affects bar applicants from low-income families. It is well documented that low-income students are disproportionately excluded from traditional higher education institutions. One

1. Jeremy B. Bernerth, et al., *An Empirical Investigation of Dispositional Antecedents and Performance-Related Outcomes of Credit Scores*, J. of Applied Psych., Mar 2012, at 469–478.

study looked at students enrolled in first tier undergraduate schools (defined by this study as the top 146 most selective universities) and found that only 10% of the enrolled students came from the bottom half of the social economic status ("SES") scale, with only 3% represented in the bottom quartile of that scale.[2] The majority of enrolled students, a whopping 74%, came from the top quarter of the SES scale. Similarly, Professor Richard Sander complied a great deal of research and reported the following: "The vast majority of American law students come from relatively elite backgrounds; this is especially true at the most prestigious law schools, where only five percent of all students come from families whose SES is in the bottom half of the national distribution."[3] As a result, a small, but important, number of students are from low-income backgrounds and, in the absence of being awarded generous scholarships, most likely will borrow substantial amounts to finance a legal education. Consequently, I find it unthinkable that bar examiners and courts would assume that law graduates in the bottom quarter of the social economic status should be viewed with suspicion just because they have substantial student loan debt.

Even before getting admitted to law school, many students from families in the bottom of the SES scale have already incurred substantial debt in undergraduate school to pay for tuition fees, book purchases, and cost-of-living expenses. In hopes of getting into a good law school, low-income applicants have to pay the relatively-high costs of taking the LSAT, which starts at $227, and of paying for a LSAT preparation course, which ranges from $600 to $2,000, depending on the length of the course. Of course, prospective law students can elect not to take this optional preparatory course to avoid debt, but that decision may place them at a distinct disadvantage and jeopardize their ability to get an admission offer from a good school. Even the act of applying for admission to law school often forces low-income students to use their credit cards to pay for the application fees that range from $60–$100 per school.[4]

Once enrolled in law school, low-income students, in the absence of substantial scholarship offers,[5] have to obtain a larger amount of student loans than their wealthier counterparts. Borrowing to cover tuition and cost-of-living expenses is very expensive, and it is incredibly difficult to manage for students without any additional financial resources or scholarships. Moreover, many schools prohibit or strongly discourage first-year law students from working, which necessitates additional borrowing by low-income students to cover living expenses. In fact, the ABA prohibits full-time first-year law students from working. Networking and job hunting are also expensive endeavors. Some law students spend money to attend events hosted by local law firms or bar associations to network for job opportunities.

---

2. Anthony P. Carnevale & Stephen J. Rose, *The Century Found, Socioeconomic Status, Race/Ethnicity, and Selective College Admissions*, *in* AMERICA'S UNTAPPED RESOURCE 102 (2003), *available at* http://tcf.org/assets/downloads/tcf-carnrose.pdf (finding that "under current affirmative action policies, racial minorities are underrepresented, and that the underrepresentation of low-income students is even greater").

3. Richard Sander, *Class in American Legal Education*, 88 DENVER U.L. REV.631, 662 (2011).

4. While many low-income students receive waivers of application fees, some are ineligible for waivers for various reasons. Jodie G. Roure, *Achieving Educational Equity and Access for Underrepresented Students in the Legal Profession*, 19 TEMPLE POL. & CIV. RTS. L. REV. 31, 53 (2009) (stating that "financial limitations impact the number of schools to which the students can apply, which can result in a decrease of opportunity for admissions").

5. Although law schools offer needs-based scholarships, merit-based scholarships are the norm. That's because law schools "use merit-based scholarships to woo applicants with high numerical credentials; those numbers yield higher points in the U.S. News [rankings] formula." Deborah Merritt & Daniel Merritt, *Responsibility-Rights in the Legal Profession*, 43 ARIZ. ST. L.J. 1257, 1266 (2011).

To be thorough in their job search, many students, at their own expense,[6] attend out-of-state job fairs, such as the annual Public Interest Legal Career Fair.[7]

Graduation does not provide any immediate financial relief for low-income students as they rely on credit cards and any remaining student loan funds to bridge the income gap while they are studying for the bar exam. Studying for the bar exam is very time consuming, making it nearly impossible for somebody to work more than part-time; and even working part-time is discouraged as it makes it harder to study for the exam and increases the likelihood of a graduate not passing the bar exam. Because most law schools do not provide any bar exam preparation services, students must pay for bar prep courses from for-profit companies, such as Barbri, Kaplan, or Supreme, which charge as much as $4,000 for comprehensive courses.

Finally, expenses for and associated with taking the bar exam can easily exceed $1,000 Allow me to use Ohio as an example. Graduates who want to take the Ohio bar exam have to follow a two-step application process. First, the one-time Application to Register as a Candidate for the Bar is due by November 15th of the second year of law school and cost $75 (or a late fee of an additional $200), which is paid to the Ohio Supreme Court. An additional $225 fee must be paid to the National Conference of Bar Examiners. Step two is the application to take the bar exam, which is due approximately 3 months before the Bar Exam. The one-time fee for the application is $330, plus a $24 fee for the Multistate Performance Test. A late application will cost an additional $100. If applicants want to use their laptops to take the exam, they must then pay an additional, non-refundable laptop fee of $110. Ohio administers the bar exam in Columbus at Veteran's Memorial Coliseum, which charges $7 per day parking fees. Because the Ohio exam takes 3 days, the test-taker will have to pay $21 for parking. Of course, test-takers can bring their own lunch. However, test-takers from out of town also have to cover the additional costs of hotel and food for three days (not to mention the gas to get to Columbus).

With all of the foregoing costs, it is no surprise that low-income students have an enormous amount of debt and face financial problems managing it. Recently students are seeing their debt problems quickly compound if they have charged expenses on their credit cards and have only made the minimum payments required over the course of three years in law school. After graduating, many find themselves unable to make payments on their student loans and other financial obligations due to an inability to find adequate employment. Although many law students get through this period of unemployment or under-employment with financial support from family members, those who lack such support are left to watch their debt load rise, while their credit scores sink.

Many struggling graduates believe that once they pass the bar exam and are licensed, they will be able to find full-time, long-term jobs as attorneys and then be able to catch up on their delinquent bills and to start rebuilding their credit. However, state bar examiners are denying them that opportunity by preventing those with high debt from even sitting for the bar exam. State bar examiners premise their denials on the basis that these students are not morally fit to practice law because of their high debt load. However, denying these

6. A few schools provide financial assistance to help defray the costs of attending a job fair. *See, e.g.*, *Interviewing[:]Career Search Travel Reimbursement*, Ohio St. Univ. Moritz Coll. of L., http://moritzlaw.osu.edu/careerservices/guides/interviewing/search_grants.php (last visited March 1, 2013) (stating that Ohio State provides travel expense reimbursement for up to $100).

7. New York University School of Law has for the past few years hosted this job fair. *2013 Public Interest Legal Career Fair*, NYU's Pub. Int. L. Ctr., http://pilcfair.law.nyu.edu/ (last visited Oct. 23, 2012).

students the opportunity to even try to repair the financial damage caused by the high costs of attending law school has lasting repercussions for both the student and his or her dependents.

Applicant Passed the NY Bar Exam But Was Denied a Law License Due to Enormous Debt

Robert Bowman[8] is an example of a modern-day "pull yourself up by your bootstraps" story. But, unfortunately, his story was discounted due to his student loan debt.[9] Mr. Bowman had all the odds stacked against him. As a child he was shuffled through foster care via various legal proceedings. He never met his biological father. His mentally unstable mother, who was eventually unable to care for him, put him up for adoption at the age of five. However, two years later his mother kidnapped him and raised her child on the run from law enforcement. The family managed to stay together until Bowman was eleven when his step-father was murdered. With that trauma proving to be too much for his mercurial mother, Bowman spent the next seven years floating between homeless shelters and friends' homes until he was able to join the army at age 18.

Bowman never let himself become a victim of his circumstances and worked to create a better life for himself. After being discharged from the military, he invested in his education and began working towards a bachelor's degree. Tragedy struck again while in school; Bowman was involved in a devastating accident that shattered his leg. This accident forced him to delay his college pursuits while he recovered in a residential rehabilitation facility. Ten years from when he first enrolled in community college, Mr. Bowman walked across the stage to accept his degree at State University of New York in Albany in 1995. This success would not have been possible without his reliance on student loans to finance his education. In 2000, Bowman enrolled in law school at the University of California Hastings School of Law. Like most students, he funded this education with student loans. Upon graduation, he enrolled in a master's of law program in London and completed this degree in December 2004.

By that point, Mr. Bowman had borrowed around $230,000. This amount may seem high at first glance, but it is important to remember that he funded his education entirely on his own, which meant he had to take out loans for his undergraduate education, law school, and the master's program as well as loans to necessary pay for the additional expenses while preparing to take the bar exam.

Mr. Bowman had a difficult time passing the bar exam. Many people would have given up, but Mr. Bowman kept trying and finally on the fourth time he passed it, making him eligible to practice law in the state of New York. He only had one final hurdle to cross, which was his character and fitness exam. In New York, the character and fitness interview is not conducted until after bar passage.

8. Mr. Bowman's identity was initially unknown due to the fact that he could make an anonymous appeal. *See* In re Anonymous, 61 A.D.3d 1214, 875 N.Y.S.2d 925 (2009). His identity was later revealed along with details about his life in an article in the New York Times. *Report on Robert A. Bowman's Application for Admission to the New York State Bar*, N.Y. Times (Jan. 2009), *available at* http://documents.nytimes.com/report-on-robert-a-bowman-s-application-for-admission-to-the-new-york-state-bar#p=1.

9. *Report on Robert Bowman's Application*, *supra* note 8.

Unfortunately for Mr. Bowman, bad luck struck again and he was involved in a second accident that shattered his good leg. He sought a medical deferment from Sallie Mae, his lender, while he recovered from the injury, but his request was denied. Sallie Mae then turned his account over to a private collections agency and tacked on fees that nearly doubled his principal amount owed to a whopping $435,000.

Finally recovered from his injury, Mr. Bowman began preparing to undergo his character and fitness evaluation and was worried that is debt may pose a problem. Mr. Bowman went to his interview prepared to honestly and openly answer all questions about his debt. He had brought with him all of his correspondence with Sallie Mae and the details of his current dispute with the lender. The Committee on Character and Fitness, comprised of three lawyers who interviewed him, found his "determination to pursue a postsecondary education remarkable."[10] As for the loans, they remarked that "it appears unconscionable that student loan indebtedness could go from $270,000 to $435,000 in four years." After gaining more information about his dispute with Sallie Mae and conducting a thorough investigation, the Committee eventually "concluded that Applicant [Mr. Bowman] has exceptional character, with exceptional perseverance, tenacity and humility." At this point, the last hurdle for Mr. Bowman to cross was for the court to approve the Committee's recommendation.

Despite the Committee's certifying Mr. Bowman for admission as a licensed attorney, the New York Supreme Court denied him admission. Because Mr. Bowman had not made substantial payments on his debt and because the Court concluded Mr. Bowman had not been "flexible" in working out a payment arrangement with the lender, the court decided he did "not presently established the character and general fitness requisite for an attorney and counselor-at-law."[11] The court's decision means that, unless Mr. Bowman is able at a future date to prove he has satisfactorily dealt with his debt, he will never be a lawyer in New York. What is most disturbing about this decision is that the State of New York Supreme Court has allowed others to become admitted as licensed attorneys despite misconduct such as solicitation of minors for sex,[12] efforts to deceive judges,[13] and possession of cocaine.[14] While the Court decided that those offenses only warranted temporary suspension, apparently Mr. Bowman's debt was just too much. Unfortunately, some will see this as a jarring example of the bias against individuals who have to finance their legal education solely from student loans.

Indebted 2008 Grad is Denied the Chance to Take the Ohio Bar Exam

Tom Smith[15] joins Robert Bowman on the list of students who were unfairly denied admission to the bar. His story is the epitome of a horrible catch-22. Like Mr. Bowman, Mr. Smith was denied admission to the bar for having student loans—student loans necessary to attend law school. Mr. Smith's story is even more surprising because his

10. *Id.*
11. http://decisions.courts.state.ny.us/ad3/Decisions/2009/D-11-09Anonymous.pdf.
12. http://www.courts.state.ny.us/reporter/3dseries/2008/2008_10230.htm.
13. http://decisions.courts.state.ny.us/ad3/decisions/2008/d-17-08arnold.pdf.
14. http://decisions.courts.state.ny.us/ad3/Decisions/2008/D-67-08Matey.pdf.
15. Although this case is a matter of public record, I have decided to use a fictitious name to prevent any further embarrassment or harm.

loans were not very high—only $170,000—an amount that is certainly within the range that an individual would have to borrow to attend law school.[16]

Mr. Smith wanted to practice law in the state of Ohio. After graduating from Ohio State University Moritz College of Law, he applied to take the bar exam. He attempted to pass the exam three times, but was unsuccessful. Despite these setbacks, he did not give up. Instead, he persevered and decided to try again by signing up for the February 2010 Ohio bar exam. Unfortunately this time, the bar exam committee denied his request, expressing a concern about Mr. Smith's finances due to his high student loans.[17]

Mr. Smith should not be regarded as a slacker when it comes to managing finances. Before enrolling in law school in 2005, he worked as a full-time stockbroker for more than five years, earning a salary that was enough to meet his living and educational expenses.[18] The timeline from the opinion shows that Mr. Smith worked as a stockbroker while pursuing an undergraduate degree from Arizona State University, obtaining his degree in 2004. However, when Mr. Smith started law school, he had to take a large salary cut. Like many law schools, Ohio State strongly discourages students from working during their first year of law school. Mr. Smith eventually started working at the Franklin County Public Defender's Office. After graduation in 2008, like many of his classmates, Mr. Smith was unable to secure full-time employment. Trying to make ends meet until he found a full-time job, he continued to work at the public defender's office part-time, but he was only getting paid $12 an hour.[19]

Mr. Smith's student loan payments became due in July of 2009, but because he was only working part-time and not getting paid very well, he was unable to make his payments. His low salary also affected his ability to pay his credit card bills. Because he was unable to make his credit card payments, one of his creditors obtained a default judgment against him.[20]

Mr. Smith thought that once he obtained his law license, it would be easier for him to find a better paying legal job. After applying to take the February 2010 bar exam, the Columbus Bar Association Admissions Committee reviewed his application and personally interviewed him. After the interview, the Committee issued a report certifying that Mr. Smith possessed the "character, fitness, and moral qualification required for admission to the practice of law and recommended that [his application] be approved."[21] Unfortunately for Mr. Smith, the Board of Commissioners on Character and Fitness (the "Board") felt otherwise. The Board members expressed their concern about the way Mr. Smith had handled his personal finances and decided to launch an investigation of his debt in accordance with the appropriate rules.

---

16. To protect Mr. Smith's privacy, I do not want to get into the specifics of his borrowing. Below are the non-resident and resident tuition amounts and budgeted borrowing amounts for the three years he attended Ohio State:

2006 tuition: $29,262	2006 budget: $49,826
2007 tuition: $17,538	2007 budget: $51,931
2008 tuition: $24,535	2008 budget: $53,858

A total of the three years of budgeted borrowing equals $155,615. A student is able to borrow more than the budgeted amount based on demonstrated need at professional judgment appeals. Mr. Smith's debt of $170,000 was within the range of indebtedness anticipated for students lacking fellowships or scholarships.

17. In re Application of Smith, 128 Ohio St.3d 300, 2011-Ohio-20, at ¶ 1.

18. *Id.* at ¶ 5.

19. *Id.*

20. I have not interviewed Mr. Smith and, therefore, have no explanation regarding what led to the entry of a default judgment against him.

21. *Id.*

Subsequently, a panel of the Board conducted a hearing that focused on Mr. Smith's debt and their perception that he lacked a plan to meet his financial obligations. The panel found that after graduating from Arizona State University and The Ohio State University Moritz College of Law, Mr. Smith owed approximately $170,000 in student loans, along with $16,500 in credit-card debt.

In light of the foregoing, Mr. Smith met with an attorney and considered filing bankruptcy. During the Board's investigation, Mr. Smith described the potential benefits of bankruptcy.

The reader may recall from my in-depth discussion in Chapter 13 that student loan debts are extremely difficult to discharge. Because Mr. Smith is a healthy, fairly young man, nothing about his life circumstances would make him eligible to receive a hardship discharge of his student loan debt. So, at best, Mr. Smith's filing for bankruptcy relief would have discharged his small amount of credit card debt but would not have discharged his $170,000 in student loan debt.

During his hearing with the Board, Mr. Smith revealed that he had never filed a bankruptcy petition. The Board held this fact against him even though filing bankruptcy would have done nothing to alleviate Mr. Smith's student loan debt. As a result, the Board decided that Mr. Smith had no plan or ability to repay his debts and, therefore, denied his bar application. The Board stated that he would be permitted to reapply at a future date should his circumstances improve.

Since his bar application had been denied, Mr. Smith appealed the denial and sought a reversal from the Ohio Supreme Court. In its opinion, the Ohio Supreme Court set forth the character and fitness standard for applicants to the Ohio bar:

> The applicant's record must justify "the trust of clients, adversaries, courts, and others with respect to the professional duties owed to them." Gov.Bar R. I(11)(D)(3). Necessarily, "[a] record manifesting a significant deficiency in the honesty, trustworthiness, diligence, or reliability of an applicant may constitute a basis for disapproval of the applicant.[22]

However, the Ohio Supreme Court never actually discussed how under this standard, Mr. Smith's student loan debt shows he is dishonest or untrustworthy or why his debt would make his clients not respect him. The Court accepted the Boards findings and concluded with the following:

> The applicant has neglected his personal financial obligations by electing to maintain his part-time employment with the Public Defender's Office in the hope that it will lead to a full-time position upon passage of the bar exam, rather than seeking full-time employment, which he acknowledges would give him a better opportunity to pay his obligations and possibly qualify him for an additional deferment of his student-loan obligation.[23]

Ultimately, the Court agreed with the Board in its assessment that Mr. Smith "failed to prove that he possesses the requisite character, fitness, and moral qualifications for admissions to the practice of law."

It strikes me that the Court is implying that Mr. Smith was somehow lazy for failing to get another job, yet the Court never takes into account or inquires about whether Mr. Smith's family arrangement limited this options due to his being a parent to his young daughter.[24]

---

22. *Id.* at ¶8.
23. *Id.*
24. Mr. Smith, his nine-year-old daughter, and the mother of the daughter live together. *Id.* at ¶10.

Mr. Smith's situation can be unpacked into several observations. First, from an academic perspective, because Mr. Smith failed to pass the bar three times, empirical research shows that he likely either graduated in the bottom 25% of his law school class or that his first semester GPA was in the bottom 25% of his class.[25] If this was true for Mr. Smith, then, as the research shows, he was already susceptible to not passing the bar exam on his first attempt. As I have explained in Chapter 6, prospective students with LSAT scores that put them in the bottom percentile should make sure the school has demonstrated a commitment to provided academic support services as well as bar exam support services.[26] Such services significantly increase the chances of a graduate passing the bar exam on the first try, and some schools that have implemented major changes in their bar support programs have seen their bar passage rates increase dramatically.[27] If students in the bottom of the class have access to bar support services, they should obviously take advantage of them because then they are much more likely to pass the bar exam.

Another observation worth noting is that Mr. Smith's student loan debt—$170,000—was not excessive in light of the cost of attending law school for three years without scholarships. He began Ohio State as a non-resident student when the tuition rate for non-residents was $29,262. I am sure he was urged to borrow only necessary amounts.

Because of the Ohio Supreme Court's ruling against him, graduates seeking to be admitted to the Ohio bar now know that an applicant with no history of criminal wrongdoing or substance abuse could be denied the chance to become a practicing attorney in Ohio solely on the basis that bar examiners and judges believe the applicant has not adequately handled his or her student loan debt. This ruling is particularly troubling when one considers that a different Ohio court reinstated in 2009 the law license of a convicted murderer Derek Farmer, whose law license was suspended for violating several provisions of the Code of Professional Misconduct.[28]

---

25. Denise Riebe, *A Bar Review for Law Schools: Getting Students on Board to Pass Their Bar Exams*, 45 BRANDEIS L.J. 269, 283 (2007) (discussing research showing that "[t]he strongest predictor of bar passage ... is law school GPAs"). In a study of 862 graduates (from 1996 to 1999) of St. Mary's University School of Law in San Antonio, Texas, researchers found that "[m]ore than 97 percent of those with at least a 3.0 grade-point average in law school passed their first Texas bar exam. In contrast, only 25 percent of those with a GPA below 2.5 passed on the first try." *Id.* at 284, n. 111. Christian C. Day, *Law Schools Can Solve the "Bar Pass Problem"—"Do the Work!"*, 40 CAL. W. L. REV. 321, 324 (2004) ("The greatest risk of failure on the bar exam is for those students in the lower half, particularly, the bottom quartile.").

26. Ohio State has both services. I decline to convey any specifics regarding Mr. Smith's use of these services to protect his privacy.

27. *See generally* Linda Jellum & Emmeline Paulette Reeves, *Cool Data on a Hot Issue: Empirical Evidence that a Law School Bar Support Program Enhances Bar Performance*, 5 NEV. L.J. 646 (2005); Donald H. Zeigler et al., *Curriculum Design and Bar Passage: New York Law School's Experience*, 59 J. LEGAL EDUC. 393 (2010); Derek Alphran et al., *Yes We Can, Pass the Bar. University of the District of Columbia, David A. Clarke School of Law Bar Passage Initiatives and Bar Passage Rates—From the Titanic to the Queen Mary!*, 14 U. D.C. L. REV. 9 (2011).

28. Dan Horn, *Murderer Wins Fight to Reinstate Law License*, CINCINNATI ENQUIRER (Cincinnati, Ohio), at B4, June 6, 2009. Mr. Farmer spent 18 years in prison for his role in the death of a police officer and civil rights activist before going on to obtain a law degree from University of Akron School of Law and passing the Ohio bar exam in 1999. His law license was suspended after the Columbus Bar Association accused him of charging excessive legal fees, failing to keep records, and misleading investigators. *See Columbus Bar Assn. v. Farmer*, 111 Ohio St.3d 137, 855 N.E.2d 462 (2006). In its opinion reinstating Farmer's law license, the United States District Court for the Southern District of Ohio stated "that Respondent [Farmer] has shown by clear and convincing evidence that he has the moral qualifications, competency, and learning in the law required for admission to practice law before this Court. This Court also finds that Respondent's resumption of the practice of law will not

I find it surprising that the Court stated that Mr. Smith did not have a strategy to pay back his debt because he actually did. He planned to pass the bar exam and to turn his part-time job at the Public Defender's Office into a full-time public defender position. That would have allowed Mr. Smith to bring in income sufficient to pay off part of his loan. Such a strategy is regularly used by recent graduates to secure permanent jobs. As the saying goes, "part-time work allows you to get your foot in the door." Some law graduates even volunteer their time at a business in hopes of networking with the right people to advance a job search or in hopes that such volunteer work will be parlayed into full-time employment at that organization. The Ohio Supreme Court's opinion failed to take into consideration that not volunteering or interning at the desired employer's office may be practically fatal to getting employed there. Consequently, low-income students, while volunteering or interning, are going to accumulate more debt than their counterparts who have financial support from family.

Unfortunately for Mr. Smith, neither the initial Board's decision nor the Court's opinion ever mentioned the loan forgiveness programs that I describe in this book. Perhaps, the judges were not aware of such programs and perhaps Mr. Smith did not know about the programs either. Had the Board and the Ohio Supreme Court been aware, perhaps they could have made approval of his bar application contingent on his getting a full-time qualifying public service job in another field that would have allowed him to take part in the payment reduction and loan forgiveness programs as a way to pay down his debt.[29] The Ohio Supreme Court, as the final arbiter who could decide Mr. Smith's fate, did not offer him any hope and essentially kicked Mr. Smith while he was already down.

Without explicitly saying so, the judges may be implying that Mr. Smith should go back to his broker job and give up on his dreams of becoming a public defender just to pay back his student loans. This is truly tragic. It begs the question: how is the legal profession served by somebody going back to a job where his goal was presumably just to make money? He left that job because it was unfulfilling. He left that broker position behind and took on the enormous challenge of attending law school. His investment clients would not be well served by someone who does not want to do the job. As others have already said, the judges put Mr. Smith in a catch-22 situation. The Ohio Supreme Court essentially said that he could not take the bar exam until he dealt with his debt, but the court banned him from the legal profession by preventing him from taking the bar exam, that when passed, would qualify him for an attorney job so that he could pay his debts.

Mr. Smith's case is the epitome of student loan debt becoming a life sentence of indebtedness. As already noted, he cannot get rid of his student loan debt in bankruptcy. Thus, he may have been forced to go back to his unsatisfying job as a stockbroker. Because

---

be detrimental to the integrity and standing of the bar or to the administration of justice, or subversive to the public interest." *In re Farmer*, No. 1:06mc85, 2009 WL 990869 (S.D. Ohio Apr. 10, 2009).

29. Under the College Cost Reduction and Access Act of 2007, the term 'public service job' means: (i) a full-time job in emergency management, government, military service, public safety, law enforcement, public health, public education (including early childhood education), social work in a public child or family service agency, public interest law services (including prosecution or public defense or legal advocacy in low-income communities at a nonprofit organization), public child care, public service for individuals with disabilities, public service for the elderly, public library sciences, school-based library sciences and other school-based services, or at an organization that is described in section 501(c)(3) of the Internal Revenue Code of 1986 and exempt from taxation under section 501(a) of such Code; or (ii) teaching as a full-time faculty member at a Tribal College or University as defined in section 316(b) and other faculty teaching in high-needs areas, as determined by the Secretary.

See 20 U.S.C. § 1087e(m)(3)(B), (2012).

of this ruling, Mr. Smith literally incurred $170,000 in debt for no good reason. The legal profession is deprived of a graduate who was dedicated enough to work a part-time job making $12 per hour just so he could represent the accused in the criminal justice system. I contacted the Ohio Supreme Court, and I can confirm that Mr. Smith has ***not*** been able to sit to take the bar exam even though he applied again after losing his appeal.

When Did State Bar Associations Become Debt Collectors?

Similar to the Ohio Supreme Court using student loan debt to deny an applicant the ability to take the bar exam, the Kentucky Supreme Court went so far as to revoke a law graduate's conditional admission due to the graduate's failure to follow a payment plan prescribed by the character and fitness committee. Lincoln Jones, a recent law school graduate with a heavy debt load, was granted admission to the bar, but it was contingent upon proof of payment of his debts. In this case,[30] in order to be admitted, the applicant was required to comply with an agreement that stated he must submit twelve proofs of payments acceptable under a specified loan program. While this outcome is certainly better than the outcome that Bowman and Smith received, it begs the question: when did state bar associations become debt collectors?

The Kentucky Supreme Court first gave lip service to the idea that they—the Court, the Character and Fitness Committee, and the Kentucky Bar Association—are not authorized to assume "the role of a collection agency for student loan creditors."[31] The Court, then, deemed Mr. Jones unfit to practice law due to his excessive student loans and, thus, took on the role of a debt collector. The court never really explained this dissonance between its stated role and its assumed role.

Realizing the absurdity of this decision, Justice Cooper, one of the dissenting judges who wanted to allow Mr. Jones to keep his license, stated: "If the creditor is not demanding payment, why should we? Implicit in this agreement is an assumption that any attorney with substantial unpaid debts is prima facie unfit to practice law. I find that assumption untenable."[32] Justice Cooper follows this with the comment that "one can only wonder how a young law graduate with poor parents and a substantial student loan debt is expected to earn the money to pay that debt if denied the opportunity to practice the profession which was the *raison d'etre* for the incurrence of the debt."[33]

Justice Cooper's criticisms strikes at the heart of a sinister problem arising in the legal community: to become a lawyer, you must incur an enormous amount debt, but to incur an enormous amount of debt means you may be declared *unfit* to be a lawyer. If the legal community continues down this fallacious circular path, the road to becoming a lawyer will be blocked for a great number of well-intentioned, eager, prospective law school students. It is astonishing to see, yet again, how much blame is put on the law student

30. Character & Fitness Comm. Office of Bar Admissions v. Jones, 62 S.W.3d 28(Ky. 2001)
31. *Id.* at 31.
32. *Id.* at 33.
33. *Id.*

while law schools are given a pass for their astronomical tuition costs that necessitates enormous borrowing in the first place.

In a separate disturbing case, *In re G.W.*, the applicant was similarly denied admission to the bar for reasons that included his high student debt. Most troubling in this case was the fact that issues regarding his student debt were put on par with his criminal record which included among other things a DWI, violating a restraining order, and a "fake robbery."[34] The Court found that G.W.'s ballooning student loan debt, which grew in the 16 years it took for him to pass the bar exam, was indicative of his "inability to handle his own affairs" which in turn indicated that he was not qualified to handle the affairs of others as a lawyer.[35] The fact that his financial problems are regarded as equally as detrimental to his bar admittance as his documented criminal conduct shows just how serious of a problem student loan debt is becoming.

It is worth taking a moment to seriously think about what is going on here: the act of going to law school can now create a character flaw in you that is comparable in gravity to that of criminal actions. Should we be telling potential law school students that you are just as likely to be denied admittance to the bar if you incur substantial student loan debt as you are if you commit a criminal act? OF COURSE NOT!

What Do These Stories Mean for the Future of the Legal Profession?

Stories like the ones of Bowman and Smith leave us with a seemingly dismal future for the legal profession. The most unfortunate interpretation of the courts' opinions in these cases is that now student loan debt has become a test for character and fitness. One can further extrapolate that the graduates who have affluent parents to help them financially have character and fitness while graduates who have cash-strapped parents do not. This line of thinking will continue to create a greater divide between the rich and the poor in the legal profession. Courts and bar examiner committees should applaud perseverance and beating the odds among *all* law graduates. I am concerned that the gatekeepers of the legal profession are sending a message to those without familial financial-backing that they should not attempt to pursue a legal education.

What does this mean for students considering law school? Prospective students must assess their current financial situation and determine how they can minimize borrowing once enrolled in law school. Prospective students must also consider the fact that debt is being heavily scrutinized and may serve as a barrier to crossing the finish line in the race to become a lawyer. I encourage undergraduate students desiring to enroll in law school to work for a year or two before enrolling. During that time, they should learn to live independently and solely on their income. By working fulltime and learning to live financially independent for a year or two, a young adult will be better prepared to borrow wisely once enrolled in law school. I am not painting all young adults with a broad brush. Many prospective law students work full-time jobs while pursuing an undergraduate degree. They pay their auto premiums and credit card bills on time. However,

34. In re G.W., 161 N.H. 401, 402, 13 A.3d 194, 195 (2011).
35. *Id.* at 200.

many prospective law students have not learned to live financially independent lives; therefore, for these students, I suggest working fulltime for a year or two before going to law school.

Although the recommendation to postpone enrollment in law school may seem to be an over-reaction, my recommendation is meant to get young adults who have never learned to live independently of help from parents to have a chance to deal with undergraduate student loan debt. Let me use myself as an example. I worked for two years as an accountant before enrolling in law school. Because my student loans became due during that two-year period, I had to learn how to budget and to spend my money wisely so that I had enough money to cover both my monthly student loan payments and my living expenses. By seeing how much the student loan debt reduced my disposable income, I realized that I could not enroll in a law school where my student loan debt would approach six figures. I knew that such debt would result in a monthly payment of around $700 or $800 and, therefore, could have eaten up half of my post-graduation monthly income. Moreover, based on what I have learned since then, unmanageable student loan debt could also become an obstacle to being able to take the bar exam or being admitted to the practice of law. Just like students must reasonably prepare themselves for the harsh reality that there is a 90% percent chance they will not be in the top ten percent of the class, they must also prepare themselves for the reality that a high debt load may preclude them from admission to the bar. We like to think that with hard work anything is possible, but try asking Mr. Bowman and Mr. Smith whether that is the case.

Prospective students who have to finance their legal education should enroll in the law school that offers the most for the least costs. Refer back to Chapter 3 to read my explanation regarding how to do sophisticated analysis of a law school. Once enrolled, students should live frugally to minimize the amount necessary to pay for a legal education. Students also need to document their lifestyle in case there is a question about it later. They should save credit card bills as proof for a board member or a judge that they were not "living high on the hog" while in law school.

Students should borrow the maximum amount of direct and Grad Plus loans, but they should *save* a substantial part of these government-backed loans to tide them over during periods of unemployment. Why? Prior to entering law school, prospective students think that they will be employed as law clerks during both summers while in law school. Except for perhaps students enrolled in one of the Top 14 law schools, the majority of law students do not find paying legal jobs during the summer between the first and second years of law school.[36] Therefore, first-year students should put themselves in the position of not having to borrow any money to cover summer living expenses and, thereby, avoid taking a *non*-legal job just to make ends meet. Students who are unable to find legal jobs but

36. The majority of legal employment for students who have completed their first year of law school comes from law firms. Since the recession, NALP has consistently reported that law firms have reduced and maintained reduced levels of summer law clerk positions since the start of the recession. Press Release, NALP, Recruiting for Entry Level Lawyers Edges Up Slightly (March 16, 2012), *available at* http://www.nalp.org/uploads/PressReleases/PerspFall2010_March11PressRel.pdf (discussing employment results for the 2010 graduates as well as the results for students working as summer associates and stating that "[a]fter having been caught in the middle of the recession with larger summer programs than they would have liked, law firms in general brought in much smaller classes this past summer"). Even though law firms increased their hiring of students for their 2011 summer program, such hiring has not returned to the pre-recession hiring levels and is not expected to return. *See Legal Summer Jobs Gaining Steam*, JD J., http://www.jdjournal.com/2012/02/08/legal-summer-j-obs-gaining-steam/ (last visited March 1, 2013).

have saved a sufficient part of their student loans are perfectly situated to volunteer their time working for a law professor or a small law firm to gain valuable legal experience and to do networking, as many jobs are still obtained through having the right connections. In this way, a law student can "plan for the worst and hope for the best." Furthermore, depending on the school's requirements, such volunteer work can count as credit hours towards the school's graduation requirements.

As they approach their last year of law school, students who find themselves ***not*** ranked in the top one-third should borrow the maximum amount of government-backed loans and save at least $10,000 of those loan funds to tide them over while they are studying for the bar exam and searching for a permanent attorney position. Students ranked in the bottom half of a *non*-Top 14 school should also save accordingly. Too many students fill this income gap by charging expenses to their credit cards or by getting private loans—both of these options frequently carry double-digit interest rates and substantially deepen the debt hole.

Assume that a student lived off their savings while studying for the bar exam but unfortunately did not pass. What can be done then? Students who do not have the option of moving in with their parents and living with them for free should consider finding a full-time, public-service job, even if it is non-legal, that satisfies the federal or state loan assistance or forgiveness programs. Such a move would be especially prudent when coupled with participation in an IBR program (discussed in Chapter 14). Recall Tom Smith, who was only working part-time at the public defender's office, was denied the chance to take the bar exam for the third time because the Ohio Supreme Court decided he lacked a plan to deal with his student loan debt. If he had obtained full-time employment in a public service position, he would have been able to participate in a PSLF program, which provides loan forgiveness of the remaining student loan balance after 10 years of payments. Such a career move would have shown the judge that he had a sufficient plan to deal with his student loan debt so that the court could have allowed him to take the bar exam again in order to pursue realization of his dream of becoming a practicing lawyer.

Taking a Public Service Job to Deal with Student Loan Debt

I recognize that a recent graduate may not be able to easily obtain a public service position at a local organization. However, AmeriCorps is a national organization that public-service-minded graduates, particularly those unable to find traditional full time employment in their field, should consider. AmeriCorps is funded by the Corporation for National & Community Service, the federal agency that oversees various national programs designed to help individuals, families, and communities. Through that funding as well as funding from various public and private partnerships, AmeriCorps has over 80,000 adults employed annually in results-driven public service positions through more than 15,000 organizations in the United States.[37] In exchange for full-time service, AmeriCorps workers, aka "members" or "volunteers," not only earn a monthly living

37. *Fact Sheet 2012*, AmeriCorps, (January 2013), *available at* http://www.americorps.gov/pdf/factsheet_americorps.pdf.

stipend, but also earn a $5,550 Segal AmeriCorps Education Award, which can be used to pay qualified student loans or help pay for additional education.[38]

While the majority of AmeriCorps opportunities are not related directly to the law, AmeriCorps does offer a limited number of opportunities that may ideal for law graduates. For example, AmeriCorps members have worked for both Advocates for Basic Legal Equality, Inc. ("ABLE") and Legal Aid of Western Ohio, Inc. (LAWO), which are law firms that represent low-income people. Through ABLE and LAWO, members of AmeriCorps provide legal representation to the homeless and other low-income individuals to help them find and maintain affordable housing.

Some of these law-related AmeriCorps members are employed as legal fellows, and they are practicing attorneys just like other licensed attorneys doing public service work. For instance, Katherine Hollingsworth, a graduate of Georgetown University Law Center, was selected as an Equal Justice Works AmeriCorps Legal Fellow to serve as an attorney in the consumer law section of the Legal Aid Society of Cleveland.[39] Legal fellows are paid salaries on par with salaries for traditional legal aid attorneys. In this capacity, Ms. Hollingsworth is able to do foreclosure defense. She finds her work rewarding and is especially gratified that she was able to help one special client, an elderly woman raising her teenage grandson, to save her home of 40 years from foreclosure. Ms. Hollingsworth's service as an AmeriCorps Legal Fellow allows her to make a real, life-saving difference for low-income families while simultaneously paying down the student loan debt she accumulated at Georgetown.[40]

Unlike the law-related AmeriCorps programs that employ legal fellows, some law-related AmeriCorps programs pay much less for non-attorney positions that allow law graduates and students to provide assistance to low-income families. For example, Legal Assistance of Western New York ("LawNY") has an AmeriCorps program called the Access to Justice Project, which employs 29 AmeriCorps members who serve as paralegals.[41] They conduct intake services that refer callers to the hotline to organizations that can provide legal assistance, they provide legal education to community groups, and they provide direct legal services, including representation of the clients at administrative hearings.

Many AmeriCorps opportunities, even though not law-related, can still help law graduates keep the enthusiasm to practice law alive as they provide non-legal assistance to individuals that they can refer to legal aid organizations. For example, there are numerous AmeriCorps programs where members provide domestic violence awareness and prevention,

38. Unfortunately, the education award is taxable; therefore, students need to be prepared to pay taxes. *Tax Implications*, AMERICORPS, http://www.americorps.gov/for_individuals/benefits/benefits_ed_award_taxes.asp (last visited March 1, 2013). However, there are ways to structure one's use of the award to minimize the tax liability.

39. LEGAL AID SOC. OF CLEVELAND, *Legal Aid Attorneys & Volunteers Work Together: Preserve Good Outcomes for Client*, POETIC JUSTICE, (Winter 2012), *available at* http://lasclev.org/wp-content/uploads/Poetic-Justice-Volume-9-Issue-1-FINAL.pdf.

40. I do not know what the tuition fee was when Ms. Hollingsworth attended Georgetown. However, tuition for the 2012–2013 year is $48,835.00 (based on fulltime tuition for each semester at $24,417.50). *Tuition Fees Per Semester*, GEORGETOWN LAW CTR., *available at* http://www.law.georgetown.edu/campus-services/student-accounts/upload/tuition-fee-schedule.pdf (last visited March 1, 2013).

41. *Snapshot of Accomplishments*, LEGAL ASSISTANCE OF WESTERN NEW YORK, INC., 2010–2011, *available at* http://www.iola.org/board/Grantee%20Annual%20Report%202010/Legal%20Assistance%20of%20Western%20New%20York%202010.pdf (last visited March 1, 2013) (stating also that LawNY has an AmeriCorps legal fellow who staffs LiveHelp, a real-time, online chat service to low-income New York residents who need legal help).

foreclosure relief assistance, and homeless transition and prevention services. Such service will uncover legal issues and law graduates serving clients in need of legal representation can facilitate that representation. Although these AmeriCorps members serving full-time will only earn a monthly income of $925, which amounts to an annual stipend of $11,100, law graduates will not have to make any payments under the IBR program because this salary is so low. Moreover, graduates will have their year of service count towards the 10-year period of payments needed for loan forgiveness under the PSLF program.

Assuming Mr. Smith did not know about the foregoing service opportunities available in Ohio, had he known about them and taken advantage of them, he would have provided needed legal service to low-income families and, at same time, he would have earned a full-time annual salary of $11,100. That may not sound like much. However, he was already earning near that amount[42] and was viewed as a deadbeat by the Ohio Supreme Court. But had he been a full-time AmeriCorps member, he would have been eligible to participate in both the IBR and PSLF programs. That means he would have had zero student loan payments and his one or two years of service would have counted towards his 10 years of service to have his qualified loans forgiven after 10 years. At the end of one-year of service, he would have also received the $5,550 education award and been able to use it to pay back a portion of his qualified student loans. Based on the foregoing, the Ohio Supreme Court would have had to conclude that Mr. Smith had a plan to repay his loans and, therefore, would allow him to take the bar exam.

I began this chapter by explaining how student loan debt is raised as a hurdle standing between you and your license to practice law. I have ended on a positive note by telling students that the inability to find a traditional law firm job or to pass the bar exam the first time should be seen not as a mountain but as stepping stone. Graduates can turn the temporary setback into an opportunity to serve. An AmeriCorps position will leave a graduate with many evening and weekend hours for a diligent graduate to study so that he or she can pass the bar exam. A graduate can minimize the risk of not being admitted to the bar due to student loan debt by *wisely* planning, borrowing, and spending. Such actions must take place before, during, and after law school. As a result of heeding the above recommendations, law students should realize that student loan debt by itself should not be an obstacle that prevents the graduate who passes the bar exam from becoming a licensed attorney.

Before closing the chapter, you should know that Mr. Bowman is still a fighter and ultimately prevailed. He appealed to the US Department of Education to dispute Sallie Mae's fixing his debt at $435,000 when it was only $270,000 just four years before. The Education Department found that Sallie Mae had made several errors processing his debt that resulted in it ballooning dramatically.[43] The Education Department concluded that Mr. Bowman's loan was not in default. That finding meant that Mr. Bowman could argue that neither the bar examiners nor the court could accuse him of not responsibly handling his student loan debt. Armed with this finding, Mr. Bowman applied again for admission and was admitted to the New York bar in 2012.[44]

---

42. Recall that he was getting paid $12 per hour in his part-time position at the public defender's office. If one assumes he was able to get 20 hours per week for 50 weeks, he would earn an annual salary of $12,000.

43. Note that the Education Department did not find Sallie Mae guilty of any intentionally wrongdoing, and Sallie Mae did not admit to such wrongdoing. See Robin Wilson, *Man Denied a Law License Because of Unpaid Loans Hopes for Another Chance*, The Chron. of Higher Ed., Nov. 14, 2010, available at http://chronicle.com/article/Man-Denied-a-Law-License/125360/.

44. Mr. Bowman's record of admission can be found by searching his name (Robert Bowman) at http://iapps.courts.state.ny.us/attorney/AttorneySearch.

Chapter 16

"Am I Stupid If I *Still* Want to Go to Law School?"

If you happened to be holding in your hot little hand a letter of admission, you may be bothered by a re-occurring, nagging question: "Should I still go to law school?" You're not stupid for having a desire to go to law school. However, by now you realize that a potentially dangerous trap for law school graduates exists due to a substantial contraction in the legal job market and due to the legal education price tag of six-figure student loan debt. Undergraduates who are unemployed or under-employed often feel like they are in the frying pan because they have too little experience and too few employment options.

Unfortunately, a steady stream of media reporting either suggests or outright claims that law school is a horrible idea. Such reporting completely ignores the fact that 11% of recent college graduates are unemployed and 48% of US college graduates—those with only a bachelor's degree—are already under-employed: holding jobs that require little-to-no skills and most that do not even require a high school diploma.[1] Furthermore, the majority of the occupations where job growth is expected will require only a high school diploma or less. Therefore, some people frightened away from attending law school are likely to remain under-employed for a long time as many undergraduate degree holders have no current viable alternatives to improving their career trajectory. As a result, reporters, if they care about responsible journalism, should paint the entire picture of the employment realities and steer clear of biased reporting against law schools.

The media should also eschew reporting that sends an elitist message that only people with high LSAT scores should go to law school. For instance, in an article titled "The Wrong People Have Stopped Applying to Law School,"[2] the author (who has never been to law school) reports about the double-digit drop in the percentage of law school applications during the 2011–2012 year from LSAT test takers scoring 165 or better. While the author does a good job of laying out the facts regarding the drop in applications, he incorrectly concludes that "smart and hard working" people are *not* applying to law school because the smallest decrease in applications was among test-takers with the lowest LSAT scores. He bases his conclusion on the fact that LSAC reported a 4.3% decrease in applications among LSAT test takers with a score below 140 but a 13.6% decrease among test takers who scored from 175 to 180 and a 20.7% decrease among those scoring from

1. *See* Chapter 12 discussing a study released by the Center for College Affordability and Productivity and a report by the US Bureau of Labor Statistics.

2. Jordan Weissmann, *The Wrong People Have Stopped Applying to Law School*, The Atlantic (Apr. 12, 2012), *available at* http://www.theatlantic.com/business/archive/2012/04/the-wrong-people-have-stopped-applying-to-law-school/255685/.

170 to 174. Based on these figures, he concludes his article by stating: "So the smart kids got the memo. Law school is largely a losing game, and they're not going to play.... Maybe that's just what makes the smart kids the smart kids."

His logic is faulty, as there are several other reasonable conclusions one could draw based on the LSAC's report. For example, contrary to his interpretation, the decrease among the high-scoring LSAT test takers could mean that many are fearful of incurring six-figure debt to get a legal education. Others who were motivated *only* by money to become lawyers could have decided to pursue other career options with a greater likelihood of *immediate* financial gain. Second, some could have taken the GMAT or the GRE[3] and chosen to pursue a master's or Ph.D. degree as a less costly route to getting an advanced degree. For the last few years, GMAT test-taking has steadily risen and reached a historic high in 2012.[4] It is very likely that some of the "smart kids" decided to go to MBA school instead of law school. Moreover, unlike law schools, traditional graduate degree programs tend to offer high-scoring test takers fellowships or graduate assistant positions that include tuition waivers ***and*** monthly stipends. In other words, by pursuing a Ph.D. instead of a JD, the "smart kid" would most likely emerge from professional school with substantially less student loan debt than if he or she had gone to law school. Finally, the author is wrong because *nearly all* students who score below 160 are very hard workers and many of them work harder than the top scorers.

The debate over whether enrollment in law school is advisable is even occurring among academics. For example, in one popular legal magazine, *The Pennsylvania Lawyer*, a debate entitled "The Rise of Dr. No: The Dilemma of Pre-Law Advising in an Unbalanced Market," is between Steven Lichtman,[5] an associate professor at Shippensburg University, and Ken Gormley, the dean of Duquesne University School of Law.[6] Dr. Lichtman likens himself to the James Bond villain "Dr. No" due to his pragmatic, some would even say pessimistic, outlook on a legal career. Embracing the role of Dr. No., he now advises undergraduate students, even those very well-suited for law school, to seek other career options. Dr. No argues that the decline in job opportunities for recent law school graduates, the increase in law school attendees, and the increase in law school tuition rates have made the idea of going to law school an almost completely inadvisable. He urges the legal academy to begin taking measures to handle the supply and demand disparity in the legal profession. Dr. No confesses that until that happens, he is left in the uncomfortable position of doing the following: "I am forced to steer my students away from law school.

---

3. The GMAT is the Graduate Management Admission Test and is taken to gain admission to graduate-level business and management schools and programs. The GRE is Graduate Record Examination and is the standard test taken to gain admission to graduate schools in general.

4. *GMAT Testing Hits Record Volume*, Market Wire, (Sept. 23, 2012), *available at* http://www.marketwire.com/press-release/gmat-testing-hits-record-volume-1704508.htm ("GMAT exam volume for the 2012 testing year (July 1, 2011, to June 30, 2012), was up 11 percent from the 2011 testing year, and 8 percent higher than the previous record of 265,613 in 2009.").

5. Steven Lichtman & Ken Gormley, *Pro/Con: Is Law School A Reasonable Choice?*, The Pennsylvania Lawyer Feb. 2012, at 5, *available at* http://webspace.ship.edu/SBLichtman/documents/Pro-Con%20on%20Law%20School%20%28PA%20Lawyer%29.pdf. Steven Lichtman is an associate professor of political science and a pre-law advisor for Shippensburg University, located in Pennsylvania. He has a law degree from New York University and a Ph.D. in politics and public law from Brandies University. *See* Steven B. Lichtman's Curriculum Vitae, *available at* http://www.ship.edu/uploadedFiles/Ship/PoliSci/LichtmanCVweb.pdf (last visited Feb. 28, 2013).

6. Ken Gormley became the dean in 2011 and has been a professor since 1994 at Duquesne Law School, located in Pittsburgh, Pennsylvania. *See* Dean Ken Gormley, Duquesne Univ., http://www.duq.edu/academics/faculty/ken-gormley (last visited Feb. 28, 2013). He is a 1980 graduate of Harvard Law School.

I am forced to tell them that they need to spend several years working, developing practical experience, before they even think of applying to law school."

"Dean Yes" (Ken Gormley) responds by stating that Dr. No's analysis is overly broad and insufficiently nuanced. The decision to go to law school is a choice that should be evaluated in relation to each student's "background, goals, dreams, intellectual capabilities and financial resources." Furthermore, Dean Yes argues that earning a six-figure salary is not the ultimate outcome for all law students and that to reference declining salaries and increasing debt as the primary justifications for advising people to not go to law school is to do a disservice to potential law school students and to miss what the legal profession is truly about.

I agree with Dean Yes on this point. Just like firefighters and school teachers, some feel a sense of calling to become a lawyer so that they can serve others even though the salary for many legal positions is not lucrative.

Both sides of this debate have merit and have insight into what sort of solutions law schools, admissions offices, and pre-law advisors across the country should be thinking about trying. Dr. No is absolutely right that law schools should be proactive in adjusting school curricula to better fit the realities of the legal job market. And he is also right to believe that we as a legal community should take the initiative to solve this problem instead of letting the market forces correct the problem. However, I also agree with Dean Yes that numerous reasons exist to pursue a legal career, and depending on the student's goals, a student may be willing to incur debt and risk obtaining only a five-figure salary to achieve a particular goal.

So who is right, Dr. No or Dean Yes? Should pre-law advisors and lawyers be advising enthusiastic prospective students against going to law school? The answer is not saying "yes" to everyone, but it certainly is not saying "no" to everyone either. The legal community should make an effort to encourage people to become lawyers, not out of a desire for a six-figure salary, but out of a desire to positively impact the legal profession by serving both businesses and disadvantaged consumers while being guided by the highest ethical standards. We should *not* be saying the legal profession is no longer a good one. We should be saying that choosing to enter a legal profession for strictly monetary gain is not a good enough reason to enroll. The legal bar and academy need to do more to attract people who really want to go to law school but are fearful of incurring six-figure debt and offer them more scholarships and loan forgiveness programs.

Closing Thoughts

Throughout this book, I've emphasized the advantages of getting a law degree. Law school has allowed many people, including myself, to find satisfying careers even when our salaries have been lower than expected or desired. In comparison to today's law graduate, we incurred manageable student loan debt or received scholarships to cover much of the cost of law school. Others have had their student loan debts reduced through various loan forgiveness and assistance programs. By pursuing a law degree, many of us happily left behind jobs that were boring, required little skills, or paid only minimum wage. Many have been able to use their legal education to make real, positive changes in the lives of others—a labor lawyer who helped an injured worker get her job back, a volunteer lawyer for the Innocence Project who got a wrongfully-convicted man exonerated, or a bankruptcy lawyer who helped General Motors reverse its financial woes. We are excited *most* days to get out of bed to see how we can use our legal education to better society.

Many recent law graduates, however, have yet to experience the career and personal transformations that a law degree can bring. Because of the prosperity years of the early 2000s, many law students have enrolled in law school with the expectation of getting a job at a mid- to large-size law firm and earning six-figure salaries. Graduates of the top law schools expected, as if by birthright, to land jobs at the nation's largest law firms.[7] I, amongst others, reveal the ugly truth that having such expectations has been unrealistic for at least the last four years and continues to be so.[8] We now know that the average starting salary is only in the mid-five-figure range and has declined in the last two years. Instead of six-figure salaries, graduates today face a seemingly insurmountable amount of student loan debt even though various loan assistance programs exist to lessen the debt load.

Rather than securing a traditional attorney job with a salary that affords a comfortable lifestyle, many recent graduates are employed in part-time legal jobs or as temp attorneys doing document review. Due to pressure from Law School Transparency and others, the ABA has adopted employment reporting standards that expose the fact that *many* of the ABA-accredited law schools are annually pumping out 100s of graduates while less than half of them have found full-time, long-term, bar-passage-required jobs. As repeated often in this book, this employment rate is the best indicator of the percentage of graduates who have found jobs as attorneys. As a result of the new reporting requirements, we now know that many graduates, even the majority of graduates at some schools, did not get what they bargained for when they enrolled in law school.[9]

I have devoted the majority of this book explaining the importance of considering a plethora of factors and how to weigh those factors when deciding whether to accept a school's offer of admission. The purpose of a sophisticated analysis of a law school is to assess whether enrolling in that school is worth incurring six-figure student loan debt. I have demonstrated that even among first-tier law schools, there are dramatic differences in the employment rates of graduates with fulltime, long-term, bar-required jobs.[10] Therefore, unless a prospective student receives an offer from a Top 14 school—almost all of which have employment rates greater than 75% in fulltime, bar passage required jobs—an enrollment decision based upon rankings alone is not a wise decision.[11]

---

7. *See, e.g.*, Gerry Shih, *Downturn Dims Prospects Even at Top Law Schools*, N.Y. TIMES, Aug. 26, 2009, at B1 (explaining that graduates of top law schools, such as Harvard, grew accustomed to landing a BigLaw position "almost like a birthright").

8. *Class of 2011 Has Lowest Employment Rate Since Class of 1994*, NALP BULLETIN, (July 2012) http://www.nalp.org/0712research; Press Release, NALP, Class of 2010 Graduates Faced Worst Job Market Since Mid-1990s: Longstanding Employment Patterns Interrupted (June 1, 2011), *available at* http://www.nalp.org/2010selectedfindingsrelease.

9. Research shows most students, at the time of enrollment, anticipate that they will practice law after graduating from law school.

10. *See* Appendix A, Table 1-1.

11. Georgetown is the only law school in the Top 14 with an employment rate for bar-required jobs that is below 75%. As previously stated, since Georgetown has a reputation for having some of its graduates be employed in politics at that state and federal level, the graduates it has employed in the "JD-Advantage" category likely have desirable jobs, thereby making Georgetown's 63% employment rate for bar-required jobs acceptable in comparison to other schools in the top 14. *See* Appendix A, Tables 1-1 and 1-2. Ultimately, the reader has to come to his or her own conclusion about how to interpret Georgetown's 63% employment rate.

Unfortunately, most law school applicants will not receive an offer from one of the Top 14 schools.

Hopefully, you are a prospective law student with multiple offers. My advice then is that you select the school with all of the following: (1) the highest percentage of graduates employed fulltime, long-term in bar-passage-required jobs, (2) the lowest number of unemployed graduates seeking employment, (3) the lowest rate of attrition, (4) the lowest number of students who transfer out, (5) the highest rate of graduates who pass the bar exam the first time, and (6) the largest scholarship offer rate. If all factors seem fairly equal at the competing schools, then let the scale tip in favor of the law school with course offerings and programs designed to prepare graduates for the actual practice of law, particularly in the solo and small-firm setting. All of the recommendations assume that the prospective students are very flexible about the geographic location in which they are willing to work in after graduation. If that is not the case, the prospective student should enroll in the best school (based on my analysis above) in the city or closest region where post-graduation employment is wanted.

Just as I was about to finish this chapter, I came across a February 2013 press release from NALP stating that hiring by law firms of students as summer associates and graduates as entry-level attorneys is mostly flat.[12] Specifically, NALP reported that when comparing 2012 to previous years, "[l]aw firms continue to bring in small summer classes, with median and average class size barely increasing from recession-era lows." As for the members of the graduating class of 2013, the news is not good. James Leipold, NALP's Executive Director, stated that "[a]s law firms battle for market share and compete within a global marketplace that is driving the price of legal services down, law firms continue to be *cautious* about bringing in more lawyers than they can confidently keep busy. I would expect flat and faltering to be characteristics of the entry-level law firm hiring market going forward, at least for the short and even medium term."[13] Note that he says the law firms continue to be *cautious.*

After reading Mr. Leipold's statement, I was reminded of Judge Gordon Quist's opinion dismissing the lawsuit filed against Cooley. Judge Quist stated that "[p]laintiffs and prospective students should have approached their decision to enter into law school with extreme *caution* given the size of the investment."[14]

Rather than summarizing each of the chapters covered in this book, I want to make a lasting impression by ending with that word "cautious" using an acronym that emphasizes the main points that I've made in this book. The acronym explains why I urge you to be cautious in deciding when and where you will attend law school!! Good Luck!

---

12. Press Release, *Law Firm Recruiting Mostly Flat After Tumbling During Recession*, NAT'L ASSOC. OF LAW PLACEMENT, Feb. 11, 2013, *available at* http://www.nalp.org/march13_perspectives_pr.

13. *Id.* (italics added).

14. MacDonald v. Thomas M. Cooley Law School, U.S. Dist. LEXIS 100785, at *9 (W.D., Mich. Jul. 20, 2012) (italics added).

C	Competition is severe among graduates for fewer traditional attorney jobs.
A	Astronomical student loan debt is necessary for most to get a legal education.
U	Unscrupulous reporting practices by some law schools enable them to hide *under*-employed grads in university-funded positions and in the "JD-Advantage" category.
T	Tuition is high and is expected to continue to rise.
I	Insufficient training offered by law schools produced ill-prepared, not "practice-ready," grads.
O	Over-abundance of law schools with low percentages of graduates employed in real attorney jobs.
U	Ushering in of more certificate and LL.M. programs that increase revenue for law schools but may not produce jobs for the graduates.
S	Salaries have decreased post-recession and average in the mid-five-figure range.

"The important thing to remember is that, for most of us, going to law school makes sense only if you're willing to make a long-term commitment to practicing law. It's not a get-rich-quick scheme[;] … some law grads may have to make do with a few years of non-legal work. But if you have a passion for the law, and if you're persistent, you will eventually succeed in the law."[15]

15. Adam Freedman, *Is Law School Worth It?*, Legal Lad, Feb. 22, 2013, http://legallad.quickanddirtytips.com/is-law-school-worth-it.aspx.

Appendix A

After submitting to the ABA the data reflected in the tables in Appendix A, three law schools made name changes in 2013. Since receiving a $55 million donation, Chapman University School of Law became the Chapman University Dale E. Fowler School of Law. After being purchased in August 2013, Texas Wesleyan University School of Law became the Texas A&M University School of Law. As a result of an official affiliation agreement signed in 2013, Thomas M. Cooley Law School is now the Western Michigan University Thomas M. Cooley Law School.

Table 1-1. Schools Ranked from Highest Percent of 2011 Grads Employed in Full-Time, Long-Term Bar-Passage Required Jobs

	Table 1-1 Schools Ranked from Highest to Lowest Employment Rate	2011 Grads Employed FT, LT Bar-Passage Required Jobs	Total No. of 2011 Grads	% of 2011 Grads Employed FT, LT Bar-Passage Required Jobs
1	VIRGINIA, UNIV. OF	357	377	94.7%
2	COLUMBIA UNIV.	429	456	94.1%
3	STANFORD UNIV.	175	192	91.1%
4	NEW YORK UNIV.	420	466	90.1%
5	HARVARD UNIV.	525	583	90.1%
6	CHICAGO, UNIV. OF	179	203	88.2%
7	YALE UNIV.	180	205	87.8%
8	PENNSYLVANIA, UNIV. OF	231	274	84.3%
9	DUKE UNIV.	170	207	82.1%
10	GEORGE WASHINGTON UNIV.	421	518	81.3%
11	LOUISIANA STATE UNIV.	143	176	81.3%
12	CALIFORNIA-BERKELEY, UNIV. OF	248	310	80.0%
13	ST. MARY'S UNIV.	195	249	78.3%
14	ALABAMA, UNIV. OF	128	164	78.0%
15	NORTHWESTERN UNIV.	221	287	77.0%
16	CORNELL UNIV.	153	201	76.1%
17	MICHIGAN, UNIV. OF	286	379	75.5%
18	ARIZONA, UNIV. OF	119	158	75.3%
19	MISSISSIPPI COLLEGE	125	166	75.3%
20	VANDERBILT UNIV.	146	198	73.7%
21	KENTUCKY, UNIV. OF	97	135	71.9%

	Table 1-1 Schools Ranked from Highest to Lowest Employment Rate	2011 Grads Employed FT, LT Bar-Passage Required Jobs	Total No. of 2011 Grads	% of 2011 Grads Employed FT, LT Bar-Passage Required Jobs
22	CAMPBELL UNIV.	95	133	71.4%
23	BAYLOR UNIV.	110	157	70.1%
24	TEXAS AT AUSTIN, UNIV. OF	267	382	69.9%
25	FLORIDA STATE UNIV.	194	279	69.5%
26	EMORY UNIV.	155	225	68.9%
27	WEST VIRGINIA UNIV.	86	125	68.8%
28	UTAH, UNIV. OF	92	134	68.7%
29	BOSTON COLLEGE	195	285	68.4%
30	NORTH CAROLINA, UNIV. OF	169	247	68.4%
31	ARIZONA STATE UNIV.	137	201	68.2%
32	LOUISVILLE, UNIV. OF	95	142	66.9%
33	MISSOURI-COLUMBIA, UNIV. OF	94	141	66.7%
34	UNIV. OF NEVADA-LAS VEGAS	85	128	66.4%
35	NEW MEXICO, UNIV. OF	68	103	66.0%
36	MONTANA, UNIV. OF	56	85	65.9%
37	TULSA, UNIV. OF	79	120	65.8%
38	IOWA, UNIV. OF	120	183	65.6%
39	SAMFORD UNIV.	97	148	65.5%
40	SOUTHERN CALIFORNIA, UNIV. OF	134	207	64.7%
41	NEBRASKA, UNIV. OF	84	130	64.6%
42	GEORGIA STATE UNIV.	120	186	64.5%
43	SOUTH TEXAS COLLEGE OF LAW	259	402	64.4%
44	INDIANA UNIV. MAURER SCHOOL OF LAW	124	195	63.6%
45	TEXAS TECH UNIV.	127	200	63.5%
46	ARKANSAS, LITTLE ROCK, UNIV. OF	95	150	63.3%
47	SOUTHERN METHODIST UNIV.	172	272	63.2%
48	MERCER UNIV.	82	130	63.1%
49	SETON HALL UNIV.	184	293	62.8%
50	WISCONSIN, UNIV. OF	159	254	62.6%
51	GEORGETOWN UNIV.	403	644	62.6%

	Table 1-1 Schools Ranked from Highest to Lowest Employment Rate	2011 Grads Employed FT, LT Bar-Passage Required Jobs	Total No. of 2011 Grads	% of 2011 Grads Employed FT, LT Bar-Passage Required Jobs
52	TENNESSEE, UNIV. OF	91	146	62.3%
53	WYOMING, UNIV. OF	46	74	62.2%
54	NOTRE DAME, UNIV. OF	118	190	62.1%
55	OKLAHOMA, UNIV. OF	101	163	62.0%
56	CALIFORNIA-LOS ANGELES, UNIV. OF	211	344	61.3%
57	GEORGIA, UNIV. OF	139	227	61.2%
58	ARKANSAS, FAYETTEVILLE, UNIV. OF	71	116	61.2%
59	MISSOURI-KANSAS CITY, UNIV. OF	94	154	61.0%
60	FLORIDA INTERNATIONAL	105	173	60.7%
61	DRAKE UNIV.	94	155	60.6%
62	HOUSTON, UNIV. OF	169	281	60.1%
63	CREIGHTON UNIV.	92	153	60.1%
64	GEORGE MASON UNIV.	102	170	60.0%
65	PENNSYLVANIA STATE UNIV.	107	179	59.8%
66	MEMPHIS, UNIV. OF	77	129	59.7%
67	OKLAHOMA CITY UNIV.	105	176	59.7%
68	RICHMOND, UNIV. OF	99	166	59.6%
69	SOUTHERN ILLINOIS UNIV.-CARBONDALE	66	111	59.5%
70	FLORIDA, UNIV. OF	243	409	59.4%
71	MINNESOTA, UNIV. OF	155	261	59.4%
72	WASHINGTON UNIV.	188	317	59.3%
73	TOURO COLLEGE	131	221	59.3%
74	OHIO STATE UNIV.	135	231	58.4%
75	NOVA SOUTHEASTERN UNIV.	176	302	58.3%
76	RUTGERS UNIV.-CAMDEN	141	242	58.3%
77	TULANE UNIV.	140	241	58.1%
78	MARQUETTE UNIV.	133	230	57.8%
79	FORDHAM UNIV.	246	428	57.5%
80	STETSON UNIV.	184	322	57.1%
81	OHIO NORTHERN UNIV.	55	97	56.7%

	Table 1-1 Schools Ranked from Highest to Lowest Employment Rate	2011 Grads Employed FT, LT Bar-Passage Required Jobs	Total No. of 2011 Grads	% of 2011 Grads Employed FT, LT Bar-Passage Required Jobs
82	RUTGERS UNIV.-NEWARK	140	248	56.5%
83	FAULKNER UNIV.	57	101	56.4%
84	CALIFORNIA-DAVIS, UNIV. OF	110	195	56.4%
85	WAKE FOREST UNIV.	89	158	56.3%
86	COLORADO, UNIV. OF	98	176	55.7%
87	GONZAGA UNIV.	89	160	55.6%
88	ELON UNIV.	55	99	55.6%
89	TEMPLE UNIV.	177	319	55.5%
90	AKRON, UNIV. OF	64	116	55.2%
91	MIAMI, UNIV. OF	212	385	55.1%
92	WASHINGTON AND LEE UNIV.	71	129	55.0%
93	MISSISSIPPI, UNIV. OF	83	151	55.0%
94	SOUTH CAROLINA, UNIV. OF	122	222	55.0%
95	WILLIAM AND MARY SCHOOL OF LAW	112	204	54.9%
96	NORTHERN ILLINOIS UNIV.	53	97	54.6%
97	PITTSBURGH, UNIV. OF	137	253	54.2%
98	INDIANA UNIV.-INDIANAPOLIS	136	252	54.0%
99	TEXAS SOUTHERN UNIV.	87	163	53.4%
100	CINCINNATI, UNIV. OF	64	120	53.3%
101	ST. LOUIS UNIV.	144	272	52.9%
102	WASHINGTON, UNIV. OF	96	182	52.7%
103	REGENT UNIV.	62	118	52.5%
104	KANSAS, UNIV. OF	88	168	52.4%
105	VILLANOVA UNIV.	132	252	52.4%
106	YESHIVA UNIV.	197	380	51.8%
107	STATE UNIV. OF NEW YORK AT BUFFALO	127	245	51.8%
108	DAYTON, UNIV. OF	88	171	51.5%
109	BRIGHAM YOUNG UNIV.	76	148	51.4%
110	CHARLESTON SCHOOL OF LAW	99	193	51.3%
111	IDAHO, UNIV. OF	52	102	51.0%

	Table 1-1 Schools Ranked from Highest to Lowest Employment Rate	2011 Grads Employed FT, LT Bar-Passage Required Jobs	Total No. of 2011 Grads	% of 2011 Grads Employed FT, LT Bar-Passage Required Jobs
112	BOSTON UNIV.	139	273	50.9%
113	ILLINOIS INST. OF TECH., CHICAGO-KENT	169	332	50.9%
114	WAYNE STATE UNIV.	103	203	50.7%
115	ILLINOIS, UNIV. OF	96	190	50.5%
116	CLEVELAND STATE UNIV.	93	185	50.3%
117	SYRACUSE UNIV.	97	193	50.3%
118	HAMLINE UNIV.	103	205	50.2%
119	LOYOLA UNIV.-CHICAGO	126	251	50.2%
120	ALBANY LAW SCHOOL	118	236	50.0%
121	ROGER WILLIAMS UNIV.	79	158	50.0%
122	WASHBURN UNIV.	71	142	50.0%
123	NORTHEASTERN UNIV.	90	182	49.5%
124	NORTH DAKOTA, UNIV. OF	40	81	49.4%
125	ST. THOMAS UNIV.	109	221	49.3%
126	TEXAS WESLEYAN UNIV.	109	223	48.9%
127	VERMONT LAW SCHOOL	85	174	48.9%
128	DENVER, UNIV. OF	140	287	48.8%
129	CONNECTICUT, UNIV. OF	86	179	48.0%
130	BALTIMORE, UNIV. OF	143	298	48.0%
131	ST. JOHN'S UNIV.	132	276	47.8%
132	HOWARD UNIV.	75	157	47.8%
133	NEW HAMPSHIRE UNIV. OF	70	147	47.6%
134	HAWAII, UNIV. OF	48	101	47.5%
135	WILLAMETTE UNIV.	61	129	47.3%
136	BROOKLYN LAW SCHOOL	215	455	47.3%
137	WIDENER UNIV.	119	252	47.2%
138	MARYLAND, UNIV. OF	140	297	47.1%
139	SAN DIEGO, UNIV. OF	149	318	46.9%
140	CASE WESTERN RESERVE UNIV.	94	201	46.8%
141	CALIFORNIA-HASTINGS, UNIV. OF	191	411	46.5%

	Table 1-1 Schools Ranked from Highest to Lowest Employment Rate	2011 Grads Employed FT, LT Bar-Passage Required Jobs	Total No. of 2011 Grads	% of 2011 Grads Employed FT, LT Bar-Passage Required Jobs
142	LEWIS AND CLARK COLLEGE	107	233	45.9%
143	LOYOLA UNIV.-NEW ORLEANS	106	231	45.9%
144	DUQUESNE UNIV.	92	206	44.7%
145	WIDENER UNIV.-HARRISBURG	55	124	44.4%
146	MICHIGAN STATE UNIV.	125	283	44.2%
147	UNIV. OF ST. THOMAS	59	134	44.0%
148	CATHOLIC UNIV. OF AMERICA	114	261	43.7%
149	WILLIAM MITCHELL COLLEGE OF LAW	123	282	43.6%
150	MCGEORGE SCHOOL OF LAW	132	303	43.6%
151	NORTH CAROLINA CENTRAL UNIV.	74	170	43.5%
152	DREXEL UNIV.	57	131	43.5%
153	JOHN MARSHALL LAW SCHOOL	174	401	43.4%
154	CHARLOTTE SCHOOL OF LAW	42	97	43.3%
155	SANTA CLARA UNIV.	127	296	42.9%
156	PEPPERDINE UNIV.	98	229	42.8%
157	LOYOLA MARYMOUNT UNIV.-LOS ANGELES	172	403	42.7%
158	MAINE, UNIV. OF	38	90	42.2%
159	VALPARAISO UNIV.	76	181	42.0%
160	OREGON, UNIV. OF	72	174	41.4%
161	ATLANTA'S JOHN MARSHALL LAW SHOOL	54	132	40.9%
162	HOFSTRA UNIV.	121	297	40.7%
163	DEPAUL UNIV.	129	319	40.4%
164	SEATTLE UNIV.	127	315	40.3%
165	CHAPMAN UNIV.	71	177	40.1%
166	CAPITAL UNIV.	70	175	40.0%
167	CALIFORNIA WESTERN SCHOOL OF LAW	112	285	39.3%
168	BARRY UNIV.	82	209	39.2%
169	SUFFOLK UNIV.	193	502	38.4%
170	SOUTH DAKOTA, UNIV. OF	21	55	38.2%
171	THOMAS M. COOLEY LAW SCHOOL	375	999	37.5%

	Table 1-1 Schools Ranked from Highest to Lowest Employment Rate	2011 Grads Employed FT, LT Bar-Passage Required Jobs	Total No. of 2011 Grads	% of 2011 Grads Employed FT, LT Bar-Passage Required Jobs
172	PHOENIX SCHOOL OF LAW	49	131	37.4%
173	SOUTHERN UNIV.	53	143	37.1%
174	CITY UNIV. OF NEW YORK	41	111	36.9%
175	DETROIT MERCY, UNIV. OF	77	209	36.8%
176	FLORIDA COASTAL	165	451	36.6%
177	TOLEDO, UNIV. OF	42	115	36.5%
178	NORTHERN KENTUCKY UNIV.	65	179	36.3%
179	PACE UNIV.	80	222	36.0%
180	AMERICAN UNIV.	167	467	35.8%
181	NEW YORK LAW SCHOOL	183	515	35.5%
182	QUINNIPIAC UNIV.	46	133	34.6%
183	SOUTHWESTERN LAW SCHOOL	103	298	34.6%
184	NEW ENGLAND SCHOOL OF LAW	106	308	34.4%
185	SAN FRANCISCO, UNIV. OF	76	222	34.2%
186	FLORIDA A&M	52	152	34.2%
187	AVE MARIA	29	88	33.0%
188	UNIV. OF LA VERNE	38	116	32.8%
189	WESTERN STATE	29	90	32.2%
190	LIBERTY UNIV.	28	90	31.1%
191	APPALACHIAN SCHOOL OF LAW	28	91	30.8%
192	WESTERN NEW ENGLAND UNIV.	46	153	30.1%
193	THOMAS JEFFERSON SCHOOL OF LAW	63	236	26.7%
194	GOLDEN GATE UNIV.	42	191	22.0%
195	DISTRICT OF COLUMBIA	16	78	20.5%
196	WHITTIER COLLEGE	21	123	17.1%
197	PUERTO RICO, UNIV. OF*	0	244	0.0%

Data Source: Employment Summary Report, http://employmentsummary.abaquestionnaire.org. FT, LT = Full-time and Long-term; * ABA did not explain Puerto Rico's figures.

Table 1-2. Employment Rate for 2011 Grads Employed in FT, LT Bar-Passage Required Jobs

Table 1-2 Schools Ranked in Alphabetical Order	2011 Grads Employed FT, LT Bar-Passage Required Jobs	Total No. of 2011 Grads	% of 2011 Grads Employed FT, LT Bar-Passage Required Jobs
AKRON, UNIV. OF	64	116	55.2%
ALABAMA, UNIV. OF	128	164	78.0%
ALBANY LAW SCHOOL	118	236	50.0%
AMERICAN UNIV.	167	467	35.8%
APPALACHIAN SCHOOL OF LAW	28	91	30.8%
ARIZONA STATE UNIV.	137	201	68.2%
ARIZONA, UNIV. OF	119	158	75.3%
ARKANSAS, FAYETTEVILLE, UNIV. OF	71	116	61.2%
ARKANSAS, LITTLE ROCK, UNIV. OF	95	150	63.3%
ATLANTA'S JOHN MARSHALL LAW SHOOL	54	132	40.9%
AVE MARIA	29	88	33.0%
BALTIMORE, UNIV. OF	143	298	48.0%
BARRY UNIV.	82	209	39.2%
BAYLOR UNIV.	110	157	70.1%
BOSTON COLLEGE	195	285	68.4%
BOSTON UNIV.	139	273	50.9%
BRIGHAM YOUNG UNIV.	76	148	51.4%
BROOKLYN LAW SCHOOL	215	455	47.3%
CALIFORNIA WESTERN SCHOOL OF LAW	112	285	39.3%
CALIFORNIA-BERKELEY, UNIV. OF	248	310	80.0%
CALIFORNIA-DAVIS, UNIV. OF	110	195	56.4%
CALIFORNIA-HASTINGS, UNIV. OF	191	411	46.5%
CALIFORNIA-LOS ANGELES, UNIV. OF	211	344	61.3%
CAMPBELL UNIV.	95	133	71.4%
CAPITAL UNIV.	70	175	40.0%
CASE WESTERN RESERVE UNIV.	94	201	46.8%
CATHOLIC UNIV. OF AMERICA	114	261	43.7%
CHAPMAN UNIV.	71	177	40.1%

Table 1-2 Schools Ranked in Alphabetical Order	2011 Grads Employed FT, LT Bar-Passage Required Jobs	Total No. of 2011 Grads	% of 2011 Grads Employed FT, LT Bar-Passage Required Jobs
CHARLESTON SCHOOL OF LAW	99	193	51.3%
CHARLOTTE SCHOOL OF LAW	42	97	43.3%
CHICAGO, UNIV. OF	179	203	88.2%
CINCINNATI, UNIV. OF	64	120	53.3%
CITY UNIV. OF NEW YORK	41	111	36.9%
CLEVELAND STATE UNIV.	93	185	50.3%
COLORADO, UNIV. OF	98	176	55.7%
COLUMBIA UNIV.	429	456	94.1%
CONNECTICUT, UNIV. OF	86	179	48.0%
CORNELL UNIV.	153	201	76.1%
CREIGHTON UNIV.	92	153	60.1%
DAYTON, UNIV. OF	88	171	51.5%
DENVER, UNIV. OF	140	287	48.8%
DEPAUL UNIV.	129	319	40.4%
DETROIT MERCY, UNIV. OF	77	209	36.8%
DISTRICT OF COLUMBIA	16	78	20.5%
DRAKE UNIV.	94	155	60.6%
DREXEL UNIV.	57	131	43.5%
DUKE UNIV.	170	207	82.1%
DUQUESNE UNIV.	92	206	44.7%
ELON UNIV.	55	99	55.6%
EMORY UNIV.	155	225	68.9%
FAULKNER UNIV.	57	101	56.4%
FLORIDA A&M	52	152	34.2%
FLORIDA COASTAL	165	451	36.6%
FLORIDA INTERNATIONAL	105	173	60.7%
FLORIDA STATE UNIV.	194	279	69.5%
FLORIDA, UNIV. OF	243	409	59.4%
FORDHAM UNIV.	246	428	57.5%

Table 1-2 Schools Ranked in Alphabetical Order	2011 Grads Employed FT, LT Bar-Passage Required Jobs	Total No. of 2011 Grads	% of 2011 Grads Employed FT, LT Bar-Passage Required Jobs
GEORGE MASON UNIV.	102	170	60.0%
GEORGE WASHINGTON UNIV.	421	518	81.3%
GEORGETOWN UNIV.	403	644	62.6%
GEORGIA STATE UNIV.	120	186	64.5%
GEORGIA, UNIV. OF	139	227	61.2%
GOLDEN GATE UNIV.	42	191	22.0%
GONZAGA UNIV.	89	160	55.6%
HAMLINE UNIV.	103	205	50.2%
HARVARD UNIV.	525	583	90.1%
HAWAII, UNIV. OF	48	101	47.5%
HOFSTRA UNIV.	121	297	40.7%
HOUSTON, UNIV. OF	169	281	60.1%
HOWARD UNIV.	75	157	47.8%
IDAHO, UNIV. OF	52	102	51.0%
ILLINOIS INST. OF TECH., CHICAGO-KENT	169	332	50.9%
ILLINOIS, UNIV. OF	96	190	50.5%
INDIANA UNIV.-INDIANAPOLIS	136	252	54.0%
INDIANA UNIV. MAURER SCHOOL OF LAW	124	195	63.6%
IOWA, UNIV. OF	120	183	65.6%
JOHN MARSHALL LAW SCHOOL	174	401	43.4%
KANSAS, UNIV. OF	88	168	52.4%
KENTUCKY, UNIV. OF	97	135	71.9%
LEWIS AND CLARK COLLEGE	107	233	45.9%
LIBERTY UNIV.	28	90	31.1%
LOUISIANA STATE UNIV.	143	176	81.3%
LOUISVILLE, UNIV. OF	95	142	66.9%
LOYOLA MARYMOUNT UNIV.-LOS ANGELES	172	403	42.7%
LOYOLA UNIV.-CHICAGO	126	251	50.2%
LOYOLA UNIV.-NEW ORLEANS	106	231	45.9%

Table 1-2 Schools Ranked in Alphabetical Order	2011 Grads Employed FT, LT Bar-Passage Required Jobs	Total No. of 2011 Grads	% of 2011 Grads Employed FT, LT Bar-Passage Required Jobs
MAINE, UNIV. OF	38	90	42.2%
MARQUETTE UNIV.	133	230	57.8%
MARYLAND, UNIV. OF	140	297	47.1%
MCGEORGE SCHOOL OF LAW	132	303	43.6%
MEMPHIS, UNIV. OF	77	129	59.7%
MERCER UNIV.	82	130	63.1%
MIAMI, UNIV. OF	212	385	55.1%
MICHIGAN STATE UNIV.	125	283	44.2%
MICHIGAN, UNIV. OF	286	379	75.5%
MINNESOTA, UNIV. OF	155	261	59.4%
MISSISSIPPI COLLEGE	125	166	75.3%
MISSISSIPPI, UNIV. OF	83	151	55.0%
MISSOURI-COLUMBIA, UNIV. OF	94	141	66.7%
MISSOURI-KANSAS CITY, UNIV. OF	94	154	61.0%
MONTANA, UNIV. OF	56	85	65.9%
NEBRASKA, UNIV. OF	84	130	64.6%
NEW ENGLAND SCHOOL OF LAW	106	308	34.4%
NEW HAMPSHIRE UNIV. OF	70	147	47.6%
NEW MEXICO, UNIV. OF	68	103	66.0%
NEW YORK LAW SCHOOL	183	515	35.5%
NEW YORK UNIV.	420	466	90.1%
NORTH CAROLINA CENTRAL UNIV.	74	170	43.5%
NORTH CAROLINA, UNIV. OF	169	247	68.4%
NORTH DAKOTA, UNIV. OF	40	81	49.4%
NORTHEASTERN UNIV.	90	182	49.5%
NORTHERN ILLINOIS UNIV.	53	97	54.6%
NORTHERN KENTUCKY UNIV.	65	179	36.3%
NORTHWESTERN UNIV.	221	287	77.0%
NOTRE DAME, UNIV. OF	118	190	62.1%

Table 1-2 Schools Ranked in Alphabetical Order	2011 Grads Employed FT, LT Bar-Passage Required Jobs	Total No. of 2011 Grads	% of 2011 Grads Employed FT, LT Bar-Passage Required Jobs
NOVA SOUTHEASTERN UNIV.	176	302	58.3%
OHIO NORTHERN UNIV.	55	97	56.7%
OHIO STATE UNIV.	135	231	58.4%
OKLAHOMA CITY UNIV.	105	176	59.7%
OKLAHOMA, UNIV. OF	101	163	62.0%
OREGON, UNIV. OF	72	174	41.4%
PACE UNIV.	80	222	36.0%
PENNSYLVANIA STATE UNIV.	107	179	59.8%
PENNSYLVANIA, UNIV. OF	231	274	84.3%
PEPPERDINE UNIV.	98	229	42.8%
PHOENIX SCHOOL OF LAW	49	131	37.4%
PITTSBURGH, UNIV. OF	137	253	54.2%
PUERTO RICO, UNIV. OF*	0	244	0.0%
QUINNIPIAC UNIV.	46	133	34.6%
REGENT UNIV.	62	118	52.5%
RICHMOND, UNIV. OF	99	166	59.6%
ROGER WILLIAMS UNIV.	79	158	50.0%
RUTGERS UNIV.-CAMDEN	141	242	58.3%
RUTGERS UNIV.-NEWARK	140	248	56.5%
SAMFORD UNIV.	97	148	65.5%
SAN DIEGO, UNIV. OF	149	318	46.9%
SAN FRANCISCO, UNIV. OF	76	222	34.2%
SANTA CLARA UNIV.	127	296	42.9%
SEATTLE UNIV.	127	315	40.3%
SETON HALL UNIV.	184	293	62.8%
SOUTH CAROLINA, UNIV. OF	122	222	55.0%
SOUTH DAKOTA, UNIV. OF	21	55	38.2%
SOUTH TEXAS COLLEGE OF LAW	259	402	64.4%
SOUTHERN CALIFORNIA, UNIV. OF	134	207	64.7%

Table 1-2 Schools Ranked in Alphabetical Order	2011 Grads Employed FT, LT Bar-Passage Required Jobs	Total No. of 2011 Grads	% of 2011 Grads Employed FT, LT Bar-Passage Required Jobs
SOUTHERN ILLINOIS UNIV.-CARBONDALE	66	111	59.5%
SOUTHERN METHODIST UNIV.	172	272	63.2%
SOUTHERN UNIV.	53	143	37.1%
SOUTHWESTERN LAW SCHOOL	103	298	34.6%
ST. JOHN'S UNIV.	132	276	47.8%
ST. LOUIS UNIV.	144	272	52.9%
ST. MARY'S UNIV.	195	249	78.3%
ST. THOMAS UNIV.	109	221	49.3%
STANFORD UNIV.	175	192	91.1%
STATE UNIV. OF NEW YORK AT BUFFALO	127	245	51.8%
STETSON UNIV.	184	322	57.1%
SUFFOLK UNIV.	193	502	38.4%
SYRACUSE UNIV.	97	193	50.3%
TEMPLE UNIV.	177	319	55.5%
TENNESSEE, UNIV. OF	91	146	62.3%
TEXAS AT AUSTIN, UNIV. OF	267	382	69.9%
TEXAS SOUTHERN UNIV.	87	163	53.4%
TEXAS TECH UNIV.	127	200	63.5%
TEXAS WESLEYAN UNIV.	109	223	48.9%
THOMAS JEFFERSON SCHOOL OF LAW	63	236	26.7%
THOMAS M. COOLEY LAW SCHOOL	375	999	37.5%
TOLEDO, UNIV. OF	42	115	36.5%
TOURO COLLEGE	131	221	59.3%
TULANE UNIV.	140	241	58.1%
TULSA, UNIV. OF	79	120	65.8%
UNIV. OF LA VERNE	38	116	32.8%
UNIV. OF NEVADA-LAS VEGAS	85	128	66.4%
UNIV. OF ST. THOMAS	59	134	44.0%
UTAH, UNIV. OF	92	134	68.7%

Table 1-2 Schools Ranked in Alphabetical Order	2011 Grads Employed FT, LT Bar-Passage Required Jobs	Total No. of 2011 Grads	% of 2011 Grads Employed FT, LT Bar-Passage Required Jobs
VALPARAISO UNIV.	76	181	42.0%
VANDERBILT UNIV.	146	198	73.7%
VERMONT LAW SCHOOL	85	174	48.9%
VILLANOVA UNIV.	132	252	52.4%
VIRGINIA, UNIV. OF	357	377	94.7%
WAKE FOREST UNIV.	89	158	56.3%
WASHBURN UNIV.	71	142	50.0%
WASHINGTON AND LEE UNIV.	71	129	55.0%
WASHINGTON UNIV.	188	317	59.3%
WASHINGTON, UNIV. OF	96	182	52.7%
WAYNE STATE UNIV.	103	203	50.7%
WEST VIRGINIA UNIV.	86	125	68.8%
WESTERN NEW ENGLAND UNIV.	46	153	30.1%
WESTERN STATE	29	90	32.2%
WHITTIER COLLEGE	21	123	17.1%
WIDENER UNIV.	119	252	47.2%
WIDENER UNIV.-HARRISBURG	55	124	44.4%
WILLAMETTE UNIV.	61	129	47.3%
WILLIAM AND MARY SCHOOL OF LAW	112	204	54.9%
WILLIAM MITCHELL COLLEGE OF LAW	123	282	43.6%
WISCONSIN, UNIV. OF	159	254	62.6%
WYOMING, UNIV. OF	46	74	62.2%
YALE UNIV.	180	205	87.8%
YESHIVA UNIV.	197	380	51.8%

Data Source: Employment Summary Report, http://employmentsummary.abaquestionnaire.org. FT, LT = Full-time and Long-term; * ABA did not explain Puerto Rico's figures.

Table 2. Schools with Attrition Rates 10% or Higher

	Table 2 Ranked from Highest to Lowest 1L Attrition Rate (column in bold)	*Academic Attrition #	*Other Attrition #	*Total #	*Total Attrition Percentage of 1L Class	*Transfer In #	*Transfer Out #	2011 Grads w/ FT, LT, Bar Passage-Required Job	Total # of 2011 Grads	% with FT, LT, Bar Passage-Required Job
1	Univ. of LaVerne Col. of Law	21	51	72	**43.6%**	1	34	38	116	32.8%
2	Western State Col. of Law	59	24	83	**34.9%**	11	16	29	90	32.2%
3	Whittier Law Sch.	60	33	93	**31.0%**	20	32	21	123	17.1%
4	Widener Univ. Sch. of Law - Pennsylvania	23	32	55	**30.9%**	1	17	55	124	44.4%
5	Nova Southeastern Univ. - Broad Law Center	66	44	110	**28.0%**	8	55	176	302	58.3%
6	Thomas Jefferson Sch. of Law	32	67	99	**28.0%**	3	43	63	236	26.7%
7	Faulkner Univ., Thomas Goode Jones Sch. of Law	20	18	38	**26.0%**	0	9	57	101	56.4%
8	Liberty Univ. Sch. of Law	19	15	34	**25.8%**	2	4	28	90	31.1%
9	Florida A&M Univ. Col. of Law	37	37	74	**25.7%**	0	9	52	152	34.2%
10	Florida Coastal Sch. of Law	26	114	200	**25.5%**	3	90	165	451	36.6%
11	Western New England Univ. Sch. of Law	7	34	41	**24.1%**	2	22	46	153	30.1%
12	Touro Col. Jacob D. Fuchsberg Law Center	14	55	69	**23.8%**	23	51	131	221	59.3%
13	Capital Univ. Law Sch.	26	31	57	**23.7%**	6	10	70	175	40.0%

	Table 2 Ranked from Highest to Lowest 1L Attrition Rate (column in bold)	*Academic Attrition #	*Other Attrition #	*Total #	*Total Attrition Percentage of 1L Class	*Transfer In #	*Transfer Out #	2011 Grads w/ FT, LT, Bar Passage-Required Job	Total # of 2011 Grads	% with FT, LT, Bar Passage-Required Job
14	Widener Univ. Sch. of Law - Delaware	34	57	91	**23.5%**	2	40	119	252	47.2%
15	Golden Gate Univ. Sch. of Law	24	50	74	**23.2%**	2	36	42	191	22.0%
16	Univ. of San Francisco Sch. of Law	18	38	56	**22.3%**	6	20	76	222	34.2%
17	Willamette Univ. Col. of Law	12	24	36	**22.2%**	4	15	61	129	47.3%
18	Pontifical Catholic Univ. of Puerto Rico Sch. of Law**	16	42	58	**21.4%**	15	36			
19	Univ. of Detroit Mercy Sch. of Law	13	45	58	**21.2%**	0	25	77	209	36.8%
20	New England Law - Boston	10	73	83	**21.2%**	2	33	106	308	34.4%
21	Barry Univ. Dwayne O. Andreas Sch. of Law	23	32	55	**21.1%**	6	28	82	209	39.2%
22	The John Marshall Law Sch.	44	63	107	**21.0%**	12	40	174	401	43.4%
23	Univ. of the District of Columbia - Clarke Sch. of Law	5	21	26	**20.6%**	8	15	16	78	20.5%
24	The Univ. of Toledo Col. of Law	6	33	39	**20.6%**	3	22	42	115	36.5%
25	Oklahoma City Univ. Sch. of Law	14	31	45	**20.0%**	3	25	105	176	59.7%
26	St. Thomas Univ. Sch. of Law	29	24	53	**19.4%**	4	12	109	221	49.3%
27	Charlotte Sch. of Law	47	48	95	**19.3%**	10	22	99	193	51.3%
28	N. Carolina Central Univ. Sch. of Law	26	12	38	**18.5%**	0	1	74	170	43.5%

	Table 2 Ranked from Highest to Lowest 1L Attrition Rate (column in bold)	*Academic Attrition #	*Other Attrition #	*Total #	*Total Attrition Percentage of 1L Class	*Transfer In #	*Transfer Out #	2011 Grads w/ FT, LT, Bar Passage-Required Job	Total # of 2011 Grads	% with FT, LT, Bar Passage-Required Job
29	Southern Univ. Law Center	54	5	59	**18.4%**	0	5	53	143	37.1%
30	Valparaiso Univ. Law Sch.	5	33	38	**18.4%**	1	28	76	181	42.0%
31	Univ. of New Hampshire Sch. of Law	4	20	24	**18.3%**	0	11	70	147	47.6%
32	Cleveland-Marshall Col. of Law, CSU	12	22	34	**17.5%**	4	3	93	185	50.3%
33	Ave Maria Sch. of Law	8	27	35	**17.4%**	2	18	29	88	33.0%
34	California Western Sch. of Law	27	30	57	**17.4%**	6	10	112	285	39.3%
35	Regent Univ. Sch. of Law	15	13	28	**16.7%**	4	6	62	118	52.5%
36	The Catholic Univ. of America, Columbus Sch. of Law	5	40	45	**16.4%**	5	33	114	261	43.7%
37	The Thomas M. Cooley Law Sch.	124	211	335	**16.3%**	11	227	375	999	37.5%
38	Santa Clara Univ. Sch. of Law	19	32	51	**15.6%**	22	9	127	296	42.9%
39	Univ. of Dayton Sch. of Law	7	24	31	**15.3%**	2	48	88	171	51.5%
40	Washburn Univ. Sch. of Law	8	17	25	**15.2%**	6	6	71	142	50.0%
41	The Univ. of Alabama Sch. of Law	4	20	24	**14.7%**	10	2	128	164	78.0%
42	The Univ. of Akron Sch. of Law	12	17	29	**14.4%**	3	7	64	116	55.2%
43	Chapman Univ. Sch. of Law	11	19	30	**14.4%**	9	10	71	177	40.1%

	Table 2 Ranked from Highest to Lowest 1L Attrition Rate (column in bold)	*Academic Attrition #	*Other Attrition #	*Total #	*Total Attrition Percentage of 1L Class	*Transfer In #	*Transfer Out #	2011 Grads w/ FT, LT, Bar Passage-Required Job	Total # of 2011 Grads	% with FT, LT, Bar Passage-Required Job
44	Northern Kentucky Univ. - Chase Sch. of Law	14	14	28	**14.2%**	3	8	65	179	36.3%
45	Texas Southern Univ. - Marshall Sch. of Law	30	0	30	**14.2%**	1	4	87	163	53.4%
46	Appalachian Sch. of Law	12	5	17	**13.9%**	0	6	28	91	30.8%
47	Syracuse Univ. Col. of Law	14	21	35	**13.9%**	3	17	97	193	50.3%
48	New York Law Sch.	32	56	88	**13.7%**	14	54	183	515	35.5%
49	The Pennsylvania State Univ., Dickinson Sch. of Law	3	28	31	**13.6%**	5	20	107	179	59.8%
50	Gonzaga Univ. Sch. of Law	6	18	24	**13.4%**	7	8	89	160	55.6%
51	Ohio Northern Univ. Pettit Col. of Law	9	7	16	**13.3%**	1	3	55	97	56.7%
52	Campbell Univ., Wiggins Sch. of Law	9	12	21	**12.8%**	1	3	95	133	71.4%
53	Roger Williams Univ. Sch. of Law	10	16	26	**12.7%**	5	11	79	158	50.0%
54	Univ. of Missouri Sch. of Law	5	14	19	**12.6%**	9	3	94	141	66.7%
55	Howard Univ. Sch. of Law	6	14	20	**12.4%**	1	7	75	157	47.8%
56	Hofstra Univ. - Deane Sch. of Law	13	31	44	**12.1%**	11	24	121	297	40.7%
57	Phoenix Sch. of Law	22	34	56	**11.8%**	11	31	49	131	37.4%
58	Texas Wesleyan Univ. Sch. of Law	18	30	48	**11.7%**	5	14	109	223	48.9%

	Table 2 Ranked from Highest to Lowest 1L Attrition Rate (column in bold)	*Academic Attrition #	*Other Attrition #	*Total #	*Total Attrition Percentage of 1L Class	*Transfer In #	*Transfer Out #	2011 Grads w/ FT, LT, Bar Passage-Required Job	Total # of 2011 Grads	% with FT, LT, Bar Passage-Required Job
59	Chicago-Kent Col. of Law, IIT	10	26	36	**11.6%**	24	7	169	332	50.9%
60	Southwestern Law Sch.	25	20	45	**11.1%**	6	19	103	298	34.6%
61	Univ. of Baltimore Sch. of Law	17	29	46	**11.0%**	22	26	143	298	48.0%
62	American Univ. Washington Col. of Law	0	55	55	**10.8%**	53	50	167	467	35.8%
63	Rutgers Sch. of Law Camden	3	26	29	**10.8%**	36	16	141	242	58.3%
64	DePaul Univ. Col. of Law	13	20	33	**10.6%**	18	17	129	319	40.4%
65	Pace Univ. Sch. of Law	3	25	28	**10.5%**	7	19	80	222	36.0%
66	Loyola Law Sch., Loyola Marymount Univ.	19	29	42	**10.3%**	44	13	172	403	42.7%
67	Seattle Univ. Sch. of Law	1	32	33	**10.3%**	23	20	127	315	40.3%
68	Univ. of San Diego Sch. of Law	4	29	33	**10.2%**	35	15	149	318	46.9%
69	Charleston Sch. of Law	3	21	24	**10.1%**	5	13	99	193	51.3%
70	The Florida State Univ. Col. of Law	1	19	20	**10.0%**	57	8	194	279	69.5%
71	Seton Hall Univ. Sch. of Law	21	15	36	**10.0%**	16	14	184	293	62.8%
	Totals	1369	2324	3747						

Data Source: Employment Summary Report, http://employmentsummary.abaquestionnaire.org.
FT, LT = Full-time and Long-term; * Data from 2012 LSAC Guide; ** ABA did not explain Puerto Rico's figures.

Table 3. Schools with Highest # of Grads Seeking Employment

	Table 3 Top 50 Schools Ranked from Highest to Lowest Number of Jobless Grads Seeking Employment	No. of 2011 Grads Unemployed and Seeking Jobs	Total No. of 2011 Grads	% of 2011 Grads Unemployed Seeking
1	THOMAS M. COOLEY LAW SCHOOL	110	999	11%
2	BROOKLYN LAW SCHOOL	108	455	24%
3	SUFFOLK UNIVERSITY	92	502	18%
4	NEW YORK LAW SCHOOL	75	515	15%
5	CALIFORNIA-HASTINGS, UNIVERSITY OF	74	411	18%
6	THOMAS JEFFERSON SCHOOL OF LAW	74	236	31%
7	BARRY UNIVERSITY	67	209	32%
8	DEPAUL UNIVERSITY	66	319	21%
9	LOYOLA MARYMOUNT UNIV.-LOS ANGELES	65	403	16%
10	AMERICAN UNIVERSITY	61	467	13%
11	FLORIDA COASTAL	61	451	14%
12	VILLANOVA UNIVERSITY	59	252	23%
13	SEATTLE UNIVERSITY	58	315	18%
14	JOHN MARSHALL LAW SCHOOL	56	401	14%
15	PEPPERDINE UNIVERSITY	53	229	23%
16	WHITTIER COLLEGE	50	123	41%
17	MCGEORGE SCHOOL OF LAW	49	303	16%
18	STETSON UNIVERSITY	43	322	13%
19	LOYOLA UNIVERSITY-NEW ORLEANS	42	231	18%
20	FLORIDA, UNIVERSITY OF	41	409	10%
21	NEW ENGLAND SCHOOL OF LAW	41	308	13%
22	TOURO COLLEGE	41	221	19%
23	FORDHAM UNIVERSITY	40	428	9%
24	ST. THOMAS UNIVERSITY	40	221	18%
25	UNIVERSITY OF LA VERNE	39	116	34%
26	OREGON, UNIVERSITY OF	37	174	21%
27	GEORGETOWN UNIVERSITY	35	644	5%
28	CALIFORNIA WESTERN SCHOOL OF LAW	34	285	12%
29	GOLDEN GATE UNIVERSITY	34	191	18%
30	SAN DIEGO, UNIVERSITY OF	34	318	11%

	Table 3 Top 50 Schools Ranked from Highest to Lowest Number of Jobless Grads Seeking Employment	No. of 2011 Grads Unemployed and Seeking Jobs	Total No. of 2011 Grads	% of 2011 Grads Unemployed Seeking
31	ILLINOIS INST. OF TECH., CHICAGO-KENT	33	332	10%
32	VALPARAISO UNIVERSITY	32	181	18%
33	WESTERN NEW ENGLAND UNIVERSITY	32	153	21%
34	ILLINOIS, UNIVERSITY OF	30	190	16%
35	SOUTHWESTERN LAW SCHOOL	30	298	10%
36	PACE UNIVERSITY	29	222	13%
37	YESHIVA UNIVERSITY	29	380	8%
38	NOVA SOUTHEASTERN UNIVERSITY	28	302	9%
39	WAYNE STATE UNIVERSITY	28	203	14%
40	CATHOLIC UNIVERSITY OF AMERICA	27	261	10%
41	HOFSTRA UNIVERSITY	27	297	9%
42	RUTGERS UNIVERSITY-CAMDEN	27	242	11%
43	SOUTHERN UNIVERSITY	27	143	19%
44	ALBANY LAW SCHOOL	26	236	11%
45	DETROIT MERCY, UNIVERSITY OF	26	209	12%
46	PITTSBURGH, UNIVERSITY OF	26	253	10%
47	PUERTO RICO, UNIVERSITY OF	26	244	11%
48	SAN FRANCISCO, UNIVERSITY OF	26	222	12%
49	CHARLESTON SCHOOL OF LAW	25	193	13%
50	DUQUESNE UNIVERSITY	25	206	12%

Data Source: http://employmentsummary.abaquestionnaire.org.

Table 4. It's A Very Small World After All

Small World Ranking	US News Ranking	Table 4 School Name—Ranked from Highest to Lowest Percentage of Grads in Solo & Very Small Firms (last column)	Total # of Grads	Grads w/ FT, LT, Bar-Passage Required	Percent w/ FT, LT, Bar-Job	Total # of Grads at Law Firms	% of Grads in Solo Firms	% of Grads in Very Small Firms (size 2–10)	% of Grads in Solo & Very Small Firms (size 2–10)[+]
1	RNP	SOUTH DAKOTA, UNIV. OF	55	21	38.2%	11	18.2%	81.8%	100%
2	RNP	APPALACHIAN SCHOOL OF LAW	91	28	30.8%	32	12.5%	81.3%	94%
3	113	CITY UNIV. OF NEW YORK	111	41	36.9%	21	4.8%	85.7%	90%
4	RNP	SOUTHERN UNIV.	143	53	37.1%	38	31.6%	57.9%	89%
5	RNP	ATLANTA'S JOHN MARSHALL LAW SCHOOL	132	54	40.9%	60	35.0%	53.3%	88%
6	RNP	ELON UNIV.	99	55	55.6%	50	12.0%	76.0%	88%
7	RNP	REGENT UNIV.	118	62	52.5%	40	17.5%	70.0%	88%
8	RNP	TEXAS SOUTHERN UNIV.	163	87	53.4%	76	40.8%	46.1%	87%
9	RNP	PHOENIX SCHOOL OF LAW	131	49	37.4%	59	8.5%	78.0%	86%
10	RNP	AVE MARIA	88	29	33.0%	27	7.4%	77.8%	85%
11	RNP	ST. MARY'S UNIV.	249	195	78.3%	153	19.0%	66.0%	85%
12	129	TOLEDO, UNIV. OF	115	42	36.5%	33	18.2%	66.7%	85%
13	RNP	WESTERN NEW ENGLAND UNIV.	153	46	30.1%	38	15.8%	68.4%	84%
14	44	FAULKNER UNIV.	101	57	56.4%	54	13.0%	70.4%	83%
15	145	MONTANA, UNIV. OF	85	56	65.9%	42	4.8%	78.6%	83%
16	RNP	WESTERN STATE	90	29	32.2%	41	14.6%	68.3%	83%

Small World Ranking	US News Ranking	Table 4 School Name—Ranked from Highest to Lowest Percentage of Grads in Solo & Very Small Firms (last column)	Total # of Grads	Grads w/ FT, LT, Bar-Passage Required	Percent w/ FT, LT, Bar-Job	Total # of Grads at Law Firms	% of Grads in Solo Firms	% of Grads in Very Small Firms (size 2–10)	% of Grads in Solo & Very Small Firms (size 2–10)+
17	RNP	HAMLINE UNIV.	205	103	50.2%	70	4.3%	78.6%	83%
18	RNP	TEXAS WESLEYAN UNIV.	223	109	48.9%	96	21.9%	60.4%	82%
19	RNP	NORTHERN ILLINOIS UNIV.	97	53	54.6%	39	7.7%	74.4%	82%
20	RNP	VALPARAISO UNIV.	181	76	42.0%	66	7.6%	74.2%	82%
21	RNP	NORTH CAROLINA CENTRAL UNIV.	170	74	43.5%	49	26.5%	55.1%	82%
22	RNP	THOMAS M. COOLEY LAW SCHOOL	999	375	37.5%	332	24.1%	57.2%	81%
23	113	QUINNIPIAC UNIV.	133	46	34.6%	47	8.5%	72.3%	81%
24	RNP	CHARLOTTE SCHOOL OF LAW	97	42	43.3%	31	29.0%	51.6%	81%
25	RNP	NEW ENGLAND SCHOOL OF LAW	308	106	34.4%	94	16.0%	63.8%	80%
26	RNP	BARRY UNIV.	209	82	39.2%	82	13.4%	65.9%	79%
27	129	WILLAMETTE UNIV.	129	61	47.3%	55	25.5%	52.7%	78%
28	69	NEW MEXICO, UNIV. OF	103	68	66.0%	50	8.0%	70.0%	78%
29	RNP	LIBERTY UNIV.	90	28	31.1%	27	18.5%	59.3%	78%
30	RNP	WASHBURN UNIV.	142	71	50.0%	58	24.1%	53.4%	78%
31	119	VERMONT LAW SCHOOL	174	85	48.9%	49	4.1%	73.5%	78%
32	129	IDAHO, UNIV. OF	102	52	51.0%	40	5.0%	72.5%	78%
33	RNP	CHARLESTON SCHOOL OF LAW	193	99	51.3%	69	1.4%	75.4%	77%

Small World Ranking	US News Ranking	Table 4 School Name — Ranked from Highest to Lowest Percentage of Grads in Solo & Very Small Firms (last column)	Total # of Grads	Grads w/ FT, LT, Bar-Passage Required	Percent w/ FT, LT, Bar-Job	Total # of Grads at Law Firms	% of Grads in Solo Firms	% of Grads in Very Small Firms (size 2–10)	% of Grads in Solo & Very Small Firms (size 2–10)+
34	82	OREGON, UNIV. OF	174	72	41.4%	56	14.3%	62.5%	77%
35	RNP	CAMPBELL UNIV.	133	95	71.4%	73	17.8%	58.9%	77%
36	106	DRAKE UNIV.	155	94	60.6%	76	14.5%	61.8%	76%
37	RNP	THOMAS JEFFERSON SCHOOL OF LAW	236	63	26.7%	75	13.3%	62.7%	76%
38	145	NORTH DAKOTA, UNIV. OF	81	40	49.4%	29	0.0%	75.9%	76%
39	RNP	SOUTHERN ILLINOIS UNIV.-CARBONDALE	111	66	59.5%	58	17.2%	58.6%	76%
40	129	SOUTHWESTERN LAW SCHOOL	298	103	34.6%	106	11.3%	64.2%	75%
41	RNP	UNIV OF LA VERNE	116	38	32.8%	44	2.3%	72.7%	75%
42	119	MAINE, UNIV. OF	90	38	42.2%	28	3.6%	71.4%	75%
43	RNP	MISSISSIPPI COLLEGE	166	125	75.3%	84	16.7%	58.3%	75%
44	RNP	SOUTH TEXAS COLLEGE OF LAW	402	259	64.4%	203	10.3%	64.5%	75%
45	RNP	CALIFORNIA WESTERN SCHOOL OF LAW	285	112	39.3%	143	7.7%	66.4%	74%
46	89	LOUISVILLE, UNIV. OF	142	95	66.9%	54	9.3%	64.8%	74%
47	119	ARKANSAS, LITTLE ROCK, UNIV. OF	150	95	63.3%	73	6.8%	67.1%	74%
48	26	ARIZONA STATE UNIV.	201	137	68.2%	86	11.6%	61.6%	73%
49	RNP	WIDENER UNIV.	252	119	47.2%	97	7.2%	66.0%	73%
50	RNP	CAPITAL UNIV.	175	70	40.0%	65	10.8%	61.5%	72%

Small World Ranking	US News Ranking	Table 4 School Name—Ranked from Highest to Lowest Percentage of Grads in Solo & Very Small Firms (last column)	Total # of Grads	Grads w/ FT, LT, Bar-Passage Required	Percent w/ FT, LT, Bar-Job	Total # of Grads at Law Firms	% of Grads in Solo Firms	% of Grads in Very Small Firms (size 2–10)	% of Grads in Solo & Very Small Firms (size 2–10)+
51	113	GONZAGA UNIV.	160	89	55.6%	61	6.6%	65.6%	72%
52	RNP	FLORIDA COASTAL	451	165	36.6%	136	9.6%	62.5%	72%
53	127	WYOMING, UNIV. OF	74	46	62.2%	27	3.7%	66.7%	70%
54	113	ALBANY LAW SCHOOL	236	118	50.0%	101	3.0%	67.3%	70%
55	58	LEWIS & CLARK COLLEGE	233	107	45.9%	76	10.5%	59.2%	70%
56	101	MCGEORGE SCHOOL OF LAW	303	132	43.6%	112	6.3%	63.4%	70%
57	119	AKRON, UNIV. OF	116	64	55.2%	39	15.4%	53.8%	69%
58	89	ARKANSAS, FAYETTEVILLE, UNIV. OF	116	71	61.2%	55	5.5%	63.6%	69%
59	89	NEBRASKA, UNIV. OF	130	84	64.6%	55	10.9%	58.2%	69%
60	RNP	ROGER WILLIAMS UNIV.	158	79	50.0%	42	11.9%	57.1%	69%
61	RNP	OKLAHOMA CITY UNIV.	176	105	59.7%	84	16.7%	52.4%	69%
62	58	GEORGIA STATE UNIV.	186	120	64.5%	86	0.0%	68.6%	69%
63	RNP	MEMPHIS, UNIV. OF	129	77	59.7%	54	13.0%	55.6%	69%
64	113	BALTIMORE, UNIV. OF	298	143	48.0%	100	7.0%	61.0%	68%
65	RNP	DAYTON, UNIV. OF	171	88	51.5%	71	14.1%	53.5%	68%
66	RNP	TOURO COLLEGE	221	131	59.3%	108	3.7%	63.9%	68%
67	82	SEATTLE UNIV.	315	127	40.3%	88	11.4%	55.7%	67%

Small World Ranking	US News Ranking	Table 4 School Name — Ranked from Highest to Lowest Percentage of Grads in Solo & Very Small Firms (last column)	Total # of Grads	Grads w/ FT, LT, Bar-Passage Required	Percent w/ FT, LT, Bar-Job	Total # of Grads at Law Firms	% of Grads in Solo Firms	% of Grads in Very Small Firms (size 2–10)	% of Grads in Solo & Very Small Firms (size 2–10)[+]
68	RNP	WIDENER UNIV.-HARRISBURG	124	55	44.4%	42	16.7%	50.0%	67%
69	76	UNIV. OF NEVADA-LAS VEGAS	128	85	66.4%	54	9.3%	57.4%	67%
70	110	CHAPMAN UNIV.	177	71	40.1%	77	6.5%	59.7%	66%
71	RNP	NOVA SOUTHEASTERN UNIV.	302	176	58.3%	170	5.9%	60.0%	66%
72	99	TULSA, UNIV. OF	120	79	65.8%	61	9.8%	55.7%	66%
73	99	RUTGERS UNIV.-CAMDEN	242	141	58.3%	58	6.9%	58.6%	66%
74	135	LOYOLA UNIV.-NEW ORLEANS	231	106	45.9%	92	5.4%	59.8%	65%
75	135	MISSOURI-KANSAS CITY, UNIV. OF	154	94	61.0%	73	8.2%	56.2%	64%
76	RNP	GOLDEN GATE UNIV.	191	42	22.0%	56	12.5%	51.8%	64%
77	106	SAN FRANCISCO, UNIV. OF	222	76	34.2%	84	6.0%	58.3%	64%
78	135	CREIGHTON UNIV.	153	92	60.1%	61	9.8%	54.1%	64%
79	62	NORTHERN KENTUCKY UNIV.	179	65	36.3%	60	8.3%	55.0%	63%
80	RNP	ST. THOMAS UNIV.	221	109	49.3%	111	10.8%	52.3%	63%
81	82	STATE UNIV. OF NEW YORK AT BUFFALO	245	127	51.8%	99	8.1%	54.5%	63%
82	96	MARQUETTE UNIV.	230	133	57.8%	107	10.3%	52.3%	63%
83	89	DEPAUL UNIV.	319	129	40.4%	138	3.6%	58.7%	62%
84	135	SUFFOLK UNIV.	502	193	38.4%	159	8.8%	53.5%	62%

Small World Ranking	US News Ranking	Table 4 School Name—Ranked from Highest to Lowest Percentage of Grads in Solo & Very Small Firms (last column)	Total # of Grads	Grads w/ FT, LT, Bar-Passage Required	Percent w/ FT, LT, Bar-Job	Total # of Grads at Law Firms	% of Grads in Solo Firms	% of Grads in Very Small Firms (size 2–10)	% of Grads in Solo & Very Small Firms (size 2–10)[+]
85	47	UTAH, UNIV. OF	134	92	68.7%	68	11.8%	50.0%	62%
86	79	LOUISIANA STATE UNIV.	176	143	81.3%	90	3.3%	57.8%	61%
87	RNP	UNIV. OF ST. THOMAS	134	59	44.0%	51	13.7%	47.1%	61%
88	135	MISSISSIPPI, UNIV. OF	151	83	55.0%	63	7.9%	52.4%	60%
89	82	MICHIGAN STATE UNIV.	283	125	44.2%	103	11.7%	48.5%	60%
90	127	WILLIAM MITCHELL COLLEGE OF LAW	282	123	43.6%	119	9.2%	50.4%	60%
91	RNP	WHITTIER COLLEGE	123	21	17.1%	32	15.6%	43.8%	59%
92	82	OKLAHOMA, UNIV. OF	163	101	62.0%	85	3.5%	55.3%	59%
93	29	ALABAMA, UNIV. OF	164	128	78.0%	75	14.7%	44.0%	59%
94	135	NEW YORK LAW SCHOOL	515	183	35.5%	164	1.2%	57.3%	59%
95	82	CATHOLIC UNIV. OF AMERICA	261	114	43.7%	82	8.5%	50.0%	59%
96	106	HAWAII, UNIV. OF	101	48	47.5%	24	0.0%	58.3%	58%
97	RNP	DISTRICT OF COLUMBIA	78	16	20.5%	12	25.0%	33.3%	58%
98	69	TENNESSEE, UNIV. OF	146	91	62.3%	64	18.8%	39.1%	58%
99	62	ILLINOIS INST. OF TECH., CHICAGO-KENT	332	169	50.9%	153	5.2%	52.3%	58%
100	69	DENVER, UNIV. OF	287	140	48.8%	87	4.6%	52.9%	57%
101	142	SAMFORD UNIV.	148	97	65.5%	87	10.3%	47.1%	57%

Small World Ranking	US News Ranking	Table 4 School Name—Ranked from Highest to Lowest Percentage of Grads in Solo & Very Small Firms (last column)	Total # of Grads	Grads w/ FT, LT, Bar-Passage Required	Percent w/ FT, LT, Bar-Job	Total # of Grads at Law Firms	% of Grads in Solo Firms	% of Grads in Very Small Firms (size 2–10)	% of Grads in Solo & Very Small Firms (size 2–10)+
102	101	TEXAS TECH UNIV.	200	127	63.5%	101	5.9%	51.5%	57%
103	135	CLEVELAND STATE UNIV.	185	93	50.3%	89	12.4%	44.9%	57%
104	142	NEW HAMPSHIRE UNIV. OF	147	70	47.6%	51	21.6%	35.3%	57%
105	RNP	OHIO NORTHERN UNIV.	97	55	56.7%	37	5.4%	51.4%	57%
106	89	KANSAS, UNIV. OF	168	88	52.4%	67	13.4%	43.3%	57%
107	129	JOHN MARSHALL-CHICAGO	401	174	43.4%	168	7.7%	48.8%	57%
108	35	WISCONSIN, UNIV. OF	254	159	62.6%	104	12.5%	43.3%	56%
109	RNP	FLORIDA A&M	152	52	34.2%	36	25.0%	30.6%	56%
110	89	INDIANA UNIV.-INDIANAPOLIS	252	136	54.0%	103	5.8%	49.5%	55%
111	39	GEORGE MASON UNIV.	170	102	60.0%	67	3.0%	52.2%	55%
112	89	HOFSTRA UNIV.	297	121	40.7%	130	2.3%	52.3%	55%
113	67	LOYOLA UNIV.-CHICAGO	251	126	50.2%	110	4.5%	50.0%	55%
114	113	FLORIDA INTERNATIONAL	173	105	60.7%	103	9.7%	44.7%	54%
115	RNP	DETROIT MERCY, UNIV. OF	209	77	36.8%	96	6.3%	47.9%	54%
116	43	ARIZONA, UNIV. OF	158	119	75.3%	63	4.8%	49.2%	54%
117	76	NORTHEASTERN UNIV.	182	90	49.5%	54	1.9%	51.9%	54%
118	51	BAYLOR UNIV.	157	110	70.1%	88	2.3%	51.1%	53%

Small World Ranking	US News Ranking	Table 4 School Name—Ranked from Highest to Lowest Percentage of Grads in Solo & Very Small Firms (last column)	Total # of Grads	Grads w/ FT, LT, Bar-Passage Required	Percent w/ FT, LT, Bar-Job	Total # of Grads at Law Firms	% of Grads in Solo Firms	% of Grads in Very Small Firms (size 2–10)	% of Grads in Solo & Very Small Firms (size 2–10)+
119	65	SAN DIEGO, UNIV. OF	318	149	46.9%	148	4.1%	49.3%	53%
120	101	ST. LOUIS UNIV.	272	144	52.9%	105	1.9%	51.4%	53%
121	110	WAYNE STATE UNIV.	203	103	50.7%	89	5.6%	47.2%	53%
122	RNP	DUQUESNE UNIV.	206	92	44.7%	78	3.8%	48.7%	53%
123	RNP	KENTUCKY, UNIV. OF	135	97	71.9%	63	4.8%	47.6%	52%
124	96	SYRACUSE UNIV.	193	97	50.3%	65	1.5%	50.8%	52%
125	62	CONNECTICUT, UNIV. OF	179	86	48.0%	69	1.4%	50.7%	52%
126	119	STETSON UNIV.	322	184	57.1%	127	9.4%	42.5%	52%
127	119	DREXEL UNIV.	131	57	43.5%	39	2.6%	48.7%	51%
128	142	PACE UNIV.	222	80	36.0%	70	1.4%	48.6%	50%
129	29	IOWA, UNIV. OF	183	120	65.6%	82	1.2%	48.8%	50%
130	39	MARYLAND, UNIV. OF	297	140	47.1%	79	0.0%	49.4%	49%
131	96	SANTA CLARA UNIV.	296	127	42.9%	114	7.0%	42.1%	49%
132	110	MERCER UNIV.	130	82	63.1%	66	3.0%	45.5%	48%
133	69	MIAMI, UNIV. OF	385	212	55.1%	177	1.1%	46.9%	48%
134	57	HOUSTON, UNIV. OF	281	169	60.1%	144	5.6%	42.4%	48%
135	51	FLORIDA STATE UNIV.	279	194	69.5%	117	7.7%	40.2%	48%

Small World Ranking	US News Ranking	Table 4 School Name—Ranked from Highest to Lowest Percentage of Grads in Solo & Very Small Firms (last column)	Total # of Grads	Grads w/ FT, LT, Bar-Passage Required	Percent w/ FT, LT, Bar-Job	Total # of Grads at Law Firms	% of Grads in Solo Firms	% of Grads in Very Small Firms (size 2–10)	% of Grads in Solo & Very Small Firms (size 2–10)+
136	109	SOUTH CAROLINA, UNIV. OF	222	122	55.0%	69	2.9%	44.9%	48%
137	44	COLORADO, UNIV. OF	176	98	55.7%	65	0.0%	47.7%	48%
138	76	PENNSYLVANIA STATE UNIV.	179	107	59.8%	60	6.7%	40.0%	47%
139	49	PEPPERDINE UNIV.	229	98	42.8%	95	7.4%	38.9%	46%
140	44	CALIFORNIA-HASTINGS, UNIV. OF	411	191	46.5%	156	7.1%	39.1%	46%
141	51	LOYOLA MARYMOUNT UNIV.-LOS ANGELES	403	172	42.7%	183	1.6%	44.3%	46%
142	79	MISSOURI-COLUMBIA, UNIV. OF	141	94	66.7%	59	6.8%	39.0%	46%
143	58	TEMPLE UNIV.	319	177	55.5%	119	5.0%	38.7%	44%
144	101	WEST VIRGINIA UNIV.	125	86	68.8%	71	5.6%	38.0%	44%
145	51	TULANE UNIV.	241	140	58.1%	97	3.1%	40.2%	43%
146	58	RICHMOND, UNIV. OF	166	99	59.6%	58	3.4%	39.7%	43%
147	67	CASE WESTERN RESERVE UNIV.	201	94	46.8%	77	1.3%	41.6%	43%
148	82	RUTGERS UNIV.-NEWARK	248	140	56.5%	52	13.5%	28.8%	42%
149	51	SOUTHERN METHODIST UNIV.	272	172	63.2%	165	3.0%	38.8%	42%
150	65	BROOKLYN LAW SCHOOL	455	215	47.3%	134	0.0%	41.8%	42%
151	19	MINNESOTA, UNIV. OF	261	155	59.4%	96	2.1%	39.6%	42%
152	34	GEORGIA, UNIV. OF	227	139	61.2%	101	0.0%	41.6%	42%

Small World Ranking	US News Ranking	Table 4 School Name—Ranked from Highest to Lowest Percentage of Grads in Solo & Very Small Firms (last column)	Total # of Grads	Grads w/ FT, LT, Bar-Passage Required	Percent w/ FT, LT, Bar-Job	Total # of Grads at Law Firms	% of Grads in Solo Firms	% of Grads in Very Small Firms (size 2–10)	% of Grads in Solo & Very Small Firms (size 2–10)[+]
153	26	INDIANA UNIV. SCHOOL OF LAW	195	124	63.6%	78	10.3%	30.8%	41%
154	44	WAKE FOREST UNIV.	158	89	56.3%	66	10.6%	30.3%	41%
155	69	PITTSBURGH, UNIV. OF	253	137	54.2%	84	4.8%	35.7%	40%
156	69	SETON HALL UNIV.	293	184	62.8%	94	4.3%	36.2%	40%
157	24	WASHINGTON AND LEE UNIV.	129	71	55.0%	52	1.9%	38.5%	40%
158	39	OHIO STATE UNIV.	231	135	58.4%	93	1.1%	38.7%	40%
159	79	ST. JOHN'S UNIV.	276	132	47.8%	115	2.6%	36.5%	39%
160	20	WASHINGTON, UNIV. OF	182	96	52.7%	69	4.3%	34.8%	39%
161	39	BRIGHAM YOUNG UNIV.	148	76	51.4%	65	1.5%	36.9%	38%
162	48	FLORIDA, UNIV. OF	409	243	59.4%	184	1.6%	36.4%	38%
163	101	VILLANOVA UNIV.	252	132	52.4%	95	1.1%	36.8%	38%
164	69	CINCINNATI, UNIV. OF	120	64	53.3%	45	15.6%	22.2%	38%
165	38	NORTH CAROLINA, UNIV. OF	247	169	68.4%	106	2.8%	34.9%	38%
166	56	YESHIVA UNIV.	380	197	51.8%	142	2.8%	34.5%	37%
167	29	CALIFORNIA-DAVIS, UNIV. OF	195	110	56.4%	92	2.2%	33.7%	36%
168	35	WILLIAM AND MARY SCHOOL OF LAW	204	112	54.9%	51	2.0%	33.3%	35%
169	23	WASHINGTON UNIV.	317	188	59.3%	134	4.5%	26.9%	31%

Small World Ranking	US News Ranking	Table 4 School Name—Ranked from Highest to Lowest Percentage of Grads in Solo & Very Small Firms (last column)	Total # of Grads	Grads w/ FT, LT, Bar-Passage Required	Percent w/ FT, LT, Bar-Job	Total # of Grads at Law Firms	% of Grads in Solo Firms	% of Grads in Very Small Firms (size 2–10)	% of Grads in Solo & Very Small Firms (size 2–10)+
170	35	ILLINOIS, UNIV. OF	190	96	50.5%	68	1.5%	29.4%	31%
171	119	HOWARD UNIV.	157	75	47.8%	33	3.0%	27.3%	30%
172	15	CALIFORNIA-LOS ANGELES, UNIV. OF	344	211	61.3%	169	0.0%	29.6%	30%
173	49	AMERICAN UNIV.	467	167	35.8%	106	0.0%	29.2%	29%
174	16	TEXAS AT AUSTIN, UNIV. OF	382	267	69.9%	186	3.8%	23.7%	27%
175	18	SOUTHERN CALIFORNIA, UNIV. OF	207	134	64.7%	118	3.4%	23.7%	27%
176	RNP	EMORY UNIV.	225	155	68.9%	102	1.0%	25.5%	26%
177	26	BOSTON UNIV.	273	139	50.9%	92	0.0%	25.0%	25%
178	20	GEORGE WASHINGTON UNIV.	518	421	81.3%	211	1.4%	22.7%	24%
179	29	BOSTON COLLEGE	285	195	68.4%	125	0.0%	20.0%	20%
180	29	FORDHAM UNIV.	428	246	57.5%	182	0.0%	17.6%	18%
181	22	NOTRE DAME, UNIV. OF	190	118	62.1%	64	0.0%	17.2%	17%
182	16	VANDERBILT UNIV.	198	146	73.7%	90	1.1%	13.3%	14%
183	10	MICHIGAN, UNIV. OF	379	286	75.5%	169	0.0%	11.2%	11%
184	13	GEORGETOWN UNIV.	644	403	62.6%	276	0.7%	9.8%	11%
185	11	DUKE UNIV.	207	170	82.1%	122	0.0%	9.8%	10%
186	7	CALIFORNIA-BERKELEY, UNIV. OF	310	248	80.0%	154	0.0%	8.4%	8%

Small World Ranking	US News Ranking	Table 4 School Name—Ranked from Highest to Lowest Percentage of Grads in Solo & Very Small Firms (last column)	Total # of Grads	Grads w/ FT, LT, Bar-Passage Required	Percent w/ FT, LT, Bar-Job	Total # of Grads at Law Firms	% of Grads in Solo Firms	% of Grads in Very Small Firms (size 2–10)	% of Grads in Solo & Very Small Firms (size 2–10)+
187	7	VIRGINIA, UNIV. OF	377	357	94.7%	197	0.0%	7.6%	8%
188	6	NEW YORK UNIV.	466	420	90.1%	240	2.1%	5.0%	7%
189	14	CORNELL UNIV.	201	153	76.1%	99	0.0%	6.1%	6%
190	5	CHICAGO, UNIV. OF	203	179	88.2%	116	0.0%	6.0%	6%
191	12	NORTHWESTERN UNIV.	287	221	77.0%	186	1.1%	4.3%	5%
192	7	PENNSYLVANIA, UNIV. OF	274	231	84.3%	179	0.6%	3.4%	4%
193	3	HARVARD UNIV.	583	525	90.1%	317	0.3%	2.5%	3%
194	4	COLUMBIA UNIV.	456	429	94.1%	309	0.0%	2.6%	3%
195	2	STANFORD UNIV.	192	175	91.1%	101	0.0%	2.0%	2%
196	1	YALE UNIV.	205	180	87.8%	71	0.0%	0.0%	0%

Data Source: Employment Summary Report, http://employmentsummary.abaquestionnaire.org.
FT, LT = Full-time and Long-term; RNP = Ranking not published by US News; + I rounded up the percentages; I removed Puerto Rico from the table because its data seemed to be incorrect.

Table 5. Employment Data for 2012 Grads of Law Schools—Ranked in Alphabetical Order

Table 5 Schools in Alphabetical Order*	Total # of 2012 Graduates	2012 Grads Employed Bar Pass Req. FT, LT	% of 2012 Grads Employed Bar Pass Req. FT, LT	2012 Grads Employed JD-Advantage FT, LT	% of 2012 Grads Employed JD-Advantage FT, LT	2012 Grads—Unemployed Seeking Jobs	% of 2012 Grads—Unemployed Seeking Jobs	2012 Grads with Unknown Employment Status	% of 2012 Grads with Unknown Employment Status
AKRON, UNIVERSITY OF	139	65	46.8%	30	21.6%	7	5.0%	0	0.0%
ALABAMA, UNIVERSITY OF	172	133	77.3%	15	8.7%	1	0.6%	4	2.3%
ALBANY LAW SCHOOL	233	121	51.9%	22	9.4%	23	9.9%	6	2.6%
AMERICAN UNIVERSITY	463	180	38.9%	68	14.7%	71	15.3%	5	1.1%
APPALACHIAN SCHOOL OF LAW	91	35	38.5%	14	15.4%	17	18.7%	5	5.5%
ARIZONA STATE UNIVERSITY	212	136	64.2%	17	8.0%	0	0.0%	1	0.5%
ARIZONA, UNIVERSITY OF	149	99	66.4%	13	8.7%	16	10.7%	2	1.3%
ARKANSAS, FAYETTEVILLE, UNIV. OF	132	93	70.5%	20	15.2%	5	3.8%	1	0.8%
ARKANSAS, LITTLE ROCK, UNIV. OF	139	84	60.4%	11	7.9%	20	14.4%	0	0.0%
ATLANTA'S JOHN MARSHALL LAW SCHOOL	177	77	43.5%	26	14.7%	4	2.3%	0	0.0%
AVE MARIA	166	59	35.5%	21	12.7%	37	22.3%	12	7.2%
BALTIMORE, UNIVERSITY OF	347	185	53.3%	66	19.0%	39	11.2%	4	1.2%
BARRY UNIVERSITY	200	97	48.5%	8	4.0%	39	19.5%	15	7.5%
BAYLOR UNIVERSITY	164	112	68.3%	8	4.9%	15	9.1%	3	1.8%
BOSTON COLLEGE	260	170	65.4%	15	5.8%	29	11.2%	2	0.8%

Table 5 Schools in Alphabetical Order*	Total # of 2012 Graduates	2012 Grads Employed Bar Pass Req. FT, LT	% of 2012 Grads Employed Bar Pass Req. FT, LT	2012 Grads Employed JD-Advantage FT, LT	% of 2012 Grads Employed JD-Advantage FT, LT	2012 Grads—Unemployed Seeking Jobs	% of 2012 Grads—Unemployed Seeking Jobs	2012 Grads with Unknown Employment Status	% of 2012 Grads with Unknown Employment Status
BOSTON UNIVERSITY	273	175	64.1%	11	4.0%	12	4.4%	7	2.6%
BRIGHAM YOUNG UNIVERSITY	147	94	63.9%	21	14.3%	7	4.8%	0	0.0%
BROOKLYN LAW SCHOOL	466	227	48.7%	40	8.6%	100	21.5%	12	2.6%
CALIFORNIA WESTERN SCHOOL OF LAW	283	124	43.8%	16	5.7%	57	20.1%	20	7.1%
CALIFORNIA-BERKELEY, UNIV. OF	312	268	85.9%	9	2.9%	9	2.9%	1	0.3%
CALIFORNIA-DAVIS, UNIVERSITY OF	202	124	61.4%	12	5.9%	12	5.9%	4	2.0%
CALIFORNIA-HASTINGS, UNIV. OF	443	205	46.3%	24	5.4%	95	21.4%	8	1.8%
CALIFORNIA-IRVINE, UNIVERSITY OF	56	47	83.9%	1	1.8%	3	5.4%	0	0.0%
CALIFORNIA-LOS ANGELES, UNIV. OF	333	240	72.1%	17	5.1%	19	5.7%	1	0.3%
CAMPBELL UNIVERSITY	145	98	67.6%	15	10.3%	5	3.4%	2	1.4%
CAPITAL UNIVERSITY	197	95	48.2%	19	9.6%	21	10.7%	7	3.6%
CASE WESTERN RESERVE UNIVERSITY	172	81	47.1%	25	14.5%	21	12.2%	2	1.2%
CATHOLIC UNIVERSITY OF AMERICA	246	90	36.6%	64	26.0%	36	14.6%	3	1.2%
CHAPMAN UNIVERSITY	178	65	36.5%	20	11.2%	43	24.2%	0	0.0%
CHARLESTON SCHOOL OF LAW	229	123	53.7%	9	3.9%	41	17.9%	0	0.0%
CHARLOTTE SCHOOL OF LAW	234	90	38.5%	22	9.4%	20	8.5%	0	0.0%
CHICAGO, UNIVERSITY OF	215	204	94.9%	4	1.9%	1	0.5%	0	0.0%

Table 5 Schools in Alphabetical Order*	Total # of 2012 Graduates	2012 Grads Employed Bar Pass Req. FT, LT	% of 2012 Grads Employed Bar Pass Req. FT, LT	2012 Grads Employed JD-Advantage FT, LT	% of 2012 Grads Employed JD-Advantage FT, LT	2012 Grads— Unemployed Seeking Jobs	% of 2012 Grads— Unemployed Seeking Jobs	2012 Grads with Unknown Employment Status	% of 2012 Grads with Unknown Employment Status
CINCINNATI, UNIVERSITY OF	140	75	53.6%	15	10.7%	14	10.0%	0	0.0%
CITY UNIVERSITY OF NEW YORK	141	77	54.6%	7	5.0%	19	13.5%	1	0.7%
CLEVELAND STATE UNIVERSITY	176	86	48.9%	20	11.4%	19	10.8%	0	0.0%
COLORADO, UNIVERSITY OF	175	90	51.4%	21	12.0%	10	5.7%	2	1.1%
COLUMBIA UNIVERSITY	469	438	93.4%	17	3.6%	5	1.1%	2	0.4%
CONNECTICUT, UNIVERSITY OF	199	108	54.3%	32	16.1%	15	7.5%	5	2.5%
CORNELL UNIVERSITY	190	163	85.8%	0	0.0%	13	6.8%	0	0.0%
CREIGHTON UNIVERSITY	165	95	57.6%	18	10.9%	15	9.1%	4	2.4%
DAYTON, UNIVERSITY OF	174	89	51.1%	13	7.5%	22	12.6%	12	6.9%
DENVER, UNIVERSITY OF	317	156	49.2%	30	9.5%	23	7.3%	4	1.3%
DEPAUL UNIVERSITY	368	149	40.5%	42	11.4%	68	18.5%	19	5.2%
DETROIT MERCY, UNIVERSITY OF	212	63	29.7%	24	11.3%	34	16.0%	7	3.3%
DISTRICT OF COLUMBIA	93	24	25.8%	11	11.8%	20	21.5%	7	7.5%
DRAKE UNIVERSITY	139	78	56.1%	26	18.7%	8	5.8%	0	0.0%
DREXEL UNIVERSITY	155	75	48.4%	13	8.4%	22	14.2%	3	1.9%
DUKE UNIVERSITY	225	192	85.3%	4	1.8%	3	1.3%	1	0.4%
DUQUESNE UNIVERSITY	201	106	52.7%	26	12.9%	31	15.4%	3	1.5%

Table 5 Schools in Alphabetical Order*	Total # of 2012 Graduates	2012 Grads Employed Bar Pass Req. FT, LT	% of 2012 Grads Employed Bar Pass Req. FT, LT	2012 Grads Employed JD-Advantage FT, LT	% of 2012 Grads Employed JD-Advantage FT, LT	2012 Grads—Unemployed Seeking Jobs	% of 2012 Grads—Unemployed Seeking Jobs	2012 Grads with Unknown Employment Status	% of 2012 Grads with Unknown Employment Status
ELON UNIVERSITY	112	57	50.9%	7	6.3%	24	21.4%	2	1.8%
EMORY UNIVERSITY	266	195	73.3%	14	5.3%	4	1.5%	0	0.0%
FAULKNER UNIVERSITY	104	52	50.0%	14	13.5%	10	9.6%	2	1.9%
FLORIDA A&M	160	61	38.1%	22	13.8%	32	20.0%	9	5.6%
FLORIDA COASTAL	510	183	35.9%	27	5.3%	92	18.0%	0	0.0%
FLORIDA INTERNATIONAL	184	117	63.6%	23	12.5%	5	2.7%	3	1.6%
FLORIDA STATE UNIVERSITY	286	190	66.4%	31	10.8%	9	3.1%	3	1.0%
FLORIDA, UNIVERSITY OF	333	189	56.8%	21	6.3%	29	8.7%	6	1.8%
FORDHAM UNIVERSITY	486	305	62.8%	30	6.2%	39	8.0%	7	1.4%
GEORGE MASON UNIVERSITY	220	112	50.9%	48	21.8%	8	3.6%	1	0.5%
GEORGE WASHINGTON UNIVERSITY	575	466	81.0%	57	9.9%	22	3.8%	0	0.0%
GEORGETOWN UNIVERSITY	626	459	73.3%	69	11.0%	29	4.6%	2	0.3%
GEORGIA STATE UNIVERSITY	199	131	65.8%	21	10.6%	21	10.6%	0	0.0%
GEORGIA, UNIVERSITY OF	229	159	69.4%	14	6.1%	21	9.2%	4	1.7%
GOLDEN GATE UNIVERSITY	186	40	21.5%	11	5.9%	38	20.4%	6	3.2%
GONZAGA UNIVERSITY	166	84	50.6%	30	18.1%	20	12.0%	2	1.2%
HAMLINE UNIVERSITY	190	81	42.6%	57	30.0%	7	3.7%	4	2.1%

Table 5 Schools in Alphabetical Order*	Total # of 2012 Graduates	2012 Grads Employed Bar Pass Req. FT, LT	% of 2012 Grads Employed Bar Pass Req. FT, LT	2012 Grads Employed JD-Advantage FT, LT	% of 2012 Grads Employed JD-Advantage FT, LT	2012 Grads—Unemployed Seeking Jobs	% of 2012 Grads—Unemployed Seeking Jobs	2012 Grads with Unknown Employment Status	% of 2012 Grads with Unknown Employment Status
HARVARD UNIVERSITY	590	515	87.3%	40	6.8%	14	2.4%	0	0.0%
HAWAII, UNIVERSITY OF	106	56	52.8%	14	13.2%	10	9.4%	10	9.4%
HOFSTRA UNIVERSITY	363	186	51.2%	24	6.6%	61	16.8%	11	3.0%
HOUSTON, UNIVERSITY OF	262	165	63.0%	32	12.2%	30	11.5%	0	0.0%
HOWARD UNIVERSITY	151	72	47.7%	13	8.6%	13	8.6%	9	6.0%
IDAHO, UNIVERSITY OF	104	59	56.7%	8	7.7%	4	3.8%	0	0.0%
ILLINOIS INST. OF TECH., CHICAGO-KENT	282	168	59.6%	16	5.7%	25	8.9%	11	3.9%
ILLINOIS, UNIVERSITY OF	213	131	61.5%	13	6.1%	22	10.3%	4	1.9%
INDIANA UNIVERSITY-INDIANAPOLIS	295	151	51.2%	31	10.5%	27	9.2%	10	3.4%
INDIANA UNIVERSITY MAURER SCHOOL OF LAW	204	111	54.4%	21	10.3%	12	5.9%	1	0.5%
INTER AMERICAN UNIV. OF PUERTO RICO	234	5	2.1%	10	4.3%	42	17.9%	5	2.1%
IOWA, UNIVERSITY OF	185	132	71.4%	11	5.9%	2	1.1%	0	0.0%
JOHN MARSHALL LAW SCHOOL	414	175	42.3%	65	15.7%	69	16.7%	5	1.2%
KANSAS, UNIVERSITY OF	154	96	62.3%	20	13.0%	20	13.0%	1	0.6%
KENTUCKY, UNIVERSITY OF	147	109	74.1%	14	9.5%	2	1.4%	1	0.7%

Table 5 Schools in Alphabetical Order*	Total # of 2012 Graduates	2012 Grads Employed Bar Pass Req. FT, LT	% of 2012 Grads Employed Bar Pass Req. FT, LT	2012 Grads Employed JD-Advantage FT, LT	% of 2012 Grads Employed JD-Advantage FT, LT	2012 Grads—Unemployed Seeking Jobs	% of 2012 Grads—Unemployed Seeking Jobs	2012 Grads with Unknown Employment Status	% of 2012 Grads with Unknown E mployment Status
LEWIS AND CLARK COLLEGE	209	117	56.0%	17	8.1%	23	11.0%	2	1.0%
LIBERTY UNIVERSITY	90	47	52.2%	7	7.8%	18	20.0%	1	1.1%
LOUISIANA STATE UNIVERSITY	223	171	76.7%	16	7.2%	7	3.1%	2	0.9%
LOUISVILLE, UNIVERSITY OF	127	85	66.9%	16	12.6%	7	5.5%	3	2.4%
LOYOLA MARYMOUNT UNIV.-LOS ANGELES	411	170	41.4%	30	7.3%	82	20.0%	0	0.0%
LOYOLA UNIVERSITY-CHICAGO	271	148	54.6%	24	8.9%	28	10.3%	0	0.0%
LOYOLA UNIVERSITY-NEW ORLEANS	278	135	48.6%	13	4.7%	75	27.0%	18	6.5%
MAINE, UNIVERSITY OF	87	37	42.5%	5	5.7%	17	19.5%	0	0.0%
MARQUETTE UNIVERSITY	218	125	57.3%	23	10.6%	19	8.7%	7	3.2%
MARYLAND, UNIVERSITY OF	319	169	53.0%	50	15.7%	19	6.0%	1	0.3%
MCGEORGE SCHOOL OF LAW	306	127	41.5%	7	2.3%	56	18.3%	8	2.6%
MEMPHIS, UNIVERSITY OF	134	76	56.7%	14	10.4%	14	10.4%	4	3.0%
MERCER UNIVERSITY	142	104	73.2%	7	4.9%	11	7.7%	3	2.1%
MIAMI, UNIVERSITY OF	461	273	59.2%	44	9.5%	8	1.7%	13	2.8%
MICHIGAN STATE UNIVERSITY	291	120	41.2%	50	17.2%	28	9.6%	16	5.5%
MICHIGAN, UNIVERSITY OF	388	320	82.5%	16	4.1%	16	4.1%	4	1.0%

Table 5 Schools in Alphabetical Order*	Total # of 2012 Graduates	2012 Grads Employed Bar Pass Req. FT, LT	% of 2012 Grads Employed Bar Pass Req. FT, LT	2012 Grads Employed JD-Advantage FT, LT	% of 2012 Grads Employed JD-Advantage FT, LT	2012 Grads—Unemployed Seeking Jobs	% of 2012 Grads—Unemployed Seeking Jobs	2012 Grads with Unknown Employment Status	% of 2012 Grads with Unknown Employment Status
MINNESOTA, UNIVERSITY OF	230	155	67.4%	18	7.8%	5	2.2%	0	0.0%
MISSISSIPPI COLLEGE	164	99	60.4%	31	18.9%	19	11.6%	1	0.6%
MISSISSIPPI, UNIVERSITY OF	165	99	60.0%	10	6.1%	18	10.9%	5	3.0%
MISSOURI-COLUMBIA, UNIVERSITY OF	147	100	68.0%	16	10.9%	6	4.1%	4	2.7%
MISSOURI-KANSAS CITY, UNIV. OF	153	101	66.0%	14	9.2%	7	4.6%	0	0.0%
MONTANA, UNIVERSITY OF	82	50	61.0%	2	2.4%	9	11.0%	1	1.2%
NEBRASKA, UNIVERSITY OF	128	84	65.6%	21	16.4%	10	7.8%	1	0.8%
NEW ENGLAND LAW | BOSTON	339	123	36.3%	44	13.0%	63	18.6%	11	3.2%
NEW HAMPSHIRE UNIVERSITY OF	138	84	60.9%	10	7.2%	7	5.1%	0	0.0%
NEW MEXICO, UNIVERSITY OF	119	80	67.2%	3	2.5%	8	6.7%	0	0.0%
NEW YORK LAW SCHOOL	601	238	39.6%	94	15.6%	82	13.6%	17	2.8%
NEW YORK UNIVERSITY	482	439	91.1%	23	4.8%	4	0.8%	0	0.0%
NORTH CAROLINA CENTRAL UNIV.	165	43	26.1%	15	9.1%	17	10.3%	74	44.8%
NORTH CAROLINA, UNIVERSITY OF	256	177	69.1%	8	3.1%	28	10.9%	7	2.7%
NORTH DAKOTA, UNIVERSITY OF	90	61	67.8%	9	10.0%	6	6.7%	2	2.2%
NORTHEASTERN UNIVERSITY	215	93	43.3%	18	8.4%	28	13.0%	11	5.1%
NORTHERN ILLINOIS UNIVERSITY	91	57	62.6%	2	2.2%	6	6.6%	3	3.3%

Table 5 Schools in Alphabetical Order*	Total # of 2012 Graduates	2012 Grads Employed Bar Pass Req. FT, LT	% of 2012 Grads Employed Bar Pass Req. FT, LT	2012 Grads Employed JD-Advantage FT, LT	% of 2012 Grads Employed JD-Advantage FT, LT	2012 Grads—Unemployed Seeking Jobs	% of 2012 Grads—Unemployed Seeking Jobs	2012 Grads with Unknown Employment Status	% of 2012 Grads with Unknown Employment Status
NORTHERN KENTUCKY UNIVERSITY	162	71	43.8%	33	20.4%	19	11.7%	10	6.2%
NORTHWESTERN UNIVERSITY	295	225	76.3%	28	9.5%	12	4.1%	2	0.7%
NOTRE DAME, UNIVERSITY OF	196	131	66.8%	20	10.2%	28	14.3%	0	0.0%
NOVA SOUTHEASTERN UNIVERSITY	354	202	57.1%	30	8.5%	53	15.0%	0	0.0%
OHIO NORTHERN UNIVERSITY	96	57	59.4%	7	7.3%	12	12.5%	4	4.2%
OHIO STATE UNIVERSITY	222	132	59.5%	28	12.6%	4	1.8%	2	0.9%
OKLAHOMA CITY UNIVERSITY	207	112	54.1%	37	17.9%	25	12.1%	14	6.8%
OKLAHOMA, UNIVERSITY OF	188	126	67.0%	20	10.6%	12	6.4%	0	0.0%
OREGON, UNIVERSITY OF	161	67	41.6%	12	7.5%	35	21.7%	5	3.1%
PACE UNIVERSITY	230	111	48.3%	16	7.0%	29	12.6%	8	3.5%
PENNSYLVANIA STATE UNIVERSITY	194	114	58.8%	12	6.2%	17	8.8%	5	2.6%
PENNSYLVANIA, UNIVERSITY OF	270	255	94.4%	7	2.6%	5	1.9%	0	0.0%
PEPPERDINE UNIVERSITY	213	99	46.5%	25	11.7%	23	10.8%	3	1.4%
PHOENIX SCHOOL OF LAW	181	79	43.6%	30	16.6%	9	5.0%	1	0.6%
PITTSBURGH, UNIVERSITY OF	222	114	51.4%	29	13.1%	37	16.7%	8	3.6%
PONTIFICAL CATHOLIC UNIV. OF P.R.	217	23	10.6%	5	2.3%	77	35.5%	78	35.9%

Table 5 Schools in Alphabetical Order*	Total # of 2012 Graduates	2012 Grads Employed Bar Pass Req. FT, LT	% of 2012 Grads Employed Bar Pass Req. FT, LT	2012 Grads Employed JD-Advantage FT, LT	% of 2012 Grads Employed JD-Advantage FT, LT	2012 Grads—Unemployed Seeking Jobs	% of 2012 Grads—Unemployed Seeking Jobs	2012 Grads with Unknown Employment Status	% of 2012 Grads with Unknown Employment Status
PUERTO RICO, UNIVERSITY OF	202	28	13.9%	26	12.9%	48	23.8%	8	4.0%
QUINNIPIAC UNIVERSITY	151	62	41.1%	41	27.2%	16	10.6%	1	0.7%
REGENT UNIVERSITY	127	65	51.2%	10	7.9%	14	11.0%	19	15.0%
RICHMOND, UNIVERSITY OF	148	84	56.8%	30	20.3%	10	6.8%	5	3.4%
ROGER WILLIAMS UNIVERSITY	181	93	51.4%	9	5.0%	31	17.1%	10	5.5%
RUTGERS UNIVERSITY-CAMDEN	270	170	63.0%	14	5.2%	42	15.6%	3	1.1%
RUTGERS UNIVERSITY-NEWARK	243	132	54.3%	26	10.7%	22	9.1%	8	3.3%
SAMFORD UNIVERSITY	166	99	59.6%	14	8.4%	15	9.0%	0	0.0%
SAN DIEGO, UNIVERSITY OF	327	154	47.1%	15	4.6%	36	11.0%	3	0.9%
SAN FRANCISCO, UNIVERSITY OF	221	50	22.6%	22	10.0%	67	30.3%	8	3.6%
SANTA CLARA UNIVERSITY	298	128	43.0%	40	13.4%	24	8.1%	14	4.7%
SEATTLE UNIVERSITY	323	152	47.1%	45	13.9%	38	11.8%	7	2.2%
SETON HALL UNIVERSITY	310	204	65.8%	31	10.0%	30	9.7%	22	7.1%
SOUTH CAROLINA, UNIVERSITY OF	226	159	70.4%	13	5.8%	19	8.4%	7	3.1%
SOUTH DAKOTA, UNIVERSITY OF	76	48	63.2%	12	15.8%	5	6.6%	0	0.0%
SOUTH TEXAS COLLEGE OF LAW	377	269	71.4%	16	4.2%	27	7.2%	16	4.2%

Table 5 Schools in Alphabetical Order*	Total # of 2012 Graduates	2012 Grads Employed Bar Pass Req. FT, LT	% of 2012 Grads Employed Bar Pass Req. FT, LT	2012 Grads Employed JD-Advantage FT, LT	% of 2012 Grads Employed JD-Advantage FT, LT	2012 Grads—Unemployed Seeking Jobs	% of 2012 Grads—Unemployed Seeking Jobs	2012 Grads with Unknown Employment Status	% of 2012 Grads with Unknown Employment Status
SOUTHERN CALIFORNIA, UNIV. OF	221	154	69.7%	6	2.7%	19	8.6%	4	1.8%
SOUTHERN ILLINOIS UNIV.-CARBONDALE	128	67	52.3%	3	2.3%	16	12.5%	10	7.8%
SOUTHERN METHODIST UNIVERSITY	293	220	75.1%	15	5.1%	6	2.0%	0	0.0%
SOUTHERN UNIVERSITY	162	70	43.2%	31	19.1%	21	13.0%	0	0.0%
SOUTHWESTERN LAW SCHOOL	324	143	44.1%	40	12.3%	34	10.5%	33	10.2%
ST. JOHN'S UNIVERSITY	281	138	49.1%	32	11.4%	45	16.0%	7	2.5%
ST. LOUIS UNIVERSITY	276	168	60.9%	34	12.3%	14	5.1%	0	0.0%
ST. MARY'S UNIVERSITY	268	181	67.5%	22	8.2%	32	11.9%	0	0.0%
ST. THOMAS UNIVERSITY	216	87	40.3%	17	7.9%	46	21.3%	17	7.9%
STANFORD UNIVERSITY	181	165	91.2%	9	5.0%	3	1.7%	0	0.0%
STATE UNIVERSITY OF NEW YORK AT BUFFALO	209	109	52.2%	17	8.1%	21	10.0%	7	3.3%
STETSON UNIVERSITY	341	204	59.8%	31	9.1%	21	6.2%	2	0.6%
SUFFOLK UNIVERSITY	517	206	39.8%	60	11.6%	80	15.5%	28	5.4%
SYRACUSE UNIVERSITY	185	85	45.9%	18	9.7%	19	10.3%	12	6.5%
TEMPLE UNIVERSITY	277	147	53.1%	31	11.2%	26	9.4%	3	1.1%

Table 5 Schools in Alphabetical Order*	Total # of 2012 Graduates	2012 Grads Employed Bar Pass Req. FT, LT	% of 2012 Grads Employed Bar Pass Req. FT, LT	2012 Grads Employed JD-Advantage FT, LT	% of 2012 Grads Employed JD-Advantage FT, LT	2012 Grads— Unemployed Seeking Jobs	% of 2012 Grads— Unemployed Seeking Jobs	2012 Grads with Unknown Employment Status	% of 2012 Grads with Unknown Employment Status
TENNESSEE, UNIVERSITY OF	155	101	65.2%	11	7.1%	18	11.6%	3	1.9%
TEXAS AT AUSTIN, UNIVERSITY OF	373	283	75.9%	21	5.6%	13	3.5%	3	0.8%
TEXAS SOUTHERN UNIVERSITY	187	104	55.6%	12	6.4%	24	12.8%	17	9.1%
TEXAS TECH UNIVERSITY	215	133	61.9%	20	9.3%	25	11.6%	1	0.5%
TEXAS WESLEYAN UNIVERSITY	207	110	53.1%	22	10.6%	23	11.1%	18	8.7%
THOMAS JEFFERSON SCHOOL OF LAW	260	75	28.8%	19	7.3%	82	31.5%	18	6.9%
THOMAS M. COOLEY LAW SCHOOL	1079	311	28.8%	122	11.3%	215	19.9%	104	9.6%
TOLEDO, UNIVERSITY OF	147	76	51.7%	19	12.9%	14	9.5%	5	3.4%
TOURO COLLEGE	244	124	50.8%	19	7.8%	52	21.3%	6	2.5%
TULANE UNIVERSITY	269	169	62.8%	25	9.3%	15	5.6%	6	2.2%
TULSA, UNIVERSITY OF	134	88	65.7%	18	13.4%	2	1.5%	1	0.7%
UNIVERSITY OF LA VERNE	104	37	35.6%	2	1.9%	31	29.8%	0	0.0%
UNIVERSITY OF MASSACHUSETTS DARTMOUTH	44	13	29.5%	6	13.6%	6	13.6%	0	0.0%
UNIVERSITY OF NEVADA-LAS VEGAS	161	98	60.9%	4	2.5%	21	13.0%	2	1.2%
UNIVERSITY OF ST. THOMAS	161	71	44.1%	25	15.5%	14	8.7%	0	0.0%

Table 5 Schools in Alphabetical Order*	Total # of 2012 Graduates	2012 Grads Employed Bar Pass Req. FT, LT	% of 2012 Grads Employed Bar Pass Req. FT, LT	2012 Grads Employed JD-Advantage FT, LT	% of 2012 Grads Employed JD-Advantage FT, LT	2012 Grads—Unemployed Seeking Jobs	% of 2012 Grads—Unemployed Seeking Jobs	2012 Grads with Unknown Employment Status	% of 2012 Grads with Unknown Employment Status
UTAH, UNIVERSITY OF	134	86	64.2%	10	7.5%	8	6.0%	3	2.2%
VALPARAISO UNIVERSITY	172	73	42.4%	21	12.2%	37	21.5%	4	2.3%
VANDERBILT UNIVERSITY	196	140	71.4%	6	3.1%	5	2.6%	3	1.5%
VERMONT LAW SCHOOL	206	93	45.1%	27	13.1%	25	12.1%	3	1.5%
VILLANOVA UNIVERSITY	256	131	51.2%	21	8.2%	58	22.7%	4	1.6%
VIRGINIA, UNIVERSITY OF	364	344	94.5%	10	2.7%	1	0.3%	2	0.5%
WAKE FOREST UNIVERSITY	156	106	67.9%	14	9.0%	15	9.6%	0	0.0%
WASHBURN UNIVERSITY	156	99	63.5%	18	11.5%	12	7.7%	4	2.6%
WASHINGTON AND LEE UNIVERSITY	130	64	49.2%	11	8.5%	25	19.2%	2	1.5%
WASHINGTON UNIVERSITY	300	205	68.3%	20	6.7%	5	1.7%	1	0.3%
WASHINGTON, UNIVERSITY OF	181	123	68.0%	20	11.0%	10	5.5%	0	0.0%
WAYNE STATE UNIVERSITY	168	92	54.8%	17	10.1%	18	10.7%	2	1.2%
WEST VIRGINIA UNIVERSITY	142	109	76.8%	6	4.2%	8	5.6%	3	2.1%
WESTERN NEW ENGLAND UNIVERSITY	160	54	33.8%	28	17.5%	26	16.3%	5	3.1%
WESTERN STATE	83	27	32.5%	6	7.2%	23	27.7%	7	8.4%
WHITTIER COLLEGE	170	58	34.1%	19	11.2%	40	23.5%	6	3.5%

Table 5 Schools in Alphabetical Order*	Total # of 2012 Graduates	2012 Grads Employed Bar Pass Req. FT, LT	% of 2012 Grads Employed Bar Pass Req. FT, LT	2012 Grads Employed JD-Advantage FT, LT	% of 2012 Grads Employed JD-Advantage FT, LT	2012 Grads—Unemployed Seeking Jobs	% of 2012 Grads—Unemployed Seeking Jobs	2012 Grads with Unknown Employment Status	% of 2012 Grads with Unknown Employment Status
WIDENER UNIVERSITY	269	104	38.7%	30	11.2%	23	8.6%	16	5.9%
WIDENER UNIVERSITY-HARRISBURG	122	57	46.7%	7	5.7%	7	5.7%	14	11.5%
WILLAMETTE UNIVERSITY	125	65	52.0%	25	20.0%	5	4.0%	0	0.0%
WILLIAM AND MARY SCHOOL OF LAW	204	150	73.5%	24	11.8%	8	3.9%	0	0.0%
WILLIAM MITCHELL COLLEGE OF LAW	303	156	51.5%	49	16.2%	32	10.6%	3	1.0%
WISCONSIN, UNIVERSITY OF	284	178	62.7%	32	11.3%	18	6.3%	2	0.7%
WYOMING, UNIVERSITY OF	75	43	57.3%	6	8.0%	10	13.3%	3	4.0%
YALE UNIVERSITY	222	182	82.0%	20	9.0%	0	0.0%	2	0.9%
YESHIVA UNIVERSITY	387	209	54.0%	25	6.5%	37	9.6%	2	0.5%

Data Source: http://employmentsummary.abaquestionnaire.org.
FT, LT = Full-time and Long-term; * Belmont, Concordia and Lincoln Memorial Law Schools have been deleted from this table as the ABA had no statistics on these schools.

Table 6. Employment Data for 2012 Grads—Ranked in Order of School with Highest # of Grads Employed in FT/LT Bar-Pass-Req. Jobs

Table 6 Schools Ranked in Order of Percent of Grads Employed in FT/LT Bar-Pass-Req. Jobs* (column in bold)	Total # of 2012 Graduates	2012 Grads Employed Bar Pass Req. FT/LT	% of 2012 Grads Employed Bar Pass Req. FT/LT	2012 Grads Employed JD Advantage FT/LT	% of 2012 Grads Employed JD Advantage FT/LT	2012 Grads—Unemployed Seeking Jobs	% of 2012 Grads—Unemployed Seeking Jobs	2012 Grads with Unknown Employment Status	% of 2012 Grads with Unknown Employment Status
CHICAGO, UNIVERSITY OF	215	204	**94.9%**	4	1.9%	1	0.5%	0	0.0%
VIRGINIA, UNIVERSITY OF	364	344	**94.5%**	10	2.7%	1	0.3%	2	0.5%
PENNSYLVANIA, UNIVERSITY OF	270	255	**94.4%**	7	2.6%	5	1.9%	0	0.0%
COLUMBIA UNIVERSITY	469	438	**93.4%**	17	3.6%	5	1.1%	2	0.4%
STANFORD UNIVERSITY	181	165	**91.2%**	9	5.0%	3	1.7%	0	0.0%
NEW YORK UNIVERSITY	482	439	**91.1%**	23	4.8%	4	0.8%	0	0.0%
HARVARD UNIVERSITY	590	515	**87.3%**	40	6.8%	14	2.4%	0	0.0%
CALIFORNIA-BERKELEY, UNIV. OF	312	268	**85.9%**	9	2.9%	9	2.9%	1	0.3%
CORNELL UNIVERSITY	190	163	**85.8%**	0	0.0%	13	6.8%	0	0.0%
DUKE UNIVERSITY	225	192	**85.3%**	4	1.8%	3	1.3%	1	0.4%
CALIFORNIA-IRVINE, UNIVERSITY OF	56	47	**83.9%**	1	1.8%	3	5.4%	0	0.0%
MICHIGAN, UNIVERSITY OF	388	320	**82.5%**	16	4.1%	16	4.1%	4	1.0%
YALE UNIVERSITY	222	182	**82.0%**	20	9.0%	0	0.0%	2	0.9%
GEORGE WASHINGTON UNIVERSITY	575	466	**81.0%**	57	9.9%	22	3.8%	0	0.0%
ALABAMA, UNIVERSITY OF	172	133	**77.3%**	15	8.7%	1	0.6%	4	2.3%

Table 6 Schools Ranked in Order of Percent of Grads Employed in FT/LT Bar-Pass-Req. Jobs* (column in bold)	Total # of 2012 Graduates	2012 Grads Employed Bar Pass Req. FT/LT	% of 2012 Grads Employed Bar Pass Req. FT/LT	2012 Grads Employed JD Advantage FT/LT	% of 2012 Grads Employed JD Advantage FT/LT	2012 Grads—Unemployed Seeking Jobs	% of 2012 Grads—Unemployed Seeking Jobs	2012 Grads with Unknown Employment Status	% of 2012 Grads with Unknown Employment Status
WEST VIRGINIA UNIVERSITY	142	109	**76.8%**	6	4.2%	8	5.6%	3	2.1%
LOUISIANA STATE UNIVERSITY	223	171	**76.7%**	16	7.2%	7	3.1%	2	0.9%
NORTHWESTERN UNIVERSITY	295	225	**76.3%**	28	9.5%	12	4.1%	2	0.7%
TEXAS AT AUSTIN, UNIVERSITY OF	373	283	**75.9%**	21	5.6%	13	3.5%	3	0.8%
SOUTHERN METHODIST UNIVERSITY	293	220	**75.1%**	15	5.1%	6	2.0%	0	0.0%
KENTUCKY, UNIVERSITY OF	147	109	**74.1%**	14	9.5%	2	1.4%	1	0.7%
WILLIAM AND MARY SCHOOL OF LAW	204	150	**73.5%**	24	11.8%	8	3.9%	0	0.0%
GEORGETOWN UNIVERSITY	626	459	**73.3%**	69	11.0%	29	4.6%	2	0.3%
EMORY UNIVERSITY	266	195	**73.3%**	14	5.3%	4	1.5%	0	0.0%
MERCER UNIVERSITY	142	104	**73.2%**	7	4.9%	11	7.7%	3	2.1%
CALIFORNIA-LOS ANGELES, UNIV. OF	333	240	**72.1%**	17	5.1%	19	5.7%	1	0.3%
VANDERBILT UNIVERSITY	196	140	**71.4%**	6	3.1%	5	2.6%	3	1.5%
SOUTH TEXAS COLLEGE OF LAW	377	269	**71.4%**	16	4.2%	27	7.2%	16	4.2%
IOWA, UNIVERSITY OF	185	132	**71.4%**	11	5.9%	2	1.1%	0	0.0%
ARKANSAS, FAYETTEVILLE, UNIV. OF	132	93	**70.5%**	20	15.2%	5	3.8%	1	0.8%
SOUTH CAROLINA, UNIVERSITY OF	226	159	**70.4%**	13	5.8%	19	8.4%	7	3.1%

Table 6 Schools Ranked in Order of Percent of Grads Employed in FT/LT Bar-Pass-Req. Jobs* (column in bold)	Total # of 2012 Graduates	2012 Grads Employed Bar Pass Req. FT/LT	% of 2012 Grads Employed Bar Pass Req. FT/LT	2012 Grads Employed JD Advantage FT/LT	% of 2012 Grads Employed JD Advantage FT/LT	2012 Grads—Unemployed Seeking Jobs	% of 2012 Grads—Unemployed Seeking Jobs	2012 Grads with Unknown Employment Status	% of 2012 Grads with Unknown Employment Status
SOUTHERN CALIFORNIA, UNIV. OF	221	154	**69.7%**	6	2.7%	19	8.6%	4	1.8%
GEORGIA, UNIVERSITY OF	229	159	**69.4%**	14	6.1%	21	9.2%	4	1.7%
NORTH CAROLINA, UNIVERSITY OF	256	177	**69.1%**	8	3.1%	28	10.9%	7	2.7%
WASHINGTON UNIVERSITY	300	205	**68.3%**	20	6.7%	5	1.7%	1	0.3%
BAYLOR UNIVERSITY	164	112	**68.3%**	8	4.9%	15	9.1%	3	1.8%
MISSOURI-COLUMBIA, UNIVERSITY OF	147	100	**68.0%**	16	10.9%	6	4.1%	4	2.7%
WASHINGTON, UNIVERSITY OF	181	123	**68.0%**	20	11.0%	10	5.5%	0	0.0%
WAKE FOREST UNIVERSITY	156	106	**67.9%**	14	9.0%	15	9.6%	0	0.0%
NORTH DAKOTA, UNIVERSITY OF	90	61	**67.8%**	9	10.0%	6	6.7%	2	2.2%
CAMPBELL UNIVERSITY	145	98	**67.6%**	15	10.3%	5	3.4%	2	1.4%
ST. MARY'S UNIVERSITY	268	181	**67.5%**	22	8.2%	32	11.9%	0	0.0%
MINNESOTA, UNIVERSITY OF	230	155	**67.4%**	18	7.8%	5	2.2%	0	0.0%
NEW MEXICO, UNIVERSITY OF	119	80	**67.2%**	3	2.5%	8	6.7%	0	0.0%
OKLAHOMA, UNIVERSITY OF	188	126	**67.0%**	20	10.6%	12	6.4%	0	0.0%
LOUISVILLE, UNIVERSITY OF	127	85	**66.9%**	16	12.6%	7	5.5%	3	2.4%
NOTRE DAME, UNIVERSITY OF	196	131	**66.8%**	20	10.2%	28	14.3%	0	0.0%

Table 6 Schools Ranked in Order of Percent of Grads Employed in FT/LT Bar-Pass-Req. Jobs* (column in bold)	Total # of 2012 Graduates	2012 Grads Employed Bar Pass Req. FT/LT	% of 2012 Grads Employed Bar Pass Req. FT/LT	2012 Grads Employed JD Advantage FT/LT	% of 2012 Grads Employed JD Advantage FT/LT	2012 Grads—Unemployed Seeking Jobs	% of 2012 Grads—Unemployed Seeking Jobs	2012 Grads with Unknown Employment Status	% of 2012 Grads with Unknown Employment Status
ARIZONA, UNIVERSITY OF	149	99	**66.4%**	13	8.7%	16	10.7%	2	1.3%
FLORIDA STATE UNIVERSITY	286	190	**66.4%**	31	10.8%	9	3.1%	3	1.0%
MISSOURI-KANSAS CITY, UNIV. OF	153	101	**66.0%**	14	9.2%	7	4.6%	0	0.0%
GEORGIA STATE UNIVERSITY	199	131	**65.8%**	21	10.6%	21	10.6%	0	0.0%
SETON HALL UNIVERSITY	310	204	**65.8%**	31	10.0%	30	9.7%	22	7.1%
TULSA, UNIVERSITY OF	134	88	**65.7%**	18	13.4%	2	1.5%	1	0.7%
NEBRASKA, UNIVERSITY OF	128	84	**65.6%**	21	16.4%	10	7.8%	1	0.8%
BOSTON COLLEGE	260	170	**65.4%**	15	5.8%	29	11.2%	2	0.8%
TENNESSEE, UNIVERSITY OF	155	101	**65.2%**	11	7.1%	18	11.6%	3	1.9%
UTAH, UNIVERSITY OF	134	86	**64.2%**	10	7.5%	8	6.0%	3	2.2%
ARIZONA STATE UNIVERSITY	212	136	**64.2%**	17	8.0%	0	0.0%	1	0.5%
BOSTON UNIVERSITY	273	175	**64.1%**	11	4.0%	12	4.4%	7	2.6%
BRIGHAM YOUNG UNIVERSITY	147	94	**63.9%**	21	14.3%	7	4.8%	0	0.0%
FLORIDA INTERNATIONAL	184	117	**63.6%**	23	12.5%	5	2.7%	3	1.6%
WASHBURN UNIVERSITY	156	99	**63.5%**	18	11.5%	12	7.7%	4	2.6%
SOUTH DAKOTA, UNIVERSITY OF	76	48	**63.2%**	12	15.8%	5	6.6%	0	0.0%

Table 6 Schools Ranked in Order of Percent of Grads Employed in FT/LT Bar-Pass-Req. Jobs* (column in bold)	Total # of 2012 Graduates	2012 Grads Employed Bar Pass Req. FT/LT	**% of 2012 Grads Employed Bar Pass Req. FT/LT**	2012 Grads Employed JD Advantage FT/LT	% of 2012 Grads Employed JD Advantage FT/LT	2012 Grads—Unemployed Seeking Jobs	% of 2012 Grads—Unemployed Seeking Jobs	2012 Grads with Unknown Employment Status	% of 2012 Grads with Unknown Employment Status
HOUSTON, UNIVERSITY OF	262	165	**63.0%**	32	12.2%	30	11.5%	0	0.0%
RUTGERS UNIVERSITY-CAMDEN	270	170	**63.0%**	14	5.2%	42	15.6%	3	1.1%
TULANE UNIVERSITY	269	169	**62.8%**	25	9.3%	15	5.6%	6	2.2%
FORDHAM UNIVERSITY	486	305	**62.8%**	30	6.2%	39	8.0%	7	1.4%
WISCONSIN, UNIVERSITY OF	284	178	**62.7%**	32	11.3%	18	6.3%	2	0.7%
NORTHERN ILLINOIS UNIVERSITY	91	57	**62.6%**	2	2.2%	6	6.6%	3	3.3%
KANSAS, UNIVERSITY OF	154	96	**62.3%**	20	13.0%	20	13.0%	1	0.6%
TEXAS TECH UNIVERSITY	215	133	**61.9%**	20	9.3%	25	11.6%	1	0.5%
ILLINOIS, UNIVERSITY OF	213	131	**61.5%**	13	6.1%	22	10.3%	4	1.9%
CALIFORNIA-DAVIS, UNIVERSITY OF	202	124	**61.4%**	12	5.9%	12	5.9%	4	2.0%
MONTANA, UNIVERSITY OF	82	50	**61.0%**	2	2.4%	9	11.0%	1	1.2%
NEW HAMPSHIRE UNIVERSITY OF	138	84	**60.9%**	10	7.2%	7	5.1%	0	0.0%
ST. LOUIS UNIVERSITY	276	168	**60.9%**	34	12.3%	14	5.1%	0	0.0%
UNIVERSITY OF NEVADA-LAS VEGAS	161	98	**60.9%**	4	2.5%	21	13.0%	2	1.2%
ARKANSAS, LITTLE ROCK, UNIV. OF	139	84	**60.4%**	11	7.9%	20	14.4%	0	0.0%
MISSISSIPPI COLLEGE	164	99	**60.4%**	31	18.9%	19	11.6%	1	0.6%

Table 6 Schools Ranked in Order of Percent of Grads Employed in FT/LT Bar-Pass-Req. Jobs* (column in bold)	Total # of 2012 Graduates	2012 Grads Employed Bar Pass Req. FT/LT	% of 2012 Grads Employed Bar Pass Req. FT/LT	2012 Grads Employed JD Advantage FT/LT	% of 2012 Grads Employed JD Advantage FT/LT	2012 Grads—Unemployed Seeking Jobs	% of 2012 Grads—Unemployed Seeking Jobs	2012 Grads with Unknown Employment Status	% of 2012 Grads with Unknown Employment Status
MISSISSIPPI, UNIVERSITY OF	165	99	**60.0%**	10	6.1%	18	10.9%	5	3.0%
STETSON UNIVERSITY	341	204	**59.8%**	31	9.1%	21	6.2%	2	0.6%
SAMFORD UNIVERSITY	166	99	**59.6%**	14	8.4%	15	9.0%	0	0.0%
ILLINOIS INST. OF TECH., CHICAGO-KENT	282	168	**59.6%**	16	5.7%	25	8.9%	11	3.9%
OHIO STATE UNIVERSITY	222	132	**59.5%**	28	12.6%	4	1.8%	2	0.9%
OHIO NORTHERN UNIVERSITY	96	57	**59.4%**	7	7.3%	12	12.5%	4	4.2%
MIAMI, UNIVERSITY OF	461	273	**59.2%**	44	9.5%	8	1.7%	13	2.8%
PENNSYLVANIA STATE UNIVERSITY	194	114	**58.8%**	12	6.2%	17	8.8%	5	2.6%
CREIGHTON UNIVERSITY	165	95	**57.6%**	18	10.9%	15	9.1%	4	2.4%
MARQUETTE UNIVERSITY	218	125	**57.3%**	23	10.6%	19	8.7%	7	3.2%
WYOMING, UNIVERSITY OF	75	43	**57.3%**	6	8.0%	10	13.3%	3	4.0%
NOVA SOUTHEASTERN UNIVERSITY	354	202	**57.1%**	30	8.5%	53	15.0%	0	0.0%
FLORIDA, UNIVERSITY OF	333	189	**56.8%**	21	6.3%	29	8.7%	6	1.8%
RICHMOND, UNIVERSITY OF	148	84	**56.8%**	30	20.3%	10	6.8%	5	3.4%
IDAHO, UNIVERSITY OF	104	59	**56.7%**	8	7.7%	4	3.8%	0	0.0%
MEMPHIS, UNIVERSITY OF	134	76	**56.7%**	14	10.4%	14	10.4%	4	3.0%

Table 6 Schools Ranked in Order of Percent of Grads Employed in FT/LT Bar-Pass-Req. Jobs* (column in bold)	Total # of 2012 Graduates	2012 Grads Employed Bar Pass Req. FT/LT	% of 2012 Grads Employed Bar Pass Req. FT/LT	2012 Grads Employed JD Advantage FT/LT	% of 2012 Grads Employed JD Advantage FT/LT	2012 Grads—Unemployed Seeking Jobs	% of 2012 Grads—Unemployed Seeking Jobs	2012 Grads with Unknown Employment Status	% of 2012 Grads with Unknown Employment Status
DRAKE UNIVERSITY	139	78	**56.1%**	26	18.7%	8	5.8%	0	0.0%
LEWIS AND CLARK COLLEGE	209	117	**56.0%**	17	8.1%	23	11.0%	2	1.0%
TEXAS SOUTHERN UNIVERSITY	187	104	**55.6%**	12	6.4%	24	12.8%	17	9.1%
WAYNE STATE UNIVERSITY	168	92	**54.8%**	17	10.1%	18	10.7%	2	1.2%
LOYOLA UNIVERSITY-CHICAGO	271	148	**54.6%**	24	8.9%	28	10.3%	0	0.0%
CITY UNIVERSITY OF NEW YORK	141	77	**54.6%**	7	5.0%	19	13.5%	1	0.7%
INDIANA UNIV. MAURER SCHOOL OF LAW	204	111	**54.4%**	21	10.3%	12	5.9%	1	0.5%
RUTGERS UNIVERSITY-NEWARK	243	132	**54.3%**	26	10.7%	22	9.1%	8	3.3%
CONNECTICUT, UNIVERSITY OF	199	108	**54.3%**	32	16.1%	15	7.5%	5	2.5%
OKLAHOMA CITY UNIVERSITY	207	112	**54.1%**	37	17.9%	25	12.1%	14	6.8%
YESHIVA UNIVERSITY	387	209	**54.0%**	25	6.5%	37	9.6%	2	0.5%
CHARLESTON SCHOOL OF LAW	229	123	**53.7%**	9	3.9%	41	17.9%	0	0.0%
CINCINNATI, UNIVERSITY OF	140	75	**53.6%**	15	10.7%	14	10.0%	0	0.0%
BALTIMORE, UNIVERSITY OF	347	185	**53.3%**	66	19.0%	39	11.2%	4	1.2%
TEXAS WESLEYAN UNIVERSITY	207	110	**53.1%**	22	10.6%	23	11.1%	18	8.7%

Table 6 Schools Ranked in Order of Percent of Grads Employed in FT/LT Bar-Pass-Req. Jobs* (column in bold)	Total # of 2012 Graduates	2012 Grads Employed Bar Pass Req. FT/LT	% of 2012 Grads Employed Bar Pass Req. FT/LT	2012 Grads Employed JD Advantage FT/LT	% of 2012 Grads Employed JD Advantage FT/LT	2012 Grads—Unemployed Seeking Jobs	% of 2012 Grads—Unemployed Seeking Jobs	2012 Grads with Unknown Employment Status	% of 2012 Grads with Unknown Employment Status
TEMPLE UNIVERSITY	277	147	**53.1%**	31	11.2%	26	9.4%	3	1.1%
MARYLAND, UNIVERSITY OF	319	169	**53.0%**	50	15.7%	19	6.0%	1	0.3%
HAWAII, UNIVERSITY OF	106	56	**52.8%**	14	13.2%	10	9.4%	10	9.4%
DUQUESNE UNIVERSITY	201	106	**52.7%**	26	12.9%	31	15.4%	3	1.5%
SOUTHERN ILLINOIS UNIV.-CARBONDALE	128	67	**52.3%**	3	2.3%	16	12.5%	10	7.8%
LIBERTY UNIVERSITY	90	47	**52.2%**	7	7.8%	18	20.0%	1	1.1%
STATE UNIV. OF NEW YORK AT BUFFALO	209	109	**52.2%**	17	8.1%	21	10.0%	7	3.3%
WILLAMETTE UNIVERSITY	125	65	**52.0%**	25	20.0%	5	4.0%	0	0.0%
ALBANY LAW SCHOOL	233	121	**51.9%**	22	9.4%	23	9.9%	6	2.6%
TOLEDO, UNIVERSITY OF	147	76	**51.7%**	19	12.9%	14	9.5%	5	3.4%
WILLAMETTE UNIVERSITY	125	65	**52.0%**	25	20.0%	5	4.0%	0	0.0%
ALBANY LAW SCHOOL	233	121	**51.9%**	22	9.4%	23	9.9%	6	2.6%
TOLEDO, UNIVERSITY OF	147	76	**51.7%**	19	12.9%	14	9.5%	5	3.4%
WILLIAM MITCHELL COLLEGE OF LAW	303	156	**51.5%**	49	16.2%	32	10.6%	3	1.0%
COLORADO, UNIVERSITY OF	175	90	**51.4%**	21	12.0%	10	5.7%	2	1.1%

Table 6 Schools Ranked in Order of Percent of Grads Employed in FT/LT Bar-Pass-Req. Jobs* (column in bold)	Total # of 2012 Graduates	2012 Grads Employed Bar Pass Req. FT/LT	% of 2012 Grads Employed Bar Pass Req. FT/LT	2012 Grads Employed JD Advantage FT/LT	% of 2012 Grads Employed JD Advantage FT/LT	2012 Grads—Unemployed Seeking Jobs	% of 2012 Grads—Unemployed Seeking Jobs	2012 Grads with Unknown Employment Status	% of 2012 Grads with Unknown Employment Status
ROGER WILLIAMS UNIVERSITY	181	93	**51.4%**	9	5.0%	31	17.1%	10	5.5%
PITTSBURGH, UNIVERSITY OF	222	114	**51.4%**	29	13.1%	37	16.7%	8	3.6%
HOFSTRA UNIVERSITY	363	186	**51.2%**	24	6.6%	61	16.8%	11	3.0%
INDIANA UNIVERSITY-INDIANAPOLIS	295	151	**51.2%**	31	10.5%	27	9.2%	10	3.4%
REGENT UNIVERSITY	127	65	**51.2%**	10	7.9%	14	11.0%	19	15.0%
VILLANOVA UNIVERSITY	256	131	**51.2%**	21	8.2%	58	22.7%	4	1.6%
DAYTON, UNIVERSITY OF	174	89	**51.1%**	13	7.5%	22	12.6%	12	6.9%
GEORGE MASON UNIVERSITY	220	112	**50.9%**	48	21.8%	8	3.6%	1	0.5%
ELON UNIVERSITY	112	57	**50.9%**	7	6.3%	24	21.4%	2	1.8%
TOURO COLLEGE	244	124	**50.8%**	19	7.8%	52	21.3%	6	2.5%
GONZAGA UNIVERSITY	166	84	**50.6%**	30	18.1%	20	12.0%	2	1.2%
FAULKNER UNIVERSITY	104	52	**50.0%**	14	13.5%	10	9.6%	2	1.9%
WASHINGTON AND LEE UNIVERSITY	130	64	**49.2%**	11	8.5%	25	19.2%	2	1.5%
DENVER, UNIVERSITY OF	317	156	**49.2%**	30	9.5%	23	7.3%	4	1.3%
ST. JOHN'S UNIVERSITY	281	138	**49.1%**	32	11.4%	45	16.0%	7	2.5%
CLEVELAND STATE UNIVERSITY	176	86	**48.9%**	20	11.4%	19	10.8%	0	0.0%

Table 6 Schools Ranked in Order of Percent of Grads Employed in FT/LT Bar-Pass-Req. Jobs* (column in bold)	Total # of 2012 Graduates	2012 Grads Employed Bar Pass Req. FT/LT	% of 2012 Grads Employed Bar Pass Req. FT/LT	2012 Grads Employed JD Advantage FT/LT	% of 2012 Grads Employed JD Advantage FT/LT	2012 Grads—Unemployed Seeking Jobs	% of 2012 Grads—Unemployed Seeking Jobs	2012 Grads with Unknown Employment Status	% of 2012 Grads with Unknown Employment Status
BROOKLYN LAW SCHOOL	466	227	**48.7%**	40	8.6%	100	21.5%	12	2.6%
LOYOLA UNIVERSITY-NEW ORLEANS	278	135	**48.6%**	13	4.7%	75	27.0%	18	6.5%
BARRY UNIVERSITY	200	97	**48.5%**	8	4.0%	39	19.5%	15	7.5%
DREXEL UNIVERSITY	155	75	**48.4%**	13	8.4%	22	14.2%	3	1.9%
PACE UNIVERSITY	230	111	**48.3%**	16	7.0%	29	12.6%	8	3.5%
CAPITAL UNIVERSITY	197	95	**48.2%**	19	9.6%	21	10.7%	7	3.6%
HOWARD UNIVERSITY	151	72	**47.7%**	13	8.6%	13	8.6%	9	6.0%
SAN DIEGO, UNIVERSITY OF	327	154	**47.1%**	15	4.6%	36	11.0%	3	0.9%
CASE WESTERN RESERVE UNIVERSITY	172	81	**47.1%**	25	14.5%	21	12.2%	2	1.2%
SEATTLE UNIVERSITY	323	152	**47.1%**	45	13.9%	38	11.8%	7	2.2%
AKRON, UNIVERSITY OF	139	65	**46.8%**	30	21.6%	7	5.0%	0	0.0%
WIDENER UNIVERSITY-HARRISBURG	122	57	**46.7%**	7	5.7%	7	5.7%	14	11.5%
PEPPERDINE UNIVERSITY	213	99	**46.5%**	25	11.7%	23	10.8%	3	1.4%
CALIFORNIA-HASTINGS, UNIV. OF	443	205	**46.3%**	24	5.4%	95	21.4%	8	1.8%
SYRACUSE UNIVERSITY	185	85	**45.9%**	18	9.7%	19	10.3%	12	6.5%
VERMONT LAW SCHOOL	206	93	**45.1%**	27	13.1%	25	12.1%	3	1.5%
SOUTHWESTERN LAW SCHOOL	324	143	**44.1%**	40	12.3%	34	10.5%	33	10.2%

Table 6 Schools Ranked in Order of Percent of Grads Employed in FT/LT Bar-Pass-Req. Jobs* (column in bold)	Total # of 2012 Graduates	2012 Grads Employed Bar Pass Req. FT/LT	% of 2012 Grads Employed Bar Pass Req. FT/LT	2012 Grads Employed JD Advantage FT/LT	% of 2012 Grads Employed JD Advantage FT/LT	2012 Grads—Unemployed Seeking Jobs	% of 2012 Grads—Unemployed Seeking Jobs	2012 Grads with Unknown Employment Status	% of 2012 Grads with Unknown Employment Status
UNIVERSITY OF ST. THOMAS	161	71	**44.1%**	25	15.5%	14	8.7%	0	0.0%
NORTHERN KENTUCKY UNIVERSITY	162	71	**43.8%**	33	20.4%	19	11.7%	10	6.2%
CALIFORNIA WESTERN SCHOOL OF LAW	283	124	**43.8%**	16	5.7%	57	20.1%	20	7.1%
PHOENIX SCHOOL OF LAW	181	79	**43.6%**	30	16.6%	9	5.0%	1	0.6%
ATLANTA'S JOHN MARSHALL LAW SCHOOL	177	77	**43.5%**	26	14.7%	4	2.3%	0	0.0%
NORTHEASTERN UNIVERSITY	215	93	**43.3%**	18	8.4%	28	13.0%	11	5.1%
SOUTHERN UNIVERSITY	162	70	**43.2%**	31	19.1%	21	13.0%	0	0.0%
SANTA CLARA UNIVERSITY	298	128	**43.0%**	40	13.4%	24	8.1%	14	4.7%
HAMLINE UNIVERSITY	190	81	**42.6%**	57	30.0%	7	3.7%	4	2.1%
MAINE, UNIVERSITY OF	87	37	**42.5%**	5	5.7%	17	19.5%	0	0.0%
VALPARAISO UNIVERSITY	172	73	**42.4%**	21	12.2%	37	21.5%	4	2.3%
JOHN MARSHALL LAW SCHOOL	414	175	**42.3%**	65	15.7%	69	16.7%	5	1.2%
OREGON, UNIVERSITY OF	161	67	**41.6%**	12	7.5%	35	21.7%	5	3.1%
MCGEORGE SCHOOL OF LAW	306	127	**41.5%**	7	2.3%	56	18.3%	8	2.6%
LOYOLA MARYMOUNT UNIV.-LOS ANGELES	411	170	**41.4%**	30	7.3%	82	20.0%	0	0.0%

Table 6 Schools Ranked in Order of Percent of Grads Employed in FT/LT Bar-Pass-Req. Jobs* (column in bold)	Total # of 2012 Graduates	2012 Grads Employed Bar Pass Req. FT/LT	% of 2012 Grads Employed Bar Pass Req. FT/LT	2012 Grads Employed JD Advantage FT/LT	% of 2012 Grads Employed JD Advantage FT/LT	2012 Grads—Unemployed Seeking Jobs	% of 2012 Grads—Unemployed Seeking Jobs	2012 Grads with Unknown Employment Status	% of 2012 Grads with Unknown Employment Status
MICHIGAN STATE UNIVERSITY	291	120	**41.2%**	50	17.2%	28	9.6%	16	5.5%
QUINNIPIAC UNIVERSITY	151	62	**41.1%**	41	27.2%	16	10.6%	1	0.7%
DEPAUL UNIVERSITY	368	149	**40.5%**	42	11.4%	68	18.5%	19	5.2%
ST. THOMAS UNIVERSITY	216	87	**40.3%**	17	7.9%	46	21.3%	17	7.9%
SUFFOLK UNIVERSITY	517	206	**39.8%**	60	11.6%	80	15.5%	28	5.4%
NEW YORK LAW SCHOOL	601	238	**39.6%**	94	15.6%	82	13.6%	17	2.8%
AMERICAN UNIVERSITY	463	180	**38.9%**	68	14.7%	71	15.3%	5	1.1%
WIDENER UNIVERSITY	269	104	**38.7%**	30	11.2%	23	8.6%	16	5.9%
APPALACHIAN SCHOOL OF LAW	91	35	**38.5%**	14	15.4%	17	18.7%	5	5.5%
CHARLOTTE SCHOOL OF LAW	234	90	**38.5%**	22	9.4%	20	8.5%	0	0.0%
FLORIDA A&M	160	61	**38.1%**	22	13.8%	32	20.0%	9	5.6%
CATHOLIC UNIVERSITY OF AMERICA	246	90	**36.6%**	64	26.0%	36	14.6%	3	1.2%
CHAPMAN UNIVERSITY	178	65	**36.5%**	20	11.2%	43	24.2%	0	0.0%
NEW ENGLAND LAW | BOSTON	339	123	**36.3%**	44	13.0%	63	18.6%	11	3.2%
FLORIDA COASTAL	510	183	**35.9%**	27	5.3%	92	18.0%	0	0.0%
UNIVERSITY OF LA VERNE	104	37	**35.6%**	2	1.9%	31	29.8%	0	0.0%
AVE MARIA	166	59	**35.5%**	21	12.7%	37	22.3%	12	7.2%

Table 6 Schools Ranked in Order of Percent of Grads Employed in FT/LT Bar-Pass-Req. Jobs* (column in bold)	Total # of 2012 Graduates	2012 Grads Employed Bar Pass Req. FT/LT	% of 2012 Grads Employed Bar Pass Req. FT/LT	2012 Grads Employed JD Ad- vantage FT/LT	% of 2012 Grads Employed JD Ad- vantage FT/LT	2012 Grads— Unem- ployed Seeking Jobs	% of 2012 Grads— Unem- ployed Seeking Jobs	2012 Grads with Un- known Employ- ment Status	% of 2012 Grads with Un- known Employ- ment Status
WHITTIER COLLEGE	170	58	**34.1%**	19	11.2%	40	23.5%	6	3.5%
WESTERN NEW ENGLAND UNIVERSITY	160	54	**33.8%**	28	17.5%	26	16.3%	5	3.1%
WESTERN STATE	83	27	**32.5%**	6	7.2%	23	27.7%	7	8.4%
DETROIT MERCY, UNIVERSITY OF	212	63	**29.7%**	24	11.3%	34	16.0%	7	3.3%
UNIV. OF MASSACHUSETTS DARTMOUTH	44	13	**29.5%**	6	13.6%	6	13.6%	0	0.0%
THOMAS JEFFERSON SCHOOL OF LAW	260	75	**28.8%**	19	7.3%	82	31.5%	18	6.9%
THOMAS M. COOLEY LAW SCHOOL	1079	311	**28.8%**	122	11.3%	215	19.9%	104	9.6%
NORTH CAROLINA CENTRAL UNIV.	165	43	**26.1%**	15	9.1%	17	10.3%	74	44.8%
DISTRICT OF COLUMBIA	93	24	**25.8%**	11	11.8%	20	21.5%	7	7.5%
SAN FRANCISCO, UNIVERSITY OF	221	50	**22.6%**	22	10.0%	67	30.3%	8	3.6%
GOLDEN GATE UNIVERSITY	186	40	**21.5%**	11	5.9%	38	20.4%	6	3.2%
PUERTO RICO, UNIVERSITY OF	202	28	**13.9%**	26	12.9%	48	23.8%	8	4.0%
PONTIFICAL CATHOLIC UNIV. OF P.R.	217	23	**10.6%**	5	2.3%	77	35.5%	78	35.9%
INTER AMERICAN UNIV. OF PUERTO RICO	234	5	**2.1%**	10	4.3%	42	17.9%	5	2.1%

Data Source: Employment Summary Report, http://employmentsummary.abaquestionnaire.org.
FT, LT = Full-time and Long-term; * Belmont, Concordia and Lincoln Memorial Law Schools have been deleted from this table as the ABA had no statistics on these schools.

Table 7. Comparison of 2011 and 2012 Grads

	Table 7 Schools Ranked from Highest to Lowest Employment Rate for 2011 Grads	2011 Grads Employed FT, LT Bar Passage Required Jobs	2012 Grads Employed FT, LT Bar Passage Required Jobs	Total No. of 2011 Grads	Total No. of 2012 Grads	% of 2011 Grads Employed FT, LT Bar Passage Required Jobs	% of 2012 Grads Employed FT, LT Bar Passage Required Jobs
1	VIRGINIA, UNIV. OF	357	344	377	364	94.7%	94.5%
2	COLUMBIA UNIV.	429	438	456	469	94.1%	93.4%
3	STANFORD UNIV.	175	165	192	181	91.1%	91.2%
4	NEW YORK UNIV.	420	439	466	482	90.1%	91.1%
5	HARVARD UNIV.	525	515	583	590	90.1%	87.3%
6	CHICAGO, UNIV. OF	179	204	203	215	88.2%	94.9%
7	YALE UNIV.	180	182	205	222	87.8%	82.0%
8	PENNSYLVANIA, UNIV. OF	231	255	274	270	84.3%	94.4%
9	DUKE UNIV.	170	192	207	225	82.1%	85.3%
10	GEORGE WASHINGTON UNIV.	421	466	518	575	81.3%	81.0%
11	LOUISIANA STATE UNIV.	143	171	176	223	81.3%	76.7%
12	CALIFORNIA-BERKELEY, UNIV. OF	248	268	310	312	80.0%	85.9%
13	ST. MARY'S UNIV.	195	181	249	268	78.3%	67.5%
14	ALABAMA, UNIV. OF	128	133	164	172	78.0%	77.3%
15	NORTHWESTERN UNIV.	221	225	287	295	77.0%	76.3%
16	CORNELL UNIV.	153	163	201	190	76.1%	85.8%

	Table 7 Schools Ranked from Highest to Lowest Employment Rate for 2011 Grads	2011 Grads Employed FT, LT Bar Passage Required Jobs	2012 Grads Employed FT, LT Bar Passage Required Jobs	Total No. of 2011 Grads	Total No. of 2012 Grads	% of 2011 Grads Employed FT, LT Bar Passage Required Jobs	% of 2012 Grads Employed FT, LT Bar Passage Required Jobs
17	MICHIGAN, UNIV. OF	286	320	379	388	75.5%	82.5%
18	ARIZONA, UNIV. OF	119	99	158	149	75.3%	66.4%
19	MISSISSIPPI COLLEGE	125	99	166	164	75.3%	60.4%
20	VANDERBILT UNIV.	146	140	198	196	73.7%	71.4%
21	KENTUCKY, UNIV. OF	97	109	135	147	71.9%	74.1%
22	CAMPBELL UNIV.	95	98	133	145	71.4%	67.6%
23	BAYLOR UNIV.	110	112	157	164	70.1%	68.3%
24	TEXAS AT AUSTIN, UNIV. OF	267	283	382	373	69.9%	75.9%
25	FLORIDA STATE UNIV.	194	190	279	286	69.5%	66.4%
26	EMORY UNIV.	155	195	225	266	68.9%	73.3%
27	WEST VIRGINIA UNIV.	86	109	125	142	68.8%	76.8%
28	UTAH, UNIV. OF	92	86	134	134	68.7%	64.2%
29	BOSTON COLLEGE	195	170	285	260	68.4%	65.4%
30	NORTH CAROLINA, UNIV. OF	169	177	247	256	68.4%	69.1%
31	ARIZONA STATE UNIV.	137	136	201	212	68.2%	64.2%
32	LOUISVILLE, UNIV. OF	95	85	142	127	66.9%	66.9%
33	MISSOURI-COLUMBIA, UNIV. OF	94	100	141	147	66.7%	68.0%

	Table 7 Schools Ranked from Highest to Lowest Employment Rate for 2011 Grads	2011 Grads Employed FT, LT Bar Passage Required Jobs	2012 Grads Employed FT, LT Bar Passage Required Jobs	Total No. of 2011 Grads	Total No. of 2012 Grads	% of 2011 Grads Employed FT, LT Bar Passage Required Jobs	% of 2012 Grads Employed FT, LT Bar Passage Required Jobs
34	UNIV. OF NEVADA-LAS VEGAS	85	98	128	161	66.4%	60.9%
35	NEW MEXICO, UNIV. OF	68	80	103	119	66.0%	67.2%
36	MONTANA, UNIV. OF	56	50	85	82	65.9%	61.0%
37	TULSA, UNIV. OF	79	88	120	134	65.8%	65.7%
38	IOWA, UNIV. OF	120	132	183	185	65.6%	71.4%
39	SAMFORD UNIV.	97	99	148	166	65.5%	59.6%
40	SOUTHERN CALIFORNIA, UNIV. OF	134	154	207	221	64.7%	69.7%
41	NEBRASKA, UNIV. OF	84	84	130	128	64.6%	65.6%
42	GEORGIA STATE UNIV.	120	131	186	199	64.5%	65.8%
43	SOUTH TEXAS COLLEGE OF LAW	259	104	402	187	64.4%	55.6%
44	INDIANA UNIV. MAURER SCHOOL OF LAW	124	111	195	204	63.6%	54.4%
45	TEXAS TECH UNIV.	127	133	200	215	63.5%	61.9%
46	ARKANSAS, LITTLE ROCK, UNIV. OF	95	84	150	139	63.3%	60.4%
47	SOUTHERN METHODIST UNIV.	172	220	272	293	63.2%	75.1%
48	MERCER UNIV.	82	104	130	142	63.1%	73.2%
49	SETON HALL UNIV.	184	204	293	310	62.8%	65.8%
50	WISCONSIN, UNIV. OF	159	178	254	284	62.6%	62.7%

	Table 7 Schools Ranked from Highest to Lowest Employment Rate for 2011 Grads	2011 Grads Employed FT, LT Bar Passage Required Jobs	2012 Grads Employed FT, LT Bar Passage Required Jobs	Total No. of 2011 Grads	Total No. of 2012 Grads	% of 2011 Grads Employed FT, LT Bar Passage Required Jobs	% of 2012 Grads Employed FT, LT Bar Passage Required Jobs
51	GEORGETOWN UNIV.	403	459	644	626	62.6%	73.3%
52	TENNESSEE, UNIV. OF	91	101	146	155	62.3%	65.2%
53	WYOMING, UNIV. OF	46	43	74	75	62.2%	57.3%
54	NOTRE DAME, UNIV. OF	118	131	190	196	62.1%	66.8%
55	OKLAHOMA, UNIV. OF	101	126	163	188	62.0%	67.0%
56	CALIFORNIA-LOS ANGELES, UNIV. OF	211	170	344	411	61.3%	41.4%
57	GEORGIA, UNIV. OF	139	159	227	229	61.2%	69.4%
58	ARKANSAS, FAYETTEVILLE, UNIV. OF	71	93	116	132	61.2%	70.5%
59	MISSOURI-KANSAS CITY, UNIV. OF	94	101	154	153	61.0%	66.0%
60	FLORIDA INTERNATIONAL	105	117	173	184	60.7%	63.6%
61	DRAKE UNIV.	94	78	155	139	60.6%	56.1%
62	HOUSTON, UNIV. OF	169	165	281	262	60.1%	63.0%
63	CREIGHTON UNIV.	92	95	153	165	60.1%	57.6%
64	GEORGE MASON UNIV.	102	112	170	220	60.0%	50.9%
65	PENNSYLVANIA STATE UNIV.	107	114	179	194	59.8%	58.8%
66	MEMPHIS, UNIV. OF	77	76	129	134	59.7%	56.7%
67	OKLAHOMA CITY UNIV.	105	112	176	207	59.7%	54.1%

	Table 7 Schools Ranked from Highest to Lowest Employment Rate for 2011 Grads	2011 Grads Employed FT, LT Bar Passage Required Jobs	2012 Grads Employed FT, LT Bar Passage Required Jobs	Total No. of 2011 Grads	Total No. of 2012 Grads	% of 2011 Grads Employed FT, LT Bar Passage Required Jobs	% of 2012 Grads Employed FT, LT Bar Passage Required Jobs
68	RICHMOND, UNIV. OF	99	84	166	148	59.6%	56.8%
69	SOUTHERN ILLINOIS UNIV.-CARBONDALE	66	67	111	128	59.5%	52.3%
70	FLORIDA, UNIV. OF	243	189	409	333	59.4%	56.8%
71	MINNESOTA, UNIV. OF	155	155	261	230	59.4%	67.4%
72	WASHINGTON UNIV.	188	123	317	181	59.3%	68.0%
73	TOURO COLLEGE	131	124	221	244	59.3%	50.8%
74	OHIO STATE UNIV.	135	132	231	222	58.4%	59.5%
75	NOVA SOUTHEASTERN UNIV.	176	202	302	354	58.3%	57.1%
76	RUTGERS UNIV.-CAMDEN	141	170	242	270	58.3%	63.0%
77	TULANE UNIV.	140	169	241	269	58.1%	62.8%
78	MARQUETTE UNIV.	133	125	230	218	57.8%	57.3%
79	FORDHAM UNIV.	246	305	428	486	57.5%	62.8%
80	STETSON UNIV.	184	204	322	341	57.1%	59.8%
81	OHIO NORTHERN UNIV.	55	57	97	96	56.7%	59.4%
82	RUTGERS UNIV.-NEWARK	140	132	248	243	56.5%	54.3%
83	FAULKNER UNIV.	57	52	101	104	56.4%	50.0%
84	CALIFORNIA-DAVIS, UNIV. OF	110	124	195	202	56.4%	61.4%

	Table 7 Schools Ranked from Highest to Lowest Employment Rate for 2011 Grads	2011 Grads Employed FT, LT Bar Passage Required Jobs	2012 Grads Employed FT, LT Bar Passage Required Jobs	Total No. of 2011 Grads	Total No. of 2012 Grads	% of 2011 Grads Employed FT, LT Bar Passage Required Jobs	% of 2012 Grads Employed FT, LT Bar Passage Required Jobs
85	WAKE FOREST UNIV.	89	106	158	156	56.3%	67.9%
86	COLORADO, UNIV. OF	98	90	176	175	55.7%	51.4%
87	GONZAGA UNIV.	89	84	160	166	55.6%	50.6%
88	ELON UNIV.	55	57	99	112	55.6%	50.9%
89	TEMPLE UNIV.	177	147	319	277	55.5%	53.1%
90	AKRON, UNIV. OF	64	65	116	139	55.2%	46.8%
91	MIAMI, UNIV. OF	212	273	385	461	55.1%	59.2%
92	WASHINGTON AND LEE UNIV.	71	64	129	130	55.0%	49.2%
93	MISSISSIPPI, UNIV. OF	83	99	151	165	55.0%	60.0%
94	SOUTH CAROLINA, UNIV. OF	122	159	222	226	55.0%	70.4%
95	WILLIAM AND MARY SCHOOL OF LAW	112	150	204	204	54.9%	73.5%
96	NORTHERN ILLINOIS UNIV.	53	57	97	91	54.6%	62.6%
97	PITTSBURGH, UNIV. OF	137	114	253	222	54.2%	51.4%
98	INDIANA UNIV.-INDIANAPOLIS	136	151	252	295	54.0%	51.2%
99	TEXAS SOUTHERN UNIV.	87	70	163	162	53.4%	43.2%
100	CINCINNATI, UNIV. OF	64	75	120	140	53.3%	53.6%
101	ST. LOUIS UNIV.	144	168	272	276	52.9%	60.9%

	Table 7 Schools Ranked from Highest to Lowest Employment Rate for 2011 Grads	2011 Grads Employed FT, LT Bar Passage Required Jobs	2012 Grads Employed FT, LT Bar Passage Required Jobs	Total No. of 2011 Grads	Total No. of 2012 Grads	% of 2011 Grads Employed FT, LT Bar Passage Required Jobs	% of 2012 Grads Employed FT, LT Bar Passage Required Jobs
102	WASHINGTON, UNIV. OF	96	205	182	300	52.7%	68.3%
103	REGENT UNIV.	62	65	118	127	52.5%	51.2%
104	KANSAS, UNIV. OF	88	96	168	154	52.4%	62.3%
105	VILLANOVA UNIV.	132	131	252	256	52.4%	51.2%
106	YESHIVA UNIV.	197	209	380	387	51.8%	54.0%
107	STATE UNIV. OF NEW YORK AT BUFFALO	127	109	245	209	51.8%	52.2%
108	DAYTON, UNIV. OF	88	89	171	174	51.5%	51.1%
109	BRIGHAM YOUNG UNIV.	76	94	148	147	51.4%	63.9%
110	CHARLESTON SCHOOL OF LAW	99	123	193	229	51.3%	53.7%
111	IDAHO, UNIV. OF	52	59	102	104	51.0%	56.7%
112	BOSTON UNIV.	139	175	273	273	50.9%	64.1%
113	ILLINOIS INST. OF TECH., CHICAGO-KENT	169	168	332	282	50.9%	59.6%
114	WAYNE STATE UNIV.	103	92	203	168	50.7%	54.8%
115	ILLINOIS, UNIV. OF	96	131	190	213	50.5%	61.5%
116	CLEVELAND STATE UNIV.	93	86	185	176	50.3%	48.9%
117	SYRACUSE UNIV.	97	85	193	185	50.3%	45.9%
118	HAMLINE UNIV.	103	81	205	190	50.2%	42.6%

	Table 7 Schools Ranked from Highest to Lowest Employment Rate for 2011 Grads	2011 Grads Employed FT, LT Bar Passage Required Jobs	2012 Grads Employed FT, LT Bar Passage Required Jobs	Total No. of 2011 Grads	Total No. of 2012 Grads	% of 2011 Grads Employed FT, LT Bar Passage Required Jobs	% of 2012 Grads Employed FT, LT Bar Passage Required Jobs
119	LOYOLA UNIV.-CHICAGO	126	148	251	271	50.2%	54.6%
120	ALBANY LAW SCHOOL	118	121	236	233	50.0%	51.9%
121	ROGER WILLIAMS UNIV.	79	93	158	181	50.0%	51.4%
122	WASHBURN UNIV.	71	99	142	156	50.0%	63.5%
123	NORTHEASTERN UNIV.	90	93	182	215	49.5%	43.3%
124	NORTH DAKOTA, UNIV. OF	40	61	81	90	49.4%	67.8%
125	ST. THOMAS UNIV.	109	87	221	216	49.3%	40.3%
126	TEXAS WESLEYAN UNIV.	109	110	223	207	48.9%	53.1%
127	VERMONT LAW SCHOOL	85	93	174	206	48.9%	45.1%
128	DENVER, UNIV. OF	140	156	287	317	48.8%	49.2%
129	CONNECTICUT, UNIV. OF	86	108	179	199	48.0%	54.3%
130	BALTIMORE, UNIV. OF	143	185	298	347	48.0%	53.3%
131	ST. JOHN'S UNIV.	132	138	276	281	47.8%	49.1%
132	HOWARD UNIV.	75	72	157	151	47.8%	47.7%
133	NEW HAMPSHIRE UNIV. OF	70	84	147	138	47.6%	60.9%
134	HAWAII, UNIV. OF	48	56	101	106	47.5%	52.8%

	Table 7 Schools Ranked from Highest to Lowest Employment Rate for 2011 Grads	2011 Grads Employed FT, LT Bar Passage Required Jobs	2012 Grads Employed FT, LT Bar Passage Required Jobs	Total No. of 2011 Grads	Total No. of 2012 Grads	% of 2011 Grads Employed FT, LT Bar Passage Required Jobs	% of 2012 Grads Employed FT, LT Bar Passage Required Jobs
135	WILLAMETTE UNIV.	61	65	129	125	47.3%	52.0%
136	BROOKLYN LAW SCHOOL	215	227	455	466	47.3%	48.7%
137	WIDENER UNIV.	119	104	252	269	47.2%	38.7%
138	MARYLAND, UNIV. OF	140	169	297	319	47.1%	53.0%
139	SAN DIEGO, UNIV. OF	149	154	318	327	46.9%	47.1%
140	CASE WESTERN RESERVE UNIV.	94	81	201	172	46.8%	47.1%
141	CALIFORNIA-HASTINGS, UNIV. OF	191	205	411	443	46.5%	46.3%
142	LEWIS AND CLARK COLLEGE	107	117	233	209	45.9%	56.0%
143	LOYOLA UNIV.-NEW ORLEANS	106	135	231	278	45.9%	48.6%
144	DUQUESNE UNIV.	92	106	206	201	44.7%	52.7%
145	WIDENER UNIV.-HARRISBURG	55	57	124	122	44.4%	46.7%
146	MICHIGAN STATE UNIV.	125	120	283	291	44.2%	41.2%
147	UNIV. OF ST. THOMAS	59	71	134	161	44.0%	44.1%
148	CATHOLIC UNIV. OF AMERICA	114	90	261	246	43.7%	36.6%
149	WILLIAM MITCHELL COLLEGE OF LAW	123	156	282	303	43.6%	51.5%
150	MCGEORGE SCHOOL OF LAW	132	127	303	306	43.6%	41.5%

	Table 7 Schools Ranked from Highest to Lowest Employment Rate for 2011 Grads	2011 Grads Employed FT, LT Bar Passage Required Jobs	2012 Grads Employed FT, LT Bar Passage Required Jobs	Total No. of 2011 Grads	Total No. of 2012 Grads	% of 2011 Grads Employed FT, LT Bar Passage Required Jobs	% of 2012 Grads Employed FT, LT Bar Passage Required Jobs
151	NORTH CAROLINA CENTRAL UNIV.	74	43	170	165	43.5%	26.1%
152	DREXEL UNIV.	57	75	131	155	43.5%	48.4%
153	JOHN MARSHALL LAW SCHOOL	174	175	401	414	43.4%	42.3%
154	CHARLOTTE SCHOOL OF LAW	42	90	97	234	43.3%	38.5%
155	SANTA CLARA UNIV.	127	128	296	298	42.9%	43.0%
156	PEPPERDINE UNIV.	98	99	229	213	42.8%	46.5%
157	LOYOLA MARYMOUNT UNIV.-LOS ANGELES	172	170	403	411	42.7%	41.4%
158	MAINE, UNIV. OF	38	37	90	87	42.2%	42.5%
159	VALPARAISO UNIV.	76	73	181	172	42.0%	42.4%
160	OREGON, UNIV. OF	72	67	174	161	41.4%	41.6%
161	ATLANTA'S JOHN MARSHALL LAW SHOOL	54	77	132	177	40.9%	43.5%
162	HOFSTRA UNIV.	121	186	297	363	40.7%	51.2%
163	DEPAUL UNIV.	129	149	319	368	40.4%	40.5%
164	SEATTLE UNIV.	127	152	315	323	40.3%	47.1%
165	CHAPMAN UNIV.	71	65	177	178	40.1%	36.5%
166	CAPITAL UNIV.	70	95	175	197	40.0%	48.2%

	Table 7 Schools Ranked from Highest to Lowest Employment Rate for 2011 Grads	2011 Grads Employed FT, LT Bar Passage Required Jobs	2012 Grads Employed FT, LT Bar Passage Required Jobs	Total No. of 2011 Grads	Total No. of 2012 Grads	% of 2011 Grads Employed FT, LT Bar Passage Required Jobs	% of 2012 Grads Employed FT, LT Bar Passage Required Jobs
167	CALIFORNIA WESTERN SCHOOL OF LAW	112	124	285	283	39.3%	43.8%
168	BARRY UNIV.	82	97	209	200	39.2%	48.5%
169	SUFFOLK UNIV.	193	206	502	517	38.4%	39.8%
170	SOUTH DAKOTA, UNIV. OF	21	48	55	76	38.2%	63.2%
171	THOMAS M. COOLEY LAW SCHOOL	375	311	999	1079	37.5%	28.8%
172	PHOENIX SCHOOL OF LAW	49	79	131	181	37.4%	43.6%
173	SOUTHERN UNIV.	53	70	143	162	37.1%	43.2%
174	CITY UNIV. OF NEW YORK	41	77	111	141	36.9%	54.6%
175	DETROIT MERCY, UNIV. OF	77	63	209	212	36.8%	29.7%
176	FLORIDA COASTAL	165	183	451	510	36.6%	35.9%
177	TOLEDO, UNIV. OF	42	76	115	147	36.5%	51.7%
178	NORTHERN KENTUCKY UNIV.	65	71	179	162	36.3%	43.8%
179	PACE UNIV.	80	111	222	230	36.0%	48.3%
180	AMERICAN UNIV.	167	180	467	463	35.8%	38.9%
181	NEW YORK LAW SCHOOL	183	238	515	601	35.5%	39.6%
182	QUINNIPIAC UNIV.	46	62	133	151	34.6%	41.1%

	Table 7 Schools Ranked from Highest to Lowest Employment Rate for 2011 Grads	2011 Grads Employed FT, LT Bar Passage Required Jobs	2012 Grads Employed FT, LT Bar Passage Required Jobs	Total No. of 2011 Grads	Total No. of 2012 Grads	% of 2011 Grads Employed FT, LT Bar Passage Required Jobs	% of 2012 Grads Employed FT, LT Bar Passage Required Jobs
183	SOUTHWESTERN LAW SCHOOL	103	143	298	324	34.6%	44.1%
184	NEW ENGLAND SCHOOL OF LAW	106	123	308	339	34.4%	36.3%
185	SAN FRANCISCO, UNIV. OF	76	50	222	221	34.2%	22.6%
186	FLORIDA A&M	52	61	152	160	34.2%	38.1%
187	AVE MARIA	29	59	88	166	33.0%	35.5%
188	UNIV. OF LA VERNE	38	37	116	104	32.8%	35.6%
189	WESTERN STATE	29	27	90	83	32.2%	32.5%
190	LIBERTY UNIV.	28	47	90	90	31.1%	52.2%
191	APPALACHIAN SCHOOL OF LAW	28	35	91	91	30.8%	38.5%
192	WESTERN NEW ENGLAND UNIV.	46	54	153	160	30.1%	33.8%
193	THOMAS JEFFERSON SCHOOL OF LAW	63	75	236	260	26.7%	28.8%
194	GOLDEN GATE UNIV.	42	40	191	186	22.0%	21.5%
195	DISTRICT OF COLUMBIA	16	24	78	93	20.5%	25.8%
196	WHITTIER COLLEGE	21	58	123	170	17.1%	34.1%
197	PUERTO RICO, UNIV. OF*	0	28	244	202	0.0%	13.9%

Data Source: Employment Summary Report, http://employmentsummary.abaquestionnaire.org.
FT, LT = Full-time and Long-term; * ABA did not explain Puerto Rico's figures.

Appendix B

Table 1. Professor Johnson's Matrix for Analyzing and Comparing Law Schools Making Admission Offers

	Criteria to Compare	School No. 1	School No. 2	School No. 3	School No. 4
1	Tuition[+]				
2	Estimated Cost of Living[+]				
3	Scholarship Award Offered to You				
4	Median Scholarship Award to FT Students*				
5	Retention Rate of Merit-Based Scholarships•				
6	1L Attrition Rate*				
7	2L Attrition Rate*				
8	No. of Transfer-Out Students*				
9	No. of Transfer-In Students*				
10	Form of Academic Support Program~				
11	School's Average Bar Passage Rate*				
12	State's Average Bar Passage Rate*				
13	Law-School-Based Bar Exam Passage Support~				
14	Total No. of Grads^				
15	# of Grads with FTLT Bar-Passage-Required Jobs^				
16	% of Grads with FTLT Bar-Passage-Required Jobs				
17	# of Grads with in FTLT JD-Advantage Jobs^				
18	% of Grads with FTLT JD-Advantage Jobs				

	Criteria to Compare	School No. 1	School No. 2	School No. 3	School No. 4
19	# of Grads Unemployed and Seeking Jobs^				
20	% of Grads Unemployed and Seeking Jobs				
21	# of Grads with Unknown Employment Status^				
22	% of Grads with Unknown Employment Status				
23	# of Grads with University-Funded Positions^				
24	Total # of Grads at Law Firms‡				
25	# of Grads who are Solo Attorneys‡				
26	# of Grads at Very Small Firms (2–10)‡				
27	# of Grads at Solo & Very Small Firms‡				
28	% of Grads at Solo and Very Small Firms				

FTLT = Full-time, Long-term; * = ABA-LSAC Guide available in print and online; ^ = ABA's Employment Summary for recent grads, http://employmentsummary.abaquestionnaire.org; + = School's Website and Promotional Materials; • = School must disclose retention rates on website and to students offered scholarships; ~ = Applicants must search a school's website and speak with the director of such programs; ‡ = Total No. of solo and/or small-firm grads working full time, part time, long term and short term.

Please read Chapters 3, 4 and 7 for full explanations of various criteria that should be considered.

Table 2. Example of Professor Johnson's Matrix for Analyzing and Comparing Law Schools Making Admission Offers[Δ]

	Criteria to Compare	Indiana University Maurer School No. 1	Loyola-LA School No. 2	Southwestern School No. 3	Wash & Lee School No. 4
1	Tuition[+]	$29,946 res.[√]	$44,230	$43,650	$48,507
2	Estimated Cost of Living[+]	$22,882	$27,472	$29,409	$14,643
3	Scholarship Award Offered to You				
4	Median Scholarship Award to FT Students*	$15,883	$22,000	$16,861	$15,800
5	Retention Rate of Merit-Based Scholarships[•]	Not evident from website	Not avail.	40 kept out of 45 - Yrs. '11–'12	1 of 315 revoked - Yrs. 2009–12
6	1L Attrition Rate*	3.3%	10.3%	11.1%	2.1%
7	2L Attrition Rate*	4.3%	0.5%	8.3%	14.2%
8	No. of Transfer-Out Students*	9	13	19	22
9	No. of Transfer-In Students*	0	44	6	15
10	Form of Academic Support Program[~]	Not evident from website	Workshops	Workshops, programs and individual assistance	Not evident from website
11	School's Average Bar Passage Rate*	82.99%	80.92%	58.57%	80.24%
12	State's Average Bar Passage Rate*	83.53%	71.24%	71.24%	79.93%
13	Law-School-Based Bar Exam Passage Support[~]	Not evident from website	Bar prep course & 3-day workshop	List of other sources[@]	List of other sources[@]
14	Total No. of Grads[^]	195	403	298	129
15	# of Grads with FTLT Bar-Passage-Required Jobs[^]	124	172	103	71

	Criteria to Compare	Indiana University Maurer School No. 1	Loyola-LA School No. 2	Southwestern School No. 3	Wash & Lee School No. 4
16	% of Grads with FTLT Bar-Passage-Required Jobs	63%	43%	35%	55%
17	# of Grads with in FTLT JD-Advantage Jobs^	19	17	53	12
18	% of Grads with FTLT JD-Advantage Jobs	10%	4%	18%	9%
19	# of Grads Unemployed and Seeking Jobs^	11	65	30	7
20	% of Grads Unemployed and Seeking Jobs	6%	16%	10%	5%
21	# of Grads with Unknown Employment Status^	1	0	25	3
22	% of Grads with Unknown Employment Status	<1%	0%	8%	2%
23	# of Grads with University-Funded Positions^	8	30	0	12
24	Total # of Grads at Law Firms‡	78	183	106	52
25	# of Grads who are Solo Attorneys‡	8	3	12	1
26	# of Grads at Very Small Firms (2–10)‡	24	81	68	20
27	# of Grads at Solo & Very Small Firms‡	32	84	80	21
28	% of Grads at Solo and Very Small Firms	41%	46%	75%	40%

Δ = These schools were chosen because of media reports regarding their innovative curricula changes; FTLT = Full-time, Long-term; * = 2012–2013 ABA-LSAC Guide; √ = information from school's website indicated that tuition is $48,020 for non-residents; ^ = ABA's Employment Summary for 2011 grads, http://employmentsummary.abaquestionnaire.org; + = School's website and promotional materials; • = School must disclose retention rates on website and to students offered scholarships; ~ = Applicants must search a school's website and speak with the director of such programs; ‡ = Total No. of 2011 grads working full time, part time, long term and short term; @ = Website provides a list of books and other resources students can consult.

Please read Chapters 3, 4 and 7 for full explanations of various criteria that should be considered.

Appendix C

List of Abbreviations

ABA	American Bar Association
FTC	Federal Trade Commission
GPA	Grade Point Average
IBR	Income Based Repayment
JD	Juris Doctor/Juris Doctorate
LLM	Master of Laws
LRAP	Loan Repayment Assistance Program
LSAC	Law School Admission Council
LSAT	Law School Admission Test
NALP	National Association for Law Placement
NYLS	New York Law School
PSLF	Public Service Loan Forgiveness

Index